SEARCHING FOR LORD HAW-HAW

Searching for Lord Haw-Haw is an authoritative account of the political lives of William Joyce. He became notorious as a fascist, an anti-Semite and then as a Second World War traitor when, assuming the persona of Lord Haw-Haw, he acted as a radio propagandist for the Nazis. It is an endlessly compelling story of simmering hope, intense frustration, renewed anticipation and ultimately catastrophic failure.

This fully referenced work is the first attempt to place Joyce at the centre of the turbulent, traumatic and influential events through which he lived. It challenges existing biographies which have reflected not only Joyce's frequent calculated deceptions but also the suspect claims advanced by his family, friends and apologists. By exploring his rampant, increasingly influential narcissism it also offers a pioneering analysis of Joyce's personality and exposes its dangerous, destructive consequences.

"What a saga my life would make!" Joyce wrote from prison just before his execution. Few would disagree with him.

Colin Holmes is Emeritus Professor of History at the University of Sheffield, UK.

Routledge Studies in Fascism and the Far Right

Series editors: Nigel Copsey, *Teesside University*, and
Graham Macklin, *University of Huddersfield*

This book series examines fascist, far right and right-wing politics
within a historical context. Fascism falls within the far right but the
far right also extends to so-called 'radical-right populism'. Boundaries
are not fixed and it is important to recognise points of convergence
and exchange with the mainstream right.

The series will include books with a broad thematic or biographical focus suitable for students, teachers and general readers. These will
be available in hardback, paperback and e-book. The series will also
include books aimed largely at subject specialists which will appear in
hardback and e-book format only.

Titles include:

Cultures of Post-War British Fascism
Nigel Copsey and John E. Richardson

France and Fascism
February 1934 and
the dynamics of political crisis
Brian Jenkins and Chris Millington

Searching for Lord Haw-Haw
The political lives of William Joyce
Colin Holmes

SEARCHING FOR LORD HAW-HAW

The political lives of
William Joyce

Colin Holmes

Routledge
Taylor & Francis Group

LONDON AND NEW YORK

First published 2016
by Routledge
2 Park Square, Milton Park, Abingdon, Oxon OX14 4RN

and by Routledge
711 Third Avenue, New York, NY 10017

Routledge is an imprint of the Taylor & Francis Group, an Informa business

British Library Cataloguing-in-Publication Data
A catalogue record for this book is available from the British Library

Library of Congress Cataloging-in-Publication Data
Holmes, Colin, 1938– author. Searching for Lord Haw-Haw : the political
    lives of William Joyce / Colin Holmes.
      pages cm. — (Routledge studies in fascism and the far right)
    Includes bibliographical references and index.
    1. Joyce, William, 1906–1946. 2. Defectors—Great Britain—
Biography. 3. Nazi propaganda—Great Britain—History. 4. World
War, 1939–1945—Germany—Propaganda. 5. Radio in
propaganda. 6. Treason—Great Britain. I. Title.
    DA587.H65 2016
    940.54'88743092—dc23
    [B] 2015012713

ISBN: 978-1-138-88884-5 (hbk)
ISBN: 978-1-138-88886-9 (pbk)
ISBN: 978-1-315-68416-1 (ebk)

Typeset in Bembo
by Apex CoVantage, LLC

In memory of my mother, Grace Mary Holmes (1902–1995), who lived through these turbulent times and to whom I owe so much.

CONTENTS

PREFACE

I first read the political writings of William Joyce when researching the history of British anti-Semitism. However, I already knew of his activities, assuming for many years I had heard his wartime voice as Lord Haw-Haw. The memory often deceives and my sister offered evidence that flattened my belief.

For some time I kept a file on Joyce. But my attempt to write seriously did not begin until the later 1990s. I had intended to write a standard biography. However, he left little by way of private papers and parts of his life remain stubbornly obscure. Some biographers, swamped with material, can tell us what their subjects ate for break-fast on any particular day or, in Beatrice Webb's case, the books she ordered from the British Museum. Such fine detail does not exist on Joyce. In one respect this absence is not a major problem. From an early age he lived his life as a political activist and this consuming interest, on which there are surviving records, amounts to his funda-mental historical legacy. His life with Margaret, his second wife, is a love story that deserves to be told. But nothing in this relationship, which he dominated and needed to control, significantly affected or changed him, certainly never seriously influenced his politics. I took a decision, therefore, to focus on Joyce's political life. At first my prog-ress proved slow on account of a disproportionately heavy teaching load. When retirement lifted that responsibility, I began to experience health problems that had their origins before I left full-time work. Nevertheless, I continued to engage with the muses.

The award of the Hartley Fellowship at the University of Southampton in 2000 afforded me access to the impressive collection of anti-Semitica and related items in the Parkes Collection. The British Library in St Pancras, its Colindale site and its colonial outpost at Boston Spa, were ransacked for their scholarly riches. I drew once more on the resources of the Wiener Library. The official files in the National Archives proved invaluable. I benefited from materials in the National Maritime Museum the London Metropolitan Archives, the Imperial War Museum and King's College, London, the last of which possesses the Arthur Bryant collection, the Hamilton papers and part of the J.F.C. Fuller archive. I worked in the less well-known Rawnsley archive in the University of Bradford. Faber and Faber generously allowed me to consult files in their possession. Sir Oswald Mosley's papers in Birmingham University Library, the Charles Saroléa collection at the University of Edinburgh, documents at the BBC Written Archives Centre at Reading, along with files at the Mass-Observation Archive at Sussex, yielded valuable information. The Manchester Central Reference Library, and public libraries in Kensington, Oldham and Sheffield, provided other sources. The Labour History Archive and Study Centre in Manchester held several useful documents.

Outside Britain, I received assistance in Germany from the Berlin Document Center, the Bundesarchiv, and the Deutsches Rundfunkarchiv. In the United States I profited from files held in the National Archives in Washington, the Special Collections at Rutgers University and the Hoover Institution at Stanford. I also benefited from manuscripts in the University of Tulsa, the Beinecke Library at Yale and the State Historical Society in Wisconsin. In Dublin I read official papers in the Irish Military Archives.

When pursuing these sources I was taken away from the University Library in Sheffield, which over many years has been an important base for my work. Even so, this study reveals a continuing link. I have drawn especially on the impressive, increasing supply of material on fascism in its Special Collections Department.

Colleagues in Sheffield were always helpful. At one point in my text coded messages become important and some University library staff prefer to have their assistance recognised in code. They include 'Jeeves' and

'The Doctor.' 'The Mouse,' proved unfailingly supportive. 'Super Sleuth,' who died recently, an excellent historical detective seriously under-rated by the institution, solved a number of problems, as she had in my earlier research. Moving into the sharper world of direct identity, I am especially indebted to Chris Jones, whose help went far beyond the call of duty. As did Alistair Allan's. I found Lawrence Aspden's support in the Library's Special Collections of enormous benefit. I remain extremely grateful to him, his successor Jacky Hodgson, and all her staff. From the University's History Department I received early help from Richard Thurlow. Later, Dr Gary Rivett made a number of decisive interventions. Dr David Martin's sharp editorial eye saved me from solecism and factual error. James Pearson performed some of his impressive computer wizardry. Dr Graham Macklin was supportive throughout. His work makes an important contribution to the history of British fascism. I benefited, too, from interventions by members of other Departments, including Professor Gerald Newton and Dr Chris Spencer. Professor Robert Russell, who helped with Russian-language material, deserves a special mention. Professor Craig Brandist and Dušan Radunović assisted with sources in the Russian State Military Archive in Moscow.

Beyond the Steel City, Professor Chris Woolgar of Southampton University and his staff provided a welcoming ambience in the Parkes Library. Other university archivists, including Sheila Noble at Edinburgh, Maureen Shettle at Surrey, Martin Killeen and Mark Eccleston at Birmingham, responded promptly to my queries. Chris Terrey at Birkbeck College and Richard Temple, archivist at Senate House, assisted with University of London materials. In the United States, Dave Kuzma at Rutgers, Ronald Bulatoff at Stanford, Becca Lloyd at Yale and Katie Lee at Tulsa deserve special mention. Academic friends have again been generous with advice. They include Dr Enda Delaney, Professor Tony Kushner and Professor Don MacRaild. The late Professor Douglas Johnson intervened significantly. Professor Lord Skidelsky undertook several initiatives on my behalf. Professor Michael Biddiss and Professor Christie Davies offered sound advice. So did Professor Richard Griffiths. Professor Sir Elihu Lauterpacht QC generously provided material from his father's archive. Professor Tim Bergfelder, Professor Charmian Brinson, Professor L. Kettenacker and the late Professor Kurt Lipstein responded to my queries. Professor Geoffrey Alderman, Professor J. J. Barnes, Professor Dr Jan

Lucassen, Dr David Mayall, Dr Matt O'Brien, Dr Jo Reilly, the late Professor Hamish Ritchie and Professor Michael Weiner were all supportive. Professor Seán Ó Coileáin assisted with a Gaelic source.

I have gained enormously from my contacts beyond the increasingly pressured institutions of higher education. Francis Beckett has been a constant source of encouragement over many years and I felt his presence in this most recent work. Bryan Clough offered some provocative ideas. Rosemary Goad, who helped to produce the first biography of Joyce, added to my thoughts. Graeme Atkinson devilled for me in Germany. Sim Smiley and John Elliott assisted in the United States. The late Nigel Acheson, once of the BBC, later an independent producer of radio programmes, granted me access to his archive. Derek Denton generously opened his collection of materials. Lorna Swire, a former BBC monitor, offered some vivid testimony. John Davies took time away from patients to help in the complex task of understanding Joyce's personality. Dr David O'Donoghue assisted with Irish matters. At a late stage so did Rik Kavanagh. Eva Neustadt of the William Morris Organisation in New York provided a copy of an unpublished but performed work on Joyce. I am grateful to Jeffrey Hatcher, its author, for allowing me to read it. In one vital instance Martin Dawes of Sheffield Newspapers brought home the continuing power of the press. I spoke several times to James Clark, who knew Joyce in the Berlin Funkhaus. The Friends of Oswald Mosley were initially interested in my work but, aware of its drift, became detached from it. Heather Iandolo, one of Joyce's daughters, shared thoughts and sources with me, and also allowed me to consult her father's prison letters, though I doubt she will cherish my considered image of him. But I have to write as I find. "Sincere thanks to the late Michael Ralf Forman, Esq of the 'Forman Archive' for his kindness in making available and supplying both unique copyright material in the form of photocopies of the unique historical original death cell letters from William Joyce to Margaret Joyce and allowing the use of extracts from the same, as well as extracts from both William Joyce and Margaret Joyce's original wartime and post-war diaries of unique unpublished copyright material. The present copyright holder is Mr Michael Adrian Forman (Forman Archive)." Michael and Angela Joyce kindly allowed me to read through materials collected by Quentin Joyce. At an early stage I received help from the late Joan Cole. The staff of Savoy Books, Manchester, made intriguing suggestions that required attention. I am also indebted to the late Kevan Bleach, the late Richard Boston, Michael Brearley, knowledgeable on psychotherapy as well as cricket, Roger Boyes, Bob Briscoe, Ken Brown, Judge Graeme Bryson, Albert Cantor, Terry Charman, the late Ronald Creasy, Nigel Fallon, Bas. Grandfield, A. Hamer, Roger Howe, Patricia Hoare, Martin Jameson, Mary Kenny, the late Richard Kupsch, Nick Lowles, John Mathew, QC, Paul Meszaros, the late Wolf Mittler, the late Sir Reginald Murley, Kenneth Nichols, Wendy Petrie, Dr Peter Pugh, Geoffrey Robertson, QC, the late Dr Jimmy Shee, Kate Temple, Dr David Turner and especially Dr Rozina Visram.

A legion of archivists and librarians, beyond the Universities, responded to my enquiries, among them Stewart Mead at the Home Office, Rosemarie Nief and Marek Jaros at the Wiener Library, Julie Snelling and Jeff Walden at the BBC Written Archives Centre, Caversham, and, closer to home, Diane, Heather, Pat, Rachel as well as the late Gerry, in Sheffield City Library. Some of this last group have since been victims of the draconian cuts the local council recently imposed on its libraries. Kath Baker in Oldham, David Taylor in Manchester and Gabriel Sewell at Lambeth Palace, also deserve to be mentioned. Captain Stephen Mac Eoin made it a pleasure to work in the Irish Military Archives. Damien Burke at the Jesuit archives in Dublin, responded quickly to a late request. Nick Mays at *The Times* patiently tracked down elusive references. The late John Bodley, Robert Brown and Victor Gray, assisted with sources at Faber. Late on, I met Andy Simons of the British Library and benefited from his vast bibliographical knowledge of British fascism. Rob Perks and Alex King at the National Sound Archive were helpful as ever. One private collection remained closed to me.

Dr Helen Carter kindly volunteered to type my original manuscript. Hilka Bronski proofread the manuscript, typed the frequent revisions, drew my attention to sources, suggested amendments, and compiled the index for all of which I am grateful. Craig Fowlie at Routledge believed in the book as soon as he read it and has been a superb editor. It has also been a pleasure to work with his assistant, Emma Chappell. Any errors are mine alone.

Finally, research requires financial support. I therefore thank the Nuffield Foundation and the Hansard Trust. The administrators have waited patiently for the outcome. At last, here it is.

Colin Holmes, Sheffield, March 2015.

ARCHIVE ABBREVIATIONS

Documents ADM; BT; CRIM; CSC; FO; GFM; HO; INF; KV; LO; LCO; PIN; TS; WO – All from The National Archives, London

DOM – National Maritime Museum

FA – The Faber Archive

NARA – National Archives, Washington DC

RWA, YCAL – Rebecca West Archive, Yale University

RWC, Tulsa SC – Rebecca West Correspondence, University of Tulsa Special Collections

USSC – University of Sheffield Special Collections

WJ to ED – Prison Letters, William Joyce to Edmund Dunkerton

WJ to ES – Prison Letters, William Joyce to Ethel Scrimgeour

WJ to MJ – Prison Letters, William Joyce to Margaret Joyce

YCAL – Yale University Archive

INTRODUCTION

Why can't the past ever leave off, why must it be forever pawing at us, like a wheedling child. [John Banville, *The Untouchable* (London, 1997), p.392.]

Political biographies usually focus on the lives of powerful personalities who lead parties, determine policy, influence the history of their country or the world. William Joyce never headed a major political movement, never sat at Westminster, was never remarkable as an ideologist. Who was he? Why is he of interest?

Joyce grew up in the United States and Ireland before coming to England where, amid the global upheaval of the inter-war years, he committed himself to a political career. His first attachment was to the Tory Party. But he soon began to operate in fascist circles. In late August 1939 this commitment propelled him on a momentous voyage to Germany where he served throughout the War as a faithful political servant of Hitler. During these years he became better known and much reviled in Britain as Lord Haw-Haw, the broadcasting voice of the Nazis. In January 1946 Joyce paid the ultimate price for his actions. The British, acting on a controversial point of law, executed him for treason.

Such details alone are intriguing. But there is more to his life than these bare bones would suggest. As a result, he has intrigued Rebecca

West, Jack Cole, Francis Selwyn, Mary Kenny and Nigel Farndale. As both William Joyce and Lord Haw-Haw he has featured in film scripts, novels, plays and radio programmes.

Rebecca West's pioneering essay failed to fully capture his short yet notorious political career and that problem has persisted in biographies of Joyce. Partly because each fights shy of delving too deeply into his complex personality. The dead cannot be psychoanalysed. However, by reflecting on his writings, speeches and actions, observing his behaviour in different situations and registering the views of his contemporaries, insights can be gained into one of the powerful forces which helped to drive his politics. Bernard Crick adopted a similar approach when writing his life of Orwell.[1]

All earlier studies of Joyce reveal another problem. He did not pursue his short career in a vacuum. But insufficient attention has been given to the social-political influences which helped to power him on his turbulent journey. Ben Pimlott rightly emphasised that biography "focuses on character," yet added, significantly, "It is not about character abstracted from environment." It is "character in environment."[2] In Joyce's case, his fascist career in Britain, a vital prelude to his years in Germany, has never been thoroughly dissected. That same narrowness characterises existing accounts of his time with the Nazis. By painting his portrait on a bigger canvas, a better understanding emerges of how and why he operated.

Joyce's fascist politics soon became dominated by a searing Jew-hatred, which also calls for more attention. His hostility partly reflected that amorphous antipathy which circulated across all classes in inter-war Britain. But it soon transcended such sentiment. By the 1930s he would be recommending Jews should be eliminated, shot in the streets or hanged from lamp-posts. They were sub-human, ripe for elimination. He came to embrace an exterminatory strand of anti-Semitism.

When exploring these neglected avenues, I have drawn on new primary sources in official archives and private collections. Also, apart from relying on published academic texts – historical, legal, medical, psychological, and sociological – I have raided literary sources, oral testimony, radio recordings and visual evidence.

Finally, importantly, I have sought to avoid a trap. Following Rebecca West's essay, Joyce's biographers have been deceived by a carefully crafted deception. He lied constantly to enhance his image, and his family and friends have since campaigned to massage his standing, smooth out his viciousness. These combined influences have distorted all existing biographies.

The task of questioning our current knowledge of William Joyce, Lord Haw-Haw, offering new perspectives on his politics, probing further into his life, raising uncomfortable questions, while placing him in the context of twentieth-century history, begins here.

Notes

1   B. Crick, *George Orwell: A Life* (London, 1980), p.xxiii.
2   B. Pimlott, "It's all in the life," *New Statesman*, 6 November 1998, p.57.

PART I

Identities

1

EARLY LIFE

It is only in spy stories that things can be arranged slickly. In real life the wheels are all jagged and rusty from long exposure, and the grooves are invariably the wrong gauge. [Simon Raven, *Friends in Low Places* (London, 1965), p.25.]

1

This saga begins with an ending. Galway burials seldom feature in the British press. But on 20 August 1976 *The Times* reported that "William Joyce, Lord Haw-Haw, the propaganda radio broadcaster for Hitler during the last war will be buried in the Irish Republic this weekend."[1] His body, undisturbed in the bleak grounds of Wandsworth prison since his execution and solitary burial in the wintry days of January 1946, had just been lifted by permission of Roy Jenkins, the Home Secretary. These decayed fragments, placed in a lead-lined coffin, were loaded onto an Aer Lingus plane and then flown to the Irish Republic. There, on 21 August, at St Patrick's Roman Catholic Church, Galway, about two hundred people attended a burial service to hear Father Padraic Ó Laoi conduct a Latin Requiem Mass.[2] These mourners, swelled by a media presence, included people who had known the young Joyce in Ireland and members of his family.[3]

Heather Iandolo, one of Joyce's daughters, dressed in deepest black, silhouetted against the brilliant sunshine of the August afternoon, had been the driving force behind these events. The previous day she had told the press: "At last I have granted his last wish. In letters he wrote in his death cell he asked to be returned to Ireland. It has taken a long time but the Home Office have always been very helpful."[4] An informed source has queried whether the remains were Joyce's.[5] But this ceremony assumed a symbolic importance for a clearly relieved Mrs Iandolo.

Joyce's new resting place is Galway's Bohermore Cemetery, the Protestant section. He has a simple gravestone, a small white cross, where the word resurrection is misspelt and his date of birth – a contentious matter, as will soon become clear – appears as 23 April 1906. His reburial, marking the end of a turbulent life's journey, left him lying beside a Rainsbury and a Tuckwell.

2

In the late nineteenth century many Irish people died far beyond their birthplace.[6] Large numbers undertook the journey to England, where important settlements developed in London and also Liverpool, that most Irish of English cities. In Scotland, Glasgow acted as a similar magnet. This continuous movement became especially heavy between 1841 and 1861, the years of the Great Hunger. As the century wore on, as steam replaced sail, a growing number of migrants ventured further afield, particularly to the United States, a country which appealed to them because it had played no part in the bloody conquest of Ireland. As a result, "between 1856 and 1921 the last great waves of Irish emigration broke on American shores" and "during this period more Irishmen and – women left their native land than in the preceding two and a half centuries." Many counties experiencing this unusually heavy emigration were situated on the western seaboard.[7]

Joyce's father featured in this growing exodus. Michael Francis Joyce, an elusive figure in this saga, was born in or near Ballinrobe in County Mayo. One claim is that he was born in 1868.[8] However, Intelligence files suggest 9 December 1866.[9] Another source has agreed on 1866 but a date of 12 December.[10] Other details are more certain. Michael's father, Martin, who had married Mary Naughton, earned a respectable living as a farmer.[11] But in 1888, rather than follow in his father's footsteps, Michael left for a new life in America. He envisaged his long-term future in the golden land and in 1892 in the Court of Common Pleas, Hudson County, New Jersey, began proceedings to become an American citizen. He completed this process on 25 October 1894, with fellow Irishman John Duane as his witness.[12]

The American economy grew strongly in the late nineteenth century, the age of the Robber Barons, those successful, ruthless capitalists who significantly influenced the country's economic development, and Michael made money in the railway and building booms. He worked for the Griffin Ironworks on the Pennsylvania railway and, underlining the importance of Irish family networks, became a partner in the Naughton Construction Company of Brooklyn.[13] America offered better prospects but from time to time Michael would return to Ireland and on one visit met Gertrude Emily Brooke, in the Skeffington Arms Hotel, Galway. She was accompanying her father on a fishing holiday. The couple kept in touch before Michael proposed by post.[14]

There is a suggestion that Gertrude, often called Queenie, was born in 1879 at Crompton in Lancashire. However, the Registrar-General's records, confirmed in a 1917 police report, have 28 August 1878.[15] She came from a prosperous family and lived at 27 Manchester Road, Shaw, with her parents William and Emily, a grandmother on her father's side, and three brothers Edgar, Gilbert and William Emile. The Brookes had long relied on having 'downstairs' young women servants to cater for their everyday needs.[16]

William Brooke, the head of the family, was born in Roscommon. A graduate of Galway, Manchester and Edinburgh, he practised as a doctor and when Gertrude expressed her wish to marry, was serving as Medical Officer of Health for the Urban District of Crompton.[17] When he died in April 1914 the local press, faithful to the language of its day, described him as "a noted practitioner" and one of the town's "most respected residents" who, "in a quiet way," had selflessly given years of service to the community. The flag flew at half-mast on Shaw's Town Hall. Joyce's parents attended his funeral, riding in the second carriage.[18] Emily, Dr Brooke's widow, followed him to the grave, much more quietly, on 28 March 1917.[19]

Dr Brooke came from the predominantly Catholic part of Ireland. But he and his family were staunch Protestants and objected to Gertrude marrying out of their faith. It would not have been unusual for the Brookes, belonging to a religious minority, to have developed this entrenched view. But class differences might also have concerned them. Their substantial wills reflected not only Dr Brooke's professional standing but also a regular flow of rental income derived from property investments. These documents also revealed in their tortuous legal prose an obsessive concern with preserving a 'dynasty.' It remained a bourgeois household to its core.

However, Gertrude possessed a decidedly steely personality. Her first-born son remarked later how stubborn she could be.[20] And in 1905, accompanied by her brother Edgar, a practising solicitor with offices in Clegg Street, Oldham, she sailed out of Liverpool on the *Campania* bound for New York and her future husband, arriving at Ellis Island on 30 April 1905.[21] She was carrying the sizeable sum of $250.[22] Her brother, now consigned to historical obscurity, travelled with her just before his life began to disintegrate. He became an alcoholic and by 1907 his name had disappeared from the Law List. Gilbert Brooke later told lawyers, teasingly, that his brother had accompanied Gertrude to America because "my mother wanted to know the thing was done properly."[23] Gertrude married Michael on 2 May 1905 in a Roman Catholic service at All Saints' Church, Madison Avenue, 129th Street.[24]

Their first child, it is said, was born at 1377 Herkimer Street, Brooklyn, on 24 April 1906 and registered on 3 May as William Joyce. When registered, his mother apparently wanted the name William Brooke Joyce.[25] He appears as such in the *Oxford Dictionary of National Biography*.[26] But Gertrude lost that struggle. Did her wish reflect a family preference, a dynastic whim? Did it suggest more? Whatever the reason, Michael objected. However, Joyce sometimes regarded himself as William Brooke Joyce – his baptised name – a preference known only to "the family and a small circle of friends."[27] Why, it must be asked, was there this need for secrecy?

And there are related questions. In later life Joyce would shift his birthplace to suit his convenience. Sometimes he offered Galway; on other occasions New York.[28] His responses underline how dissembling he could be.

More puzzling, much harder to understand, is the confusion surrounding *when* he was born, a problem his biographers have persistently ignored. After Michael and Gertrude had disembarked from the *Lusitania* on 13 September 1907 following a visit to England, they told staff at Ellis Island that their son, travelling with them, was born in November 1906.[29] When Joyce applied for a British passport in 1933 he gave his birthdate as 24 April 1906. But his 1944 German passport suggested 11 March 1906.[30] Sometimes 1906 disappears altogether. When admitted to Lambeth Hospital in 1924 for a severe facial wound, a traumatised Joyce informed staff he had been born in 1904.[31] An even earlier date appeared in 1939 when he contacted Gabbitas Thring regarding a teaching post. The interviewer disbelieved Joyce's claim to be thirty-three, writing on the company's record card that the applicant was in fact thirty-six.[32] What exactly did this interviewer know?

Moving onto surer ground, a document from 1906 records Joyce's birth in New York, on 24 April of that year. Gertrude and Michael received a copy of this certificate in 1917, just after the death of Emily Brooke, when Gertrude became a beneficiary of her mother's estate. And there is a curiosity here. Emily's will, dated 29 October 1916, referred to only one grandchild, though other grandchildren alive on her death were eligible to inherit. Gertrude probably requested a copy of the US birth certificate to prove she had a child. Yet when Dr Brooke had died three years earlier, a wreath had been sent by "Queenie, Michael and Sonny."[33] Why could Emily Brooke not bring herself to recognise William directly in her will? It is all extremely strange.

The US certificate registered a home birth in Brooklyn and bore the signature of Dr Charles Francis Yerdon, a physician practising at 1276 Herkimer Street. American medical records record his death in 1937, but he appears to have been absent during all US census returns between 1900 and 1930.[34] To have missed one, but to have missed more . . . ? There is a mystery here, too. Gertrude and Michael were so fortunate to have found him at home. Joyce eventually acquired a copy of the certificate signed by Yerdon. Exactly when is uncertain, but he knew of it during his early politicking in England.

Joyce's responses when asked about his place, and especially his date of birth, are therefore puzzling. And why did his parents mirror this inconsistency? Why erect 'Keep Out' signs? All families have their secrets; what was the 'ghost' in Joyce's case?[35] What should be made of his statement to Lambeth Hospital and the suspicions at Gabbitas Thring, both of which suggest he was born before his parents had married?

Whenever, wherever he was born, no-one has disputed that Michael Joyce, an American citizen since 1894, was William's natural father. Any child of Michael's born subsequently in the United States would have been American.[36] In English law, so would any child he fathered, who during its infancy lived in America even if born in Ireland or in England. The 1870 Naturalisation Act was clear on that point.[37] And William certainly spent part of his early life in New York.

An American admirer has described the Brooklyn where Joyce lived as now being "a nest of Puerto Ricans."[38] Another has called it "a black hell hole not fit for Aryans to live in."[39] However, in the early twentieth century it had a different ambience.[40] During their time there the family lived in "a substantial house standing at the corner of a tree-lined street in an Irish neighbourhood."[41] In this predominantly Roman Catholic area everyday life was largely moulded by "the dictates of a superannuated [church] hierarchy"; as a result, "creativity was suspect, independent thinking anathema."[42] Joyce's early days were therefore tightly ordered, hedged in by social-religious restrictions.

3

Joyce spent only a short time in Brooklyn. The family crossed the Atlantic quite frequently. They have been noticed in 1907 on the *Lusitania*. The following year William and his mother sailed on the *Mauritania*.[43] This 1908 Atlantic journey, which returned them to the bosom of the Brooke family, is probably significant. In teeming, throbbing, multi-ethnic America Gertrude soon began to experience intense feelings of loneliness.[44] She needed to escape. Her situation partly explains why in the following year the family returned to the old world, to Ireland. Michael left first. William and his mother followed.[45]

Their return from America might also have reflected other pressures. William Brooke did not stand at Gertrude's side when she married. But arriving in New York on the *Carmania* on 25 July 1906 carrying a generally recognized considerable sum of $1000, he told the immigration authorities he had come to visit his daughter. By providing this money was he showing that he had become reconciled to Gertrude's marriage? Or were Gertrude and Michael experiencing money problems? Disembarking later from the *Cedric* on 28 August 1909, he informed immigration staff that on this occasion he had travelled to meet his son-in-law.[46] Had a business dispute involving Michael in New York put him in some financial difficulty?[47] Significantly, Edgar Brooke's will, drawn up in 1917, specifically, though not by name, excluded Michael Joyce as a possible beneficiary. Did this condition reflect no more than yet another Brooke interest in the family's dynasty? Did Edgar cast out his Catholic brother-in-law on religious grounds? Or had Michael not always revealed a sure touch with money?[48] In the Brookes' unyielding commercial gospel any such stumbling alone would have been sufficient reason to exclude him.

In Ireland, Michael, Gertrude and William settled first in County Mayo, where the ever-adaptable Michael bought a pub at Ayle.[49] Did Brooke family money help here? Then in 1913 the family uprooted to Galway.

This city where they stayed for the remainder of their time in Ireland still carried architectural traces of its earlier links with Spain, especially its once-flourishing trade in wine and salt. However, in 1912 a traveller lamented the progressive loss of the old whilst noticing the new. "The old houses require looking for," he wrote, and "in recent years many of them have sunk into complete dilapidation, or have been destroyed in the ordinary course of street alterations or rebuildings."[50] Galway had almost doubled in size and, with his New York business experience, Michael Joyce probably welcomed this transformation. Every age presents investment opportunities and, for the enterprising with a little capital, there was money to be made. Michael bought up houses and acted as a landlord to the Royal Irish

Constabulary. In 1920 he also became a shareholder in and general manager of the local bus company.[51]

The Joyces lived at various addresses in Galway before buying 1 Rutledge Terrace, Rockbarton, Salthill, outside the city centre and quite close to the beach. Michael retained this property until 1930.[52] He and Gertrude later bought other houses in the terrace which they rented out to tenants.[53] By accumulating their Galway properties they were perhaps consciously following the example of Dr and Mrs Brooke, hoping to succeed as comfortably-off rentiers. Chez Joyce was once described as "a two-storey comfortable-looking house with a tiny walled garden, in a pleasantly-secluded position just off the promenade."[54] Today it remains an attractive property and in that sense William grew up in a generous environment.

He first attended the Convent of Mercy School before enrolling in 1915 at the Jesuit-run St. Ignatius's College, which in 1861 had left its premises in the centre of Galway and moved out to Sea Road. Here he gave the impression of being an intelligent pupil but with a consummate ability to get under the skin of his contemporaries. One of them, Brendan Fox, later an Augustinian, disliked him on account of his showy cleverness.[55] Even a sympathetic source has described Joyce as "a boy with an air of childish arrogance."[56]

However, his teachers were impressed and Billy Naughton, a schoolboy contemporary, recalled an essay by the fourteen-year-old Joyce that was read out to the entire school. "It was a superb day, the summer sun shone on the tranquil waters of Lough Corrib," the young author began. Jimmy Shee, another schoolboy, never forgot those opening lines.[57] Joyce also became proficient in Latin, French and German. Yet he was more than a grubber of academic detail. He sailed, skated and became competent with his fists.[58]

Shee became a doctor and his unvarnished recollections, which reflected his later medical training, paint a picture of the young William never before brought before the public. He recalled that Joyce, whom he described as "of quaint but not of rebarbative aspect," was "less than five feet and six inches in height" and had "noticeably short arms and legs." His complexion was sallow and, Shee remarked, "his cranium commodious, noticeably so compared with his small jaws and pouting lips." He also pictured Joyce's eyes having "transverse ridges of skin running across his upper lids" which "gave him a slightly oriental cast of countenance." This distinctive appearance was enhanced by a broken nose sustained during a schoolboy brawl.[59]

Billy Naughton, also drawing on school memories, described Joyce as being scruffy, with hardly any interest in clothes.[60] There might have been some backward projection here, with Naughton's memory being influenced by Joyce's later disordered dress sense. In any case, it all depends what is meant by scruffy. Different, certainly, as other evidence suggests. Jimmy Shee noticed that Joyce invariably wore "a sort of connemara tweed, with knee britches fastened with buckles over thick woolen stockings below his knees" and a "disproportionately long" jacket.[61] This style gave him a strikingly quaint appearance. But was it precisely that impression his mother intended? Was she deliberately separating him from the everyday, the commonplace?[62]

That suggestion of being different surfaced at other times. On Sundays, when Gertrude left for a Protestant service, Michael took William in the family's pony and trap to worship at a Roman Catholic church.[63] Many childhood contemporaries had to walk. William was being raised as a special little boy.

4

Joyce's family life affected his development in other ways. Gilbert Brooke remarked that religious differences between his sister and Michael made for "a most unhappy" marriage.[64] The nature of Michael's and Gertrude's relationship is impossible now to recreate in any detail. But strong religious tensions were certainly present. Gertrude now lies in an unfindable plot in a Chadderton graveyard, close to her Lancashire roots, not at the side of the man she had married in New York in 1905.[65] The young William soon found himself caught between two opposing forms of Christianity and his emotional closeness to his mother proved critical here. The Roman Church's view that she was damned soon alienated him from Catholicism and Christianity generally. His parents' relationship might also have been affected by the long shadow cast by the influential Brooke family, who had disapproved of Gertrude's marriage. Such pressures alone guaranteed Joyce did not enjoy that "certainty, trust, and quietude" which make for an individual's psychological balance.[66] A throwaway remark to his "slightly strained" home circumstances is significant.[67]

While his father remained throughout a "remote and authoritarian figure" his mother effectively appropriated William.[68] Her boy provided the emotional support she desperately needed, isolated in New York and Galway. He quickly became "the whole focus for her daily life."[69] Gertrude undoubtedly, understandably, cherished her son but, without necessarily realising it, rather than being responsive to his needs was busy imposing her agenda on their relationship.[70] She imprisoned him in her world. His school attendance was affected by illness but his absences also probably reflected her reluctance to let him go, hand him over to his teachers. She needed him.[71] He belonged to her, not to anyone else. "Probably thoroughly spoiled from conception," William was "much fussed over."[72]

Joyce – the first and for some time only child – was helping his mother at this time through her dark emotional nights.[73] They thus became attached, "comme la bouteille à l'ivrogne," as Baudelaire wrote of another relationship, which led him to bubble over "with self-importance."[74] And it had its effect. "I never could suffer fools gladly," he later remarked.[75]

His mother not only clung to him. Coming from a more cultured background than her husband, she doubtless encouraged her son's scholarly interests, which created such a seething mixed stew of admiration, envy and hostility among his school contemporaries. With his "very precocious" intellectual development, he would surely become important.[76]

Behaving thus, she might have been seeking a compensatory life through William. One day she would bathe contentedly in all the reflected glory of 'Sonny,' the apple of her eye, her young literary dazzler. When lonely in the west of Ireland, did she murmur softly he was the sugar in her tea? Did she whisper soothingly, "Without you at the center . . . there is no empire"?[77] From what can now be gleaned of their relationship, such imaginings carry a ring of truth.

Gertrude's abiding influence was felt in another sense. Marooned in a fiercely nationalist part of Ireland, she remained determined to raise an English gentleman. A playwright's portrayal of her saying to

William, "We may not be in England but we carry England in our heart. We are loyal to the idea," is quite believable.[78]

5

Joyce's outlook on life was further influenced during these years by his teachers. They puffed up his talents. The likes of Father Nolan, a Jesuit schoolmaster at St. Ignatius's, initially had him under their sway as a bright boy to be encouraged in his cleverness, and he must have grown taller when hearing his essay read to the entire school. The priests believed if he stepped out of line the swishing cane would quickly return him to their fold. However, he rebelled and rejected their religion. Why could they not accommodate his Protestant mother? But their influence remained.[79] His photographic memory retained all their praises.[80] If told repeatedly he was a clever boy, how could he deny his distinctiveness?

6

In a crime novelist's words, "You [cannot] wash out memories completely, no matter how unpleasant. They [leave] their traces everywhere in the overlooked corners of your mind, and in the sensations of your body."[81] Joyce's family life and school days helped to create a little god, with an overbearing sense of self-importance who always believed he knew best about everything.[82]

7

Joyce took forward not only these influences. Political conflicts then building up in Galway which pressed upon him – and his entire family – also had their consequences. According to a perceptive foreign commentator, early twentieth-century Ireland "[was] at a turning point in her history." He continued: "The Constabulary in Ireland is a military force, an army of occupation encamped in a foreign country," it is "a supplementary corps of the regular army ... stationed in Ireland as a main guarantee of the security of British rule."[83] Joyce's pro-British family welcomed their presence.[84] But many neighbours felt differently. Fierce landlord and tenant disputes flared up in Kerry, Mayo and Galway and in 1916, as tensions grew during the Easter Rising in Dublin, Irish nationalists could frequently be seen drilling in the Galway area.[85]

By 1919 the Black and Tans, special constables recruited to support the Royal Irish Constabulary, had appeared in the city to control the restive local population and in July 1920 they were supplemented by the Auxiliary Division, made up of ex-British Army officers. "Heavily armed, absurdly lacking in police experience or training, and unrestrained by the discipline normally imposed on armed men under military law, the 'Auxies' pushed violent response to the level of counter-terrorism."[86]

In these increasingly uncertain days, in May 1920 the British appointed Ormonde de l'Epée Winter, an ex-soldier who had served in India and in the Great War, as Deputy Chief of Police and Director of Intelligence in Ireland. His brief was to penetrate and neutralise the ranks of the nationalists. Joyce was about to step outside the influences of home and school and gain his first taste of political activity.[87] This experience proved crucial in how his life developed. Joyce's opposition to Irish nationalism drew him into the net of the security service and he began to assist the British Army in dangerous, lonely work against the nationalists. Years later, recalling their Galway days, Miles Webb wrote, "I am afraid that I . . . was a bit proud of being the more or less only friend of such a firebrand pro-Britisher."[88]

Did the monocled Winter, a cigarette perpetually dangling from his lips, and who sometimes appeared in disguise with a "chestnut moustache and wig, trench coat, flannel trousers and bowler hat" – thereby looking, in a civil servant's words, "the most complete swine" – ever directly recruit any pro-British assets?[89] In Joyce's case, certainly, someone else brought him on board. Captain Patrick William Keating was to die in May 1922 when HMS *Egypt* went down off Ushant, but had served earlier as head of British Army Intelligence in Galway.[90] His two sons attended St. Ignatius's and these personal links probably brought Joyce and Keating together.[91] Later, when Joyce applied to join the OTC (Officers Training Corps) at the University of London he claimed to have served under the British officer in an Intelligence capacity.[92]

Contemporaries would recall Willie Joyce gaily, brazenly, associating with British soldiers, riding imperiously alongside them through the streets of Galway.[93] He also fraternised with the Black and Tans on the outskirts of the town at Lenaboy Castle.[94] But did his activity amount to anything significant?

Joyce's version of his life at this time has been dismissed as "youthful bombast."[95] He has been called a nuisance, more than anything.[96] He would certainly not have been involved in any high-level intelligence gathering. More likely – evidence is elusive – he acted as a courier and, keeping his eyes and ears open, reported on overheard conversations that wafted through the air amid the curl of men's tobacco smoke.

Even a minor role carried risks, particularly since Joyce's political activities became an open secret in Galway and, following the July 1921 Truce and the Anglo-Irish Treaty of December 1921, which paved the way for the country's eventual partition, his position became precarious. Dangerous to a degree that the IRA deputed a lieutenant to kill the young lad. The would-be assassin has never been named. A hint, but no more, of his identity appeared recently.[97] More than eighty years on, he can be identified as Michael Molloy. On a darkening December afternoon in '21 he lay waiting. His Lee Enfield was primed. The young lad would come into range as he went home from school. One shot. The nuisance would be eliminated. Fate seldom smiled on Joyce. But for once it did. Michael Joyce, alert to danger, had moved his family to another, safer, house he owned in Victoria Place. His son dodged the would-be assassin's bullet.[98]

The early '20s were also frightening days for his family. A property leased by Michael to the Royal Irish Constabulary was torched and destroyed.[99] The pro-British Joyces – feeling completely abandoned – retained an abiding sense of bitterness at their treatment. In the acidulous word of Quentin Joyce, a younger brother, "my parents and the family were forced out of Ireland . . . at the point of the gun on account of our love and loyalty towards the British Crown."[100] Michael retained property in Salthill for some time, but his hopes had taken a severe battering. So had Gertrude's. She had inherited quite substantial sums from her mother and brother Edgar, but these dramatic events in Ireland proved devastating.[101] Twenty years on, the estates of Gertrude and Michael, though respectable, would reveal how far their bourgeois dreams had crumbled.[102]

8

Captain Keating's conscience was pricked, or possibly he felt a sense of indebtedness about using Joyce, because soon after the 1921 Truce it became "widely known" in Galway that he had arranged for his courier and informant to be mustered into the Worcestershire Regiment. "In Galway there was no-one but Keating . . . who would have had the authority or motivation" to put this plan into operation.[103] Joyce left Ireland with the Worcesters on 9 December 1921, bound for their barracks at Norton. His military life would prove brief, however. He was discharged within a few months on health grounds and because he was underage. He had informed the military authorities he was born on 6 December 1903.[104]

9

Joyce would remain a fierce opponent of Irish nationalism. He also carried with him a bigger and linked fear, that the events in Ireland would have a disastrous domino effect. "He and his family . . . were . . . the casualties of failing Empire," and "Out of this experience grew a counter-revolutionary creed."[105] The "obsolete England" he had been brought up to worship, almost blindly, was being destroyed by its "shabby" and "dishonest" politicians.[106] The Liberals, weak on Ireland, were particularly dangerous; his initial political commitment would be to the Conservative Party.

His political activity in Ireland affected him in another sense. It "brought him to early maturity as a willing recruit for the politics of the street fight."[107] The power, the terror, and the violence he experienced when mixing with the military in Galway, all that the testosterone-fuelled excitement and euphoria, never left him.[108] He had witnessed a neighbour, a policeman, with a bullet in his head. He had seen a Sinn Féiner captured and killed by the police. He had known "Battle, murder and sudden death" from "an early age."[109] These vivid impressions burnt their way into his young psyche.

Politics was more than a sophisticated form of drawing-room activity. Someone who knew him well remarked his youthful immersion in Irish politics, its perpetual violence and constant treachery, also made him extremely calculating.[110] He was certainly watchful. At London University in the 1920s he once brought his OTC rifle into lectures and sat menacingly with it on the front row. Enemies might descend at any time, from any direction. You had to be prepared. He would remain ever-alert for political foes, find them in so many places, and display boundless energy for plotting against them.[111]

10

Joyce spent only about a quarter of his short life in Ireland and none of it as an adult. But his experiences at home, in school, and with the British army, the guardians of his Empire, seriously affected him. Knowing the child helps us to know the man. Even if later pressures influenced his political outlook.

Joyce's thoughts often returned to Ireland. Yet to claim his reburial there in 1976 reflected his deepest wish is one of the many myths surrounding him. He had other ideas. However, a condemned man does not choose his burial site. He was despatched to the prison grounds at Wandsworth and remained there until his symbolic transfer to Ireland, where our search for him has just begun.

Notes

1 *The Times*, 20 August 1976. *Daily Mirror*, 9 January 1976, on earlier developments. Anticipating his reburial *The Sunday Post*, 11 January 1976 carried a feature on him.

2 *The Times*, 21 August 1976; *Daily Telegraph*, 21 August 1976; *Galway Advertiser*, 26 August 1976. Following Joyce's reburial, John Amery's family petitioned for his body to be removed from Wandsworth. He too had been executed for treason. His ashes were subsequently scattered in the Dordogne, close to the remains of a former lover. D. Faber, *Speaking for England. Leo, Julian and John Amery: The Tragedy of a Political Family* (London, 2005), p.534.

3 *Daily Telegraph*, 21 August 1976; *Daily Mail*, 21 August 1976; private information.

4 *The Times*, 20 August 1976. *The Guardian*, 6 January 1976, for the Home Office consenting to her request. See her later reflections in the *Daily*

Express, 11 February 1995; *Jewish Chronicle*, 17 February 1995; *Sunday Telegraph*, 20 October 1996.

5 Private information.

6 R. F. Foster, *The Oxford History of Ireland* (Oxford, 1989), p.175.

7 K. A. Miller, *Emigration and Exiles: Ireland and the Irish Exodus to North America* (New York.1995), pp.345, 349.

8 J. A. Cole, *Lord Haw-Haw: The Full Story of William Joyce* (London, 1987. First ed.1964), p.18. All subsequent references are to the 1987 paperback. The first edition carried the title, *Lord Haw-Haw and William Joyce. The Full Story*.

9 KV 2/246/406.

10 M. Kenny, *Germany Calling: A Personal Biography of William Joyce, 'Lord Haw-Haw'* (Dublin, 2003), p.26.

11 KV 2/246/395A.

12 KV 2/246.

13 KV 2/246/479c.

14 "Dear Old Daddy," RTÉ, 15 September 1999.

15 Cole, *Lord Haw-Haw*, p.19, offers 1879. But see CRIM 1/483, Police Superintendent, Rochdale to Lancashire's Chief Constable, 25 June 1917.

16 RG 12/3324, Folio 78 (1891 census) and RG 13/3830 Folio 122 (1901 census).

17 *The Medical Directory*, 1905.

18 *Oldham Standard*, 22 April 1914.

19 Emily Brooke left just over £7000. Probate Records, General Register Office, England and Wales.

20 WJ to ES, 11 July 1945.

21 www.libertyellisislandfoundation.org. Record 0456. Last accessed 31 March 2015. KV 2/245/338a; NARA, FBI File RG 65, Box 26.

22 www.libertyellisislandfoundation.org. Record 0456. Last accessed 31 March 2015.

23 Statement of Gilbert Brooke, Curtis-Bennett Archive.

24 J.W. Hall (ed.), *Trial of William Joyce* (London, 1946), p.102.

25 Cole, *Lord Haw-Haw*, p.19.

26 H.C.G. Matthew and B. Harrison (eds), *Oxford Dictionary of National Biography*, Vol.30 (Oxford, 2004), pp.803–804. Henceforth *ODNB*.

27 Cole, *Lord Haw-Haw*, p.19.

28 Hall (ed.), *Trial*, pp.85–86.

29 www.libertyellisislandfoundation.org. Records 0061–0062. Last accessed 31 March 2015.

30 Hall (ed.), *Trial*, pp.85–86.

31 London Metropolitan Archive, HL/L/B24/109 case no.72146.

32 Photocopy of record card at Gabbitas Thring.

33 *Oldham Standard*, 25 April 1914.

34 Detail on Yerdon (1867–1937) from National Genealogical Society in the United States to author, 9 September 2005.

35 J. Lanchester, *Family Romance* (London, 2007), on family lies and deceptions.

36 Hall (ed.), *Trial*, p.133.

37 The Public General Acts passed in the thirty-third and thirty-fourth years of the reign of her Majesty Queen Victoria . . . (London, 1870), p.114; Hall (ed.), *Trial*, p.100.

38 Joseph Quinlan, "William Joyce, Martyr and Model" (National Vanguard Tape).

39 John Metzger, in *War. White Aryan Resistance*, September 1993.

40 K. T. Jackson (ed.), *Encyclopaedia of New York City* (New Haven, 1988), pp.148–153.

41 F. Selwyn, *Hitler's Englishman: The Crime of Lord Haw-Haw* (London, 1993), p.13. R. West, *The Meaning of Treason* (London, 1949), p.14. All subsequent West references to this edition unless stated.

42 D. T. Casey, "Heresy in the Diocese of Brooklyn: An Unholy Trinity," in D.T. Casey and R. E. Rhodes (eds), *Irish-American Fiction. Essays in Criticism* (New York, 1979), pp.153–154.

43 www.libertyellisislandfoundation.org. Records 0698–0699. Last accessed 31 March 2015.

44 *Hamburger Fremdenblatt*, 6 October 1944.

45 Cole, *Lord Haw-Haw*, pp.19–20.

46 William Brooke's journeys appear in the passenger lists. www.liberty ellisislandfoundation.org. Records 0235 and 0190-0191. Last accessed 31 March 2015.

47 Kenny, *Germany Calling*, p.39 notes business problems in America.

48 Edgar Brooke's will, 13 October 1917, National Archives of Scotland, SC53/47/17.

49 Kenny, *Germany Calling*, p.41.

50 J. Cooke, *Handbook for Travellers in Ireland* (London, 1912), p.254.

51 HO 144/22707, Advisory Committee to consider Appeals against Internment, 19 December 1940, Frank Joyce. Kenny, *Germany Calling*, p.55.

52 Kenny, *Germany Calling*, p.70.

53 KV 2/249/54b records Michael Joyce owning the other properties. WJ to MJ, 30 December 1945, suggesting former tenants might assist Margaret in writing her husband's biography.

54 Cole, *Lord Haw-Haw*, p.20.

55 Interview, 1 April 1992.

56 Kenny, *Germany Calling*, p.49.

57 J. Shee, unpublished typescript, p.103. Shee's recollections stretched back to 1919 when he came to know Frank Joyce. Altogether Michael and Gertrude had five children. Francis Martin, known as Frank, was born in 1912. Quentin in 1917, Joan in 1920 and Robert in 1922. Kenny, *Germany Calling*, pp 55, 69, on family members.

58 Cole, *Lord Haw-Haw*, pp.20–21.

59 Shee, ts, pp.104, 115.

60 Kenny, *Germany Calling*, p.52.

61 Shee, ts, p.115, spelling as in original.

62 O. Kernberg, *Borderline Conditions and Pathological Narcissism* (New Jersey, 1990), p.235.

63 Kenny, *Germany Calling*, p.43.

64 KV 2/245/230.

65 Burial recorded in the parish register of St Matthew's, 22 September 1944.

66 J. M. Glass, "Hobbes and Narcissism. Pathology in the State of Nature," *Political Theory*, Vol.8 (1980), p.350, on "certainty trust and quietude."

67 N. Farndale, *Haw-Haw: The Tragedy of William and Margaret Joyce* (London, 2006), p.48. All later references are to this edition.

68 *Ibid*. p.46 on Michael's remoteness.

69 Kenny, *Germany Calling*, p.38.

70 *Ibid*. notes Joyce being "hugely cherished." P. Mollon (ed.), *The Fragile Self: The Structure of Narcissistic Disturbance* (London, 1993), p.85 on likely personality effects.

71 Kenny, *Germany Calling*, p.46.

72 *Ibid*. p.37, draws back from exploring how such treatment affected his personality.

73 Kernberg, *Borderline Conditions*, p.235, for the likely effect on him.

74 KV 2/249/54b.

75 KV 2/250, 24 March 1945.

76 KV 2/245/1b.

77 J. Hatcher, "Hanging Lord Haw-Haw," unpublished typescript, p.8.

78 *Ibid*.

79 James Clark claimed whenever Joyce discussed politics he reflected the influence of the Jesuits. James Clark to A. Weiss, 27 March 1995 (private archive).

80 USSC, MS 238/7/11, John Macnab, "Material for a work on William Joyce," p.3.

81 S. Booth, *Dancing with the Virgins* (London, 2007), p.67.

82 James Clark to Derek Denton, 12 June 1997, for Joyce's persistent egotism and pedantry.

83 L. Paul-Dubois, *Contemporary Ireland* (Dublin, 1908), pp.512, 196.

84 Cole, *Lord Haw-Haw*, pp.21–22 on Michael Joyce's politics.

85 C. Townshend, *Political Violence in Ireland: Government and Resistance since 1845* (Oxford, 1983), p.301. F. Campbell, *Land and Revolution: Nationalist Politics in the West of Ireland, 1891–1921* (Oxford, 2005) on land issues.

86 Townshend, *Political Violence*, p.350. S. C. Mason (pseud.), *"Bloody Murder": A Story of Ireland* (London, 1937), for an Auxiliary's account.

87 C. Townshend, *The British Campaign in Ireland 1919–1921: The Development of Political and Military Policies* (Oxford, 1975), p.82, generally. O. Winter, *Winter's Tale: An Autobiography* (London, 1955). Winter remarked stereotypically, "agents and informers were difficult to obtain, for the Irishman's appetite for gold had been replaced by a surfeit of terror. . . ." (*ibid*. p.295). *The Times*, 15 and 20 February 1962 carried obituary notices. He features heavily in P. Hart, *British Intelligence in Ireland, 1920–21. The Final Reports* (Cork, 2002). P. McMahon, *British Spies and Irish Rebels: British Intelligence and Ireland, 1916–1945* (Woodbridge, 2008), also picks up on his activities.

88   KV 2/249/54b.
89   Cameo drawn from McMahon, *British Spies*, p.37 and R. F. Foster, *Modern Ireland 1600–1972* (London, 1989), p.521.
90   Keating, commissioned into the Royal Irish Rifles in 1916, appears in the Army List (1921) in the ranks of "officers holding Military and other Appointments not remunerated out of Army Funds." He was now involved in Ormonde Winter's activities (p.2526). Brief career details are in WO 372/11. Surviving evidence suggests before his death he had attained the rank of major.
91   Shee, ts, pp.105–106.
92   HO45/25780/25.
93   "Dear Old Daddy," RTÉ, 15 September 1999.
94   KV 2/249/54b, testimony of A. Miles Webb.
95   Selwyn, *Hitler's Englishman*, p.19.
96   D.V. Duff, *May the Winds Blow! An Autobiography* (London, 1948), p.82.
97   Kenny, *Germany Calling*, p.59.
98   *Ibid*.
99   USSC, MS 238/7/12, John Macnab's critique of Rebecca West's work, p.3.
100 HO 45/25690, letter, 6 September 1939.
101 National Archives of Scotland, SC53/41/26 and SC53/47/17, for Edgar Brookes's will, 13 October 1917. Joyce's mother is referred to, strangely, perhaps significantly, as "Gertrude Emily Brooke or Joyce."
102 Probate Records, General Register Office, England and Wales, 1943 and 1947 for Michael Joyce leaving £650 and Gertrude Joyce £550.6s.4d.
103 Shee, ts, p.106. *Worcester Evening News*, 2 March 1996.
104 Kenny, *Germany Calling*, p.62.
105 R. Skidelsky, *Oswald Mosley* (London, 1975), p.343.
106 West, *Treason*, pp.19, 21.
107 Selwyn, *Hitler's Englishman*, p.20.
108 Cole, *Lord Haw-Haw*, p.23. "Dear Old Daddy," RTÉ, 15 September 1999.
109 KV 2/245/1b.
110 KV 2/245, report, 21 September 1934.
111 Cole, *Lord Haw-Haw*, p.31.

2

A NEW BEGINNING

I will be a different person when I live in England and different things will happen to me. [Jean Rhys, *Wide Sargasso Sea*, Harmondsworth, 1968, p.92.]

1

Joyce had often been isolated in Ireland, where his political views had alienated many contemporaries and few could tolerate his swaggering self-importance. It is no accident that as a young boy he was impressed by Napoleon. He was already creating gods, identifying with powerful figures from history.[1] However, in his isolation he drew comfort from his mother, as she did from him. In England, at first he could no longer turn to her. He found himself alone.

2

After being rejected by the armed forces he attended a military school in Aldershot before enrolling in October 1922 at Battersea Polytechnic. He had just made his first move in building a new life in big, surging London, the most heavily populated city in Europe, so different in many ways from the Galway he had come to know so well.

In 1923 his family – no longer safe in Ireland – followed him to England and settled close to Gertrude Joyce's roots in Lancashire. An Oldham resident with whom they stayed until 1 Brompton Street was ready, said William was "a very nice boy at that time."[2] Before they left the town the family appear to have lived in several different houses, to which Joyce would return periodically when enjoying a break from his student lodgings in London.[3]

When Gertrude Joyce had come to Shaw following her mother's death in 1917, the police had treated her as an alien. But when the Joyces arrived later from Ireland it is said they lived "as British subjects."[4] The War had ended; they kept a low profile; and, doubtless at Michael's bidding, suppressed details of their American ties.[5]

Neither Joyce nor his family remained long in Oldham and little is known about his days there. But he would have observed that King Cotton ruled in the North-West, with many families dependent on the mills which, Lowry-like, imposed themselves on the townscapes. In 1920 the town had been badly hit by a slump in trade and Joyce's later interest in the cotton industry, especially the threat posed by Asian imports to British textile workers, must have drawn something from his time in Lancashire.

Oldham had provided the Joyces with a bolt-hole. But Michael, Gertrude and their children soon joined William in London, the dream city, to which many migrants, immigrants and refugees have been drawn. As ever, the capital had its attractions. "You cannot imagine just how dizzying, terrifying and fascinating London is," the Italian novelist Giuseppe di Lampedusa exclaimed in 1926.[6] There is also a suggestion this move was encouraged by the state of Michael's health, which had been adversely affected in Lancashire – a claim which might contain some truth.[7] The North-West's climate can be quite unforgiving. But how comfortable did Michael feel in Oldham, close to the roots of a family that had treated him as an outsider, not one of their dynasty? The failure of Gertrude's parents to attend her wedding in 1905 and Michael's exclusion from Edgar Brooke's will in 1917 were not long distant. Tensions between professions, trades, different faiths, were not unusual in the early twentieth century.

3

London became Joyce's base between the early 1920s and the summer of 1939, and his fortunes changed dramatically during these years.

At first he attempted to pursue a conventional professional career. Yet significantly for his future politics he never fulfilled his ambitions. He would constantly, effortlessly, tirelessly, promulgate the myth of his own brilliance, and this self-created image has persisted. He "flew through exams," according to one biographer.[8] This claim exaggerates. In 1923 he failed the intermediate science examinations at Battersea – which had implications for his hopes to practise medicine.[9]

In any case Joyce would have found the financial burden of studying for a medical degree extremely taxing. He therefore transferred his academic interests and in September 1923 registered at Birkbeck College, in the University of London, close to the British Museum.[10] It offered evening study – its motto is "In Nochte Consilium" – and seemed ideally suited to his current circumstances. He followed intermediate courses in English, French, Latin and History, passing his language subjects in June 1924, and History, his subsidiary course, in 1926.[11] In June 1927 he graduated with a first-class honours degree in English.[12] He now appeared to be fulfilling that academic promise first evident as a schoolboy in Ireland.

Joyce was no more a cloistered undergraduate in London than he had been a mere inky swot in Galway. He enjoyed boxing and between 1923 and 1924 served as assistant secretary of the Birkbeck Boxing Club.[13] He can be observed participating in college debates.[14] He pursued his military interests, too, and when writing on 9 August 1922 from 10 Longbeach Road, Battersea, to join the University's Officer Training Corps, claimed to be of pure British descent.[15] Who might doubt him, dressed as he often was in plus-fours and a black sweater emblazoned with a Union Jack?[16] However, he could offer no documents to support this claim and Michael Joyce proved remarkably vague when the OTC Adjutant requested him to clarify matters.[17] But Joyce was permitted to join and in the 1926 Spring term emphasised the OTC's virtues in Birkbeck's student magazine, *The Lodestone*.[18]

Also in *The Lodestone*, Joyce turned his hand to poetry and when responding to a piece by P. Loftus Ryan mounted a fierce attack on trends in modern literature. In "Verses to an Impolite Reformer," he pounced on "that impious reptile Shaw" and "the sickly, putrid, maggot-eaten Coward." Student reaction was swift. Loftus Ryan, apart from deploring his critic's "gratuitous rudeness," claimed his oratory stank " unpleasantly of the soap-box" and suggested his literary opponent was "unworthy to unlace" the shoes of the "lowliest peasant" in the nation. F. Oxley Read, another student, objected to what he called Joyce's "ill-bred and unprovoked effusions."[19] No-one sprang to Joyce's defence.

In this busy undergraduate life Joyce can be found acting in student drama productions, once playing Kestrel in Ben Jonson's *The Alchemist.*[20] And he was constantly reading. Encouraged by J. H. Lobban, Head of English, he found John Dryden, who became one of his favourite, much-quoted authors.[21] He also discovered Thomas Carlyle and soon incorporated the author's image of man triumphing over circumstance into his developing political thought. Carlyle's message gave him hope. Joyce believed that with his own iron will he would ultimately win through, would fully realise his ambitions.

Amid this constant whirl he became chairman of the Conservative Student Society, and in the 1926 Spring term reported that on his watch it had "grown very considerably in strength and importance."[22] He would remain in the Tory Party for some time, but beyond university had already become involved with Britain's early fascist group. His mounting disappointments would hasten his transition to fascism.

About this time Hazel Kathleen Barr entered his life and they soon decided to marry – which they did at Chelsea Register Office on 30 April 1927.[23] No Catholic wedding for him. The Roman Church had damned his mother; he was finished with it. No parents were present at this distinctly low-key ceremony.[24] Joyce had already obtained a part-time teaching post and appeared on the marriage certificate as a Tutor.[25] After getting married the couple returned to their respective homes. Soon, though, they began living at 44 Jubilee Place, Chelsea.[26]

The bride's father, Edward Reginald Barr, has been described as a dentist who had served in the Scots Guards during the First World War, which might suggest Joyce had married into a well-heeled middle-class family.[27] Quite in keeping with the young ambitious man he had become. It has also been claimed both sets of parents were alive when the wedding took place.[28]

However, some of this evidence is suspect. Edward Barr had died on 23 February 1927, before his daughter's wedding, and his death certificate reveals he worked only as a dental mechanic.[29] His marriage had disintegrated, he was living apart from his family and his sister rather than wife registered the death in Hammersmith. He left all of his insignificant £60 to Edith Mary Smith, presumably related to his executor Jesse Smith, a roadman.[30] And another claim, that the Barrs provided the newly-weds with a marital home, needs to be questioned.[31] Mrs Emma Barr can be traced to 44 Jubilee Place as far back as 1915 and Hazel was living here when she married.[32] But her mother did not own the flat; it belonged to R. Carter, a Brighton-based businessman. Rate books would suggest Joyce came to share his mother-in-law's rented apartment.[33]

No-one can doubt Joyce's initial feelings for Hazel. Tucked away in *The Lodestone* is a poem by him which dwelt on her "matchless loyal mood of pride and love" and extolled her as "the woman of my life's great dream." The young poet proclaimed their love would last unto eternity:

> This is no tie of earthly love sublime
> 'Tis bond-heroic of immortal time.[34]

Hazel had two daughters by Joyce whose names reflected the continuing influence of his mother. Heather Brooke, later the prime mover behind the transfer of her father's remains to Galway, was born on 30 July 1928 and Diana Patricia Brooke on 20 July 1931.[35] Their mother has remained a mere whisper in Joyce biographies, mainly because the marriage failed. After which Joyce largely expunged her memory. His second wife, Margaret, acting on his instructions to promote an authorised, sanitised version of his life, then virtually obliterated Hazel's place in the historical record.

These domestic upheavals are to anticipate. Now with a degree, newly married, saddled with growing responsibilities, what would be his next step? Beatrice Marjorie Daunt, who had an interest in Old and Middle English, had taught at Birkbeck since 1920 and with

R. W. Chambers was to publish a well-known work on London English.[36] She suggested Joyce begin research on medieval petitions. However, he was unable to discover sufficient sources, a not uncommon problem for postgraduates, and this project lapsed. Nevertheless, his article on the importance of vowel sounds published in 1928 in the prestigious *Review of English Studies* clearly suggests his academic potential.[37]

Following this first research disappointment Joyce supposedly applied for a higher degree at Birkbeck under C.E.M. Joad, Reader in Philosophy, later better known as a member of the BBC's radio programme, "The Brains Trust."[38] "A disgusting toad" to one critic, Joad championed progressive causes and pursued political interests.[39] He served for a time as Director of Propaganda for Oswald Mosley's New Party.[40] He also wrote on the fascist phenomenon.[41] But London University's archives contain nothing to suggest any such application by Joyce.[42] He fantasised this episode as he did much else in his life. However, in May 1932, he did register as a part-time Psychology postgraduate at King's College to work with Professor F.A.P. Aveling, whose interest in higher thought processes and the power of the will had caught his attention.[43] This registration was cancelled in 1933–34.[44] By now Joyce had also become impressed by the research into human inequality being pursued by Professor Charles Edward Spearman, another London University psychologist, whose work *The Abilities of Man* had appeared in 1927.[45]

These steps reveal an academic manqué, dipping his toes into different intellectual pools. But not only academia came into his sights. In 1928 he applied to the Foreign Office.

In its telling this episode has become seriously distorted. It is one of many occasions Joyce fabricated details of his life. He claimed to have passed the written examination brilliantly. He was never reticent at proclaiming his genius. That story has been slavishly repeated by his acolytes. He also put it about that his application had nevertheless failed because he lacked a private income.[46] He was gilding the lily here.

His provisional application went before the Selection Board on 30 March 1928. Since applicants should normally have been born in the United Kingdom or one of the self-governing dominions, how could he proceed? He offered the United States as his birthplace but informed the Commission that "business reasons" had prevented his mother crossing the Atlantic, as she had hoped, to ensure he was born in England.[47] He did not gloss this comment. However, the Commission allowed his application to stand.[48] An early reference, more of a character sketch, from the Rev. C. C. Keet, Vicar of St James's, Hampstead, was brief but satisfactory. Yet Joyce never sat the written examination. Interviewed at the beginning of May, he was rejected two days later.[49]

Jack Cole, Joyce's first biographer, enquired whether information he had received on the application was accurate. However, in the early 1960s the official file remained closed and he never secured the detail he sought.[50] This source – now available – reveals why Joyce was unsuccessful.

When G. F. O'Riordan, the newly appointed Principal of Battersea Polytechnic, returned the Commission's questionnaire on 17 April 1928, he added, "I think it right to give you in this letter some special and confidential information." He had enquired among colleagues and their image of Joyce turned out to be less than flattering. According to one:

> Mr William Joyce was merely an ordinary student during one session. He failed to pass the Intermediate Science Examination in Chemistry and Applied Mathematics. We are unable to report any distinctions.

Here is further proof his genius did not always manifest itself. O'Riordan continued:

> He seemed to hold rather extreme views on politics and upheld the use of force as a method of spreading opinions.

Hardly the smoothly elegant individual to be our man in Moscow or Paris.

O'Riordan had still more to say. Warming enthusiastically to his task he effectively damned Joyce's chances by reporting:

> Our very vivid recollection . . . is that he was entirely unfitted for a responsible position, and particularly for the Foreign Office or Diplomatic Service.[51]

Joyce's application, one official noted much later, possessed a "distinctly oily" appearance which did it no favours.[52] But O'Riordan's letter proved decisive.

Joyce knew he had lied when telling friends and family he had passed the written examination. But unaware of why he had been rejected he constructed an explanation that aligned with his developing paranoid view of the world. His disappointments were mounting. He had not been allowed to serve as a soldier. His ambition to practise medicine had come to nothing. His academic research interests had been frustrated. His hopes of becoming a civil servant had just been cruelly dashed. He seemed to be travelling along a barren, stony road. He wanted to be accepted, make an important contribution to society. But he faced constant rejection. These frustrations go some way towards explaining his later politics.

Where could he turn? In September 1926, before graduating, he had been appointed a tutor at the Victoria Tutorial College, Eccleston Square, SW1.[53] And teaching occupied him during his remaining time in London. He became a Licenciate of the College of Preceptors and on 13 November 1931, by now experienced in the classroom, was accepted as a full member.[54]

Few snapshots survive of him as a teacher. But Maurice Kinmouth remembered Joyce from a crammer course in English for first MB students. The would-be doctor was now assisting others to gain their medical qualifications. Kinmouth recalled him as "a smallish man, very bright and alert and not much else."[55] Another pupil, apart from observing Joyce's doodling habit, thought him "clever, sarcastic and supercilious."[56]

Borland's, as students at Victoria College knew it, did not absorb all Joyce's energies. He worked part of his time at the Institute of Political Secretaries, based at 5 Woodstock House, London. Directed by Colonel Philip J. Woods, it coached its paying clients for political positions.[57] Tutors set exercises on current affairs, taught pupils the art of public speaking and introduced these aspirants to a range of hopefully useful contacts.

Joyce's efforts can be traced in the papers of Captain C. C. Lewis. Lewis, an author – his *Culinary Notes for Sind* had appeared in Karachi in 1928 — lawyer, and soldier, had just returned to England from service overseas and was now anxious to find work. In 1932 Joyce wrote to him, "I appreciate your position as well as any human being can appreciate it," adding, "I have a wife and two small daughters; and thanks to my own wild folly I have had, am having, and shall have, a strenuous fight."[58] At Borland's in 1927, with Hazel pregnant, Joyce had become sexually entangled with Mary Ogilvy, a sixteen-year-old pupil. He also knew her from the Junior Imperial League in Chelsea. This "wild folly" had created absolute havoc in his recent marriage and even beyond.[59]

With the Institute committed to fostering its students' political careers, Joyce wrote to Lewis in early 1932: "We must get you into good favour with the important Conservatives in a good constituency such as Chelsea."[60] He was boasting here. A contemporary recalled that he cut a rather lonely figure among the local party – the Ogilvy business had damaged him – and far removed from any influence.[61] Within a few years, however, both men would be sharing a political career; not in the Tory Party, but the British Union of Fascists.[62]

Joyce's marking of Lewis's essays show him as a conscientious and demanding teacher. More importantly, his marginalia offer a glimpse into his early political thinking.[63] On one occasion when Lewis referred to Black and Tan reprisals on innocent people Joyce – bearing in mind his contact with the security forces – would have none of it. He quickly counter-attacked: "I do not know personally of any such cases," even though he admitted "nice discrimination" could not "always be observed." Another of Joyce's observations – "Long before the 'Black and Tans' appeared, my parents had been reduced to abject poverty by Sinn Fein burnings " – offered a further reminder of his troubled past.[64]

Lewis probably anticipated similar criticism when writing on the violence surrounding events near Galway in September 1920. "Can it honestly be suggested," he asked, "that *every* man, woman and child who suffered from any of the above burnings was a Sinn Feiner, and had encouraged murder?" Joyce replied laconically: "It is quite possible."[65] To claim that by the 1920s he was already distancing himself from his experiences in Ireland and softening his opposition to Irish nationalists is clearly wrong.[66]

An oblique reference to Joyce's traumatic, troubled past appeared on another essay in his remark that ex-soldiers had been condemned to walk Britain's streets "looking for work because financiers believed in buying in the cheapest market and selling in the dearest."[67] He believed the British Government had sold short these deserving veterans. Just as he and his loyal family had been betrayed in Ireland.

Lewis, a diligent, enquiring mature student, refused to take such criticism without fighting back. But he had just met an arrogant, condescending tutor. When Joyce trespassed beyond teaching English at Victoria Tutorial College and turned to political themes at the Institute, he exposed another side to his personality. "Thanks very much for the statement of your views," he once wrote to Lewis. "You are certainly trying to understand the conditions of 1920–21. With my help, you will, mon chèr élève, ultimately succeed," before adding disingenuously, "Indeed, I do appreciate the pains which you take to enlighten me."[68] Joyce seldom took advice from anybody.

Other feedback Joyce gave Lewis reflected his growing authoritarianism. "I cannot infer that democracy is a good system," he once wrote. "No system presuming universal suffrage can be based on any psychology but a bad one."[69] By now his beliefs were taking him in a different direction: "Biology demands that the strong must profit by the weak: but one mustn't say so, What! What!"[70] When that great day dawned he would be among the leaders of society. Not fit to unlace a peasant's shoes, indeed.

4

Joyce had arrived in England as an eager lad, keen to succeed in the world but a succession of career disappointments had soon soured him. His activities at Birkbeck, and his comments on Lewis's essays show him throughout this time thinking politically. But his political ambitions had also been thwarted. He once remarked ruefully to Lewis – hinting at the Ogilvy affair – on his "awful tactlessness, general recklessness, and general disregard of others," which had damaged his political career, though he consoled himself with "I am quite young as yet."[71]

His most dynamic years did indeed lie ahead. Beyond Birkbeck's lecture theatres, Borland's chalky classrooms, his teaching at the Institute, he became exposed to, and significantly influenced by, certain ideological currents then flowing through London. This exposure would seriously affect his future politics.

Notes

1 Kenny, *Germany Calling*, p.51.
2 *Oldham Evening Chronicle*, 27 February 1976.
3 KV 2/250, diary, 8 March 1945.
4 Cole, *Lord Haw-Haw*, p.27.
5 CRIM 1/483 on the 1917 visit.
6 G. T. di Lampedusa, *Letters from London and Europe* (Richmond, 2001), p.171 (letter, 29 May 1925).
7 HO 144/22707, p.2.
8 Kenny, *Germany Calling*, p.5.
9 Interview, Hazel Brooks, 15 April 1992; letter, University of London to author, 21 April 1997.
10 Only fragments of his registration forms, relating to 1926 and 1927, have survived in the University's archives.
11 University archives; Cole, *Lord Haw-Haw*, p.33.
12 Interview with Hazel Brooks, 15 April 1992. USSC, MS 238/7/11 carries comment by Macnab.
13 CSC 11/150.
14 *Irish Times*, 21 June 1945.
15 Selwyn, *Hitler's Englishman*, pp.24–25.
16 *Irish Times*, 21 June 1945.
17 KV 2/249/70a.
18 *The Lodestone*, Vol.20 (Spring Term, 1926), p.101.
19 *Ibid*. Vol.22 (Summer Term, 1927), pp. 126–127 and *ibid*. Vol.23 (Autumn Term, 1927), pp.45–47.
20 Cole, *Lord Haw-Haw*, p.32.
21 WJ to MJ, 15 November 1945, 19 December 1945.
22 CSC 11/150. *The Lodestone*, Vol.21 (Spring Term, 1926), p.102.
23 Interview, Hazel Brooks, 15 April 1992.
24 Cole, *Lord Haw-Haw*, p.33. Kenny, *Germany Calling*, p.82.
25 Marriage Certificate, General Register Office, England and Wales.
26 Kenny, *Germany Calling*, p.82.
27 Selwyn, *Hitler's Englishman*, p.37; Farndale, *Haw-Haw*, p.59
28 Kenny, *Germany Calling*, pp.81–83; Farndale, *Haw-Haw*, p.61.
29 Death certificate, Hammersmith and Fulham Registration District.
30 Probate records, General Register Office, England and Wales.
31 Kenny, *Germany Calling*, p.82 carries the more favourable gloss.
32 The Joyces' marriage certificate in General Register Office, England and Wales, has Hazel Barr living at Jubilee Place. Communications from the British Dental Association, 5 May 2006, and Guildhall Library, 5 May 2006. London Metropolitan Archives, 17 May 2006 for other detail. Hazel died in 2001.
33 Rate books, Kensington Public Library.
34 *The Lodestone*, Vol.22 (Summer Term, 1927), pp.118–119.
35 Both birth certificates describe Joyce as a "Tutor." General Register Office, England and Wales.

36 University of London to author, 21 December 1997. R. W. Chambers and B. M. Daunt, *A Book of London English, 1384–1425* (Oxford, 1931).

37 W. Joyce, "A Note on the Mid Back Slang Unrounded Vowel [a] in the English of To-day," *Review of English Studies*, Vol.4 (1928), pp.337–340.

38 Cole, *Lord Haw-Haw*, pp.38–39. Joad is in Matthew and Harrison (eds), *ODNB*, Vol.30, pp.132–134.

39 Count Potocki in *The Right Review*, May 1946, p.2.

40 M. Worley, *Oswald Mosley and the New Party* (London, 2010) and C.E.M. Joad, *The Case for the New Party* (sl., 1931?).

41 "Prolegomena to Fascism," *Political Quarterly*, Vol.2 (1931), pp.82–99.

42 University of London student records.

43 *Who Was Who 1941–1950* (London, 1952), p.42.

44 University of London to author, 21 December 1997.

45 USSC, MS 238/7/11, notes by J. Macnab and A. K. Chesterton. Matthew and Harrison (eds), *ODNB*, Vol.51, pp.762–764, on Spearman.

46 Cole, *Lord Haw-Haw*, p.35.

47 CSC 11/150, letter to Selection Board, 30 March 1928.

48 CSC 11/150, Civil Service Commission Report, 12 April 1928.

49 CSC 11/150, references of 4 April 1928 and other detail.

50 CSC 11/150, 9 August 1961.

51 All from CSC 11/150, communication by O'Riordan, 17 April 1928.

52 CSC 11/150, internal memo, 8 April 1961.

53 Cole, *Lord Haw-Haw*, p.38.

54 Minutes, College of Preceptors' Council Meeting, May 1929–May 1932.

55 Letter to author, 31 July 1996.

56 KV 2/245/257A.

57 USSC, MSS 166/2/X/i–ii. On Woods, see N. Baron, *The King of Karelia. Colonel P.J. Woods and the British Intervention in North Russia 1918-1919. A History and Memoir* (London, 2007).

58 USSC, MS 166/1/I, Joyce to Lewis, 5 April 1932.

59 Farndale, *Haw-Haw*, p.63.

60 USSC, MS 166/1/iii, Joyce to Lewis, 20 May 1932.

61 Letter, 9 May 1991 (private archive).

62 *Fascist Week*, 29 December 1933–4 January 1934, for Lewis's profile. He became a legal advisor to the movement.

63 USSC, MS 166/2/I, Exercise XV.

64 USSC, MS 166/2/V.

65 USSC, MS 166/2/V.

66 The error appears in Cole, *Lord Haw-Haw*, p.33.

67 USSC, MS 166/2/I, Exercise XV.

68 USSC, MS 166/2/V.

69 USSC, MS 166/2/I, Exercise XXII.

70 USSC, MS 166/2/I, Exercise XV.

71 USSC, MS 166/I/V, incomplete letter.

PART II
Ideologies

3

JOYCE AND THE BRITISH FASCISTS

'Poor old Daddy – just one of those sturdy old plants left over from the Edwardian Wilderness that can't understand why the sun isn't shining any more.' [John Osborne, *Look Back in Anger and Other Plays*, in *Collected Plays, Volume 1* (London, 1993), p.65.]

1

Britain faced major challenges after the First World War. "Ill fares the land . . ." Goldsmith had written much earlier and, glancing at his new surroundings, Joyce would have agreed.

Ranks of traumatised, disillusioned men, victims of the '14–'18 War, became a familiar sight on Britain's streets. The mass slaughter had also resulted in an army of unmarried women. To make matters worse, unemployment rates climbed in the early '20s as key sectors of the economy encountered problems. In 1926 the General Strike then cast a dark, lingering shadow over the country. Three years later the crash on Wall Street created further havoc. Would the capitalist system collapse? Significant developments were already underway in Europe, where countries also faced major problems. Italy had turned fascist under Mussolini. In Germany Hitler's National Socialist movement was stirring. In Russia Communism had come to power. Which path would Britain take in this "morbid age"?[1] Joyce's politics would no longer be fashioned by events in the west of Ireland, but played out on this much bigger canvas.

2

Joyce's feet had hardly touched English soil before he threw himself into politics. Jack Cole's pioneer biography skimmed over his political activity in the '20s and early '30s.[2] Mary Kenny's work never rectified this silence.[3] Nigel Farndale proved equally reticent.[4]

Evidence from beyond Birkbeck confirms Joyce's early links to the Conservative party. Alan Livesey Stuart Todd, one-time Tory MP for Kingswinford in Staffordshire, recalled Joyce as a member of the Chelsea branch of the Junior Imperial League who had won an annual speaking competition.[5] Further detail is elusive. But Joyce's correspondence with C. C. Lewis suggests his links to that branch of the party, and he certainly possessed considerable public-speaking skills.[6]

Yet the Tories failed to satisfy him.[7] In the early 1930s he wrote on one of Lewis's exercises at the Institute of Political Secretaries: "Believe me, I care nothing for the Tory Party."[8] A little later, getting firmly, more confidently, into his political stride and revealing his fondness for delicate prose, he dismissed it as "one loathsome, fetid, purulent, tumid mass of hypocrisy."[9] How significantly his outlook had shifted since leaving Ireland. Nevertheless, as an acute political operator he maintained his links with the Conservatives for some time.[10]

Some opponents have latched onto Joyce's Toryism to divert attention from his career in British fascism. Oswald Mosley's lingering supporters remain ever-anxious to distance themselves from his memory. But his first step into fascism came soon after arriving in London. Viewing them as an extreme form of High Toryism, he was drawn into the British Fascisti (later the British Fascists), which Rotha Beryl Lintorn-Orman, a prominent Girl Guider who had served with distinction in the Women's Reserve Ambulance in the First World War, formed in May 1923. Joyce signed up the following December, soon after he had enrolled at Birkbeck.[11]

To suggest he never became a full member – an impression which might have arisen because the Fascisti created different categories of membership – is misleading.[12] Joyce not only joined. A 1924 Intelligence report referred to him as a district officer.[13] Similar sources identified his membership in the group's inner organisation – "K" or "Z" – populated by "some of the wilder and more youthful elements," including demobbed Black and Tans.[14] He would have known these sorts of men from his time in Galway.

The pre-war Die-Hard Tories acted as one influence on the group.[15] As did Sir Henry Page Croft's "imperialist, protectionist, xenophobic and anti-Semitic" National Party.[16] The Britons, the racial nationalist body Henry Hamilton Beamish established in 1919, sharpened its anti-Jewish focus.[17]

Not all influences were home grown. Mussolini was portrayed as Italy's saviour, who had repelled "the barbarous and destructive tyranny of the alien despots of Moscow."[18] The Italian dictator might be "bombastic, inconsistent, shallow and vainglorious," but even beyond fascist circles he was sometimes viewed as "a true prophet."[19] The British Fascists therefore promoted works by James Strachey Barnes and Harold Goad, both associates of the Centre International d'Etudes sur le Fascisme, which from 1927 acted as a propaganda outlet for Mussolini.[20] By the early 1930s the group was also drawn increasingly towards National Socialism.[21] Which led it to advertise some vicious anti-Semitic comment translated from the *Völkischer Beobachter*.[22] This political camaraderie was further revealed in 1935 when members of the NSDAP (Hitler's National Socialist German Workers' Party) were invited to attend Lintorn-Orman's funeral service at St Giles-in-the-Fields.[23]

Lintorn-Orman's group was soon awash with conflict, and one clash in 1924 led to the formation of the National Fascisti, a short-lived splinter organisation.[24] It has been suggested Joyce joined this breakaway group.[25] With his passion for intrigue, he might have done. However, his first biographer is adamant he never did.[26] Two years later the General Strike resulted in another important fracture.[27] Fascism's tendency to fragment had soon become evident.

Joyce's serious involvement in the British Fascists can be traced in the early and mid-1920s, after which financial problems compounded the group's ideological splits. Lintorn-Orman possessed plenty of 'tin' and with the group's original upper-class recruits managed for some time to keep her enterprise afloat. By the late 1920s, though, it had become strapped for cash, a problem increasingly evident in its ragged, episodic publications.[28]

As a remnant staggered on, it gradually adopted a more pronounced fascist ideology, a development traceable in three manifestos of 1926, 1927 and 1933. By the early '30s it was calling for the parliamentary system to be replaced by a corporate state of "Guilds and Corporations of workers, traders, employers and owners," claiming this new political arrangement was vital for the country's future.[29] Here was fascism speaking the anti-democratic language which sharply separated it from the Tories who shared parts of its ideology.[30] Those advertisements for fascist Christmas cards, fascist cigarettes, fascist cufflinks, fascist matches, fascist ties, the group's rousing hymn, "Hail! The nation sprung from heroes, Hail! Britannia's race immortal!" as well as its commercial slogan, "Buy British goods," masked another developing image.[31] But the end was near. After Lintorn-Orman, increasingly dependent on drink and drugs, died in Las Palmas in 1935, far away from the political strife that had once troubled her, the movement was quickly wound up.[32]

Joyce, always in a hurry, had already moved away. Between 1923 and 1925 he had engaged with the group's activities, but soon realised it did not offer him a longer-term political future. Was he, nevertheless, influenced by his time with Lintorn-Orman? If her group was merely a "quixotic and eccentric" confection, he would have been little affected.[33] The same would be true if, as a Joyce biography states, the British Fascists revealed a distinct "lack of policies."[34]

However, arguing to the contrary, his early exposure to fascism influenced his future political career in three significant ways. He encountered an ideology, some of it shared by Die-Hard Tories, which chimed with the political beliefs he brought from Ireland and introduced him to new ideas he would champion throughout the 1930s and '40s. He extended his range of contacts. Far more was on offer in London than in Galway's small world. Finally, in 1924 he was severely wounded when on duty for the cause, an incident that became tightly woven into his emerging political outlook.

3

Joyce was not alone in maintaining links with the Tory Party while serving in the British Fascists.[35] Arnold Leese once dismissed Lintorn-Orman's group as "Conservatism with Knobs On," a remark that overlooks its later commitment to a recognisable fascism.[36] But, particularly in its early days, the group did attract Tory supporters.

Colonel Sir Charles Burn, Tory MP for Torquay, sat on the Grand Council, the group's ruling body.[37] Patrick Hannon, Conservative MP for Birmingham (Moseley) between 1921 and 1950, and Oliver Locker-Lampson, Conservative MP for Birmingham (Handsworth), from 1922 to 1945, also became involved.[38] Hannon served as President of the group's Birmingham branch and, like Burn, sat on the Grand Council.[39] The "teetotal, sabbatarian, solicitor-MP" William Joynson-Hicks, Home Secretary between 1924 and 1929, though never a member of the British Fascists, exercised a key role in oiling these channels.[40]

Aware that Tory support carried political benefits, Lintorn-Orman persistently tried to woo this constituency. She co-operated therefore with *The Patriot*, which the Duke of Northumberland founded in 1922 to alert Britain to the dangers of Jewish Bolshevism.[41] She also cultivated the *Morning Post*.[42]

Joyce's contact with such sources increasingly exposed him to a paranoid version of politics.[43] What the poet Charles Hamilton Sorley called the loss of "millions of mouthless dead" during the Great War was bad enough. But the British Fascists and their Tory allies worried over other matters.[44]

They believed the pre-1914 power structure was slipping away. Where would it end? Joyce's recent experiences in Ireland led him to identify with this sentiment. His old world had vanished, to be replaced by the grubbing uncertainty of life in Oldham and London. Back in the refined atmosphere of the university after his rough and tumble involvement in London's street politics, he never ceased to remind his more cushioned student contemporaries that the end of the '14–'18 War had not resulted, as he would have wished, in the restoration of British influence. The country was "going to the dogs." It was in danger of suffering the fate of Greece and Rome.[45]

Reflecting her fears for a weakened and vulnerable Britain, Lintorn-Orman's group focused increasingly on events in Russia. Conservative political circles – the *Morning Post* and, more briefly, *The Times* – likewise detected a dangerous, dark political storm gathering there. They viewed the 1917 Bolshevik Revolution as the first organised step in a plot to gain world power and regarded Britain's disaffected groups as offering the Soviets a lush recruiting ground.[46] The election of Britain's first Labour Government in 1924 only increased their fears. Would these people get into political bed with the Bolsheviks? The Zinoviev Letter, one of history's most notorious forgeries, which circulated during the second election of that year, invited voters to draw that conclusion.[47]

Joyce was eagerly receptive to these messages. Socialism had no place in the world he and his family had believed was theirs in Ireland. He would have agreed that this virulent "red poison" had to be neutralised.[48] And he would soon be writing of Marx in similar terms to the *Fascist Bulletin*, which in 1926 described Communism's father figure as "a repulsive looking object."[49]

The British Fascists believed a growing trade union movement added to the Red Peril.[50] As a result, during the 1926 General Strike they threw their political weight behind Baldwin's Government.[51] It was now vital "to build up a body of loyal citizens" to "stem the tide of impending revolt."[52]

And Bolshevism's triumph was not inevitable. The British Fascists were influenced here by the writings of F.J.C. Hearnshaw, who taught at King's College, London, and held a Chair of History in the university between 1913 and 1934.[53] In *A Survey of Socialism*, published in 1929, he presented Bolshevism as "the inversion of normal society" and dismissed its "perverse over-emphasis" on "environment" as the driving force in history. "Character," he claimed, "can mould environment" and "intelligence and will can often convert calamity to success."[54] Joyce would soon be arguing in similar vein. He might not have met Hearnshaw when at Birkbeck but he certainly came to know of his work. His eyes were being opened wide by London's political-cultural scene. It is uncertain how right-wing Hearnshaw was. But a glowing reference to Nesta Webster's work suggests he had moved some way along that political spectrum.[55]

When British Fascists and their Tory supporters considered the "greater Britain," they became obsessed by the loss of Imperial power and would often describe Ireland as the Achilles' heel of the Empire. Marx's writing had not been entirely in vain.[56] Lintorn–Orman's group had no sympathy therefore for Irish nationalism.[57] Joyce must have felt a deep sense of pleasure in now being surrounded by activists arguing for British as opposed to Irish interests. London was so different, more welcoming politically than Galway.

Ireland was not the only problem. When Lintorn-Orman and her Tory allies of the *Morning Post* constituency – the Northumberlands, the Londonderrys, and the Page Crofts – surveyed the wider Imperial scene, they perceived British power under threat in so many places.[58] They scented trouble in India following the 1919 Amritsar massacre.[59] Egypt and Iraq were "fast slipping away." In Ceylon, British authority had been reduced by a "pseudo-democratic constitution" with power passing to local "political cliques."[60] In this increasingly uncertain, fragile world the fate of India remained crucial; "if we lose [it] the Sun of the Empire will have set."[61] So claimed Sir Michael O'Dwyer, a former Governor of the Punjab, now a supporter of the British Fascists and soon to be shot in London by an Indian nationalist who had apparently witnessed the Amritsar tragedy.[62] Joyce deeply mourned O'Dwyer, whom he regarded one of his "very great heroes."[63]

With his Irish experiences, Joyce would have agreed that British statesmen had been beating a steady retreat from the Empire.[64] He believed Indian nationalists in particular should have been put firmly in their place long ago and was soon coveting a major post charged with Indian affairs, even hankering after the post of Viceroy.[65] In fact, on India he became "a sort of Die-Hard fanatic" and his delusional self-regard convinced him he would have quickly tamed those nationalist forces.[66] "I have always been for a strong Empire," he was to remark later, and sympathised with the dyspeptic Brigadier-General Dyer, who had commanded the British forces at Amritsar.[67] Joyce would have known from the *Morning Post*, one of his preferred dailies in the '20s, that its redoubtable editor H. A. 'Taffy' Gwynne had publicly defended Dyer's actions and raised a considerable sum to help ease him into retirement.[68]

These problems in Britain, Europe and the Empire must reflect a guiding force, Joyce and others believed. There must be an international agency at work, exerting a malign world influence. It did not take long to find it. Many European and American commentators began to portray the Bolshevik Revolution as Jewish-inspired. In Britain, the *Morning Post* vigorously advanced this claim and in 1920 its editor orchestrated the publication of *The Cause of World Unrest* with its pronounced conspiratorial overtones.[69] The British Fascists followed this line. This hostility became sharper after Joyce had left the group. Stalin's camps were then being described as sites where "Judeo-Bolshevism" practised torture.[70] It was also being gleefully, shakily, asserted, that "The triumph of anti-semite and Fascist ideals in Germany is the first knock out against the International Jew," and Hitler's struggle was "the first stride towards the liberation of the whole Aryan race from the yoke of the hook-nosed sons of Israel."[71] But earlier anti-Jewish sentiment, when Joyce politicked with Lintorn-Orman, can easily be found.[72] In the political salons where he felt most comfortable, and even beyond, the Jews were perceived, particularly after the Bolshevik Revolution, as a damnable problem.[73]

4

Joyce's newly acquired contacts during his time with Lintorn-Orman, included upper-class types who exercised an important role in fascism's early history. Apart from Sir Michael O'Dwyer, they included Lord Garvagh,[74] Lord Ernest Hamilton[75] and Sir Arthur Hardinge.[76] Joyce also met military men, including Brigadier-General R.G.D. Blakeney.[77] Ormonde Winter – known to Joyce from Ireland – soon became involved.[78] Winter's rabid fear of "disgruntled aliens and moral perverts" guaranteed he soon assumed a key role in the group.[79]

Joyce was not alone among fascists in having Lintorn-Orman's group as an early training ground. Heather Donovan later joined the BUF.[80] As did the schoolmasterish, wax-moustachioed Mandeville Roe. He wrote for the British Fascists and composed their hymn, which he dedicated to Lintorn-Orman and set to the "inspiring tune of 'Giovinezza.'"[81] However, he would soon dismiss her initiative as nothing more than a "little tea party at Earl's Court."[82]

He doubtless said something similar about the BUF after leaving it to spy on the likes of Joyce for the Board of Deputies of British Jews.[83] Neil Francis-Hawkins, later the BUF's Director-General, also served Lintorn-Orman, though Mosleyite histories quickly pass over this detail as if it were some gross political indiscretion.[84] In the BUF this puffy-cheeked bureaucrat took himself extremely seriously and he and Joyce were to fight for the soul of the movement. However, earlier, Francis-Hawkins had shown a lighter touch. On 4 April 1930 he acted as MC at a Carnival Dance in the Northumberland Rooms, Trafalgar Square. Presumably the group's "Frivolity Ball" held no terrors for him.[85] The degree of Joyce's contact, if any, with such activists at this time is unclear. But two people who now entered his world exercised a special effect on his later career. One is obscure; the other well-known.

Through links the British Fascists forged with The Britons, he met G. P. Mudge, the race scientist, an invisible figure in Joyce biographies, from whom he drew ideas on anti-Semitism, Bolshevism and race. Before he died in September 1939, Mudge became an important figure in the early Eugenics Society and, apart from The Britons, participated in various extreme nationalist groups in the 1920s.[86] Joyce kept in touch with him until as late as August 1939.

Joyce also encountered Maxwell Knight, aspiring novelist, "eccentric and amateur naturalist," fascist, jazz-lover, MI5 officer and student of the occult.[87] Hazel, Joyce's first wife, had known Max since she was a schoolgirl and had seemingly entertained hopes he might propose. He never did, but after she had married Joyce, Knight would often descend on the young couple at their home in Chelsea.[88]

Max joined Lintorn-Orman early, served as Deputy Chief of Staff and Director of Intelligence and received the Order of the Fasces 2nd Class.[89] In late 1927 the *British Lion* announced "with regret" that on health grounds he was required to leave London "for a considerable time" but added reassuringly, "Mr Knight's enforced departure from GHQ will in no way affect *his other Fascist activities* which will continue as before."[90] Max wrote in the same issue: "I *am* going where I can still keep an eye (or even two) on any undesirables, inside or outside the movement who may seek to make trouble for us."[91] All exceedingly Delphic. He did not remain active much longer, though.

His involvement ended in 1932 and the British Fascists denuded him of his Order.[92]

Was Knight on MI5's payroll when busy organising the group's Intelligence activities?[93] This claim is not as conspiratorial as might first appear. After 1917, the Home Office, the security service and Special Branch, all seriously concerned about a perceived Communist threat, found in the British Fascists a group which had a similar loathing for Communism, and some MI5 officers felt at ease with its ideology.[94] To a degree, "the BF appeared to be honeycombed with intelligence agents."[95] In Knight's case, he joined SIS in 1929, concentrating on domestic subversion, and entered MI5 in 1931.[96] Was he therefore pursuing more than one agenda after 1929? He would later play down his fascist background, claiming that throughout his time with Lintorn-Orman he was serving the interests of the state. MI5's official historian was not persuaded.[97]

Once in the service, Knight, who operated initially from his flat in Sloane Square and later Dolphin Square, was soon successfully running agents charged with penetrating a range of Britain's extremist political groups.[98] And throughout this time he never forgot "Joycey," who appeared as "a young cub" in one of Max's novels.[99] However, the fine detail of their relationship remains tantalisingly obscure.[100]

5

Joyce's early days in London are also important in his political life because of what he would proclaim as his near-martyrdom in the fascist cause. His most distinguishing physical trait resulted from a clash when on duty for the British Fascists. It left him with a prominent scar stretching from behind the lobe of his ear to the corner of his mouth on the right-hand side of his face. This trauma, it has always been claimed, influenced the future direction of his politics. What is known of this incident?

6

It is the evening of 22 October 1924. Jack Lazarus, Conservative candidate for the Lambeth North constituency, is holding a meeting at the local baths.[101] Joyce is a steward, commanding an 'I' squad of the British Fascists, a role which underlines his importance in the group and Lintorn-Orman's close links with the Conservatives. He and his colleagues are 'guards of honour,' charged with safeguarding the meeting from the Reds.[102] They are the British Fascists' thugs, the forerunners of Mosley's 'biff boys' and the equivalents of the Italian *squadristi*. It is no surprise Joyce features: he knows all about political violence from Galway. According to a Special Branch officer, "Men like Joyce . . . rather enjoy a fight for its own sake."[103]

Lazarus is a Jew, which indicates that at this stage the British Fascists are prepared to support a patriotic Jewish Conservative. Joyce will soon be viciously damning all Jews. But in 1924 he turns up to support Lazarus. Ormonde Winter has apparently informed the British Fascists it will be a "big show."[104] It certainly proves a traumatic evening in Joyce's life.

His account of events that evening in Lambeth "never varied":

> Someone jumped him from behind, a man he later identified as 'a Jewish Communist'. Something struck his face, though he did not at first realise what it was. The man who jumped him had gone and the crowd about him was drawing back in horror. He felt blood on his face but still did not realise the full extent of the wound. Someone handed him a 'filthy handkerchief' to staunch the flow. Others cleared a way through the crowd and he was helped outside to Lambeth Infirmary.
>
> The name of his assailant was never discovered but Joyce was adamant in repeating that he was a 'Jewish Communist.' There is every indication that he believed it to be true whether it was or not.[105]

Now he not only has a broken nose, a legacy of his Galway school-days, but also a livid facial scar.[106] He will call it his "Lambeth honour" or later, "die Schramme."[107]

7

Richard Reynell Bellamy's massive unpublished official history of the BUF described the incident rather differently, claiming the "badly healed wound was a legacy of the days when [Joyce] had spoken from Conservative platforms in East London."[108] This geographical switch from Lambeth is revealing. If a Jew had wielded the razor, Bellamy believed the attack must have occurred in the East End, which at that time was a major area of Jewish settlement.

He then dwelt on the scar's wider significance:

> "[Joyce] told how at a meeting broken up by Reds, mostly Jews and aliens, he had been seized, held down in the road, a razor inserted in his mouth then drawn up towards his ear. This had left him with a frightful cicatrice and an aversion to Jews."[109]

A political enemy had discovered Joyce and seriously damaged him. The implication is that his payback, his anti-Semitism, can be fully understood.

Another version of events drawn from a BUF source has Joyce walking away alone from the meeting only to be suddenly waylaid by a gang of vicious Jewish Reds:

> If this were true, the incident acquired a still darker and more ignoble quality. To a man of Joyce's stamp it added a degree of humiliation and defeat, in that the wound was not sustained in the course of open battle but as a captive of what he soon called his 'sub-human' enemy. The recurrent memory of that humiliation and agony might well account for his near-hysterical loathing.[110]

More bizarrely, one ex-Mosleyite believed Joyce had been attacked by Jews outside a café near Victoria Station in Manchester.[111]

Whatever their differences, these accounts underline the trauma of what happened and present Joyce as someone almost felled for his beliefs.[112] Fact, though, must be separated from fiction. Nothing offered so far explains what happened that fateful evening in south London.

A personal note is called for here. One afternoon in 1992, a student entered my university room and put me in touch with Hazel, Joyce's first wife. When I spoke to her she suddenly said: "You know his scarred face didn't result from an assault by a Jew, don't you? Oh no, it wasn't a Jewish Communist who disfigured him. He was knifed by an Irish woman."[113] My surprise can be imagined. Was she fantasising? Was her memory playing a trick? Was there any independent confirmation? How did the local press report the incident?

The disturbance began when the anti-Labour campaigner, Victor Fisher, was speaking from the platform:

> The tumult was terrific and the speaker could not be heard. A few young men commenced to sing, "Come back to Erin" and in this particular corner a scene of indescribable confusion ensued. A couple of men apparently came to blows and the crowd surged forward. Women became alarmed and made for the exit doors and stewards rushed to the scene. The excitement was tremendous and from out of the crowd there suddenly emerged a young steward with blood streaming from a nasty gash on the cheek. He was led to the rear and subsequently taken to Lambeth Infirmary for treatment. His condition was said to be serious. It is stated that the man was slashed with a razor. He was still at hospital yesterday (Thursday). His name is given as Mr Wm Joyce of Allison Grove, Dulwich.[114]

The key part of this report is "'Come back to Erin." Joyce's Galway activities had followed him to London. The IRA had missed killing him in Ireland. But he was not forgotten. Irish nationalists had found him in London.

This cumulative evidence destroys the fantasy Joyce spun about his scar, which has become firmly implanted in all existing biographies.

8

In 1945, revisiting his past, he recalled that following the Lambeth incident a photographer had appeared at his hospital bedside. Had he taken the widely distributed press image? If so, this "bug headed Yid," completely misunderstanding events, had remarked, "Ach these Fascist Blackguards – damn swine to carve you up like that. Should be shot."[115] Joyce had laughed, but reflecting on the visit, said he should have kicked him out of the ward. His comment shows how far he had travelled in his Jew-hatred. By 1945 all Jews were loathsome creatures.

In fact, within a few years of his scarring Joyce would constantly be attacking the Jews. But the emergence of his scorching hatred should not be linked to what actually happened in Lambeth. With the betrayal of his 'more-British-than-the British' family in Ireland and his later career disappointments – why could others not recognise what he believed were all his prodigious talents? – he proved particularly susceptible to those anti-Jewish feelings that wafted across society in inter-war Britain.[116] However, his journey to anti-Semitism was driven by more than a sense of British nationalism betrayed, mounting professional frustrations and his exposure to anti-Jewish antipathy in London. Already with an authoritarian, self-regarding rigid personality – recall some comments on Captain Lewis's essays – he was increasingly unable to tolerate difference. His fiction of a Jewish attacker in Lambeth, a story he willingly, enthusiastically retailed in the 1930s, and his endlessly repeated claim that his university research career had been choked off by a Jewish woman tutor stealing his notes, reflected these combined influences.[117] After he had found anti-Semitism, he found the Jews.[118] He soon placed them at the opposing centre of his political life.

9

Joyce had joined the Fascisti in December 1923. Several years later, before the group skidded to a halt, he had secured an excellent degree, married and started a family. Less positively, he had suffered a litany of professional setbacks. How psychologically gruelling it must have been. He had survived as best he could through teaching. But he soon came to regard a conventional career as less significant than the cut and thrust of politics. Such activity excited him. It captured his energies. Even here, he appeared trapped in a cul-de-sac. Following his traumas in Ireland, his early days in London had provided an important stage on which to expand his horizons, absorb new ideas, meet like-minded activists, and push himself further along the political road. But he had not yet made the decisive breakthrough he yearned for and believed was his due.

Notes

1   R. Overy, *The Morbid Age: Britain between the Wars* (London, 2009).
2   Cole, *Lord Haw-Haw*.
3   Kenny, *Germany Calling*, p.74 offers a passing reference.
4   Farndale, *Haw-Haw*, pp.54–55, 57, 58 reveals only a glancing interest.
5   John Warburton to author, 27 February 1992.
6   Private information.
7   Cole, *Lord Haw-Haw*, p.35.
8   USSC, MS 166/2/I, Exercise XV. The date is probably 1932.
9   *The Blackshirt*, 24 May 1935.
10   USSC, MS 166/1/iii.
11   Cole, *Lord Haw-Haw*, p.29.
12   Kenny, *Germany Calling*, p.74. T. P. Linehan, *British Fascism 1918–39: Parties, Ideology and Culture* (Manchester, 2000), p.63 on membership.
13   KV 2/245/1b and KV 3/57 (memo, 23 November 1924), for Joyce as a district officer in Chelsea.
14   KV 3/57, report, 23 November 1924.
15   K. Lunn, "Political Anti-Semitism before 1914: Fascism's Heritage?" in K. Lunn and R. C. Thurlow (eds), *British Fascism: Essays on the Radical Right in Inter-War Britain* (London, 1980), pp.20– 40.
16   M. Pugh, *'Hurrah for the Blackshirts!' Fascists and Fascism in Britain between the Wars* (London, 2005), p.76; W. D. Rubinstein, "Henry Page Croft and the National Party 1917–1922," *Journal of Contemporary History*, Vol.9 (1974), pp.129–148.
17   L. W. Bondy, *Racketeers of Hatred* (London and Leicester, 1946); B. A. Kosmin, "Colonial careers for Marginal Fascists – A Portrait of Hamilton Beamish," *Wiener Library Bulletin*, Vol.27 (1973–4), pp.16–23 and G. C. Lebzelter, "Henry Hamilton Beamish and the Britons: Champions of Anti-Semitism", in Lunn and Thurlow (eds), *British Fascism*, pp.41–56. S. Woodbridge, "The Nature and Development of the Concept of National Synthesis in British Fascist Ideology 1920–1940," PhD thesis, Kingston University, 1997, pp.237–243, for the interest of Beamish's group in Lintorn-Orman's. KV 2/246 notices Joyce and Beamish as correspondents.
18   R.B.D. Blakeney, "British Fascism," *The Nineteenth Century*, Vol. XCVII (1925), p.132. See more generally R.J.B. Bosworth, "The British Press, the Conservatives and Mussolini, 1920– 34," *Journal of Contemporary History*, Vol.5 (1970), pp.163–182. The well-thumbed J.A.R. Marriott, *The Makers of Modern Italy* (London, 1931), revealed the sympathies of a leading historian.
19   P. Brendon, *The Dark Valley. A Panorama of the 1930s* (London, 2000), p.21.
20   J. S. Barnes, *Fascism and the International Centre of Fascist Studies* (Lausanne, 1929). *British Fascism*, No.14, September 1931 for comment on Barnes's "exceedingly interesting" work. Goad's thoughts featured earlier in *ibid*. No. 3, August 1930 and continued over two issues. Goad published *What is Fascism?* (Florence, 1929) and *The Making of the Corporate*

State (London, 1932). On the Italian connection generally, see "Practical Fascism in Italy," *Fascist Bulletin*, 20 June 1925 and "Fascists in Italy and England," *ibid.*, 29 August 1925. Further detail on Barnes appears in WO 204/12841. He wrote *Half a Life* (London, 1933) and *Half a Life Left* (London, 1939). C. Baldoli, *Exporting Fascism: Italian Fascists and Britain's Italians in the 1930s* (Oxford, 2003), for more on Italian influences. The novel by A. Preston, *In Love and War* (London, 2014), also explores the British-Italian fascist connection in 1930s Florence.

21 B. Granzow, *A Mirror of Nazism: British Opinion and the Emergence of Hitler 1929–1933* (London, 1964) and I. Kershaw, *Making Friends with Hitler: Lord Londonderry, the Nazis and the Road to War* (London, 2004), provide the broader context.

22 *British Fascism*, No.17, January 1932 and No.23, February 1933 offer this evidence on Nazi links.

23 NARA, microfilm, T-81 Roll 35, Folder 20, Hoffmann and Bene exchange, 3–5 April 1935.

24 R. Griffiths, *Fellow Travellers of the Right: British Enthusiasts for Nazi Germany* (London, 1980), p.88. Woodbridge, "British Fascist Ideology," pp.243 ff on the National Fascisti. Pugh, '*Hurrah!*' p.53. KV 3/57 for *England's Reveille*, its manifesto of November 1924. KV 3/121 for an Intelligence report on the National Fascisti.

25 Linehan, *British Fascism 1918–39*, p.126. But he provides no source. Neither does Farr, *The Development*, p.56.

26 Cole, *Lord Haw-Haw*, p.31.

27 Linehan, *British Fascism*, p.65.

28 R. Thurlow, *Fascism in Britain. A History, 1918–1985* (Oxford, 1987), p.53. Linehan, *British Fascism*, p.68

29 *British Lion*, late June 1926 and October–November 1927; *British Fascism*, Summer 1933; Linehan, *British Fascism*, p.66. It also adopted a more defined 'fascist feminism': Farr, *The Development*, pp.73–80 and J. Gottlieb, *Feminine Fascism: Women in Britain's Fascist Movement, 1923–1945* (London, 2000).

30 Linehan, *British Fascism*, p.55.

31 *Fascist Bulletin*, 5 December 1925 [Christmas cards]; *ibid.* 26 September 1925 [Fascist cigarettes]; *British Lion*, No.25 nd [matches]; *Fascist Bulletin*, 29 August 1925 [ties]; *British Fascism*, No.15, October 1931 [cufflinks]. For the British Fascist Hymn, see *British Fascism*, No.18, February 1932. *British Lion*, 23 October 1926 on buy British.

32 Oxford Dictionary of National Biography Online. Accessed 30 June 2013.

33 R. Thurlow, "The Failure of British Fascism 1932–40," in A. Thorpe (ed.) *The Failure of Political Extremism in Inter-War Britain* (Exeter, 1989), p.67. D. Baker, "The Extreme Right in the 1920s: Fascism in a cold climate, or 'Conservatism with knobs on,'" in M. Cronin (ed.), *The Failure of British Fascism* (London, 1996), pp.12–28.

34 Farndale, *Haw-Haw*, p.57.

35 Pugh, '*Hurrah!*' pp.59 ff

36 A. Leese, *Out of Step* (Hollywood, nd. First published Guildford, 1951), p.49. See generally, J. E. Morell, "The Life and Opinions of A. S. Leese: A Study in Extreme Antisemitism," MA Thesis, University of Sheffield, 1974. *The Times*, 16 April 2009, obituary of Colin Jordan, emphasised Leese's role as an ideological influence on British fascism. Linehan, *British Fascism*, p.55 and K. Lunn, "The Impact and Ideology of British Fascism in the 1920s," in T. Kushner and K. Lunn (eds), *Traditions of Intolerance: Historical Perspectives on Fascism and Race Discourse in Britain* (Manchester, 1989), pp.140–154, on this ideological drift.

37 Pugh, '*Hurrah!*' pp.55 ff. is valuable on linkages.

38 *British Lion*, No.29, March 1929 and No.30, April 1929; *British Fascism*, No.1, June 1930 and *ibid*. No.19, 1 March 1932.

39 Patrick Hannon papers, House of Lords, HNN 123, Box F, diary 29 December 1924. Farr, *The Development*, p.49.

40 Linehan, *British Fascism*, p.45 for general comment. Pugh, '*Hurrah!*', p.59 on Jix's key role. The portrait derives from M. Cowling, *The Impact of Labour 1920–1924: The Beginning of Modern British Politics* (Cambridge, 1971), p.75 which is generally useful on High Tory opinion. D. Cesarani, "The anti-Jewish Career of William Joynson-Hicks, Cabinet Minister," *Journal of Contemporary History*, Vol.24 (1989), pp.461–482 on Jix's anti-Jewish politics. Matthew and Harrison (eds), *ODNB*, Vol.24, pp.38–41.

41 Woodbridge, "British Fascist Ideology," pp.155–160. M. Ruotsila, "The Antisemitism of the Eighth Duke of Northumberland's the *Patriot*, 1922–1930," *Journal of Contemporary History*, Vol.39 (2004), pp.71–92.

42 Linehan, *British Fascism*, p.49

43 Paranoid as in R. Hofstadter, *The Paranoid Style in American Politics* (London, 1966).

44 J. M. Wilson (ed.), *The Collected Poems of Charles Hamilton SORLEY* (London, 1985), p.91.

45 *Irish Times*, 21 June 1945.

46 *Fascist Bulletin*, 20 June 1925, "Possible Cheka Troops in England."

47 G. Bennett, '*A most extraordinary and mysterious business:' The Zinoviev Letter* (London, 1999).

48 *British Fascism*, No.21, Summer 1932.

49 "No dealings with Diabolus," *Fascist Bulletin*, 27 March 1926.

50 "The TUC Humbug, 1927 Brand," by M. K. in *British Lion*, October–November 1927, attacked "the Trade Union tricksters". M. K. was Maxwell Knight.

51 *British Fascism*, 1 March 1932.

52 *Fascist Bulletin*, 29 August 1925.

53 *British Lion*, No.27, nd, pp.13–14.

54 F.J.C. Hearnshaw, *A Survey of Socialism* (London, 1929), pp.18, 338. He appears in *Who Was Who 1941–1950*, p.521.

55 Hearnshaw, *Survey of Socialism*, p.14. See N. H. Webster, *World Revolution* (London, 1921), *Secret Societies and Subversive Movements* (London, 1924),

The Socialist Network (London, 1926), and her autobiography, *Spacious Days* (London, 1949). See also R. Gilman, *Behind 'World Revolution': The Strange Career of Nesta Webster* (Ann Arbor, 1982).

56 *British Lion*, No.29, March 1929; *British Fascism*, No.20, Spring 1932; J. Loughlin, "Rotha Lintorn-Orman, Ulster and the British Fascists Movement," *Immigrants and Minorities*, Vol. 32 (2014), pp.62–89. See generally, R. M. Douglas, "'The Swastika and the Shamrock': British Fascism and the Irish Question, 1918–1940," *Albion*, Vol.29 (1997), pp.57–75.

57 *Fascist Bulletin*, 11 July 1925; *British Lion*, December 1927; *British Fascism*, February 1933.

58 Northumberland appears in Matthew and Harrison (eds), *ODNB*, Vol.43, pp.677–678, "Everywhere he saw danger, betrayal, and plots" (p.678). Kershaw, *Making Friends with Hitler*, on Londonderry. Matthew and Harrison (eds.), *ODNB*, Vol.14, pp.235–238 on Croft and H. P. Croft, *My Life of Strife* (London, 1948). See generally, Cowling, *The Impact of Labour*.

59 A. Draper, *Amritsar: The Massacre that Ended the Raj* (London, 1981).

60 *British Fascism*, Special Propaganda Issue, nd.

61 M. O'Dwyer, "The Surrender of an Empire," *British Fascism*, Special Summer Propaganda Issue, nd, p.1.

62 Matthew and Harrison (eds), *ODNB*, Vol.41, pp.538–540.

63 KV 2/2474, Macnab before the Advisory Committee, 29 July 1940, p.35.

64 *British Fascism*, Special Propaganda Issue, nd.

65 KV 2/245/1a.

66 KV 2/2474, Macnab before the Advisory Committee, 29 July 1940, p.35.

67 C. Bewley, *Memoirs of a Wild Goose* (Dublin, 1989), pp.205–206. Matthew and Harrison (eds), *ODNB*, Vol.17, pp.488–490, on Dyer. N. Collett, *The Butcher of Amritsar* (London, 2005) and N. Lloyd, *The Amritsar Massacre: The Untold Story of a Fateful Day* (London, 2012).

68 MS Gwynne, DEP8, Bodleian Library. Matthew and Harrison (eds), *ODNB*, Vol.24, pp.366–368 for Gwynne. I. Colvin, *The Life of General Dyer* (Edinburgh and London, 1929), gives the *Morning Post's* line. Kenny, *Germany Calling*, p.72 on Joyce's preference for the paper.

69 C. Holmes, *Anti-Semitism in British Society 1876–1939* (London, 1989), ch.9; K.M. Wilson, *A Study in the History and Politics of the Morning Post 1905–1926* (Lampeter, 1990), ch.6.

70 C. G. Philipoff (pseud? Capel Pownall?), "The Death Camps of the Soviet," *British Fascism*, Extra Autumn Issue, 1933?

71 C. G. Philipoff (pseud? Capel Pownall?), "Germany and the Jewish Question," in *ibid*. Special Summer Propaganda Issue, nd. Philipoff was almost certainly Pownall.

72 *Fascist Bulletin*, 20 June 1925.

73 J. Vincent, "The Case for Mosley," *The Times Literary Supplement*, 4 April 1975, p.351.

74 *Who Was Who 1951–1960* (London, 1961), p.409.

75 "What is Fascism?" *Fascist Bulletin*, 25 July 1925. *Who Was Who 1929–1940* (London, 1941), p.583.

76 A. Hardinge, *A Diplomatist in Europe* (London, 1927) and *A Diplomatist in the East* (London, 1928). *Who Was Who 1929–1940*, pp.591–592.

77 *Who Was Who 1951–1960*, p.111. Joyce wanted him as a source when contemplating his own biography. WJ to MJ, 30 December 1945.

78 Winter, *Winter's Tale.*

79 *Fascist Bulletin*, 13 June 1925 for a Hyde Park meeting where, as officer commanding the London area, he made a speech. See also "A Statement on Fascist Policy," *ibid.* 29 August 1925. *Manchester Guardian*, 26 November 1924 for aliens and perverts.

80 Thurlow, *Fascism in Britain*, p.53. G. Macklin, *Very Deeply Dyed in Black: Sir Oswald Mosley and the Resurrection of British Fascism after 1945* (London, 2007), p.13.

81 *British Fascism*, No.18, 1 February 1932.

82 *The Blackshirt*, 23–29 September 1933.

83 R. Griffiths, *Patriotism Perverted: Captain Ramsay, the Right Club and British Anti-Semitism 1939–40* (London, 1998), pp.29–30, 45.

84 *Fascist Week*, 2–8 March 1934.

85 *British Fascism*, No.1, June 1930; *ibid.* No.9, March 1931.

86 G. P. Mudge, *The Menace to the English Race and its Traditions of Present-day Immigration and Emigration* (np nd 1919–1920?), p.2. This work also appeared in the *Eugenics Review*, 11, Vol. 4 (1920). See his contributions to *Jewry ueber alles* (May 1920), p.7 and June 1920, pp.5–6, *Jewry ueber alles or The Hidden Hand Exposed* (July 1920), pp.6–7, *The Hidden Hand or the Jewish Peril* (February 1924), pp.21–22, March 1924, pp.70–71, June 1924, pp.86–87, and November 1924, pp.161–162. Associated with Regent Street Polytechnic, his more acceptable face appeared in *A Textbook of Zoology* (London, 1901). G. Schaffer, *Racial Science and British Society, 1930–62* (London, 2008), is excellent on race scientists.

87 A. Masters, *The Man who was M: The Life of Maxwell Knight* (London, 1986). Matthew and Harrison (eds), *ODNB*, Vol.31, pp.919–920.

88 Private information.

89 *British Lion*, No.28, nd.

90 *Ibid.* December 1927. My emphasis.

91 *Ibid.*

92 *British Fascism*, Special Summer Propaganda issue, 1933.

93 J. Hope, "Fascism, the Security Service and the Curious Careers of Maxwell Knight and James McGuirk Hughes," *Lobster*, No. 22, November 1991, pp.1–5. See also *idem*, "Surveillance or Collusion? Maxwell Knight, MI5 and the British Fascisti," *Intelligence and National Security*, Vol.9 (1994), pp.651–675.

94 J. Hope, "British Fascism and the State 1917–1927: A Re-Examination of the Documentary Evidence," *Labour History Review*, Vol.57 (1992), pp.72–83; *idem*, "Fascism and the State in Britain: The Case of the British Fascisti 1923–31," *Australian Journal of History and Politics*, Vol.39 (1993), pp.367–380. See also more recently, V. Madeira, *Britannia and the Bear: Anglo-Russian Intelligence Wars, 1917–1929* (Woodbridge, 2014).

95   R. Thurlow, "State Management of the BUF in the 1930s," in Cronin (ed.), *Failure of British Fascism*, p.31. R. Thurlow, *The Secret State: British Internal Security in the Twentieth Century* (Oxford, 1994), pp.203–213.

96   B. Clough, *State Secrets: The Kent–Wolkoff Affair* (Hove, 2006), p. 25. S. Dorril, *Blackshirt: Sir Oswald Mosley and British Fascism* (London, 2006), p.200. Since confirmed in C. Andrew, *In Defence of the Realm: The Authorized History of MI5* (London, 2009), pp.124, 128–131.

97   Andrew, *Defence of the Realm*, pp.123–124.

98   HO 283/40, Neil Francis-Hawkins before the 18B Advisory Committee. Masters, *The Man who was M*, p.29, for the start of his career; Hope, "British Fascism," p.73. See also Andrew, *Defence of the Realm*, and C. Pincher, *Treachery* (London, 2009).

99   M. Knight, *Crime Cargo* (London, 1934), for "Mr Joycey."

100   Andrew, *Defence of the Realm* stays silent.

101   *The Times*, 23 October 1924 reports the meeting but does not mention Joyce.

102   Farr, *The Development*, p.65 for their defence of a meeting held by Locker-Lampson.

103   HO 144/20144/130, report, 11 March 1935.

104   KV 2/346, notes by Margaret Joyce.

105   Selwyn, *Hitler's Englishman*, p.28.

106   *Ibid.* p.31.

107   WJ to MJ, 30 December 1945. See photograph in the *Daily Mirror*, 25 October 1924.

108   USSC, R. R. Bellamy, "We Marched with Mosley," p.510, unpublished ts. In 2013 Black House Publishing brought out an abridged version of Bellamy's work.

109   Bellamy, "We Marched with Mosley," p.510.

110   Selwyn, *Hitler's Englishman*, p.29.

111   Rawnsley Collection, Bradford University, BUF Interviews, Testimony of A. Fawcett.

112   M. Burleigh, *Sacred Causes: Religion and Politics from the European Dictators to Al Qaeda* (London, 2006), pp.60, 114, on the cult of fascist martyrdom.

113   Hazel Brooks interviewed by author, 15 April 1992.

114   *Lambeth Free Press*, 24 October 1924. J. O. Stubbs, "Lord Milner and Patriotic Labour," *English Historical Review*, Vol.87 (1972), pp.717–754. R. Douglas, "The National Democratic Party and the British Workers' League," *Historical Journal*, Vol.15 (1972), pp.533–552. Obituary in *The Times*, 4 February 1952. Matthew and Harrison (eds), *ODNB*, Vol.19, pp.723–724 on Fisher.

115   WJ to MJ, 13 October 1945.

116   Vincent, "The Case for Mosley," p.351.

117   Cole, *Lord Haw-Haw*, p.34.

118   F. A. Voigt, *Unto Caesar* (London, 1938), pp.133–134.

4

MARCHING WITH MOSLEY

I felt as if I were in a room filled with old men and with mirrors
on all sides, so that their faces were repeated in endless facsimile –
Baldwin, Ramsay MacDonald, Chamberlain, Simon, Hoare, Lord
Broadacres and Lord Coalmine and Lord Dailydope, Sir Puffin
Tory, Colonel Dividend, and all the rest of that cackling coterie.
[Douglas Reed, *A Prophet at Home* (London, 1941), p. 171.]

1

Joyce was a frustrated, virtually unknown politician in the late 1920s.
However, he became much better known in the 1930s, at first through
his association with Sir Oswald Mosley. They came from strikingly
different backgrounds, but until 1937 marched together in the British
Union of Fascists. Both were desperately hungry for political power.

'Tom' Mosley had been a Conservative member of parliament
before crossing the floor to Labour and throughout his time at Westminster craved the influence those parties denied him.[1] Reflecting
this deep dissatisfaction, in 1931 he established the New Party.[2] Its
failure in that year's general election, and the victory of those he
scornfully dismissed as dead political souls, proved the last straw. In
January 1932 he went off impatiently to Mussolini's Italy. He was

impressed, as many political travellers had been.[3] Politically fired up, on 1 October 1932 he formed the British Union of Fascists. The BUF had a better-known leader, more followers, more resources, and a more rounded programme than any earlier fascist organisation in Britain.[4] Mosley was heading a movement rather than a pressure group.

Supremely self-obsessed – just like Joyce – Mosley believed the BUF would sweep him to power.[5] In 1933 he told an American journalist that by the time he was forty he would be in charge of a fascist government.[6] He was giving himself three years. The reporter remained sceptical.[7] Mosley peddled similar enthusiasms to the Nazis: they, too, would come to disbelieve him. To strike out anew in British politics will always carry high risks. For now, though, he fired himself, Joyce and other converts, with the belief nothing ventured, nothing gained.

Joyce's background in the British Fascists might have led him to regard Mosley, a denizen of Westminster's corridors, with some suspicion, a Johnny-come-lately to fascism. But he stifled any doubts and enlisted six months or so after the movement had started.[8] It marked a decisive moment in his political life. He gained more contacts, became involved in a dynamic organisation and quickly emerged as a fully fledged fascist politician.

2

Early twentieth-century fascism is widely regarded as a small tear on the smooth fabric of British politics. A novelist, echoing others, has dismissed it as "a complete irrelevance to the heart of political life in this country."[9] Admittedly, it never achieved its yearned-for break-through. But the BUF attracted sympathisers beyond its hard-core members. It raised important political questions, posed serious problems and became a marked feature of the country's historical landscape.[10]

The British Fascists showed many signs of being a Tory hybrid when Joyce was an active member. But picking up where Lintorn-Orman's organisation had left off, the BUF advanced a comprehensive fascist alternative.[11] Fascism is a term often used to smear political opponents and more serious attempts to define it have proved controversial.[12] But it perceived a "pervasive crisis of liberalism, free market capitalism, [and European] and Western Civilisation." The solution lay in "a palingenetic form of populist ultra-nationalism," in other words, a programme of economic, political and social-cultural renewal.[13]

In simpler language, the BUF believed that "The weakness and ineptitude of [Britain's] governing class (the 'old gang')" had resulted in the country's "decline as a manufacturing and trading nation." In parallel, it was suffering from "spiritual and cultural anarchy," decaying at its core.

The democratic political system presiding over this regrettable national degeneration had served its time. Britain now needed "a new strong state led by an inspired leader."[14] In fascism's corporate political structure, representing the country's sectional interests and working for the common good, "a new technocratic elite" would revitalise industry and operate the economy on "behalf of a national community of 'true' Britons."[15] Joyce, a totally self-absorbed first-class honours graduate, sniffed the prospect of self-interest here. So far his life had disappointed: he had been betrayed in Ireland; his career had constantly been thwarted in London. Under fascism it would be different. At last he would be able to forget his dismal past. He would become an important political figure. And could anyone seriously doubt he should exercise more influence than the miserable majority who lacked all his insights and talents?

The BUF argued that in this new world British labour must be protected against low-priced, job-threatening imports. Joyce's knowledge of Lancashire had already impressed on him how mill workers had been badly affected by Asian competition, and he and other fascists often viewed this problem as the consequence of overseas loans organised by a parasitic City.[16] The British economy must be organised for the benefit of industry and commerce rather than finance – there are shades of some early Socialist economic thinking here – which would be revived by stimulating domestic demand.

To recover Britain's position as a world power – and the likes of Mr 'Safety First' Baldwin were not equipped for that task – the Empire must remain a self-contained trading unit, controlled from its metropolitan centre. The British Fascists had been keen to prevent any Imperial scuttle, and the BUF followed that line.[17] Radio links and improved transport systems, including air power, would make the Empire a seamless unit. "Southern Ireland" had already been surrendered – in Joyce's words to "a gang of gunmen" – and did not feature heavily in BUF thinking, whereas independence for India and other Imperial territories was off the agenda.[18] Still smarting at his family's betrayal in Galway, Joyce readily identified with this policy and soon appropriated the "tall" and "gaunt" Edward Carson, the defender of Ulster, as a political god.[19] "In bearing, will, act, and thought," he declared, "Carson was a Fascist."[20] And the Ulster Volunteer Force – Carson's Own – intended to defend the province against Dublin's jurisdiction, was "the first real and tangible resistance that Liberal Plutocracy had to encounter in Britain."[21] More Carsons were needed to save the Empire. Joyce, who never sold himself short, has already been observed thinking he was fitted for such a major role.

When Britain's fascists reflected on the country's cultural problems, they argued that here too a fresh start was needed, a spiritual rebirth. Believing as much, a contemporary of Joyce's wrote: "One of the first duties of Fascism will be to recapture the British cinema and the British theatre for the British nation." At present both outlets were described as under the control of Jews, mainly America-based, preoccupied as ever by materialism and exhibiting no 'feel' for Britain's great historical past. These forces held the arts in an "alien stranglehold."[22] More generally, one of the BUF's leading figures proclaimed that fascism would sweep away the "cult of ugliness and distortion" to be found in so much contemporary art, music and literature and only when it did would a truly British culture emerge.[23]

When enthusiastically promoting these messages, Joyce spoke to fascist audiences, addressed open public meetings across Britain, wrote in the movement's newspapers and thumped out pamphlets on his typewriter. His interest in publishing academic articles in English language journals was fading fast. He was now a dedicated political missionary, delivering the fascist message, seeking converts, fully committed to smashing his enemies. "You're a Soldier of the Plan, a son of Greater Britain," the playwright wrote.[24] He was just that. As a fascist soldier he would always be ready to battle his enemies, pitch into the rough and tumble of physical combat. The BUF's black shirt might not have quite the cut, the style, of the officer's army uniform for which he had yearned. It might not allow the proud military swagger. But it had its compensations.[25]

He would soon be expressing his vision in near-religious terms. His political beliefs provided a substitute for his lost Catholicism. In his case – as with many others – fascism "metabolised the religious instinct."[26] The old world would be replaced by "a new heroic spirit of patriotism, community and historical purpose."[27] The country would be reawakened, reborn. A secular utopia would emerge.[28] And rightfully, he thought, he would be operating at the centre of it.

The BUF's programme, which reflected British and European influences, amounted to an authoritarian, anti-democratic vision of politics.[29] Even a passing glance towards Continental Europe makes that quite clear.[30] Fascism, like Communism, devoured its own while deliberately, ruthlessly, systematically, liquidating legions of political opponents. Bodies littered the political landscape. The ideology was always more than a form of contemporary chic; the BUF was never "perfectly harmless and even worthy."[31] Katharine Burdekin, writing as Murray Constantine, soon realised the real and potential horrors of fascism, which she transmitted to readers of her dystopian novel, *Swastika Night*, as early as 1937.[32] In Britain, the BUF's Jew-baiting was certainly never harmless for East London's Jews, some of whom had escaped only recently from Tsarist persecution.[33] But Joyce, schooled in the violent politics of Ireland, never hesitated to back this policy. He would soon be recommending Jews should be shot in the streets or hanged from lamp-posts.[34]

3

Who marched alongside Joyce?[35] Mosley's shadow fell everywhere, over everybody. The slogan went: "Mosley for ACTION! Mosley for UNITY! Mosley for DISCIPLINE! Mosley for a NEW and VIR-ILE Britain!"[36] The BUF soon succumbed to the personality cult. As the worshipped political boss – though Joyce predictably thought he could make a better fist of it – 'The Leader' wrote in the cause.[37] He also held public meetings and in an age of pre-television poli-tics always attracted large audiences. Contemporary photographs and newsreels capture the pageantry of these minor Nuremberg rallies. Spotlight-fixed, eyes ablaze, he would confidently proclaim that "moments of truth, moments of destiny" arose in every great nation and assure his fascist foot soldiers and black-dressed lieutenants like Joyce that the country had reached this decisive turning point. Mosley, the Valentino of British politics, demanded star billing in this orchestrated attempt to package the message and sell it to the public.[38] "He loves parades, uniforms, flags and music," H. R. Knickerbocker observed, all of which made up the political brand.[39] And it had the desired effect. "Albert Hall – Wonderful!" one supporter recorded in his diary in 1936.[40]

To 1936, when the movement became the British Union of Fascists and National Socialists, indeed, until 10 July 1940, when the government declared it a proscribed organisation, Mosley stayed centre stage, safe from challenge by the likes of Joyce, the little men, as he dismissively called them. After the Second World War his ambitions continued through the Union Movement.[41] And he retained his worshippers. Ronald Creasy, whose Suffolk weather vane with its fascist symbol reflected his adoration of 'The Leader', wrote in 1980, "I am always with you in dedication and application."[42] John Charnley, an early convert, also continued to venerate Mosley as a political god.[43] After 'The Leader's' death in 1980, ageing supporters and new followers have continued to worship his exalted memory, most recently through the Friends of Oswald Mosley.[44]

Joyce's senior position in the movement – he soon replaced Wilfred 'Bill' Risdon as Director of Propaganda in the BUF – often brought him into Mosley's close company.[45] But who else would he have met or known of? Financial backing came from tycoons like Viscount Rothermere and Lord Nuffield and other wealthy members of the upper-class who lamented what they viewed as Britain's decline since its Victorian heyday. They feared for their interests in an uncertain post-war world; Bolshevism, the rise of British labour, worried them.[46] Alexander Scrimgeour, an affluent Sussex stockbroker, soon to become one of Joyce's few close friends, had no confidence that the current crop of Westminster politicians would ever restore the country's greatness. They were totally lacking in 'fizz.' Fascism was the answer. Dorothy Wilding's soft-focus photograph of Mosley in

The Tatler, with its caption suggesting he alone could take the country forward, played to these supporters.[47]

Joyce mixed with such wealthy backers when they fund-raised at expensive London venues, but socially he was closer to recruits from another constituency. He had been uprooted from America, forced out of Ireland, frustrated when trying to establish himself in London. He readily identified therefore with those displaced professional types who joined the BUF. Some had attempted fresh starts in the Empire, oiling "the machinery" of British rule or scratching a living in far flung parts of the world, often "moving on, trying something else, somewhere else": these were restless people who knew all about "loneliness, longing, debt, disease, disaster and death."[48] Richard Reynell Bellamy, formerly an Imperial planter and later the BUF's official historian, featured in their ranks.[49] As did John Macnab, soon to become Joyce's closest ally. After Oxford he had tried his hand in Northern Rhodesia. Back in England after his colonial dreams crumbled, he ran into more financial problems.[50] It requires no great leap of the imagination to understand why Joyce and he were attracted to each other.

Joyce brushed against former soldiers who felt sold short after the First World War.[51] They represented action, which typified the movement. When attacking the Jews he found a ready ally in 'Boney' Fuller, the highly respected military strategist, who resented having to resign from the active list in 1933.[52] Captain Robert Gordon Canning MC discovered in fascism "a certain barbaric splendour," a "warrior spirit," necessary for the country's rebirth, "the Spirit of Everest as opposed to that of the night club."[53]

Working-class recruits marched alongside them. The mill worker Nellie Driver – author of an unpublished autobiography and also a novel on fascism – would have reminded Joyce of social problems in the North-West.[54] In the South of England, workers in the long-neglected, economically depressed areas of East London offered a rich recruiting ground for his knuckle-duster fascism.[55] He was soon busy among them.

These supporters were joined by men who had served at Westminster. Joyce became a close associate of the ex-Labour MP John Beckett. Robert Forgan and 'Bill' Risdon also had Labour backgrounds, before transferring their allegiances to Mosley.[56] Alexander Raven Thomson, the movement's key ideologist, had been a Marxist.[57]

During his time with Mosley Joyce grew to love Sussex. But he was essentially an urban type based in London. He showed little interest in the seasons' patterns. Yet he went on recruiting missions to the countryside as the BUF strained to capitalise on the problems faced by Britain's farmers, an initiative Ernest Shepard captured in *Punch*.[58] The movement also emphasised the role that rural life had to play in Britain's spiritual recovery. One convert was Henry Williamson, ex-soldier, writer, and now a Norfolk farmer, who in his sequent novels, *A Chronicle of Ancient Sunlight*, introduced readers to "Philip Maddison," who marched for fascism.[59] Robert Saunders, a farmer in Dorset, joined up.[60] Sylvia Morris, a doctor's daughter in rural Lincolnshire, and familiar with countryside issues, enlisted with Mosley and soon became close to Joyce in more ways than one.[61]

When focusing on rural values, the fascists were positing an implicit or explicit distinction between a squalid, broken urban environment, often populated by foreigners such as rootless cosmopolitan Jews, and a rooted, healthy countryside. Like its arguments on film and theatre, distinctions were overdrawn, as they often are in politics. But the message was similar. Recovering Britain's greatness required a rural rebirth, too.[62]

At the same time, the BUF never lost sight of the importance of the creatively destructive power of science and technology, reflected in its interest in aeroplanes, motorised transport, motorways and radio.[63] 'Fabulous' Fay Taylour, who raced cars and speedway bikes, provided a personal reminder of this belief in the regenerative, transforming power of the machine.[64] It is no surprise the BUF became associated with Malcolm Campbell's *Blue Bird*.[65]

The British Fascists had attracted Arthur Gilligan, England's cricket captain.[66] The BUF's emphasis on physical activity – creating fine specimens for the fascist utopia – also captured sporting personalities. Joyce's boxing interests went down well. Ted 'Kid' Lewis and Joe Beckett both joined, though Lewis's time with Mosley proved short-lived. These boxers, like Joyce, were useful men to have in support when combatting Red opposition.[67] The movement had its clergymen supporters, too.[68]

To describe the BUF as full of "cranks, criminals, alcoholics and worse," is a distortion.[69] Youth heavily outnumbered deviants.[70] Joyce, and many like him, gravitated towards Mosley, hoping to benefit personally and politically from fascism's programme of national renewal.[71] The road ahead would not be easy. But Joyce never hesitated. "I am no pessimist," he once declared.[72] If others harboured doubts, they had only to open their leather pocket diaries to read:

> Britain awake! Arise from slumber!
> Soon comes the daybreak of Rebirth.

These followers have been overshadowed by the excessive attention lavished on Mosley in history books, literary fiction and television programmes.[73] Yet fascism's hero-worship with leaders transformed into gods – a status Joyce desperately craved – should not obscure those faceless men and women who every day quietly turned the wheels of the BUF's machinery.

When Joyce glanced across the ranks he would have recognised some colleagues from his days in the British Fascists. Other faces would have been new. Some comrades would soon intrude dangerously into his life. But for now, full of expectation and hope, he swam alongside them, hoping to reach the political shore he was urgently seeking.

Notes

1 Dorril, *Blackshirt*, is the latest Mosley biography.
2 See generally Worley, *Oswald Mosley*.
3 Dorril, *Blackshirt*, pp.191 ff. Cassius (M. Foot), *The Trial of Mussolini. Being a Verbatim Report of the First Great Trial of War Criminals held in London, sometime in 1944 or 1945* (London, 1943), on prominent British admirers of Mussolini. Alfio Bernabei's play based on Foot's polemic was staged in London in 2007.
4 Pugh, '*Hurrah!*' p.73. D. Stone, *Responses to Nazism in Britain, 1933–1939* (Basingstoke, 2003), pp.169–188.
5 Skidelsky, *Oswald Mosley*, remains the standard biography. Skidelsky recognises Mosley's hubris in Matthew and Harrison (eds), *ODNB*, Vol.39 (Oxford, 2004), p.474. See also Macklin, *Deeply Dyed*, for Mosley's

"overweening egoism and the monumental self-delusion that he, and he alone, was capable of defeating Stalin's bloodthirsty Asiatic hordes" (p.49). This belief is similar to Joyce's claim, soon to be emphasised, that at Hitler's side he would have won the War for the Nazis. See also Mosley as "Arthur Clayton" in W. Holtby and N. Ginsburg, Take *Back Your Freedom* (London, 1939), p.124 especially.

6 H. R. Knickerbocker, *Die Schwarzhemden in England und Englands wirtschaflichen Aufstieg* (Berlin, 1934), p.18.

7 *Ibid.* p.39.

8 *Fascist Week*, 26 January–1 February 1934, p.5.

9 K. Ishiguro, *The Remains of the Day* (London, 1990), p.137.

10 F. Mullally, *Fascism inside England* (London, 1946) and C. Cross, *The Fascists in Britain* (London, 1961), provided pioneer studies. See later, Thurlow's *Fascism in Britain*, revised as *Fascism in Britain: from Oswald Mosley's Blackshirts to the National Front* (London, 1998), and his *Fascism in Modern Britain* (Stroud, 2000).

11 R. Griffiths, *An Intelligent Person's Guide to Fascism* (London, 2000).

12 See the debate involving Roger Griffin and others in the *Journal of Contemporary History*, Vol.37 (2002), pp.21–43, 259–269. See also R. Griffin et al., *Fascism Past and Present. West and East* (Stuttgart, 2006).

13 R. Griffin, "British Fascism: The Ugly Duckling," in M. Cronin (ed.), *The Failure of British Fascism*, pp.141–165, especially p.143.

14 *Ibid.* pp.143–144.

15 *Ibid.* p.143.

16 S. J. Rawnsley, "Fascism and Fascists in the 1930s. A Case Study of Fascism in the North of England in a Period of Economic Change." PhD thesis, University of Bradford, 1981, p.127, observes Joyce campaigning in the textile areas. Rawnsley Collection, University of Bradford, BUF Interview, Bob Row, 24 August 1978, on Japanese and Indian competition.

17 Griffin, "British Fascism," p.143. Pugh, *'Hurrah!'* ch. 10.

18 *The Blackshirt*, 29 June 1934 for Joyce referring to the gunmen during a speech at the January Club. Douglas, "'The Swastika and the Shamrock,'" pp.70–72 on the BUF and Ireland.

19 A.T.Q. Stewart, *Edward Carson* (Belfast, 1997). G. Lewis, *Carson: The Man Who Divided Ireland* (London, 2005).

20 W.J. (W. Joyce), "Quis Separabit?" *Fascist Quarterly*, Vol.II, (1936), p.28. Joyce's interpretation was influenced by W.E.D. Allen. On Allen and the Ulster Movement, see his J. Drennan, *BUF: Oswald Mosley and British Fascism* (London, 1934), p.292.

21 W.J., "Quis Separabit?" p.28.

22 A.K. Chesterton, *Oswald Mosley. Portrait of a Leader* (London, 1936), p.159.

23 A. Raven Thomson, "Why Fascism," *Fascist Quarterly*, Vol. 1 (1935), p.235. For a wider discussion, see T.P. Linehan, "Reactionary Spectatorship: British Fascists and Cinema in Inter-War Britain" and R. Griffin, "'This Fortress Built against Infection:' The BUF Vision of Britain's Theatrical and Musical Renaissance," in J. V. Gottlieb and T. P Linehan (eds),

The Culture of Fascism. Visions of the Far Right in Britain (London, 2004), pp.27–44 and 25–65, respectively.

24 Holtby and Ginsburg, *Take Back Your Freedom*, p.120.

25 S. J. Rawnsley, "Fascism and Fascists in the 1930s," p.120 emphasises "the lure of the uniform."

26 Burleigh, *Sacred Causes*, p.xii. Voigt, *Unto Caesar*, on fascism and Marxism as religions.

27 Griffin, "British Fascism," pp.143–144.

28 P. M. Coupland, "The Blackshirted Utopians," *Journal of Contemporary History*, Vol.33 (1998), pp.255–272.

29 R. Eatwell, "Towards a New Model of Generic Fascism," *Journal of Theoretical Politics*, Vol.4 (1992), pp.161–194 provides a political science perspective. G. Love, "'What's the big idea?' Oswald Mosley and the British Union of Fascists and Generic Fascism," *Journal of Contemporary History*, Vol.42 (2006), pp.447–468, discusses home-grown and external influences.

30 P. Morgan, *Fascism in Europe 1939–1945* (London, 2003). Biographies illustrate the phenomenon: R.J.B. Bosworth, *Mussolini* (London, 2002); I. Kershaw's two volumes, *Hitler 1889–1936: Hubris* (London, 1998) and *Hitler 1936–1945: Nemesis* (London, 2000); P. Preston, *Franco: A Biography* (London, 1993) and F. R. de Meneses, *Salazar. A Political Biography* (New York, 2009). On Mosley, there is now Dorril, *Blackshirt*.

31 Kenny, *Germany Calling*, p.98.

32 M. Constantine, *Swastika Night* (London, 1940. First ed., 1937).

33 Mullally, *Fascism*, p.71. L. Birch, *Why They Join the Fascists* (London, 1937), p.29.

34 DPP 2/407 (Leeson's report). W. Joyce, *Twilight over England* (Metairie, La nd), p.70. All subsequent references are to this edition.

35 Birch, *Why They Join*, for a contemporary discussion of membership.

36 Mullally, *Fascism*, p.25.

37 *The Greater Britain* (1932 and 1934), *Fascism – One Hundred Questions Asked and Answered* (1936) and *Tomorrow We Live* (1938).

38 The Valentino image originated with A. J. Cummings in the *News Chronicle*, 23 April 1934. His looks did not impress Admiral Sir Barry Domvile: to him Mosley did not "look English . . . but a touch of something east of Suez. Perhaps his ma stayed out late," YCAL, MSS Box 13, Folder 598, Domvile to Ezra Pound, 13 September 1954. In coded form here was another suggestion Mosley was part Jewish. J. Gottlieb, "The Marketing of Megalomania: Celebrity, Consumption and the Development of Political Technology in the British Union of Fascists," *Journal of Contemporary History*, Vol.41 (2006), pp.35–55, on packaging fascism.

39 Knickerbocker, *Die Schwarzhemden*, p.16. "Er liebt Paraden, Uniformen, Flaggen und Musik."

40 USSC, MS 119/F7/2, Robert Saunders, diary, 22 March 1936.

41 Skidelsky, *Mosley* (1995), ch.26, 27; Dorril, *Blackshirt*, pp.544 ff. Macklin, *Deeply Dyed* is more comprehensive.

42 Mosley Papers, University of Birmingham Special Collections, OMD/ 1/1/7/61, Creasy to Mosley, 21 June 1980. Creasy's wartime agitation, after being released from internment, is discussed in KV3/3800.

43 J. Charnley, *Blackshirts and Roses: An Autobiography* (London, 1990), pp.233, 234, 237, 238 exudes hero-worship as does his contribution to Anon (ed.) *Mosley's Blackshirts: The Inside Story of the British Union of Fascists* (London, 1986), pp.31, 35.

44 *Comrade* generally.

45 J. L. Risdon, *Black Shirt and Smoking Beagles: The Biography of Wilfred Risdon: an unconventional Campaigner* (s.l, 2013), pp.99–100, 158, touches on the change.

46 Dorril, *Blackshirt*, pp.277–278.

47 *The Tatler*, 30 May 1934.

48 R. Bickers, *Empire Made Me: An Englishman Adrift in Shanghai* (New York, 2003), pp.43, 242.

49 KV 2/1747 and KV 2/1748. Bellamy's Imperial reflections appear in *The Real South Seas* (London, 1933) and *Mixed Bliss in Melanesia* (London, 1934).

50 KV 2/2474/91a, pp.2–3 (29 July 1940).

51 S. R. Ward, "Great Britain: Land fit for Heroes Lost," in his edited *The War Generation. Veterans of the First World War* (Port Washington, 1975), pp.31ff. M. Petter, "'Temporary Gentlemen' in the Aftermath of the Great War; Rank, Status and the ex-Officer Problem," *Historical Journal*, Vol.37 (1994), pp.127–152. P. Coupland, "The Black Shirt in Britain: The Meanings and Functions of Political Uniform," in Gottlieb and Linehan (eds), *Culture of Fascism*, pp.100–115.

52 A. J. Trythall, *'Boney' Fuller: The Intellectual General, 1978–1966* (London, 1977). B. Holden Reid, *J.F.C. Fuller: Military Thinker* (London, 1987). Fuller was a fierce anti-Semite. See "The Cancer of Europe," *Fascist Quarterly*, Vol.1 (1935), pp.66–81 and *ibid*. Vol.1, No.2, pp.232–242.

53 *Action*, 30 December 1937. HO 45/25706 and KV 2/878, for official files.

54 N. Driver, "From the Shadows of Exile," unpublished ts (Author's possession), and D. Mayall, "Rescued from the Shadows of Exile: Nellie Driver, Autobiography and the British Union of Fascists," in T. Kushner and K. Lunn (eds), *The Politics of Marginality: Race, the Radical Right and Minorities in Twentieth Century Britain* (London, 1990), pp.19–39. Rawnsley Collection, Bradford University, contains her novel, "The Mill."

55 T. P. Linehan, *East London for Mosley: The British Union of Fascists in East London and South West Essex* (London, 1996).

56 F. Beckett, *The Rebel who Lost His Cause: The Tragedy of John Beckett* (London, 1999). C. Holmes and B. Hill, "Robert Forgan," in J. Saville and J. M. Bellamy (eds), *Dictionary of Labour Biography*, Vol.6 (London, 1982), pp.111–114. Skidelsky, *Oswald Mosley*, pp.248–249, 325, 344 and Risdon, *Black Shirt and Smoking Beagles* on Risdon. See generally P. Coupland, "'Left Wing' Fascism in Theory and Practice: the Case of the British Union of Fascists," *20 Century British History*, Vol.13 (2002), pp.38–61.

57 P. Pugh, "A Political Biography of Alexander Raven Thomson," PhD thesis, University of Sheffield, 2002. M. McMurray, "Alexander Raven Thomson, Philosopher of the British Union of Fascists," *The European Legacy*, Vol.17 (2012), pp.33–59.

58 R. Moore-Colyer, "'Towards Mother Earth'?: Jorian Jenks, Organicism, the Right and the British Union of Fascists," *Journal of Contemporary History*, Vol.39 (July 2004), p.353. J. Daniels and M. Freeman, *Pershore People* (Malvern, 2004), p.65, notices Joyce as recruiter. "Fascism infects the farm," *Punch*, 23 May 1934 for Shepard's drawing.

59 Matthew and Harrison (eds), *ODNB*, Vol.59, pp.344–345. M. E. Romanovitch, "Henry Williamson as a 'Romantic Fascist'? The Origins, Context and Application of Henry Williamson's Aesthetic and Political Ideas," PhD thesis, Kingston University, 1991. H. Williamson, *The Story of a Norfolk Farm* (London, 1941). A. Williamson, *A Patriot's Progress: Henry Williamson and the First World War* (Stroud, 1998). See generally, A. Mitchell, "Fascism in East Anglia: The British Union of Fascists in Norfolk, Suffolk and Essex," PhD thesis, University of Sheffield, 1999.

60 USSC, MS 119/E3, "A Tiller of Several Soils: The Memoirs of Robert Saunders OBE."

61 Martin Jameson is working on her life (2012). She wrote on countryside issues for the BUF press.

62 D. Stone, "The Far Right and the Back-to-the-Land Movement," in Gottlieb and Linehan (eds), *Culture of Fascism*, pp.182–198.

63 P. G. Zander, "Right modern technology, nation, and Britain's extreme right in the interwar period (1919–1940)," PhD thesis, Georgia Institute of Technology, 2009, on modernism and technology in British fascism.

64 USSC, MS 5/13, F. Taylour, "Your attention is arrested," is an autobiographical fragment. KV 2/2146 for a heavily weeded internment file. See also KV2/2143–2144; Gottlieb, *Feminine Fascism*, p.342; B. Belton, *Fay Taylour: Queen of Speedway* (London, 2006). And see S. Cullen, "Fay Taylour: a Dangerous Woman in Sport and Politics," *Women's History Review*, Vol.21 (2012), pp.211–232.

65 Skidelsky, *Oswald Mosley*, p.320 notices the *Blue Bird* connection.

66 *British Lion*, 28 August 1926; 25 September 1926; June 1927.

67 HO 144/21840 for Beckett's internment file. M. Lewis, *Ted Kid Lewis: His Life and Times* (London, 1990).

68 H.E.B. Nye, "Egoists," *Action*, 28 May 1938 and *ibid*. 5 March, 21 May 1938. He last appeared in *Crockford's Clerical Directory 1977–79*. The cleric C. A. Maginn wrote in *The Blackshirt*, 26 December 1936. He featured in *Crockford's* in 1938 and died that year.

69 Thurlow, *Fascism in Britain*, p.130.

70 Birch, *Why They Join*, p.14. K. H. Galinsky, *British Fascism. The British Union of Fascists* (Leipzig and Berlin, 1935), p.7.

71 Skidelsky, *Oswald Mosley*, pp.317–321. J. D. Brewer, "The British Union of Fascists: Some Tentative Conclusions on its Membership," in S. U. Larsen, et al., *Who Were the Fascists?* (Bergen, 1980), p.543.

72 KV 2/250, 9 March 1945.

73 G. Walters, *The Leader* (London, 2004). H. Charteris, *The River Watcher* (London, 1965), for an earlier fictional work that Mosley thought actionable. An unflattering portrait of OM as "Roderick Spode," had appeared in P. G. Wodehouse, *The Code of the Woosters* (Harmondsworth, 1953. First ed. 1938), p.54; "That chin. . . . Those eyes . . . that moustache." Winifred Holtby, Aldous Huxley, Nancy Mitford, and H. G. Wells are other writers to portray OM in fiction. The television series starring Jonathan Cake is available on DVD as "Mosley" (Alomo Productions for Channel 4, 1998).

5

DEEPER INTO FASCIST POLITICS

Remarkable what glamour a uniform can impart to anyone.
[Nellie Driver, "The Mill," unpublished novel on fascism by a
Mosleyite.]

1

George Bowling reflects in Orwell's *Coming up for Air*, "There's something that's gone out of us in these twenty years since the end of the
war."[1] Joyce believed as much when he joined the BUF. What subsequently happened to someone who, apart from Mosley, was "the most
remarkable personality in the Movement?"[2]

Joyce's profile with soft-focus photograph, which soon appeared
in *Fascist Week*, declared in code, carefully avoiding mention of the
British Fascists, that he had been "a Fascist by conviction for many
years." Lintorn-Orman's group was excised from the historical
record. He was described as an Area Administrative Officer, Director of Research at National Headquarters and "one of the most able
speakers in the Movement," whose "chief job" involved "holding
meetings in all parts of the country, and assisting in the promulgation
of Fascist policy."[3] When joining Mosley, Joyce had gaily declared
on his membership form, "I the undersigned, being a British citizen,
loyal to King and Empire, desire to become a member of the British
Union of Fascists."[4]

He was soon out on the road. In January 1934 he debated with the historian A. L. Rowse at the Fabian Society.[5] On 16 February he spoke at Bedford Town Hall and appeared on 23 February in Ealing.[6] In March a Brighton meeting heard him claim, "Mosley's place in European history" would be second to none. That same month he visited Longton, Chelsea and Reading. The following April it was the turn of Harrow and Chichester.[7] In May his schedule took him to Beaconsfield, then Sutton in Surrey.[8] In June he conducted meetings in Evesham and Eastbourne and later that month at Southend. In July he descended on Croydon, dealing vigorously with hecklers, again praising Mosley and also enjoyed a quieter moment in Cromer. December 1934 saw him keeping an engagement at Hayling Island and debating fascism with Labour MP Fenner Brockway at Aberdeen University. Later that month commitments took him to Barnard Castle and Durham.[9]

A letter from Robert Saunders adds to this picture. On 27 June 1935 he wrote that Joyce had regaled a meeting in Bournemouth for one hundred and ten minutes, telling his "not very large audience" that "apathy" had to be fought "in exactly the same way as the Red Front"; it was "just as much a menace," indeed a greater threat than Communism. To lift his audience, Joyce had proclaimed: "Make the public politically conscious and your battle will be won."[10] So much optimism prevailed. The political breakthrough beckoned. The promised utopia was near.

Joyce featured almost two years later in a letter from Saunders to Eric Burch, district treasurer of the BUF's Dorset West branch:

> We had a wonderful time during the weekend. And also learnt so much! About 25 at the school – a number which Joyce was very pleased with. Joyce was wonderful! Even those who [used] to think little of him now regard him as almost a demigod!! The least one can say is that he is a very remarkable man.[11]

He was still spreading the gospel and, in Saunders's opinion, effectively. Yet in the soon-to-erupt 1937 conflict in the BUF this Dorset fascist never hesitated to pledge his personal loyalty to 'The Leader.'[12]

Joyce not only spoke in the cause. He advised others. At one BUF speakers' school Nellie Driver watched this "cold and egotistical" man, as she later called him, behave in a way that stayed in her memory:

> One of his pupils stood by his table out at the front with a handful of notes of his practice speech. William Joyce coldly leaned forward – took the notes from his hand – and deposited them on the fire! The would-be speaker had to continue extempore.

This "man without a soul" – she had glimpsed his personality without labelling it – doubtless believed that by burning the notes he had done his comrade a favour.[13]

Frank Lee recalled another training course at Colchester in 1936 when each participant had to speak for five minutes. "My tutor was William Joyce," Lee reminisced, "and he was (justifiably) very critical of my effort . . . One thing I remember him saying about speaking was: 'It's better to be rightfully wrong than wrongfully right.'"[14] Joyce gave Lee the impression of being a "very forceful personality" and "a powerful orator, second only to Sir Oswald Mosley."[15]

Joyce left his mark not only on young recruits but also on more seasoned campaigners. John Beckett, no mean speaker himself, and with parliamentary experience to draw upon, recalled being impressed when hearing him in Paddington. "Here was one of the dozen finest orators in the country. Snowden's close reasoning and unerring instinct for words were allied with Maxton's humour and Churchill's daring . . . After that meeting I joined the British Union of Fascists."[16]

Beckett's admiration continued after they went their separate political ways. This former Labour MP was always reaching for gods, and during his colourful political life believed he had encountered several. In the Labour Party he had worshipped John Wheatley and Jimmy Maxton, socialists with Scottish roots. As a fascist, he fell for Mosley and Joyce. All were to disappoint him. He turned finally to the Roman Catholic Church and wrapped himself in its comforting, authoritarian folds. It too failed to satisfy him. He had so much potential, showed so much promise but achieved so little.[17]

Perhaps Beckett exaggerated when linking his conversion to Joyce's speech in Paddington. Certainly no mention of it appeared when early in 1934 *Fascist Week* discussed Beckett's enlistment in the BUF.[18] But Mosley's hand lay across its pages and OM and his submissive lieutenants had no interest in singing Joyce's praises too highly.

Other witnesses were to remark on Joyce's speaking skills. Cecil Roberts, novelist and one-time fascist fellow traveller, has left a powerful vignette of him in action:

> Thin, pale, intense, he had not been speaking many minutes before we were electrified by this man. I have been a connoisseur of speech-making for a quarter of a century but never before, in any country, had I met a personality so terrifying in its dynamic force, so vituperative, so vitriolic. The words poured from him in a corrosive spate. . . . We listened in a kind of frozen hypnotism to this cold, stabbing voice. There was the gleam of a Marat in his eyes, and his eloquence took on a Satanic ring when he invoked the rising wrath of his colleagues against the festering scum that by cowardice and sloth had reduced the British Empire to a moribund thing, in peril of annihilation.[19]

The young fascist clearly made an impression on at least one sympathetic member of his audience.

However, the temptation to buy unreservedly into these flattering views of Frank Lee, John Beckett, and Cecil Roberts, must be resisted.[20] Joyce was essentially unpredictable. He was certainly capable of delivering "a magnificent oration," but could sometimes alienate audiences with "his aggressiveness, pomposity, and sheer bad manners." His obsessive self-regard guaranteed he could also become "dull and interminable." An evening in Evesham devoted to four hours on India must have seemed to listeners like an eternity.[21] However, despite his faults, Joyce often spoke for the movement.

Mosley was convinced of the way forward. He had to persuade others, and at the beginning of 1934 launched the January Club. It has been called "a dining group which, although not specifically a front organization, nevertheless was designed to influence politicians, businessmen and members of the armed forces towards the fascist cause."[22] This description does not go anywhere near far enough. The Club was undoubtedly a front organisation. It fished for sympathisers and aimed to smooth the transition from parliamentary democracy to fascism.[23] Permeation featured among Mosley's strategies as it had Rotha Lintorn-Orman's.

The Club attracted right-wing Conservative MPs, including Alan Lennox-Boyd and Duncan Sandys, both government ministers after the Second World War.[24] Viscount Rothermere, who had encouraged Mosley in his fascism, was a member.[25] As were Robert Forgan, then the BUF's Director of Organisation, and the "mystically inclined" Major Francis Yeats-Brown, author of *Bengal Lancer* and *Golden Horn*.[26] Forgan and Yeats-Brown would soon leave Mosley.[27] But in 1934 they rowed in the same political boat. Captain H. W. Luttman-Johnson, ex-Indian Army and Scottish landowner, appeared alongside them. He was an early fellow traveller.[28] Sir John Squire, editor of the *London Mercury*, served as chairman.[29]

Joyce spoke at its first meeting and in the plush surroundings of the Hotel Splendide in Piccadilly delivered a powerful after-dinner speech to an audience of hardened fascists, possible converts and the politically curious. "Mr Joyce was at his best," a report emphasised, and remarked on "his withering contempt for the Old Gangs" who had presided over "the present disintegration of democracy the world over." He promised that fascism would cure these problems and usher in "a saner, cleaner, safer world." He ended to great applause. It amounted to a risk to employ him in this role. As a speaker he appealed to many rank-and-file BUF members and ideologically inclined fellow travellers. But if the aim were to reach a wider constituency, his difficult-to-control viciousness could prove counter-productive. On this occasion he managed to restrain himself. The same audience heard a well-received speech by Dr Hans Galinsky, of the Hitler Youth.[30] It is often claimed that the early BUF hovered closer to Italian Fascism than German National Socialism, but Galinsky's presence underlines that it was soon forging links with Berlin.[31]

What impression did Joyce leave on the novelist Gilbert Frankau and, more particularly, George Ward Price of the *Daily Mail*?[32] 'Wardy,' "tall, bronzed, handsome ... monocled," and sporting a duelling scar, had numerous BUF contacts and helped to promote Mosley in the press.

Back from his roving commissions in Central Europe, where he enjoyed close connections with influential Nazis, he operated as the vital conduit between Rothermere and 'The Leader.' Reflecting that link, he became involved in a Rothermere initiative to raise funds for Mosley by marketing a BUF brand of cigarette.[33] He was certainly "a useful man" to have in support, as John Macnab once put it.[34]

Joyce also busied himself in the Windsor Club at 23 Grosvenor Place, another route for the permeation of the political Right. Mosleyites believed the Prince of Wales was sympathetic to their cause; the naming of the Club reflected as much. They portrayed the future Edward VIII as "fascism's ideal king, young, unconventional, anti-Establishment who stood for friendship with Germany and action on unemployment."[35] The Prince's interest in Nazi Germany encouraged the German Chancellor to believe he, too, had secured a friend.[36] Detail on Joyce's involvement in the Windsor Club remains slight. But the son of Captain H. W. 'Billy' Luttman-Johnson believed a photograph in his father's papers showed Joyce at one meeting alongside Sir Charles Petrie, the historian, and the "superficial, silly, frivolous and viciously anti-Semitic" Edward 'Fruity' Metcalfe, who served as aide to the Prince of Wales.[37]

Joyce's growing portfolio also included promoting fascism at British universities, which saw him debating immigration at Imperial College, London.[38] And passing himself off as 'Professor' – another sign of his incessant self-advertisement – in the 1934 Hilary Term he spoke at the Oxford University Fascist Association on "Fascist £.s.d."[39] His official role doubtless guaranteed his attendance on 20 November of that year at the group's First Annual Dinner in the Clarendon Hotel, to enjoy among other delights the Sole Véronique and the Poulet de Surrey Rôti au Lard.[40]

The same year Mosley, recognising Joyce's talents, appointed him Director of Propaganda. His yearly salary of £300, later increased to £364, was "respectable."[41] But he came cheap compared with the slippery Dr Robert Forgan, who drew £600 as Director of Organisation and £750 as Deputy Leader.[42] John Beckett also appears to have collected a larger salary.[43]

As an evidently rising star, Joyce came to the attention of the security service, in particular his old contact Maxwell Knight. In a profile Max wrote for MI5 in September 1934 he emphasised Joyce's "basic patriotism" as well as his violent opposition to Bolshevism and predicted that if fascism were to progress in Britain his young friend would play a "very prominent part in affairs." One source has claimed that at an uncertain date Knight had offered Joyce's name to the security service as a candidate for employment but retracted it after Joyce had "made a fool of himself" over a girl.[44] Had his affair with Mary Ogilvy become an issue here? Max's September 1934 assessment was written after the Ogilvy relationship had gone cold. Was he tempted yet again to think Joyce might be a useful asset to the security service, now as a mole within the BUF? His report reads almost like a character reference for someone who might be cultivated for that task.[45] And Joyce was easily tolerant of double dealing.

2

As a schoolboy Joyce had displayed a precocious facility with words and as a young graduate had featured in a respectable academic journal. He now harnessed these talents to the promotion of fascism, producing a corpus of written work which has never received much attention.

He pontificated in *Fascist Week* on conquest and empire.[46] He wrote combative essays for *The Blackshirt* including "We are intolerant and proud of it"; the same newspaper also saw him attacking "the Knights of the Razor and the Esquires of the Broken Bottle."[47] He wrote more considered articles for the *Fascist Quarterly* aimed at the intellectual element in the BUF.[48] He treated readers of *Action* to his columns, "Searchlight over Britain" and "The World, the Flesh and Financial Democracy."[49] Such issues were discussed at greater length in BUF pamphlets, in *National Socialism Now* – published after he had split from Mosley – and *Twilight over England*, which he completed in wartime Germany.

In the '30s Joyce displayed little originality as a fascist thinker. He was no Raven Thomson. In *Dictatorship* he presented the image of a trapped, stagnating Britain and called for a corporate state to replace those "exhausted volcanoes" currently exercising power.[50] Contemporary democracy he dismissed as "refined nonsense." Society must be controlled by "a new aristocracy," based "on merit alone."[51] Here he was serving up standard fare from the political menu of British fascism.[52] As he did when writing on the Empire.[53] His *Fascism and India* proclaimed a fascist Britain would never grant independence to the sub-Continent; India's destiny was to remain bound to Britain "like the rods of the Fasces," its resources exploited for the benefit of Europeans.[54] Still thinking long-term, in *Fascist Educational Policy* he emphasised that fascism must set the highest value on the promotion of personal happiness, but there was a bigger educational goal − "to make citizens worthy of Fascist civilization."[55] Fascism, like Communism, aimed at creating a new breed of men and women for the future secular utopia.[56]

Joyce's writings concentrated not only on Britain and the Empire. He also focused on Europe.[57] In the course of which he became obsessed by the battle between Fascism and Communism.[58] From its powerful base in the Soviet Union he believed that Bolshevism posed a constant danger and "*white* civilization" was in grave danger of being surrendered "to the Orient."[59] This outcome was not inevitable. If their voices were heard, Joyce argued "those Aryan men and women who [believed] in the unconquerable greatness of the human spirit and the subordination to it of all economic and material considerations" would eventually defeat those deluded "worshippers of materialism and the haters of higher human values."[60]

His reading of history and literature buttressed this belief. When concluding that "material resources" would never overcome "the will to win," he was echoing F.J.C. Hearnshaw, whose writings he first encountered in the '20s.[61] Carlyle, "first amongst British heralds of the Fascist revolution," also intruded into his thinking here.[62]

Joyce looked to psychology for further intellectual support − recall his 1932 application to work under Professor Aveling at King's − and implicitly incorporated Aveling's emphases on the power of mental energy, the role of higher thought processes and the influence of the will into his political thinking. Joyce's postgraduate career had proved brief, but his supervisor's ideas lodged in his photographic memory.

Whenever he discussed this struggle between Fascism and Communism, this crucial battle between spiritual and material forces, Joyce's writings became saturated with anti-Semitism. His *Fascism and Jewry* promoted the well-worn anti-Semitic image of Jews having no sense of patriotism and presented readers with an image of a "secret but mighty [Jewish] state" perpetually busy plotting its way towards world power under the aegis of Bolshevism.[63] Jews and Bolshevism linked symbiotically in Joyce's mind, as they did in Hitler's.[64] Along with many anti-Semites he believed that these worldwide ambitions were underwritten by Jewish finance.[65] This union was in no sense paradoxical. All Jews worked for a Jewish end. In isolating this phenomenon Joyce – and others so convinced – believed they had uncovered "the grim truth of the European situation."[66] He was influenced here by that conspiratorial Jew-hatred in *The Protocols of the Elders of Zion*, which gained worldwide currency in the 1920s.[67] Yet he was no pessimist. Hitler had rolled back Jewish influence and Joyce argued that Britain should ally with Germany in this crusade.[68]

Joyce's increasingly obsessive anti-Semitism amounted to an overt, unrestrained gutter hatred; it had none of the fancy calculated trimming which characterised some inter-war anti-Jew hostility. Mosley prided himself on being a rational anti-Semite.[69] But Joyce had no time for those coded references to "alien finance," "cosmopolitans" and "wanderers over the face of the earth."[70] Marxism, he declared, was that "verminous old Hebrew's system," a political creed spawned by "the lousy old Jew."[71] He also emphasised – soon to become tiresomely evident – that biology rather than culture was the essential signifier of difference. Jews were programmed to behave as they did.

His anti-Semitic world-view had become fully formed and totally congealed well before he left for Germany in August 1939. When still marching with Mosley it is doubtful whether Nazi anti-Semites could have taught him very much. Writing in 1936 on those Jews who had dared to attack the BUF, he proclaimed:

> These little sub-men are a nuisance to be eliminated, but their wealthy instigators and controllers, well known to us, are, in sum, a criminal monstrosity, for which not all the gold of Jewry can pay the just compensation which we will demand and obtain.[72]

These are chilling, ominous sentiments by any standards.

3

After its launch in October 1932, the BUF had become Britain's largest ever fascist party. How large has been debated. By mid-1934 it might have attracted 40,000 followers.[73] It had published *The Blackshirt* and *Fascist Week*, which were soon followed by *Action*. In 1935 it had created its in-house journal, the *Fascist Quarterly*, later the *British Union Quarterly*. It had formed political clubs. From early on it had held large banner-parading, searchlight-lit public meetings where black-shirted BUF members and a curious public could listen to Mosley and his leading lieutenants.[74] Fascists found it exhilarating, wonderful, and in these early days Mosley remained fully confident of a major political breakthrough.[75] Yet his burgeoning ambitions became thwarted. Even by the mid-'30s serious barriers blocked his way.[76]

Mosley's opponents, Communists particularly, aware of events in Hitler's Germany, soon fought back and on 7 June 1934 a meeting at Olympia witnessed scenes of remarkable violence. The fighting within the hall, which also spilled over into the surrounding streets, left some participants bloodied and bruised. In Berlin, Mosley was seen as standing up to the Reds. Some Conservative circles in Britain felt the same.[77] However, other influential quarters viewed events differently. The Chief Commissioner of the Metropolitan Police warned the government that fascism posed a danger. It is further said the BBC banned Mosley and starved him of publicity.[78] It never did. But since the BUF had no MPs it did not receive any air time. However, the big blow came when Mosley lost the support of Viscount Rothermere. On 15 January 1934 the *Daily Mail* had proclaimed: "Hurrah for the Blackshirts!" and soon drenched its columns with such sentiment. But that summer it withdrew its public backing.[79] Mosley's political spirits had soared with his dazzling coup in bringing onside the *Mail* and its sister papers, including the *Sunday Dispatch*. He was understandably deeply wounded when in July 1934 they suddenly changed course. Their proprietor, he fumed, had meekly surrendered to pressure from Jewish businesses.[80] Mosley believed Northcliffe, the *Mail's* founder, would have shown more backbone. Even though support from the Rothermere press was brief, it has never been allowed to forget its public excursion in the company of Britain's putative Füh-rer. Its proprietor became especially tainted since well-placed sources believed that privately he continued to have "more than a sneaking admiration" for Mosley.[81]

The BUF soon faced other problems. In the early summer of 1934 it lost some supporters and potential recruits when Hitler liquidated Ernst Röhm and others in the Night of the Long Knives, an early sign of Nazi brutality. Was this political creed to be welcomed in Britain?[82]

By the mid-1930s Britain had also started to recover from the global economic dislocation of the 1920s and early '30s. The develop-ment of suburbia stimulated the building industry and encouraged the marketing of new household products. The growth of the car indus-try and its ancillary trades provided another major economic boost.[83] The aspirational "middle-class house-and-car culture," was starting to take root.[84] Why opt for the untried, draconian, fascist alternative?[85] The political crisis Mosley believed – and hoped – would follow from the failings of a rotten economic system had not occurred. Britain remained scarred by problems of structural and regional unemploy-ment. There remained too many "sordid streets, foetid alleys, mephitic courts, decaying houses and suffocating rooms."[86] Readers of Wal-ter Brierley, Walter Greenwood, George Orwell and J. B Priestley can vicariously experience some of that pain. But even in depressed areas the BUF, an untested, untried political newcomer, struggled to recruit.[87] A nagging fear must have taken hold in some Blackshirt circles that their best days were already behind them. Mosley's ear-lier boast – that he would be in Downing Street by the time he had reached forty – was looking increasingly hollow.

Faced with these problems, the BUF made greater use of anti-Semitism as a political weapon. This hostility had always been present in the movement.[88] But it increased after the Olympia meet-ing in June 1934, when many BUF members claimed that respon-sibility for the disruption and violence lay with the Jewish Reds, and it became even sharper the following month when Rothermere withdrew the backing of the *Daily Mail*. By that autumn 'The Leader,' throwing away all public restraint, began to attack Jews directly. *The Blackshirt* reported his Albert Hall speech on 28 October 1934 under the headlines: "They Will It! They Shall Have It!! The Folly of Jewry. THEY HAVE CHALLENGED THE SPIRIT OF THE MODERN AGE."[89] Mosley was here defending his anti-Semitism as a measured response to a group that had questioned his vision for Britain. How dare they. Audiences would hear a good deal more on these lines right to the end of 'The Leader's' life.

Early the following year, a BUF policy meeting instructed Joyce to prepare material on the pernicious international influence of the Jews.[90] He doubtless relished every minute of it and in this highly charged political atmosphere sections of the movement closely linked to him assumed an increasing prominence.

Joyce's columns in *Action* in '36–'37, characterised by their persistent drip of a vituperative anti-Semitism, testified to his growing influence. He attacked individual Jews, especially the Ostrer brothers, who had cinema and newspaper interests.[91] They possessed too much economic power and wielded an excessive political influence. He tore into Sigmund Freud, still living at Berggasse 19, Vienna, but soon to settle at 28 Maresfield Gardens, London. 'Professor' Joyce, would-be doctor, intending researcher in human psychology, accused him of undermining society's cultural values through "pornography in the guise of scientific treatises." Britain, he argued, was also having to contend with the complex market manipulations of international Jewish financiers, whose self-enriching activities created such havoc in the lives of British workers. These dark satanic forces, acting in concert, were totally destructive. There it was, all laid out on a weekly basis. The Jews were our difficulty, our problem. They stood in the way of "the British race." BUF members, who never reached for Joyce's pamphlets or persisted with them, could quickly grasp the core of his ideology through his journalism.[92]

John Macnab's "Jolly Judah" column in *The Blackshirt*, which began on 28 February 1936, and "Behind the News" in *Action*, first attributed to him on 11 June 1936, peddled similar sentiments: the malign influence of Jews reached everywhere.

This anti-Semitism occurred in parallel with the anti-Jewish programme being unleashed by the Nazis and can be related to it. Mosley, Joyce and other leading BUF figures believed mistakenly that if Hitler's policy in identifying and attacking a Jewish enemy were copied, it might carry them to their political goal. The BUF had not been swept to power on the back of the economic crisis in the early 1930s. The amorphous tradition of anti-Semitism in Britain, which cut across society, suggested a focus on the Jews might prove more effective.[93] The antipathy towards refugees from Nazism trickling slowly into the country further suggested political dividends might accrue from this strategy. Joyce and his disciples could be let loose.[94]

In this atmosphere, a decision was taken in 1935–36 to concentrate resources on East London, where Russian-Polish Jews had settled in the late nineteenth and early twentieth century. This initiative met with fierce opposition from anti-fascist groups, which became strikingly evident on 4 October 1936 at the battle of Cable Street. Finding his path defiantly blocked by political opponents, Mosley, acting on police advice, retreated from what had been intended as a major demonstration of the BUF's strength in East London.[95] It was humiliation on a grand scale, even though the movement remained active in the area.[96]

Joyce was absolutely infuriated by Mosley's response. That much as becomes clear from Police Constable Leslie Leeson's shorthand notes of a speech he delivered in Hammersmith Town Hall on 9 October 1936. Referring to Cable Street, Joyce told his audience, "Sunday was their day," however "the days to come are our days and we shall use them."[97] He placed Jewry at the centre of the BUF's problems:

> because we believe in the greatness of Britain and not in the greatness of Palestine we have no right to march or walk through the streets of London.[98]

He went further in comments the Police Commissioner drew to the attention of the Director of Public Prosecutions:

> If the government does lay down its title to govern, and if the Communist Party here attempts to reproduce the havoc wrought in Spain – if the Communist Party here tries to burn our churches and murder ministers of religion, then communism will be met by us on the streets and if communist machine guns are good our machine guns will be better.[99]

Strong meat; but after the failure the previous September to convict Arnold Leese on a charge of seditious libel against Jews, the Attorney-General advised any similar charge would fail.[100] Yet Joyce's stark comments underlined that Cable Street had unleashed strong feelings and dangerous passions.

Worried by such developments, on 1 January 1937 the government passed the Public Order Act. It banned the wearing of political uniforms in public, provided the police with powers to prevent marches likely to result in a breach of the peace, strengthened the law against verbal insults and prohibited the deployment of stewards at open-air meetings. Britain's Communists and the National Unemployed Workers' Movement came within its scope. But the fascists were its clear targets. John Macnab wrote to Ezra Pound, "you cannot kill a man's faith by taking a piece of cotton off his chest." But such controls were hardly helpful.[101]

After being humiliated at Cable Street, Mosley decided to fight the 1937 local elections in East London. Joyce, described in a BUF source as "second only to Mosley in national reputation," stood in Shoreditch with J. A. 'Bill' Bailey.[102] Bailey, from Islington, and Richard Allistair 'Jock' Houston, from Highbury, had formed a BUF branch in Shoreditch in August 1935.[103] Both men were rabid anti-Semites and attacks on Jews in the area became commonplace. These hardened activists proved difficult for national headquarters to control and in East London the Shoreditch fascists developed a fearsome reputation.[104] Joyce, however, was always ready for such political rough trade and some locals strongly identified with his brand of fascism:

> "And of course we in Shoreditch started grabbing William Joyce ... Well Joyce come down, done a few ... meetings in the street. He loved what he saw. Because the boys he saw down there was practically his way of thinking."[105]

The BUF put up Alexander Raven Thomson and E. G. 'Mick' Clarke in Bethnal Green. Clarke had a reputation as one of Mosley's ablest lieutenants in East London.[106] Anne Brock-Griggs and Charles Wegg-Prosser contested Limehouse (Stepney).[107]

Mosley's followers hoped to draw political capital from the anti-Semitism that circulated in East London and exploit the vigilante traditions which erected a sharp distinction between 'them' and 'us.' They also gambled that the BUF could successfully capitalise on the area's structural problems.[108] Charles Booth's magisterial late-nineteenth-century survey had revealed the extent to which poverty and squalor pressed daily on the lives of this area's teeming inhabitants and a follow-up study in the 1930s achingly exposed the massive economic and social deprivation that still affected this troubled, if vibrant, slab of London.[109]

Mosley urged Londoners to choose between the British Union of Fascists and "the party of Jewry."[110] Full of expectation, he opened Joyce's election campaign. "The fight's on," *Action* boldly proclaimed.[111] Photographs of Joyce in February 1937 show him eager for the fray in his long belted raincoat, one of his political trademarks. He relished going into battle and, with Bailey, exploited anti-Semitism as a political weapon.[112] Even a sympathetic source recognised as much.[113] As the degree of Jew-hatred in the BUF's East London campaign continued to grow, and fearful of its consequences, the National Council for Civil Liberties and the Jewish People's Council called a protest meeting in Shoreditch Town Hall, chaired by the historian R. H. Tawney.[114] Joyce paid no attention to it. He revelled in this atmosphere and remained buoyant throughout, telling an audience at Cromwell Street School that "on March the 4th the insults of October 4th will be flung in the face of Jewry."[115] The election results would compensate for the humiliation at Cable Street.

Yet in a heavy turnout the BUF was to be disappointed. In Bethnal Green North-East, Raven Thomson secured 3028 votes and 'Mick' Clarke 3022. They polled more than the Liberals but Labour's two candidates with 7777 and 7756 votes comfortably saw them off. In Limehouse (Stepney) Brock-Griggs and Wegg-Prosser came bottom of the poll, each with 2086 votes. The successful Labour representatives secured just over 8000 votes. The Municipal Reform Party also fared better than the Mosleyites. The BUF failed to take Shoreditch:[116]

Mrs H. Girling (Labour)	11098
Dr S. Jeger (Labour)	11069

S. L. Pace (Municipal Progressive)	3303
R. S. Falk (Municipal Progressive)	3217
W. Joyce (BU)	2564
J. A. Bailey (BU)	2492
C. E. Taylor (Independent Labour)	385

In defeat Joyce remained defiant.[117]

The movement clutched at thin straws. Political resilience was called for. Comrades had to be reminded of their great enemy.[118] 'Mick' Clarke roundly declared: "THE BRITISH ARE NEVER BEATEN."[119] Mosley even detected National Socialism rising phoenix-like from East London. And an optimistic Joyce wrote that "a Communist sage in Shoreditch, incidentally, but naturally, a Jew" had told him he would be fortunate to secure 500 votes. "To poll a vote five times as good as the enemy expects," he mused, "is no mean beginning."[120] But the reek of political failure rose above this bravado. Would the breakthrough ever come? Writing in *The Blackshirt* in early 1937 Joyce had been expectant. "MOSLEY SHALL WIN. WHAT WE HAVE WON – AND WHAT WE WILL WIN IN 1937" and Henry Gibbs's "BLACKSHIRTS HAIL THE NEW YEAR" mirrored such optimism.[121] A couple of months later these hopes appeared to be crumbling fast.

The BUF was now in some difficulty. Britain's economy and political system had not collapsed. The later tactic of anti-Semitism had failed to deliver political dividends. Hitler had successfully exploited a fear of Jewish Bolshevism – the perceived threat was closer to Germany's borders and memories survived of the failed Communist revolution in 1919 – but in Britain the Communist Party remained small and it proved harder to 'sell' this message. Even if some quarters feared Socialism, in whatever form.

Joyce's new wife shared his political disappointment. His marriage to the woman whose many virtues he had extravagantly, proudly announced to Birkbeck's students ended in 1935. He was "terrible to live with," had a "vile temper," was often "very sarcastic," she remarked later.[122] His new wife, the attractive, vivacious Margaret Cairns White, was twenty-two when she first met Joyce. Her Lancashire family, with Irish connections, had moved to Carlisle where her father was once manager at Todd's Mills. They lived here in Nelson Street, Denton Holme. Margot, as she was known, worked as a secretary at Morton Mills, a local textile firm.[123] Older residents would recall a "charming" and "compassionate" young woman, interested in dancing, and once romantically linked with a local doctor.[124] But this relationship did not last. Instead, her family's fascist sympathies brought her into Joyce's bullying, domineering orbit. They first met on 7 February 1935 at a BUF meeting in Dumfries and kept in touch. The following year she became full-time secretary to the BUF's Manchester branch. She later moved to Bramerton Street, Chelsea, to live with Joyce in a property he shared with John Macnab.[125]

The couple married at Kensington Register Office on 13 February 1937, five days after Joyce's decree absolute, and during the build-up to the East London elections. Ever self-obsessed, he appears on the marriage certificate as "University Tutor (retired)" and "of independent means."[126] Macnab and BUF member Mrs Hastings Bonora acted as witnesses. Bonora threw a cocktail party for the newly-weds, who later returned to a flat in Fawcett Street, once again shared with Macnab. However, they were soon out canvassing in Shoreditch. Margaret Joyce's married life would prove turbulent, to say the least, and she secured an early glimpse of that future when her husband "gave no thought to a honeymoon or, indeed, to any celebrations at all."[127] She had good reason to be grateful for Hastings Bonora's cocktails.

Notes

1 G. Orwell, *Coming up for Air* (Harmondsworth, 1975. First ed.1939), p.168.
2 Skidelsky, *Oswald Mosley*, p.343.
3 *Fascist Week*, 26 January–1 February 1934.
4 Membership Form, British Union of Fascists, 1, Great George Street, SW1. Author's possession.
5 *Fascist Week*, 19–25 January 1934, p.3. *Manchester Guardian*, 13 January 1934, reported Mosley "was ably represented" by Joyce.
6 *Fascist Week*, 2–8 February 1934.
7 *Ibid*. 9–15 March 1934, 23–29 March, 6–12 April 1934, respectively.
8 *Ibid*. 4–10 May 1934, 11–17 May 1934.
9 *The Blackshirt*, 1 June 1934, 29 June, 27 July, 7 December, 14 December, 21 December 1934 respectively.

10 Saunders to Fitzgerald, 27 June 1935, USSC, MS 119/A5/184. *Islington and Holloway News*, 8 December 1933 reported another mammoth speech when for two hours Joyce attacked democracy and the Jews.

11 USSC, MS 119/A6/153, Saunders to Burch, 11 January 1937.

12 USSC, MS 119/A6/427, Saunders to NHQ, 2 April 1937; USSC, MS 119/A8/234(i)and (ii), Saunders to D. F. Thomson, 15 August 1939.

13 Driver, "From the Shadows of Exile," pp.40–41.

14 Frank Lee, written evidence to John Warburton, 9 March 1992.

15 Lee, evidence.

16 J. Beckett, Introduction to W. Joyce, *National Socialism Now* (London, 1937), pp.6–7.

17 Beckett, *The Rebel who Lost His Cause*.

18 *Fascist Week*, 2–8 March 1934.

19 C. Roberts, *And so to America* (London, 1947), pp.22–23. Like many others he retreated from his fascist political leanings after the War. See *Sunshine and Shadow: Being the Fourth Book of an Autobiography 1930–1946* (London, 1972), pp.111–112.

20 Skidelsky, *Oswald Mosley*, p.343 and Kenny, *Germany Calling*, p.109 emphasise Roberts's portrait of Joyce.

21 USSC, MS 238/7/7, "The Enigma of William Joyce," by One Who Knew Him, p.3.

22 Thurlow, *Fascism in Britain*, p.100. Charles Petrie to Luttman-Johnson, 28 June 1934, suggesting John Boyd-Carpenter, Quentin Hogg and Derek Walker-Smith should be contacted as "the brightest of the Conservative Jeunes" regarding their possible membership. Imperial War Museum, Papers of Captain H.W. Luttman-Johnson, Documents, 1995, Box no. 92/32/1, HWL-J 1/23. Imperial War Museum, HWL-J 5/8 for a membership list.

23 Pugh, *'Hurrah!'* p.146.

24 P. Murphy, *Alan Lennox-Boyd: A Biography* (London, 1999); *The Times*, 27 November 1987, respectively. Matthew and Harrison (eds), *ODNB*, Vol. 48; pp.911–914 on Sandys. See also G. Love, "The British Movement, Duncan Sandys and the Politics of Constitutionalism in the 1930s," *Contemporary British History*, Vol.23 (2009), pp.543–558.

25 Skidelsky, *Oswald Mosley*, p.283. Dorril, *Blackshirt*, pp.191, 258.

26 Forgan has already been noticed as a convert from the Labour Party. HO 144/20144/267 on Yeats-Brown's mysticism. J. E. Wrench, *Francis Yeats-Brown, 1886–1944* (London, 1948), is massively discreet. See also Matthew and Harrison (eds), *ODNB*, Vol.8, pp.28–29. G. Martel (ed.), *The Times and Appeasement: The Journals of A. L. Kennedy 1932–1939* (Cambridge, 2000), p.208 for *Bengal Lancer* as a favourite film of Hitler's.

27 Griffiths, *Fellow Travellers*, pp. 17–18, 56–57 on Yeats-Brown: Forgan's departure is noted in Saville and Bellamy(eds), *Dictionary*, Vol.VI, p.113

28 R. Hoffmann to O. Bene, 3 January 1935 and O. Bene to R. Hoffmann, 19 January 1935, NARA Microcopy, T-81 Roll 35, Folder 20.

29 Griffiths, *Fellow Travellers*, pp. 24, 51.

30 *Fascist Week*, 16–22 February 1934.

31 USSC, MS 5/10, F. Burdett, "A Modern Statesman and his Work: Il Duce," reflects the Italian influence on the early BUF. Burdett was fifteen when he wrote his powerful eulogy. His "'Giovinezza . . . Giovinezza . . .' Song of Youth Triumphant," *The Blackshirt*, 16 November 1934 offers more of the same. Galinsky's presence at the January Club is merely one example of the BUF's early Nazi links.

32 *Fascist Week*, 16–22 February 1934. Joyce read Frankau's work in prison prior to his execution. *The Blackshirt*, 29 June 1934, notes a later address by Joyce.

33 S. Scaffardi, *Fire under the Carpet. Working for Civil Liberties in the 1930s* (London, 1986), p.68. O. Mosley, *My Life* (London, 1968), p.346 on the cigarette venture. 'Wardy's' physical appearance is from *The Times*, 29 April 1961. For his writings on contemporary Europe, see G. W. Price, *I Know These Dictators* (London, 1937) and *Extra-Special Correspondent* (London, 1957).

34 YCAL, MSS 43, Box 32 Folder 1337, John Macnab to Ezra Pound, 17 December 1936. Ward Price's "Mosley – Britain's Political White Hope," *Sunday Pictorial*, 22 April 1934, has him 'selling' Mosley to the public.

35 Skidelsky, *Oswald Mosley*, p.329.

36 H. von Kotze (ed.), *Heeresadjutant bei Hitler 1938–1943. Aufzeichnungen des Majors Engel* (Stuttgart, 1974), p.85, diary, 15 July 1940. See also GFM 33/2514 and GFM 33/3001, for Nazi opinions. C. Higham, *Mrs Simpson: Secret Lives of the Duchess of Windsor* (London, 2004); A Roberts, *Eminent Churchillians* (London, 2004), pp.5–53; A Massie, The Royals and the Nazis, *The Independent*, 14 January 2005; "Britain's Nazi King," Channel 5 TV, 2 August 2009; and, more recently, A. Morton, *17 Carnations: The Royals, the Nazis and the Biggest Cover-Up in History* (London, 2015), carry further comment.

37 USSC, Defence Regulations 18B Research Papers, MS 287/3, Hugo Luttman-Johnson to Brian Simpson, 24 June 1991, on the photograph at the Windsor Club. See also a shot, which includes Metcalfe, at a January Club dinner in the Savoy: Joyce, wine glass in hand and dressed in fascist uniform rather than the coat and tails of other diners, is seated with Dr Robert Forgan and Miss M. Aitken, *The Tatler*, 30 May 1934, p.395. Higham, *Mrs Simpson*, p.95, on Metcalfe.

38 Imperial College Archives, Imperial College Literary and Debating Society, File SG3/1.

39 Imperial War Museum, HWL-J, II. Cross, *The Fascists in Britain*, p.97, generally and *The Blackshirt*, 13 July 1934, specifically. A national newspaper's investigation into Joyce's unauthorised use of a professorial title led to some embarrassment in the BUF.

40 Dinner menu at the Clarendon Hotel, 20 November 1934. Author's possession.

41 Cole, *Lord Haw-Haw*, p.44.

42 In 1934 Forgan's thirst for funds led him to the Board of Deputies of British Jews. He offered, even if obliquely, to inform on the BUF. He

also allegedly pocketed intended BUF funds. G. Alderman, "Dr Robert Forgan's Resignation from the British Union of Fascists," *Labour History Review*, Vol.57 (1992), pp.37–41, and HO 144/20144/75–6, respectively. Cole, *Lord Haw-Haw*, emphasises Joyce's lack of materialism but in wartime Germany – and earlier – he developed a taste for living well.

43   R. Benewick, *Political Violence and Public Order: A Study of British Fascism* (London, 1969), p.195.

44   G. Bennett, *Churchill's Man of Mystery: Desmond Morton and the World of Intelligence* (Abingdon, 2007), p.129.

45   KV 2/245, 21 September 1934.

46   *Fascist Week*, 5–11 January 1934, 11–17 May 1934.

47   *The Blackshirt*, 1 June 1934, 8 June 1934, respectively.

48   "Britain's Empire shall live," *Fascist Quarterly*, Vol.I (1935), pp.91–107.

49   "Searchlight over Britain" appeared between 21 February and 7 May 1936 and was attributed to Joyce on 28 February: "The World, the Flesh and Financial Democracy" featured in *Action* between 14 May 1936 and 13 March 1937.

50   "Exhausted volcanoes" belongs to Disraeli, a criticism he made of Gladstone's front bench.

51   W. Joyce, *Dictatorship* (London, 1933), p.8.

52   Thurlow, *Fascism in Britain*, pp.153–155.

53   Joyce, "Britain's Empire Shall Live," pp.91–107.

54   W. Joyce, *Fascism and India* (London, 1933?), pp.16, 19. See L. Vaughan-Henry's critique of this "cheap," "windy," "rather pretentious," "priggish" production with its "insufferable condescension." Mosley Papers, University of Birmingham Special Collections, OMN/B/7/2/10–13, letter to Mosley, 25 July 1934.

55   W. Joyce, *Fascist Educational Policy* (np, nd. First published London, 1933), pp.16, 2–3.

56   M. A. Spurr, "'Playing For Fascism': Sportsmanship, Antisemitism and the British Union of Fascists," *Patterns of Prejudice*, Vol.37 (2003), pp.359–376; T. Collins, "Return to Manhood. The Cult of Masculinity and the British Union of Fascists," *International Journal of the History of Sport*, Vol.16 (1999), pp.145–162, on the physical fitness cult; I. Zweiniger-Burgielowska, "Building a British Superman: Physical Culture in Inter-War Britain," *Journal of Contemporary History*, Vol.41 (2006), pp.595–610. See more generally, P. and R. Fisher, "Tomorrow We Live: Fascist Visions of Education," *British Journal of the Sociology of Education*, Vol.30 (2009), pp.71–82.

57   HO 144/20144/130, report on Policy Meeting of BUF, 7 March 1935.

58   For further evidence on BUF thinking see H. Gibbs, *The Spectre of Communism* (London, 1936). Joyce reviewed it in *Fascist Quarterly*, Vol.2 (1936), pp.578–579.

59   W. Joyce, "Collective Security," *Fascist Quarterly*, Vol.1 (1935), p.422. Author's italics.

60   W. Joyce, "Analysis of Marxism," *ibid.* Vol.2 (1936), p.542.

61   *Ibid.*

62 W. Joyce, "Thomas Carlyle – National Socialist," *Ibid*. Vol.2 (1936),1936, p.427, and his review of Liselott Eckloff, "Bild und Wirklichkeit bei Thomas Carlyle," in the *British Union Quarterly*, Vol.1 (1937), pp.121–122. J. D. Rosenberg, *Carlyle and the Burden of History* (Oxford, 1985), on Carlyle's writings. S. Heffer, *Moral Desperado: A Life of Thomas Carlyle* (London, 1995). For other fascist interest in Carlyle see *Mosley's Blackshirts*. p.78, and at various points in D. Baker, *Ideology of Obsession: A. K. Chesterton and British Fascism* (London, 1996).

63 W. Joyce, *Fascism and Jewry* (London, 1936?), p.6.

64 *Ibid*. p.7. Hitler's linkage appears in a speech to the 1937 Nuremberg Parteitag. See N. H. Baynes (ed.), *The Speeches of Hitler*, Vol.1 (London, 1942), pp.695 ff.

65 Joyce, "Britain's Empire," pp.96, 105.

66 Joyce, *Fascism and Jewry*, p.7. Holmes, *Anti-Semitism in British Society*, ch.9 discusses this conspiratorial slant.

67 N. Cohn, *Warrant for Genocide* (London, 1967).

68 Joyce, "Collective Security," pp.427–429.

69 W. F. Mandle, *Anti-Semitism and the British Union of Fascists* (London, 1968), p.9.

70 Mosley's *My Life* (1970 ed.), ch.18, continued to present his Jew-hatred in the best possible light. Mandle, *Anti-Semitism*, for his darker side.

71 Joyce, "Analysis of Marxism," pp.535, 539, respectively.

72 Joyce, *Fascism and Jewry*, p.8.

73 G. Webber, "Patterns of Membership and Support for the British Union of Fascists," *Journal of Contemporary History*, Vol.19 (1984), pp.575–606.

74 USSC, MS F 7/2, Saunders, diary, 22 March 1936, "Albert Hall – Wonderful."

75 M. Pugh, "The British Union of Fascists and the Olympia Debate," *Historical Journal*, Vol.41 (1998), pp.529–542.

76 R. Thurlow, "The Failure of British Fascism 1932–40," in Thorpe (ed.), *Failure of Political Extremism*, pp.67–84, on the issue of Mosley's failure.

77 Dorril, *Blackshirt*, p.299.

78 Pugh, '*Hurrah!*' p.167.

79 *Daily Mail*, 15 January 1934; *The Blackshirt*, 20 July 1934. K. Martin, "Fascism and the 'Daily Mail,'" *Political Quarterly*, Vol.5 (1934), pp.273–276, for a contemporary critique of Rothermere's politics.

80 Mosley, *My Life*, p.346.

81 HO 144/20144/268.

82 Brendon, *Dark Valley*, p.172. Dorril, *Blackshirt*, p.303.

83 S. Pollard, *The Development of the British Economy* (London, 1983), p.52 (GDP figures), and pp.58–66 ("new industries").

84 Brendon, *Dark Valley*, p.165

85 A. Booth, "Corporatism, Capitalism, and Depression in Twentieth-Century Britain," *British Journal of Sociology*, Vol.32 (1982), p.215. See also J. Stevenson and C. Cook, *The Slump* (London, 1977), pp.214–215.

86 Brendon, *Dark Valley*, p.167.

87 Thurlow, *Fascism in Britain*, pp.122–130.

88 *The Blackshirt*, 5–11 April 1933, "Fascism and Justice." *Ibid.* 22–28 July 1933 for "Little Laski." *Ibid.* 30 September–6 October 1933 on "Britain for the British" and *ibid.* 4–10 November 1933, "Shall Jews Drag Britain to War?"

89 *Ibid.* 2 November 1934.

90 HO 144/20144/115–116.

91 H. Pollins, *Economic History of the Jews in England* (London, 1982), pp.203–204, on the Ostrers.

92 *Action*, 28 February, 12 March, 26 December 1936 and 16 January 1937 (Ostrer brothers). *Ibid.* 16 April 1936 (Freud). *Ibid.* 30 April 1936 (alleged Jewish manipulation of the Orient and its consequences). *Ibid.* 21 February 1936 (Joyce's belief in 'the British race').

93 J.Vincent, "The Case for Mosley," pp.350–351 and the inter-war novel, R. Westerby, *Wide Boys Never Work* (London, 2008. First ed. 1937).

94 Linehan, *East London for Mosley*, p.8 on more overt anti-Semitism. Holmes, *Anti-Semitism*, ch.11.

95 T. Kushner and N.Valman (eds.), *Remembering Cable Street: Fascism and Anti-Fascism in British Society* (London, 1999). The opposition attracted a gangster element; W. Clarkson, *Hit 'em Hard: Jack Spot, King of the Underworld* (London, 2003), pp.31–39

96 Linehan, *East London for Mosley*, generally. See also his "Fascist Perspectives of Cable Street," *Jewish Culture and History*, Vol. 1(1998), pp.23–30. D.Tilles, "'Some Lesser Known Aspects.' The Anti-Fascist Campaign of the Board of Deputies of British Jews," in G.Alderman (ed.), *New Directions in Anglo-Jewish History* (Boston, 2010), p.143, which suggests Cable Street boosted support for the BUF. See finally D. Rosenberg, *Battle for the East End. Jewish Responses to Fascism in the 1930s* (Nottingham, 2011).

97 DPP 2/407, Leeson's report of a meeting at Hammersmith Town Hall, 9 October 1936, p.1.

98 *Ibid.*

99 *Ibid.* p.2. Joyce gave a more measured response to the *Evening Standard*, 4 November 1936.

100 DPP 2/407, DPP to Commissioner of Police, 13 October 1936. C. Holmes, "The Ritual Murder Accusation in Britain," *Ethnic and Racial Studies*, Vol.4 (1981), pp.272–273, on Leese and seditious libel.

101 YCAL, MSS 43, Box 32, Folder 1337, Macnab to Pound, 30 November 1936.

102 Mandle, *Anti-Semitism*, pp.57–58. *Action*, 12 June 1937, carried a later election cameo of Bailey. He was described as forty-one, an ex-soldier, a woodworker in the furniture trade and "something of a popular hero in Shoreditch."

103 Linehan, *East London for Mosley*, p.22. KV 2/2899–2901 for more on Houston. He appears in P. Briscoe, *My Friend The Enemy: An English Boy in Nazi Germany* (London, 2007). *East London Pioneer*, Vol.1, No.4, January 1937, carries the description of Joyce.

104   Linehan, *East London for Mosley*, pp.42–56.

105   Taped interview of G.T.in *ibid.* p.46.

106   Obituary in *Comrade*, No.47 (1996), pp.1, 5; KV 2/2476–2481.

107   In early 1938 Wegg-Prosser left the BUF, citing the "increasingly dicta-
torial and un-English" drift of Mosley's movement, and his disenchantment with a leader surrounded by "a small narrow-minded group of
ex-army officers" (HO 144/21381/14, Metropolitan Police report,13
June 1938).

108   C. Husbands, "East End Racism 1900–1980: Continuities in Vigilantist
and Extreme Right-Wing Political Behaviour," *London Journal*, Vol.8
(1982), pp.3–26. *The Times*, 20 October 1936 carried a contemporary
assessment of East London's problems.

109   *The New Survey of London Life and Labour*, 9 Vols. (London, 1930–35).
J.White, *London in the Twentieth Century: A City and its People* (London,
2001), pp.217–231.

110   *The Blackshirt*, 6 February 1937.

111   *Action*, 6 February 1937.

112   *The Blackshirt*, 6, 13, 20 February 1937.

113   Cole, *Lord Haw-Haw*, p.67, relying on Margaret Joyce's testimony.

114   *Jewish Chronicle*, 26 February 1937.

115   *The Blackshirt*, 13 February 1937.

116   Mandle, *Anti-Semitism*, pp.57–58; *The Times*, 5 March 1937, for the election results.

117   *Action*, 13 March 1937.

118   Following the Shoreditch election *The Blackshirt*, 13 March 1937,
reported R. Gordon Canning's reference to Jews as "locust hordes" that
"blight the fields of the Gentile race."

119   *Ibid.*

120   *Action*, 13 March 1937.

121   Both sentiments from *The Blackshirt*, 2 January 1937.

122   *Daily Herald*, 2 March 1940.

123   Cole, *Lord Haw-Haw*, p.49.

124   *Cumberland News and Star*, 15 November 2000. Private information.

125   Cole, *Lord Haw-Haw*, pp.49 ff.

126   Marriage Certificate, General Register Office, England and Wales.

127   Cole, *Lord Haw-Haw*, p.66.

6

THE GODS IN CONFLICT

There are no true friends in politics. We are all sharks circling, and waiting, for traces of blood to appear in the water. [Alan Clark, *Diaries* (London, 1993), p.373, entry 30 November 1990.]

1

Mosley's failure to capture East London in 1937 dealt a devastating political blow to his grandiose ambitions. But he refused to capitulate. Many young supporters not yet ratepayers had been unable to vote and he reasoned that when they became eligible his fortunes would change.[1] He therefore decided to fight the municipal elections scheduled for that autumn. By then Joyce no longer marched alongside him. On 11 March 1937, 'The Leader' carried out a sacking spree.

Mosley's knife amounted to a mild act of political butchery compared with Stalin's periodic purges and the intra-party terror which gripped Hitler's NSDAP. "Lord Horatio Bohun's" latest biographer passes over the incident at some speed.[2] But Joyce and many members of the BUF were abruptly cut adrift.

Tensions had always washed through the movement.[3] As Special Branch soon noticed.[4] Joyce schemed against J.F.C. Fuller.[5] Alexander

Raven Thomson came within his sights.[6] The Friends of Oswald Mosley recall Thomson as a "Writer, philosopher, soldier, politician: A loyal comrade and great British and European patriot."[7] Joyce saw him as a political rival who had to be removed.[8] Shortly after joining the BUF, Joyce had plotted against Ian Hope Dundas, hoping to replace him as Mosley's Chief of Staff.[9] He always wanted be in control. He also intrigued against the BUF's Director of Organisation, Dr Robert Forgan.[10] G. A. Pfister was another of his targets. Born in Naples to Swiss parents, Pfister had arrived in Britain from Australia in the 1920s and soon assumed an important role in the BUF's secretive Foreign Relations and Overseas Department.[11] He worked at the Reliance Translations Bureau but politics occupied much of his time. Nazi representatives in Britain were impressed by his cosmopolitan background and, noticing this connection, one police report described him as "an agent of the Nazi Party on the staff of the Headquarters of the British Union of Fascists."[12] Mosley made use of his international connections.[13] Joyce, however, soon felt the need to attack his supremely confident rival.[14] He quickly moved against him in the autumn of 1934, after Pfister had overstepped the mark in dealings with Austrian Nazis.[15]

Joyce's obsession with power – his interfering everywhere, attempting to dominate the BUF's agenda – led one member to claim as early as 1934 that "to all intents and purposes" he was widely perceived as personifying the entire movement.[16]

Sexual conflicts also surfaced when Frederick Burdett and Alexander Raven Thomson fought for the body and soul of Olive Hawks, fascist, novelist, and would-be poet.[17] Sometimes these sexual intrigues entwined with political ambitions. Eric Piercy, commander of the Fascist Defence Force, the BUF's hit squad, sombre-faced and decorated with a slim moustache, began an affair with Joyce's first wife, seemingly with his connivance.[18] From which Joyce hoped to benefit politically by discrediting Piercy.[19] And when Mosley's gargantuan sexual appetite led him into an entangled adventure with the actress and fascist supporter, Mary Russell Taviner, sometimes called Baroness Marovna, it could have had serious political consequences.[20] Some BUF members had obtained her letters to 'Tom.' Joyce had kept copies.[21] There could be ammunition here.

However, the tensions in 1937, which resulted in "a widespread reduction in Headquarters personnel" and "a fundamental restructuring of the movement's organisational machinery," proved far more serious than any earlier conflict.[22]

Financial problems have been cited as the catalyst of the purge.[23] Mosley, a wealthy man, always put in his twopenn'orth. W.E.D. Allen, with interests in advertising, was another backer: one MI5 report described him as the main financier of the young BUF.[24] Industrialists including Lord Nuffield, Viscount Rothermere, Sir Alliot Verdon Roe, and, probably, Sir Henry Deterding, provided additional funding.[25] A number of companies and City firms opened their purses.[26] However, following the Olympia meeting, the Conservative Research Department made a concerted successful effort to retrieve its business and City donors.[27] The loss of such support created a problem for Mosley. Rank-and-file members, worker-fascists who bought *The Blackshirt* and other publications, put in what they could afford. But their contributions alone could never provide enough. Joyce, always scrambling for funds, often kept afloat by Macnab, was no use at all in this respect.

In its early days the BUF could rely on funds from Europe. Italian money had arrived during the 1935 Abyssinian crisis, when Mosley had supported Mussolini's African ambitions.[28] This contribution, estimated at £3000 per month, allegedly came with conditions. John Beckett claimed that the Italian dictator "expected political and military espionage."[29] A special account at the National Westminster Bank, Charing Cross Road, served as a deposit for some, if not all, foreign donations. However, when closed in May 1937, it was showing a balance of only £1.17s.9d.[30]

Just as Britain's Communists could count on Moscow's 'gold,' surely Mosley could rely on Berlin as well as Rome to keep his political show on the road. For some time MI5 was unclear about such monies.[31] Yet the flow of income into the BUF between 1934 and 1936 suggests Hitler was probably bankrolling Mosley during these years.[32] One Intelligence report claimed Bill Allen not only put in his own money and acted as a signatory to the Charing Cross account, but also operated as a courier for Nazi monies. Some of what he raised there travelled through anonymous ledgers in Europe before finishing up in a Belfast bank account.[33] 'Front' businesses linked to the crooked Dr Albert Tester were other conduits through which German funds came to Britain.[34] Meantime, Diana Mosley was busy soliciting support in Berlin.[35]

Yet by 1937 money had become tight. A hitherto unnoticed sign of these growing troubles had appeared earlier in a letter Joyce sent to Mosley in December 1936. Adopting a decidedly oily tone similar to his unsuccessful Civil Service application, he began:

> My dear Leader
>
> When you have been giving all your time and energy to affairs of grave national importance, I hate to trouble you with a mere personal detail; but as all my personal allegiance is to you, I hope to be forgiven.

Still fawning towards 'The Leader,' writing "my pledge is not to be broken until you tell me I am of no use to you personally," he bridled at being treated as "a paid hand" rather than a "brother officer" and destined for a pay cut. How could someone with his talents, be treated like this? Did he think of his earlier disappointments? Why could life be so unforgiving?

His letter is revealing for other reasons. His proposed salary reduction came when, with his impending second marriage, he would be shouldering many more commitments, He was also in dispute with the Inland Revenue. Friends have always portrayed him as completely uninterested in money.[36] But Joyce told Mosley quite openly, "I do not conceive myself to be following a mendicant's course." More importantly, faced with pressing financial problems, he never lost sight of his chief ideological enemy. "I am content to do no less than my best," he wrote. However, "my best is not likely to be very brilliant if I have to cope with the Inland Revenue as well as the Jews."[37] That Jewish threat would not go away. It followed him into the deepest nooks and crannies of his private life. Already it possessed him.

Joyce's letter confirms that by late 1936 the BUF had become pinched financially. The savage cuts implemented a few months later left only fifty-seven out of one hundred and twenty-nine paid and voluntary personnel still in post at national headquarters.[38] On hearing that his salaried services were no longer required, Joyce created difficulties and Mosley expelled him.[39] 'The Leader' often acted like an over-zealous prefect or, better, the bully of the Remove. But matters did not end there. Bad blood continued to flow, not surprisingly given Joyce's estimate of his own worth, and according to an Intelligence report he proceeded to sue – successfully it would appear – for wrongful dismissal.[40] Mosleyites, keen to control the BUF's historical record, have suppressed this embarrassment. In addition to Joyce, all the paid National Staff speakers under his direction in the Policy Propaganda Department were cast aside. John Beckett fell in this political cull. The new focus of power appeared when Joyce's rival, Neil Francis-Hawkins, assumed control of the BUF's administrative and political machinery.[41]

A funding crisis evidently influenced events in '37. However, the purge also reflected a power struggle within the upper echelons of the BUF. Joyce claimed he had been manoeuvred into that disastrous election contest in Shoreditch by Francis-Hawkins, in order to be humiliated.[42] He might have been attempting to shift responsibility for his failure to capture the seat. But his allegation reveals the movement's internal tensions.

The victory of the Francis-Hawkins faction was a triumph for those members wedded to a bureaucratic and quasi-military form of organisation over the likes of Joyce and Beckett, whose chief interest lay in propaganda activities. In John Macnab's words, "the bureaucrats" had defeated "the brains trust"; he added "All this is, of course, not FASCISM but STALINISM."[43] Special Branch reported the conflict rather differently, claiming the "body of fighters which, three years ago, smashed the terror of red hooliganism on the streets and in the halls" had now themselves been vanquished.[44] The purge had an intra-political as well as a financial dimension.

By removing Joyce and Beckett and their supporters it has been argued that Mosley was signalling "a re-orientation away from the more violent forms of anti-Semitism."[45] Even by 1936 some leading figures had become concerned about the level of Jew-hatred in the movement.[46] Such tensions increased following the failure of the BUF's anti-Jewish campaign in the 1937 local elections, and some individuals were certainly encouraged to tone down their anti-Semitism. J. A. Bailey, who had stood with Joyce in Shoreditch, faced censure on this account and resigned from the BUF in acrimonious circumstances the following December.[47]

However, anti-Semitism continued to circulate within the BUF during 1937 well after Joyce and his supporters had been ejected. The "Jolly Judah" column in *The Blackshirt*, written originally by John Macnab, appeared until the end of July, and was still characterised by a vituperative Jew-hatred.[48] From the autumn of '37 until the spring of '38, readers were also treated episodically to "The Kronikles of Klemens Brunovitch." Its author, Clement Bruning, was unashamedly anti-Semitic.[49]

Joyce and his supporters were not isolated bearers of anti-Semitism, whose excommunication cleansed the BUF of its Jew-hatred and purified its political soul. Such sentiment permeated all the way up to Mosley, in whom it usually appeared in a more dissembling form. The BUF's anti-Semitism, evident as early as 1932, continued throughout its brief political life; it featured in its East London politics; it characterised its campaign in 1938 and 1939 against British involvement in a European war allegedly fomented by Jews to serve Jewish interests; it persisted until 1940 when the BUF became proscribed.[50]

Like so much of the movement's history, the accounts of 1937 have been drawn from Mosley's perspective. The organisation had to be knocked into better financial shape; exhausting personal conflicts had to stop; centralised control had to prevail; overt anti-Semitism had to be diminished. The views of Joyce and Beckett have been virtually ignored.

Their evidence confirms they had little time for Francis-Hawkins and his bureaucratic allies. Beckett, always good for a choice turn of phrase, said they were a "comical little circus of ex-peddlers and humourless ex-officers."[51] But his testimony suggests more. By 1937 Joyce and Beckett had developed serious doubts regarding Mosley's grip on political events. Would he ever lift fascism into power? Two incidents in particular encouraged their concern.

During the 1936 Abdication Crisis Mosley invited them to join him at the cavernous Adelphi Hotel in Liverpool where he announced the King would soon accept Stanley Baldwin's resignation as Prime

Minister and turn to him to form a government. 'The Leader's' great political gamble would have paid off. Both men, taken aback, aghast even, left Liverpool convinced Mosley's "power of self-delusion had conquered his sanity."[52]

The second incident arose after the 1937 London local elections. Joyce and Beckett drove from Shoreditch to inform Mosley of the result there. The outcome had not met his expectations. But convinced of his political destiny, he claimed that the votes in Bethnal Green and Limehouse would "mend matters." Once again failure stared straight back at him. Yet his political imagination knew no bounds. He put the most extravagant gloss on the outcome. He loftily announced that the BUF's percentage of the vote was higher than Hitler had achieved in his first big election battle. However, the National Socialists had campaigned across the whole of Germany, whereas the BUF's votes had been accumulated merely in three local elections.[53] Mosley's deluded defiance was translated into his movement's 'understanding' of these elections.

Joyce and Beckett kept to the party line in public but neither was relaxed about it. Joyce knew by now that he was out of favour with Mosley.[54] He and Beckett prepared for a "final showdown."[55] It soon came.

Beckett's evidence suggests that far from being a resolute leader, Mosley had lost touch with political realities; he was a busted flush. In such testing circumstances he surrounded himself with fawning admirers rather than activists of ability who on occasions might prove troublesome. This was not surprising for someone who expected human beings "to react in the same simple and inevitable way as a crankshaft is driven by a piston rod."[56] Mosley could never manage 'difficult' people. He demanded fawning admirers. The purge reflected his political weakness rather than his strength. Joyce and Beckett might be well rid of his close political company, even if not all ties had to be severed: after all, each continued to work for fascism.

Beckett's testimony provides a new, much-needed dimension on the events of '37 even if, like its Mosleyite equivalent, it is self-serving. His assessment of Mosley can now be probed further – which involves discussing Mosley's relations with Berlin, his changing image there and its political implications.

From the start 'The Leader' had edged ever closer to the Nazis. Their courtship can be gleaned particularly from one important collection of documents which for many years could be found only in the Russian State Military Archive. When the Nazis occupied Paris they seized French Intelligence files and transported them to Berlin.[57] When an exhausted, wrecked Berlin fell to the Red Army in 1945, these documents, along with German files, were scooped up and transported to the Soviet Union to become part of the 'Trophy Archive.'

These sources, historical loot, are significant. Mosley always claimed publicly – his admirers still slavishly repeat it – that he remained a staunch patriot. Unlike Joyce, the Nazi, who finished up in Germany. 'The Leader's' claim is a deception.

German documents record early visits by Nazi representatives to Britain.[58] In 1934 one delegate met Mosley and also Pfister, then charged with special responsibility for the BUF's external and international links.[59] In a clear attempt to impress, Mosley claimed his movement would sweep to power at the next general election.[60] Political traffic also took place in the reverse direction and on 12 May 1934 several BUF members were warmly received in Cologne.[61]

In October 1934, in a gesture further designed to suggest his political significance as a partner in European fascism, 'The Leader' sent Hitler a signed copy of the German edition of James Drennan's *BUF: Oswald Mosley. Portrait of a Leader*. Making the most of the occasion, he attached a letter emphasising the need for their continued close co-operation.[62]

These contacts continued and when Colin Ross, a personal friend of Hitler's, arrived in Britain in early 1936 to gauge the BUF's progress, Mosley advised him he was heading "an active and virile movement which was steadily gaining ground in Great Britain."[63] Once again he was promoting himself as the horse Berlin should back: he would soon be galloping into government. The same year more significant secret meetings, organised by Rudolf Hess, took place in Germany. That autumn in Munich Mosley met with leading members of the Nazi hierarchy – Hess, Himmler, von Ribbentrop – along with French and Spanish fascists.[64] He was placing himself and the BUF within the confines of the Brown International. It seemed perfectly proper that in October 1936 he re-married in Joseph Goebbels's house on Hermann–Göring-Strasse: Berlin had become his spiritual home.[65]

While presenting himself as a virile leader on the cusp of greatness, Mosley never hesitated to dance to Hitler's tune and in March 1935 he abruptly suspended Joyce's rival, Pfister, as head of the BUF's external relations department. Pfister had given offence to Berlin.[66] Such deference appeared again in 1935 when Julius Streicher, pathological anti-Semite and editor of *Der Stürmer*, complained of BUF policy towards the Jews. 'The Leader' replied:

> Please accept my very best wishes for your kind telegram . . . I value your advice greatly in the midst of our hard struggle. The power of Jewish corruption must be destroyed in all countries before peace and justice can be successfully achieved in Europe. Our struggle in this direction is hard but our victory is certain.[67]

Would he have written to any of his British comrades in such deferential terms?

Clearly, relations between the BUF and Berlin did not always run smoothly; MI5 knew of a number of specific irritants.[68] However, political self-interest dictated that such contact continued and in 1936 the BUF became the British Union of Fascists and National Socialists; its symbol now assumed a more Nazi appearance with the flash within the circle replacing the fasces Mosley had adopted earlier from the Italians.[69]

In this atmosphere Mosley can be tracked meeting Nazis, trying to bond with and impress them. In return Berlin offered advice, support and funding.[70] But political dreams and reality often collide. At meetings in Britain and Germany 'The Leader' had boasted of what he would achieve. But his standing up to the Reds at the 1934 Olympia meeting had not been followed through.[71] The débâcle at Cable Street which infuriated Joyce must have led the Nazis to question Mosley's leadership. Then came the failure in the 1937 East London elections results. It requires no great leap of political imagination to realise that by early '37 — Joyce would have been well aware of it – 'The Leader's' political stock in Berlin had plummeted alarmingly. What price now the politician on the threshold of power? His machismo had yielded nothing. Why should the Nazis keep throwing money into his lap?[72]

As late as 1940, Hitler viewed Mosley as a political thinker whose historical role had not yet been fully played out. But the Führer's sensitive antennae told him Mosley would never become a popular leader.[73] Hitler doubtless pondered how he personally would have dealt with the Jewish-Communist rabble – as he would have regarded them – who had defiantly blocked the BUF's path in East London.[74] 'Tom' Mosley was not the man to build the Nazi satellite state in Britain. He was too much a product of the old system which had nurtured him and he had once served.

Aware of 'The Leader's' difficulties in late '36, early '37, Joyce, a politico to his fingertips, was encouraged to plan for a future without him. He could not challenge for control of the BUF: no structure allowed for it. Another group was needed to move Britain more decisively towards fascism. Evidence, never before recognised, suggests he had planned in advance for this eventuality.

It appears in correspondence between John Macnab, then associate editor of the *Fascist Quarterly*, and Ezra Pound.[75] On 11 January 1937, well before the great political fallout that spring, he was writing to Pound on the official notepaper of the National Socialist League, to express his exasperation about the "total torpor of English people", who would never to be stirred politically until "a big bolshie comes & whacks them on [the] head."[76] The group was being organised from 190 Vauxhall Bridge Road and 83 Onslow Gardens.[77]

The Friends of Oswald Mosley will be delighted to hear "the little man's" double dealing had depths previously unrecognised.[78] But to Joyce it made sound political sense to plan along these lines. He and his followers hoped a fair chunk of the BUF's membership would follow them and, though seldom emphasised, following the rupture with Mosley, they attracted "an appreciable degree of sympathy."[79] But to survive, the NSL would need funds; and Joyce had expectations. Apart from possible Nazi support, he knew that the stockbroker Alexander Carron Scrimgeour, who had previously invested heavily in Mosley, would back him.

Joyce would need to do more than secure money. He would have to distance himself publicly from the fading Mosley. 'The Leader' could have his local campaigns in East London. Joyce believed, correctly, the future of European fascism would be determined by events in Berlin. He would operate outside the BUF, refrain on tactical grounds from challenging Mosley to become the leader of British fascism and wait on the much bigger developments unfolding in Europe. Against this background of uncertainty and promise, the National Socialist League amounted to another new political beginning for him.

Notes

1 *The Blackshirt*, 6 March 1937; *Action*, 13 March 1937.
2 Dorril, *Blackshirt*, pp.413–414. "Bohun" is Mosley in H. G. Wells's *The Holy Terror* (London, 1939).
3 A. C. Miles, *Mosley in Motley* (London, 1937), pp.11–13.
4 HO 144/20144/234, report, 17 December 1934.
5 KV 2/245/1a, report, 3 April 1935.
6 Pugh, "A Political Biography"; HO 45/25701; HO 283/70.
7 *Comrade*, No.21 (1989), p.6. *Fascist Week*, 8–14 December 1933 for an early impression.
8 KV 2/245, report, 3 April 1935.
9 KV 2/245/1a.
10 HO 144/21063/10, Special Branch report, 29 June 1937. Alderman, "Dr Robert Forgan's Resignation," pp.37–41 traces Forgan's manoeuvrings.
11 Knickerbocker, *Die Schwarzhemden*, p.12 carries a vignette. See also USSC MSS, 366/7/20.
12 HO 45/25385/39. FO 371/17730/165 for Nazi views on Pfister drawn from a Special Branch report, 3 September 1934. KV 3/218 for him under surveillance. See also A. Bauerkämpfer, *Die "radikale Rechte" in Grossbritannien* (Göttingen, 1991), p.229.
13 Dorril, *Blackshirt*, p.288.
14 YCAL, MSS43, Box 5, Folder 251, letter, 5 April 1934, for Pfister soon putting Ezra Pound in his place.
15 HO 144/20142/221.
16 Mosley Papers, University of Birmingham Special Collections, OMN/B/7/2/8.
17 Gottlieb, *Feminine Fascism*, p.308 offers brief biographical details. Hawks's *What Hope for Green Street?* (1946), is one of the few fictional remains of British fascism. To J. Suh, *Fascism and Anti-Fascism in Twentieth-Century British Fiction* (London, 2009), p.46 it is "a boring mess." See also

J. Gottlieb, "A Mosleyite Life stranger than Fiction. The Making and Remaking of Olive Hawks," in R. Toye and J. Gottlieb (eds), *Making Reputations: Power, Persuasion and the Individual in Modern British Politics* (London, 2008), pp.70–91. Pugh, "A Political Biography," pp.190–192 on Thomson and the struggle for Hawks's affections. HO 45/25703 on Burdett.

18 HO 144/21564 on Piercy. HO 144/20144/242–243, Special Branch report, 17 December 1934, refers to Hazel's pregnancy and attributes her condition to Piercy.

19 HO 144/20144/243 reported Piercy's transfer out of National HQ to avoid a scandal. KV 2/245/1a, 3 April 1935, on Joyce's encouragement of their relationship for political gain.

20 Her name often appears as Taverner. The International Movie Database has it Taviner and I have retained that version.

21 J. Dalley, *Diana Mosley: A Life* (London, 2000), pp.156–157.

22 Linehan, *East London for Mosley*, p.110.

23 Linehan, *British Fascism*, p.110.

24 KV 2/879/7g.

25 Dorril, *Blackshirt*, pp.277–278,306 and Skidelsky, *Oswald Mosley*, p.330.

26 Skidelsky, *Oswald Mosley*, p.330.

27 Dorril, *Blackshirt*, pp.312–313.

28 Baldoli, *Exporting Fascism*, on Italian and British fascism.

29 HO 144/21247/18.

30 HO 45/25393/33–4. J. J. Barnes and P. P. Barnes, *Nazis in Pre-War London, 1930–1939* (Brighton, 2005), p.135 emphasises Italian money drying up by 1937.

31 Dorril, *Blackshirt*, p.377.

32 *Ibid*; Barnes and Barnes, *Nazis in Pre-War London*, p.136.

33 KV 2/880/110a and KV 2/879/35A, 91, for Allen's involvement.

34 KV 2/618.

35 KV 2/879/35A and Barnes and Barnes, *Nazis in Pre-War London*, p.136. J. Richter (ed.), *Die Tagebücher von Joseph Goebbels 3/11, März 1936–Februar 1937* (München, 2001), pp.68, 362, 24 April 1936 and 7 February 1937, on the begging bowl activities in Berlin. On Diana, see Dalley, *Diana Mosley*, and A. de Courcy, *Diana Mosley* (London, 2003). See also D. Mosley, *A Life of Contrasts: The Autobiography of Diana Mosley* (London, 1977). Also on the Mitfords see D. Pryce-Jones, *Unity Mitford: A Quest* (London, 1976). M. Lovell, *The Mitford Girls: The Biography of an Extraordinary Family* (London, 2001).

36 Cole, *Lord Haw-Haw*, p.71, reflecting testimony from Margaret Joyce. Kenny, *Germany Calling*, p.7.

37 Mosley Papers, University of Birmingham Special Collections, OMD/1/1/2, William Joyce to Oswald Mosley, 14 December 1936, for this correspondence, and a letter from Joyce to the Chief Accountant detailing his financial problems.

38 Linehan, *East London for Mosley*, p.12.

39 *Ibid*. See also HO 144/21063/10–12, Special Branch report, 29 June 1937. A BUF document carried the observation: "Mr Joyce on being informed that he could no longer be retained as a salaried member of HQ staff immediately refused either to speak or to write for the Movement or to give any voluntary service. He even went so far as to write and cancel his weekly order for Action." He refused to appear before Mosley to argue his case and the termination of his membership followed. Report headed "PRIVATE DOCUMENT – FOR PERSONAL USE AND INFOR-MATION ONLY." (Various locations).

40 KV 2/245/266b, Kimpton to Stamp, 5 March 1941; KV 2/1513/246a.

41 HO 144/21063/252–6.

42 HO 144/21063/11, Special Branch report, 29 June 1937.

43 YCAL, MSS 43, Box 32, Folder 1338, Macnab to Ezra Pound, 11 April 1937.

44 HO 144/21247/82, Special Branch report, 26 October 1937, recorded the victory of bureaucrats over fighters.

45 Linehan, *East London for Mosley*, p.12.

46 D.S. Lewis, *Illusions of Grandeur: Mosley, Fascism and British Society 1931–81* (Manchester, 1987), p.76.

47 Linehan, *East London for Mosley*, p.47. Bailey remained a fascist. See "A Workman Speaks," in *The New Pioneer*, Vol.1 (1939), p.173. In 1939 he formed the Nationalist Association with Jock Houston. See Griffiths, *Patriotism Perverted*, p.62.

48 Columns by Margaret Collins and Sandy McDougall were followed by unsigned articles in *The Blackshirt* until the summer of 1937.

49 "The Kronikles" began on 2 October 1937 as "The Diary of Klemens Brunovitch" and then appeared as "The Kronikles etc." Klemens was sometimes Klemenz.

50 Mandle, *Anti-Semitism and the British Union of Fascists* and Holmes, *Anti-Semitism*, ch.11, on the BUF's anti-Jewish sentiments. The later Jew-hatred is particularly apparent in *Action* between 1937 and 1940.

51 USSC, MS 5/1, J. Beckett, "After my Fashion; twenty post-war years," unpublished ts, p.374, The reference to peddlers is a cruel jibe at the expense of Neil Francis-Hawkins, a former salesman.

52 Beckett, "After my Fashion," p.372.

53 *Ibid*. pp.375–376.

54 HO 144/21062/347–50.

55 Beckett, "After my Fashion," p.375.

56 HO 144/20144/266, MI5 report, 13 December 1934.

57 French agents monitored fascism in both Britain and Germany. P. Jackson, *France and the Nazi Menace: Intelligence and Policy Making 1933–39* (Oxford, 2000). His emphasis is on operations against Germany.

58 Russian State Military Archives, Moscow (RGVA) 500–1–244, p.3; RGVA 519–4–34a, p.8; RGVA 1355–1–7, p.4.

59 RGVA 519–4–34a, p.8.

60 RGVA 519–4–34a, p.8.

61 RGVA 500–1–244, p.3.
62 RGVA 1355–1–7, p.4. Drennan was the pseudonym of W.E.D. Allen. His book had appeared in 1934.
63 HO 144/20147/236, Special Branch report, 24 April 1936. KV 2/532 on Ross. See his "Englische Reise," *Völkischer Beobachter*, 28 April 1936.
64 RGVA 1361–1–2106, p.113.
65 Skidelsky, *Oswald Mosley*, p.341 and Dorril, *Blackshirt*, pp.392–394, refer to the marriage in Berlin. As does Mosley, *A Life of Contrasts*, pp.142–143.
66 HO 144/20144/109, Special Branch report, 20 March 1935. Pfister's fascism was not diminished by such brusque treatment. Dorril, *Blackshirt*, p.338, notes his leaving for Germany to continue his work but misses his later involvement in the Anglo-German Fellowship. Did he serve here as a Nazi agent?
67 *Jewish Chronicle*, 17 May 1935. *Daily Herald*, 11 May 1935, for a slightly different version. See also KV 3/218/13a.
68 HO 144/20144/109, MI5 to Home Office, 20 March 1935.
69 Skidelsky, *Oswald Mosley*, p.292.
70 This symbiosis led to articles such as "Bei dem Führer den Blackshirts," *Völkischer Beobachter*, 26 August 1934.
71 *The Observer*, 10 June 1934, on Nazi approval for Mosley's confronting the Reds at Olympia.
72 Barnes and Barnes, *Nazis in Pre-War London*, pp.134–136 trace the BUF's fluctuating finances. Richter (ed.), *Tagebücher*, p.362, 7 February 1937, for Berlin's growing frustration at Mosley's inability to make political progress.
73 von Kotze (ed.), *Heeresadjutant*, 14 June 1940, pp.82–83.
74 *Frankfurter Tageszeitung*, 5 October 1936, "Juden terrorisieren London," and *Völkischer Beobachter*, 6 October 1936, "Judentumulte in Londoner Osten," offer a flavour of Nazi opinion.
75 KV 2/875 and KV 2/876, on MI5 and Pound.
76 YCAL, MSS 43, Box 43, Folder 1338, Macnab to Pound, 11 January 1937, on "Unemployment going up rapidly, 160,000 extra *last two months Xmas and all*" [my italics].
77 YCAL, MSS43, Box 32, Folder 1337, Macnab, undated to Pound, for their new address.
78 A tediously familiar Mosleyite put-down of Joyce.
79 KV 2/1507/14a, Special Branch report, 12 April 1937. KV 2/1507/24a, Clement Bruning to Beckett, 23 March 1937.

7

THE NATIONAL SOCIALIST LEAGUE

> In the street [he] bought a copy of the *Volkischer Beobachter* and read with a sense of relief of Hitler's triumph at the polls. That at last might convince Europe. That at last might silence the mercurial foreign correspondents who at their masters' bidding maintained a vicious barrage of Press criticism against a nation striving to climb to its feet. Put an end to that suspicion, hate and fear engineered by the powerful irresponsible section of world opinion and there might be hope for international co-operation, understanding, peace. [Raymond Burns, *Turncoat. A Political Thriller* (London, 1937), p. 29.]

1

By 1937, despite Lintorn-Orman's best efforts, Oswald Mosley's many talents and the strivings of like-minded activists, such as Arnold Leese, fascism had not assumed power in Britain. A Nazi later remarked that the soil was simply not conducive to that ideology.[1]

Historians of British fascism in the 1930s have focused attention mainly on the BUF and, to a lesser extent, the Imperial Fascist League.[2] They, and Joyce's biographers, have treated the National Socialist League as no more significant than the little coterie described by Richmal Crompton in her children's story of fascism and dictatorship.[3] The conventional narrative of Joyce's life suggests that after the

BUF his political career lapsed into insignificance until he achieved notoriety as a wartime broadcaster for the Nazis.[4]

Yet that period between the spring of '37 and the summer of '39 witnessed the next important phase in his political life. Through the National Socialist League (the NSL) he began to align himself increasingly with Nazi Germany.

2

Interviewed by the *Morning Post* on his new group, Joyce renounced the ethos of personal autocracy. This statement is misleading. Autocratic arrangements, provided he were in charge, suited him admirably. Another emphasis, his rejection of Continental models of fascism, would likewise soon become threadbare.[5] The *Morning Post* identified at certain points with Britain's fascists. The *Jewish Chronicle* knew its enemy and it, too, pursued Joyce for an interview.[6] The Nazi press was equally quick to report on the League.[7]

For many years little was known about the group.[8] Joyce destroyed certain records in 1939, just before leaving for Germany, which hardly helps. When hunting for him that late summer, not realising he had left the country, the police seized other papers which appear to have vanished off the face of the earth.[9] However, at the time the authorities already knew a good deal. Joyce and his colleagues were under surveillance and these reports have now been made public.

Contrary to all histories of British fascism and Joyce biographies the League existed before Mosley's purge but its official life did not begin until the evening of 2 April 1937 when Special Branch reported that about fifty people attended an open meeting at the Prince Albert Hotel, in Wood Street, Westminster. It made for such a contrast with the serried BUF assemblies at Olympia and the Albert Hall. If Joyce and Beckett had counted on attracting support from Mosley's movement – as opposed to sympathy – they must have been disappointed. Interestingly, however, and never before noticed, 'Mick' Clarke, a key BUF figure in East London, spent some time in the NSL.[10]

At least one interesting nuance emerged at the Prince Albert. The BUF had already issued a statement suggesting the NSL would create trouble.[11] Yet that scenario was not immediately evident. Joyce and Beckett emphasised that anyone believing Mosley would lead British fascism to power should remain with him. These noises recognised, as much as politically possible, that both groups marched together for fascism. This shared vision might explain why, in the aftermath of '37, the BUF had not necessarily closed the door on Joyce and Beckett. In September 1938 Special Branch reported on "a delicate approach" to bring Joyce back into the fold, but not Beckett.[12] In October MI5 claimed Mosley would have reinstated Beckett but not Joyce.[13] In the event, no reconciliation took place.

At its first public meeting Captain A.V. Collier proposed the formation of the NSL. John Macnab seconded.[14]

Collier, an elusive figure who was a casualty of the BUF's 1937 purge, served briefly as the NSL's first Chief National Propaganda Officer. Beckett believed he was a Mosleyite agent.[15] He was never interned and several years ago it was suggested he might have worked for MI5.[16] This claim has re-appeared more recently.[17] Under the name Captain Hawke, this former Sinn Féiner probably monitored Britain's fascists for the Board of Deputies of British Jews.[18] His activities, even if not fully visible, are a further reminder that Britain's fascist groups were often penetrated by agents.[19]

Macnab, 'Master,' as Joyce would call him, was the son of a distinguished Harley Street ophthalmologist bayoneted to death in November 1914 while attending the wounded at Messines.[20] Reflecting on his loss, Macnab turned to poetry, lamenting the tragic human waste of the War and regretting that after it many brave men had been consigned "to fill the Nation's need for Bootlace Hawkers and itinerant Bands."[21] He attended Rugby School and entered Christ Church, Oxford, as a scholar before going into business. After commercial failure struck him down he became a schoolmaster.[22] He joined the BUF in April 1934 aged twenty-seven, served alongside Joyce in its propaganda wing and became his closest, adoring friend. Like Joyce, Macnab was a rabid anti-Semite. He has been noticed as the original "Jolly Judah" in *The Blackshirt*. Both men also regarded the truth as an infinitely flexible commodity.[23] Socially, they shared a passion for alcohol, chess, classical music, particularly Wagner, and literature. They also had sporting interests, Joyce in boxing, his friend in mountaineering. With such ties they often lived together in London, with Macnab putting up the money.[24] He was Joyce's Engels.

Special Branch soon reported that the NSL, based at 28 Fawcett Street, had appointed Joyce and Beckett as National Directors and Macnab as National Propaganda Officer. What had happened to Vincent Collier? This report also latched onto a remark, almost certainly Joyce's, that "if we march without Mosley, it is because he gladly permits his pace to become a dawdle, lest perchance the unwieldy functionaries who cling to him should be left behind."[25]

By early April a number of local officials had been appointed, including Joyce's brother Frank in Camberwell.[26] Quentin Joyce had become a member.[27] Their mother had joined.[28] Sylvia Morris, a former BUF parliamentary candidate, had been charged with NSL activities at Holland with Boston – another reminder fascism sought recruits in the countryside.[29]

The group soon published a policy statement. Its constipated prose argued for "A people thoroughly united as an organic being – National in spirit and Socialist in achievement, free from class war, free from snobbery, and free from exploitation by privileged pirates." To this end it called for a "scientific government based on authority," as opposed to the "party intrigue" of contemporary politics and absolutely "free from the domination of international finance and Jewish money power." Its economic policy emphasised the importance of "real wealth" and full employment "in a nation free from poverty, free from fear of economic insecurity, and free from cut-throat competition, whether domestic or foreign." In external affairs, it emphasised the need for a strong Empire "free from exploitation by international finance." Finally, and significantly, it urged an alliance of a well-armed Britain with National Socialist countries, "to shield Europe from the danger of Bolshevism and the oppression of international finance."[30] Joyce never doubted that "red violence" had to be fought "to the finish."[31] This programme reflected the ideology he had been preaching for years.

The British public showed little enthusiasm for these policies. However, Joyce and Beckett claimed they had attracted recruits "of a good type." As promised, they had kept their political distance from East London and concentrated on other parts of the capital, as well as

Birmingham, an important centre for Nazi sympathisers, where they held weekly meetings in the Bull Ring.[32]

A leaflet issued in May 1937 emphasised the group's intention to build a federated structure. Joyce and Beckett, the National Directors, would be assisted by a National Council. Further appointments included National Finance Officers and local officials in London and Birmingham. *The Helmsman*, a four-page penny publication, was announced for June and small membership badges inscribed with "Steer Straight" had been ordered.[33]

That summer *The Helmsman* encouraged members' spirits, by emphasising: "Already a fine band of Englishmen and Englishwomen stand behind the League and the sign of the Helm and the speakers of the League become every day a more noticeable feature of our national life."[34] But Macnab's correspondence with Ezra Pound was telling a different story.[35] In September 1937 Special Branch confirmed that members were drawn almost entirely from London, Birmingham and Manchester.[36] Next month the same source portrayed the group as staggering on its last political legs.[37] In these circumstances rumours began to circulate in some quarters, possibly within the BUF, that Joyce and Beckett had quarrelled. However, Special Branch dismissed such speculation; the men and their wives were often seen together in public and appeared quite friendly.[38]

Throughout this time Joyce kept himself busy. His column "Out and About" in *The Helmsman* provided him with a platform to attack Jews, including Leslie Hore-Belisha, the newly appointed Secretary of State for War, and the butt of much anti-Jewish sentiment.[39] Joyce claimed that with its anti-Jewish agenda National Socialism had attracted "the implacable enmity of Jewry." But he saw no alternative. He had arrived at a view of the world and could not be shifted. Macnab believed the same. Writing on "Our Hebrew Bailiffs" for *The Helmsman*, he suggested ominously: "The only great service that Jewry can do to Britain is to reveal itself. The British people can do the rest." The NSL's newspaper also carried advertisements for well-known anti-Semitica.[40]

With the League just stuttering along, Special Branch reported that Joyce had written *National Socialism Now*. John Beckett's effulgent preface to this political 'novella' claimed that in the future his colleague would "exercise a very great influence upon the life and thought of our people."[41] He could hardly have known how prophetic his words would be.

Joyce's book emphasised that despite its current failure to appeal to the British electorate, fascism remained as relevant as ever. National Socialism, he declared, was no "temporary grievance" but "the revolutionary yearning of the people to cast off the chains of gross, sordid, democratic materialism without having to wear the shackles of Marxian Materialism." It amounted to the ideology of the hour.

He offered no policy surprises, but a more reflective summary of key ideas he had expounded both in the BUF and also the League's policy statement. He argued for a Keynesian expansion of the economy within a planned and protectionist framework: any return to the mass unemployment of the early 1930s was unthinkable. Once again mirroring his fascist contemporaries, he advocated the dismantling of parliamentary democracy in favour of a new corporate political arrangement. He chimed with them, too, when claiming: "Our National Socialist League is openly and unashamedly imperialist." India must be organised in Britain's interests rather than the incessant demands of "noisy fakirs" and "chattering babus." Joyce added haughtily, "If the policy seems brutal, it has at least the merit of being understood and a little plain speaking in India a few years ago would have saved many lives and much trouble." Here is the Joyce who knew best, writing like a schoolmaster or, as he would prefer, a professor. His observations on foreign policy proved equally consistent. The overriding need here was for "firm friendship" with National Socialist Germany and Fascist Italy. These alliances were vital to guarantee the future he wanted.

In stressing his patriotism, Joyce claimed the NSL was no mirror image of Hitler's NSDAP. "His way is for Germany, ours is for Britain," therefore "let us tread our paths with mutual respect, which is rarely increased by borrowing."[42] However, as Hitler's popularity grew, Joyce increasingly regarded Nazism as the only political vehicle through which his ideal Britain could finally emerge.[43]

Joyce believed that the power of financial interests lay at the core of the economic and political systems he wanted to replace. "The existing order of Parliamentary incumbents," he wrote, "is too closely linked to High Finance to desire revolutionary change." Even "the political leader" [was] "but the slave of international money interests." But who controlled international finance?

He gave his answer when discussing foreign policy. When the National Socialists in Germany had resolved to be "entirely independent of international finance," what he called "the tremendous forces of Jewry in Britain" had mounted a furious counter-attack. In other words, Jews were the fascists' core enemy. They strived relentlessly for power. Their tentacles reached everywhere, touched virtually everything. Even India was controlled by "international Jewish finance." This malign octopus-like force manipulated British politicians and Indian nationalists, profited from the exploitation of Indian workers, and severely damaged British labour.

These international financiers found their ally in Bolshevism, with Jews, dominant in both, scheming ultimately for Jewish interests. Support for Hitler, who understood this 'truth,' was therefore vital. Joyce then declared: "If Germany needs help in hurling Orientals back to the Orient" then "she is entitled to receive it from those who prefer *white manhood* and government to any other." Joyce's emphasis on "white manhood" reveals him persisting with his racial opposition to Jews. He proclaimed, "The [Jewish] question is pre-eminently racial and religion does not enter into it," adding: "The Hebrews are distinctly a race, possessing greater unity and cohesion than nearly all others. Their salient characteristic is inveterate materialism." How different from the spirituality present in the Aryan.

This constant struggle lay at the heart of his politics. He believed that eventually National Socialism would smash the power of Jewish finance. Even then Jews would exist and "any well-disposed foreigner" in Britain "whose presence could harm nobody and benefit some" would be tolerated. But the majority would have to be settled elsewhere. Since they could not be despatched to Palestine "without injustice to the Arabs" where could they be sent? In formulating his most benign response to Jews, he told his curious readers only that: "There are . . . great tracts of territory in this world wherein the necessary accommodation could be found."

When National Socialism finally defeated this Jewish threat it would enjoy a glorious lasting triumph. A new society would emerge.

Joyce scoffed at Oswald Spengler's gloomy outlook, then in vogue in fascist circles, with its emphasis on cycles in civilisation and the decay of all empires. The road to victory would not be easy. Joyce had experienced too many bruising political encounters to believe otherwise. But, doubtless projecting himself as the ideal National Socialist, he announced:

> In the whole world there is no power or obstacle that he regards as unconquerable. He is the true rebel, the divinely inspired revolutionary who lives to make destiny, not to be enslaved by it.[44]

These stirring and frightening words have been treated as a major ideological breakthrough:

> The familiar Joyce of the wartime German radio had already appeared – speaking English but oddly alien in manner, employing extravagant figures of speech which obscured rather than emphasized his message ... plugging ... the Wall Street-Moscow conspiracy.[45]

Jack Cole's assessment can be defended only by overlooking Joyce's earlier writings. *National Socialism Now* reflected ideas he had nurtured for years. In the short time ahead, he added little to them.

This excursion into Joyce's political ideas can now be put aside, to return to the National Socialist League. In October '37, Special Branch reported it was "quite unable to make any material progress."[46] Relations between Joyce and Beckett, rumoured earlier to be under strain, now became frostier.[47] The group's activities continued, however, sometimes in the face of stiff opposition. In January 1938 the BUF interrupted a meeting at Chelsea Town Hall.[48] The following November Joyce appeared before Paul Bennett, magistrate at the West London Police Court. It was alleged that at one meeting a League supporter had been arrested. When Joyce intervened a heckler had jostled him. He then retaliated.[49] He never shirked a fight.[50] The magistrate dismissed the case. On 21 May 1939 he faced another assault charge arising from an NSL meeting. Once again it was thrown out.[51] He was no stranger to the courts; he had been in the dock during his time in the BUF when in 1935 along with Mosley and Charles Bentinck-Budd he was acquitted at Lewes Assizes on a charge of "riotous assembly."[52] But these latest incidents suggest his group was not making the smooth progress he might have hoped.

3

Soon after forming the NSL, Joyce's political ambitions were hit by a stroke of misfortune. Intelligence files suggest the Nazis provided some funding.[53] But they were hardly likely to meet all his needs. He might turn out to a disaster, like Mosley.

Joyce's fund-raising work for the BUF had brought him into contact with the movement's donors, including the stockbroker Alexander Scrimgeour, and he came to view Scrimgeour as crucial to his own plans.[54] Their hitherto obscure relationship now needs to be unscrambled.

The stockbroker owned Honer Farm, at South Mundham near Chichester, and Joyce sometimes stayed there. He also became a friend of Scrimgeour's sister, Ethel, who owned a cottage at Pigeon Hill near Midhurst. In the 1920s and 1930s Joyce wandered about London from one rented flat to another without forming any strong attachments. But he developed a particular liking for Pigeon Hill and its comfortable life-style.

Joyce generally despised finance capitalists. But Scrimgeour, whose bold handwritten letters – echoing Voltaire – usually ended with "Écrasez l'infâme," proved the exception. The stockbroker despatched occasional missives to the BUF's newspapers but exerted greater influence behind the scenes, especially when funds were required to combat the Jews.[55] And it is easy to imagine his and Joyce's discussions in Sussex, when they put the political world to rights. Here is Scrimgeour writing to Joyce in November 1936:

> Baldwin and his vile gang of corrupt paid pimps and ponces will hang themselves, only give them rope....We here at Honer are always delighted to see you, and all good and true Blackshirts, whenever you find it convenient to use this villa as a temporary rest house. . . . The Jews have fairly got Yankee land

in their grip and so their bought man Baldwin speaking to order talks of Britain and USA coming together . . . what a filthy, stinking poxy leprous bugger the creature is.[56]

Both men viewed the world in similar terms and cultivated a brutal style. Joyce, always consumed by his own importance, had no difficulty ejecting people from his life. But he remained fond of 'Scrim.'[57]

Early in 1937, with the BUF strapped for cash, Mosley had despatched his Director of Propaganda to see Scrimgeour. However, scheming as always, and fully aware of Mosley's sliding political reputation, Joyce harboured plans of his own. Remember that contrary to all received opinion, the NSL was not formed in April 1937, but the previous January when Joyce anticipated a big fall-out with Mosley. Aware he would need funds to pursue his ambitions, he urged his City friend to resign from the BUF.[58] 'Scrim's' deep pocket would prove invaluable in promoting the new movement. On 29 January Joyce duly received a letter from the stockbroker, which declared he would no longer finance Mosley and also attacked George VI's accession following Edward VIII's abdication:

> I am really sorry but my views are such that I find it impossible to support Sir Oswald Mosley any longer.
> I look upon the present occupier of the throne as a contemptible disloyal traitor unworthy of respect or loyalty, who deserves to be hanged.
> You must know that the Jews have placed him on the throne.[59]

It is likely that this unnoticed letter in the Mosley archive did not arise spontaneously from 'Scrim's' pen but from a seed Joyce had planted in his mind and from which he hoped to benefit politically. He would use Scrimgeour's money, which Mosleyites believed should have been theirs.[60] With his lack of soul, as Nellie Driver described it, he would have felt no pangs of conscience in treating the £2000 as his political slush fund.[61]

This cosy and for Joyce potentially lucrative arrangement was suddenly shattered, however. The second issue of *The Helmsman* carried the black-edged sombre notice: "Alexander Carron Scrimgeour, great patriot, true gentleman, and unassuming scholar, died at Honer, Sussex, on August 20th."[62]

Scrimgeour's substantial estate was valued at £73,298 17s. 8d. He added a codicil to his will as late as 1937, but made no provision for the National Socialist League. Some have said that the will instructed his sister to continue funding Joyce. This claim, based on a Special Branch report, is misguided.[63] He laid down no such condition.[64] Nevertheless, Ethel Scrimgeour, wealthy on her own account and holding convinced fascist and anti-Semitic opinions, remained loyal to Joyce and can be found corresponding with him just before his execution. She also supported Margaret at this difficult time, attempting to soothe and console her with: "He [Joyce] was too great a man to be allowed to live and I felt sure the Jews were too powerful to allow him to."[65] By her own wish she almost certainly continued to help finance the League.

Political groups are constantly consuming cash, the search for wealthy backers remains constant and 'Scrim's' death was undoubtedly a blow. Without Ethel Scrimgeour dipping into her ample funds, the financial consequences of her brother's passing would have been even more severe. Special Branch and MI5 remained alert therefore to political gossip on other possible donors. Their reports identified several.

Mary Taviner's affair with Mosley, which ended in acrimonious circumstances, has already attracted our attention. There were compromising letters – copies of some of which were in Joyce's hands – a nude photograph, and suggestions of slander. And when in July 1937 Taviner was observed visiting the NSL's headquarters the Intelligence services claimed blackmail was now involved.[66] Was she attempting to draw in Joyce and Beckett? These are dark waters, indeed. Joyce, who later described the actress as a "preposterous obscenity," apparently offered her no encouragement.[67]

About this time the authorities also reported on John Beckett's link to W.E.D. Allen.[68] *Who Was Who* recorded Allen's birth in 1901 and his death in 1973. It noted his role as chairman, between 1925 and 1970, of the advertising firm David Allen and Sons Limited. He was also described as a historian, associated with the Hakluyt Society and the Royal Asiatic Society, whose publications focused especially on Russia and Turkey. It reported his representing West Belfast for the Unionist Party since 1929 and his resignation from that Party in 1931. The entry also referred to service in the Irish Guards early in the Second World War and his various governmental posts.[69] Allen's obituary in *The Times*, headed "Traveller and Scholar," proved equally discreet, informing readers that after the Second World War he had returned to "his beloved Ireland" and built up "a splendid library at his residence, Whitechurch House, County Waterford." He enjoyed membership of The Turf in London and the Kildare Street in Dublin.[70] There it was, neatly laid out; a gentleman scholar.

But Allen's politics had another dimension. "He saw Mosley as an aristocratic adventurer in the Elizabethan tradition" and after ceasing to be a Unionist MP joined the New Party. On its collapse he went on to serve the BUF as "a propagandist writer of great flair."[71] His hand appeared in "The Letters of Lucifer" in *The Blackshirt*. He wrote in the *British Union Quarterly*.[72] He contributed to the *Quarterly Review*.[73] As James Drennan in *BUF: Oswald Mosley. Portrait of a Leader* published in 1934, he attempted to 'sell' Mosley to the British public. Allen also helped to establish the January Club.[74]

He did more than make an intellectual contribution. In 1938–39 he became centrally involved in the Air Time project, 'The Leader's' plan to establish a radio station in collaboration with the Nazis.[75] Mosley, like Hitler, soon recognised the political potential of the wireless and Allen's commercial background in advertising encouraged Mosley to seek his advice on various radio schemes.[76] Allen has also been noticed dipping into his pocket to support the BUF and ferrying funds from Europe. MI5 reported, too, on a Mosleyite scheme to capture the Labour MPs, George Buchanan and John McGovern, whose defections would have been sweetened by their receiving attractive retainers from Allen's business.[77]

Allen clearly played a key role in the BUF. He never held any official position in the movement – would Joyce have schemed against him if he had? – but an undated Intelligence report claimed he was "the power behind Mosley."[78] For some time he and 'The Leader' enjoyed a close personal relationship and in 1936 Allen was a guest in Berlin when Mosley married Diana Guinness.[79] Free from the newly-weds, did he indulge his taste for *le vice anglais* at the party-protected brothel on the Kurfürstendamm? This special interest was merely one of his activities that intrigued the British security service.[80]

Were they concerned because he was one of their own and might become vulnerable? Convention has it that before the War Allen had Intelligence connections and the omniscient Mosley exploited these links for his own ends.[81] This claim, often recycled by 'The Leader's' present-day admirers, cannot be sustained. Previously secret files reveal Allen's security work began only in late 1939 when he entered Military Intelligence. Even then clearance proved difficult. Suspicions lingered, particularly because of his involvement in the Air Time project.[82] MI5 concluded he was a political chancer, "completely amoral and politically unstable," and his alleged interest in Joyce's National Socialist League might have been yet another adventure.[83]

Allen was a complex figure. But he held fascist sympathies, had Nazi contacts, knew about money, possessed it in some quantity, was well-versed in the complex international movement of funds. He was someone Joyce would recognise as worth cultivating.

In April 1937, when Special Branch reported Allen's possible interest in the NSL, he was still involved with Mosley. However, next year they fell out dramatically and savagely over money, particularly the radio ventures.[84] His role in the BUF began to fade.[85] This breach was not easily repaired, though to some extent the two were reconciled after the War.[86] Had the seeds of their earlier conflict been simmering in 1937? Had it encouraged him to flirt with Joyce and the NSL?

Allen has not previously been linked with funding the National Socialist League. What, if anything, he contributed remains elusive. But in 1937 political chatter evidently suggested some contact between the parties. In any discussions Joyce would doubtless have reminded Allen how valuable he had found his views on Ireland.[87]

More obscure fascists might have backed the Joyce's group. Special Branch mentioned "a wealthy young man named Bainbridge," almost certainly Emerson Muschamp Bainbridge, who had business connections in the North-East.[88] Articles by him in praise of Nazi Germany, a political line calculated to appeal to Joyce, had appeared in 1936 in *The Blackshirt*.[89] The security service also knew of him as "a generous donor to the exchequer of the British Union of Fascists."[90] He later joined the Anglo-German Fellowship Society.[91] Bainbridge's money might have helped to fund *The Helmsman*. But hard evidence is difficult to find.

In the autumn of 1937 another possible source of funding, the flamboyant 'Count Potocki,' or "John Penis," flitted briefly across the scene.[92] Geoffrey Wladislas Vaile Potocki de Montalk, born in New Zealand in 1903, had arrived in Europe in 1928.[93] He posed as a poet. However, the police viewed him as "a sexual pervert" and suspected him of what they called "procuration."[94] He was graphically described by them as:

> a familiar figure in the West End, where he may sometimes be seen parading bare-headed with hair falling down almost to his shoulders and wearing a flowing red velvet cloak and sandals.[95]

How could this eccentric with a bizarre life-style possibly relate to Joyce and the NSL?

Surprisingly, there were potential links. Not through the 'Count's' obsession with the divine right of kings – which in 1943 saw him crowned King of Poland during a ceremony at Little Bookham – but through his other activities.[96] He owned printing facilities and on behalf of the League produced A. K. Chesterton's *Why I Left Mosley*.[97] His anti-Semitism provided another bridge. His journal, the *Right Review*, started in 1936, became an important outlet for such sentiment in wartime Britain.[98] Joyce and Potocki clearly shared an ideological affinity and the 'Count,' now 'King,' kept in contact until Joyce's execution.

Potocki did make a small personal donation to the NSL.[99] More important, though, Joyce and Beckett knew of his connections to Bryan Guinness, who with Aldous Huxley had bought the press which printed the *Right Review*.[100] Strange to say, Potocki had acted for Guinness in a number of business matters. Might Potocki now be able to interest him in supporting the NSL? If he did donate – nothing has yet emerged to say he did – Joyce would have rejoiced if only because until 1934 Guinness had been married to Diana Freeman-Mitford, subsequently Lady Diana Mosley.[101] What a sweet revenge that would have been.

4

With the NSL faltering and backers hard to find, how did Joyce and Margaret survive? Years later she would claim that "in urgent domestic conferences," which translates as violent arguments, he "flatly refused to get a job." He pontificated "if he had to work purely for money," then "he would do so only part-time." He told her quite firmly "his main energies were to be devoted to politics."[102]

He did devote some time to Macnab and Joyce, Private Tutors, an enterprise started before their 1937 split with Mosley.[103] At 83 Onslow Gardens, South Kensington, it offered "expert private tuition for university entrance and professional preliminary examinations" and also provided English lessons "to foreigners of suitable character" interested in "acquiring a knowledge of our speech and customs." However, not everybody was welcomed. Joyce refused to teach Black or Asian students. Nor would he admit Jews.[104] Macnab's journalism suggests he would also have agreed to bar Jews. Principle clearly came before profit.

Margaret, Macnab, possibly both, have claimed that Joyce remained quite untroubled by his increasingly fragile circumstances; he totally rejected the ideal of "some beastly little semi-detached villa in Putney, with hire-purchase furniture and a portable radio and an aspidistra in the window."[105] Cole writes:

> The sole amenities he needed were books, cigarettes, alcohol and agreeable companions. He was not interested in dressing well, getting a home together or living in a good district; all he noticed about a flat was whether there were trees in the neighbourhood.[106]

Whether that assessment hits all the right notes is questionable. Joyce had not been reticent in fighting for money in 1936 when Mosley insisted he take a pay cut, even though political power mattered to him far more than a steady income.

By the summer of 1939, however, with political and personal funds hard to muster, Joyce and Macnab — essentially the latter — could no longer afford to keep on their South Kensington flat. Macnab took himself off to Pimlico. The Joyces went to a basement dwelling in Earls Court. From 38a Eardley Crescent on 8 August 1939, Joyce returned a set of forms to the teaching agency Gabbitas Thring. It was his final job application in Britain.

Joyce appeared on the agency's handwritten record card as a "Gent" with an "Irish accent." His age, we have remarked, was given significantly as thirty-six, even though at interview he claimed to be thirty-three.[107] He offered to teach shooting and drill tactics which reflected his military interests, as well as boxing, a passion he had brought from Ireland and later pursued at university. His academic subjects included phonetics and languages.[108] He lied when telling the interviewer he was planning a visit to America. He was certainly thinking of travelling – but in a rather different direction.

Notes

1 W. von Oven, *Mit Goebbels bis zum Ende* (Buenos Aires, 1949–50), Vol. 1, p. 182, diary, 25 January 1944.

2 Thurlow, *Fascism in Britain*; Griffiths, *Patriotism Perverted*, is a noticeable exception.

3 R. Crompton, *William – the Dictator* (London, 1938).

4 Note the silences in Cole, *Lord Haw-Haw*; Kenny, *Germany Calling*; Farndale, *Haw-Haw*.

5 *Morning Post*, 13 April 1937.

6 *Jewish Chronicle*, 16 April 1937.

7 *Die Neue Zeit*, 4 June 1937.

8 USSC, MS 238/7/2, "The Future of National Socialism in Great Britain," 29 March 1937, by Joyce and Beckett, justifying the new group.

9 KV 2/1508/50b.

10 KV 2/2476/29a, interview with Frederick Burdett, 21 July 1937.

11 PRIVATE DOCUMENT. FOR PERSONAL USE AND INFORMATION ONLY. (Various locations).

12 KV 2/1507/27a, Special Branch report, 1 September 1938.

13 KV2/1507/29a.

14 HO 144/21247/8.

15 HO 144/21247/85, Special Branch report, 11 November 1937; HO 144/21064/50.

16 A. W. B. Simpson, *In the Highest Degree Odious: Detention without Trial in Wartime Britain* (Oxford, 1994), p. 135.

17 Dorril, *Blackshirt*, p. 454.

18 Griffiths, *Patriotism Perverted*, pp. 142, 56, discusses his later activities in the British People's Party.

19 HO 144/21247/5–8.
20 *The Times*, 12 November 1914. He specialised in diseases of the cornea. *British Medical Journal*, 21 November 1914, p.897.
21 Leonard Wise to author, 3 May 1991.
22 KV 2/2474/91A, pp.2–3 (29 July 1940).
23 KV 2/2474 and KV 2/2475.
24 Anon, *Fascism in England* (London? 1997?), p.38. The detail came from Macnab. See also KV 2/2894 on Quentin Joyce, 20 September 1939, p.3.
25 HO 144/21247/5, Special Branch report, 5 April 1937 (copy to MI5). The attack on OM's functionaries was partly directed at Neil Francis-Hawkins, who had supplanted Joyce and Beckett in the BUF.
26 HO 144/21247/23.
27 KV 2/2894/14a, 37a, 46a.
28 HO 144/21247/5, Special Branch report, 5 April 1937.
29 HO 144/21247/23, Special Branch report, 17 April 1937.
30 HO 144/21247/25.
31 HO 144/21247/82, Special Branch report, 26 October 1937.
32 HO 144/21247/30, Special Branch report, 31 May 1937 (Copy to MI5).
33 *Ibid.*
34 *The Helmsman*, Vol.1, No.2, p.1.
35 YCAL, MSS 43, Box 32, Folder 1338, letters, 18 July 1937, 27 July 1937.
36 HO 144/21247/34, Special Branch report, 15 September 1937.
37 HO 144/21247/81, Special Branch report, 26 October 1937.
38 HO 144/21247/34. Beckett's 'wife' – at this stage they had not married – was Anne Cutmore. A member of the BUF, she wrote for its publications. Beckett, *The Rebel who Lost His Cause*. HO 144/21247/34, Special Branch report, 15 September 1937, dismissed rumours of a Beckett-Joyce split as "baseless."
39 A. J. Trythall, "The Downfall of Leslie Hore-Belisha," *Journal of Contemporary History*, Vol.16 (1981), pp.391–411. *The Helmsman*, Vol.1 No.2, p.2 for Joyce attacking Hore-Belisha.
40 All NSL comment from *The Helmsman*, Vol.1, No.2.
41 Joyce, *National Socialism Now*, p.6.
42 *Ibid.* pp.15, 55, 58, 59, 63, 15 for the above arguments.
43 KV 2/245/62x and /134a.
44 Details of these latest claims from Joyce, *National Socialism Now*, pp.21,23,66,58,64 (my emphasis),66,68,67,70.
45 Cole, *Lord Haw-Haw*, p.76.
46 HO 144/21247/81, Special Branch report, 26 October 1937 (Copy to MI5).
47 HO 144/21247/85, Special Branch report, 11 November 1937.
48 HO 144/21242/88–95, Special Branch report of meeting at Chelsea Town Hall, 14 January 1938 (Copy to MI5).
49 KV 2/245/96a.
50 R. W. Jones, "I was a Blackshirt Menace," *The Spectator*, 6 August 1983, p.11.

51 Joyce in the courts is from Cole, *Lord Haw-Haw*, p.79.
52 Cross, *The Fascists in Britain*, p.142 and N. Mosley, *Beyond the Pale: Sir Oswald Mosley and Family 1933–1980* (London, 1983), p.82. See also the file on Bentinck-Budd, KV 2/2309/8a,9x.
53 KV 2/2894, statement of case against Edwin Quentin Joyce, p.3.
54 HO 144/20144/75–6, Special Branch report, 11 April 1935; HO 144/21247/9, Special Branch report, 5 April 1937. Mosley, *My Life*, remains silent.
55 *Fascist Week*, 25–31 May 1934. *Action*, 7 November 1936 for Scrimgeour's letters.
56 KV 2/245/254a, letter, 12 November 1936.
57 WJ to ES, 11 July 1945.
58 USSC 238/7/7, "The Enigma of William Joyce," p.6.
59 Mosley Papers, University of Birmingham Special Collections, OMD/11/2/2, A. Scrimgeour to Joyce, 29 January 1937.
60 KV 2/880/129A. Joyce pocketed £2000.
61 KV2/880/129A.
62 *The Helmsman*, Vol.1, No.2; *Bognor Regis Observer*, 1 September 1937.
63 HO 144/21064/49. Farndale, *Haw-Haw*, p.109 is the latest to repeat it.
64 Probate Records, General Register Office, England and Wales, will of 14 March 1937.
65 KV 2/346, letter, 18 December 1945.
66 KV2/1507/17a. USSC MSS, 366/22/5, carries intriguing Delphic evidence.
67 WJ to MJ, 20 August 1945.
68 KV 2/879/31b.
69 *Who Was Who 1971–1980* (London, 1981), p.15.
70 *The Times*, 21 September 1973. Matthew and Harrison (eds), *ODNB*, Vol.1, pp.835–837 is only a little less discreet.
71 Skidelsky, *Oswald Mosley*, p.342.
72 KV 2/879/7a, for the Lucifer letters. See, among other work, "Why not 'Drang nach Osten'?" *British Union Quarterly*, Vol.II (1938), pp.16–27.
73 W.E.D. Allen, "The Fascist Idea in Britain," *Quarterly Review*, No.518 (1933), pp.223–238. Reprinted as *Fascism in Relation to British History and Character* (London, 2002).
74 Imperial War Museum, HWL-J, 1/6, Forgan to Luttman-Johnson, 23 December 1933.
75 J. J. and P. P. Barnes, "Oswald Mosley as Entrepreneur," *History Today*, Vol.40 (1990), pp.11–16. See also Dalley, *Diana Mosley*, pp.217–220 and also Mosley, *Beyond the Pale*, pp.134–137.
76 KV 2/879 and KV 2/880.
77 KV 2/879, memo, 6 September 1934 on Allen funding the BUF. KV 2/879/20a on the plan to attract the Labour MPs.
78 KV 2/879/7a.
79 KV 2/880/129a.
80 KV 2/880/141a.

81　Mosley, *Beyond the Pale*, pp.174–175.

82　KV 2/880, KV2/879/82a, 83a, 89a.

83　KV 4/185, Guy Liddell's diary, 8 April 1942. KV 2/880/135a for more on Allen the adventurer.

84　Mosley Papers, University of Birmingham Special Collections, OMN/B/2/2/15, Allen to Mosley, 22 August 1938. See also KV 2/879/66a. MI5 memo, 1 November 1939, claimed Allen would have "cut Mosley's throat if he had the chance." Dorril, *Blackshirt*, pp.415–416, 435, 459–460.

85　Cross, *Fascists in Britain*, p.187.

86　Dorril, *Blackshirt*, p.571.

87　Reflected in Joyce, "Quis Separabit?" p.28.

88　HO 144/21247/20, report, 22 April 1937.

89　"Hail Mosley," *The Blackshirt*, 4 April 1936; "Germany's Olympiad," *ibid.* 8 August 1936; "The Spirit of Nuremberg," *ibid.* 26 September 1936.

90　HO 144/21247/20.

91　KV 5/3 notices members in 1935–1936.

92　G.W.V. Potocki, *Here Lies John Penis* (Paris, 1932), on his early life.

93　R.T. Risk, "*It is the choice of the Gods." The Remarkable Life of Count Potocki of Montalk* (Francestown, New Hampshire, 1978).

94　HO 144/21247/84, 11 November 1937.

95　*Ibid.* See also HO 144/21064/49 and D.A. Callard, "The Trial of John Penis," *London Magazine*, Vol.39 (1999), pp.34–41.

96　Risk, "*It is the choice,*" p.10.

97　A. K. Chesterton, *Why I Left Mosley* (London, 1938). For his earlier eulogy see *Oswald Mosley: Portrait of a Leader.* Joyce reviewed it in the *British Union Quarterly*, Vol.I (1937), pp.108–109.

98　T. Kushner, *The Persistence of Prejudice: Antisemitism in British Society during the Second World War* (Manchester, 1989), p.46.

99　HO 144/21247/84, report, 11 November 1937.

100　Callard, "Trial of John Penis," p.39.

101　See Guinness's obituary, *The Times*, 7 July 1992. HO 144/21247/84, report, 11 November 1937 on the possibility of Potocki tapping Guinness.

102　Cole, *Lord Haw-Haw*, p.70.

103　YCAL, MSS 43, Box 32, Folder 1338 has Macnab writing on its notepaper on 22 January 1937.

104　Cole, *Lord Haw-Haw*, p.70–71. *Daily Telegraph*, 14 October 2000 for comment, some of it questionable, on these premises.

105　G. Orwell, *Keep the Aspidistra Flying* (Harmondsworth, 1973. First ed., 1936), p.122

106　Cole, *Lord Haw-Haw*, p.71.

107　Photocopy provided by the late Richard Boston. The original is missing.

108　*The Guardian*, 20 January 1990.

8

WORSHIPPERS OF HITLER

Hero-worship is strongest where there is least regard for human freedom. [H. Spencer, *Social Statics* (London, 1868), pt.4, ch.30, sec.6, p.461.]

1

Between '37 and '39, in addition to his activities in the National Socialist League, Joyce involved himself in several pro-Nazi pressure groups.[1] His eventual departure for Berlin cannot be understood without taking into account all these activities.

2

From the mid-1930s European fascism began to flex its political muscles. In 1935 Italy invaded Abyssinia. Between 1936 and 1939 Spain was ripped apart by Civil War. But Hitler's ambitions to redress the European political status quo quickly moved centre stage. In 1938 he annexed Austria. Between 1938 and 1939 he took control of Czechoslovakia. In September 1939 he turned savagely on Poland. Here was the immediate political landscape against which Joyce's politics now unfolded.

Sympathy for Germany's treatment after the First World War transcended Joyce's circle of Britain's fascists and Nazi fellow travellers. Some believed that in 1919 the country had been harshly treated at Versailles, and in 1931 Sir Ian Hamilton had founded the Anglo-German Association to foster friendship between the two countries. However, with the NSDAP triumphant, the Association soon went "to pieces over the Jewish Question."[2]

The views of leading public figures who grappled with Germany's role in inter-war Europe have remained controversial.[3] Viscount Rothermere, the press baron, probably influenced by G. Ward Price, his chief foreign correspondent, wrote saccharine letters to a beloved Führer.[4] Geoffrey Dawson, editor of *The Times* – and his colleague Robert Barrington-Ward – constantly watered down criticism of the Nazis.[5] Michael Burn, reporting from Central Europe, was frustratingly alert to this censorship.[6] Lloyd George revealed his willingness to sup with Hitler.[7] In fact, during Edward VIII's brief reign many leading public figures expressed sympathy for Europe's dictators. There were plenty of "Guilty Men."[8] And until the Munich agreement in September 1938, which ceded control of the German-speaking Sudeten territory of Czechoslovakia to Hitler, their voices were influential.[9] The writer Robert Byron, who conducted a personal crusade against appeasement, once even asking a Chamberlainite MP over dinner at a London club, "Are you in German pay?" was a remarkable exception.[10] Before Munich even Churchill's views were not simple or straightforward.[11] The appeasers believed that having restored Germany's self-respect Hitler provided a powerful first barrier against Bolshevism.[12] The Führer should therefore be allowed space in Europe while Britain preserved its Empire. Many such voices argued that in any case Britain was militarily unprepared for war, even though it had greater resources than Germany.[13]

Neville Chamberlain, Prime Minister from May 1937, had to grapple with this increasingly tense European situation and, heavily influenced by Joseph Ball, that "quintessential *éminence grise*," believed he should do business with Hitler in Britain's interest.[14] Here we find a domestic autocrat trying to conciliate Europe's most powerful dictator.[15] When Chamberlain returned from Germany on 30 September 1938, after signing the Munich Agreement, waved a piece of paper at Heston aerodrome and announced later in Downing Street he had secured "peace for our time," an immediate sense of relief was palpable. Hitler had already been accommodated by many of the British public who, recalling the horrors of the Great War, dreaded the prospect of yet more carnage.[16] A repeat was simply "unthinkable, unspeakable, inconceivable."[17] By sacrificing the Czechs at Munich Chamberlain had just abolished this threat and became affectionately associated with *The Umbrella Man* a pop song of that year.[18] A celebratory commemorative plate was fired. These hopes were soon to fade.

3

What opinions on Hitler's Germany circulated at the more extreme end of British politics? Mosley's supporters have often exploited Joyce's ejection from the BUF in 1937 to improve the image of their venerated icon. How much insight 'The Leader' showed by removing a future traitor. Yet throughout the later 1930s the Blackshirt press expressed pro-German sympathies. During those important political crises involving Austria, Czechoslovakia and then Poland – "this rotten confederacy of cash and corruption," as *Action* once scathingly described it – the BUF consistently adopted a pro-Nazi stance.[19] Britain must not become involved in defending Jewish interests in Central Europe. For the BUF it was not a case of accommodating Hitler; all his initiatives called for support. One Intelligence report emphasised: "In questions of foreign policy they follow the German Führer as blindly and uncritically as does the Nazi Party in Germany."[20] This political stance followed on from the BUF's earlier Nazi sympathies.[21] Such sentiments mirrored Joyce's, though he was no longer in the movement. By the late '30s he was yearning for a Hitler triumphant and a Nazi future.

These darkening events in Europe and the belief that a war with Germany should be, must be, avoided, "helped to take the BUF back towards the political mainstream . . . thereby strengthening its links with the political establishment."[22] By 1939 it had made "a significant recovery [from its crisis in 1936 and 1937] which was checked only by the outbreak of war."[23]

Joyce's National Socialist League never developed such momentum and this contrast must have irritated him intensely. He remained persona non grata in the BUF. But from the mid-'30s, pro-Nazi fellow-travelling groups including the Anglo-German Fellowship, The Link, the Nordic League, the British Council against European Commitments and the Right Club, were sprouting up in Britain. Philip Larkin's father, who lived comfortably with a mechanical bust of Hitler on the mantelpiece which 'spoke' of his political sympathies, was far from alone.[24] These groups and their key figures add to the context of Joyce's political life in the late '30s.

4

In 1935 Ernest Tennant, assisted by his friend Joachim von Ribbentrop, a future Ambassador to Britain, founded the Anglo-German Fellowship "to promote good understanding between England and Germany and thus contribute to the maintenance of peace and the development of stability."[25] It had a twin organisation in the Berlin-based Deutsche-Englische Gesellschaft. The unashamedly elitist Fellowship sought out the rich and powerful. Joyce, ever scrambling for funds to keep the National Socialist League afloat, did not become a member. The group preferred to cultivate business and city groups, as well as public figures including Lord Redesdale and his daughter Unity,[26] Lord Londonderry,[27] Duncan Sandys, MP,[28] Sir Ernest Bennett, National Labour MP for Central Cardiff,[29] and Sir Raymond Beazley, formerly Professor of History at Birmingham University.[30] Joyce would have been kept informed, though, since two of his contacts, Alexander Scrimgeour and Emerson Bainbridge, were active members.[31] Dorothy Eckersley who—as will soon be shown— was politically close to Joyce, also appeared at its functions.[32] As did Kim Philby. Already operating for Moscow, the AGF provided him not only with information on Britain's fellow travellers, but also a degree of political camouflage.[33]

Tensions soon surfaced in the group. Lord Mount Temple, chairman until 1938, agonised over Nazi anti-Semitism. So did Tennant.[34] Others, more in tune with Joyce's views, proved less squeamish.[35] His old BUF rival, G.A. Pfister, would hardly have felt any qualms over Hitler's

Jew-hatred. Nor would C. E. Carroll, the obsessively anti-Semitic editor of the Fellowship's *The Anglo-German Review*.[36] These personal
differences sometimes proved difficult to resolve and more extreme
members of the AGF gravitated towards fellow-travelling groups such
as The Link, which was even more closely aligned with the Nazis.

The Link was founded in September 1937 by Admiral Sir Barry
Domvile, a former Director of Naval Intelligence and ardent believer
in a Jewish-Masonic world conspiracy.[37] Its aim was described as "to
foster the mutual knowledge and understanding that ought to exist
between the British and German peoples," and to counteract "the
flood of lies" on Anglo-German matters allegedly appearing in the
British national press.[38]

In a 1937 Intelligence report Domvile appeared as "an amiable little Irish man with an unduly trusting spirit." He drank too much, had
mistresses, and could not resist boasting about 'touching' the bookies
at Kempton and other courses. But he put himself about a good deal,
apparently even having a channel to the Prime Minister through Lady
Austen Chamberlain.[39] He organised visits to marvel at the wonders
of Nazism and contributed to the German press. "Berliner Tageblatt
has asked me to write for [the] anniversary of Hitler's arrival on the
scene. A great compliment," he wrote in 1938, rather pleased with
himself.[40] He would soon be relishing Joyce's evening broadcasts from
Berlin. They had much in common and shared similar aims.

Domvile's group was "more openly pro-Nazi" than the AGF,
but some crossover of members occurred.[41] Reflecting this closeness, funds from The Link, some deriving from Berlin, spilled over
to support the AGF and sustain the *Anglo-German Review*.[42] Dorothy
Eckersley doubtless kept Joyce up-to-date with developments here as
well as in the Anglo-German Fellowship.[43]

The Link soon developed a national network.[44] By May 1939
it claimed to have 4000 members.[45] Looking ahead, it provided a
meeting ground for some of Joyce's future wartime colleagues. Dorothy Eckersley, Margaret Bothamley, secretary of the Central London branch, and the lesser-known Diana Hardwick, were all actively
involved before leaving to broadcast for the Nazis.[46]

Where did Joyce connect to these increasingly busy pro-Nazi
manoeuvres? The Nordic League, formed in 1937, provided one

point of contact. MI5 described it as "an association rather than an organisation of race-conscious Britons" through which fascists and anti-Semites aimed to co-ordinate their activities.[47]

The Board of Deputies of British Jews recruited Cecil Burlie Pavey, a retired police inspector, to monitor developments; E.G. Mandeville Roe, formerly of the British Fascists and the BUF, also provided it with confidential reports.[48] It has been noticed that Captain Hawke, the 'cover' of Vincent Collier, formerly involved in Joyce's National Socialist League, probably acted as another agent of the Board.

The Nordics did not have a recognised leader. But Captain Elwin Wright, one-time Secretary of the Anglo-German Fellowship, the Rev. S. Coverdale Sharpe – father of the novelist Tom Sharpe – and 'Professor' Edward Ralph Serocold Skeels, sometimes called Cecil Serocold Skeels, were prominent figures on its Council.[49] Captain A.H.M. Ramsay, the Tory MP for Peebles, described by Malcolm Muggeridge as having "the benighted innocence of the crazed," operated at the centre of the group.[50] Obsessed by what he viewed as the malign Jewish influence on British politics and keen to gain favour with the Nazis, the Nordics afforded Ramsay an outlet beyond Westminster.[51]

Joyce, who held an opinion on everything, was soon invited to speak and delivered a predictable effort on 1 May 1939. An agent, probably Pavey, described it as "a clever but scurrilous oration, impassioned and full of fire." Joyce called the Prime Minister "a liar"; he attacked "a lying Jew-corrupted press"; he savaged that "slobbering, bastardised mendacious triumvirate" of Winston Churchill, Duff Cooper and Anthony Eden; in full flow he portrayed Maisky, the Soviet Ambassador, as "this evil little Asiatic," with blood dripping from his "fangs"; still far from exhausted, he summoned up a dose of sheer venom to attack the "whore-mongering, wine-besotted" King of Roumania "and his Jewish concubine." He can be heard here at his violent worst, well calculated to please his select, hardened audience. He also gave them hope:

> We had a great Empire yearning for active leadership. We had much in fact that Hitler lacked in 1933. He had to fight the 'red

flag' in Berlin, Hamburg and Munich. He had to fight starvation and a depleted treasury. He won through to a glorious victory: what Hitler had done for Germany the Patriots of Britain can do for this country and for the Empire.[52]

Joyce was again affirming his longstanding belief in the power of the will. It went down well. Captain Elwin Wright replied with "a flattering tribute" and hoped Joyce would return "very soon."[53] He required little encouragement. He probably expected no less. Three weeks later he offered more of the same.[54]

Some meetings were held in private.[55] From mid-1939, however, reflecting Ramsay's influence, the group adopted a more public profile.[56] The Nazis keenly monitored its progress and according to one agent it was the only body of its kind in Britain which attracted Hitler's attention.[57] Berlin's views on British politics were sometimes bizarre. But the Führer's interest carried an important implication.[58] In National Socialism Now, Joyce had claimed to have distanced himself from Nazism. His participation in the Nordics showed him quite clearly in Hitler's camp.

By the late 1930s, key figures in the Nordics, including Commander E. H. Cole, Oliver C. Gilbert, Serocold Skeels and T. Victor Rowe, had developed close personal links with Nazis in Britain and also with Berlin.[59] In the words of an Intelligence report: "it is Germany and not England which occupies the prior position in the thoughts and exercises the first claim upon the 'loyalty' of these people."[60] Joyce now actively worked alongside them. They were small in number and powerless in Britain, but glancing towards Europe, felt part of a more powerful political surge, which pointed ultimately towards a fascist victory. The Nazis understandably financed such activity, with Erich Hetzler sometimes acting as a financial middleman.[61] He and Joyce would soon become close colleagues in Berlin. Had Hetzler earlier supplemented his future companion's slim finances?

In September 1938, Joyce extended his growing range of his activities by helping to form the British Council against European Commitments, where he served for a time as vice-president.[62] For a short period John Beckett acted as honorary secretary.[63] Viscount

Lymington, its president, was the group's key figure and its principal funder.[64] Consigned now to history's obscure footnotes, Lymington had been Tory MP for Basingstoke between 1929 and 1934 before resigning over what he called the polluted atmosphere at Westminster. Deeply involved in organic farming, much of his career can be said to have embraced "muck, mysticism and the more esoteric reaches of British fascism."[65]

The group reflected Lymington's belief that European conflicts must never result in war between Britain and Germany.[66] At its meetings Joyce would have encountered Captain George Lane-Fox Pitt-Rivers, a substantial West Country landowner, crashing bore and racist, who believed obsessively in an international Jewish conspiracy.[67] They knew each other from the BUF.[68] Others he knew included A. K. Chesterton and J.F.C. Fuller.[69]

Joyce soon drifted away. Did his overt Nazism alienate Lymington?[70] Possibly. But was it so straightforward? The Hampshire grandee might have protested he was pro-British; that a war with Germany would be suicidal and lead to a Bolshevik triumph; that Britain must develop its agriculture and arm itself to guard against any such outcome. But when the War began, he drifted towards a collaborationist position.[71] Other pressures might therefore have contributed to Joyce's decision. He always needed to be in charge and became intensely irritated, "sometimes to the point of insanity," by anyone above him.[72]

Beckett also soon left Lymington's group for the British People's Party, which he had helped to establish in April 1939. It quickly attracted the Marquess of Tavistock (later the Duke of Bedford) who in effect became Beckett's political patron.[73]

In May 1939, as a war seemed increasingly likely, Captain Ramsay formed the Right Club.[74] It has been portrayed as an anti-war pressure group which also focused on "infiltrating and influencing the establishment" to lessen "the alleged Jewish influence on the Conservative party."[75] But is that all? It is highly unlikely. Who knows how members might assist the Nazis in the event of an invasion? Joyce soon joined this latest initiative.

Ramsay painstakingly entered the names of one hundred and thirty-five men and one hundred women in a gilt-edged, padlocked red membership book.[76] Joyce already knew many of them. Margaret

Bothamley, A. K. Chesterton, Dorothy Eckersley, her husband Captain P. P. Eckersley, 'Billy' Luttman-Johnson, Serocold Skeels, Major Francis Yeats-Brown were all familiar figures. Anna Wolkoff, later to intrude dramatically into Joyce's life, was another member.

These hard-core activists sat alongside aristocrats. The Duke of Wellington, Lord Redesdale (another reminder of the recurring Mitford involvement in fellow-travelling activities), Lord Sempill – who also politicked in the Anglo-German Fellowship and The Link – as well as Lord Ronald Graham, second son of the Duke of Montrose, and his elder brother, the Marquess of Graham, were all listed as members.

The Club attracted a handful of MPs. Sir Ernest Bennett, fiercely anti-Communist, pro-German and pro-Arab, circulated here and in the Anglo-German Fellowship. Others included Lt-Commander Peter Agnew, the Tory member for Camborne, Captain the Hon. John Joseph Stourton, Conservative MP for South Salford, and James McKie, who had represented Galloway since 1931.[77]

Some members appear not to have had any links with fascist, anti-Semitic or fellow-travelling groups.[78]

Agents lurked among the names. Was Vincent Collier one of these? Marjorie Amor (Marjorie Mackie), certainly was. The scheming and dangerous Captain J. M. Hughes, otherwise known as P. G. Taylor, appeared on Ramsay's list.[79]

Joyce soon assumed a leading role in the group. His involvement in the Nordic League, the British Council against European Commitments and the Right Club, suggests that in fascist and fellow-travelling circles he remained a prominent political operator. He sent his five shillings subscription to Ramsay on 1 July 1939, writing, "I am very sorry indeed that I cannot spare any more at present; but you will probably understand that my political activities have had certain repercussions on my private affairs."[80] Financial problems constantly pursued him as earlier they had Marx, his great ideological enemy. But he had his uses. Ramsay despatched him on expeditions to enlist new members and appointed him a warden, one of the Club's sixteen senior figures.[81]

When the War began, the increasingly secret activities of Ramsay's group began to alarm the authorities. By then Joyce was no longer involved. He had left for Berlin.

5

The NSL had clearly not brought Joyce the political success he desperately craved, though the Nazi press continued to smile on his initiative, and being his own boss must have gone some way towards satisfying him.[82] But after 1937 his political life involved far more than the National Socialist League. His belief in the future triumph of fascism led him to bond with key Nazi groups in Britain and, as the clouds of war continued to gather, Nazism featured increasingly in his day-to-day thoughts.

Notes

1 Cole, *Lord Haw-Haw*; Selwyn, *Hitler's Englishman*; Kenny, *Germany Calling*; Farndale, *Haw- Haw*, remain largely silent.

2 Hamilton to Lady Downe, 20 March 1936, King's College, London, Hamilton Archive, 14/2/8.

3 Pugh, '*Hurrah!*' and, more specifically, J. Charmley, *Churchill: The End of Glory* (London, 1993); R.A.C. Parker, *Chamberlain and Appeasement: British Policy and the Coming of the Second World War* (Basingstoke, 1993); N. J. Crowson, *Facing Fascism: The Conservative Party and the European Dictators* (London, 1997); R.A.C. Parker, *Churchill and Appeasement* (London, 2000); D. Dutton, *Neville Chamberlain* (London, 2001).

4 Stanford University, Jacques de Launay Archive, Box 1 "La correspondance secrète, Hitler–Rothermere," p.48.

5 J. E. Wrench, *Geoffrey Dawson and Our Times* (London, 1955), p.361; Martel (ed.), *The Times and Appeasement*.

6 "Tourists of the Revolution," BBC2, TV, 18 March 2000. M. Burn, *Turned towards the Sun: An Autobiography* (Wilby, Norwich, 2003).

7 K. O. Morgan, *The Age of Lloyd George* (London, 1971), p.105. R. Hattersley, *The Great Outsider: David Lloyd George* (London, 2010), pp.623–627.

8 Cato (Michael Foot, F. Owen, P. Howard), *Guilty Men* (London, 1940).

9 I. Kershaw, *Fateful Choices: Ten Decisions that Changed the World, 1940–1941* (London, 2007), ch.1. On Munich see D. Faber, *Munich* (London, 2008) and the novel, G-M. Benamou, *The Ghost of Munich* (London, 2008).

10 Quoted in Matthew and Harrison (eds), *ODNB*, accessed online 27 November 2014.

11 Dutton, *Chamberlain*, p.111.

12 Wrench, *Dawson*, p.362.

13 D. Edgerton, *Britain's War Machine* (London, 2011).

14 Dutton, *Chamberlain*, pp.70, 71, 126, 139, 156, 183. Ball had MI5 connections. See Robert Blake's entry in Matthew and Harrison (eds), *ODNB*, Vol.3, p.567.

15 Brendon, *Dark Valley*, p.522 on Chamberlain's authoritarianism.

16 D. Pryce-Jones, *Treason of the Heart: From Thomas Paine to Kim Philby* (New York and London, 2011), p.169–170.

17 M. Muggeridge, *Chronicles of Wasted Time*. Part 2. *The Infernal Grove* (London, 1973), p.73.

18 www.songwritershalloffame.org, accessed 10 July 2013.

19 *Action*, 8 April 1939.

20 KV 4/140, "The British Union of Fascists," July 1939.

21 *Fascist Week*, 22–28 December 1933, and the *British Union Quarterly* after 1935.

22 Pugh, '*Hurrah!*' p.261. Mosley might have been further helped by the sharp recession in 1937 and unemployment rising into 1938. Pollard, *British Economy*, p.155.

23 Pugh, '*Hurrah!*' p.261.

24 J. Kenyon, "Larkin at Hull," *About Larkin*, No.6, *The Newsletter of the Philip Larkin Society* (Winter 1998/9), p.5. Pryce-Jones, *Treason*, p.170.

25 University of Southampton, Ashley Papers, BR/81/1.

26 Griffiths, *Patriotism Perverted*, pp.35, 37. Pryce-Jones, *Unity Mitford*. She is the subject of a song by The Indelicates, "Like Romeo and Juliet/In a bunker, shot through the head," on her attempted suicide and relationship with Hitler. She had appeared earlier in A. G. Macdonell's novel, *Lords and Masters* (London, 1936). She features there as "Veronica."

27 Kershaw, *Making Friends with Hitler*, generally. Griffiths, *Patriotism Perverted*, p.36 for his AGF membership.

28 Pugh, '*Hurrah!*' p.270.

29 Griffiths, *Fellow Travellers*, p.185. Matthew and Harrison (eds), *ODNB*, Vol.5, pp.126–128.

30 The Labour History Archive and Studies Centre (LHASC), LP/JSM (INT), Box 8, contains a January 1936 membership list, which includes Beazley's name. See also Griffiths, *Fellow Travellers*, pp.35–39.

31 KV 5/3.

32 *The Anglo-German Review*, Vol.2 (1938), p. 62 and *ibid*. Vol I (1937), p.135.

33 *Ibid*. Vol. I (1937), p. 138.

34 University of Southampton, Ashley Papers, BR/81/15. See also Tennant to Ribbentrop, 7 September 1935, and his report on a visit to the seventh National Socialist Party Rally, BR/81/9 and BR/81/10, respectively.

35 LHASC, LP/JSM (INT), Box 8 lists members at January 1936.

36 *Ibid* on Pfister and Carroll's involvement. See generally Griffiths, *Patriotism Perverted*, pp.35–39.

37 J. S. Wiggins, "The Link," MA Dissertation, University of St Andrews, 1985.

38 B. Domvile, *From Admiral to Cabin Boy* (London, 1947), p.64, and his *By and Large* (London, 1936). Griffiths, *Patriotism Perverted*, pp.39–42 provides an outline of The Link. KV 2/836/247A, Admiral Sir Barry Domvile KBE, CB, CMG, 6 March 1944, contains a career summary. HO 283/31 carries additional detail.

39 KV 5/2, memo, 30 November 1937. The personality sketch derives from KV2/835/60z and his diaries at the National Maritime Museum.

40 DOM 55, Domvile diary, 13 January 1938.

41 Griffiths, *Patriotism Perverted*, p.39 for its Nazism. *The Anglo-German Review*, from 1938 onwards for personal linkages. National Maritime Museum, DOM 55, Domvile diary, 19 January 1938.

42 KV 2/835/41a.

43 HO 45/25776, Statement of Dorothy Eckersley at Libenau Camp, 2 July 1945.

44 KV 5/2.

45 KV 2/836/247A.

46 *The Anglo-German Review*, Vol.3 (1939), p. 94, notices Bothamley speaking to the branch on the Jewish Question.

47 KV 4/140, memo on the Nordic League, November 1939 and HO 144/21381/184, 214–217, 219–222, 224–228, 275–293.

48 Griffiths, *Patriotism Perverted*, p.45. Pavey appears in Wiener Library, Board of Deputies of British Jews, File 1658/2/1/5. His Metropolitan police file is 100508. Tilles, "The Anti-Fascist Campaign of the Board of Deputies," on agents. See more generally, D. Tilles, "'Jewish Decay against British Revolution.' The British Union of Fascists' Antisemitism and Jewish Responses to it," University of London PhD thesis, 2011, which has since appeared as *British Fascist Antisemitism and Jewish Responses, 1932–40* (London, 2014).

49 KV 4/140, Nordic League, November 1939. University of Southampton, Ashley Papers, BR 81/1 for Wright and the AGF.

50 KV 4/140, Nordic League, November 1939. HO 144/21381/272 on Ramsay's role. See also Griffiths, *Patriotism Perverted*, p.47. Muggeridge, *Chronicles*, p.109 for the crazed Ramsay.

51 There is no Ramsay biography, but his politics can be gleaned from his *The Nameless War* (London, 1952). A circular from Final Conflict misspells Ramsay's name but refers to it as "A 'must read' book." Press cuttings on him appear in Wiener Library, Board of Deputies of British Jews, File, 1658/9/3/2.

52 HO 144/21381/289, meeting, 1 May 1939.

53 *Ibid.*

54 HO 144/22454/79–80.

55 HO 144/21381/214–217, 219–222, 224–228, 275–293 and Wiener Library, Board of Deputies of British Jews, "Memorandum on the Nordic League and other organisations," file 1658/2/1/5

56 Griffiths, *Patriotism Perverted*, p.47.

57 HO 144/21381/284.

58 World Service, 1/1, 1 December 1933 where the Imperial Fascist League, under "the Stalwart Leese," was regarded as more vital to the success of British fascism than the BUF. G. Strobl, *The Germanic Isle: Nazi Perceptions of Britain* (Cambridge, 2000), discusses Nazi opinion on Britain.

59 FO 321/17731/35, circular from Otto Bene, 9 October 1934, to Germans in Britain. KV 4/140, Nordic League, November 1939, reports

on leading Nordics. Thurlow, *Fascism in Britain*, p.78, treats the group as a branch of International Nazism but his source does not support that claim. KV 4/14, p.1, comments more cautiously that the League was "probably a branch of the Nordische Gesellschaft, although actual proof of this has not been obtained."

60 KV 4/140, "Nordic League," November 1939. FO 371/18868/155–163 notices individuals involved with the Golden Eagle Publishing Company, another Nazi front organisation.

61 KV 2/836/247A, pp.5, 6, 15, for example. *Ibid.* pp.1 and 2 for more on Domvile's and Carroll's Nazi links. DOM 56, Domvile diary, 5 March 1939 and KV 2/835/40a are useful.

62 Cole, *Lord Haw-Haw*, p.78.

63 Griffiths, *Fellow Travellers*, p.322. HO 144/21247/103, Special Branch report, 14 October 1938.

64 Obituary, *The Times*, 1 October 1984.

65 Matthew and Harrison (eds), *ODNB*, Vol.57, pp.26–27. Kushner, *Persistence of Prejudice*, p.43; Griffiths, *Patriotism Perverted*, pp.52–53. For more detail, see Stone, "Back to the Land Movement," in Gottlieb and Linehan (eds), *The Culture of Fascism*, pp.182–198. Note also G. V. Wallop, *A Knot of Roots. An Autobiography* (London, 1965), and P. Conford, Organic society: agriculture and radical politics in the career of Gerard Wallop, ninth Earl of Portsmouth (1898–1984), *Agricultural History Review*, Vol.53 (2005), pp.78–96.

66 See *Should Britain Fight? The British and some facts on the Sudeten Problem* (London, 1938) and Griffiths, *Fellow Travellers*, pp.317–329.

67 G. Pitt-Rivers, *The World Significance of the Russian Revolution* (Oxford, 1920); *The Clash of Cultures and the Contact of Races* (London, 1927) and *Czecho-Slovakia: The Naked Truth about the World-War Plot* (London, 1938). Griffiths, *Fellow Travellers*, pp.322 ff comments. Simpson, *In the Highest Degree Odious*, pp.217–218 and E. Barkan, *The Retreat of Scientific Racism: Changing Concepts of Race in Britain and the United States between the World Wars* (Cambridge, 1992), pp.291–292 for further detail. Schaffer, *Racial Science*, p.31 describes him as a "loose cannon." Pitt-Rivers is the subject of HO 45/25725.

68 TS 27/5141A.

69 Griffiths, *Patriotism Perverted*, p.54. Beckett eventually left the NSL to firm up his links with Lymington, in December 1938 becoming editor of *The New Pioneer*, a well-produced monthly journal, a further sign of the Viscount's willingness to invest in his political agenda.

70 KV 2/245/62X for Joyce's growing Nazism.

71 Griffiths, *Patriotism Perverted*, pp.70, 201–202, 220, 222. Joyce's friend Fritz Krüger advised Lymington on European politics. Hampshire Record Office, Lymington Archive, 15M84/F255/17.

72 KV2/245/24a. See also KV 2/245/1b, report, 21 September 1934, "His greatest failing is that his mental balance is not equal to his intellectual capacity."

73 *The New Pioneer*, Vol.1 (1939), p.188 discusses Beckett's departure.

74 Pugh, *'Hurrah!'* p.281.
75 Thurlow, *Fascism in Britain*, p.83.
76 R. Saikia (ed.), *The Red Book: The Membership List of the Right Club, 1939* (London, 2010).
77 Bennett, the most significant of the MPs in this connection, appears in Matthew and Harrison (eds), *ODNB*, Vol.5, pp.126–128.
78 Griffiths, *Patriotism Perverted*, chapter 9.
79 *Ibid.* chapters 8 and 9.
80 Joyce to Ramsay, 1 July 1939. Wiener Library, Right Club File, 1369. This letter is now missing from the file. The Library is aware of its loss.
81 Wiener Library, The Red Book, Document 1369. Griffiths, *Patriotism Perverted*, p.130.
82 "Antisemitismus in England," *Der Stürmer*, No.14, April 1939.

9

NAZI GERMANY BECKONS

In the week which preceded the outbreak of the Second
World War – days of surmise and apprehension which cannot,
without irony, be called the last days of peace ... [Evelyn Waugh,
Put Out More Flags (London, 1959 ed. First edition 1942), p.13.]

1

How quickly lives can change. In 1921 Joyce had been brought
to England by events in Ireland and by the mid-'20s had become
involved in fascist politics. In 1933 he was marching with Mosley. In
1937 his feet were pounding London's streets, campaigning for the
National Socialist League. That same year he was busy with Britain's
fellow-travelling groups. In the late summer of 1939 he left all this
behind and stepped into Hitler's world.

2

In late 1938, as the prospect of a near-term war increased, it is claimed
that Joyce, Margaret and Macnab planned to leave for Ireland and
actually purchased tickets. If true, his hatred of Irish nationalism did
not preclude Ireland serving as a temporary refuge. He would have

wound up the National Socialist League before joining the other two across the water.[1]

By 1938 MI5 was advising that in the event of war Joyce's loyalty could not be guaranteed.[2] And by now he had started to think increasingly of going to Germany. When contemplating that retreat to Ireland he had apparently considered leaving there later for Berlin.[3] Against this background, a sequence of events began that significantly shaped his life. Engaging in pro-Nazi activity in Britain was one thing; working for Hitler in Berlin was far more significant.

Any such move needed a passport, for which he had first applied on 4 July 1933, when, describing himself as "a British subject by birth" born in Galway, he declared his intention to undertake a touring holiday. On one level it might have been true. But it could hide a good deal. The National Bank in Grosvenor Gardens, Belgravia, where Joyce held an account, had no reason to disbelieve him when supporting his application.[4]

When interrogated at Huyton internment camp in 1941, Frank Joyce claimed his brother had never been abroad before leaving for Germany in 1939.[5] Yet a Special Branch report of an unknown date, though almost certainly before 1937, noticed Joyce and Margaret Cairns White, as she then was, in Boulogne. Was it a lovers' holiday break, an opportunity to drink French wine and purchase Gitanes? Margaret would describe it later as a "one-day no-passport excursion"; but can her evidence be trusted?[6] That question cannot be answered because, in yet another act of cultural barbarism, the weeders of the official records have destroyed the file.[7]

But did Joyce make use of his 1933 passport? There is allegedly a photograph of him at that year's Nuremberg rally.[8] In 1941 Frank Joyce would have been anxious to overlook this detail suggesting his brother's early identification with Nazism. After the War, Margaret and Macnab would have been equally keen to suppress such evidence.[9] In the 1930s, British fascists and Nazi sympathisers never hesitated to grace Nuremberg with their presence. Some indeed were indecently anxious to receive their invitations. Attendance there and visits to Germany tended to fire-up Hitler's fan club.[10] George Ward Price, "a Nazi heart and soul," swooned in political and sexual ecstasy when seeing those athletic young men who might one day rule Europe.[11] The schoolboy James Clark was fully swept along by this political pageant. Hitler's revitalised Germany had so much "go" about it.[12] But the evidence for Joyce featuring in the 1933 photograph is not to be trusted. The face does not match up. The detritus of Oswald Mosley's movement vehemently deny his presence in the BUF delegation.[13] On this occasion they are right.

Yet Margaret knew of an early visit to Germany, though the exact date remains uncertain. When they arrived in Berlin in August '39 he apparently remarked that the place had changed.[14] Had he visited in the '20s on a student expedition?[15] Or later on political business? It is impossible to say.

Joyce next applied for a passport in 1938, as tensions increased between Britain and Germany over Czechoslovakia. By now he was even more firmly focused on Hitler's role in determining Europe's future. He affirmed he was a British subject and his application was successful. This document expired on 1 July 1939.

He submitted his third and final application on 24 August 1939, declaring: "I, the Undersigned William Joyce, at present residing at 38a Eardley Crescent, SW5, London, hereby make application for the renewal of British passport No 125943 issued to me in London on the 6th July 1933, for a further period of one year." He affirmed: "I am a British subject by birth and I have not lost that national status, and that the whole of the particulars given by me in respect of this application are true." Once again his application received an endorsement from the National Bank in Belgravia. Once again it proved successful. Once again he secured an extension, this time until 1 July 1940.[16]

3

Fascism in Britain had not progressed as Joyce had hoped. And by late '39 he was under close surveillance by the authorities. In the event of war he would have known that detention beckoned and, if his US links become known, he could face deportation. Germany offered a more sympathetic political environment and his passport would allow him to move there. But before leaving for Berlin he wanted certain assurances from the Germans. These negotiations began in

August 1939 when, it is claimed, Macnab happened to be visiting Germany. Seizing this unexpected but welcome opportunity, Joyce asked him to take up matters on his behalf.[17] 'Master' and the Joyces had shared peripatetic lives in London and Macnab claimed he had also considered going to Naziland.[18]

Such is Margaret and Macnab's agreed, carefully crafted story. It reflects their attempt to control the writing of history. Nuances have been added later.[19] Yet what we have been encouraged to believe falls far short of what is required.

Macnab's mission, for contrary to his own testimony he almost certainly went as Joyce's emissary rather than as a tourist or a political pilgrim, raises the question: whom would he approach?[20]

Various interested parties, Mosleyites particularly, have talked down the degree of contact between Britain's fascists and the Nazis in the 1930s. However, those captured files in Moscow provide conclusive evidence to the contrary.[21] British reports on Mosley's involvement – with Dr Arthur Tester – in a Nazi plan to buy into the Belgian press confirm such links.[22] We also know some members of the Nordic League and the Right Club allegedly served as agents.[23] In view of events between 1939 and 1945, today's fascist sympathisers are keen to suppress such evidence.

Joyce is said to have had "remarkably few" Germans contacts when in the BUF.[24] However, even then he sometimes gave the impression of having "an actual working arrangement with the Nazis."[25] He was certainly in touch with Otto Bene, who after 1927 spent considerable time in Britain, eventually becoming Landesgruppenleiter [National Leader].[26] In 1934 Joyce, then charged with the BUF's university recruitment drive, had probably arranged Bene's lecture to the Oxford University Fascist Association.[27] The Landesgruppenleiter regarded 'The Leader' as an adventurer and, through Bene, Joyce would have glimpsed the enticing prospect of increasing his influence with the Nazis at Mosley's expense.[28]

Their link appeared again in 1935, when Joyce wrote a report for Bene on the current state of British fascism.[29] His intercepted typescript exaggerated the movement's strength and, predictably, was full of anti-Jewish, anti-Communist sentiments. The British authorities picked off its wilder comments with some relish. But Joyce's intended audience lay elsewhere. He believed this report would do him, and British fascism, no harm at all in influential circles in Berlin. But did he write it independently? Put differently, could he have compiled it without Mosley's knowledge? Security sources believed not.[30] If their assessment is well-founded, its exaggerated account of the BUF's strength can be viewed as 'The Leader' yet again advertising his movement. Its strong anti-Jewish tone further undermines Mosley's position that he harboured no such sentiment. The survey is of more than passing interest, therefore.[31]

Joyce also knew Lisa and Fritz Paul Heinrich Krüger. The latter is an important yet neglected figure in the history of fascism in Britain. He joined the NSDAP in 1932 and the SS in 1933 before being sent to Britain where, the security service believed, from 1935 he was entrusted with "a special mission to study the Jewish question" and "engage in anti-Jewish propaganda among English circles."[32] He could often be seen burrowing away in the British Museum and as Peter Aldag wrote the well-known anti-Semitic work *Das Judentum in England*.[33] But Krüger might have had other strings to his bow. He soon developed a bulging address book.[34] On 27 May 1939 the British authorities, increasingly suspicious of his activities, refused to allow him back into the country.[35] At Oswald Mosley's wartime internment hearing it became clear MI5 regarded Krüger as a Nazi Intelligence agent.[36] Did he, as alleged, try to recruit Edward Whinfield of the BUF?[37] Did he attempt to enlist Joyce?[38]

By the late '30s Joyce had increased his German contacts, who now included R. H. Hoffmann of the Auslandsdienst in Munich, a recognised conduit for Britain's fascists linking up with the Nazis.[39] MI5 believed that through such links he had secured funds from Germany and reported his boast that he could bankroll similar activities.[40] His changed physical appearance, his closely cropped hair, his Prussian parade-ground manner, reflected his developing Nazism.[41] The source is questionable but it has been claimed that by now he was recruiting and organising Hitlerite sympathisers in Britain.[42]

Ernst Ulrich von Bülow, "tall and gracious and speaking unaccented English," was another of Joyce's London contacts. They would meet up again in Germany.[43] Joyce, we already know, also had dealings with Erich Hetzler, then busily transferring funds to Britain's fellow travellers.

However, Christian Bauer, "a young man who spoke good English and cultivated an English appearance," was a closer contact.[44] He came to England in 1934 as a nineteen-year-old and lived at several addresses including Tennyson Mansions, Queens Club Gardens, W14, and 88 Castellain Mansions, W9.[45] He talked a good tale and quickly assessed the weaknesses in Joyce's personality, which he then exploited.

Between 1934 and 1937 Bauer worked as a journalist for several newspapers, including Goebbels's *Der Angriff*. At the same time, he kept his eyes and ears open for the Nazis. But in 1937 he made a big mistake. He returned to Germany and that autumn, the British government, convinced he was a Nazi agent, barred his re-entry.[46] Bauer's personal file in the Berlin Document Center suggests he did not belong to the National Socialist Party.[47] But it is clear why the authorities had become concerned.

On 30 March 1937 Joyce had invited him to the inaugural meeting of the National Socialist League, doubtless hoping Bauer would relay this latest development in British fascism to Berlin.[48] The Intelligence services intercepted more of their correspondence, which Joyce signed off: "Heil Hitler."[49]

This Bauer connection also brought Joyce's brother, Quentin, to MI5's attention. Quentin had enlisted in the BUF and later served as communications officer in the National Socialist League[50] He was one of the first fascists to be detained in 1939.[51] He worked in the Air Ministry and MI5 feared that through the Joyce brothers, official secrets might find their way into enemy hands.[52] This concern dominated Quentin's early internment interrogations. But his links to Bauer also exercised the authorities.[53] He passed off his pre-war German contact as no more than "a newspaper correspondent."[54] And, according to a later source, Quentin had merely done "a couple of favours" for his German friend, "a bit of entirely innocent personal shopping."[55] The Advisory Committee on Internment did not believe his defence. Quentin's correspondence with Bauer, which appears strange in parts even now, encouraged their belief the journalist was engaged in espionage. Bauer's deft ability to manoeuvre his way through Nazi Germany's stringent currency regulations and engage in other shady activities added to these concerns.[56]

When 'Q', as his older brother called him, was released from internment in 1943, the Committee withdrew virtually all charges. But his contact with Bauer had created a problem for him.[57]

These suspicions of Bauer were heightened following a major indiscretion by John Macnab, a seriously naïve political operator. His full importance in the saga of Joyce's life has gone unrecognised. He has been presented as a mere boxwallah, anxious to please but otherwise of little significance.[58] To portray him as "full of Latin scholarship and jolly japes" misses both his fanatical fascism and corrosive anti-Semitism.[59] And, significantly, serious slip-ups made by him had profound implications for Joyce, his god.

He made his first mistake in the autumn of 1938. En route to Germany, allegedly on a commercial matter – once again as Joyce's emissary? – he stopped off in Brussels. There, of an evening, deep in his cups, he let slip he was journeying to Cologne to meet Bauer, whom he described as an influential Nazi. Next day Macnab begged his drinking companion, the ex-gaucho and adventurer Charles Thurlow Craig, "For God's sake, forget that I ever mentioned such a man or such a name."[60] Too late. Unknown to him, he had been boozily keeping the company of "a casual informant" and his indiscretion quickly found its way to MI6 in London.[61] The authorities, knowing the Joyces' connections to Bauer, now seemingly had concrete evidence of the young journalist's importance. This detail created a major problem for both the Joyce brothers.

Bauer's name surfaced again on 10 June 1940, when John Beckett appeared before the Advisory Committee on Internment. Answering Norman Birkett KC, the Committee's chairman, Beckett admitted writing to Bauer to give his and Joyce's account of the 1937 split with Mosley, because both were anxious "*our German friends should know the truth*."[62] He also acknowledged that in September 1938 he had provided Quentin with a letter of introduction to Bauer in Berlin.[63] But, returning to the wider links between British fascism and Nazism, Beckett claimed he had first been introduced to the young journalist by Mosley.[64] Was it true? Or was he attempting to smear 'The Leader'?

Bauer is clearly important, and in August 1939 he was the contact with whom Macnab raised those concerns harboured by Joyce should he decide to leave for Germany. 'Master' found Bauer luxuriating in the opulent Adlon Hotel, near the Brandenburg Gate. What a sharp contrast to the Prince Albert, where a few years before they had attended the public launch of the National Socialist League.[65] The art moderne Adlon was a favourite haunt of the Nazi elite. Macnab would doubtless have been impressed.

Macnab's account of their meeting appeared in Jack Cole's biography of Joyce. But with his capacity to deceive, 'Master' did not reveal everything.[66] He claimed Joyce wanted to sound out the Germans on the prospect of his and Margaret's immediate naturalisation should they begin afresh in Berlin. Bauer allegedly envisaged no problems and offered Macnab a similar assurance.[67]

At his 1940 internment hearing Macnab claimed he had decided against going to Germany because he had no German.[68] He preferred "Latinist" to "Germanist" cultures.[69] An Intelligence reports casts doubt on this evidence. He was not fluent, but he did have some German.[70] What he never said, but knew quite well, both in 1940 and later when offering evidence to Jack Cole, was that he had no intention of going to Germany. It will soon become apparent he had another important mission to carry out for Joyce – in Britain.

Macnab's account of that Adlon meeting raises a number of questions which Joyce's biographers have conveniently sidestepped. Why this alleged interest in *immediate* naturalisation? Did it reflect Joyce's fear that if he went over to the Nazis, had not become a German citizen and war broke out, the British might charge him with treason? That argument is unconvincing. He had a British passport tucked in his pocket. But he also had his American birth certificate. He was entitled to believe that if he threw in his lot with Hitler, as a US citizen he would remain beyond the reach of the British authorities. In 1945–1946 they did charge him. But his case established a legal precedent which in 1939 neither he nor anyone else could possibly have predicted.

References to Joyce's US birth certificate appear in wartime evidence from his 'spokesmen.' It is often said he remained guarded on his origins; his family had more than its share of secrets. But

John Beckett knew some details, possibly from Macnab.[71] And in July 1940 he drew Joyce's American links to the attention of the Advisory Committee on Internment, indeed appeared to do it deliberately.[72] The British authorities already knew Joyce was broadcasting on Nazi radio, and Beckett was declaring that his former comrade lay beyond their reach. John Macnab made the same point at his hearing.[73] Its reappearance suggests this tactic had been discussed either before or after Joyce's departure. And when in November 1941 the "tall ... domineering ... slightly deaf and irrepressibly garrulous" Cecil Serocold Skeels appeared at the Old Bailey accused of encouraging David Esme Vaughan to contact Joyce via the Spanish Embassy, and with other matters, he, too, emphasised Joyce's American roots.[74]

Evidence from US sources in wartime Berlin will soon underscore Joyce's belief that, should his personal circumstances turn nasty, his American card would trump anything the British might play against him.

Was his alleged interest in immediate naturalisation motivated by something else? Had he calculated that if war started, by becoming a German citizen he would be spared internment as an enemy alien?[75] Some British exiles in wartime Germany, even Nazi sympathisers, were to be interned.[76] A number of them apparently betrayed by fellow renegades.[77] It was not only Stalin's Communists who stabbed their own. But Joyce could once again have brandished his American card. And when Macnab met Bauer, no-one envisaged the United States ever entering a European conflict.

This emphasis on immediate naturalisation is highly questionable. However, Macnab's reason for suggesting it is easily understood. He did so after Joyce had been executed. 'Master' desperately wanted to present him as a victim of circumstances. If Joyce had become German straightaway – he did not assume German citizenship until 1940 — it would have been impossible for the English legal system to convict him of treason. His story searches for our sympathy.

Joyce, through Macnab, probably did express an interest in becoming German at some future point. He would soon take that step. Passports, official documents mattered, even if he had to lie to obtain them. His life's early uncertainties had instilled a need for order.

In 1938 he had been reluctant to travel to Ireland without a British passport – though no such document was needed.[78]

However, above all, Joyce's primary interest in naturalisation sooner rather than later – though not immediately – reflected the fact he was a politico. It would signify his total commitment to Germany. He would rise above the raggle-taggle renegades who during a war would drift to Berlin yet remain British. He would position himself far beyond those faint-hearted political souls who hovered in Britain watching the incremental growth of Hitler's power, hoping eventually to sit down, admittedly below the salt, at Nazi tables.

4

On 21 August, Macnab informed Joyce he had concluded his business with Bauer, checked out of the Hotel Minerva, Saarlandstrasse 68, and left Berlin.[79] Two days later Germany and Russia signed a non-aggression pact in Moscow.[80] Joyce had never anticipated this *rapprochement*. Who had? Bill Shirer, reporting for CBS from Berlin, wrote later: "At first I could scarcely believe it. There had been no inkling that such an amazing deal was in the works."[81] Public figures in Britain were shocked. 'Chips' Channon fumed: "A historic day . . . the Russians have double-crossed us . . . They are the foulest people on earth."[82] Harold Nicolson, sailing off southern England, remarked bluntly: "I felt rather stunned."[83]

Arnold Leese was dumbfounded:

> This pact of Hitler's with Russia is an ideological blow of the worst description, and no amount of explaining away that he was driven to it is much comfort to me . . . Hitler has been a marvel but he is no longer one . . . Such a pity.[84]

How frustrating politics could be.

Particularly now for Joyce. Maxwell Knight's 1934 Intelligence assessment had remarked that as a student his young friend had often come close to a mental collapse.[85] MI5's reports in the '30s continued to emphasise his instability.[86] Joyce's family also remarked on his "mental flips."[87] And a contemporary observed that his nerves were

"frequently frazzled."[88] None of which is surprising. He was a per-
fectionist. He drove himself hard.[89] He needed to be in control, and
in the late '30s the rapidly changing, increasingly uncertain European political situation posed acute problems for him. By 1939 he
was living in emotional turmoil and began to experience recurrent
"forebodings of disaster." Once he "talked wildly, shook off attempts
to calm him, shouted and, finally, in a terrifying burst of temper, raved
at his bewildered wife." Not until the following morning had he
calmed down, become "tranquil."[90] Here was someone unable from
his small London base to influence the big political events determining Europe's future. Margaret must have endured a wretched time.
The failure in mid-summer '39 of Macnab and Joyce, Private Tutors,
hardly helped. But its collapse alone would not have unhinged him in
this way. He would soon have picked himself up, started afresh.

News then broke of the agreement signed in the Kremlin by
Molotov and Ribbentrop in the presence of an avuncular-looking
Stalin. When it came over the wires from Moscow, Joyce simply
collapsed.

> In his tiny basement dwelling he brooded . . . numbed by this
> wholly unexpected blow. He had enraged hostile street-corner
> groups and aroused Fascist cheers by maintaining that Hitler was
> the far-seeing statesman who had recognised the Jewish-Bolshevik
> menace.[91]

Yet Hitler and Stalin now shared the same political bed. For days
Joyce "did nothing but read the papers and sit about smoking."[92] He
probably 'put away' many bottles, too. MI5 knew by now he had
begun drinking heavily.[93]

However, political figures can usually rationalise the unexpected.
In the summer of 1941 Britain's Communists had to perform a political cartwheel when Hitler attacked the USSR, which led the Soviets
to abandon their wartime neutrality and become allies in the fight
against Nazism. This change of strategy, initially a problem for British
comrades, lifted 'Red Russia' to unimagined heights of popularity in
Britain and secured some much-needed political capital for Harry
Pollitt and his friends.[94]

In 1939 Joyce eventually convinced himself that since the Western European powers would not join with Germany against the Soviet threat, political expediency had driven Hitler to conclude a strategic pact with the Bolshevik Devil.[95] As someone who lived politics, his struggle to rationalise the unexpected should not be underestimated. These psychological pressures might have been heightened by his longstanding thyroid problems.[96]

Initially unbalanced by the Moscow agreement, Joyce realised it did nothing to lessen the prospect of war.[97] Hitler now had the time and the strategic security to pursue his ambitions in Eastern Europe. Britain, which in March 1939 had offered guarantees to Poland, would duly respond. Joyce would finally have to clarify his position. He would never fight against Hitler.[98] "Fascism is such a sacred thing to us that we should regard it as a crime to fight a fellow Fascist," he had told the Fabian Society in 1934.[99] What would he do?

On 24 August, the day after the signing of the pact, he renewed his passport. Margaret said he did it "reluctantly." He had not finally decided on his next step. But late that night something allegedly happened. Margaret let it be known later and it has since been widely repeated:

> At about midnight the telephone rang. Startled, they looked at each other. Joyce, his expression strained, lifted the receiver, announced himself, listened for a few seconds and replaced it.

Jack Cole, heavily influenced by Margaret, wrote that:

> The actual text of the curt message Joyce never revealed. The call came from the Intelligence officer to whom he had reported on Communist activities and who had (or so he said) sounded him on his willingness to go to Germany as an agent. Its purport was that the clause covering the detention of security suspects in the Emergency Powers (Defence) Act had not been modified, that it could, or would, apply to him, but that the machinery for detaining suspects would not operate before Saturday, August 26th. In other words, if Joyce wanted to get way, he had less than two days.

Joyce is said to have remarked despondently, "We must now make a final decision."[100] Next morning when they sat down to breakfast, the die had been cast. They would leave for Berlin.

Margaret's unsupported account suggests Joyce's fear of detention finally overcame his reluctance, his dithering.[101] But did it? His name did feature on the list of fascists destined for internment.[102] His "unbridled fanaticism" guaranteed it.[103] But would that prospect alone have caused him to leave?

Margaret's motive when claiming the threat of internment rather than Joyce's belief in National Socialism, his craving to serve Hitler, took him to Berlin was clear. She was skewing the historical record to present him as persecuted by the British authorities.

Jack Cole did not name the MI5 officer allegedly responsible for that phone call. He has since been identified as none other than Maxwell Knight.[104] It has even been argued Max might have wanted Joyce out of the way to avoid awkward questions being asked about his own involvement in fascism.[105] It is unlikely Max ever worried over any such revelation. He had initially been recommended to SIS by none other than Nesta Webster, that arch conspiracy theorist and member of the British Fascists.[106] The security service could hardly have been unaware of his political past – which arguably could be turned to their advantage. At some uncertain point he had even declared it.[107]

Joyce had a long-standing connection with Intelligence sources.[108] And some telephone contact did occur between the parties at this critical juncture – by whom from MI5 is unknown.[109] However, at present no firm evidence supports the claim of a tip-off and, whatever that phone call involved, nothing can be found to suggest it was made by Knight, even though he pursued a "somewhat independent" style in his operations.[110] By now he would have been well aware of Joyce's increasingly strident Nazism, and MI5's assessment of him as a danger to the state.[111]

5

Why, everything considered, did Joyce leave for Germany in 1939? Rather than believing it was Margaret's initiative, the focus must remain on Joyce himself.[112] His growing Nazism, rather than his inability to carve out a political career in Britain or his pressing fear of internment or deportation, provides the answer. Joyce was not essentially *pushed* to Berlin. The Nazi state *pulled* him into itself. A 1938 Intelligence report presents him as hysterical, tears streaming down his face, proclaiming: "I am convinced that one day we shall see Germany the master of Europe."[113] Britain had to be destroyed, put under Nazi tutelage before it could be revived. Joyce hoped his full commitment to Nazism would guarantee him a major role in this process.[114] With his vanity, his ever-present, overpowering sense of self-importance, he never doubted his ultimate destiny was to act as a key agent in the triumph of fascism. Believing as much, it made so much political sense to go to Germany, where he would mix with influential figures at the centre of fascist politics. And unlike fellow-travelling contemporaries in Britain he could move with impunity. He kept the card close to his chest, but, if the wheels of history did not turn the way he anticipated, he believed his US birth certificate would protect him against the British authorities. It was definitely a risk worth taking.

6

Joyce would have known that in the late '30s other fascists from Britain were ingratiating themselves with the Nazis. The "tall, dark and handsome" Clement Bruning, close to Joyce in the BUF's propaganda wing – he would have welcomed Joyce's return after the 1937 split – had made a big decision.[115] In the spring of 1938 his photograph appeared in the fascist press outside his café in Green Street, Bethnal Green, an establishment which catered exclusively "for white men"; it was a 'cover' for his politics.[116] But he soon left East London for Erfurt, and a propaganda post in the World Service. He was returning to his roots: his father had been naturalised in 1903.[117] Bruning had been Joyce's junior in the BUF. By moving first he might outflank his old boss, who would have bridled at the prospect.

To a fanfare of Nazi publicity the obsessive and paranoid Henry William Wicks, who felt persecuted in Britain because of a criminal libel case, had also reached Germany.[118] In 1939, when meeting

Bauer in the Adlon, Macnab had handed over a message from Joyce warning the Germans about employing Wicks. Bauer expressed his gratitude. Joyce was attempting to demonstrate his usefulness to the Nazis, whilst fouling Wicks's new-found nest.[119] He simply could not resist any opportunity for intrigue, particularly if he believed he might benefit politically.

Margaret Bothamley, Nordic Leaguer and convinced pro-Nazi, had likewise been busy.[120] This committed member of the Brown International wrote in the cause. She knew Otto Bene. The Commandant of Oranienburg concentration camp was a friend.[121] In 1934 Bothamley defended such camps in *The Times*.[122] She would soon be working alongside Joyce on Nazi radio.

Dorothy Eckersley, an associate of Joyce's in the Right Club and other groups, was another who had been gathering contacts. She, it will become clear, was playing an important role behind the scenes in his currently developing plans to leave for Germany.

7

The biggest gamble of Joyce's life now begins. After breakfast on 25 August 1939 Margaret says their goodbyes to Ethel Scrimgeour.[123] Joyce closes their joint bank account. He puts his hands on funds belonging to the National Socialist League. He dissolves the group and the Carlyle Club, its political think-tank. He writes a Special Notice to members, urging them to hold fast, "despite the barrage of Jewish propaganda." That enemy still haunts him.[124] Macnab is their future point of contact.[125] Joyce is ready to go.

8

This version of events, first advanced by Jack Cole, has persisted.[126] Yet it omits one significant detail. Macnab offered any number of reasons why he never left for Germany with the Joyces. But he never told the truth. When Joyce wound up the National Socialist League and instructed members to remain in touch with Macnab, the authorities had a "strong suspicion" he had entrusted 'Master' with a crucial role for the future. Under his direction the League's diehards would become a fifth column, committed to undermining Britain while waiting for the arrival of the Wehrmacht when they would continue their supporting activities.[127] By their actions they would raise Joyce's profile and further help to secure an important role for him in a Nazi Britain. Macnab remained reluctant to admit to any of this arrangement. He would quote his dearest friend as saying, "I am going to Germany for good . . . to throw in my lot with Germany for good or ill."[128] He always knew Joyce never intended to remain on the Continent.

9

The Joyces have just made their preparations to leave. It is a Bank Holiday weekend when on 26 August they arrive at a bustling Victoria Station accompanied by the ever-faithful Macnab. Their luggage is labelled 'Berlin.' They purchase two single tickets. No immediate return is envisaged. Queenie and Frank Joyce see them off. Leonard Sinclair, Operations Officer in the National Socialist League, arrives.[129] Quentin is not at Victoria; work detains him in Bristol. Michael Joyce is a more noticeable absentee, which says much about the dynamics of the Joyce household.[130] For Queenie and her William, who had shared so much in New York, Galway and London, and are so close emotionally, it is a final parting.

As the small party walks purposefully across the platform, the porter carrying their luggage, noticing the destination, remarks dryly, "That's a funny place to be going to!" or words to that effect.[131] But to Joyce it is neither strange nor paradoxical. He joins the long queue for the boat train which snakes virtually from the ticket barrier to the rear of the station.[132] Anxious but undeterred, leaving behind families, friends, political colleagues and enemies, the couple are soon speeding on their way. First they travel to Dover. There they board the packet to Ostend. From its upper deck on a beautiful late summer's day they watch the white cliffs fade into the distance.[133] Joyce is leaving what he views as a decaying, Jew-infested country and sailing hopefully into a bright future. From Belgium they journey by train to Berlin where the next crucial chapter in his life will be played out.

10

Two years earlier, in *National Socialism Now*, Joyce had written of his love for Britain in terms similar to George Orwell's lyrical hymns to England.[134] They were opposed politically, and Joyce never had the "Crystal Spirit's" literary style. But his writing reads as if it sprang straight from his heart:

> For all of us British people there is a land in which we have played our part, great or humble, in the drama of life, a land where we have had our happy days as well as the sad. We generally forget the spring morning, with the splendid sun sparkling on the dew in the green fields, the white lanes with their smiling hedges in summer, the rich tint of the leaves in the declining autumn afternoon, the first nip of winter, the English Christmas with our nearest and dearest, the mists on the fens, the gigantic bustle of our great cities, the fire-breathing giants of the night in the Black Country or by South Shields, the long snaky monsters that bring happiness, sorrow, hope or anxiety into Euston or King's Cross, the ocean battering away at the rocks of Devon, the Cockney with his Shoreditch barrow, making fun of every moment in his struggling little life, the broad Mersey restively bringing the challenge of the sea into the heart of Liverpool, the godly majesty of the Highlands, the serene power in the mountains of North Wales, even the rain blending so strangely with the romance of our early days, when, as children we played in it – all these things are most often out of our minds; but if it ever happens to us to see the chalk cliffs receding for the last time as the water widens between us and our homeland, then the memories will come in a choking flood, and we shall know our land when it is too late.
>
> This is the land for which better than we have died. For it, we are asked not to die but to live; it is ours, it belongs to us in every spiritual and sensuous way; it must be ours in every other way, completely and utterly ours, not for some but for all of us. Know this truth, feel it, live it, and the victory shall be ours.

> Some there are who will call the sentiment cheap; but it has been again and again redeemed in the blood of heroes, whose spirit the cheap alone can never understand.[135]

"Kitsch"?[136] No. Overdone? Perhaps. But a powerful reminder of his literary flair, first shown as a Galway schoolboy.

His writing displayed all the signs of an ardent patriot. Several years later he was still expressing his affection for Britain. He loved its landscape. He genuinely wanted what he considered a better deal for its people. But he could never embrace what he viewed as its rotten Jew-ridden political system. It must be liberated from being "a colony of Palestine."[137] Any suggestion that by August 1939 his reasoning had also fired him up to draw the sword on his Bolshevik enemies should be treated with caution.[138] That struggle between West and East for the defence of western civilisation, had been averted temporarily by the Molotov–Ribbentrop pact. But when that surprising accord crumbled, as Joyce believed it would, he knew exactly where he would stand. All the resources and resourcefulness of Nazi Germany would be needed to hold back that wave of subhumans carrying with them the dreaded disease of Jewish Bolshevism. But other important struggles had to be fought first.

Notes

1 Selwyn, *Hitler's Englishman*, p.74.
2 KV 2/245/62x, report, 27 September 1938.
3 Cole, *Lord Haw-Haw*, p.77.
4 *Ibid*. p.42.
5 HO 144/22707. Commandant of Huyton Camp to Home Office, 17 March 1941.
6 Cole, *Lord Haw-Haw*, p.76.
7 KV 2/235/6a.
8 Pryce-Jones, *Unity Mitford*, photograph 6; Farndale, *Haw-Haw*, p.70 and photograph.
9 Influenced by them, Cole, *Lord Haw-Haw*, remains silent.
10 A. Schwarz, "British Visitors to National Socialist Germany: In a Familiar or a Foreign Country?" *Journal of Contemporary History*, Vol.28 (1993), pp.487–509.
11 *Daily Mail*, 14 September 1936. This comment on 'Wardy' is A. L. Kennedy's in Martel (ed.), *The Times and Appeasement*, p.265 (19 March 1938).

12 "Tourists of the Revolution," BBC2, TV, 25 March 2000. Evident too in J. R. Clark, "Open Wounds. A Berlin Memoir, 1939–1945," unpublished ts.

13 *Comrade*, No.60 (2006), pp.17–18, review of Nigel Farndale's biography of Joyce.

14 Cole, *Lord Haw-Haw*, p.92.

15 USSC, MS 238/7/11. Comment by Macnab.

16 Cole, *Lord Haw-Haw*, p. 85.

17 *Ibid.* pp.78–80.

18 *Ibid.* p.87.

19 Kenny, *Germany Calling*, pp.123–125; Farndale, *Haw-Haw*, pp.107,116.

20 HO 45/25780/22 on Joyce sending Macnab to Berlin. Kenny, *Germany Calling*, p.125, almost recognises their arrangement.

21 A. Prokopov, *Fashisty Britanii* (St Petersburg, 2001), pp.264–275, a suggestive account based largely on captured sources held in Moscow.

22 KV 4/118, report on Tester.

23 Some appear in Griffiths, *Patriotism Perverted*, ch.7.

24 Cole, *Lord Haw-Haw*, p.59.

25 KV 2/245/1a, report, 8 January 1935.

26 D. M. McKale, *The Swastika outside Germany* (Kent, Ohio, 1977), pp.27, 77, 115, 212, on Bene; Barnes and Barnes, *Nazis in Pre-War London*, especially ch.3.

27 Imperial War Museum, HWL-J, II, Brochure.

28 FO 371/17730/165, Special Branch report, 3 September 1934, for Bene on Mosley.

29 HO 45/25385.

30 HO 45/25385/41.

31 If true, the claim that Joyce provided Berlin with a confidential assessment of the novelist Dennis Wheatley as a potential collaborator would further confirm his Nazi links. Their connection might have arisen through Maxwell Knight. Max and Wheatley sometimes attended the meetings of Aleister Crowley, the Occultist, and the Great Beast. A. Masters, *Literary Agents: The Novelist as Spy* (Oxford, 1987), p.201 on Joyce in Wheatley's company. Wheatley held extreme political views but never succumbed to Nazism. He assisted British Intelligence during the War and, crucially, in 1940 advised on how to stem a possible German invasion. Joyce remarked later, perhaps irked he had misread Wheatley, "He is fiercely anti-Nazi without knowing how to be." WJ to MJ, 29 October 1945. On Wheatley, see Matthew and Harrison (eds), *ODNB*, Vol.58, pp.411–412 and C. Cabell, *Dennis Wheatley: Churchill's Storyteller* (Staplehurst, 2006). His activities featured on BBC4, TV, 11 March 2006. D. Wheatley, *The Deception Planners* (London, 1980) is a posthumous account of his wartime activities. See also Wheatley's *The Time Has Come: The Memoirs of Dennis Wheatley* (London, 1981).

32 FO 272/3345/128.

33 P. Aldag, *Das Judentum in England* (Berlin, 1943).

34 FO 372/3345/127.

35 FO 372/3345/122–131.

36 HO 283/13/97–98.

37 KV 4/140/13X.

38 KV 2/245/190a (now destroyed) noticed the Joyce–Krüger pre-war connection. C. C. Aronsfeld, "Anglo-Jewry through Nazi eyes," *Jewish Chronicle Literary Supplement*, 7 February 1986, is the fullest study of Krüger, though not entirely to be trusted. For years Aronsfeld tried unsuccessfully to secure the relevant Home Office file (K7691). See *The Times*, 16 April 1977. I accessed it in 2011 after an FOI request.

39 KV 2/247/504A.

40 KV 2/245/134a, report, 30 March 1939.

41 KV 2/245/24a, report, 24 January 1937.

42 *Evening Standard*, 21 March 1941. The source was Mary Taviner.

43 Clark, "Open Wounds," p.37.

44 Cole, *Lord Haw-Haw*, p.59.

45 KV 2/245/45a; KV 2/1507/10a.

46 FO 371/20741/208–209, 11 October 1937.

47 Berlin Document Center. Personal File; Ernst Ferdinand Harri Christoph Bauer.

48 KV 2/1507/11a.

49 KV 2/245/167.

50 HO 283/43/148–149, KV 2/2894/37a, KV 2/2895/253a.

51 HO 283/43 generally on his internment. See also KV 2/2894 and KV 2/2895. Quentin died in 1989.

52 HO 45/25690 Advisory Committee Report, 25 October 1939 on Air Ministry matters.

53 KV 2/2894.

54 HO 283/43/20 and elsewhere.

55 Kenny, *Germany Calling*, pp.131–132.

56 HO 283/43 is full of such detail.

57 HO 283/43/14 reports his release and exoneration (pp.14–19).

58 Cole, *Lord Haw-Haw*; Kenny, *Germany* Calling; Farndale, *Haw-Haw*, project this image.

59 Kenny, *Germany Calling*, p.102.

60 KV 2/245/96b. KV 2/2474/91A, (29 July 1940), p.13, adds little to Macnab's time in Belgium, except identifying Craig as his drinking partner. Macnab lied throughout this hearing.

61 KV 2/245, extracted 28 September 1938 from SIS report.

62 HO 283/26/78. My italics.

63 HO 283/26/113.

64 HO 283/26/78.

65 HO 283/43/22.

66 Cole, *Lord Haw-Haw*, pp.82–83.

67 *Ibid*. p.83.

68 KV 2/2474/91A, p.24.

69 KV 2/2474/91A, p.18.

70 KV 2/245, memo, 2 May 1935.

71 HO 283/26/12 for a Christmas card to Macnab with an attached verse, December 1943.

72 HO 283/26/74. Conversations with Francis Beckett.

73 KV 2/2474/91A, p.17.

74 WO 339/15154 for details of his early military career. *The Fascist*, No.55, December 1933, on his days in the Imperial Fascist League. He often featured in the press in 1934. See *Manchester Guardian*, 11 January 1934 and the *Daily Herald*, 18 June 1934. HO 45/25746, reports the attempt to reach Joyce through the Spanish Embassy and contains a transcript of the trial.

75 H.J.P. Bergmeier and R. Lotz, *Hitler's Airwaves: The Inside Story of Nazi Radio Broadcasting Propaganda* (New Haven and London, 1997), p.100, hints at Joyce's fear of possible internment.

76 M.A. Doherty, *Nazi Wireless Propaganda: Lord Haw-Haw and British Public Opinion in the Second World War* (Edinburgh, 2000), pp.11, 16, 17, 21.

77 KV 2/622/1y on Anthony Cedric Sebastian Steane furnishing a list of 'enemies.'

78 Cole, *Lord Haw-Haw*, p.77.

79 *Ibid*. p.83.

80 G. Roberts, *The Unholy Alliance: Stalin's Pact with Hitler* (London, 1989) and his *Stalin's Wars* (New Haven and London, 2006). L. Rees, *World War Two: Behind Closed Doors. Stalin, the Nazis and the West* (London, 2008), ch.1. And, later, R. Moorhouse, *The Devil's Alliance: Hitler's Pact with Stalin* (London, 2014). N. Davies, *Europe: A History* (London, 1997), pp.991–998, provides a Polish perspective.

81 W. L. Shirer, *20th Century Journey: A Memoir of a Life and Times*. Vol.2: *The Nightmare Years 1930–1940* (Boston and Toronto, 1984), p.425.

82 R. Rhodes-James, *"Chips." The Diaries of Sir Henry Channon* (London, 1993), p.208.

83 H. Nicolson, *Diaries and Letters 1930–39*, ed. N. Nicolson (London, 1971), p.404.

84 HO 45/24967/3.

85 KV 2/245/1b, report, 21 September 1934.

86 KV 2/245/24A, report, 24 January 1937, which contrasts with /1b written on 21 September 1934.

87 HO 45/25690, report on a family visit to Quentin Joyce.

88 USSC, MS 238/7/8.

89 "Just perfect . . . or perfectly mad?" *The Times*, 28 July 2004.

90 Cole, *Lord Haw-Haw*, p.80.

91 *Ibid*. p.83.

92 *Ibid*. p.84.

93 KV 2/245/24a.

94 F. King and G. Matthews, *About Turn: The Communist Party and the Outbreak of War* (London, 1990).

95 Cole, *Lord Haw-Haw*, pp.83–84.

96   HO 283/43/147.

97   Cole, *Lord Haw-Haw*, p.84.

98   Farndale, *Haw-Haw*, p.116.

99   *Manchester Guardian*, 13 January 1934.

100 Cole, *Lord Haw-Haw*, pp.84,86.

101 Farndale, *Haw-Haw*, pp.114–115.

102 Marginal note, 25 October 1939, HO 45/25690.

103 KV 2/245/160a.

104 Kenny, *Germany Calling*, pp.121, 123. Knight is also named in Farndale, *Haw-Haw*, p.114; W. J. West, *Truth Betrayed* (London, 1987), p.234; S. Murphy, *Letting the Side Down: British Traitors of the Second World War* (Stroud, 2003), p.106.

105 Murphy, *Letting the Side Down*, p.106.

106 Andrew, *Defence of the Realm*, pp.123–125.

107 *Ibid*. p.123

108 On fascism and the security service see Hope, "British Fascism and the State" and his "Fascism and the State in Britain," pp.367–380, on MI5 and fascism. Thurlow, discusses P. G. Taylor, otherwise known as J. McGuirk Hughes, in *Fascism in Britain*, pp.203–204, and in *The Secret State*, ch.5. Dorril, *Blackshirt*, pp.197–198, 262–263, is useful. Andrew, *Defence of the Realm*, is disappointing.

109 KV 2/245/179X.

110 Knight's alleged traits based on Simpson, *In the Highest Degree Odious*, p.144 and D. Stafford, *Roosevelt and Churchill. Men of Secrets* (London, 1999), p.41. Clough, *State Secrets*, adds new, intriguing detail.

111 KV 2/245/62x. See also KV 2/245/64a and 65a, on MI5's attitudes and actions.

112 Farndale, *Haw-Haw*, pp.113–114, tries unconvincingly to talk up her role.

113 KV 2/245/62x, B5b report, 22 September 1938.

114 KV 2/1513, Kimpton memo, 5 March 1941.

115 Driver, "Shadows of Exile," p.40.

116 See the photograph in *The Blackshirt*, April 1938. *Action*, 2 April 1938, carried one of the advertisements for 243 Green Street, "The café which caters for White Men."

117 HO 45/25568, report 119.

118 *Der Angriff*, 18 and 25 July 1939 on this "English refugee" with tales of corruption in high places. On Wicks generally see J. R. Spencer, "Criminal Libel in Action – The Snuffing of Mr. Wicks," *Cambridge Law Journal*, Vol.38 (1979), pp.60–78.

119 KV 2/419/69a.

120 *Frankfurter Tageszeitung*, 23 November 1934, carried "Was ich in Deutschland erlebte." *Deutsche Freiheit*, 18 May 1939, for "Mrs Bothamley reist nach Deutschland."

121 See her 'selling' Nazism in *An English Statement about National Socialism in Germany. As Broadcast from Berlin by M. F. Bothamley* (London, nd)

and *"What's going on in the Saar?"* (London, 1934). Bothamley's fierce anti-Marxism appears in *Hungary* (London, 1934), p.106. See also FO 371/18868/158–160.

122 *The Times*, 6 April 1934.
123 Cole, *Lord Haw-Haw*, p.86.
124 Mosley Papers, University of Birmingham Special Collections, OMD/11/2/1, Special Notice to all Members, date as postmark, written from 177 Vauxhall Bridge Road.
125 Special Notice, etc.
126 Farndale, *Haw-Haw*, pp.115–116.
127 KV 2/2474/91A, pp.20–21.
128 Cole, *Lord Haw-Haw*, p.88. Offered uncritically in Farndale, *Haw-Haw*, p.115.
129 KV 2/247/518 for Sinclair writing to Joyce in prison. HO 283/26/68 on his role in the NSL.
130 Kenny, *Germany Calling*, p.126 notices Michael's absence. Had he attended his son's recent marriage? Cole, *Lord Haw-Haw*, p.66 says he had. So does Kenny, *Germany Calling*, p.106. Farndale, *Haw-Haw*, p.116 claims he was absent.
131 Cole, *Lord Haw-Haw*, p.88.
132 Mass-Observation Archive, University of Sussex TC23, Box 1: 23/1/B, Air Raids 1938–45: Observations on Victoria Station, 26 August 1939..
133 KV 2/245/340b, transcript of German European Service broadcast by William Joyce, 28 August 1944.
134 G. Orwell, *Homage to Catalonia* (London, 1970. First ed. 1938), p.211 and *The Lion and the Unicorn* (Harmondsworth, 1982. First ed. 1941), pp.36–37.
135 Joyce, *National Socialism Now*, p.71.
136 Cole *Lord Haw-Haw*, p.90.
137 KV 2/245/340b, transcript of broadcast, 28 August 1944.
138 Cole, *Lord Haw-Haw*, p.77 for his interest in defending the West against Bolshevism.

PART III
Speaking

10

ANOTHER NEW LIFE. A SERVANT OF THE THIRD REICH

You choose your side once for all – of course it may be the wrong side. Only history can tell that. [Graham Greene, *The Confidential Agent* (London, 1971), p.68.]

1

Between the late summer of 1939 and the early spring of 1945 Joyce lived and worked in Germany. He no longer breathed in 'Tom' Mosley's shadow. As the detested voice of Nazi radio propaganda, Lord Haw-Haw became in Britain the country's "Number One traitor."[1]

2

When the Marxist economist Maurice Dobb first entered the Soviet Union, a wave of euphoria apparently surged through him. He had reached the sacred land with the truest political ideology. But when the Joyces disembarked at the Friedrichstrasse station just off the Unter den Linden on that "hot and sultry" Sunday, 27 August 1939, it is claimed Nazi Germany did not act as an immediate political aphrodisiac.[2] According to Margaret, rather than reaching their ideological heaven, they were soon tempted to return to England. However, they had converted all their English money into Reichsmarks and found German travel agents unwilling to accept this currency for journeys beyond the frontier. For help they turned to the British Embassy. They were directed to the British Consulate. Nothing was on offer. They had no escape route.[3]

Terence Rattigan, commissioned in 1971 to write a film script on Joyce's life which would have starred Peter Finch and Glenda Jackson, took on board her evidence and transformed it into one his most dramatic sequences:

> amid the confusion attendant on a large Mission preparing for an imminent departure, with a bonfire of secret documents visible outside, they are interviewed by a languid and effeminate young Attaché . . . who is the epitome of all that Joyce most despises. They really are rather *naughty*, he says, to have come to Berlin anyway in these circumstances. Anyway, war is by no means certain – Joyce glances at the bonfire outside – indeed Sir Neville is still most hopeful that he can get these *tiresome* Poles to see reason – but as for changing marks into sterling, it just isn't on dear Mr – what was that name again? . . . . If he did it for them [he] would. . . . Never live it down. Of course they *could* try and get to Cologne, so much closer to the French frontier. . . . But then there are hardly any civilian trains going, at the moment, and they might be *weeks* before they got on one. Still, worth a shot if they really feel they must get back, despite what he's told them about there not going to be a war.[4]

It is so delicately nuanced. But does it have any historical basis?

Mary Kenny and Nigel Farndale have repeated this story.[5] But Margaret's claim deceives us. Five years after setting out on his momentous journey, Joyce recalled a haze drawing over the cliffs at Dover as he sailed away from England. He likened it to an "impenetrable veil" which symbolised "the end of an old life and the beginning of a new."[6] He certainly expected it would be. His political adventures in Britain would become the faded fabric of yesterday. War seemed inevitable. He hoped and expected Fascism would quickly triumph. His fifth column would play its part in Britain's collapse.

On board the packet to Belgium he was doubtless eagerly anticipating such events. First though, he needed to be at the centre of the action, where Britain's fate would be decided. These anticipations had sent him on his messianic mission. Now was not the time to slink back.

The ever-unreliable Margaret was pleading a case. How convenient to portray an impetuous, naïve young couple devoured by circumstances beyond their control. It is her attempt to seize and manipulate the historical record.

When Joyce sent Macnab a postcard with a Latin message announcing his safe arrival in Berlin, life there in some respects was proceeding quite normally.[7] In those scorching days of late August '39, Berliners strolled languidly through the Tiergarten, shopped on the bustling Leipziger Strasse, sought out the shade of a café-bar or film-theatre on Friedrichstrasse or bathed in the surrounding lakes. It contrasted sharply with black-out-practising, gasmask-fitting, trench-digging London. Nevertheless, it had just been announced that with the deteriorating state of German–Polish relations rationing controls would be introduced.[8] Berliners, including the Joyces, would also have noticed field-grey troops moving through the capital on their way East. A few days later, on 1 September, the German army invaded Poland.[9] On 3 September Britain and France declared war on Germany. In the words of *McAlpine's Fusiliers*, the sky suddenly became "full of lead." Or, in Auden's, "the unmentionable odour of death" began to offend "the September night."[10]

Joyce had spoken at political meetings across Britain, written newspaper articles, pamphlets and a book. He yearned now for an opportunity to serve the Reich, display his commitment, and advance his prospects. Such eager thoughts had propelled his journey Eastwards. Once in Berlin he had hoped Christian Bauer would smooth his way forward. Yet Bauer proved incapable of finding him any work. What a thoroughly damp squib he had turned out to be. So insignificant was Bauer in Berlin, he did not even qualify for a special petrol allowance.[11] Joyce's obsessive self-regard had led him totally to misjudge his young German friend. His way forward was advanced instead by a contact from Britain.

Dorothy Stevens was born in 1893 and worked as an actress. In 1921 she had married Edward Clark, who was to become the BBC's music adviser.[12] But she fell for Captain Peter Eckersley, the Corporation's Chief Engineer, and in 1929 their open liaison contributed to his forced resignation.[13] They married in 1930. Peter Eckersley was a fascist who a few years later would be employed by Oswald Mosley in 'The Leader's' European radio plans.[14] Such activity alone guaranteed that MI5 kept a close watch on this renowned wireless expert. Eckersley's membership of the Right Club added to their suspicions.[15] His technology columns in the *Daily Mail* constituted his more acceptable public face.

Political activity also fascinated Dorothy Eckersley and, once bitten, she "sampled the ideologies on offer one by one."[16] Eckersley's actressy vein had led her through Zionism and Communism before she, too, took up with Fascism.[17] In this latest obsession she joined the Anglo-German Fellowship, attended meetings of The Link and appeared in the Red Book as a member of the Right Club.[18] She also became involved in Joyce's National Socialist League and helped to finance his political activities.[19] An MI5 report claimed their closeness was such she employed him to tutor her son, James Clark, though the latter remains reticent on the matter.[20] German archives reveal she stood bail for Joyce when he was arrested during the declining days of the National Socialist League.[21]

A Nazi source claims "it was probably her advice that led the Joyces to turn to Berlin in August 1939."[22] British Intelligence files carry a more likely emphasis, that Joyce enlisted her help at an early stage in his plans.[23] She was familiar with the political scene in Germany and as a swooning admirer of his politics would have been only too willing to assist him.[24]

Since 1935, and by now a "convinced pro-Nazi," Dorothy Eckersley had indulged in political pilgrimages to Germany.[25] She and James Clark viewed it as a magic wonderland where they could bask in all the glories of Nazism.[26] She absolutely adored the Führer, once remarking, "I went with Unity [Mitford] to the restaurant . . . [where Hitler was going to drink tea] . . . and there I gazed upon him."[27] How wonderful it was, how truly inspiring. Here was the future in the present.

Joyce doubtless knew that not only did she have useful contacts in Germany. She had also played host to well-known Nazi visitors to

Britain, including in 1934 Lothar Streicher, son of the editor of *Der Stürmer*, whom she had probably met through the Mitfords.[28]

Several people knew of Joyce's intentions to leave for Berlin. They included his politically active family. They saw him off. Ethel Scrimgeour had been informed. John Macnab had been at Victoria. Leonard Sinclair from the National Socialist League was at the station. Sylvia Morris and Mercedes Barrington from the NSL knew what was afoot.[29] 'Ma' Eckersley, as Joyce generally called her, was undoubtedly in the picture. Rather than being some hasty response, as Margaret and Macnab would want us to believe, and others have uncritically repeated, his departure was coldly calculated. From the beginning Eckersley assumed a key role in this unfolding drama.

Supportive of Joyce's plan to leave for Germany and doubtless offering guidance, how did she assist him once he had reached Berlin? According to Margaret, 'Raz', as Eckersley was sometimes known, had just returned to Germany to deal with family matters. In August 1939 her son James Clark was about to attend the Humboldt School in Berlin-Tegel and this matter had allegedly brought Eckersley from Budapest to Berlin. Joyce, it has always been claimed, just happened to recall she would be in town. And did he vaguely remember her saying she would be staying at the Hotel Continental? He managed eventually to find that hotel. Amazingly, quite by chance, he then spotted her, much to their mutual delight and total surprise.[30] How fortunate. They were incredibly lucky to have met up in this way. What a small world it was. Their encounter might have been a stroke of good fortune. But Margaret's account seriously strains the evidence. Eckersley had been involved in Joyce's plans and knew he was in Berlin. He now needed her help to begin his new political life. A meeting beckoned. If only she would introduce him to her German contacts his problem might be solved. She, hopefully, would serve his purposes better than the wretchedly ineffectual Christian Bauer. She would 'sell' him to the Nazis, act as his agent.

Dr Erika Schirmer of the Hochschule für Politik was one of Eckersley's contacts. She had helped to place James Clark in his Berlin school.[31] Described by Charles Saroléa in a pre-war letter to Douglas Chandler as "extraordinarily well-informed on all subjects pertaining to the Third Reich," Schirmer had a particular interest in fostering

Anglo-German connections and, prompted by Eckersley, took up Joyce's case.[32] She arranged a meeting with her brother Hans, an official in the German Foreign Ministry, "a young bespectacled chap, who looked like a university professor."[33] In turn, he fixed up other appointments. In this byzantine process Joyce was vetted by, among others, the suave E. U. von Bülow, known to him from pre-war London.[34] However in late August, after what he must have viewed as a succession of tedious, tiresome, interviews, it seemed part-time translation work might be his lot. Joyce's horror at this prospect can easily be imagined. Was he facing a repeat of that depressing sequence of job rejections he had suffered in Britain in the 1920s?

He was soon able to banish such unwelcome thoughts. Hans Schirmer activated his Foreign Ministry connections and a meeting followed with Erich Hetzler. Nazi records suggest Hetzler had enrolled as a student at the London School of Economics in 1929 and spent two terms there. However, the LSE has no record of his attendance under that name. His life, like Joyce's, is shrouded by some misty uncertainty. According to his Party file, Hetzler joined the NSDAP on 1 March 1932 and the SS in September 1935. He has already been observed visiting London before the War to liaise with Britain's fellow-travelling groups and in 1937 carried out unspecified business there for the Foreign Ministry.[35] Joyce had probably met him on at least one occasion in the late '30s.[36]

In 1939, and holding a post in the Propaganda Ministry, Hetzler passed Joyce to Walter Kamm, a senior broadcasting official, charged with foreign-language services. On 11 September Joyce, then suffering from a cold, was asked to undergo a voice test by reading a news item.[37] His assessors were unimpressed. Terence Rattigan pictured this scene beautifully, with Kamm saying: "I am most sorry . . . News-reading is not for you. It is a most difficult job – and needs a professional touch you see. I feel that is a voice they will never listen to."[38] However, the Nazis decided to employ him. Always convinced of his talents, Joyce had wanted a directing role during what he anticipated would be a decisive phase in European and world history.[39] But beggars cannot be choosers.

A few days earlier the police in London had gone looking for him. They had a warrant to detain him. They sought him here.

They sought him there. They swooped on Onslow Gardens, Eardley Crescent and Vauxhall Bridge Road. To no avail.[40] The place to search would have been Berlin. Following his first broadcast he secured a radio contract on 18 September 1939.[41]

Joyce's German State Workbook, stamped 4 October 1939, revealed he and Margaret had moved from their accommodation near the Friedrichstrasse station to a flat in the Charlottenburg district, close to the broadcasting studios in Masurenallee. It recorded that from 1926 he had worked for nine years as a lecturer at the Victoria Tutorial College in London. It referred to his membership of the BUF and the National Socialist League. It repeated detail on his British passport that he was a British citizen, born in Galway.[42] This Workbook was to feature as vital evidence at his trial.[43] Joyce had few regrets in life, but remarked he had been a "prime idiot" for so carelessly letting it fall into Allied hands. It linked him to the Nazis while holding a British passport.[44]

3

State-organised propaganda had become a vital political tool for authoritarian governments by the early twentieth century. The written word remained important. But newer initiatives emerged. The Bolsheviks harnessed Eisenstein's prodigious filmic talents; both *Battleship Potemkin* and *October* carried striking political images. The Nazis turned to Leni Riefenstahl, whose *Triumph of the Will* deified the 1934 rally in Nuremberg, the kind of political choreography that entranced Dorothy Eckersley, James Clark and other British observers. Photography, by the likes of Khaldei in Russia and Hoffmann in Germany, served a similar purpose.

Music offered other possibilities. In Nazi Germany, Charlie and his Orchestra personified its popular form. In the USSR, Shostakovich's Seventh Symphony on the traumas of the Leningrad Siege reflected its more serious dimension.[45]

The power of radio broadcasting, "the greatest export industry of modern times," was also soon recognised.[46] Its immediacy alone gave it a key role.[47]

In Germany and the Soviet Union all such activity occurred under the ever-watchful eye of the state.[48] This controlled yet brave new world which influenced the Second World War on all fronts now provided the base for Joyce's political activities.

The Nazis had established the Ministry for Public Enlightenment and Propaganda in mid-March 1933. Its early formation underlined the significance they attached to it, and Joseph Goebbels soon created what a contemporary American reporter called a "high-powered 12-cylinder propaganda machine."[49] One division had the specific brief of overseeing the RRG, the German equivalent of the BBC. The reasoning here was straightforward. The Nazis needed to bring this organisation under Party control to ensure the success of their radio offensive. However, in a polycentric state such administrative arrangements did not always run smoothly. The Foreign Ministry wanted to influence messages beamed abroad and power struggles often occurred between it and the Propaganda Ministry.[50] Despite such internal battles, the radio remained a powerful weapon throughout the War.

4

Joyce soon achieved notoriety in his new role. A contemporary remarked, "His strange story is a pulp melodrama come to life."[51] He achieved a degree of public exposure his unremitting toil for the BUF in draughty halls, often speaking to sparsely attended meetings across the length and breadth of Britain, had never given him. Millions came to know his voice. Many knew of him, though they had never even heard him.[52] Few had ever met him. In what Alan Coren called the "Golden Age of Ears," he became a radio pop star. He featured as such in 1940 in *Life* magazine.[53]

Notes

1 H. Ettlinger, *The Axis on the Air* (New York, 1943), p.39.
2 W. L. Shirer, *Berlin Diary: The Journal of a Foreign Correspondent 1934–1941* (London, 1941), p.150, experienced the sultriness "which makes for an increase in tension."
3 Cole, *Lord Haw-Haw*, pp.98, 99.
4 British Library, Add MS 74490, f.27, T. Rattigan, "Lord Haw-Haw. A Memorandum," and FA, File OE 3/7. Spelling as in original. Sir Nevile Henderson was British Ambassador to Germany.

5   Kenny, *Germany Calling*, p.137; Farndale, *Haw-Haw*, p.124.

6   KV 2/245/96b, transcript, 28 August 1944.

7   KV 2/246/391A; KV 2/246/399A.

8   W. L. Shirer, *This is Berlin* (London, 1999), p.61, broadcast from Berlin, 26–27 August 1939.

9   M. Hastings, *All Hell Let Loose: The World at War 1939–1945* (London, 2011), ch.1.

10 J.Wain (ed.), *The Oxford Anthology of English Poetry*,Vol.2. *Blake to Heaney* (Oxford, 2005), p.696 for W. H. Auden's "September 1 1939".

11 Cole, *Lord Haw-Haw*, pp.93–95.

12 Matthew and Harrison (eds), *ODNB*,Vol.2, pp.792–793. J. Doctor, *The BBC and Ultra-Modern Music 1922–1936* (Cambridge, 1999).

13 *The Times*, 6 June 1929. C. Stuart (ed.), *The Reith Diaries* (London, 1975), p.147 on their divorce.

14 IIO 45/23741, MI5 report, 1 November 1939. Barnes, "Oswald Mosley as Entrepreneur," pp.11–16, especially p.12. M. Eckersley, *Prospero's Wireless: A Biography of Peter Eckersley* (Romsey, 1998), pp.389 ff.

15 His Right Club membership is confirmed in the Red Book, now in Wiener Library. Eckersley wrote *The Power Behind the Microphone* (London, 1941). He was the subject of "Radio Lives. Peter Eckersley," BBC Radio 4, 7 July 1994. *The Times*, 19 March 1963, carried a discreet obituary. See also, Matthew and Harrison (eds), *ODNB*,Vol. 17, pp.645–646.

16 Eckersley, *Prospero's Wireless*, p.316.

17 *Ibid.* p.329.

18 Wiener Library, Red Book of the Right Club; HO 45/25776, statement of Dorothy Eckersley at Libenau Camp, 2 July 1945; Griffiths, *Patriotism Perverted*, p.141.

19 CRIM 1/1736/37, statement, 2 July 1945. KV 4/118, for instructions to Lloyds Bank, 117 Brompton Road, written from Berlin, 25 August 1939.

20 HO 45/25775, MI5 report on Clark, 24 September 1945. Clark, "Open Wounds," carries several references to Joyce but none in this connection.

21 Bundesarchiv, R55/181, memo, 25 November 1942, and R55/184, memo, 17 March 1943.

22 Bundesarchiv, R55/230.

23 KV 2/245/167a.

24 KV 2/880/96X, MI5 Interview with Peter Eckersley, 12 December 1940.

25 HO 45/25776, MI5 report, 24 September 1945.

26 "Tourists of the Revolution," BBC2, TV, 25 March 2000.

27 CRIM 1/1736/37.

28 FO 371/17730/157, Special Branch report, 25 August 1934. R. L. Bytwerk, *Julius Streicher* (New York, 2001), p.35 on the Mitfords and the Streichers.

29 KV 2/245/175.

30 Cole, *Lord Haw-Haw*, p.97 records the Joyces hardly believing their good fortune and Eckersley's "exclamation of surprise." Evidence derived from Margaret Joyce. Repeated uncritically in Murphy, *Letting the Side Down*,

p.106 and Farndale, *Haw-Haw*, pp.124–125. Clark, "Open Wounds," p.34 also comments.

31 Clark, "Open Wounds," p.26.

32 University of Edinburgh, Saroléa Collection, Box 85, D. Chandler to C. Saroléa, 9 February 1938. Chandler, an American, broadcast for the Nazis during the War. J. C. Edwards, *Berlin Calling: American Broadcasters in Service to the Third Reich* (New York and London, 1991), ch.5, pp.115–147. Saroléa was a distinguished but 'difficult' Edinburgh University Professor and Nazi fellow traveller. S. T. Johnson, "'A good European and a sincere racist.' The Life and Work of Professor Charles Saroléa 1870–1953," Keele University, PhD thesis, 2001.

33 H. W. Flannery, *Assignment to Berlin* (London, 1942), p.267. Schirmer's Nazi Party card, 3143496, revealed he had joined on 1 May 1933. He defended Nazi concentration camps in *The Spectator*, 14 December 1934. After the War he served as Ambassador in Canberra, Cairo and Vienna. J.de Launay, *Histoires secrètes de la Belgique de 1935 à 1945* (Paris, 1975), p.74.

34 Clark, "Open Wounds," p.35 on von Bülow. Cole, *Lord Haw-Haw*, p.59 on Joyce knowing him in pre-war London.

35 Berlin Document Center, Hetzler's NSDAP file.

36 Bergmeier and Lotz, *Hitler's Airwaves*, pp.203–204; Cole, *Lord Haw-Haw*, p.59.

37 Bergmeier and Lotz, *Hitler's Airwaves*, pp.96, 99–100, 203–205; Cole, *Lord Haw-Haw*, p.113.

38 Rattigan, British Library, Add MS 74490, f.29.

39 *Ibid.* f.32.

40 KV 2/245/172b, 175a and 176a reports the frantic police search.

41 HO 45/22405/1275–1283 for his Workbook.

42 *Ibid.*

43 Hall, (ed.) *Trial*, pp.81–82.

44 WJ to MJ, 15 November 1945.

45 The former can be heard on "German Propaganda Swing," Harlequin CD, 03 and "I got rhythm," Harlequin CD, 09. Shostakovich's symphony was first performed in 1942. See generally E. C. Blake, *War, Dictators and the Gramophone 1898–1945* (York, 2004), and A. Ross, *The Rest is Noise* (London, 2009).

46 C. Siepmann, *Radio in Wartime* (London, 1942), p.4.

47 R. Taylor, "Goebbels and the Function of Nazi Propaganda," in D. Welch, *Nazi Propaganda: The Power and the Limitations* (London, 1983), p.39.

48 E. Hadamovsky, *Propaganda und Nationale Macht* (Oldenburg, 1933), emphasises this theme from a Nazi perspective. Until 1942, when he fell from favour, he played a crucial role in propaganda. Volunteering for action, he was killed on the Eastern front. Margaret Joyce's diary, 10 March 1945, recorded "HADAMOWSKI gefallen," KV2/346.

49 H. K. Smith, *Last Train from Berlin* (London, 1943), p.36. See also D. Irving, *Goebbels. Mastermind of the Third Reich* (London, 1996) and A. J. Mackenzie, *Propaganda Boom* (London, 1938), p.23.

50 Bergmeier and Lotz, *Hitler's Airwaves*, ch.1, 2, particularly; Doherty, *Nazi Wireless Propaganda*, ch.1; A. A. Kallis, *Nazi Propaganda and the Second World War* (London, 2005), ch.2 on competing departmental interests; Kershaw's *Hitler: Hubris* and *Hitler: Nemesis*, emphasise the polycentric state.
51 C. J. Rolo, *Radio Goes To War* (London, 1943), pp.55–56.
52 Siepmann, *Radio*, p.3.
53 *Life*, 22 April 1940.

11

A RADIO STAR

Germany is furiously bitter that these stubborn English dogs do not know when they are beaten. Hitler has peered across the narrow English Channel just as Napoleon had. He has seen the cliffs of Dover and gone back to Berlin, frustrated. [Harold Ettlinger, *The Axis on the Air* (Indianapolis, New York, 1943), p.15.]

1

The War did not unfold as Joyce had anticipated. In early September 1939, after the German military had crushed Poland, neither Britain nor France launched a retaliatory offensive. And Hitler showed no signs of moving Westwards.[1] Where was this much-threatened war? The British public had expected an apocalypse. All they had was an anti-climax. At this surreal time Joyce became known as Wilhelm Fröhlich, the latter a German translation of Joyeux, which he claimed was his family's Norman name.[2]

These were "strange somnambulistic" days.[3] And during this "phoney war" Nazi radio propaganda attempted to demoralise the British public by capitalising on the country's appeasement and defeatist sentiments. Why not sue for peace with Germany?[4] In Mosley's words, why fight in a Jews' war?[5] This period did not afford Joyce an ideal context. His politics had always thrived on aggression. But still learning his radio trade he can be heard as Jacob Goldstein in an anti-Semitic radio sketch, a role which allowed him to indulge in some crude verbal mimicry.[6]

However, in 1940 as Hitler's Imperial ambitions turned Northwards and Westwards, Nazi radio became much more threatening to British listeners. The War was coming ever closer home.[7] Joyce now came into his element. Some broadcasts can be linked to him even though he did not identify himself on air until 1941. On 9 April 1940, following the invasion of Denmark and Norway, he portrayed an invincible German military with all operations progressing according to plan.[8] He repeated this emphasis a few days later in a broadcast remarkable for its fierce attack on Winston Churchill – generally treated as a bête noire in the Propaganda Ministry – and now described by Joyce as the "supreme war Lord of Whitehall." The bulldog who the following month became Prime Minister might splutter. But the British had hardly rushed to Europe's aid. Joyce claimed Europeans were beginning to understand the meaning of "Perfidious Albion."[9] He probably recalled his youth, when British politicians had sold out their friends in Ireland, including his own family, by capitulating to the nationalists.

German military victories which quickly followed in the Low Countries guaranteed he could taunt his British listeners even more.[10] Their country might have a new Prime Minister – Churchill, the "whisky-guzzling, cigar-chomping, bovine decadent liar," had entered Downing Street on 10 May, the day the Low Countries had been invaded – but what had changed?[11] Nothing. German plans remained well on course.

After German forces had swiftly scythed through Belgium, Holland and Luxembourg, they began sweeping almost effortlessly through France.[12] Ragged, frightened refugees were soon crowding promiscuously on the country's roads.[13] Between late May and early June, after the British army had failed to restrain the Wehrmacht's advance, its tattered remnants had to be evacuated from Dunkirk. This pull-back was – and still is – portrayed in Britain as a magnificent defensive action, rather like Sir John Moore's "not a drum was heard" retreat from Corunna in 1809.[14] To a Nazi commentator it smacked of a "death dance."[15]

German troops soon arrived in Paris. A swastika flag could be seen fluttering above the Eiffel Tower. On 14 June, in control of the capital, jackboots stamped in a victory march through the Arc de Triomphe. On 22 June France officially surrendered, confirming Germany's growing European power.[16] Werner Bartels, one of the first German pilots to walk down the Champs Elysées, fantasised that soon he would be strolling down Bond Street.[17] A contemporary American writer speculated Hitler might not only win the War but also the peace and reorganise Europe.[18]

"The full blast of [Goebbels's] vituperation" could now be unleashed on England. Dutifully, effortlessly, Joyce's broadcasts slipped into a higher gear.[19] Hitler's time had come. The Führer had every reason to slap his thigh, an obsessive trait he performed whenever his spirits soared.[20] Every campaign had proved strikingly successful. Who could doubt Leni Riefenstahl's deified image in *The Triumph of the Will*? Even a hard-nosed American reporter had to admit, "God's been pretty good to Hitler so far."[21]

Berlin lived in a state of near-ecstasy.[22] On 18 July its citizens were treated to a stage-managed parade of "tanned-hard-looking" veterans through the Brandenburg Gate, down a garlanded Unter den Linden. If inclined, they could watch the exultant film *Sieg im Westen*.[23] The New Order would soon become a reality.[24] No wonder Berlin's language institutes reported a roaring trade in learning English and French. Germans would soon be working among colonised peoples.[25] Londoners, by contrast, were "gloomily, grimly, grumpily settling down for a fight that might well last four years, (or fourteen or forty)."[26]

This optimism in Berlin was reflected in Joyce's broadcast on 23 June, when he told listeners that the French capitulation, underwritten by Marshal Pétain, the old hero of Verdun, amounted to a decisive moment in world politics. But what had the gods of war decreed for England? The "irresistible strength" of the German Army, the "dizzy rapidity" of its successes, guaranteed if the country held out, it would suffer. However, Joyce emphasised that Churchill, "the dictator of Britain," the personification of Perfidious Albion, would nevertheless resist. In hock to "Jewish International Finance," he had little option.[27] "Patriotic Englishmen" who had urged "the wisdom of peace" had been thrown into jail. Yet this stifling of opposition would not affect the War's outcome one iota. He claimed that the rich sensed it. As he spoke they, typically, were slipping silently out of the country. A twilight was spreading rapidly all over England.[28] The country's cause was lost. This still-powerful broadcast must have sent a frisson of anxiety and fear through his many British listeners, who heard it coming over the airwaves in 1940.

Still clearly relishing the victory in France, he remarked on 7 July that Churchill, "the degenerate of Downing Street," might have sunk the French fleet at Oran to prevent it falling into German hands, thereby forfeiting any claim to be called a civilised human being. But Hitler had triumphed. It mattered nothing a French Government-in-Exile had been established in London. These miserable souls no more represented France than they did China. Britain now had to ponder when she would face an offensive on her own soil. Taunting, teasing, tormenting listeners gathered anxiously around their sets, Joyce said the day, the hour, were Hitler's closely-guarded secrets. But the assault would come soon. When it did, the country's hastily erected papier-mâché defences would prove useless. "The smell of decay" distinctly wafting over the entire country would precipitate its rapid collapse.[29] He never breathed it over the airwaves, but in private probably fantasised about the role he hoped then to assume.

His remarks exaggerated. Hitler viewed any invasion of Britain as risky. Far better to tame it by other means. That summer the assault came through the air. Small-scale bombing raids occurred in June and by next month the RAF had become engaged in regular dog fights with the Luftwaffe over Southern England. This fighting intensified in August and September. On 11 and 12 August Bill Shirer, broadcasting to America for CBS, remarked, "Well, it looks as if the war on Britain, at least in the air, has started in earnest."[30] German pilots, evoking the First World War spirit of Manfred von Richtofen, began arriving over Britain in considerable numbers.[31] The BBC's Charles Gardner reported the resulting aerial skirmishes like a sporting event: ". . . and there he goes – sma-a-sh. Oh boy, I've never seen anything so good as this – the RAF fighters have really got these boys taped."[32] While down below in the Kent countryside the business of the Women's Institute went ahead as usual: "'I am afraid we have not *everybody* here . . . several of our members had to be up all night . . . but we have quite a little show all the same."[33] Life has always had its surreal side. Behind such gung-ho radio journalism, despite the continued daily round, a deadly battle with high stakes was being fought in the skies. And for Britain it showed no signs of getting any better. By that autumn the country was enduring a terrifying blitz on its major cities. For obvious reasons, the capital became an early target. *London can Take It!* Humphrey Jennings proclaimed in his 1940 film. But it was a close run thing. "Night after night the bombardment of London continues," Harold Nicolson wrote, "It is like the Conciergerie, since every morning one is pleased to see one's friends appearing again."[34] Coventry, Glasgow, Hull, Manchester, Portsmouth, Plymouth, above all Sheffield, took a massive pounding as bombers growled overhead and circled like dogs trying to pick up a scent before discharging their lethal cargoes.[35] Belfast, with its important shipyards, also suffered serious damage.[36] This concerted campaign continued into the late spring of the following year.

Joyce vigorously defended this devastating aerial assault which, with its civilian deaths and damage to property, was a reminder of Guernica. German air space had already been penetrated. It was payback time. Revenge was sweet, and he blamed British politicians for their country's suffering:

> those who drove their nation into a senseless war . . . just in order to save the interests of a small group of Jewish financiers and inveterate warmongers with Winston Churchill at their head – these men are responsible, not Germany.[37]

James Clark claimed later that the Luftwaffe's raids deeply troubled him.[38] He, who had earlier believed: "I want to be part of your lovely, neat Heimatstil homeland. I want to help fight off the mean, the greedy, the squalid-materialistic enemies," found himself "sliced down the middle."[39] However, he soon recovered his poise. Joyce showed a deeper sense of commitment. He never trimmed. He was no "bobbin' John."[40]

The Nazis were now exploiting their clandestine radio techniques acquired during the Spanish Civil War.[41] Büro Concordia, established in October 1939, had focused initially on France. But from 1940 it concentrated increasingly on Britain. The New British Broadcasting Station, one secret outlet, went operational on 25 February 1940 and, with British listeners specifically in mind, other stations were established under the Concordia umbrella. Workers' Challenge, Radio Caledonia, Christian Peace Movement, and Radio National, were joined briefly by Welsh National Radio.[42] Erich Hetzler, Sammy, as Joyce called him, assumed an important day-to-day role here.[43] This early contact of Joyce's became a close wartime friend, and Margaret kept in touch with him after the War.[44]

These secret stations, together with Radio Metropol, launched in 1942 by Interradio, registered by the German Foreign Office, formed part of a comprehensive broadcasting system designed to project Nazism to a wide range of countries. Wireless had quickly become a powerful psychological weapon.[45] Since the G-sender claimed to be operating from within Britain, no-one with a familiar radio voice could be put before the microphone. Joyce was therefore excluded. However, other renegades from Britain were recruited.[46] Joyce brought in some of them.[47] He also wrote and edited scripts.[48]

Whether in Berlin or a POW camp, potential recruits would have met a menacing, scarred figure who always carried "a fairly large automatic" and was capable of physical violence.[49] Behind him, ready to deal with difficult cases, stood the sadistic Hetzler.[50] Is it any wonder 'volunteers' felt threatened?[51]

Joyce usually worked at Concordia in the mornings, often with Hetzler, before turning to other duties.[52] With his "considerable authority," he could exert some influence over what was transmitted.[53] And he devoted himself totally to this routine.[54] Self-obsessed personalities know all about driving themselves hard and affirming their importance.[55]

Ursula Kruse, a fellow radio employee, regarded Joyce as an unpleasant, distasteful colleague.[56] But in the summer of 1940 a well-pleased Margaret wrote, "Dr Goebbels has sent him some cigars and congratulations on his work."[57] Her account is not entirely accurate. In defence, she might have been repeating what Joyce had told her when finessing his importance. He had actually requested the gift.[58] The Propaganda chief did not have to respond, but Joyce had clearly impressed him. "Eine Perle ist dieser Mann!" Goebbels remarked on 14 March 1940.[59] Joyce was a real gem. The following day he apparently praised him again in a meeting with the Führer.[60]

"That boy's all right!" and "totally incorruptible," Goebbels exclaimed the following August.[61] By now Joyce had become an invaluable servant of the Reich.[62] The young recruit from London was simply "magnificent," the Propaganda Chief wrote on 11 September.[63] And soon he afterwards described Joyce as "the best polemicist in our foreign language service."[64]

2

Joyce's broadcasts kept him busy, but he had no interest in the fly dying in the inkwell. The schoolboy with a talent for words, and later the BUF's Director of Propaganda – its Goebbels, in effect – continued to write during his time in Germany.

January 1940 saw him complete his major political work, *Dämmerung über England*. "Will has finished his book," Margaret entered in her diary.[65] It appeared that September under the imprint of Cesare Santoro's Internationaler Verlag, "a camouflaged publishing department of the Foreign Office."[66]

It attracted little interest at first, but sales increased after the state distributed an English version – *Twilight over England* – in POW camps, with the aim of winning over Allied captives.[67] On the back of this initiative Joyce eventually secured a substantial author's fee, though not without pressure on his part and lobbying by Fritz Hesse, a leading Foreign Office official.[68]

Joyce claimed he had been given a free hand in writing it.[69] But he deceived once again. With the Nazi-Soviet pact in force, attacks on Bolshevism were not encouraged. He must have found that a strain. His treatment of Irish nationalism, another political obsession, was similarly muted. The country's nationalists might assist the Nazi War effort.[70]

In what his old contact Peter Aldag called "this welcome book" with its "brilliant rhetoric" and "biting irony," Joyce concentrated on other themes.[71] He portrayed Britain – his thoughts slipped easily between Britain and England – as catapulting into steep decline.

Industries, formerly world leaders, had sunk to a critical condition. When Polish coalmines offered rich pickings, city investors had starved Britain's pits of capital. The cotton trade told a similar depressing story. "Pounds shillings and pence," what he called "money power," held Britain firmly in its grip.[72] In parallel, the country was groaning under a corrupt political system sacrificed to materialism.[73]

When discussing who ultimately controlled Britain, he revealed again the consistent thread in his political 'philosophy.' The Jews, who possessed "more influence than any other element in the population of Britain," were the real power. To a degree the government was "Jewish in purpose."

Joyce continued to present his everlasting enemy as a distinct race, writing "whether the Jew is orthodox, atheist, or Christian, he remains a Jew." His behaviour was therefore programmed. "If only the Hebrew would use his pelf like a vulgar merchant he would be easier to tolerate," he affirmed. However, the ever-slippery Oriental always employed it "to permeate into every stratum of society, carrying with him his racial consciousness, his racial character, his racial purpose and his monstrous materialism."[74] Joyce's observations reflected yet again his belief in a Jewish world conspiracy.[75]

His analysis of this alleged threat carried an international dimension.[76] German Jewry had opposed Hitler. However – the delight of it – the Führer had removed their influence and immediately the "most industrious and able people in the world were lifted .... right out of the domain of the Hebrew system." He claimed – as he had earlier in *National Socialism Now* – that Jews elsewhere, including Anglo-Jewry, were therefore determined to retaliate. As a result, a conflict between Britain and Nazi Germany was always likely.[77] Political developments in Czechoslovakia and Poland had finally persuaded Anglo-Jewry that the only way to protect "international Mammonism" lay in a Holy War.[78] This outcome could have been prevented, only if "some hundreds of Jews were to swing in timely fashion from the lamp-posts of Westminster."[79] The consequences of avoiding this action had proved disastrous. Europe had become drenched in blood. Irrespective of European Jewry's subsequent fate – and Joyce could not have anticipated the Holocaust – his sentiments, which built on his earlier remarks that Jews should be eliminated, Jewish Communists shot in the streets, possess their own chilling quality. He had embraced an exterminatory form of anti-Semitism.

This Jewish-created conflict constituted a decisive historical moment, "the greatest turning point in world history."[80] And his book assumed the character of a religious text, which portrayed Hitler in his determined effort to remove Hebrew influence as "the servant of a Higher Destiny."[81] For Joyce a new god was taking the place of the God he had lost in Galway. At this stage he never doubted how the War would end. He had long believed in "the transcendental ability of the human non-material will to overcome all material obstacles," in other words, the Aryans would triumph over Jewry.[82] With this victory society would be lifted to a higher phase of human development.[83] He offered this confident scenario to justify his leaving for Germany:

> If an Englishman cannot fight in his own streets against the domination of international finance, it were better for him to go elsewhere and impede by every means in his power the victory of his Government: for the victory of such a Government would be the everlasting defeat of his race: it would put an end to all prospects for ever of social justice and fundamental economic reform.[84]

Here was the stark choice now facing the world. His argument has shades of Marxism shorn of its materialism, a vision of a new society born out of the unfolding of irresistible historical forces. The secular utopia would finally come into being.

3

In 1940, by now well-established as a propagandist, Joyce bonded himself even more closely to the Nazis. He applied for naturalisation. He dealt with the matter directly. His British passport, renewed in 1939, had expired on 2 July 1940. Shortly afterwards, on 26 September, just over a year after arriving in Berlin, the German authorities granted his request.[85] He and Margaret lunched at the prestigious Kaiserhof to celebrate. "No raid that day," she wrote.[86]

Early in the War, certainly up to the early summer of 1940, when Britain stood alone in Western Europe – "the last that dare to struggle with the foe" – Joyce must have believed he had backed an odds-on winner. The Jesuits who had taught him in Galway could keep their belief in the hereafter. He and his Fascist comrades were embarked on a different mission, creating a worldly paradise. By the end of 1939 the Nazis had become dominant in Eastern-Central Europe. By April 1940 they had a presence in Scandinavia. The following May and June the Wehrmacht had swept through Belgium, Holland, Luxembourg and France in less than six weeks. They had taken casualties, materiel had been lost, but they had virtually raced to victory.[87] A triumphant nation, anticipating the next phase of the War, roared out a stream of martial songs, including *Wir fahren gegen Engeland*.[88] Joyce's pre-war prediction of Germany becoming the master of Europe seemed close to being fulfilled. How different from fascism's lack of progress in Britain. How perceptive he had been to throw in his lot with the Nazis. But he had always possessed special gifts. His mother had frequently told him so.

When Joyce believed a bright future dawned and it was bliss to be alive, contemporaries have left snapshots of him in Berlin. Bill Shirer of CBS, who later wrote a bestseller on the history of the Third Reich, referred to several of their meetings in his wartime diary.[89]

He first spotted "the British traitor who goes here by the name of Froehlich at the Funkhaus in December 1939" and clearly disliked him.[90] Soon afterwards he noticed Joyce "attacking his typewriter with gusto or shouting in his nasal voice against 'that plutocrat Chamberlain.'"[91]

However, in the summer of 1940 following an RAF raid on Berlin, Shirer wrote more approvingly:

Lord Haw-Haw [Joyce] I notice, is the only other person around here except the very plucky girl secretaries who does not rush to the shelter after the siren sounds. I have avoided him for a year but have been thinking lately it might be wise to get acquainted with the traitor. In the air-raids he has shown guts.[92]

Joyce's physical courage had clearly not deserted him – here was something else he took to Berlin.

They became better acquainted during yet another bombing, when Shirer left an air-raid shelter and took refuge with the Joyces in an unfrequented underground tunnel. Here, probably without too much effort, they demolished between them a litre of schnapps before returning to the Rundfunk building.[93]

During their brief contact Shirer found it impossible to escape his companion's decided political opinions. Joyce was ever a speaker searching for an ear and, the reporter soon realised, was consumed both by "a titanic hatred for Jews" and a fierce antipathy towards capitalists.[94] Shirer had his impressions reinforced when reading *Twilight over England*, which Joyce gave him in exchange for Brett Rutledge's 1940 novel *The Death of Lord Haw-Haw*.[95]

When the two met, so much power had accrued to the Nazis. Yet apparently Joyce feared his influence was already waning.[96] He need hardly have worried. The Nazis were to make ever-increasing demands on him.

Shirer would soon leave Berlin.[97] Years later, when trying his hand at a novel, Joyce appeared in *The Traitor* as "Sir Walter," an "inordinately ambitious" and scar-faced anti-Semite who envisaged himself as "the Fuehrer of Britain when it passed under Hitler's control." No longer would this "fanatical Fascist" have to tolerate the constant rebuffs, the frequent rejections, of his earlier years.[98] Their relationship had been fleeting. But Shirer had grasped a good deal about his companion's politics and ultimate ambitions.

Joseph C. Harsch, another American journalist, could not recall the date but it would be 1940, almost certainly, when he too shared the experience of an air raid. In a letter written just before he died, he reminisced:

> I was at the short wave sender station doing a broadcast. . . . The air raid siren sounded. I was supposed to go to the basement . . . but I preferred to stay topside . . . I became aware of another person standing by me. . . . He remarked on the bravery of the lads up there who had flown all the way from England. . . . The all clear sounded, the lights came on and I recognized Haw-Haw.[99]

Joyce was never slow to recognise courage in others.[100]

Harry Flannery, who replaced Shirer for CBS in Berlin, also encountered the Joyces. When they met – strangely he would sometimes refer to "Lord Ha Ha" – Joyce would often talk about Ireland and his fascist career in Britain.[101] Flannery was a fierce anti-fascist, but believed his acquaintance was "sincere" in his political views and "not unlikeable." When in each other's company on New Year's Eve, 1940, he thought Haw-Haw betrayed a certain sourness. However, as the clock moved inexorably into 1941, life offered some compensation. A bottle of champagne lay to hand, Cologne cathedral's bells rang out over the radio and a Nazi band played the *Horst-Wessel-Lied*. Joyce's spirits were duly lifted, and he and Margaret brought in the New Year with a Nazi salute.[102]

Looking back, it had been a successful year. Following his hesitant beginnings, everything had turned out well. He had become a star broadcaster, sowing fear among British audiences, garnering praise from within the Nazi hierarchy. Britain had not been battered into abject submission from the air. By late September 1940 it had become clear Hermann Göring's gamble – that the Luftwaffe could finish the job – had failed. But Joyce, like Hitler, still believed that ultimately victory was certain.[103] Who might prevent it? The Soviet Union had been neutralised. America was thousands of miles away, preoccupied with itself, uninvolved. Whole swathes of Europe were being Nazified. In this bigger context, Britain's stubbornness was an insignificant, temporary difficulty. Soon the real business, to defeat and reform it, would begin. A Jew-ridden country would have to be purged. The politicians Joyce despised would have to be decisively dealt with. The detested Churchill would have to confront his fate. So many new tasks would beckon. For now, though, he could sit back, relax, draw on his cigar, drink his champagne, wait on events, and congratulate himself on always doing his bit for the Nazis.

Notes

1 R. J. Evans, *The Third Reich at War 1939–1945* (London, 2008), p.112 for the British and French positions. T. Charman, *Outbreak 1939* (London, 2009), pp.374–379. A. Beevor, *The Second World War* (London, 2012), ch.3. N. Davies, *God's Playground: A History of Poland*. Vol.2, *1795 to the Present* (Oxford, 1986), ch.20 on Polish perspectives.

2 Cole, *Lord Haw-Haw*, p.120.
3 M. Panter-Downes, *London War Notes 1939–1945* (London, 1971), p.21 for the sleep imagery.
4 Doherty, *Nazi Wireless Propaganda*, pp. 6, 43–44.
5 R. Griffiths, "A Note on Mosley, the 'Jewish War' and Conscientious Objection," *Journal of Contemporary History*, Vol.40 (2005), pp.675–688.
6 "Germany Calling. The Voice of the Nazis," BBC Radio 4, 9 May 1991.
7 M. Mazower, *Hitler's Empire: Nazi Rule in Occupied Europe* (London, 2008) discusses Nazi Imperialism.
8 Imperial War Museum, Tape 13435, broadcast, 9 April 1940.
9 Imperial War Museum, Tape 13439, broadcast, 13 April 1940. H. D. Schmidt, "The Idea and Slogan of Perfidious Albion," *Journal of the History of Ideas*, Vol.14 (1953), pp.604–616, analyses the concept.
10 E. Murawski, *Der Durchbruch im Westen. Chronik der holländischen, belgischen und franzöischen Zusammenbruch* (Oldenburg, 1940).
11 J. W. Baird, *The Mythical World of Nazi War Propaganda* (Minneapolis, 1974), p.121.
12 Hastings, *Hell*, pp.53–77.
13 I. Némirovsky, *Suite Française* (London, 2007), p.50.
14 M. Hastings, *Finest Years: Churchill as Warlord, 1940–45* (London, 2009), pp.36–44. A Roberts, *The Storm of War* (London, 2009), pp.64–68.
15 C. Cranz, "Der Totenkranz von Dünkirchen," *Völkischer Beobachter*, North German edition, 4 June 1940. Hastings, *Hell*, pp.64–67.
16 F. Götz, "So marschierten unsere Truppen in Paris ein," in W. Weiss (ed.), *Der Krieg im Westen. Dargestellt nach den Berichten des "Völkischen Beobachters"* (Munich, 1941), pp.167–169. Shirer, *Berlin Diary*, pp.297–336 particularly, offers another perspective. M. Bloch, *Strange Defeat* (London, 1949), originally published 1940, for a French perspective. J. Jackson, *The Fall of France: The Nazi Invasion of 1940* (Oxford, 2003) has later comment.
17 J. Steinhoff, P. Pechel and D. Showalter (eds), *Voices from the Third Reich* (London, 1991), p.83.
18 R. G. Waldeck, *Athene Palace* (Oxford, Portland, 1988), p.5.
19 E. K. Bramsted, *Goebbels and National Socialist Propaganda 1925–1945* (London, 1965), p.417.
20 Kershaw, *Hitler: Nemesis*, p.297.
21 Shirer, *Berlin Diary*, p.360, entry, 22 July 1940.
22 G. Mak, *In Europe: Travels through the Twentieth Century* (London, 2007), p.387.
23 Shirer, *This is Berlin*, pp.353–354, broadcast, 18 July 1940.
24 Mazower, *Hitler's Empire*.
25 Shirer, *This is Berlin*, p.317 broadcast, 8 June 1940. *Ibid.* p.347, broadcast, 12 July 1940 for the German government's call for colonial officials.
26 Rattigan, British Library, Add MS, 74490, f.33.
27 If anyone doubted it, they had only to turn to the detailed study by his old friend Fritz Krüger. See P. Aldag, *Juden beherrschen England* (Berlin, 1939).

28 Imperial War Museum, Tape 13433, broadcast, 23 June 1940.

29 Imperial War Museum, Tape 13434, broadcast, 7 July 1940.

30 Shirer, *This is Berlin*, p.375, broadcast, 11–12 August 1940.

31 Baird, *Nazi War Propaganda*, p.131, for the von Richtofen image. Hastings, *Churchill*, pp.79–110 on the Battle of Britain.

32 Leslie Baily's *Scrapbook 1940* (gramophone record, Fontana FDL493 014).

33 J. Betjeman, "Coming Home, or England Revisited," BBC Home Service talk, 25 February 1943. Reprinted in J. Betjeman, *Trains and Buttered Toast*, ed. S. Games (London, 2006), p.135.

34 S. Olson (ed.), *Harold Nicolson: Diaries and Letters 1930–1964* (Harmondsworth, 1984), pp.193–194, entry, 19 September 1940.

35 T. Harrisson, *Living through the Blitz* (London, 1976. Republished 2010), a classic study based on Mass-Observation sources and J. Gardiner, *The Blitz: The British Under Attack* (London, 2010). For London, see P. Ziegler, *London at War* (London, 1995), pp.113–178 particularly and V. Hodgson, *Few Eggs and No Oranges: The Diaries of Vere Hodgson 1940–45* (London, 1999. First ed.1971), pp.66–67 for "The Devils" from Germany. White, *London in the Twentieth Century*, pp.38–39 carries later comment. The attack on Coventry in November 1940 featured on BBC2, TV, 6 October 2009, in "Blitz: the Bombing of Coventry." This bombing led to a new word, "coventrated." It is less well-publicised but J. L. Hodson, who travelled the country, remarked, "I have seen no ruins so spectacular as those in Sheffield," *Towards the Morning* (London, 1941), p.102. War artist Henry Rushbury graphically captured the damage. Goebbels recorded that the city had been more badly hit than Coventry. E. Fröhlich (ed.), *Die Tagebücher von Joseph Goebbels*, Vol.9, December 1940–July 1941, p.51 (München, 1998), entry 14 December 1940. The dog imagery is from N. Last, *Nella Last's War: A Mother's Diary* (London, 1983), p.72, entry, 2 September 1940, on the bombing of the Barrow yards.

36 A. Calder, *The Myth of the Blitz* (London, 1991), pp.168–169.

37 BBC Monitoring Service, ZEE IEFE, 22.15, 9 September 1940.

38 "Germany Calling. The Voice of the Nazis," BBC Radio 4, 16 May 1991.

39 Clark, "Open Wounds," pp.21, 86–87.

40 *Scotland on Sunday*, 20 February 2005, for the 6th Earl of Mar, known as "bobbin' John" for his changeable political positions.

41 J. B. Whitton and J. H. Herz, "Radio in International Politics," in H. L. Childs and J. B. Whitton (eds.), *Propaganda by Short Wave* (Princeton, 1942), pp.24–27. W. A. Boelcke (ed.), *The Secret Conferences of Dr Goebbels. The Nazi Propaganda War* 1939–43 (New York, 1970), p.69 (20 July 1940).

42 Boelcke (ed.), *Secret Conferences*, p.69 (20 July 1940). See generally M. Doherty, "Black Propaganda by Radio: the German Concordia broadcasts to Britain," *Historical Journal of Film, Radio and Television*, Vol. 14 (1994), pp.167–197.

43 Bergmeier and Lotz, *Hitler's Airwaves*, pp.203–205 particularly for Hetzler's involvement. See also E. Howe, *The Black Game: British Subversive Operations against the Germans during the Second World War* (London, 1982), p.68, and D. MacLeod, "Germany Calling Scotland: The Büro Concordia

and Scottish Nationalism in World War II," *Journal for the Study of British Cultures*,Vol.2(1995), pp.173–186.

44 CRIM 1/1735, statement, Leonard Banning, at Brussels, 13 May 1945, described Hetzler as "cunning," as well as "extremely narrow-minded," and a "tyrant" (p.2). In KV 2/631, statement to Intelligence Officers, 16 May 1945, Benson Freeman regarded him as "a scoundrel of the deepest dye, a complete rotter and a despicable coward in the air raids to come: he was hated by German and English alike." See also KV 2/426, para.5, interview, G.P.S. Hewitt, US Army Prison, Caserne Mortier, Paris, 2 October 1945.

45 "The Radio War," Minnesota Public Radio, 4 September 1995.

46 Bergmeier and Lotz, *Hitler's Airwaves*, pp.191–193, 216–220.

47 KV 2/246/397A, "JOYCE. Attempts to Corrupt Service Personnel." Boelcke (ed.), *Secret Conferences*, p.58 (22 June 1940) and, less reliably, J. Brown, *In Durance Vile*, rev. ed. J. Borrie (London, 1981), ch.6.

48 KV2/246/384Z, Joyce as scriptwriter. HO 45/25792, statement, J. G. Lingshaw, 16 and 17 June 1945, on Joyce as editor.

49 HO 45/25775, statement, 15 June 1945, p.8 for James Clark's awareness of Joyce carrying a gun. See also N. Baillie-Stewart, *The Officer in the Tower* (London, 1967), p.152.

50 KV 2/442.

51 W.H.Griffiths, in WO 71/1110.

52 WO 71/1112. Court Martial of Rifleman Ronald Spillman, 2 November 1945. KV 2/423, statement, Susan Hilton, 30 June 1945.

53 HO 45/25775, statement, James Clark, 15 June 1945, p.8.

54 Cole, *Lord Haw-Haw*, pp.136–137, testimony which probably reflects Margaret's feelings of neglect. Howe, *The Black Game*, p.69.

55 S. Vaknin, *Malignant Self Love: Narcissism Revisited* (Prague and Skopje, 2007), p.118.

56 Ursula Kruse to author 3 December 2002.

57 KV 2/346, 22 August 1940.

58 Boelcke, *Secret Conferences*, p.80 (21 August 1940).

59 E. Fröhlich (ed.), *Die Tagebücher von Joseph Goebbels* (München, 1998), Vol.7, July 1939–March 1940, p.348, 14 March 1940.

60 *Ibid*. p.350, 15 March 1940.

61 *Ibid*. p.284, 22 August 1940.

62 E. Fröhlich (ed.), *Die Tagebücher von Joseph Goebbels* (München, 1998),Vol 8, April–November 1940, p.75, 26 April 1940.

63 *Ibid*. p.320, 11 September 1940.

64 *Ibid*. p.339, 22 September 1940.

65 KV 2/346, 14 January 1940.

66 KV 2/249/92a, statement, Fritz Hesse. KV 2/346, Margaret Joyce's diary, 14 January 1940, 10 February 1940, and 29 February 1940 on the book's progress. Santoro wrote *Vier Jahre Hitler–Deutschland von einem ausländer gesehen* (Berlin, 1937).

67 The translation did not circulate in wartime Britain.

68 KV2 /249/92a. The preface to Hesse's *Hitler and the English* (London, 1954), describes him as rapporteur and advisor on British affairs at Hitler's HQ between 1939 and 1945.See also KV 2/ 915.

69 Joyce, *Twilight*, p.11.

70 See, therefore, propaganda films such as *Der Fuchs von Glenavon* (1940) and *Mein Leben fuer Irland* (1941).

71 *Die Judenfrage in Politik, Recht, Kultur und Wirtschaft*, 15 December 1942, p.285.

72 Joyce, *Twilight*, pp.19, 34

73 *Ibid.* chs. 1 and 3.

74 *Ibid.* p.94, 47, 104, 73, 75–76, 76.

75 Cohn, *Warrant for Genocide*, remains the best full-length study of *The Protocols of the Elders of Zion*.

76 HO 144/20144/130, MI5 report, 11 March 1935, on Joyce's international approach to fascism.

77 Joyce, *Twilight*, p.71.

78 His "international Mammonism" is from *ibid.* p.128 and p.118 for his description of Czecho-Slovakia.

79 *Ibid.* p.70.

80 *Ibid.* p.140.

81 *Ibid.* p.140.

82 *Ibid.* p.139.

83 *Ibid.* pp.141–142.

84 *Ibid.* p.134. Joyce is once again passing as English.

85 Cole, *Lord Haw-Haw*, p.176.

86 KV 2/346, 26 September 1940. Three years later Rudolf Semmler noted that the Kaiserhof, the unofficial HQ of the Nazi Party in Berlin, was blazing fiercely after an Allied air-raid. R. Semmler, *Goebbels – the Man next to Hitler* (London, 1947), diary, 24 November 1943. Semmler became press officer to Goebbels in 1940.

87 Shirer, *Berlin Diary*, p.272, 18 May 1940.

88 Baird, *Nazi War Propaganda*, p.121; R.Ní Mheara-Vinard, *Cé hí seo Amuigh? Cuimhni Cinn Ag Roisin* (Coiscéim, 1992), p.145.

89 Obituary in *The Times*, 30 December 1993. S. Wick, *The Long Night: William L. Shirer and the Rise and Fall of the Third Reich* (Basingstoke, 2012). *This is Berlin* for a sample of Shirer's wartime broadcasts. W. L. Shirer, *The Rise and Fall of the Third Reich* (London, 1963), for his history of Nazi Germany.

90 Shirer, *Berlin Diary*, p.210, 24–25 December 1939.

91 *Ibid.* p.232, 4 March 1940.

92 *Ibid.* p.385, 29 August 1940.

93 *Ibid.* pp.411–413, 26 September 1940.

94 *Ibid.* p.411.

95 *Ibid.* p.412. Brett Rutledge was the American writer Elliot Paul.

96 *Ibid.* p.413. Shirer wrote up his recollections in the *Sunday Chronicle*, 14 September 1941.

97 He volunteered to give evidence at Joyce's trial. FO 369/3173/925, 18 July 1945.

98 W. L. Shirer, *The Traitor* (New York, 1950), pp.197–198 especially. The renegades Jack Trevor and Norman Baillie-Stewart appeared as "Billy Williams" and "Reggie Alden" respectively. Shirer referred to the novel's origins in his *20th Century*, ch.2.

99 Joseph C. Harsch to author, 19 February 1998. See his *At the Hinge of History* (Athens, Ga., 1993), pp.39–63 on Berlin.

100 M. Stuart, *Manna in the Morning. A Memoir 1940–1958* (Dublin, 1984), p.23 described Joyce as "courageous" during a similar air raid experience.

101 Flannery's "Ha Ha," "young, sweatered, scarred," appeared in his Notebook on Spain, Germany and France, 1941. State Historical Society of Wisconsin, MS 80AF,Vol.8.

102 Flannery, *Assignment to Berlin*, p.95.

103 Goebbels, diary, 12 December 1940, for Hitler believing "der Krieg ist militärisch so gut wie gewonnen." Fröhlich (ed.), *Tagebücher*, Vol.9, December 1940–July 1941, p.48.

12

THE GREAT GAMBLE

On Sunday, June 29 [1941] the Nazis unleashed their propaganda. They had erected loudspeakers at intervals along all the main thoroughfares, such as the Unter den Linden and the Kurfürstendamm in Berlin. From these and over radios in all parts of the Reich they began early in the morning to release communiqués. An announcer would interrupt whatever programme was on the air to tell the people that a communiqué would be heard in *zehn Minuten*. Military band music and marching songs followed. Five minutes later the announcer said the communiqué would be heard in *fünf Minuten*. Finally, after the stirring music, came a fanfare, a blast of trumpets and a roll of drums, and the dramatic announcement beginning; 'Aus dem Führerhauptquartier gibt das Oberkommando der Wehrmacht bekannt: . . .'

After that, of course, the communiqué, and *Deutschland über Alles*.

Everyone was ordered to stand in silence during the reading. Along the Kufürstendamm the milling crowds halted and those at the café tables rose. [Harry W. Flannery, *Assignment to Berlin* (London, 1943), 262.]

1

It is 1941. Joyce is enjoying his champagne. Allied bombers have inflicted some damage on Berlin. But life continues much as before.[1]

Not quite as it had in August 1939 when he stepped onto the Fried-richstrasse station. Clothes, soap and food are rationed.[2] However, compared with what followed . . .

2

The year Joyce began in Flannery's company is one of the most deci-sive in recent history. In the early spring Joyce, still oozing confidence, told Leonard Banning, working alongside him in radio propaganda, the War would be over by the following August. Banning was not so sure.[3]

A few months later something dramatic happened. Contrary to Nazi expectations, Britain had not been beaten in the air; the Doug-las Baders, the Richard Hillarys, with their comrades-in-arms from the Empire, Czechoslovakia and Poland, had seen off Göring's finest. The Wehrmacht with its "mass of German metal," had not ventured across the Channel.[4] Britain remained a piece of unfinished busi-ness. Yet Hitler now decided to wage war on two fronts. On Sunday 22 June 1941, the Nazis tore up the 1939 non-aggression pact with the USSR which, when signed by "the scum of the earth" and "the bloody assassin of the workers," had thoroughly disorientated Joyce.[5] Hitler switched his attention from Britain and launched Operation Barbarossa.[6] It was a decisive historical moment. German troops crossed into Russian territory "on almost the same day as Napoleon 129 years before."[7] The Nazi elite held differing views on the Soviet Union and its national sub-groups. But Hitler – and many colleagues – viewed the invasion as a Western crusade against the Orient which, potentially, offered huge rewards. He would decisively root out Jewish Bolshevism, gain access to exploitable labour and essential raw mate-rials, acquire a vast European empire, and all which that implied.[8] Adding to his eager anticipation, this just-begun campaign would take only a few weeks. He knew it. He sensed it. So did Tank Gunner Karl Fuchs, who wrote home shortly after the invasion, "This war will soon be over." Russian soldiers, "the mere scum of the earth," were no match for the Wehrmacht.[9] With Stalin defeated, Britain would be even more exposed.[10]

The Nazi press rationalised the invasion by emphasising that the Soviets had not remained faithful to the 1939 pact, but had been traitorously intent on extending their influence in Poland and the Baltic states. The sheer brazenness of it, they had even harboured plans to invade the Reich.[11]

The ferocious assault on the Soviet Union allowed James Clark to recover his faith in Nazism. "At last it's all right again! THE CRUSADE TO LIBERATE THE SOVIET UNION BEGINS!" he wrote much later, attempting to project himself faithfully into his past life. "The first of the great eastern front bulletins of 1941 has been launched on the airwaves to the arching fanfares and seismic drum rolls of Liszt's *Les Préludes!*"[12] Margaret Joyce wrote more sparingly, "Germany marched into Russia." She then added, "We had supper at home – then out for a drink."[13] In faraway Moscow Rosa Rust's life was to be turned completely upside down by the invasion. "Suddenly one morning," she recalled, "I was listening to some beautiful music on the radio . . . Then Molotov . . . announced that Germany had attacked."[14] Operation Barbarossa would eventually prove fateful for the Joyces. Indeed, all Germany would suffer. The waiter who remarked with some relish to a Swedish reporter, "It's what we expected. . . . Now we'll kick Stalin in the pants," was to be disappointed.[15] His apprehensive fellow citizens showed far more insight.[16]

3

On 12 February 1941 Joyce had registered as a military reservist and received a German military passport where his nationality appeared as "German, formerly English."[17] However, he was not called upon to serve. He continued with his propaganda work, and the invasion of the Soviet Union allowed him to unleash his long-standing venom against Communism in a broadcast on 27 June 1941. These events created "a propaganda paradise" for him.[18] He told his many listeners that Bolshevism, "fortified by Jewish shekels," posed a threat to any sense of national self-respect. Using imagery students of his pre-war style would have recognised instantly, Joyce gleefully, viciously, pounced on his long-standing enemy as a species of "sub-men from Moscow."[19] Finally, though, this problem would be solved and Germany's actions would decide Europe's future.

With most of Europe effectively colonised by the Germans and now as the Wehrmacht with its "Fantastic! Unbelievable! Wonderful!" victories penetrated rapidly, ruthlessly, ever further into the unending vastness of the Soviet Union, Joyce remained fully occupied.[20] His fear, expressed to Bill Shirer in 1940, that he might be a waning star, had proved quite unfounded.

On the contrary. The month before the attack on the Soviet Union, Ezra Pound, working on Italian radio, wrote in idiosyncratic style seeking Joyce's advice on propaganda matters. 'Esrapunto' had contributed earlier to BUF publications and conducted a correspondence with John Macnab in which 'Master' had puffed Joyce's qualities.[21] 'Unkle Ez', as he described himself, or the American Haw-Haw to his critics, now wrote at some length.[22] However, "The poor old coot" received little in return.[23] Joyce claimed a busy work schedule precluded his writing real letters.[24] In any case, the poet was not worth cultivating. He had too "many screws loose."[25] Rather than waste time on Pound, he was better employed devoting all his energies to the Nazi state.[26] James Strachey Barnes, now broadcasting on Italian radio, also reached out to Joyce.[27]

Pound was not the only American working for the Axis powers. Before the United States entered the War, Bill Shirer noticed the Nazis had recruited Fred Kaltenbach as a broadcaster; he was "probably the best" of the Americans at this stage to have offered their services. Shirer also spotted Edward Leopold Delaney, otherwise known as E. D. Ward, and Constance Drexel, "the only woman in town who will sell her American accent to them."[28] Other US citizens soon joined them.[29]

Jane Anderson, sometimes called the Georgia Peach, was arguably the most intriguing of such recruits.[30] After being arrested by Republicans during the Spanish Civil War, she had become a passionate anti-Communist and later allegedly served as one of Franco's agents.[31] Anderson first went on air in Germany in April 1941 and broadcast regularly until 6 March 1942 when, rashly, she described her luxury lifestyle in an increasingly austere Berlin. That faux pas resulted in her 'retirement' until 12 June 1944.[32]

Her speciality lay in live interviews and on 21 November 1941, with the invasion of the USSR in full swing, Joyce, customary cigar in hand, appeared on her evening programme. She, "coy and unctuous," and he, "quieter than usual," soon established a rapport.[33] She knew how to stroke him, just as Christian Bauer had done. *Twilight over England*, she gushed, was no mere manuscript: it was "a confession of faith."[34] He must have swelled on hearing it.

Joyce informed listeners why he had gone over to the Nazis – not that he told the full story:

> I lived for months with friends who loved England and could not get enough to eat from her. . . . These men all hoped that out of their sacrifice a greater England would be born. Their misery was indescribable when it seemed that all their efforts would be wiped out by war. They were benumbed at the thought that there was to be a conflict between their country and all the beliefs that they had held dear.[35]

He told them that Jewish international finance – which controlled Britain – had created this present conflict. He had constantly dwelt on a pernicious Jew power before the War. He had emphasised it in *Dämmerung über England*. Now he did so again.

When this broadcast went out, everything on the surface seemed to be going well for him. But success came at a price. He had started drinking heavily in Britain. In wartime Germany, under increasing pressure, and taking only short breaks from his demanding daily routine, his cravings grew.[36] The cost of living soon became measured by the price of a drink. His first transaction when crossing into Germany in 1939 – buying two bottles of beer – was to become symbolic.[37] "If a light does flame up in him," James Clark wrote, "it's the Steinhaeger, the good white hard stuff that comes in the tall earthenware hollands flask."[38] Contemporaries in wartime Berlin remarked Joyce invariably reeked of alcohol, even when on duty.[39] "Drink, tobacco and food are the main desiderata . . . there is some connection between physical satisfaction and mental effort," he wrote towards the end of the War.[40] Which he soon followed with, "am now on my way to the club where I mean to drink farewell."[41] And, in similar vein, "I very much want to get drunk tonight, won't somebody oblige me?"[42] Human warmth and personal contact are strikingly absent from this equation.

A slave to routine and addicted to the bottle, he began to lose sight of Margaret. Her diary often refers to their domestic arguments. "Had a shouting match because It thought It's breakfast was late," she jotted down in early 1940.[43] As these tensions festered, they started to go their separate ways.

An icy chastity had never appealed to Joyce. He had always had affairs. He could dominate these passing relationships. They were not time-consuming and could be ended whenever they became inconvenient.[44] Margaret, known to renegades as a "loose" woman, also took lovers, though Joyce thrashed her for it.[45] His Berlin contemporaries knew he was a wife-beater.[46] Margaret's diary confirms it.[47] At the same time, he derived a voyeuristic pleasure from knowing men wanted her. Almost in a reprise of his earlier encouragement of Eric Piercy's relationship with Hazel, he actually *made* Margaret flirt.[48] He tried nevertheless to impose boundaries but, defiantly, she became keen on Nicky von Besack, a younger Wehrmacht Intelligence officer, and their relationship continued after the War.[49]

In August 1941, recognising their problems, Joyce and Margaret divorced, an event she graphically recorded in her diary.[50] She cited his cruelty. He counter-petitioned on grounds of her adultery. Their marriage ended. The young woman from Carlisle had run aground in Berlin.

This turmoil came soon after the sudden death of Joyce's father in London on 19 February 1941. Gertrude Joyce followed him three years later.[51] Michael's life must have been full of disappointments. Once an aspiring young capitalist, he had worked latterly as a door-to-door salesman of vacuum cleaners. He never received adequate compensation for his losses during the struggle for Irish independence. His eldest child had become a traitor. So much dust had been thrown in his eyes.

People like Joyce and Margaret who undertake great adventures together can sometimes drift apart. However, in their case they were officially reconciled. They remarried on 11 February 1942 at Berlin-Charlottenburg register office and that autumn took a delayed honeymoon, or possibly holiday, in Norway and stayed together.[52] But old patterns of behaviour continued, which led Margaret to write in March 1942: "W. lost his temper and nearly had a stroke."[53] And after she had linked up again with Besack, Joyce when broadcasting from Luxembourg stayed at the Hotel Alfa with a Finnish girlfriend.[54] He and Margaret clearly had difficulty living exclusively and harmoniously together. They found it even harder to be apart.

When they remarried, Germany was facing massive challenges. More than anyone had ever envisaged. Hitler had believed that when he invaded Russia and kicked in the door the whole rotten edifice would come crashing down. At first the advance proceeded at a furious pace. In October 1941 in faraway Lancashire, Nella Last read in the *Daily Express* that the German army was "only forty miles from Moscow." Trying to make sense of it, she was shocked to realise that forty miles was "just about the distance to Blackpool across the Bay from Barrow."[55] In London, the young Bryan Magee, reading the *Daily Mirror*, followed Hitler's advance with wonder and amazement, remarking later: "I can still remember some of the cartoons and maps."[56]

With the Wehrmacht's seemingly unstoppable victories, until the autumn of 1941 Berlin was gripped by an exuberant optimism.[57] It was the successful French campaign all over again. A map on the wall of the former Wertheim's department store enabled Berliners to look up, gauge the extent of these latest remarkable advances, and admire the bravery of their soldiers.[58] With their stunning victories, the boys would soon be back home. There would be more triumphant parades of seemingly invincible grey-clad warriors. But at the year's end, German troops remained embroiled in the Soviet Union. The Wehrmacht's dashing, dramatic push could not be sustained, and the massive counter-offensive mounted by the Red Army on the outskirts of Moscow in December 1941 amounted to "a key moment" in the War.[59] "The winning war was over."[60] Boris Yefimov's cartoon depicting bedraggled, retreating, wounded Wehrmacht officers carrying the coffin of an invincible German army was crude propaganda, but it carried an accurate message.[61] Those breathless, enthusiastic bulletins James Clark heard on his radio, proclaiming military success after success, had ceased. The War's tide had not yet turned fully against Hitler, but the Soviets were mounting a fanatical resistance to save Mother Russia.[62]

By the year's end even more dramatic political developments had occurred. On 8 December 1941, the United States declared war on

Japan after the Japanese attack on Pearl Harbor. Three days later, in Berlin, Hitler announced that in accordance with the German, Italian and Japanese Tripartite Pact, Germany now found itself at war with America.[63]

4

In 1942 a catchy, kitschy, popular German song had the lyrics: "Nothing lasts forever/It'll soon go away/Although it's December/It'll soon be May."[64] This lovers' lament carried a bigger message. A new, less-certain phase in the War had begun, but hopefully the future would bring a change in fortunes. But would it?

In these more testing times when Joyce's broadcasts occupied an important slot in the evening schedules, the Propaganda Ministry issued a number of co-ordinated press releases on his work. His voice was described as "dark, deep and full of secrets." And his "Views on the News" came in for much praise.[65] It was also emphasised how, before revealing it on air, his identity had constantly intrigued so many British listeners. Who was this broadcaster so often serving up "a pretty dish of salty truths for them to savour" in the evenings, someone seemingly better informed than *The Times*?[66]

> Lord Haw-Haw! The name raced through Britain . . . through the Empire . . . Professors became excited whether he had studied at Oxford or Cambridge, reporters attempted to tear away the mask of anonymity.[67]

In June 1942, consistent with such praise, Joyce was appointed Chief Commentator in the English language service and assumed this position the following month.[68] The "Struttin, chinjuttin, fingerpokin . . . Nicotinal . . . pullover-and-blacksuited . . . schoolmasterish [Joyce] . . . The lord expectant of the Britannic Isles, *Adolpho gratia* . . ." had finally been fully recognised.[69] How appropriate his office door should carry the sign: "Bitte Klopfen" (please knock).[70] He could now strut more than ever.[71] He could eat and drink the best Berlin offered.[72] And if, as he expected, Germany regained its early momentum and Britain fell, there would be even more to savour.

By August 1942 he had become the "anchor of announcers," an effective warrior for Germany, always totally inspired by a "holy belief" in National Socialism and Adolf Hitler.[73] How far, how quickly, he had travelled since his early uncertain contact with Nazi radio officials in September 1939.

Official reports, not made public, struck a similar note. Successful propaganda never came easily. By now the number of Americans employed by the Propaganda Ministry had increased, but since recruiting broadcasters with an accent-free and intelligible approach had proved difficult, the Nazis remained disappointed by their material beamed to the United States.[74] Joyce's efforts were in a different league. His broadcast on 30 November 1942 was classified as "ausgezeichnet" (excellent), that on 4 December "fabelhaft" (fabulous), three days later his talk was "vorbildlich" (exemplary), and on 11 December "erstklassig" (first class).[75]

Outside the broadcasting studios Joyce assisted the Nazis in other ways – which have gone unrecognised.[76] In late 1942 he was introduced to readers of *Die Judenfrage in Politik, Recht, Kultur und Wirtschaft* as a pioneer anti-Semite – "antijüdischer Vorkämpfer" – and well-equipped therefore to offer a current analysis of Anglo-Jewry. He proceeded to tell them of a Britain groaning under the sheer weight of Jewish control, citing Viscount Rothermere's withdrawal of support for the BUF as convincing proof of their long-standing malign influence. "In ihrer Hand liegt eine ungeheure Macht," he wrote.[77] How pleasurable it was to be working in a country where Hitler had tamed this formidable enemy.

Joyce had by now evidently succeeded in building a new base in Berlin. Unlike a Cold War defector to East Germany, he had no reason to ask: "Where is the omelette?"[78] He seemed to have gambled successfully. The Germans had not achieved their hoped-for knock-out victory in the east. But they remained powerful and dominated much of Europe. And importantly for him, he was at the centre of the action. He had also done well financially. He earned far more than other broadcasters and many German workers.[79] Moreover, his salary provided only part of the picture. Eduard Dietze, head of the North-West Broadcasting Zone – which between 1941 and 1945 included Britain – declared Margaret Joyce's payment was essentially a supplement to her husband's income. She offered nothing to the Reich. In Dietze's blunt words, she "was not a very good speaker."[80]

When Joyce was luxuriating in his new, successful, well-paid life, patting himself on the back for his foresight in going to Berlin, did images of former comrades now interned in Britain flash his mind? His privileged access to British sources guaranteed he knew of their fate. As did Margaret. On 23 May 1940, she noted in shaky spelling, "Mosley, Ramsey and Becket have been interned."[81] Did he believe some deserved their detention because, lacking backbone, they had not followed him to Berlin? He would hardly have worried over his old rival, Neil Francis-Hawkins. Did he envisage being reunited with certain former comrades in a Nazi Britain? Did he recall John Macnab and how, when in August 1939 they had dissolved the National Socialist League, he had instructed 'Master' to continue with his activities in a fascist underground?

4

Until 1942 Joyce must have felt well pleased by his momentous decision to make Berlin the centre of his operations. But his circumstances were about to change dramatically. He would soon be operating in a far more challenging environment.

Notes

1 A. Fredborg, *Behind the Steel Wall* (London, 1944), p.215. Fredborg lived in Berlin until May 1943.
2 Shirer, *Berlin Diary*, pp.179, 180, 240.
3 KV 2/433, Banning to M. Dulige, 7 April 1941 (his Gestapo file). "Haw Haw sagte mir heute dass der Krieg in Europa im August beendet sein wird, aber ich habe meine zweifel."
4 E. Hadamovsky, "Warum London fallen muss. Stationen des deutschen Luftsieges," *Das Reich*, No.27, 24 November 1940. The metal imagery is in Shirer, *Berlin Diary*, p.273.
5 Descriptions of Stalin and Hitler from Low's *Evening Standard* cartoon, 20 September 1939.
6 Kershaw, *Fateful Choices*, pp.272 ff discusses the build-up. D. M. Glantz, *Barbarossa: Hitler's Invasion of Russia 1941* (Stroud, 2001), on the military campaign. A. Clark, *Barbarossa* (London, 1965), is an earlier controversial account. See also Evans, *Third Reich at War*, pp.178–190, Hastings, *Hell*,

ch.6, Beevor, *War*, ch.12. C. Bellamy, *Absolute War. Soviet Russia in the Second World War: A Modern History* (New York, 2007), discusses the War from the Soviet side.

7 R. Andreas-Friedrich, *Berlin Underground 1939–1945* (London, 1948), p.64, diary, 23 June 1941. Napoleon launched his attack on 24 June 1812.

8 Mazower, *Hitler's Empire*, pp.139–140.

9 H. F. Richardson (ed.), *Sieg Heil! The War Letters of Tank Gunner Karl Fuchs 1937–1941* (Hamden, Conn., 1987), letters of 5 July 1941 (p.116) and 3 August 1941 (p.123).

10 Hesse, *Hitler and the English*, p.107.

11 *Berliner Morgenpost*, 22 June 1941, paraded the headline, "Russlands Verrat an Europa entlarvt" (Russia's European treachery unmasked).

12 Clark, "Open Wounds," p.107.

13 KV 2/346, 22 June 1941.

14 F. Beckett, *Stalin's British Victims* (Stroud, 2004), pp.100–101.

15 Fredborg, *Steel Wall*, p.33.

16 Evans, *Third Reich at War*, pp.189–190.

17 KV2/250 for details in German and English.

18 Baillie-Stewart, *Officer in the Tower*, p.151.

19 BBC Monitoring Service, BREM IEFE, 13.30, 27 June 1941.

20 Flannery, *Assignment to Berlin*, p.262.

21 YCAL, MSS 43, BOX 32, Folder 1337, correspondence Macnab and Pound, especially an undated letter from Onslow Gardens. Folder 1338 for letters of 23 March 1937, 11 April, 1937, 18 July 1937, 27 July 1937.

22 YCAL, MSS 43, Box 26, Folder 1117, Pound to Joyce, 18 July 1941. KV 2/875/33a, 34a, 35a, for Pound as the American Haw-Haw.

23 WJ to MJ, 5 December 1945.

24 YCAL, MSS 43, Box 26, Folder 1117, Joyce to Pound, 30 July 1941.

25 WJ to MJ, 26 December 1945.

26 H. Carpenter, *A Serious Character. The Life of Ezra Pound* (London, 1988), pp.592–594, reproduces letters.

27 WO 204/12841, memo, 24 September 1944.

28 Shirer, *Berlin Diary*, p.414.

29 Edwards, *Berlin Calling* discusses. See also R. Lucas, *Axis Sally: The American Voice of Nazi Germany* (Newbury, 2010).

30 Digitalcommons.law.uga/edu accessed 31 March 2015, which cites *Athens Observer*, 1 June 1995. Edwards, *Berlin Calling*, pp.41–56.

31 Rolo, *Radio Goes to War*, p.83.

32 Edwards, *Berlin Calling*, pp.41–56, particularly pp.51–56.

33 It appears in KV 2/249/91a and BBC Monitoring Service, ZEE IEFNA, 21 November 1941.

34 KV 2/249/91a emphasises.

35 BBC Monitoring Service, ZEE IEFNA, 21 November 1941.

36 KV 2/245/60a for his drinking in England.

37 Cole, *Lord Haw-Haw*, p.91

38 Clark, "Open Wounds," p.82. The drink was Westphalian gin.

39 KV 2/246/370B, 377B. Richard Kupsch, who worked with him, also commented in "Germany Calling," Historia Video, 1997.

40 KV 2/250, 28 February 1945.

41 KV 2/250, 13 March 1945.

42 KV 2/250, 16 April 1945.

43 KV 2/346, 26 January 1940.

44 KV 2/245/24a, report, 24 January 1937, for his playing around with women.

45 KV 2/246/382b. Eric Pleasants of the British Free Corps claimed to have had a relationship with her. See his *I Killed to Live* (London, 1957), p.51, for "Eileen Joyce" as he called her. *Hitler's Bastard*, eds. I. Sayer and D. Botting (Edinburgh, 2003), for a later account of his life.

46 KV 2/246/382B. KV 2/264, proceedings of a general court martial on Monday 26th November 1945. Gunner Francis Paul Maton, p.12.

47 KV 2/346, 15 April 1942.

48 KV 2/346, 13 January 1943.

49 Bergmeier and Lotz, *Hitler's Airwaves*, pp.103, 107.

50 KV 2/346, 12 August 1941.

51 *South London Observer*, 28 February 1941 reports his passing. His death certificate described him as "Formerly salesman. Electrical cleaners." When Joyce's mother died on 15 September 1944 she appeared as "widow of retired grocer." Queenie was concerned with status to the end.

52 KV 2/346/1 has Margaret Joyce's passport with the relevant stamp.

53 KV 2/346, 10 March 1942.

54 Cole, *Lord Haw-Haw*, p.213

55 Last, *Nella Last's War*, p.176, entry, 27 October 1941.

56 B. Magee, *Growing up in a War* (London, 2007), pp.126–127.

57 J. Goebbels, *Die Zeit ohne Beispiel: Reden und Aufsätze aus den Jahren 1939/40/41* (München, 1941).

58 Mak, *In Europe*, p.388.

59 Kershaw, *Fateful Choices*, p.290.

60 C. Malaparte, *Kaputt* (New York, 2005. First ed. 1944), p.214.

61 Obituary, *The Times*, 3 October 2008.

62 J. Erickson, *The Road to Stalingrad* (London, 2003), ch.7.

63 Roberts, *Storm of War*, p.193, emphasises that since Japan was the aggressor at Pearl Harbor, Germany was under no obligation to declare war on the United States.

64 "Hits of the 40s," tape (private archive).

65 *Kattowitzer Zeitung*, 1 May 1942. *Strasburger Neuste Nachrichten*, 2 August 1942.

66 *Kattowitzer Zeitung*, 1 May 1942.

67 *Schlesische Tageszeitung*, No.210, 1 August 1942.

68 KV 2/250 provides details of his appointment by Anton [Toni] Winkelkampner on 26 June 1942 at a salary of 1200 RM.

69 Clark, "Open Wounds," p.82.

70 Evidence, R. Kupsch, a fellow broadcaster, "Germany Calling," BBC Radio 4, 9 May 1991.

71 Imperial War Museum, Tape 10938, G. Vassiltchikov.

72 Kenny, *Germany Calling*, p.168; Farndale, *Haw-Haw*, p.149.

73 *Neue Zürcher Zeitung*, 12 July 1942.

74 Bundesarchiv, RKK 2100, Box 0486, File 07. Personal file of Dr Toni Winkelkempner, includes "Eine Denkschrift über die deutsche Rundfunkpropagand nach USA," 11 December 1942.

75 Bundesarchiv, R55/409, "Unsere Auslands Propaganda," Tendenzdienst, 30 November–12 December 1942.

76 Cole, *Lord Haw-Haw*; Kenny, *Germany Calling*; Farndale, *Haw-Haw*, remain silent.

77 W. Joyce, "England als Judenstaat," *Die Judenfrage in Politik, Recht, Kultur und Wirtschaft*, No.23, 1 December 1942, pp.257–258.

78 J. Peet, *The Long Engagement* (London, 1989), p.242.

79 Doherty, *Nazi Wireless Propaganda*, p.27; *New York Times*, 9 July 1945.

80 KV 2/428, Dietze to Skardon, 29 May 1945, p.5.

81 KV 2/346.

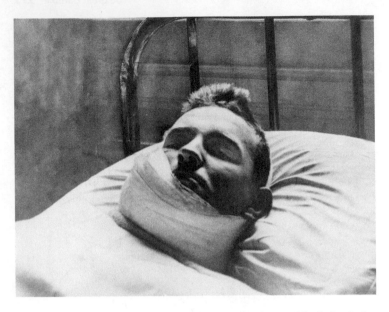

William Joyce. Here Joyce can be found in his hospital bed after being attacked during a 1924 election meeting in Lambeth. Then a member of the British Fascists, he was present there to support a Conservative candidate. Out of this incident Joyce created one of the many myths in his life.

Source: Getty Images – Bentley Archive/Popperfoto/Contributor

Margaret Joyce. William Joyce's second wife. They met through their joint involvement in British fascist politics and married in 1937. She went with Joyce to Germany and broadcast without distinction for the Nazis. She survived the War, was never put on trial, and died in London in 1972.

Source: The National Archives UK, KV 2/346

William Joyce. Some surviving photographs of Joyce soften his pronounced facial scar or present him in alternative profile. This picture makes no attempt to hide what Joyce would often call his "Lambeth honour," or at other times "die Schramme."

Source: The National Archives UK, KV 2/246

John Macnab. Macnab, whom Joyce would often call 'Master,' met Joyce through the British Union of Fascists when they attached themselves to Oswald Mosley. He became Joyce's closest friend and truly believed his beloved William was a man of destiny. Unlike Joyce, Macnab did not depart for Berlin. He left England after the War and died in 1977 in Spain.

Source: Robert Vavra Photographs and Correspondence, James A. Michener Special Collections, University of Northern Colorado.

John Beckett. This former Labour MP became one of Joyce's close political allies for much of the 1930s. Here he is shown addressing a meeting called by the BUF candidate, Charles Wegg-Prosser, during the 1937 East London elections.

Source: Photo. obtained from Francis Beckett

Leonard Banning. Banning, a former language teacher who had arrived in Germany before the start of the Second World War, became one of Joyce's broadcasting colleagues in wartime Berlin. He is one of the most intriguing and elusive of these renegades.

Source: The National Archives UK, WO 204/12856

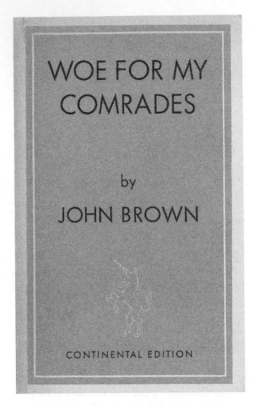

WOE FOR MY
COMRADES

by

JOHN BROWN

CONTINENTAL EDITION

Woe for my Comrades. Leonard Banning wrote this book in 1944
as part of the Nazi war effort. The text proved difficult for the security
service to trace at the end of the War and it remains a rare commodity.
When MI5 eventually secured a copy it seriously impressed its officer
Gilbert Wakefield then working on Banning's case.

Source: Continental edition of the book, 1944.

John Amery [second on left]. He was the rackety son of the well-known Conservative politician Leo Amery. During the War Amery was instrumental in forming the British Free Corps. He also broadcast and involved himself in other work for the Nazis. Here he is seen drinking with German officers and Belgian collaborators. After the War he pleaded guilty to treason and was executed.

Source: The National Archives UK, HO 45/25773

Theodore Schurch. Schurch was born into an Anglo-Swiss family in London. He developed some fascist links in the 1930s and then during the War worked for the Axis powers. Subsequently, he went on trial in Britain and was one of the three renegades to be executed.

Source: The National Archives UK, WO 204/13021

Jonah Barrington and Haw-Haw. The dust cover of a book published in 1939 by Jonah Barrington who created the character Lord Haw-Haw. The work was found in Joyce's possessions after he had been wounded and seized by British troops in 1945.

Source: Published by Hutchinson, 1939.

Witnesses. Captain Alexander Lickorish (left) was in charge of the soldiers who captured Joyce at Flensburg. He is shown here with Jim Skardon, a police officer seconded during the War to MI5, who had interrogated Joyce at Lüneberg. Both men gave crucial evidence at Joyce's trial.

Source: Photo. obtained from Mrs Heather Lickorish

Professor Hersch Lauterpacht. Lauterpacht, a distinguished authority on International Law, played a vital, behind-the-scenes role in identifying the legal arguments presented against Joyce at his trial in 1945. To an extent the prosecution's case became heavily reliant on his advice. He continued to believe Joyce was guilty of treason.

Source: Cambridge Law Library. With thanks to Sir Elihu Lauterpacht

Mr Justice Tucker. During a sensational case in 1940 Tucker had declared that Joyce was traitor. In 1945 when Joyce stood before him at the Old Bailey Tucker's interpretation of the law on passports and treason told powerfully against the arguments of the defence.

Source: Trial of William Joyce edited by J. W. Hall (London, 1946). William Hodge publishers.

The grave in Galway. In 1976 Joyce's remains were taken from the grounds of Wandsworth prison and reburied in Galway where in the early twentieth century he had lived with his parents and siblings. The grave is to be found in the Protestant section of Bohermore cemetery.

Source: Photo. taken by the author

William Joyce the Nazi. By 1939 Joyce had become totally swept up in Nazism and Hitler's political career. He was bonding increasingly with the Nazis, adopting a Prussian parade ground manner, and even modelling himself physically on the Führer.

Source: The National Archives UK, KV 2/346

13

THE BEGINNING OF THE END

To every *thing there* is a season, and a time to every purpose under the heaven. . . . A time to kill and a time to heal . . . A time to get and a time to lose; a time of war and a time of peace. [*Ecclesiastes*, 3, verses 1–8. (Italics in the original.)]

1

Berlin, 3 February 1943. The sounds of Beethoven on the radio begin to fade. Then there is silence. An important announcement is imminent. The Sixth Army under Field Marshal Friedrich Paulus has surrendered at Stalingrad.[1] A wave of utter disbelief sweeps the country. Three days of national mourning are ordered and Horcher's and other luxury restaurants are officially closed down.[2] This defeat is a monumental setback to all Hitler's ambitions and plans.

2

Paul Briscoe, son of British fascist Norah Briscoe, now living with German foster parents, was stunned.[3] In contrast, the news pleased Victor Klemperer in Dresden, but he worried that in revenge the Nazis might launch a pogrom.[4] Miles from home, an unknown soldier in Stalingrad recognised that "the hell on the Volga" was "the writing on the wall."[5]

This "great turn of the tide on the Eastern Front" posed a major challenge for the Nazis.[6] How could this defeat be presented to a home front suffering from increased Allied bombing, growing food shortages and, to make matters worse, the onset of a Siberian-style winter?[7] When German troops had marched expectantly, if apprehensively, into Soviet territory, Goebbels had remarked that in their hands they held the flame of humanity.[8] He recognised, however, the invasion was a high risk venture.[9] Now it had come adrift, Nazi propagandists faced "one of their most delicate wartime assignments."[10]

Goebbels quickly decided to steel the nation's resolve.[11] On 18 February 1943, at a stage-managed meeting in the Sportpalast, he urged the nation to engage in total war – whatever that might mean. His rallying cry, "Nun Volk, steh auf, und Sturm brich los" [People rise up and let the storm break loose], received a rapturous standing reception. In this defiant mood, he finally ordered the shooting of *Kolberg*, with its image of Prussians battling against Napoleon and securing victory against all the odds.[12] In private, however, he was far less sanguine. That autumn he was telling Hitler the Reich had never won a war on two fronts.[13]

Joyce acknowledged later that Stalingrad was a monumental tragedy.[14] When closer to that defeat, he responded by drawing on sentiments he had nurtured for years. Soldiers could be replaced. The key to victory lay in the moral rather than the physical sphere:

> the German people . . . . believe with a confidence not to be shaken, with a faith not to be weakened, that it is their honour and privilege to deliver this Continent forever from the menace of Bolshevism, and henceforth, with the help and guidance of their Government, under the leadership of their beloved Fuehrer, they will wage total war with a grim and terrible strength which, if it cannot bring back the men of Stalingrad, will none the less gain what they died to win. The whole of the German people today do not regard these heroes as gone, as vanished, as erased. They do not regard their gallant defenders as gone like the ripples on the surface of a pond, but rather do they think that these warriors are marching with them in spirit, watching over them and waiting to see their work accomplished, waiting

before they take their rest on the fulfilment of their trust by the many millions who are left behind.[15]

His rhetoric, cheap sounding on reflection, was a clutching at straws.

3

Soon after Stalingrad, problems increased for the arrogant, seemingly invincible Germans. They were shaken at Pesach 1943 by the Warsaw ghetto uprising. The following July the Wehrmacht failed to break the Soviets in the massive tank battle at Kursk.[16] That month Allied planes firebombed Hamburg.[17] Other major cities, including Berlin, faced unrelenting air attacks.[18] The same year British forces vanquished Rommel in North Africa and increased their grip in the Mediterranean; they could now begin to push into Italy. On 8 September 1943 the Italian government surrendered. On 6 June 1944 the D-Day landings were launched. The Second Front, the invasion of occupied Western Europe, was finally underway. On 1 August 1944, as Rokossovsky's Red Army troops closed in on their city, the Poles in Warsaw, sensing German vulnerability, rose up against their oppressors; it took "sixty-three days of savagery" to crush them.[19] These fast-moving events on land, growing Allied supremacy at sea and unrelenting air attacks tightened the noose around Nazi Germany's neck.[20] But between 1943 and 1945 the Allies had to fight many hard battles, endure major setbacks. Victory was not inevitable. The charismatic rule of the Third Reich proved remarkably resilient.[21] Joyce became caught up in these decisive events; his life moved forward at an increasingly rapid pace and his fortunes underwent a dramatic change.

4

Despite mountainous, sometimes self-inflicted casualties, after Stalingrad the Red Army had started to inch Westwards. In 1812 Napoleon had retreated from Russia, his dreams of conquest vanquished. Would Hitler face a similar fate? Nazi propaganda had long dwelt on the Bolshevik threat to Europe. The recent Soviet advance heightened such fears and Joyce and other propagandists were instructed to focus attention on this Red threat.[22] The barbarism and tyranny of the Steppes would rip the heart out of European civilisation.[23] He duly presented the many sacrifices in Stalin's city as part of the price that had to be paid for "the salvation of Europe."[24]

Just when the Nazis needed to reinforce their claims on the Bolshevik threat, they received help from an unexpected quarter. News began to break of the Katyń massacre.

Back in 1940 an estimated 22,000 members of the Polish elite had been brutally murdered in an area close to Smolensk, but their bodies lay undiscovered until 1943. The Soviets accused the Nazis. The latter charged the Soviets and exploited the massacre to emphasise the hideous nature of their foe. A film, *Im Wald von Katyn*, Nazi newspapers and radio, all emphasised it. Katyń must be converted into a cause célèbre. Hitler and Goebbels agreed on this point.[25] It was just what they needed.

Joyce never doubted the Bolsheviks were culpable, and Soviet materials released under *glasnost* confirmed the killings had indeed been carried out on Stalin's orders, a fact graphically conveyed in Andrzej Wajda's 2007 film *Katyń*.[26]

When the massacre was uncovered in 1943, Joyce viewed the brutality in the woods near Smolensk as a terrible warning:

> Never has there been a move flagrant abuse of human credulity than the Jewish attempt to convince the British people that Bolshevism is harmless. How harmless it is the thousands of corpses dug up in that pine forest near Smolensk will testify, with a silence more expressive than words could be.[27]

This Red threat, heavily emphasised in his pre-war speeches and writings, had assumed an even more threatening shape.[28] He conveniently overlooked the atrocities committed by the Nazis.

5

In 1943, with the Nazis under increasing pressure, it has been suggested Joyce might have assumed more responsibilities than previously realised.

An Irish radio service from Germany went on air in 1939 and began transmitting in English in 1941. This small-scale operation was staffed by German academics, Irish expatriates, including the novelist Francis Stuart, and a smattering of other nationalities.[29]

Susan Hilton, captured en route from Britain to Burma, appeared on the station from January 1942 as Susan Sweeney – having worked since September 1941 on Radio Caledonia as Ann Tower. Described as 'unstable', probably a coded reference to her lesbianism, and a heavy drinker, she proved vulnerable to Nazi pressures. But she also had a fascist past. Some Mosleyites went over to Hitler quite easily. Hilton had joined the BUF in 1936, resigned in 1938, rejoined in 1940, and with Charlie Watts edited *Voice of the People*.[30] She and Joyce had known each other in Britain.[31] Hilton not only broadcast; in Vienna she also allegedly assisted the Gestapo.[32]

Francis Stuart was the biggest name among the broadcasters to Ireland. In *Black List, Section H* he recalled visiting the Irish Ambassador's Berlin residence to hear Nazi radio.[33] But he did more than listen. He began broadcasting on St Patrick's Day 1942 and continued until 1944.[34] The German Foreign Ministry also employed him to write scripts for Joyce. However, since he focused on British atrocities in Ireland, their relationship never warmed.[35] Joyce's dealings with other Irish recruits were, for the most part, equally cold.[36]

Speculation surrounding Joyce's work has centred on talks a Patrick Joseph Cadogan delivered between 2 May and 1 October 1943. David O'Donoghue, who diligently assembled this evidence, remained uncertain whether the broadcaster was Joyce, and concluded: "Half a century after the war, mystery still surrounds the phantom broadcaster's true identity."[37] Official sources, released later, reveal he had been following a potentially important yet false trail.[38] Cadogan was Patrick Joseph Dillon, born in Glasgow in 1906 and captured by the Germans in 1940.[39]

6

Joyce was not Cadogan but the last two years of the War saw him keeping up an impressive schedule of work. On 7 June 1944, speaking after D-Day, he warned of a disaster awaiting the British, and

Churchill personally. He made no direct reference to Churchill's ill-fated First World War Gallipoli adventure, but implicitly forecast a similar humiliation:

> Naturally it must be allowed that the German Supreme Command is in a superior position with regard to the appreciation of the military situation on the Normandy coast. The defences have been systematically prepared for more than three years. The German commanders have perfected their knowledge of the country and have organised their communications with the thoroughness which the enemy sometimes likes to describe as 'Prussian'.... In dealing with the German Supreme Command, Mr Churchill is not dealing with the class of junior field officers at Camberley.[40]

Joyce filed additional comment on D-Day for the *Voelkischer Beobachter*, which introduced him to its readers as Oswald Mosley's former propaganda chief and the world's most widely-heard radio commentator. He wrote of a Britain heavily weighed down by war-weariness ("kriegsmüdigkeit") but offered no hope it would suddenly collapse. However, if only the German people held on, they might win through.[41] All that earlier euphoria fuelled by the scent of victory had gone. One of his tasks now was to raise the spirits of the German people.

7

This tactic further became evident when Joyce and other Nazi propagandists began to claim that Germany would regain the initiative in the War by exploiting its expertise in military technology.[42] In 1944 "miracle weapons propaganda" became the vogue.[43] The young Paul Briscoe's hopes soared on hearing of such weaponry.[44] Goebbels also had his spirits lifted.[45] Capturing this optimism, Joyce told British audiences in June that year:

> Germany's military policy in this war is based ... upon a scientific economy and application of energy. .... It can reasonably

be assumed that the battle in the East against the Bolshevik foes of civilisation will be hard and fierce and there is every reason to believe that the battle in the West against the capitalist agents of Jewish international finance will attain a climax of violence possibly without precedence. But in the closing rounds of this war it will be seen that Germany has conserved her strength to a degree that will confound her enemies.[46]

Ursula von Kardoff remained sceptical; people had been reading too much Jules Verne.[47]

This propaganda played on understandable British anxieties. During the summer of 1944 southern England was suddenly gripped by fear as cigar-shaped V-1 missiles fired from Europe began hitting the country, leading Harold Nicolson to write on 14 June: "There have been mysterious rocket-planes falling in Kent. The thing is very hush at the moment."[48] That autumn V-2 rockets, another awesome threat, sped silently through the skies before their power cut out and they fell to the ground to wreak their random destruction.[50] As these missiles continued to land, James Lees-Milne — architectural historian, conservationist, and in the '30s fascist fellow traveller — whose typewriter was always chattering away, wondered how much more "sheer damnable devilry" awaited the country.[51]

8

While striving to raise civilian morale, Nazi propaganda attempted to divide the Allied coalition.[52] As early as 6 November 1941, before America had entered the War, OSS monitors had recorded Joyce suggesting that the US was neatly positioned to capitalise on Britain's weakness. In a radio sketch allegedly set in London's clubland he claimed the conflict would lead to Britain becoming the forty-ninth state of the American Union. "Apart from giving them colonies, shares, bases, and our trading rights in South America and the Empire, the cads are asking for cash, as well." The Star of Zion had triumphed; what he typically called "a swindle of financiers" in New York had every reason to be pleased.[53] His inference was clear; Britain would be less damaged in a Nazi Europe.[54]

By 1944 Britain's financial indebtedness to the US had increased enormously and that autumn Joyce claimed a major conflict of interests was therefore brewing. American troops were fighting alongside 'Tommy,' but the US could not be trusted. That same year in a Hamburg publication he recalled his mother's dislike of Americans – her influence never left him – and suggested the British would soon become similarly disaffected. But, as in 1941, he added a Jewish dimension. Unless Britain woke up to the peril of sharing a political bed with America, he reiterated it would become reduced to the status of a mere colony controlled by Hebrew finance.[55]

The growing contemporaneous emphasis by Nazi propaganda on the Soviet threat was not only for domestic consumption. It, too, was aimed at splitting of the Allies. And as fears grew regarding Stalin's future intentions some politicians, including Churchill, contemplated a pre-emptive post-war strike to save the world from Communism.[56] Had he known of "Operation Unthinkable," Joyce would have welcomed these discussions but doubtless complained it was all 'too little, too late.'

9

In these difficult days for the Reich, Joyce's services were recognised by a civilian honour when on 1 September 1944 he received the Cross of War Merit, First Class. However, the occasion was marred for him because Hitler did not present it personally. He was "not flattered" by having to receive it from the "quick-witted, keen, ambitious" Dr Werner Naumann, Secretary of State in the Ministry of Propaganda, who earlier, responding to Joyce's request, had despatched him "a few cases of very good cigars."[57] Naumann had long been influential in Goebbels's circle and Hitler's political testament of 29 April 1945, which nominated Goebbels as Chancellor, also had Naumann as the new Propaganda Chief.[58]

By late '44 the Führer had far weightier matters than award ceremonies pressing on his increasingly fragile frame. Germany's situation was becoming increasingly dire and in these deteriorating circumstances Joyce was conscripted into the Volkssturm, the equivalent of the British Home Guard. From 21 December 1944 he was attached to the District V Battalion, Wilhelmplatz.[59] The would-be British Army recruit, once ready and eager to draw his sword on the King's enemies, was now swearing allegiance to "the Führer of the Greater German Reich" and being assigned to defend a Germany pushed back in the West and menaced from the East by the Red Army.[60] His boast in early 1941 to Leonard Banning that the War would soon be over and a victorious Germany would take charge of Europe, now appeared completely hollow.[61] The odds-on favourite was looking increasingly like a rank outsider.

10

By early 1945 Germany's position was becoming ever more desperate. The Red Army was still rolling relentlessly forward. On 27 January it had liberated Auschwitz. Berlin still lay miles ahead, but Soviet military thinking remained sharply focused on capturing it. In Western Europe the Allies were also fiercely engaged in land battles. While overhead American and British bombers loaded with their heavy instruments of death and destruction clogged the skies, now even in the hours of daylight.

That February, a fortnight after the heavy bombing of Dresden, Joyce, gnawingly hungry and desperate for alcohol, can be found huddling for safety in an underground shelter:

> It is 12.08. There seems to be a never-ending raid on Berlin. A whole procession is passing over us . . . I think that the proceedings may be very lengthy. It seems as if the whole bloody menagerie were being paraded. What worries me is lunch. I could almost eat the fxxxxxx Bunker. Whilst some bombers are over here, the tail of the procession is near Bremen.[62]

Earlier raids he had bravely watched above ground, with American reporters Bill Shirer and Joseph Harsch, curious, fascinated, admiring, had been no more than preliminary pinpricks. In the War's final stages Ruth Andreas-Friedrich, living in Berlin, remarked on the "toppling and crashing, quaking, bursting [and] trembling" that became a feature of everyday life.[63] Another ominous problem also loomed. "Zhukoff has issued street maps of Berlin," Joyce recorded in his notebook on 3 March 1945.[64] The Red Army's assault on the capital would not be long delayed.[65] Berlin would soon be at the mercy of the dreaded Soviets.[66]

Initially a rather surreal mood might have prevailed there.[67] Which was probably a fatalistic acceptance.[68] But many Berliners soon began to shudder at what might lie ahead.[69] Why not, when Katyń had been followed in October 1944 by the Nemmersdorf massacre?[70] Why not, considering the ceaseless anti-Soviet propaganda with which the German public had been drenched since Stalingrad? How would women survive face to face with Red Army soldiers seeking revenge for the barbarism committed on the Soviet Union and hearing the dreaded command: "Komm Frau!"?[71]

11

By March 1945 conditions in bombed-out, falling-apart, tottering Berlin had deteriorated still further. Most people there found that many basic necessities had simply disappeared or were in short supply. The heavily camouflaged Funkhaus, with its mock rural roof scene, designed to fool enemy bombers, remained unscathed. But by now the state of the capital was such that radio personnel were transferred to Apen near the Dutch frontier.[72] Joyce did not relish this move in the slightest. "The lack of alcohol . . . will be AWFUL."[73]

In a rapidly changing military situation, he, Margaret and other radio staff, were soon on the move again, this time from Apen to Hamburg.[74] With the Reich collapsing around him, Joyce received his final false passport. He became Wilhelm Hansen, a German citizen and language teacher, born in Galway on 11 March 1906.[75] To allay suspicion, it was backdated: "Hamburg, 3 November 1944."[76] Mrs Hansen shared this passport. He was advanced three months' salary; 'on the run' he would need resources.[77] This arrangement suggests no special plans were in place to save them. They did not feature among that elite group for whom devious rat lines were constructed. In 1921 Joyce had secured a safety route out of Ireland, courtesy of Captain Keating; the Nazis offered him nothing beyond a fabricated passport. He and Margaret would have to scramble to survive as best they could among an ever-growing mass of former Nazi servants cast adrift as Germany fragmented and Europe descended into ever-increasing chaos. Even Erich Hetzler, that inter-war middleman between British fellow travellers and Berlin, and later Joyce's important close broadcasting colleague, had to grab something as basic as a bicycle to reach greater safety.[78]

12

The final days of the Reich were now rapidly approaching. On 21 April 1945 Margaret scribbled in her diary: "RUSSIANS SHELLING BERLIN." Her capital letters speak volumes.[79] By this time Joyce fully recognised his great gamble had failed. "I shall be glad when this damned war is over," he wrote resignedly on 22 April. With "no alcohol, no tobacco – not enough food – why life is no better than penal servitude."[80]

Eight days later a fragile Hitler, pinned down by the Red Army, committed suicide in his Berlin bunker. Joyce heard the news the following day.[81] On the first of May Goebbels killed himself. "Goebbels is a genius – brilliant beyond words," Joyce had written shortly before.[82] He would later describe 'the little doctor' as "the greatest hero of the Götterdämmerung."[83] With the deaths of these new-found gods, who had succeeded the likes of Edward Carson, Joyce must have felt totally abandoned.

13

On 30 April, Joyce is still in Hamburg. To the East a fierce, bloody battle is raging for Berlin. His options are rapidly narrowing. He is worse for drink as he enters the broadcasting studios to make his "final, drunken, evidently extemporaneous, defiant, still sardonic and rather . . . magnificent" recording of the War.[84] His drink-oiled voice acknowledges Germany's loss of influence. The resurgent Soviets now threaten Western civilisation and he wonders – often thumping the desk for emphasis – how Europeans will survive without the determined support of the German legions. Britain, lukewarm about containing Bolshevism, deserves to suffer. By contrast, he confidently proclaims "Germany will live," rasping defiantly, "No coercion, no oppression, no measures of tyranny that any foreign foe can introduce, will shatter Germany" because the German people possess "the secret of life." He ends this infamous recording with the uncompromising cry: "Es Lebe Deutschland! Heil Hitler! And farewell!"[85]

Joyce makes no more recordings or broadcasts. That distinctive voice, which has sent shivers of fear through many British listeners, falls silent. In faraway Caversham Lorna Swire breathes a long-delayed sigh of relief. She and a colleague no longer have to monitor Joyce's efforts. "The end of his broadcasts meant that *both* of us could get early transport home."[86]

14

Joyce had different priorities. When he made his last, slurred recording, the War was continuing. With Allied troops relentlessly closing on Hamburg, the time had come for yet another move. In hasty retreat he and Margaret made their way along the increasingly crowded roads through the "flat uninteresting" countryside to Flensburg.[87] The literary Joyce might have recalled its association with Erskine Childers's *The Riddle of the Sands.* The conventional narrative has painted it as a necessary journey to assist their escape to neutral Scandinavia.[88] More likely they were again part of a general staff migration. General Jodl surrendered to General Eisenhower on 7 May 1945. But from Flensburg – "the last Nazi bolthole" – Admiral Doenitz administered the rump of a German government until 23 May.[89] Joyce, the fervent Hitlerite, stayed here with the Nazis to the end.

When Doenitz capitulated, the town was in turmoil. Thousands had descended, travelling as best they could, on foot, by horse, in motorised transport. This surging sea of disordered humanity included refugees, released POWs, criminals and fugitive Nazis, all desperately seeking a way out. Where would the Joyces run to? They did cross into Denmark. But the growing chaos in the Baltic prevented their passage to Sweden. They returned to Flensburg and stayed initially at the Bahnhofhotel. Ejected from there, they spent several days with Edward Bowlby, ex-BUF and fellow broadcaster, also trying to avoid capture. Bowlby's German girlfriend disliked the company that, unannounced, had suddenly descended and insisted he ask them to leave.[90] Normally, Joyce would never have tolerated such dismissive treatment. But these were hardly normal times. He and Margaret, abandoned, constantly arguing, trudged about, desperately seeking somewhere to stay. Eventually, they secured lodgings in the nearby hamlet of Kupfermühle. Their landlady was the English-born widow of a German she had married in England in 1914.[91] For the Joyces their War was over.

Notes

1 Bellamy, *Absolute War*, pp.507–553. Evans, *Third Reich at War*, pp.409–425. A. Beevor, *Stalingrad* (London, 1998). J. Erickson, *The Road to Berlin* (London, 2003), ch.1 is an excellent summary. Kershaw, *Hitler: Nemesis*, pp.543–550 discusses Stalingrad through Hitler's eyes. V. Grossman, *A Writer at War* (London, 2006) provides a Soviet eye-witness account. See generally, Hastings, *Hell*, pp.315–318, 320.

2 H-G. von Studnitz, *While Berlin Burns* (London, 1963), pp.7–9, diary, 1, 2, 4, February 1943.

3 Briscoe, *My Friend The Enemy*, p.139. On 16 June 1941 his mother, Norah Briscoe, was convicted at the Central Criminal Court under Defence Regulations and sentenced to five years' penal servitude. She had earlier been detained under Regulation 18B but released (HO 45/25741, KV 2/898–899 and KV 4/227). As Catherine Dee she later wrote novels and left an unrevealing unpublished autobiography, "Daemons and Magnets."

4 V. Klemperer, *To the Bitter End: The Diaries of Victor Klemperer 1942–45* (London, 2000), p.235, entry, 27 January 1943.

5 A. G. Powell (trans), *Last Letters from Stalingrad* (London, 1956), p.69.

6 G. Weinberg, *A World at Arms: A Global History of World War II* (Cambridge, 1994), p.454.

7 Stuart, *Manna in the Morning*, p.30. Klemperer, *To the Bitter End*, p.228, entry, 13 January 1943, on the "snow-covered icy streets in Dresden" and a temperature of minus 18 degrees.

8 Goebbels, *Die Zeit ohne Beispiel*, p.525, written 6 July 1941.

9 R. G. Reuth, *The Life of Joseph Goebbels: The Mephistophelean Genius of Nazi Propaganda* (London, 1993), p.291.

10 Baird, *Nazi War Propaganda*, p.187.

11 Boelcke (ed.), *Secret Conferences*, p.324 (27 January 1943).

12 Reuth, *Goebbels*, pp.342–343 reports Goebbels's belief in the strength of the will. R. Taylor, *Film Propaganda: Soviet Russia and Nazi Germany* (London, 1979), pp.216–218 on Kolberg and J. Fox, *Film Propaganda in Britain and Nazi Germany: World War II* (Oxford, 2007), pp.261–265. R. Moorhouse, *Berlin at War: Life and Death in Hitler's Capital 1939–45*

(London, 2010), pp.353–356 notes its premiere at the UFA cinema, Alexanderplatz, on 30 January 1945.

13   M. Kittel (ed.), *Die Tagebücher von Joseph Goebbels*, Vol.9, July–September 1943 (München, 1993), p.583, 23 September 1943.

14   WJ to MJ, 28 December 1945.

15   BBC Monitoring Service, BRES IEFUK, 22.30, 2 February 1943. See his "Analysis of Marxism," *Fascist Quarterly*, Vol.2 (1936), p.542.

16   Bellamy, *Absolute War*, pp.560–595; Hastings, *Hell*, pp.287–393; Beevor, *War*, ch.31.

17   K. Lowe, *Inferno: The Devastation of Hamburg, 1943* (London, 2007).

18   von Studnitz, *While Berlin Burns*, p.143, diary, 30 November 1943.

19   Davies, *God's Playground*, p.475. See A. Richie, *Warsaw 1944* (London, 2013), for a more recent account.

20   Weinberg, *World at Arms*, pp.667 ff, and Hastings, *Hell*, chs 14–24 particularly, on these developments.

21   I. Kershaw, *The End: Germany 1944–45* (London, 2011).

22   Ettlinger, *Axis on Air*, pp.71 ff.

23   J. Goebbels, *Der Steile Aufstieg: Reden und Aufsätze aus den Jahren 1942/43* (München, 1944), pp.172–173.

24   BBC Monitoring Service, BRES IEFUK, 22.30, 3 February 1943. See generally Kallis, *Nazi Propaganda*, ch.6.

25   H. Mehringer (ed.), *Die Tagebücher von Joseph Goebbels*, Vol.8, April–June 1943 (München, 1993), p.119, 17 April 1943. Semmler, *Goebbels*, pp.82–83, 12 April 1943 for comment from within Goebbels's circle.

26   Davies, *God's Playground*, pp.334–335, notes Soviet recognition of responsibility in 1990. See also *The Times*, 29 April 2010. J. K. Zawodny, *Death in the Forest* (New York, 1962), carries earlier comment. See more recently E. Maresch, *Katyń 1940* (Stroud, 2010).

27   BBC Monitoring Service, BRES IEFUK, 22.30, 15 April 1943.

28   On Katyń, he remarked later, "Who is going to try the Russkis for their K2 lager alone, not to say their Katyns?" WJ to MJ, 5 November 1945.

29   D. O'Donoghue, *Hitler's Irish Voices: The Story of German Radio's Wartime Irish Service* (Belfast, 1998), p.xii.

30   *Ibid*. pp.77 ff and Appendix II. S. Hilton, *Eine Irin erlebt England und den Seekrieg* (Hamburg, 1942).

31   KV 2/423, statement, 30 June 1945.

32   HO 45/25778 and KV 2/423. KV 2/423, MI5 report, 14 November 1945. Marietta Smart, also ex-BUF, engaged in similar work in France. See HO 45/25828, WO 204/12326 and WO 204/12697.

33   G. Elborn, *Francis Stuart: A Life* (Dublin, 1990), p.125.

34   B. Barrington (ed.), *The Wartime Broadcasts of Francis Stuart 1942–1944* (Dublin, 2000). Stuart can be heard reminiscing on tape, BBC Archive, 910630, National Sound Archive.

35   Stuart was interviewed in "Germany Calling," Historia Productions video, 1997. And see J. Cowley's profile of him in *Prospect*, February 1997, pp.26–29.

36 O'Donoghue, *Hitler's Irish Voices*, pp.43 and 57 on Stuart and Joyce. Elborn, *Francis Stuart*, p.125 for further confirmation. See also Ní Mheara-Vinard, *Cé hí seo Amuigh?* pp.197–202 and KV 2/423, statement by Susan Hilton, 30 June 1945.

37 O'Donoghue, *Hitler's Irish Voices*, p.125.

38 D. O'Donoghue to author, 20 June 2006.

39 KV 2/434, 435, 436 on Dillon.

40 BBC Monitoring Service, DES IEFUK, 22.30, 7 June 1944.

41 W. Joyce, "Die Stimmung in England," *Voelkischer Beobachter*, Muenchen und Sueddeutsche Ausgabe, No. 215, 2 August 1944.

42 Bramsted, *Goebbels*, pp.316–325 and Evans, *Third Reich at War*, pp.660–666. M. J. Neufeld, *The Rocket and the Reich: Peenemünde and the Coming of the Ballistic Missile Era* (New York, 1995).

43 Baird, *Nazi War Propaganda*, pp.218 ff.

44 Briscoe, *My Friend the Enemy*, p.154.

45 von Oven, *Mit Goebbels bis zum Ende*, Vol.2, p.54; Semmler, *Goebbels*, pp.128–131, 9,16,17 June 1944.

46 BBC Monitoring Service, DES IEFUK, 22.30, 24 June 1944.

47 U. von Kardoff, *Diary of a Nightmare: Berlin 1942–1945* (London, 1965), p.84, entry, 19 January 1944.

48 Nicolson, *Diaries and Letters 1939–45*, p.382.

49 Roberts, *The Storm of War*, pp.514–519; N. Longmate, *The Doodlebugs: The Story of the Flying Bombs* (London, 1981); A. Calder, *The People's War: Britain 1939–45* (London, 1986. First ed.1969); pp.562–563; J. Gardiner, *Wartime: Britain 1939–1945* (London, 2004), pp.547–564.

50 Photograph reproduced in *The Times*, 4 December 2008.

51 J. Lees-Milne, *Prophesying Peace* (London, 1986), p.80, writing on 18 June 1944 after a German rocket had hit the Guards' Chapel during a service. Lees-Milne appears in Matthew and Harrison (eds), *ODNB*, Vol.38, pp.298–299.

52 Ettlinger, *Axis on Air*, p.68.

53 NARA RG226 (OSS), entry 16, Box 42, Document 9763.

54 Ettlinger, *Axis on Air*, p.69.

55 *Hamburger Fremdenblatt*, 6 October 1944.

56 "After the War. Conquering Germany," BBC2, TV, 16 August 2005. Hastings, *Finest Years*, pp.571 ff, for more.

57 Boelcke (ed.), *Secret Conferences*, p.80, on Naumann's task. Irving, *Goebbels*, p.169, describes his qualities. Cole, *Lord Haw-Haw*, p.217, for Joyce's reaction to the ceremony.

58 Bergmeier and Lotz, *Hitler's Airwaves*, p.237 particularly. Naumann survived the War and, resuming his Nazi career, came into contact with Sir Oswald Mosley. J.W. Baird, "The Memoirs of Goebbels's Deputy, Dr Werner Naumann," is an unpublished account of his career. For his 1953 arrest, following his attempt to revive Nazism, see I. Kirkpatrick, *The Inner Circle. The Memoirs of Ivone Kirkpatrick* (London, 1959), pp.252–255 and P. Biddiscombe, *The Last Nazis: Werewolf Guerrilla Resistance in Europe*

1944–1947 (Stroud, 2000), pp.122–123. See, more substantially, G. J. Trittel, *"Man kann ein Ideal nicht verraten." Werner Naumann-NS-Ideologie und politische Praxis in der frühen Bundesrepublik* (Göttingen, 2013). A number of files on Naumann have recently been deposited in the National Archives at Kew.

59 His Volkssturm certificate is in KV2/250. See also Cole, *Lord Haw-Haw*, p.218.

60 Moorhouse, *Berlin at War*, pp.350–353.

61 KV 2/433, Banning to Dulige, 7 April 1941.

62 KV 2/250, 27 February 1945, for this dramatic entry. On Dresden, see the graphic eye-witness evidence in Klemperer, *To the Bitter End*, pp.496–507, written on 22–24 February 1945. See also Evans, *Third Reich at War*, pp.699–702.

63 Andreas-Friedrich, *Berlin Underground*, p.119, 21 June 1944.

64 KV 2/250, 3 March 1945. Zhukov, Deputy Commander-in-Chief of the Red Army, received the final capitulation of German forces.

65 A. Beevor, *Berlin: The Downfall 1945* (London, 2002).

66 Moorhouse, *Berlin at War*, pp.357 ff.

67 M. Hastings, *Armageddon: The Battle for Germany 1944–45* (London, 2004), p.504.

68 Kershaw, *The End*, pp.293–294.

69 Beevor, *Berlin*, Erickson, *Road to Berlin*; Hastings, *Armageddon*; Bellamy, *Absolute War*; Beevor, *War*; and C. Duffy, *Red Storm on the Reich: The Soviet March on Germany, 1945* (London, 1991), discuss the Red Army's progress.

70 Kershaw, *The End*, pp.112–117 on Nemmersdorf.

71 Anon, *A Woman in Berlin* (London, 1955). Discussed in *The Observer*, 5 October 2003, and *Sunday Telegraph*, 28 August 2005, it tells one woman's story and became a film in 2008. See *The Times*, 21 October 2008. Many Soviet soldiers carried a photograph of Zoya Kosmodemyanskaya, a teenage resistance fighter tortured and hanged by the Germans. They could then easier rationalise their revenge (Mak, *In Europe*, p.575). Kershaw, *The End*, pp.177–184, comments on fear of the Red Army. C. Merridale, *Ivan's War: The Red Army 1939–1945* (London, 2005), chapter 9, on attitudes of Soviet soldiers. See also M. Jalowicz Simon, *Gone to Ground* (London, 2015), for a Berlin Jewish woman having to survive danger from both the Nazis and the Soviets

72 KV2/250 on Joyce going to Apen on 29 March; Cole, *Lord Haw-Haw*, p.224.

73 KV 2/250, 13 March 1945.

74 Cole, *Lord Haw-Haw*, pp.228–229.

75 HO 45/25780/Exhibit 9.

76 Cole, *Lord Haw-Haw*, p.230.

77 KV2/250 provides some evidence of funds at the Flensburger Privatbank.

78 His bicycle escape features in Bergmeier and Lotz, *Hitler's Airwaves*, p.223.

79 KV 2/346, 21 April 1945.

80 KV2/250, diary entry for that day.

81 KV 2/250, 1 May 1945, "On this tragic day the death of Adolf Hitler was reported." For the Bunker in the final days see T. Junge, with M. Müller, *Until the Final Hour: Hitler's Last Secretary* (London, 2005), pp.158 ff. Her account provided the text for the film *Downfall*.

82 KV 2/250, 14 March 1945.

83 WJ to MJ, 2 October 1945.

84 Rattigan, British Library, Add MS 74490, f.3.

85 Imperial War Museum, Tape 5224, recorded 30 April 1945.

86 Lorna Swire to author, 22 January 2005.

87 E. Taverner, *These Germans* (London, 1937), pp.147–148.

88 Cole, *Lord Haw-Haw*, p.236.

89 Mazower, *Hitler's Empire*, pp.531 ff. D. Stafford, *Endgame 1945. Victory, Retribution, Liberation* (London, 2007), p.382.

90 KV2/346, 19 May 1945.

91 Cole, *Lord Haw Haw*, ch.27, discusses the Flensburg interlude.

14

HISTORY'S LOSER

All political lives, 'unless they are cut off in midstream at a happy juncture, end in failure, because that is the nature of politics and of human affairs. [J. Enoch Powell, *Joseph Chamberlain* (London, 1977), p.151.]

1

Joyce's new world had just collapsed. Not long before, Goebbels had lavished praise on his work. "The best horse in our stable," the Propaganda Minister had remarked in 1941.[1] But the one-time radio star could no longer strut in the broadcasting corridors. He was now a ragged fugitive, on the run from the Allies. Why did the wheel of history have to turn this way? In his deserted old office, Studio No. 8 in the Funkhaus, Red Army soldiers found scripts and letters which today are presumably in the 'Trophy Archive' in Moscow. Some correspondents wrote from England. Who were they? What did they say? Littered across this forsaken den the military also discovered newspaper cuttings, material for future broadcasts, including extracts from the *Catholic Herald* and the *Financial News*.[2] Here lay the literary detritus of Joyce's short but spectacular radio career.

2

Charles Chevenix Trench, or possibly C. C. Lewis, informed the British authorities that his broadcasts were "practically identical with his old speeches."[3] His impatience with the stuffy declining society, which he believed had sold him short; his hostility towards its smug politicians, especially Winston Churchill; his hatred of Bolshevism; these beliefs and emotions had travelled with him to Berlin. So had his titanic anti-Semitism. He continued to believe Britain was being thoroughly exploited by the Jews, a truly despicable race, a social misfortune. "The Great Day," which he wrote in 1944, contained the lines:

> Oh D-Day was a great day, when they gathered up the loot
> These money-grubbing Hebrews who'd never launched a 'chute
> While England's lads were dying amidst the hellish roar
> And their heroes' blood was drying on the fatal Norman shore.[4]

Here the former student of English literature was drawing inspiration, perhaps subconsciously, from Hilaire Belloc. His effort also carried shades of a literary effort by his old contact, Captain Ramsay.[5] Joyce, like the Nazi pornographer Julius Streicher, never wasted an opportunity to attack the Jews.[6]

3

Early in 1945, realising defeat was imminent, Joyce began to record his everyday thoughts, which are revealing, politically and personally.

He continued to believe National Socialism was "a splendid doctrine" but concluded the Germans lacked the capacity to convert others. "I am afraid that, rather against my will," he wrote, "I have become cynical."[7] With Germany certain to lose the War – "we have made a complete balls of it" – and his protectors gone, he recognised that the victors would demand revenge.[8] Confronted by this grim prospect, he protested, "I still love England and hate to think that I am to be regarded as a traitor to her, which, in my opinion I am not."[9] Never lacking courage, he also remarked, "I can take any punishment that is coming to me."[10] And to think too, it could have turned out so differently. "If only I had been near the old man [Hitler], it [Germany's defeat] would never have happened," he declared, massively self-regarding as ever. "The war would have been over 4 years ago."[11] Germany would have been victorious and Joyce would have secured his due political legacy.

The Nazis, though, had not appreciated his enormous ability, all his unremitting "horsework."[12] "My employers," he wrote in March 1945, "are *mean*, undiscerning buggers. They have *no* idea how to get good work out of a man. They have the proletarian mentality – poor things."[13] A few days later, he even dared to ask himself the key question: "Has it all been worthwhile?" To which he gave a brief, honest, revealing answer: "I think not."[14] His biggest political bet had failed.

Margaret lived through these growing pressures and frustrations. But especially towards the end of the War, Joyce drew little comfort from her. Even after they had remarried his thoughts turned to other lovers, to happier times. He recalled life with Hazel.[15] He mused on his affair with the young, impressionable Mary Ogilvy, and remarked," I think I am luckier in the marriages I did not contract than in those I did."[16] More than his political hopes and aspirations had run aground.

The following month, still thinking of Margaret, he sermonised in his blue-backed notebook: "She always wants to be clever and is too clever," before adding, "Her cheap repartee is very derogatory to her own dignity. . . . I may be most unjust but much as I love her subjectively I find her objectively not merely difficult but almost impossible."[17] Soon afterwards he returned to the attack: "She does not know it but she has quite lost her hold on me and once I have got her out safe, well – she can exercise her sex-appeal for what it is worth!" He must have paused here before writing, "I am sorry to be bitter, but now that she is sexually useless, it is possible for me to judge her character on its merits and it is not the sort of character that suits me. She constantly over-bids her trumps."[18] And why was he, an important person with so many talents, keeping the company of a woman with a memory like a sieve?[19] She had clearly, decisively, failed the tests he had set for her. He would certainly not have been amused had he noticed an entry in her diary to "FAT WILL'S 38th BUFFDAY."[20] Where was the reverence he deserved and demanded?

He did not restrict these bruising assaults to his notebook. He told Margaret to her face in the summer of 1943, not long after they had remarried, that it was "too late" for her "to become a whore."[21] And remarked quite brutally the following year she was now just "an old hag."[22]

When surveying all this accumulated emotional debris he wondered whether their relationship was "pathological."[23] Perhaps he never realised it consciously, but he needed a docile political disciple who would also submit to his sexual demands whilst telling him how wonderful he was. Present-day social science would say he required an "undefined, absorbable, moldable, sometimes rescuable" woman, an object, a receptacle for his needs.[24] His ideal was a worshipping "trophy wife."[25] Margaret was not that person. But he did not discard her, as threatened. A reconciliation of sorts – previously much misunderstood – did come about. He resolved to recreate their relationship. But only for his ends. He would appoint her as his biographer. In which role she would hopefully guarantee his rightful place in history and, at the same time, might just manage to redeem herself.[26]

When he compiled his notebook, sometimes in an erratic drunken scrawl, the Third Reich lay in ruins, physically and metaphorically. His private life was in turmoil. How dramatically his world had changed since he and Margaret had arrived so optimistically at the Friedrichstrasse station in late August 1939. Two years earlier, Edward Windsor and Mrs Wallis Simpson had alighted at this terminus.[27] They had their later difficulties. But hardly on the same scale as the Joyces.

4

With the milling chaos in Flensburg Joyce might easily have avoided detection. Some leading Nazis proved remarkably elusive. Margaret would have been even more invisible. Yet the gods conspired against them, devoured them for their sport, with a little help from Joyce himself.

5

It is the evening of 28 May 1945. He quarrels – yet again – with Margaret. He needs time on his own. Wearing his brown tweed suit he sets off for a walk.[28] He sees some British army officers gathering firewood. The conventional account mentions two but, puzzlingly, a detailed MI5 report refers to three, one of them unnamed.[29]

Joyce simply cannot resist an opportunity to take centre stage. He needs to talk.[30] For him, as for Hitler, talking is "like a drug."[31] He speaks to the soldiers in French. "Il y a des morceaux ici". He gathers wood. He places it on their vehicle. Reverting to English, he tells them where they can find some more. It is a suicidal mistake.

The senior officer, the sharp-eared Captain Alexander Adrian Lickorish, formerly in the London Scottish and now in Army Intelligence, turns to his junior, Lieutenant Geoffrey Perry, saying he thinks he recognises the voice. There is a suspicion Joyce is somewhere in the area.[32] They might have stumbled on him.[33] But they need to be sure. Perry says to their helper, "You wouldn't be William Joyce, by any chance, would you?" or words to that effect. Joyce's hand dives instinctively towards his pocket intending to produce his German passport as Wilhelm Hansen. Perry, thinking he is reaching for a gun, points his own revolver and fires. Joyce falls wounded, exclaiming, "My name is Hansen."[34]

Lickorish dashes over to the seriously wounded man.[35] Who says "I am not armed."[36] His captors find on him the German civilian document in the name of Hansen and the military passport for William Joyce.[37] As befits an Intelligence Officer engaged on censorship duties, Lickorish remains discreet when writing to his wife, saying only that she might soon hear news of a prisoner he and Perry had just detained.[38]

6

After the War, Lickorish resumed his career in hotel administration before dying aged forty-six when managing the George Hotel at Hathersage.[39] He never capitalised on his role in Joyce's capture and refused all offers of lucrative after-dinner speeches. But he remained critical of his junior officer's trigger-happy action, believing Perry was fortunate to escape a court martial.[40] The events that day in Flensburg evidently stayed with him.[41]

Margaret was soon found, told of her husband's fate and arrested.[42] She complained: "They did not give me a chance to arrange my hair."[43] Thoroughly tired of the War and its traumas, she recorded its latest twists with a degree of resignation.[44] She had lasted longer than some renegades. But now sighed: "Thank God that's over."[45]

Her husband's future lay in the hands of the British authorities who, for some time, had been assembling a growing file on his activities. The omens were not good. He had speculated heavily and lost heavily. What strategies were open to him? What would happen to him? To answer these questions requires more to be said about Joyce's activities in Berlin and his related image in wartime Britain.

Notes

1 Fröhlich (ed.), *Tagebücher*, Vol. 9, December 1940–July 1941, p.210, "das ist auch unser bestes Pferd im Stall," 29 March 1941.
2 *Soviet Monitor*, 6 and 12 June 1945.
3 KV 2/247/487a. The *Irish Times*, 6 December 2003 carried a gentle obituary of Trench, whom Joyce knew in the Oxford University Fascist Association. Lewis, a political colleague and one-time friend, has already appeared in this story.
4 BBC Monitoring Service, DES IEFUK, 22.30, 22 June 1944.
5 H. Belloc, "Verses to a Lord who, in the House of Lords, said that those who opposed the South African Adventure confused soldiers with Money Grubbers"(1910?). Griffiths, *Patriotism Perverted*, pp.169–170, for Ramsay's effort, written 4 September 1939 on House of Commons notepaper.
6 WJ to MJ, 21 December 1945. L. Goldensohn, *The Nuremberg Interviews: An American Psychiatrist's Conversations with the Defendants and Witnesses*, ed. R. Gellately (London, 2006), pp.252–253, meeting held 24 January 1946, recorded Streicher's continuing anti-Semitism.
7 KV 2/250, 24 March 1945.
8 *Ibid.* 20 March 1945 on losing the War.
9 *Ibid.* 29 March 1945 and 25 March.
10 *Ibid.* 22 April 1945.
11 *Ibid.* 29 March 1945.
12 *Ibid.* 31 March 1945, for his "horsework."
13 *Ibid.* 20 March 1945.
14 *Ibid.* 22 April 1945.

15 *Ibid.* 4 March and 11 March 1945.
16 *Ibid.* 9 March 1945.
17 *Ibid.* 15 April 1945.
18 *Ibid.* 26 April 1945.
19 *Ibid.* 15 April 1945.
20 KV 2/346, 24 April 1944.
21 *Ibid.* 28 July 1943.
22 *Ibid.* 29 Nov 1944.
23 KV 2/250, 27 March 1945.
24 E. Young-Bruehl, *The Anatomy of Prejudices* (Cambridge Mass., 1996), p.233.
25 Farndale, *Haw-Haw*, p.150.
26 Glass, "Hobbes and Narcissism," p.338 on personalities who constantly use people as a supply of emotional fuel to fire themselves. Vaknin, *Malignant Self Love*, pp.101–102.
27 J. Bryan III and C.J.V. Murphy, *The Windsor Story* (London, 1979), p.361.
28 KV 2/346, 28 May 1945.
29 HO 45/25780, report, 13 June 1945. If a third man were present, if not actually involved in the incident, might it have been Carl Aschan, of British Intelligence, then involved in the capture of leading Nazis in Northern Europe? Obituary in the *Daily Telegraph*, 23 August 2008, for him detaining both Albert Speer and Joyce. *The Times*, 22 September 2008, offers another obituary.
30 James Clark in conversation with A. Weiss, 27 March 1995.
31 Kershaw, *Hitler: Nemesis*, p.553, notes Hitler's compulsion.
32 "WW2 People's War – World War Two Memories," submitted 10 November 2003 by Peter Lundgren (bbc.co.uk). Accessed 10 November 2004.
33 Private information for much of this detail.
34 KV 2/248/39A. Statement by Captain Alexander Adrian Lickorish, 23 June 1945. Perry claims Joyce said, "Fritz Hansen." G. Perry, *When Life Becomes History* (London, 2002), pp.54–57, 60–61. Perry's obituary appeared in *The Times*, 16 September 2014.
35 The MI5 report, HO 45/25780, has it as Lickorisch.
36 KV 2/248/39A.
37 Cole, *Lord Haw-Haw*, p.247.
38 Private information.
39 *Sheffield Telegraph*, 10 March 1960.
40 Private information. For Perry's own fears of a court martial, see Perry, *When Life*, p.55.
41 Perry, *When Life*, pp.54–57.
42 Arrest report, 28 May 1945, KV 2/346/No7.
43 *Manchester Guardian*, 30 May 1945.
44 KV 2/346, 28 May 1945.
45 *Irish Times*, 4 June 1945.

15

KAMERADSCHAFT

"To betray you must first belong. I never belonged." [Kim Philby, interviewed by Murray Sayle, *Sunday Times*, 17 December 1967.]

1

By one estimate, six million foreign nationals lived and worked in wartime Germany.[1] This situation was fully reflected in the Funkhaus, which employed persons "of nearly every race and colour."[2] By 1941 Nazi radio was transmitting in thirty-one languages, and as the War progressed that number increased.[3] Apart from Joyce, other broadcasters from Britain became involved.[4]

2

Jack Cole knew of these people, and his publisher encouraged him to incorporate them into his biography of Joyce. He ducked this challenge. Later biographers have proved equally reticent.

Some recruits were social misfits escaping their personal problems. Others shared Joyce's background in British fascism. Its universalism guaranteed as much.[5] A sprinkling of adventurers climbed on board and a number of POWs threw in their lot. One of Joyce's tasks involved enrolling such renegades.[6]

By painting these individuals – some at least – into the picture of his wartime life adds a necessary degree of context. Also, his relationships with them reveal much about his personality. His endless taste for intrigue and renowned ruthlessness travelled with him: he never hesitated to undermine colleagues if he believed they threatened him. By considering their careers it also soon becomes clear why at the end of the War Joyce proved of special interest to the British authorities. A notorious pre-war politico, he achieved even greater notoriety in Berlin, where he hugely overshadowed all these other broadcasters from Britain.

3

Various sources alerted the British government to Joyce and the other renegades. Two of his associates, missing from existing biographies and barely featuring in histories of British fascism, provided some early information.[7]

The Sandhurst-educated Denyss Chamberlaine Wace, born in 1886, had been invalided out of service in the Great War.[8] He was one of the ex-military figures attracted to British fascism and knew Joyce in the BUF.[9] In the 1930s – it is not clear when – Wace went to Germany and apparently broadcast for the Nazis.[10] He carried out other work for the Propaganda Ministry and was still in Berlin early in the War.[11] In October 1939 MI5, anticipating his eventual return, advised he should be kept away from all confidential military files.[12] When repatriated in 1943 he was interned for a time and debriefed by the security service.[13] He informed on Norman Baillie-Stewart, Margaret Bothamley and W. E. Percival.[14] He reported on the garrulous Henry Wicks.[15] Exactly what he revealed about Joyce is unknown.

On 28 June 1944 Wace was killed when a German bomb hit the Criterion Restaurant in Acre Lane, Brixton, where he was dining with fellow informer Philip Spranklin, another fatality of that raid.[16] Joyce would later recall the incident in one of his prison letters.[17]

In 1936, Spranklin, seemingly close to mental collapse, had sought to reduce his role in Mosley's movement. "I beg you not to think I am deserting you," he wrote to Joyce, "for whom I have greater regard than for any other man in the BUF." Joyce, taking it all in, probably itched to wave this compliment in Mosley's face. The following year, by now strangely recovered, Spranklin was appointed correspondent of *The Blackshirt* in Germany. In the late '30s he would often return to Britain before leaving the Reich for good in October 1940.[18] As a privileged Nazi supporter, he had been allowed to wear an SS badge and it is clear his commitment remained strong. "Ich bin und bleibe National Socialist," he wrote to Miranda Domvile in a wartime letter. On his return, however, he was soon feeding information to the British authorities.[19] Much of it, if not all, apparently derived from Wace.[20]

Wace's continuing BUF links appeared in his will, witnessed in 1943 by Neil Francis-Hawkins, ex-Director-General and Joyce's former arch-rival, now cited as a "company director," and B.D.E. Donovan, another similarly described Mosleyite. Oswald Squire Hickson was appointed executor and trustee: his firm had often acted for Mosley. Major Wace, as a report on the restaurant raid described him, left all of £70.14s.3d.[21]

Details the security services obtained from a number of sources during the War supplemented this evidence from Wace and Spranklin. Post-war testimony from the renegades and German co-workers added to such information.[22] By 1945 the files on Joyce had grown considerably.

4

When that "venomous and unscrupulous egotist" Henry William Wicks arrived in Berlin in July 1939, he posed as a victim of British justice.[23] Joyce had left for Germany fired up by fascism to advance his political career. But Wicks, who had some contact with fascists in Britain, travelled there essentially to escape his problematic past.[24] In the War the Nazis interned him. However, he was released in 1942 and next year began writing scripts for Radio Metropol.[25]

We already know Joyce had warned the Nazis against Wicks, who was recognised by others as a bad lot and not to be trusted.[26] This strange fluttering nonentity had little to offer. Yet he knew about raw survival and when the War ended claimed never to have met Joyce.[27] He was not alone in saying so. "As for Master William Joyce I never set eyes on the swine, thank God," another renegade remarked.[28]

Joyce knew other social misfits in Berlin. Existing narratives have Cedric Sebastian Samuel Steane, educated at Westminster School and New College, Oxford. However, neither institution knows of him.[29] Gazetted in 1915, two years later he was cashiered for fraud.[30] To say he was invalided out of service is too generous.[31] He later adopted the name Jack Trevor but is not to be confused – as some have – with the novelist Jack Trevor Story.[32]

When Joyce was delivering his exuberant undergraduate stage performances, Trevor, who had left for Germany in 1924, was working as an actor with some prestigious film directors.[33] He can be seen in *Champagne*, which Hitchcock shot in a Berlin studio in 1928.[34] When the War came he was interned. But after an actor friend had secured his release he went over to Hitler.[35] His route was again quite different from Joyce's and his commitment questionable. MI5 viewed him an adventurer rather than a dedicated Nazi.[36]

Trevor never developed much of a radio presence. Joyce, the enthusiastic fascist, soon put him in the shade. But he staggered on, delivering talks on Dürer, Goya and Molière and appearing in Nazi propaganda films, including the well-known anti-British production *Ohm Krüger*.[37]

In 1940 – to her evident surprise and delight – Trevor sent Margaret Joyce a bouquet of flowers on her wedding anniversary. Its accompanying dedication suggests he might have been angling to become one of her wartime lovers.[38] By 1945, however, and needing to safeguard his future, he held out against American interrogators, admitting only reluctantly to any Joyce connections.

Before leaving for Berlin Joyce would have known of Norman Baillie-Stewart, "the Officer in the Tower," who had been imprisoned in 1933 for passing sensitive military information to the Germans.[39]

In prison, he wrote some second-rate poetry:

> I divide my world into blacks and whites and laugh
> while the world is gay.
> But sink to the gloom of despondency when the clouds
> and life are grey.[40]

But he needed to do more than write verse. To rebuild his life Baillie-Stewart left for the Continent and from about 1937 became entangled in Nazi espionage activity. The following year he applied for German nationality, a process which took almost two years to complete.[41] He first broadcast for the Nazis on August 1939 and when the War broke out showed no qualms about serving them, "in a voice . . . seeming to parody Noel Coward at his most strangled."[42]

Baillie-Stewart lacked Joyce's political background but hoped to occupy a major wartime role. He was to be sorely disappointed. At the end of 1939 several problems led to his transfer to the German Foreign Ministry.[43] Simplifying matters, he would continue to blame Joyce for this unwanted move.[44] He deeply resented his young colleague's overweening attitude, and this hostility was reciprocated.[45] Renegade circles were soon awash with talk of their fractious relationship.[46] Baillie-Stewart not only broadcast. He helped to produce *The Camp*, a weekly tabloid printed by the Nazis aimed at British POWs, and also recruited other renegades.[47]

Joyce came from a downwardly mobile social background, but John Amery, feckless son of the Conservative politician Leo Amery, was born into the English upper class.[48] This indulged child, had given his father, though probably not his mother, too many sleepless nights.[49] After the War Rebecca West painted a damning portrait of Florence Amery, remarking savagely, "I felt that the value of John to this woman had been that he went out into the world and did all the wicked things that she had wanted to do."[50] But what had he done?

In the 1930s, when Joyce was submitting himself to a punishing schedule as a fascist politician, Amery was hugely enjoying himself in the West End. He went heavily bankrupt.[51] He drank to excess. He sought out prostitutes, married one, delicately described as an actress.[52] He always lived life on the dangerous edge. But his family continued to back him financially and in other ways. Sailing close to treason, their support even continued even during the War when he worked for the Nazis. The British Embassy in Madrid acted as one conduit for their funds.[53]

'Exiled' to Europe to save family face, Amery had developed a loathing for Communism and his feelings strengthened during the War when, living at first in France, he fell under the influence of local fascists Marcel Déat and Jacques Doriot. Despite his part-Jewish background, he was also anti-Semitic. His father claimed – strangely, given the family's continued financial support – that this antipathy originated in the 1930s when poor young John had fallen prey to moneylenders.[54]

In late September 1942, after working for the Nazis in France, Amery was taken to Berlin. German officials would have been well aware of that famous parliamentary occasion on 7 May 1940 when his father, echoing Cromwell's exhortation to the Long Parliament, had famously urged Neville Chamberlain to quit as Prime Minister.[55] Yet Leo's son, a prime catch for Hitler, would now be operating at the centre of Nazi power.

By September 1942 Joyce was well-established and impressing his Nazi bosses. His early uncertainties had vanished. He had become a radio star. How ironic that someone who "could hardly succeed in receiving a powerful station on the wireless and could never get the tuning right, even for the BBC," should have achieved this status – and so quickly.[56] Goebbels had praised him and responded to his request for favours. But when Amery arrived in Berlin insisting he could make a better fist of radio propaganda, the Nazis allocated him air time.[57] He first broadcast in the November.[58] He failed miserably.[59]

Amery not only appeared on Nazi radio. From 1943 he attempted to recruit British POWs into the Legion of St George, known later as the British Free Corps, designed to bolster Germany against Bolshevism. This grand project proved a disaster. Joyce, drawing on his Irish experiences and regarding himself as a military expert, always viewed the BFC with total bemusement. To him it was a Fred Karno's Army.[60]

When not deeply depressed or roaring drunk, Amery transacted other business with the Nazis.[61] But he never delivered politically. The playwright's words on this traitor's life, "can't remember the details, doesn't matter, drinking I suppose, fucking everything in sight, I don't know," sum up Amery's efforts and character.[62] He had none of Joyce's political grip or ability.

Joyce and Amery had apparently crossed swords before the War when the latter had visited BUF headquarters.[63] And they were soon in conflict in Berlin.[64] Apart from fearing Amery might usurp his position, Joyce knew of his rival's Jewish background. That alone guaranteed trouble. He would never concede to "a quarter Yid."[65]

He had attacked Jews for years. Why not shoot them? Why not hang them from lamp-posts? Joyce also resented the largesse the Nazis lavished on a "playboy traitor."[66]

An unbridgeable ideological difference underwrote these tensions. Joyce wanted Britain crushed, defeated, which would allow the Nazis to cleanse the Augean stables, whereas Amery advocated an alliance of Britain and Germany against the Soviet Union. In Amery's arrangement the old gang would have retained power.[67] Joyce would have none of it. They must be removed. He had always said as much since his BUF days.

When the dust had barely settled on their failed Berlin adventures, Joyce sympathised on hearing Amery was to hang, believing his guilt was no greater than that of more leniently treated renegades.[68] But he would have been mightily displeased to learn that in a 2005 diary the German Right recalled Amery as a fascist martyr, yet his own name was nowhere to be found.[69] What an ungrateful lot these Germans could be.

5

Did ex-members of fascist parties in Britain serve the Nazis any better? Mosleyites are reluctant to hear it, but Joyce met a number of renegades in Berlin who had served in the BUF. Edward Bowlby, with whom he lodged briefly at Flensburg, was one of them.

Leonard Banning, another of Mosley's men, far from being "colourless," is especially intriguing.[70] In the '30s he had been a BUF organiser in Brighton and a contributor to *The Blackshirt*.[71] Joyce had often ventured into Sussex on political business, and they might have met down there.

Banning, who was a qualified language teacher, had gone to Germany before the War, and as early as 9 September 1939 offered his services to the Nazis, proclaiming immodestly, unashamedly: "My literary ability and my intimate knowledge of English psychology and politics would prove valuable."[72] His brazen offer effectively demolishes the claim that it took Joyce's best efforts to recruit him.[73] Not that Banning ever wanted to be reminded of his early burst of enthusiasm. On trial in 1946 he echoed Margaret

Joyce in claiming that if possible he would have left Germany before the War began.[74]

When Banning had second thoughts about volunteering, he was interned and released only after agreeing to engage in propaganda work. He required little prompting. He spoke mainly on the New British Broadcasting Station.[75] For this station he delivered talks entitled "Between Ourselves."[76]

Joyce had only recently been teaching pupils in London, building a portfolio of work, and passing himself off as 'Professor.'[77] Now in Berlin, revelling in his new status, he remained busy advising colleagues and writing radio scripts for Banning and others.[78] Joyce, we know, not only broadcast. In *Twilight over England*, newspapers and journals, he composed tracts for the times. Banning also had an itch to write, but harboured more literary aspirations, and late in the War Erich Hetzler was instructed to release him from broadcasting duties to allow time for an anti-war novel critical of the British political elite.[79] *Woe for my Comrades* appeared in 1944 under the pseudonym John Brown and seriously impressed MI5's Gilbert Wakefield.[80] The security service experienced great difficulty finding a copy for Wakefield and sixty years later this forgotten classic of British fascism remains hard to track down.

Towards the close of the book Lionel, probably Banning, says:

"We, the people were unwanted – two million were unemployed, and many of the rest went hungry, while the politicians and financiers lived on the fat of the land . . .
If war is for the rich against the poor – the haves against the have-nots – then I will have none of it. Come what may, I shall not fight for the old order against the new!"[81]

Joyce had repeated these same sentiments in *Dämmerung über England* and his radio broadcasts. There was a meeting of minds with Banning, which carried over from their time in the BUF.

Banning gave the Nazis little trouble. On the contrary, he soon began to enjoy himself. "I'm still going strong . . . it's all very pleasant here. Plenty of everything," he wrote to his parents in May 1941.[82] The War seemed to be going Germany's way – as Joyce often reminded his British listeners at this time. Unlike many renegades, Banning also remained steadfast. Here he is writing to Susan Hilton in April 1944:

> The war doesn't effect me as it effects you – that is to say – I don't find it repulsive. I don't think we should allow one's self to be repelled by the working out of history, however grim it may be. Instead one must take a deep breath and dive into the midst of it.[83]

This letter, which hinted at his homosexuality – he identified with her on this account – also said he continued on the "up and up."[84] Joyce would have welcomed this degree of continuing commitment.

When Joyce helped Banning to develop a radio profile and wrote scripts for him, he was underlining his important role in the propaganda network.[85] On that account he was often called upon to act as a recruiting sergeant among POWs. It was difficult, often thankless work, as he discovered in March 1944 at Dulag Nord camp when Navy officers gave him a particularly "rough reception."[86] But he did bring in some new faces.

Joyce's prize recruit was probably Walter Purdy, ex-BUF, sometimes known as Ronald Wallace or Pointer. This junior officer on HMS *Vandyck* had been captured off Narvik in 1940. Captain G.F.W. Wilson, the senior British officer in Marlag POW camp, later described him as "a truculent bully of a sly and cunning disposition."[87] But in 1943 the Nazis badly needed recruits and Joyce signed him up. That summer Purdy appeared on Radio National (Büro F) which operated under the direction of Peter Adami, formerly an official in the Foreign Office.[88] He broadcast until 1944.[89]

Joyce and Purdy were soon in conflict. The latter even alleged he tried to kill Joyce. But there might have been some special pleading here. He made this claim when fighting for his life in the British courts.[90] Was he tactically distancing himself, as Wicks and Trevor had done? Whatever the truth, there is no doubt that Joyce's personality – which before the War had led MI5 to describe him as "an expert at intrigue" – made him an exceptionally difficult colleague in Berlin, where so much more was at stake.[91]

Purdy's progress to an easier life was followed by Benson Railton Metcalfe Freeman, who had joined Mosley in 1937. In the War he entered the RAF and, following his capture in France, defected to the Nazis and worked in wireless propaganda.[92] He refused to broadcast but never hesitated to write scripts. In October 1944 he also joined the Waffen SS as an ideological officer.[93] Their shared BUF connections might have brought Joyce and Freeman together. But by writing scripts he was trespassing on Haw-Haw's domain. To make matters worse, he fancied himself in this role. During his post-war interrogation he called Joyce "a hate monger of the worst possible kind," whose broadcasts were "a howling disaster."[94] But did he say as much at the time? Freeman would have known that Joyce's closeness to the "merciless, unscrupulous and cruel" Erich Hetzler meant he could make life difficult for 'problem' colleagues.[95] And as an unrepentant admirer of Mosley, Freeman would have been an obvious target. No wonder the two hated each other.[96] Joyce would later dismiss him as a "skunk."[97]

None of these recruits had been especially prominent in the BUF. But in 1941 a more significant figure unexpectedly threatened Joyce's newly created world. With his senior position in the movement Joyce would have known of those shady intermediaries involved in the BUF's clandestine foreign funding. Dr Arthur Albert Tester, born in Germany but with a British passport, a figure strangely absent from general histories of British fascism and Joyce biographies, was one of them.[98] Tester's sham companies – European Press Agency, and British Glycerine Manufacturers – were conduits through which Nazi gold travelled to Britain.[99] James 'Java Joe' Ruston, father of Audrey Hepburn, sometimes operated alongside him.[100] None of this activity was apparent on the surface. Tester cultivated the image of a respectable, successful businessman, occupied an expensive suite of offices in central London, had an investment in a well-known restaurant in Piccadilly and lived in some style at Broadstairs in Kent. He "dressed in expensive suits, smoked expensive cigarettes, spoke excellent English (with a foreign accent) and habitually wore a monocle."[101]

He left England before the War to work for the Nazis in Europe.[102] In *England – Quo Vadis?* published in Roumania Tester pronounced that only Mosley and fascism could raise Britain from the ashes of its decline.[103] To this end, in 1941–42, he set up a Revolutionary Committee of the BUF in Exile.[104]

Joyce became concerned in April 1941 when this convicted fraudster attempted to establish a radio station in either Roumania or Bulgaria to beam messages into Britain. When promoting his project Tester emphasised his major role in pre-war British fascism.[105] He was probably looking for a new commercial money-making venture. But Joyce smelt trouble. How dare any renegade trespass near him, particularly someone close to Mosley? From BUF gossip Joyce would also have known that Tester had a Jewish father.[106] That link alone fired his hostility, as it did with Amery.

Joyce's responded by informing the Nazis Tester could not be trusted. This charge could have carried serious consequences. But Joyce had never worried when scheming earlier against colleagues. Why start now? Tester's project was not taken up. But this chameleon-like crook continued to work for the Nazis.[107] Surprisingly, however, he did not survive the War. Late on, Roumanian anti-fascists shot him near the Hungarian border.[108] Or did they?[109] The British treated reports of his death as highly suspect.[110] So did the Roumanians.[111] Dead, but how? He intrigues to the end.

Margaret Joyce, identified by British Intelligence as a broadcaster in October 1939, also came out of the BUF stable.[112] Until May 1942 she delivered weekly talks to women and appeared later on "Back Numbers," a Nazi attempt to expose what they treated as lies in the British press. She revealed her identity on air in December 1942.[113]

The claim she was an effective speaker is, to say the least, quite remarkable.[114] Haw-Haw could seriously unsettle an audience – think back to when France fell quickly and dramatically to the Wehrmacht – but no-one fretting about the world and listening to Nazi radio by a British fireside would have paid Margaret the slightest attention. Fascist comrades in Britain would certainly not have had any fire put in their bellies. MI5 recordings reveal just how poor she was.[115] She had no microphone presence and was often merely reading scripts – without much enthusiasm – Joyce had written for her. He even signed her broadcasting claims forms.[116]

"Usual boring day," she scratched in her diary in early 1940.[117] Her politically obsessed work-driven husband never gave her the attention and excitement she craved; to compensate, she turned increasingly to copious amounts of alcohol, and the transient thrills of romance and sex.[118]

6

Joyce mixed not only with social misfits seeking a safe harbour and former followers of Mosley, but also with people he knew from his Nazi fellow-travelling days in London. They had spoken up for Hitler before the War. They had cultivated the Nazis. How would they follow through their commitment alongside him?

Dorothy Eckersley, deeply implicated in his plans to leave for Germany and easing him into the Nazi radio network, broadcast for the Nazis, but without distinction. She was soon shunted into archives.[119] Whatever she did, she often complained and proved 'difficult.'[120] Before long Joyce probably began to scheme against her.[121] What further use was she? He had sucked the lemon dry. They kept in touch, though.[122]

Eckersley's son, James Clark, who initially prayed for Hitler to be victorious, delivered radio talks and read news reports. He would claim later his Nazi faith was destroyed when the Luftwaffe blitzed Britain's cities.[123] Or was it his disenchantment with the Russian campaign? Or having the Japanese as allies?[124] Or German treatment of the Baltic States?[125]

But is something missing in all these suggestions? Was it Stalingrad that acted as the final game-changer for Eckersley and Clark?[126] It seemed to have hastened their sliding away from Hitler. Was the glorious Nazi regime they had worshipped before 1939 now worth saving; could it be saved? And if not…?[127] This final breakdown of their commitment – Clark had shown his windiness during the RAF's early raids on Berlin – contrasted sharply with Joyce's continuing resilience.[128] He had more backbone. He had no interest in reneging on his commitment, crawling into a protective shell and staying there until he could safely emerge, hopefully unscathed.[129] Aware of Eckersley's and Clark's plans, Joyce began to view them with utter contempt.[130] Since Mrs Eckersley was an ineffective broadcaster and a backslider, no wonder he was "rude" to her.[131]

Margaret Bothamley, an assiduous pre-war propagandist for Hitler who had brought Dorothy Eckersley into the fascist fold, also appeared on Nazi radio.[132] She would later claim it happened by accident; she had been stranded in Berlin at the beginning of the War.[133] She was not alone in spinning that unconvincing story.

Between July 1940 and March 1945 this contact of Joyce's from the Right Club broadcast as The Lady in the Mirror.[134] Operating at the centre of the British renegade web, she might well have been the first Lady Haw-Haw.[135] Bothamley also assisted Joyce's friend Fritz Krüger, now broadcasting, writing and promoting anti-Jewish propaganda, when he wanted help with translations.[136] She claimed to have completed about six exercises for him and allegedly refused other commissions because of their anti-British sentiment.[137] It is hard to believe her.

Bothamley was a woman of independent means, with a passion for large hats, suggesting status, and had a large portrait of Queen Mary prominently displayed in her Berlin flat. It was hardly a traditional Nazi image. But she soon settled into her new role, working away steadily for the triumph of National Socialism. Her calculated move Eastwards did not put her beyond the reach of former comrades in Britain.[138] But Germany was now her base, where she became the chief figure among the women broadcasters from Britain. Not, though, as Joyce would soon have reminded her, the most important renegade from there. He coveted that role for himself.

Joyce tolerated Bothamley. She provided more congenial company than the lazy, slippery Eckersley and her son. Yet he was struck by her political naivety. As Nazi power crumbled all about them, she remarked: "Surely they can't just leave us in the lurch? Can they?"[139] How misguided, he believed. He knew how ruthless politics could be. His family's betrayal in Ireland had taught him a sharp lesson at an early age.

Joyce and Bothamley would often lunch together.[140] Yet for some obscure reason he refused to travel with her during the transfer of radio personnel to Hamburg in April 1945.[141] When Bothamley's world finally collapsed she soon distanced herself from him.[142] Even ardent pro-Nazis knew how to save their skins.

7

Those POWs who worked on Nazi radio have become virtually invisible.[143] Who recalls William Humphrey Griffiths, one of Joyce's recruits?[144] Or W. A. Colledge, who volunteered for service with the Nazis? This "burly six-foot soldier with the mind of an adolescent boy" and a radio name of Winter, would later describe Joyce as "a clever man . . . in fact probably a genius."[145] Ex-POWs were not alone in floating into historical oblivion. Ralph Baden Davenport Powell was quickly forgotten.[146] John Alexander Ward never appeared before a British court and soon disappeared from public view.[147] Who remembers Diana Hardwick, a pre-war member of The Link, as a broadcaster?[148] Or the serial fantasist W. E. Percival? He appeared on German radio before and during the War, wrote in the Hitlerite cause, and had links to the British Free Corps. He was interned, seemingly at Joyce's instigation, and twice refused Nazi offers to repatriate him, presumably fearing how the British might treat him. He featured as No. 45 on an official renegades' list but the authorities showed little post-war interest in him.[149] Following the War he drifted off into obscurity. As did Kenneth Lander, who showed great courage by refusing to read a script by Joyce which had described George VI as "that stuttering imbecile."[150] Joyce's difficulty in controlling his language, evident since his university days, was something else he took to Berlin. But what had happened to the young Royalist, once ready to spring to attention at the faintest sound of the National Anthem?[151]

8

Joyce wrote and recruited for the Nazis, but radio gave him his greatest exposure. He delivered news items and talks. He introduced listeners to characters including the hypocritical clergyman, the incompetent British diplomat, and the millionaire Jew. He continued with his acting interests but now with a committed political purpose.[152]

The new wireless technology had quickly brought him to international prominence and in contrast to Amery's and Tester's threatening interventions, Purdy's recalcitrance and Freeman's antagonism, some renegades felt flattered to have his company. Francis Paul

Maton – who had served with British commandos in Norway and Crete and later often appeared as Manxman on Nazi radio – hero-worshipped him.[153] Joyce wrote scripts for Maton and, off duty, they would drink deep together, sampling the best from a conquered Europe, especially fine wines from France. On these convivial occasions Joyce revelled in having the captive audience he had always craved.[154] Maton became entranced, believing he was drinking with "the most outstanding" renegade broadcaster, "the king pin of the whole show."[155] He was. Joyce did the work of six men for his new bosses.[156]

10

Radio renegades were not alone in revealing British fascism's treasonable strand. Theodore John William Schurch, from a "highly respectable" and "constitutionally minded" Anglo-Swiss family, had joined Mosley in 1936 and later carried out operations for the Axis in North Africa.[157] This chain-smoking, mournful-looking character with "high cheekbones, sunken face, protruding ears, crooked protruding teeth" and "small bland moustache," was executed just after Joyce.[158] The professed Jew-killer Thomas Heller Cooper, and the aspirant ideologist Francis MacLardy, who both fought in the British Free Corps, also had BUF links.[159] Cooper saw action on the Eastern front and had the dubious distinction of becoming the only British soldier decorated by the Nazis for military services.[160] They were joined in this rackety enterprise by other ex-Mosleyites and a number of shifty adventurers.[161]

There is finally a mystery. Clement Bruning, Joyce's junior colleague in the BUF, has been noticed leaving his café in Bethnal Green to work for the Germans in the World Service. MI5 believed he spoke on Nazi radio early in the War.[162] However, he was soon dead. Interned in Stalag XIIIA in 1940, he died there on 17 August 1942. He now lies in a Kraków cemetery.[163] Did he fall foul of the Nazis on ideological grounds? Was he interned merely because he was British? Why did he never secure his release by offering his services? Joyce could have testified to his political soundness. Was he betrayed from within the renegade community? If so, by whom? There are many questions, but the answers remain elusive.

11

Joyce's life in Berlin saw him tower above his renegade colleagues but his growing influence as a radio star was felt not in Germany but among listeners in the country he had deserted in the late summer of 1939. In Britain he became widely reviled on account of his broadcasts. How and why did this unsavoury image emerge?

Notes

1 J. H. Fried, *The Exploitation of Foreign Labour by Germany* (Montreal, 1945), p.41 especially; E. Kulischer, *Europe on the Move* (New York, 1948), pp.361 ff; T. Judt, *Postwar: A History of Europe since 1945* (London, 2005), pp.14, 24; S. Longden, *Hitler's British Slaves* (London, 2005), p.12. See also Moorhouse, *Berlin at War*, pp.44, 117–135 and Kershaw, *The End*, pp.225 ff.

2 J. M. Raleigh, *Behind the Nazi Front* (London, 1941), p.268.

3 *Stuttgarter Neues Tageblatt*, 23 February 1941, "Deutsche Rundfunkarbeit im Kriege." See also M. Balfour, *Propaganda in War 1939–1945: Organisations, Policies and Publics in Britain and Germany* (London, 1979), pp. 133, 136

4 Bergmeier and Lotz, *Hitler's Airwaves*, and Murphy, *Letting the Side Down*, touch on a number of these figures. A captured German document, RGVA, 1363/1/118/209, provides some detail

5 West, *Treason*, p.214.

6 WO 204/12326 is one of the many lists of renegades.

7 KV 2/185/1891A. Thurlow, *Fascism in Modern Britain* remains silent. As does Griffiths, *Patriotism Perverted*. They are absent from Cole, *Lord Haw-Haw*, Kenny, *Germany Calling* and Farndale, *Haw-Haw*.

8 WO 339/20628/3a, 16a, 17and PIN 26/22636.

9 KV 2/245/194a, now destroyed, noticed Wace's contact with Joyce.

10 KV 2/429/65a.

11 KV 3/218/17a.

12 WO 339/20628, minute, October 1939.

13 KV 2/258, refers to an interrogation on 25 April.

14 KV 2/429. Wace offered thirteen names. Twelve were confirmed as renegades. KV4/118 for Wace on Bothamley and Baillie-Stewart. HO 45/25781, confidential report, nd, for his information on Percival.

15 KV 2/419/73a.

16 Death notice, *Daily Telegraph*, 30 June 1944.

17 WJ to MJ, 20 August 1945.

18 All from HO 45/25571, report 91, including a letter of 9 November 1936.

19 KV 2/621, General Correspondence, for his letter to Domvile. For more on Spranklin, see University of Edinburgh, Saroléa Collection, File 85,

R. Hoffmann to Charles Saroléa, 7 October 1938; see also KV 2/419/74b and KV 2/622/35b. *Daily Telegraph*, 30 June 1944 carried a death notice. Pryce-Jones, *Unity Mitford*, pp.189–193,234 for some detail.

20 KV 4/118.

21 KV 2/258 and KV 4/118. Wace's will, Probate Records, General Register Office, England and Wales.

22 KV 2/3581, continuing reports on the British renegades.

23 KV 2/419/130b, "Henry William Wicks (Short Summary and Opinion)," 16 April 1945 by Gilbert Wakefield [MI5]. *The Star*, 6 December 1939 and 20 January 1940, reported his remarks on reaching Berlin. *Der Angriff*, 18 and 25 July 1939 for the publicity on his arrival. See also *The Times*, 29 May 1946. See Wicks's *A Case for Explanation* (London, 1938?) and *The Prisoner Speaks* (London, 1938).

24 KV 2/418/25a, KV 2/419/69a, 73a and CRIM 1/1767.

25 KV 2/419, "Henry William Wicks," p.2. R. Griffiths, "Antisemitic Obsessions: the Case of H. W. Wicks," *Patterns of Prejudice*, Vol. 48 (2014), pp.94–113, discusses this period of his life. Wicks wrote an unreliable memoir, "A Non-Pareil Case," now at Selwyn College, Cambridge.

26 FO 371/26509, British Embassy, Madrid, to Foreign Office, 24 February 1941.

27 KV 2/246/370b.

28 KV 2/619/236.

29 Emails, both institutions to author, 3 August 2006.

30 KV 2/622, 26A, 35A and WO 339/2668.

31 Bergmeier and Lotz, *Hitler's Airwaves*, p.93, 'buy' the story of his being invalided out.

32 He appears in Shirer, *Berlin Diary*, pp.210–211, "much in his cups." Raleigh, *Behind the Nazi Front*, p.267, offers another wartime portrait. James Clark, who knew Trevor in Berlin, writes unflatteringly in "Open Wounds," p.43. See also I. Adamson, *The Great Detective: Reginald Spooner of Scotland Yard* (London, 1966), p.128. Bergmeier and Lotz, *Hitler's Airwaves*, p.94 for confusion with Jack Trevor Story.

33 KV 2/622/21b, MI5 report, 27 November 1943, presents Trevor as a "poisonous influence" in the film industry.

34 Jack Trevor in H-M. Boch (ed.), *Cinegraph: Lexikon zum deutschsprachigen Film* (Munich, 1984).

35 FO 371/2564/161, for internee Number 16680, released in early 1940.

36 KV 2/624/213A. As late as 1943 he still believed his adventurism would pay off, declaring "The British army, led by drunkards, cannot stand up against the mighty forces of the Fuehrer ... the British are doomed" (KV 2/622/1Y).

37 GFM 33/449, propaganda broadcasts, Names of Participants. British.

38 KV 2/346, 14 February 1940.

39 KV 2/184 for the early Baillie-Stewart.

40 N. Baillie-Stewart, *I Lean on my Sword* (London, 1938), p.54.

41 Baillie-Stewart, *Officer in the Tower*, facing p.224 and p.233.

42 Panter-Downes, *London War Notes*, p.17, on his voice. KV 2/187/1998a notes his pre-war work.

43 Bergmeier and Lotz *Hitler's Airwaves*, p.92, refer to the fact he lectured at Berlin University, worked as a translator and produced programmes for the Foreign Ministry. He can be heard on 1 CDR0023717 and 1 CDR0023721, National Sound Archive. For his activities as a recruiting sergeant bringing in speakers such as Edward Bowlby, see HO 45/25789. See also Murphy, *Letting the Side Down*, pp.50–60.

44 Injudicious remarks on air in December 1939 would have provided sufficient grounds to move him (Bergmeier and Lotz, *Hitler's Airwaves*, p.92). He was also unreliable and unpunctual (KV 2/186/1969aa, Diettrich, statement, 20 October 1945). Joyce would have been quite prepared to exploit this situation. See KV2/185/1923C.

45 Baillie-Stewart, *Officer in the Tower*, p.151.

46 Clark, "Open Wounds," pp.53–54; KV 2/631, Freeman, statement, 16 May 1945.

47 KV2/165–187 for a flavour of his activities.

48 Faber, *Speaking for England*, discusses the political Amerys.

49 J. Keene, *Treason on the Airwaves: Three Allied Broadcasters on Axis Radio during World War II* (Westport, Conn. and London, 2009), p.2. *The Times*, 18 August 1937, recorded his brazen attitude towards creditors and finance generally.

50 Rebecca West to Theobald Mathew, 20 December 1947 (private archive).

51 L. S. Amery, *John Amery. An Explanation* (s.l., 1946), p.5.

52 KV 2/78/23b on Wing, "the common prostitute." Faber, *Speaking for England*, paints a more sympathetic portrait.

53 KV 2/78/12a for SIS report, 5 August 1942; Keene, *Treason*, p.57; J. Burns, *Papa Spy: Love, Faith and Betrayal in Wartime Spain* (London, 2009), pp.313–314.

54 Amery, *John Amery*, p.5 on money lenders. Faber, *Speaking for England*, pp.12–13 notices Leo Amery's Jewish background. See also W. D. Rubinstein, "The Secret of Leopold Amery," *History Today*, Vol.49, February 1999, pp.17–23.

55 *Parliamentary Debates* (Commons), Vol.360, col. 1150, 7 May 1940 for Leo Amery's intervention.

56 USSC, MS 238/7/11 for Macnab's observation on Joyce's lack of technical ability.

57 Bergmeier and Lotz, *Hitler's Airwaves*, p.115.

58 Keene, *Treason*, p.59.

59 INF 1/292/303, 26 November 1942.

60 WJ to MJ, 4 September 1945. On the BFC there is R. Seth, *Jackals of the Reich: The Story of the British Free Corps* (London, 1972); Marquis de Slade (pseud.), *The Frustrated Axis* (Withen, 1978) and *Yeomen of Valhalla* (Mannheim, 1984); A. Weale, *Renegades* (London, 1994), pp.54–69 particularly; KV 2/2828 has now become available. See also the novels P. MacAlan, *The Judas Battalion* (London, 1988), and G. Walters, *The Traitor* (London, 2002).

61 *John Amery Speaks* (np, nd) for seven lectures delivered in December 1942 and *England and Europe* (London, 1994. First ed. 1943), a text distributed among British POWs. His activities are discussed in HO 45/25773/66–73. He features in A. Weale, *Patriot Traitors: Roger Casement, John Amery and the Real Meaning of Treason* (London, 2001), pp.54–70, and briefly in M. Weinreich, *Hitler's Professors: The Part of Scholarship in Germany's Crimes against the Jewish People* (New York, 1946), p.232.

62 R. Harwood, *An English Tragedy* (London, 2008), p.94. Premiered, Watford Palace Theatre, 14 February 2008.

63 Dorril, *Blackshirt*, p.530.

64 Brown, *In Durance Vile*, p.113.

65 KV 2/250, 6 March 1945.

66 The playboy reference appears in J. Bulloch, *Akin to Treason* (London, 1966), p.35.

67 *Ibid.* p.47. Faber, *Speaking for England*, ch.20, especially pp.450–451, 453.

68 WJ to MJ, 14 December 1945.

69 *Taschenkalender des Nationalen Widerstande* (Riesa, 2004), notes Amery's execution on 18 December 1945. Joyce would have drawn some consolation, however, from his appearance in the "commemorative dates" section of the WUNS (World Union of National Socialists) *Bulletin*, No.11 (1968), where it was written, "3 January 1946—William Joyce, the first British National Socialist Martyr is murdered at Wandsworth Prison in London."

70 Bulloch, *Treason*, p.60, for him lacking colour.

71 KV 2/433, letter, Sussex police to MI5, 6 December 1945. *The Blackshirt*, 8 June, 17 August, 12 October 1934.

72 CRIM 1/1735, Banning to Gestapo, 9 September 1939.

73 Kenny, *Germany Calling*, p.171.

74 HO 45/24475, trial transcript, 21 January 1946.

75 R. Schnaubel, *Missbrauchte Mikrofone: Deutsche Rundfunk-propaganda im Zweiten Weltkrieg* (Wien, 1967), p.127, quoting official sources, notes his employment from 10 April 1940.

76 WO 71/1112, court martial of Rifleman [Lance Corporal] Ronald Spillman, 2 November 1945, pp.7, 22. KV 2/424/73a.

77 *News Chronicle*, 26 January 1934.

78 KV 2/432, statement by Banning, 13 May 1945.

79 Schnaubel, *Missbrauchte Mikrofone*, pp.127–130.

80 KV 2/432 and 433, detail his activities. KV 2/433/26–28 contains Wakefield's review. Rebecca West tried to obtain a copy but it is unclear whether she succeeded. YCAL, Gen MSS, 105, Theobald Mathew to Rebecca West, 22 February 1946.

81 J. Brown, *Woe for my Comrades* (Berne, 2nd ed., 1944), p.308.

82 KV 2/432/15a.

83 KV 2/432/61b. Spelling as in original.

84 *Ibid.* Rebecca West commented on the "softness of his voice" and his gait, which suggested "his sexual habits were unorthodox," *Treason*, p.119.

85 CRIM 1/1735, statement by Banning, 13 May 1945, on Joyce providing the John Brown scripts.

86 D. Rolf, *Prisoners of the Reich: Germany's Captives 1939–1945* (London, 1988), p.169. Imperial War Museum, Tape 12362, E. S. Truman. Imperial War Museum, Document 3653/85/29/1, diary of Captain E. Monckton, pp.30, 44.

87 ADM 1/30079.

88 Bergmeier and Lotz, *Hitler's Airwaves*, pp.216–218.

89 HO 45/25798; KV 2/259–260.

90 *Daily Worker*, 20 December 1945.

91 KV 2/245/24a reports his scheming in Britain.

92 KV 4/118.

93 *The Times*, 5,7,8,10,11 September 1945. Personal file, Berlin Document Center, for the SS connection. See also KV 2/631 and Weale, *Renegades*, pp.144–150.

94 KV 2/631, Freeman, statement, 17 May 1945, p.3.

95 Kenneth Gilbert in KV 2/442.

96 KV 2/631, Freeman, statement, 16 June 1945, p.1.

97 WJ to MJ, 20 December 1945.

98 KV2/616/1b on his background.

99 Bauerkämpfer, *Die "radikale Rechte,"* p.232.

100 KV 2/226/709ba SIS document from a Belgian contact, 27 June 1947. KV 2/3190–3191 for heavily weeded Intelligence files on Ruston. A. Walker, *Audrey: Her Real Story* (London, 2000), pp.20–22.

101 D. Seabrook, *All the Devils Are Here* (London, 2002), p.83.

102 KV 2/2266.

103 A. Tester, *England–Quo Vadis?* (Bukarest, nd), in German. GFM 33/736.

104 KV 2/2266 and GFM 33/470, memo, 12 June 1942, from Tester, outlining his plans.

105 KV 2/618/535, reveals Tester's interest in self-promotion. He emphasised that unlike his erstwhile British comrades, he remained free and able to act in Europe. USSC MSS, 366/19/1 and 366/19/8, contain some details.

106 KV 2/616/511b.

107 de Launay, *Histoires Secrètes*, pp.70 ff on the radio project. Tester does not feature in the standard histories of British fascism. But see P. Henri (pseud.), "Voice of Treason," *Searchlight*, No.171 (1989), pp.10–12.

108 KV 2/618/591A.

109 KV 2/618/596b, 634a. J. Hope and D. Turner, "The Curious Case of Dr Tester," *Searchlight*, No. 336 (1995), pp.12–13, and *ibid*. No.33 (1995), pp.14–15, remain the fullest published accounts.

110 KV 2/2266, carries detail on the mystery. The full extent of his activities has never emerged.

111 GFM 33/470, intercepted telegram, Roumanian legation in Lisbon, to Ankara, 14 December 1944. WO 204/12556/40a.

112 KV 2/253/75a and /81.

113 KV 4/118, Policy re Compilation – Distribution of list of UK renegades to be handed over under the terms of an armistice with Germany.
Surrender list.

114 Farndale, *Haw-Haw*, pp.222–223, refers to her quality as a broadcaster.
But see, more reliably, KV2/428, Dietze's statement, 29 May 1945.

115 National Sound Archive, ICDR 00 33647-BDS1–2, 7–8.

116 GFM 33/449.

117 KV 2/346, 2 January 1940.

118 As her diary shows. KV 2/346.

119 Bundesarchiv, R55 /184, memo, 17 March 1943, for her "weinerliche"
behaviour.

120 Bundesarchiv, R55/181, memo, 25 November 1942.

121 KV 2/346, 2 March 1940 for the plotting.

122 KV 2/346, 10 January and 13 January, 16 February, 22 February, 23 July,
25 July, 20 August, 21 August, 23 August, 13 October 1941, as well as 21
March 1942, 4 April and 11 April 1942.

123 He referred to his prayers in "Germany Calling," BBC Radio 4, 16
May 1991. D. Blakeway, memo, 15 November 1990 (private archive),
based on Clark's testimony, discusses the impact of the Blitz. Clark
would like to be known purely as a newsreader but German documents
carry details of receipts for other broadcasts. See GFM 33/449.

124 K. Muir, "The Englishman who felt Nazi Germany calling," *The Times*,
3 May 1991, for both sentiments.

125 "Germany Calling," Historia Video 1997.

126 Bundesarchiv, R55/182, memo, 4 March 1943.

127 Bundesarchiv, R55/181, /182, /184, /186, /189, /190, /192, on the
saga. KV 2/346, 11 March 1940 on "young Clark." For some of Clark's
later reflections, see D. Blakeway's memo, 15 November 1990 (private
archive). In "Germany Calling," Historia Video, the widow of Eduard
Dietze, a key figure in wartime propaganda in Germany, suggested
Clark's retreat occurred when he and his mother realised the game was
up. He quickly denied it. HO 45/25775 for Clark's official file.

128 Shirer, *Berlin Diary*, entry 20 August 1940, p.379, for Clark as "a frightened English lad" crying "Flieger alarm" during one raid.

129 Imagery from Clark's brilliant talk, "Hits of the 40s" (private archive).

130 Clark, "Open Wounds," p.165.

131 CRIM 1/1736/38–39.

132 HO 45/25776, statement, Dorothy Frances Eckersley, 2 July 1945, on
Bothamley's role in converting her to fascism.

133 CRIM 1/1763/41.

134 CRIM 1/1763, statement, Margaret Bothamley, 2 February 1946. KV
2/247/504a, refers to her pre-war writings.

135 Bergmeier and Lotz, *Hitler's Airwaves*, p.108.

136 CRIM 1/1763/43.

137 CRIM 1/1763, statement, 2 February 1946.

138 KV 2/840, Special Branch report, 14 March 1940.

139 KV 2/250, 4 April 1945.

140 KV 2/346, 10 January, 13 January 1941.

141 KV 2/250, 7 April 1945.

142 CRIM 1/1763/44.

143 WO 70/1110, KV 2/246/365b, KV 2/246/382b and KV 2/442 respectively. KV 2/266/397a "JOYCE. Attempts to corrupt Service Personnel," for names.

144 WJ to MJ, 9,10,24,25 October 1945 on Guardsman Griffiths.

145 WO 71/1131. Bulloch, *Treason*, p.55.

146 KV2/2075.

147 HO45/25826.

148 HO 45/25785; KV 2/247/504a.

149 KV 2/429/65a; and HO 45/25781.

150 HO 45/25827.

151 USSC, MS 238/7/11.

152 E. R. Chamberlain, *Life in Wartime Britain* (London, 1972), pp.177–178.

153 KV 2/264, Maton's statement. WO 204/ 2828 has Maton also joining the BFC.

154 WO 71/1117.

155 KV 2/264, court martial proceedings at Woolwich, 26 November 1945.

156 KV 2/250, 31 March 1945.

157 After joining Mosley he was instructed to await espionage instructions. He was later approached by Italian fascists – presumably with BUF connivance – and embarked on this career. Captured at Tobruk, he carried out his duties as Captain John Richards. See WO 204/13201, interrogation report, 9 May 1945 and KV 2/76/99a, Top Secret (interrogation report of Theodore Schurch, April 1945). The family description is from KV 2/76, Special Branch to MI5 26 June 1936.

158 His physical appearance is in WO 204/13021. See also WO 71/1109; WO 141/103; KV 2/76; KV 2/77, *Manchester Guardian*, 5 January 1946. His execution, unlike the hangings of Joyce and Amery, created little stir. But see T. A. Ende, *Racial Discrimination in the Armed Forces*, Supplement 1 (sl., 1946?).

159 Weale, *Renegades*, pp.111 ff presents some details. Murphy, *Letting the Side Down*, ch.5.

160 HO 45/25805; *Sunday Times*, 16 June 1996; Murphy, *Letting the Side Down*, p.215.

161 KV 2/2828; Weale, *Renegades;* Murphy, *Letting the Side Down*; Pleasants, *Hitler's Bastard*.

162 KV 4/117, B5b note, 12 July 1941.

163 *Comrade*, No.14 (1988). FO 371/2564/100 notes his detention on 29 January 1940, as internee Number 16687. His death on 17 August 1942 appears on www.cwgc.org. Accessed 6 July 2006. See also oswaldmosley.com. Accessed 26 March 2015.

PART IV

Connecting

16

JOYCE, HAW-HAW, AND BRITISH OPINION, 1939–1945

As I write, highly civilized human beings are flying overhead, trying to kill me. [George Orwell, "England your England," *Inside the Whale and other Essays* (Harmondsworth, 1957), p.63. First published in his "The Lion and the Unicorn" (1941).]

1

For Joyce talking was like a drug and Nazi radio offered him a perfect wartime platform. However, his nightly ration of news and comment, his incessant need for an audience, helped to determine his short-lived future.

2

Listening to the Nazis was never illegal in wartime Britain. Details of German wavelengths appeared in the press and at first some journalists encouraged their readers to tune in. Cassandra (William Connor) can be found advising his *Daily Mirror* readers in September 1939: "I earnestly ask all of you who are able to listen to the broadcasts from Germany to this country to do so."[1] Many did. A British audience would wait, often impatiently, sometimes anxiously, to hear the news from Berlin.[2] By contrast, those intrepid Germans caught listening to Allied radio stations faced the prospect of severe punishment.[3]

The British public was soon speculating on the identity of Nazi broadcasters, especially someone with an "upper-class English accent" delivering talks in a "very public school" and "posh" voice.[4] A "hoity toity", radio personality had entered their lives.[5] Jonah Barrington, otherwise Cyril Carr Dalmaine, of the *Daily Express* fanned this growing interest.[6] He called one Nazi propagandist "Winnie the Whopper of Warsaw." But he made his most significant intervention on 18 September 1939 when creating "Lord Haw-Haw – No. 1, non-stop English-speaking announcer of German Radio."[7]

> I imagine him as having a receding chin, a questing nose, thin yellow hair brushed back, a monocle, a vacant eye, a gardenia in his button hole. Rather like P. G. Wodehouse's Bertie Wooster. . . .[8]

Barrington proceeded to act as his publicity agent: "Remember, sir – all England hangs on your words. The butcher, the baker, the candlestick maker – all demand their nightly ration of Haw-Haw."[9]

Maxwell Knight knew this voice was not that of his former friend.[10] Joyce read a news item at his interview on 11 September 1939, but did not assume a bigger role until after receiving his radio contract on 18 September, the day Lord Haw-Haw was created.[11] Barrington had possibly latched onto the voice of Norman Baillie-Stewart or, more likely, Wolf Mittler. The former, had a cultivated upper-class accent which sometimes betrayed a slight lisp. The latter, "Handsome, six feet two inches tall . . . with snobbish manners," had a smooth, educated voice and a large vocabulary of mannered English.[12] "Hearty Cheerios" tripped off his tongue quite easily.[13] Both suspects later denied any Haw-Haw connection.[14] Baillie-Stewart claimed it was Mittler.[15] The latter, in an interview that left much unsaid, graciously brushed away that suggestion.[16] Another possibility, never before mentioned, is that Barrington might have been listening to Jack Trevor, whose role as the early Lord Haw-Haw featured in a contemporary Intelligence report.[17]

Since German radio did not identify its broadcasters early in the War, the British public's musings knew little restraint. Was he "public school educated Yorkshire"?[18] Or, in Harold Hobson's words, "Cholmondley-Plantagenet out of Christ Church?"[19] In December 1939 this same fascination encouraged Peter Crook Limited, cotton spinners, to refer to Haw-Haw, the "World Champion Spinner of Yarns," when advertising its goods in the *Manchester Guardian*.[20]

How did Joyce's connection to this phenomenon unravel? After one broadcast in late 1939, his ex-wife told a reporter; "I knew it was William Joyce ... the moment I listened to his voice," adding:

> One night I turned on the wireless while they (the children) were in the room. Joyce was speaking. My eldest daughter turned pale and when I asked what was the matter, she said, 'That's W.J. isn't it?' – she always called her father W.J.

She continued:

> I am positive he is the man. He even tells the same stories he used to tell me.[21]

This daughter said later she had not recognised her father's voice; there had been no contact for some years. But her mother had remarked, "That's your Daddy."[22] John Macnab knew his friend was broadcasting.[23] By late '39 other Nazi sympathisers had recognised Joyce as part of the Nazi radio network; "Did you hear JOYCE'S broadcast at 10.15 last night?" Richard Findlay asked 'Billy' Luttman-Johnson that December.[24] By now MI5 had noted Joyce's involvement.[25]

Not until early 1940, however, did the British press begin to link Joyce to the Haw-Haw phenomenon. The *Catholic Herald*, using an anonymous source, reported the connection that February.[26] The *Daily Mirror* followed suit next month carrying a photograph of Joyce and soon afterwards published an item on Margaret.[27] "Very angry about it!!" she wrote.[28] M. Kelly, writing from Galway to the *News Review* the following April, said that the voice now featuring prominently on German radio carried a reminder of her past.

> As one who knew Willie Joyce ... from the time he arrived in Galway [an infant] until he left rather hurriedly in 1922, I am quite certain that he is the 9.15 p.m. and 11.15 p.m.

English Announcer from Hamburg, Bremen etc. Ever since these broadcasts started I was struck by the familiarity of that voice. I often mentioned that I had heard that voice before but could not place it, but the minute I saw your photograph, and read your paragraph I knew at once it was 'Willie'.[29]

This voice was not public school, upper-class, but "sneering, smarmy [and] creepy"; quite "horrible."[30] Haw-Haw's persona had changed, and Joyce had become linked to this more disturbing phenomenon.

In '40 and '41 speculation continued on this speaker's identity with George Orwell informing readers of the *Partisan Review* in January 1941 – with "fair certainty" – that Joyce, "a very bitter personal enemy of Mosley," was delivering the Haw-Haw broadcasts.[31]

The matter was finally settled on the evening of 2 April 1941, when British listeners tuned into the Bremen station heard the following:

I William Joyce will merely say that I left England because I would not fight for Jewry against the Fuehrer and National Socialism. And because I believed most ardently, as I do today, that victory with a perpetuation of the old system would be an incomparably greater evil for England than defeat coupled with the possibility of building something new, something really national, something truly socialist.[32]

Even after 1941, however, the British public did not necessarily have Joyce in mind when referring to the Haw-Haw broadcasts. The title continued to be used quite promiscuously.[33]

3

Berlin's early wartime broadcasts certainly lifted the spirits of Britain's Nazi sympathisers. Fr Clement Russell could not be prised from his radio when Joyce came over the airwaves. He was listening to his "evening prayers."[34] Sir Barry Domvile, another fan, wrote early in 1940: "We generally listen to Haw Haw." Indeed, it became a family ritual at 'Robin's Tree,' Roehampton Vale. "Our usual rubber after dinner and Haw Haw," he jotted down soon afterwards. Chez Domvile, the broadcasts provided an encouraging, and sometimes amusing, interlude on the dark winter evenings of 1940.[35]

Their keen interest and evident enthusiasm were understandable. The Nazis appeared to be winning the War. British sympathisers were listening to the future. In this fevered atmosphere John Beckett contacted the Marquess of Tavistock in early 1940 with a list of names for an alternative government. Tavistock would become Prime Minister, James Maxton, Foreign Secretary, Oswald Mosley, Lord President of the Council, and J.F.C. Fuller would manage the defence portfolio. John McGovern, Labour MP, was recommended as the Minister of Labour, W.E.D. Allen, Gauleiter for Scotland and Peter Eckersley, Minister of Information.[36] A few days later MI5 reported that details of Beckett's alternative government might have been sent to Berlin.[37] Neither Beckett nor Macnab, the guardian of Joyce's plan, would have been under any illusions.[38] When the invasion came, as they hoped and believed it would, an almighty scramble would begin for leverage in the new Nazi world.

Beckett and others waited eagerly, expectantly, for the news from Berlin. But in some households bitter tensions flared up. James Leonard Stott, a seventeen-year old Birmingham youth, excited at the prospect of a Nazi victory, committed suicide after his father had refused him permission to listen to Nazi radio. He put on a swastika armlet, picked up a copy of *Mein Kampf*, went to a patch of waste ground and swallowed potassium cyanide.[39]

4

Apart from raising the spirits of British fascists and fellow travellers, what did the wider public generally make of Joyce's broadcasts?

Surrounded today by computers, the internet, television and instant news, it requires a degree of historical imagination to appreciate the significance of radio in the 1930s and '40s. But Tom Harrisson, Humphrey Jennings and Charles Madge, who in 1937 founded Mass-Observation, the social listening post, knew how important it had become in helping to form public opinion.[40]

Mass-Observation's findings in 1939 underlined the public's interest in Nazi radio propaganda. But at this time was Haw-Haw always Joyce? By 1940 there is much greater certainty. He had been 'outed' in the press. Haw-Haw was still being used as a generic term, but it is likely Joyce was the broadcaster mentioned in one important survey that year. Few listeners believed everything they heard. However, comment by a member of the RAF showed his message sometimes hitting home.

He talks a lot of cock and 75 per cent of his statements are either lies or propaganda, but occasionally he hits the nail on the head. It's then that he makes you think. You wonder whether a lot of his statements are also true.

Another interviewee remarked:

I think that, secretly, we are rather terrified by the appalling things he says. The cool way he tells us of the decadence of democracy and so on. I hate it; it frightens me. Am I alone in this? Nobody has confessed as much to me.[41]

Here, the speaker was almost certainly Joyce, sneering at democracy as he often did. And it worked. An angry working-class woman in Lambeth exclaimed: "He makes my blood boil. I feel inclined to smash the set."[42] The often-heard claim that his broadcasts never amounted to more than "a good laugh" – a crude version of "Britain can take it" – has no credibility.[43]

Terence Rattigan, who lived through these dark days, fully recognised Joyce's powers. His abortive screenplay imagined "a blacked-out pub in London filled with the usual crowd of complaining customers," fearful of invasion, resigned to defeat at Hitler's hands:

Christ, pal, I tell yer – he don't need invasion barges. He can *walk* across the bloody water. And what's to stop him when he does? My Aunt Flossie with her four-ten? . . . Oh yes, she's a good shot Flossie is. Reckon she'll take a couple with her if it's one of her good days and she's been off the gin. . . . Yes, please,

love. Two more mild and bitters . . . oh no – we're for it all right.
Well, cheers.

They paid little attention when Churchill's voice crackled over the
wireless. But when Haw-Haw's distinctive tones penetrated the
bar-room fug, these garrulous topers listened in "thoughtful silence."[44]

That same feel for these difficult times appeared in 1940 in a proposal for a radio play Graham Greene sent to the BBC, in which he
and Kenneth Clark – later drawn into the project – fantasised about
a Britain under the Nazis.[45] In their "Gestapo in England" one scene
portrayed a public school headmaster tuning into a broadcast to be
greeted by:

> This is Reichsender London. Here is the news and this is Wil-
> liam Joyce reading it. The Prime Minister in his farewell address
> to Parliament explained the circumstances which forced him to
> surrender to overwhelmingly superior German forces. This is
> the Reichsender London – you will now hear a concert by the
> Band of the Adolf Hitler Regiment from Green Park.[46]

Joyce would never have gained such notoriety had he remained in
Britain.

Greene and Clark were exploring the boundary of artistic licence.
But some people believed such fantasies were a distinct, terrifying near-possibility. In January 1940 Sarah Ann Bellamy, aged 53, a
working-class housewife of Nottingham Street, Sheffield, depressed
after listening to Haw-Haw on German radio, allowed her husband
to go to bed, washed up the supper pots, then gassed herself. He
found her the next morning.[47]

By early 1940 Mass-Observation was reporting a decline in British listeners to Nazi radio.[48] However, in March that year a letter
from Percy Goff to Robert Vansittart suggested Haw-Haw still commanded an audience: "I am appalled at the accumulating and increasing interest . . . in this swine's broadcasts," he declared, "even my own
maids and charwoman are becoming infected."[49]

When Joyce did lose listeners, it was often because he had unsettled
them.[50] F. Tennyson Jesse, writing to American friends in May 1940,

said she no longer tuned in; the transmissions were no longer a laughing matter.[51] The following month Nella Last in Barrow refused to hear the "horrifying" news her husband had just picked up from Berlin. It would have upset her too much.[52] Observers remained alert to this self-censorship.[53]

Evidence from March 1941, however, emphasised that Joyce retained listeners in the Glasgow area.[54] Reports that same year from Portsmouth revealed an audience also existed in England. This important naval base had just been battered by the Luftwaffe and it was widely claimed Haw-Haw had threatened they would soon return to finish the job on the North End of the city.[55]

Ministry of Information files are bursting with such reports.[56] Almost everywhere stories circulated of Haw-Haw predicting future Luftwaffe attacks on businesses, military installations and schools. Wartime Britain became a hoaxer's paradise, and sometimes these fantasies developed a particularly bizarre twist.[57] One even claimed that Haw-Haw had announced Hitler would be crowned King of England.[58] Another suggested he was transmitting coded messages from Berlin to fifth columnists.[59] Such extravagance was not special to the Second World War. After Al-Qaeda's 2001 attack on New York, people apparently received phone calls and emails from "a friend of a friend" warning that their city would soon face a terror attack.[60] Fear breeds fantasy.

Nazi broadcasts which revealed detailed local knowledge were particularly unsettling, though the sources were not difficult to trace.[61] British newspapers, which reached Berlin through neutral countries, provided much of this local colour.[62] Propaganda staff there could also listen to the BBC.[63] Dolly Eckersley failed dismally as a broadcaster, but even she could extract such information for those with better radio skills. However, suspicions of a Nazi espionage network active in Britain proved hard to shift. The seemingly omniscient Joyce, operating out of Berlin, encouraged this belief.[64]

5

How best to respond to the unsettling Haw-Haw broadcasts? In 1939 Jonah Barrington, his creator and 'agent,' countered in the *Daily*

Express with a strong dose of British humour. In different vein, in 1940 the *Daily Mirror* enlisted the versifier Patience Strong who attacked "The hired liar of the Reich/Paid piper of the State!"[65] It even started "an Anti-Haw-Haw League."[66] However, not all press responses were unambiguous. How should we interpret "Haw-Haw in the villages," which appeared in *Truth*, a paper associated with appeasement and anti-Semitism?

> Beware, beware! To-morrow night
> Great Snoreham's going to get a fright
> We've heard about that gun concealed
> In Farmer Jackson's turnip-field
> The gossip in the village inn
> Has reached headquarters in Berlin
> And (even if it's quite untrue)
> The Führer's got his eye on you
> Beware, beware! 'Ere morning break
> Great Snoreham's for it. No mistake![67]

There is some uncertainty here.

In 1939 and 1940 well-known entertainers, echoing Barrington, also poked fun at Nazi propaganda. In October 1939 'Stainless Stephen,' the Sheffield comedian, introduced his Manchester Hippodrome audience not only to Lord Haw-Haw but also to Oily Alf and Horace the Humbug from Hamburg.[68] The following month Arthur Askey appeared as Baron Hee-Haw on the BBC's "Bandwaggon" programme.[69] Between December 1939 and July 1940 Max Miller, "the cheeky chappie," starred in "Haw-Haw" a "delicious fantasy" which played at the Holborn Empire.[70] And Kenneth and George, the so-called Western Brothers, would often feature the song *Lord Haw-Haw, the Humbug of Hamburg, the comic of Eau-de-Cologne* in their old-school-tie music hall and radio routine.[71]

The Jewish community naturally became concerned at the anti-Semitism in Nazi broadcasts and, by way of rebuttal, the Defence Committee of the Board of Deputies once considered a proposal for a station in Palestine. The Committee also became involved in Christopher Stone's Home Service broadcast on 30 March 1940 which attacked "the oily, snarling, glib, sneering Lord Haw-Haw of Hamburg."[72]

Stone's broadcast went out over the BBC, and the Corporation clearly had a vital role to play in combating Nazi propaganda. But it was not always up to the task. The Reich's propagandists were assisted in the early days of the War not only by the Wehrmacht's stunning victories but also by the BBC's inefficiency. German radio was often first with the news. "I expect we shall hear it first from Haw Haw," one member of the public sighed when awaiting details on the defeat of France in 1940.[73]

The Corporation's sclerotic nature had become apparent well before 1939. The snappy jingle of a popular radio station started in 1931 by Captain Leonard Plugge MP, and transmitting from Fécamp, welcomed its Sunday listeners with:

> Radio Normandie calling you
> Bringing you music from out of the blue.[74]

Lord Reith's taste did not stretch to such light-heartedness.

The War's challenges proved even greater. The Corporation, dismissed by Arnold Leese as the "Blah and Boredom Confederacy," could assess the audience for Nazi propaganda and roughly calculate its size. In early 1940 an estimated 6 million people in Britain listened regularly to the Hamburg station and 18 million were occasional listeners. This large audience would have been hearing more than one Nazi broadcaster. But the chief reason for many tuning in was to hear Haw-Haw, which by now would have meant Joyce.[75] Assessing the size of this constituency was one thing. The way to respond proved more difficult.[76] "Large doses of Sandy MacPherson . . . unruffled and inviolate at the Theatre Organ" hardly lifted spirits.[77]

Several strategies were considered. Should Nazi broadcasts be jammed? Or would it suggest the British had something to hide? Should popular entertainers – Gracie Fields perhaps – go on air and hopefully spoil the audience? Should the focus be on a comprehensive, accurate news service, rather than a policy of rebuttal? Should prominent public figures promote the Allied cause through news commentaries?[78]

This uncertainty reflected a lumbering Corporation now required to heave itself into an unprecedented conflict. It also underlined the country's general unpreparedness for the War, which led Robert Bruce Lockhart to write:

> Incredible to think that today, May 1940, we have not enough rifles and not enough small ammunition for the training of the army, much less of the Defence Corps. Tonight on the radio the announcer requested everyone who had any stocks of cartridges for 12-bore guns to bring them to a police station! What jam for Haw-Haw![79]

Britain's survival demanded change and gradually it met the challenge. In 1940 the Corporation recruited refugees who could broadcast fluently to listeners in occupied Europe. The likes of Ernst Gombrich and George Weidenfeld played a vital role here.[80] Moreover, from January 1941 the V Campaign carried the propaganda battle to the Germans by encouraging disaffection in occupied Europe.[81] The following summer, after the USSR and the USA had entered the War, the Government established the Political Warfare Executive (PWE).[82] Robert Bruce Lockhart, director of this body, which combined propaganda and Intelligence functions, finally had a tool to lift his despair at Britain's lack of preparedness. He was a Foreign Office appointee, but the PWE contained representatives from bodies outside government, including the BBC.[83] Its focus on 'black' propaganda, beamed from Britain but ostensibly transmitted from occupied Europe, was Britain's answer to the Geheimsender for which Joyce was busily recruiting speakers and writing scripts.[84]

Neither the government nor the BBC showed any interest in creating a Joyce-like rival. They avoided the personality cult. Had they succumbed, Goebbels would have rubbed his hands with delight. His early wartime diary reflected his relish at the prospect of Haw-Haw taking on any such broadcaster in a battle over the airwaves.[85] Rather than going head-to-head, a more collective effort followed.

Sir Norman Birkett, who in 1939 assumed a major role in internment policy, was later drafted into service as a broadcaster.[86] However, his "Onlooker" talks proved less effective than hoped. Fluency at the Bar did not automatically translate into talking to, attracting and retaining an invisible radio audience.[87] Other recruits enjoyed more success. Until J. B. Priestley fell foul of the authorities, his tobacco-stained, Bradfordian tones were immensely reassuring.[88] He perfected a completely different approach from Joyce's hectoring style.[89] The barrister-broadcaster Edgar Lustgarten, known as Brent Wood to mask he was Jewish, also proved effective in "Listening Post," transmitted nightly to English-speaking audiences overseas.[90] The journalist Sefton Delmer – a "huge Falstaffian figure" who allegedly said "I can only think clearly in a five-star hotel" – assumed a central role in the PWE's 'black' propaganda initiative.[91] He also worked on Soldatensender Calais, the 'grey channel,' beamed from Crowborough, which offered German troops a mixture of popular music and light listening. Other individuals, British and foreign, contributed to this greater effectiveness, whether as monitors or broadcasters.[92]

These responses, which recognised successful propaganda demanded a fine attention to detail and an awareness of human psychology, were assisted by changing circumstances.[93] As Germany's wartime dominance slipped away, British broadcasters operated in an increasingly favourable context. For the Nazis "the final two years of the war were in general a period of decreasing propaganda effectiveness," which culminated in a "sense of failure."[94] Joyce's loss of influence at this time was felt not only in Britain but also in Ireland.[95] In fact, his star had started to wane before the turn of the military tide. In May 1942 Goebbels, the master tactician, observed that the time for "scharfen polemick" had gone.[96] We have seen Joyce being appointed the following month as Chief Commentator in the English language service – but he was ill-suited to the new challenges. Subtlety had never been his strong suit.

6

Few members of the wartime British public would have been unaware of Joyce's broadcasts. And his frequent boasting of Nazi successes, his steady succession of threats, were hardly likely to generate any sympathy for him when he was captured and then put on trial. But a wartime incident in 1940, largely shielded from view, though well-known to powerful forces in Britain also helped to shape how events in his life would unfold. What did it involve and why was it significant?

Notes

1 *Daily Mirror*, 25 September 1939.

2 A. Briggs, *The War of Words: The History of Broadcasting in the United Kingdom*, Vol.3 (London, 1995), p. 128.

3 Boelcke (ed.), *Secret Conferences*, p.108 (30 October 1940) and p.289 (22 October 1942), reflect official Nazi attitudes and policy. See also E. T. Lean, *Voices in the Darkness: The Story of the European Radio War* (London, 1941), pp.54–58. D. Sington and A. Weidenfeld, *The Goebbels Experiment: A Study in the Nazi Propaganda Machine* (London, 1942), pp.145–148. Germans nevertheless listened to British broadcasts. See J. F. Slatterly, "'Oscar Zuversichtlich': A German's Response to British radio propaganda during World War II," *Historical Journal of Film, Radio and Television*, Vol.12 (1992), pp.69–85.

4 "Germany Calling. The War in the Ether," BBC Radio 4, 9 May 1991.

5 *Daily Mirror*, 4 January 1940.

6 J. Barrington, *And Master of None: Autobiographical Reminiscences* (London, 1948).

7 *Daily Express*, 18 September 1939. J. Barrington, *Lord Haw-Haw of Zeesen* (London, 1939), p.9.

8 Barrington, *Lord Haw-Haw*, p.9. The reference to Wodehouse carries an unintended irony.

9 *Ibid.* p.126.

10 KV 4/117, note, 12 July 1941.

11 Cole, *Lord Haw-Haw*, p.113.

12 Baillie-Stewart, *Officer in the Tower*, pp.148–149.

13 Mittler featured in "Germany Calling: The Voice of the Nazi", BBC Radio 4, 16 May 1991. See his autobiography, *Anzac Tattoo: Eine Reise durchs Niemandsland* (Percha, 1987).

14 KV 2/246/377B for their good life (evidence, Phyllis James, 30 April 1945).

15 Baillie-Stewart, *Officer in the Tower*, p.153.

16 Wolf Mittler talking to D. Blakeway, nd. Private Collection.

17 KV 2/245/220a.

18 E. S. Turner, *The Phoney War on the Home Front* (London, 1961), p.129.

19 *The Times*, 29 December 1939.

20 *Manchester Guardian*, 21 December 1939.

21 *Sunday Pictorial*, 17 December 1939.

22 *Daily Express*, 11 February 1995.

23 USSC, MS 238/7/10.

24 HO 45/25719, intercepted letter, 28 December 1939.

25 KV 2/247/497a. HO 45/25780/95.

26 *Catholic Herald*, 16 and 23 February 1940.

27 *Daily Mirror*, 2 March, 9 March 1940, respectively.

28 KV 2/346, 15 March 1940.

29 *News Review*, 4 April 1940. The journal had raised the issue on 7 March. See KV 2/245/247a, Terminal Mails report, on Joyce's activities being recognised in Galway.

30 "Germany Calling. The War in the Ether," BBC Radio 4, 9 May 1991.

31 Letter, 3 January 1941 to *Partisan Review*, printed S. Orwell and I. Angus (eds.), *The Collected Essays, Journalism and Letters of George Orwell*. Vol.2 *My Country Right or Left 1940–1943* (Harmondsworth, 1980), pp.69–70.

32 Summary of World Broadcasts, No.624, part 1B, Bremen.

33 Orwell and Angus (eds.), *Collected Essays*, Vol.3, p.490. Diary, 24 June 1942, for Orwell listening to a Haw-Haw broadcast not delivered by Joyce.

34 J. Hamm, *Action Replay* (London, 1983), p.154.

35 National Maritime Museum, DOM 56, Domvile, diary, 8, 15 and 27 January 1940. KV 2/836/247A, p.20 for his letter to Olive Baker, 1 April 1940, describing the NBBS as a "grand" development.

36 KV 2/1511/143BC, 22 May 1940.

37 KV 2/1511/145a.

38 KV 2/1511/73x on Beckett and Macnab in contact.

39 *Manchester Guardian*, 18 September 1939.

40 Mass-Observation Archive, University of Sussex, Radio Listening 1939–1945, Box 1 and A. Calder and D. Sheridan (eds), *Speak for Yourself: A Mass-Observation Anthology 1937–49* (Oxford, 1984), ch.1.

41 Mass-Observation Archive, University of Sussex, File Report 64 US 9, "Public and Private Opinion on Lord Haw-Haw," 29 March 1940, p.74.

42 *Ibid.* See also An Englishman, *War Letters to America* (London, 1940), p.70, relating to 22 October 1939.

43 M. Waller, *London 1945* (London, 2004), p.277.

44 Rattigan, British Library, Add MS 74490, Part Two, f.34. Spelling as in original.

45 BBC Written Archives, R34/639/2, internal memo, 17 January 1940.

46 Broadcast on BBC Home Service, 21 August 1942.

47 *Daily Telegraph*, 18 January 1940.

48 Mass-Observation Archive, University of Sussex. File Report 64 US 9, "Public and Private Opinion on Lord Haw-Haw," 29 March 1940, p.75.

49 BBC Written Archives, R34/639/3, letter, 2 March 1940.

50 Thompson, *1940*, captures some of the atmosphere.

51 F. M. Tennyson Jesse and H. M. Harwood, *London Front. Letters Written to America August 1939–July 1940* (London, 1941), p.140.

52 Last, *Nella Last's War*, pp.59–60.

53 Mass-Observation Archive, University of Sussex, File Report 64 US 9, p.76.

54 Mass-Observation Archive, University of Sussex, File Report 600, "Morale in Glasgow," March 1941, p.9.

55 Mass-Observation Archive, University of Sussex, File Report 606, "Ports-mouth: Reaction to the Blitz," 15 March 1941. Gardiner, *Wartime*, pp.354 and 359–360, notes the devastation.

56 I. McLaine, *Ministry of Morale: Home Front Morale and the Ministry of Information in World War II* (London, 1979). P. Addison and J. Crang (eds), *Listening to Britain* (London, 2011), offers various Ministry of Information reports covering May–September 1940 from the National Archives.

57 Turner, *The Phoney War*, p.280, for an "extremely serious" hoax in Mansfield. *News Chronicle*, 5 June 1940, carries the original report. *Punch*, 4 October 1939, cartoon, "Let's see who can invent the best rumour" and *ibid.* 10 July 1940 for more of the same.

58 Briggs, *War of Words*, p.215.

59 INF 1/264/247, 24 May 1940.

60 *The Times*, 9 October 2001.

61 INF 1/264/204, 5 June 1940, on Joyce knowing the time on a Darlington clock.

62 Bergmeier and Lotz, *Hitler's Airwaves*, p.96.

63 Wolf Mittler in conversation with D. Blakeway, nd. Private Collection.

64 J. Langdon-Davies, *Fifth Column* (London, 1940), pp.52–53. E. Stebbing, *Diary of a Decade 1939–50* (Sussex, 1998), p.42, suggests Joyce's broadcasts showed Germany must have an excellent spy system. The Nazis had British sympathisers, including well-known public figures but never much of an organised espionage network. See A. Roberts, "Double-Barrelled Traitors of 1942," *The Spectator*, 23 January 1993, pp.19–20, on some of the more prominent suspects and R. Thurlow, "The Evolution of the Mythical British Fifth Column, 1939–46," *Twentieth Century British History*, Vol.10 (1999), pp.477–498, on the lack of organisation.

65 *Daily Mirror*, 29 February 1940.

66 *Ibid.* 6 and 10 June 1940.

67 *Truth*, 5 July 1940.

68 *Manchester Guardian*, 17 October 1939.

69 Barrington, *Lord Haw-Haw*, p.9.

70 Reviewed in *The Times*, 23 December 1939. See J. M. East, *Max Miller: The Cheeky Chappie* (London, 1977), pp.114–115.

71 T. Charman, "William Joyce Lord Haw-Haw 1906–1946," introduction to Joyce, *Twilight over England* (London, 1992), p.iv and illustration facing p.v.

72 Wiener Library, Board of Deputies of British Jews, File 1658/9/1/8.

73 INF 1/264/169, 19 June 1940.

74 "The First Pirate." BBC, Radio 4, 14 January 2000. Matthew and Harrison (eds), *ODNB*, Vol. 44, p.602.

75 BBC Written Archives, "Hamburg Broadcasting Propaganda. Summary of the results of an enquiry into the extent and effect of its impact on the British public during mid-winter 1939/40," LR/98, 8 March 1940; "The British Audience for German Bulletins in English," LR/74, 16 May 1939; "Listening to Enemy Broadcasts," LR/120, 20 January 1941; "Listening

to Enemy Broadcasts," LR/1459, 12 January 1943. Doherty, *Nazi Wireless Propaganda*, pp.93–95,119–120. *Weekly Angles*, No.103, 13 January 1939 for Leese's comment.

76 BBC Written Archives, Frederick Ogilvie to Sir Campbell Stuart, R 34/639/1, 26 December 1939.

77 Briggs, *War of Words*, p.88.

78 *Ibid.* parts I and II. Doherty, *Nazi Wireless Propaganda*; S. Nicholas, *The Echo of War: Home Front Propaganda and the Wartime BBC* (Manchester, 1996).

79 K.Young (ed.), *The Diaries of Sir Robert Bruce Lockhart*,Vol. 2, *1939–1965* (London, 1980), p.58.

80 W. E. Mosse (et al.), *Second Chance:Two Centuries of German-Speaking Jews in the United Kingdom* (Tübingen, 1991), pp.271, 202 respectively. M. Stenton, *Radio London and Resistance in Occupied Europe: British Political Warfare 1939–1943* (Oxford, 2000), ch.6.

81 R.H.S. Crossman, "Psychological Warfare," *Journal of the Royal United Service Institution*,Vol.97 (1952), p.320. Ettlinger, *Axis on Air*, pp.309 ff on the V campaign.

82 Young (ed.), *Diaries*, pp.18–34 on PWE's origins.

83 R. H. Bruce Lockhart, *Comes the Reckoning* (London, 1949).

84 Howe, *The Black Game*, on British responses.

85 E. Fröhlich (ed.), *Die Tagebücher von Josef Goebbels*, Vol.1/7, July 1939–March 1940 (München, 1998), p.259, 5 January 1940.

86 Birkett features in Simpson, *In the Highest Degree Odious*.

87 Contrast H. M. Hyde, *Norman Birkett. The Life of Lord Birkett of Ulverston* (London, 1964), p.471, with Briggs, *War of Words*, p.140, though the latter is discreet.

88 Briggs, *War of Words*, pp.292–294, refers to the conflict. So does S. Hylton, *Their Darkest Hour:The Hidden History of the Home Front 1939–1945* (Stroud, 2003), p.176. For Priestley's account, see his *Margin Released: A Writer's Reminiscence and Reflections* (London, 1962), pp.221–223. See also *J. B. Priestley's Postscripts* (London, 1940).

89 *Priestley's Postscripts* and N. Hanson with T. Priestley, *Priestley's Wars* (Ilkley, 2008), Part III.

90 E. Lustgarten, "The Time of My Life," BBC Script, 28 December 1969. BBC Written Archives.

91 Matthew and Harrison (eds), *ODNB*, Vol. 15, pp.744–745. S. Delmer, *Black Boomerang* (London, 1962).

92 Briggs, *War of Words*, on these years and their challenges. *The Times*, 9 January 2009,Vladimir Rubinstein's obituary, for a reminder of émigré involvement.

93 Crossman, "Psychological Warfare," pp.319–332.

94 I. Kershaw, "How effective was Nazi Propaganda?" in Welch, *Nazi Propaganda*, p.198.

95 D. O'Drisceoil, *Censorship in Ireland 1939–1945* (Cork, 1996), p.143.

96 E. Fröhlich (ed.), *Tagebücher*, Vol.4, April–June 1942 (München, 1995), p.339, 23 May 1942.

17

BERLIN CALLING.
CALLING BERLIN.

Anna Wolkoff has come perilously close to high treason . . . There is little doubt that Captain Ramsay is cognisant of her activities. [Guy Liddell Diary, 31 May 1940, in Nigel West (ed.), *The Guy Liddell Diaries*, Vol. 1, 1939–1942 (London, 2005), p. 83.]

1

Early in the War, when German military successes seemed virtually guaranteed and a Hitlerite future beckoned, British fascists can be traced contacting former comrades now working for the Nazis on the Continent. These messages often passed through the diplomatic bags of countries whose staff did not ask too many inconvenient questions. Sympathisers in Europe sometimes acted as go-betweens.[1]

Mary Stanford engaged in such activity through the agency of Jean Nieumanhuys, a second secretary at the Belgian Embassy in London.[2] Stanford was first detained by the British authorities in July 1940, released that September, collared in March 1941 and restricted until October 1944.[3] However, even in internment she attempted to reach her Berlin-based friend Margaret Bothamley.[4] In one of her letters in the summer of 1942 she described the War as a contest between Light and Darkness, before remarking, "I prefer Light for *all* our sakes." Later that year in another letter, still clearly praying for a Nazi victory, she wrote, "One's whole heart is with the crusade."[5] F. Gerald Gough was also believed by the security service to be in touch with Berlin.[6] Richard Findlay came under suspicion.[7] As did Edward Whinfield.[8]

In view of Joyce's prominence on Nazi radio it is hardly surprising he featured in some of these exchanges. Correspondents would sometimes write to him via 'HP' at the Hotel Meran in Maribor, Yugoslavia.[9] 'HP' is likely to have been Herbert Pullar, ex-soldier, fascist, member of the Anglo-German Fellowship and political pilgrim, who had journeyed to pre-war Germany to gaze at the wonders of National Socialism.[10]

An important episode in 1940 involving Joyce overshadows all these clandestine dealings. It is a complex affair which grew out of a larger context of fascist plotting and subversion and seriously influenced the outcome of his subsequent trial. Strangely, one Joyce biography virtually ignores it.[11] Another, caught up in "voodoo history," completely misreads it.[12]

2

A return is needed first to events in Europe. Recall that in 1939 the Wehrmacht had rapidly smashed its way through Poland. In April 1940 Norway and Denmark had fallen under German occupation. Victories had quickly followed in Belgium, Holland and Luxembourg. The main German thrust could now be directed towards France, the biggest prize of all. By late May the Wehrmacht was scything through French positions towards the English Channel.[13] Britain appeared increasingly exposed.

Joyce could finally allow himself to believe that the mottled old hands who had long ruled the country where he felt he had been denied were about to lose their grip on power. On Nazi radio he was threatening Britain with a near-certain defeat.

The legendary Ed Murrow, reporting for CBS from London, brilliantly captured this growing threat, telling his American listeners on 14 May 1940, "there is no repetition of the easy optimism that characterised the early days of the fighting."[14] Sir Alexander Cadogan at the Foreign Office doubted the country could survive. "A miracle might save us," he confided in his diary on 21 May, "otherwise we're done."[15] He was not alone in thinking it.[16] As the War unravelled further, the new Cabinet – Churchill had replaced Neville Chamberlain in Downing Street on 10 May 1940 – deliberated in late May whether to negotiate a peace settlement with Germany.[17] In the event, the country fought on. But the imminent fall of France and the soon-to-be-unleashed German air assault would test its resolve even more.[18]

Nazi fellow travellers who salivated at the prospect of Britain going under and dared to dream of Hitler's triumphal entry into London, pursued ever more ambitious plans to bring about the country's collapse.

These threatening circumstances, combined with pressure on MI5 to root out fifth columnists, formed the background to an incident in London. At about 11am on 20 May 1940 Maxwell Knight of MI5, police inspectors Harold Keeble and J. W. Pearson and American diplomat Franklin C. Gowen, raided the flat of Tyler G. Kent, a code and cipher clerk in the US Embassy who had just moved to London from Moscow. On entering 47 Gloucester Place W1, they found him entertaining Irene Danischewsky, one of his lovers.[19] The officers were not easily distracted by the sight of the semi naked couple. "It was such a gorgeous day," Mrs Danischewsky wrote later, "and we had planned to go to Kew."[20] But obviously they had a more immediate priority.

Kent, one of those Americans "who wear well-cut suits, with waistcoat and watch-chain, drink wine instead of high-balls, and easily become furiously indignant," might have appeared harmless enough on the surface.[21] A minor diplomat, an excellent linguist and something of ladies' man, might say it all. But all was not as it seemed.

In September 1939, en route from Moscow to take up his appointment in London, Kent had disembarked at Newcastle upon Tyne in the company of Ludwig Matthias. On 4 October they were seen together in the lounge of the Cumberland Hotel near Marble Arch. Matthias, a German Jew in origin but now a Swedish citizen – "5'4"; stout; dark rather Turkish appearance; well dressed" – was believed by Swedish sources to be a Gestapo agent.[22] MI5 became suspicious. Their wariness increased when Kent began seeing Anna Wolkoff, already known to us – and to MI5 – as a member of the Right Club.

They had become friendly by March 1940.[23] One fascist contact might be explained away, but two?

MI5's suspicions were justified. Knight's raiding party found in Kent's flat a large cache of official documents including Churchill-Roosevelt correspondence on possible Anglo-American co-operation in the War. Churchill began this correspondence when serving as First Lord of the Admiralty and continued it briefly after he had entered Downing Street. If this sympathetic exchange had ever become public, FDR would have been deeply embarrassed in the run-up to the Presidential election in November 1940. Any exposure would also have created a likely breach in relations between the two countries and might have helped to keep America out of the War. After all, the official US position, reflecting powerful isolationist sentiment there, was that of studied neutrality.[24] The cipher clerk, who had purloined other important confidential documents, had accumulated a potentially damaging political archive. Significantly, Kent also had in his rooms the locked membership book of 'Jock' Ramsay's Right Club.[25] Which suggested he was in contact with Britain's Nazi sympathisers, eager in any way to assist Hitler's plans. If such material ever reached Berlin, Goebbels and Joyce would have regarded it as a veritable propaganda feast, which they would have been delighted to exploit. And in view of the American's Nazi and fellow-travelling contacts there was a fear in 1940 that it might travel along this route.

Kent was arrested. The US authorities, alarmed and fearful at this grave security lapse, dismissed him and stripped him of diplomatic immunity.[26]

An American source claims Counselor Herschel Johnson, charged with security at the Embassy, later "spoke strongly" to Knight because, he claimed, MI5 had not alerted him to its suspicions.[27] This lapse, if it occurred, might have been deliberate. The British believed with good reason that Joseph Kennedy, the US Ambassador, regarded their country as finished.[28] Knight's initiative, whilst demonstrating the government's vigilance, would fire a warning shot across Kennedy's bows. Significantly, and conveniently, the Ambassador left his post in London the day Kent went on trial. He took a flight to Portugal before boarding a transatlantic clipper to New York. He was thereby spared the embarrassment of giving evidence.[29]

Why had Kent amassed this archive? One view is that he was an isolationist and also broadly sympathetic to Nazi Germany.[30] This argument has not convinced everybody. Fine details regarding his transfer from the Moscow Embassy to London remain unclear. Had his persistent womanising in Moscow made him vulnerable?[31] In other words, was he a Bolshevik agent who had moved to London at the bidding of the Soviets? Was he collecting information for them on Britain's Nazis? William Bullitt, US ambassador to Russia, certainly claimed Kent was on Stalin's payroll.[32] Or was he a maverick, who knew confidential documents had considerable value, enhanced the image of whoever possessed them, and were a tradeable commodity?[33] Five years after Kent's arrest, Maxwell Knight told his MI5 colleague Graham Mitchell the American had no sense of honour but espionage was not his game.[34] The authorised history of MI5 sheds no light on the matter.[35] Kent retains his air of mystery.

His contact, Anna Wolkoff, "short, compact, and, though still quite young already white-haired," is of more interest here.[36] She was arrested earlier the same day as Kent at 18a Roland Gardens, the Wolkoff family home.[37] The young Len Deighton, whose mother cooked for the Wolkoffs, witnessed her arrest.[38] She was charged with having US Embassy documents allegedly supplied by Kent and a more serious matter – that she had tried "to send a coded message to William Joyce, containing advice on radio propaganda."[39] She was aware that Joyce, whom she knew from the Right Club, was now in a position on Nazi radio to assist in undermining Britain and creating the society they both wanted.

Wolkoff was born in St Petersburg in 1902. But following the Bolshevik Revolution the family settled in London, where her father had served as the last tsarist Naval Attaché.[40] In 1935 she began an *haute couture* business which attracted royalty and Mrs Wallis Simpson.[41] But this commercial success was short-lived; by 1939 the firm had gone into liquidation.[42] It is not these business dealings that have given Wolkoff a place in the history books, however, but her right-wing political activities.

She held "fanatically anti-Semitic and anti-communist" views.[43] Her involvement alongside Joyce in the Right Club is no surprise. Her friend Enid Riddell said Wolkoff acted there as a "bonne à tout faire"; she served as its chauffeur and secretary and found time to display its anti-war stickybacks.[44] She could explode with "Hitler is a god . . . and it would be wonderful if he could govern England."[45] She sounds here rather like Joyce. Both wanted to 'save' the country and envisaged the same kind of future. Bolshevism crushed, the old political gang cast out, fascism triumphant. In March 1940 Maxwell Knight had described her as a "first-class liar" with "a considerable amount of superficial charm."[46] Wolkoff had to be watched.

Her family had a history of clandestine activity. After the Bolshevik Revolution Madame Wolkoff had ferried "special messages" to Russia. Admiral Wolkoff, a "good for nothing – very fond of wine, women and cards," according to a 1918 American Intelligence report, might appear less significant.[47] But he knew of his daughter's fellow-travelling activities, notwithstanding his telling Sir Vernon Kell, head of MI5 until May 1940 that her arrest had hit him "like a thunderbolt."[48] Nikolai Wolkoff appeared to know Kell. He also knew Admiral Reginald 'Blinker' Hall, formerly Director of the Intelligence at the Admiralty.[49] Had he transacted business with them? Whichever masters Admiral Wolkoff served – in the early 1920s he might have worked for the Bolsheviks – by the 1940s he leaned towards the political Right.[50]

From 1923, with financial help from other émigrés, the Wolkoffs had run the Russian Tea Rooms at 50 Harrington Road, South Kensington, a meeting place for Russian exiles.[51] First impressions do not reveal everything, however.

British fascists and fellow travellers conducted their anti-British intrigues there.[52] The small twelve-seater establishment offered more than caviar and black tea. Mary Stanford patronised it.[53] In the 1930s, before she left for Germany, Margaret Bothamley could often be found at the Tea Rooms.[54] Pre-war German Embassy staff descended to pick up gossip and develop contacts.[55] Sigismund FitzRandolph, an attaché who liaised with fascists in Britain, was seen there "fairly often."[56] Did the Nazis provide discreet funding? Captain Ramsay, who lived nearby, certainly did.[57] Did Joyce visit Harrington Road? He preferred stronger forms of liquid refreshment, but would have found a sympathetic, receptive audience.

In 1940 as the War's fortunes rapidly shifted against Britain, the Tea Rooms became a hive of fellow-travelling activity; here was the fevered ambience against which Anna Wolkoff attempted to make contact with Joyce.

3

The official papers on Wolkoff's case remain closed. But key elements of the episode can be prised open.[58]

Wolkoff always maintained she was not the author of the coded message but had received it from the mysterious J. McGuirk Hughes. As P. G. Taylor, he was Mosley's 'Chief Snoop' in Department Z of the BUF and through its Industrial Department had placed fascist agents within the trade unions.[59] Joyce would have met him not only in the BUF but also in the Right Club. However, this elusive soldier of fortune pursued another life. He worked for Special Branch and MI5. To add a further layer of complexity, he was sometimes known as Captain Cunningham.[60] He appears in Max Knight's pulp novel, *Crime Cargo*, as McGuirk, "a bald-headed, pig-eyed Irishman."[61] Whatever he called himself, here is further evidence of the still largely obscure links between the security service and British fascism.

Wolkoff alleged that when Taylor transferred the message he said it came from a friend interested in contacting Joyce. He passed it to her when Lord Ronald Graham, whose company they were both keeping, had momentarily turned his back. Graham's membership of the Right Club, the fact he knew Joyce and Kent, and displayed Nazi sympathies, might suggest he was not a completely innocent party.[62] He had apparently offered earlier to despatch the letter through his friend, the Spanish Ambassador, the 17th Duke of Alba – and 10th Duke of Berwick – Jacobo María del Pilar Carlos Manuel Fitz-James Stuart y Falcó, known unsurprisingly to his British intimates as 'Jimmy.' Wisely, Graham thought better of it.[63]

Once in possession of the letter, Wolkoff had to decide how to send it. To contact Joyce and other fascists in Germany, she needed a discreet post-box, and much speculation has centred on her connection to Duke Francesco del Monte Marigliano, a member of the Italian Embassy staff in London.[64] Not that the British authorities ever fathomed the nature of the link between them.[65] On this occasion her normal contact at the Italian Embassy – was it del Monte Marigliano? – had fallen ill and was unable to help. She thought of using Kent, but abandoned this plan. At which point Maxwell Knight's agents conveniently stepped forward.

Marjorie Joan Mackie, sometimes known as Marjorie Amor, had been watching Wolkoff since December 1939. As Amor she appeared in the membership book of the Right Club. Her involvement there took place at Knight's bidding.[66] By February 1940 Hélène de Munck, another of Max's officers, had been brought into the surveillance team.[67] Joan Miller, one of Knight's former lovers, also cultivated Wolkoff.[68]

Wolkoff was persuaded to believe that de Munck, whom she naively regarded as a new-found friend, could assist in getting the letter despatched. The MI5 officer led Wolkoff to understand the Roumanian legation might be able help.[69] Such is part of this complex story, though discrepancies remain in the fine detail. No matter these shades on the picture, a number of the key players and the complex manoeuvres to contact Joyce are starting to take shape.

When de Munck received the letter on 9 April 1940 she allegedly passed it to Maxwell Knight.[70] It was returned to Wolkoff, through de Munck, to allow for the addition of a few lines in German – which included a reference to an alleged link between Lord Ampthill and freemasonry – as well as the letters P.J. (Perish Judah) and, as a seal of its authenticity, the emblem of the Right Club.[71] Joyce would have recognised its significance immediately. The message was then despatched with MI5's connivance or direct involvement, probably through "one of the Balkans Legations."[72]

4

What does the coded letter contain?[73] Dated 2 April 1940 and headed, "Alphabetische System: Schuesselwort: Weiss-Reich-Spitzname" it began:[74]

> Talks effect splendid but news bulletins less so. Palestine good but IRA etc defeats object stick to plutocracy avoid King ...

As Joyce worked his way through it, turning serried rows of letters into understandable prose, he would have read first of all its advice on the best radio reception frequencies. He would then have come across:

Here Kriegshetze only among Blimps workers fed up, wives more so troops not keen antisemitism spreading like flame everywhere all classes.

Note refujews in so-called Pioneer Corps guaranteed in writing to be sent into firing line.[75]

Churchill not popular keep on at him as Baruch tool[76] and war-theatre-extender sacrificer Gallipoli etc. stress his conceit and repeated failures with ex-proselites [sic] and prestige.

Altmark atrocities debunked by Truth this is only free paper, circulation bounding editor fearless anti-warmonger and lie exposer big man behind paper, no fear ruin.[77]

Nearly all your friends still sound eg pay gay /00 hundred per cent, though Lewis wants murder you all league sound.[78]

Family not persecuted by public but only by Anderson who keeps Q imprisoned without trial and got F and R sacked BBC[79] still family not in distress, master teaching school again.[80]

Baphomet [or B.A.P home T.] very friendly wife also.[81]

Ironside believed very anti-Jewish, not so anti-German possible future British Franco[82] if things reach that stage here.[83]

Anyone searching for more detail would have been dependent until recently on information from Earl Jowitt. Fourteen years after participating in Wolkoff's trial he recalled her case in *Some were Spies*.[84] Quite unexpectedly, and irritatingly for him, she reappeared at this point and objected to his version of events. He had therefore to amend his text, while claiming it remained consistent with his "telling the truth."[85]

He noted that the message also contained:[86]

> Butter ration doubled because poor can't buy admitted by Telegraph bacon same cost living steeply mounting shopkeepers are suffering suits PEP.[87]

> Regret must state Meg's Tuesday talks unpopular with women[88] advise alter radically or drop God bless and salute to all leaguers[89] and CB.[90]

This detail has since been confirmed in Intelligence files.[91]

Addressed to Joyce at the Radio Building in Berlin, the communication ended with the suggestion that its arrival be confirmed by a broadcast reference to Carlyle. On Saturday 27 April 1940 the NBBS commented: "We thank the French for nothing; where is their Shakespeare? Who is their Carlyle?"[92] The letter had seemingly reached its destination.[93]

How would Joyce have interpreted this dense complex message? Who compiled it? What is its historical importance?

5

The letter was not rich in highly confidential detail. Joyce would have recognised it as an attempt to inform him on fascist thinking in a Britain that might soon collapse. The message clearly created problems for Hugh Foss of the War Office, acting as MI5's decoder. He misread the section on Jews and the Pioneer Corps and the "Baphomet" reference defeated him. Joyce, however, would have been able to understand all of it. He would have welcomed those claims that the War was unpopular, anti-Semitism was spreading and Churchill was widely disliked. He would have been relieved to hear his family – "Q, F and R" – were not "in distress" even though they had their problems. The news John Macnab ("master") had secured a teaching post would have pleased him. He was unlikely to lose any sleep on being told that "Lewis" (Captain Lewis) was hostile. What he made of "Baphomet's" (Mosley's) Nazi sympathies was likely to be more complex. And what would he think of Ironside as a British puppet ruler? He would have agreed Political and Economic Planning was a problem. Finally, if "CB" were Christian Bauer, it is doubtful Joyce would have been interested in passing on any good wishes. Bauer had proved a dreadful disappointment.

The British authorities viewed the letter differently. It went further than dangerous or careless talk, the kind of gossip that posters by Fougasse (Kenneth Bird) warned against. It involved more than distributing anti-war propaganda. Here was a serious, deliberate attempt to contact one of the enemy's emerging radio stars.

6

Who compiled this complex message? Admiral Sir Barry Domvile's name has been mentioned. So has that of Vincent Collier, Joyce's former colleague in the National Socialist League.[94]

These suggestions have now been imperiously swept aside with the claim that MI5 and Maxwell Knight had been at work, a suggestion heard recently in the television programme "Churchill and the Fascist Plot."[95] What a persistent thread is Max in Joyce's life. He then operated, it is said, through P. G. Taylor, Marjorie Amor and Hélène de Munck to compromise Wolkoff and, by implication, other British fascists.[96] These people must not remain at liberty even if it took a dirty tricks initiative to detain them. Facing intense government pressure to crack down on Britain's Nazi sympathisers, Max would have demonstrated how effective he could be.[97] The absent "Joycey," would be seriously compromised. In this version of events, since Knight wrote the letter and employed Taylor as go-between, it was unlikely to have reached its destination.[98]

A soon-to-be-undertaken forensic examination will demolish the claim that MI5 wrote the message. And, we already know, the suggestion it was never sent is difficult to sustain. Admittedly it contained detail not readily available to Joyce in Berlin, but none of it was especially sensitive; there was no reason to block its despatch. The case against Wolkoff and her kind – Joyce especially – would be stronger if it were known the letter had reached him.

This attempt to place the security service at the centre of events, and Knight as the spidery thread, is a conspiracy theory. Who, then, put it together?[99] Who desperately wanted to contact Joyce?

Its writer moved in fascist circles and remained closely in touch with their current thinking. The person had probably been involved with the National Socialist League. The Carlyle reference brings to mind the Carlyle Club, the NSL's discussion group. The compiler wanted Joyce to know "all league sound," in other words, reassure him his former political comrades in England, his fifth column followers in waiting, were still active. "God bless and salute to all leaguers" (probably a reference to former members of the National Socialist League, or members of the Nordic League now in Germany), hinted at the author's religious belief. The writer was anti-Semitic. The attack on Bernard Baruch; the claim that British anti-Semitism was rampant; the hostility towards refugee Jews, all suggested it. The P. G. Taylor ("pay gay") reference hinted at a BUF connection at some point, even if the author was unaware of Taylor's security service connections. The obscure "Baphomet" emphasis suggested the correspondent and intended recipient enjoyed an extremely close relationship; the former was even alert to the idiosyncrasies of Joyce's vocabulary. That closeness was underlined by addressing the message to William Brooke Joyce: only a handful of people know of his preference for this name. Whoever constructed it was aware Joyce had gone to Berlin, had recognised his voice over the airwaves, and was familiar with the tones of "Meg." With absolute confidence, the letter was sent to the Funkhaus.

Working through this evidence there are compelling grounds for believing that John Macnab's hand had been at work.

His role is further suggested by the drip of detail appearing in Intelligence files. One crucial document reads: "The story really starts when MacNAB approached a certain individual known to him as a sympathiser and asked this person if he knew of any means by which a letter could be got through to Germany to William JOYCE."[100]

A wartime meeting between Maxwell Knight and Bryan Donovan, a leading BUF member who knew Macnab quite well, is also suggestive. On 25 August 1940 at Latchmere House interrogation centre, Max asked: "Do you happen to know whether he [Macnab] was interested in codes and ciphers?" Rather than answering directly, Donovan remarked that his former political comrade was an excellent chess player and "there would be ground for thinking that he would be interested in at least the academic side of ciphers and codes."[101] Knight was probing further into Macnab's involvement.

The nature of the text and scattered clues in official documents point the finger at Macnab, a claim which is strengthened by evidence in his internment interrogation file, which was released in March 2007. In 2001 the then Home Secretary claimed this document had been destroyed. Had he asked MI5 he would have known differently.[102] The puzzle which had defeated all earlier investigations could be resolved.[103]

Macnab proved massively indiscreet in his political dealings. His drunken faux pas in 1938 in Brussels, his telling a casual MI6 informant he was to meet Christian Bauer, an important Nazi, had been followed by another major blunder. The coded message made Joyce of even more interest and significance to the authorities.

The security service became involved in events and encouraged it. But Macnab initiated the process. Whilst massaging his fascist contacts, keeping in touch with the Joyce family, protesting about censorship of his mail, dating the elusive "Judy," he compiled the coded message. With Joyce he had obviously worked on this prospect, Hackenschmidt code and all, which further reveals Joyce's leaving Britain in 1939 was not a spur-of-the-moment decision but the result of careful thought and planning.[104] 'Master' was "an unrepentant traitor" who always prayed for a Nazi victory.[105] The message reflected his unwavering commitment to the fifth column project his dear William had hatched before leaving for Berlin.

7

Content and authorship are important, if teasing, questions. But does this attempt to contact Joyce when Britain was at its most vulnerable amount to more than an intriguing detective story for historians? It certainly did for its key figures, for whom the consequences were serious. Tyler Kent, the stealer of diplomatic documents, went to jail for seven years, first in Wandsworth and later at Camp Hill on the Isle of Wight, before being deported to the United States.[106] After indulging in some unfortunate Mexican investments, he died in 1988 in reduced circumstances in a US trailer park, leaving behind a host of unanswered questions.[107] Anna Wolkoff also paid a heavy price. She received a ten years' prison sentence and lost the British nationality she had taken out in 1935.[108] She died in a car accident in Spain in 1973.[109]

Joyce was to be deeply affected by the incident. When delivering judgement in the Tyler Kent case in 1940, Mr Justice Tucker labelled him a traitor.[110] It is difficult to imagine a more unsavoury image. Yet five years later, Tucker presided over Joyce's trial at the Old Bailey. It can hardly be said, quoting Joyce, that he approached these later proceedings in a state of "mental virginity."[111] The Wolkoff letter helped to determine that Joyce should be executed.

And Macnab? He was interned as part of the larger round-up of fascists triggered by the Wolkoff letter.[112] This cull was approved on 22 May 1940, two days after Kent and Wolkoff had been arrested. Joyce's mother took temporary charge of his possessions.[113] Detention strengthened his belief that a thoroughly rotten Britain was governed by Blimpish and Jewish forces. But he was fortunate to have avoided a charge of treason. The state hesitated only because any prosecution could have compromised McGuirk Hughes.[114]

Macnab's internment was not the only consequence. It is understandable why later he devoted himself slavishly to Joyce's defence. His unstinting support reflected not only their long close friendship but also his crushing sense of guilt, which must always have gnawed away at him. If only he had never written that letter. If only it had not been intercepted. Macnab shared much of his life with Joyce. He loved him. Tragically, he helped to destroy him. A devout Catholic convert, he never received the satisfaction of Joyce rejoining the Church.[115] Soon after Joyce's execution, 'Master' headed for Franco's Spain and died there.[116]

Frank Joyce was detained as the bigger cull of fascists began.[117] Quentin had been collared earlier. John Beckett was arrested.[118] And so was Captain Ramsay MP.[119] Deeply implicated in all kinds of anti-war agitation, hand-in glove with Kent – even handing over the Right Club ledger – close to Wolkoff, anxious to treat with the Nazis, he could hardly have expected to remain at liberty.[120]

More faceless people, suspected of even a tenuous Joyce connection, were suddenly swept up. Leslie Orton, absent from the annals of British fascism, was arrested even though claiming he had last spoken to Joyce 1935.[121] John Sidney George Crosland, likewise invisible in that history, was detained after pressure from the West Sussex Constabulary who tried to establish a connection between him and Joyce in the summer of 1939, just before Joyce had left for Berlin.[122]

Key BUF figures, including Raven Thomson and Francis-Hawkins, were interned.[123] But Mosley, the buccaneering "Captain Jack," was the biggest catch.[124] When MI5 perused the Wolkoff letter it might not have identified "Baphomet." But when Britain stood increasingly exposed it knew enough of Mosley's activities to regard 'The Leader' as potentially dangerous. If, acting on Macnab's letter, a fifth column had to be crushed, Mosley was a clear target.

Some of 'Master's' coded observations were extravagant. But his claim that "Baphomet" and his wife retained the Nazi sympathies they had nurtured during the 1930s was well-founded.

Through the summer and autumn of 1939 Mosley, like Joyce, glimpsed an increasingly vulnerable Britain which offered an unrivalled political opportunity. If on the way he had to treat with some lesser mortals, so be it. They could easily be swept aside later. On 26 July 1939 Barry Domvile, Philip Farrer, ex-Intelligence officer and now a well-known Nazi sympathiser, Neil Francis-Hawkins, J.F.C. Fuller, A. P. Laurie and Captain Ramsay were among guests at a Mosley dinner party, given at 129 Grosvenor Road. George Ward Price, *persona grata* with the Leader-in-Waiting and a useful conduit for transmitting his views to a wider audience, also arrived to enjoy the five courses as well as the brandy, champagne, and sherry which accompanied the food and the evening's politics.[125] The following month Collin Brooks, another well-placed Rothermere-linked journalist, with an ear firmly glued to London's political gossip, even speculated whether he might become Mosley's appointee as Governor of the Bank of England.[126] There was obviously chatter in certain well-connected sections of London society of Britain soon having a fascist government. Fired by that prospect, in September 1939 'The Leader' edged close to Ramsay to co-ordinate their anti-war activities.[127] Next month MI5 reported on a *rapprochement* between the BUF and the Nordic League.[128] The prospect and then reality of war led to convenient partnerships in this increasingly expectant political dance.[129]

Mosley continued plotting until his internment.[130] Would the crisis sweep him to power? Would the anticipated Nazi invasion do the trick? Might he secure the key prize without having to be as drastic as Joyce and decamp to Berlin? In December 1939 John Coast, fascist veteran, friend of Anna Wolkoff and member of the Right Club – who enjoyed a remarkably different post-war career – wrote to Henry Hamilton Beamish, founder of The Britons and now a figure in the Nazi International, querying whether Mosley had the necessary credentials for any such future role:

> Mosley, I feel sure more than ever, is a conscious or unconscious Jew or Jew-tool. His paper Action is now quite useless, and his egotism nauseating. Under no circumstances can he be considered as a serious political proposition, but merely a dago comic who is a safety valve. Blast him, for he has likeable qualities, including a fine straight left, and a wrist and nerve of steel in a scrap![131]

'The Leader' seldom harboured any self-doubts.

While creating various expedient alliances, Mosley never forsook the BUF. At a meeting of its district officers on 30 January 1940 he confidently proclaimed, "Our time is approaching." A discreet police observer also reported 'The Leader's' emphasis on the success of our "brother parties" in other countries when their moment of destiny had struck. The same officer then remarked on Mosley telling his audience to prepare even for the "supreme sacrifice." This startling emphasis would have left listeners in no doubt what he was anticipating. "Underlying the whole of his speech there was a strong hint of a march to power by armed force."[132] He had no interest in Britain being reduced to "a dung heap" by its present effete political bosses.[133] Joyce noticed a twilight spreading over the country; Mosley glimpsed it disappearing under a pile of its own political excrement. Both messages were the same. Britain was finished, staggering on its last legs. The two were as one in envisaging a fascist future.

On the first day of March 1940, "Baphomet" appeared in similarly buoyant mood at London's Criterion restaurant when addressing a large audience of BUF members, other fascists and prominent members of society.[134] He uttered similar sentiments at secret private meetings.[135] His unashamed vaulting ambitions when Britain faced a battle for survival doubtless stirred the political fantasies of others. Mosley fantasising in London, Joyce fantasising in Berlin, where was the difference?

Mosley had long awaited his date with destiny. His personal tragedy was that it never came. Circumstances worked against him. He also lacked deep political insight and sensitive judgement. He was too 'flash,' too impetuous. It is hard to disagree with an MI5 officer's devastating portrait of him as "immensely vain" and "a bad judge of men," someone "entirely lacking in sincerity" whose "excessive vanity" made it "difficult for him to take an objective view of any situation."[136] No matter; his intentions were clear. By the autumn of 1939, one senior Intelligence source advised that Mosley was pursuing a pro-Nazi strategy.[137] To a degree which brought him close to treason.[138] How much insight Macnab showed when telling Joyce that "Baphomet" was "very friendly." What are the odds now on Mosley the patriot? He was desperate to be Britain's Laval.[139]

Joyce would not have been surprised. But he must have hoped his own dramatic uprooting to start anew in Berlin would guarantee him a warmer place in the Nazi sun. However, from the British Government's point of view, anyone behaving like Mosley in 1940 must be interned.[140]

"Baphomet's" wife also had to be detained.[141] When the Friends of Oswald Mosley gathered for their post-war dinners, the elegant symbol of the BUF would regally descend as their honoured, fragrant guest and after her death in 2003 would be mourned by them as "DIANA, OUR FRIEND."[142] Earlier, the British authorities had viewed her as dangerous:

> Diana Moseley [sic] wife of Sir Oswald Mosley, is reported on the best authority, that of her family and intimate circle, to be a public danger at the present time. Is said to be far cleverer and more dangerous than her husband and will stick at nothing to achieve her ambitions – she is wildly ambitious.[143]

When the Wolkoff episode triggered a further round of internment, the Mosleys amounted to the big catch.

This seemingly small fragment of wartime history decisively influenced Joyce's post-war fate. It affected the rest of 'Master's' life, though publicly he never breathed a word of his involvement. It significantly shaped the treatment of Britain's fascists, including Mosley, as well as the country's fellow travellers.[144]

7

A few years later Joyce was still out of the country. But he was no longer in Berlin. He was no more a star broadcaster on Nazi radio, someone his fascist comrades in Britain were anxious to involve in their plans. His high hopes of 1940 had vanished. In May 1945 he was a badly wounded man in the hands of the British army.

Notes

1 Griffiths, *Patriotism Perverted*, pp.256–257. KV 2/840, Special Branch report, 14 March 1940, on friends of Margaret Bothamley keeping in touch with her in Berlin. See also HO 45/25724, MI5 report, 8 March 1942, for Colonel F.W.R. MacDonald as a conduit for some correspondence. He had close links to the Imperial Fascist League. An intercepted letter from "Maurice" in Virginia, dated 17 April 1941, might suggest correspondence involving Joyce flowed in the reverse direction. Joyce had seemingly provided his correspondent with details of bomb damage in Berlin and hinted he might consider leaving Berlin. However, Whitehall remained unsure if it were genuine. FO 371/26572/6645 for details. Less uncertainty surrounds an alleged letter from Joyce in 1943 designed to assist British anti-Semites, and now in the Wiener Library. It is a clear forgery. See Wiener Library, File 1658/2/1/13g

2 KV2/832–833.

3 HO 45/25731.

4 KV 2/677/141a and KV 2/840. Special Branch report, 14 March 1940.

5 Letters, Stanford to Bothamley, 9 July 1942 and 27 September 1942, respectively, in HO 45/25731, extract from MI5's summary of "Acts Prejudicial" cases, January 1944. Their continuing link was further revealed when in 1944, on release from internment, Stanford's address appeared as 67 Cromwell Road, SW7, which Bothamley had occupied before leaving for Germany (HO 45/25731, Special Branch report, 24 October 1944). After Bothamley's departure it might have been Stanford's decision to secrete her possessions in Harrington Road before "destroying or removing" any "incriminating" documents (HO 45/25731, MI5 memo, December 1943). There is a degree of planning here which

further suggests Bothamley was not the 'stupid old woman' some have described – and which after the War she wanted the British authorities to believe. For Bothamley's papers in the Tea Rooms, see KV 2/2258/99a. Before the War's end and aware of what Bothamley was doing in Germany, Stanford defended her friend as "a devoted person to Great Britain" (HO 283/65/58). Briscoe, *My Friend the Enemy*, pp.119–136, for some of Stanford's activities. See also KV2/832–833, for more official detail.

6 KV 2/245/254a.
7 KV 2/245/221A. HO 45/25719 on Findlay.
8 KV 4/185, Guy Liddell's diary, 2 December 1939; HO 283/13/96. HO 45/25747, for prominent detainees under 18B.
9 KV 2/245/221a.
10 N. Stewart, "Fellow Travellers of the Right and Foreign Policy Debate in Scotland," PhD thesis, University of Edinburgh, 1995, p.217, notices him. Barry Domvile thought Pullar a "bore" but the address in the Balkans doubtless offered some compensation. DOM 54, Domvile diary, 29 July 1937.
11 Kenny, *Germany Calling*, pp.173 and 234.
12 Farndale, *Haw-Haw*, ch.11. D. Aaronovitch, *Voodoo Histories: The Role of Conspiracy Theory in Shaping Modern History* (London, 2009), on the attractions and pitfalls of this explanatory tool.
13 Weinberg, *World at Arms*, pp.113 ff and ch.3 *passim*.
14 E. R. Murrow, *This is London* (London, 1941), p.106, broadcast of 14 May.
15 D. Dilks (ed.), *The Diaries of Sir Alexander Cadogan OM, 1938–1945* (London, 1971), p.288, entry, 21 May 1940. Matthew and Harrison (eds), *ODNB*, Vol.9, pp.412–415 on Cadogan.
16 J. Lukacs, *Five Days in London, May 1940* (New Haven and London, 1999) pp.27–38, on the public's mood.
17 Kershaw, *Fateful Choices*, pp.24–47. Ben Brown's play, "Three Days in May" premiered at the Theatre Royal Windsor, in August 2011.
18 W. S. Churchill, *War Speeches*, ed. C. Eade, Vol.1 (London, 1951), p.207, speech 18 June 1940. Calder, *The People's War*, chs 3 and 4, brilliantly captures the atmosphere from April 1940 to September 1941, the "Spitfire Summer" and the "Blitz", respectively.
19 P. Rand, *Conspiracy of One* (Guildford, Conn., 2013), pp.110–114 is excellent on the raid. *Ibid.* chs 10 and 13 for fascinating detail on Danischewsky.
20 *Ibid.* p.152
21 Muggeridge, *Chronicles*, p.108.
22 KV 2/543/3a for Matthias.
23 KV 2/543/1ab.
24 Rand, *Conspiracy*, p.66. R. Bearse and A. Read, *Conspirator: The Untold Story of Churchill, Roosevelt and Tyler Kent* (London, 1991). J. H. Shaw, *The Case of Tyler Kent* (Chicago, 1947), for an isolationist perspective.
25 Simpson, *In the Highest Degree Odious*, p.147.
26 *Ibid.* p.146. Rand, *Conspiracy*, pp.117, 167, 170.

27 KV 2/543/8a refers to Knight consulting with Johnson. But see NARA RG 59 Box 481, General Records of the Department of State 1930–1939, memorandum of 28 May 1940.

28 FO 371/24251/60 (his idea of peace was a German victory) and /101 for his view that by 1940 Britain was "through." More comment is in FO 371/26217.

29 Rand, *Conspiracy*, p167.

30 Griffiths, *Patriotism Perverted*, p.258.

31 A. Lownie, "Tyler Kent," in R. Jeffreys-Jones and A. Lownie (eds) *North American Spies: New Revisionist Essays* (Edinburgh, 1991), pp.51 ff flags up some uncertainties. See also N. West, "Moscow's Moles and the Nazi Spy," *The Times*, 10 December 1983; R. Kessler, *Moscow Station* (New York, 1989), p.22; C. Andrew and O. Gordievsky, *KGB: The Inside Story of its Foreign Operations from Lenin to Gorbachev* (London, 1990), pp.180–181.

32 KV 2/543, memo, 10 June 1940.

33 Simpson, *In the Highest Degree Odious*, p.149.

34 KV 2/545/135a.

35 Andrew, *In Defence of the Realm*, pp.224–226, carries only the briefest details on the incident and related issues.

36 Muggeridge, *Chronicles*, p.108.

37 Bearse and Read, *Conspirator*, p.132.

38 Masters, *Literary Agents*, p.257.

39 Simpson, *In the Highest Degree Odious*, p.154.

40 KV 2/2257–2259 on Nikolai Wolkoff.

41 Higham, *Mrs Simpson*, p.92 on the Duchess of Windsor as a client.

42 BT 31/33602.

43 Simpson, *In the Highest Degree Odious*, p.148. Wolkoff père's signature appears in John Beckett's copy of R. H. Bruce Lockhart's *Retreat from Glory*, signed in internment by fellow internees. USSC, MS 238.

44 KV 2/1698/26B.

45 KV 2/677/726 on her deification of Hitler.

46 KV 2/840, memo, 20 March 1940.

47 KV 2/2257, Office of MID, New York to Director of Military Intelligence, 9 December 1918 on Madame and Admiral Wolkoff. *The Times*, 10 March 1954, contains a short unrevealing obituary of the Admiral.

48 KV 2/2258/96d notes his awareness of Anna's manoeuvres. KV 2/1117/5a for his 20 May 1940 letter to Kell expressing surprise at her arrest – "I can only suppose that her outspoken feelings against the Jews must have led to it" – and requesting Kell's assistance.

49 Matthew and Harrison (eds), *ODNB*, Vol.24, pp.646–648. Hall (1870–1943) is prominent in C. Andrew, *Her Majesty's Secret Service: The Making of the British Intelligence Community* (London, 1986). Hall supported Anna's application for naturalisation (HO 382/13).

50 KV 2/2258/123a.

51 KV 2/2257/80a. Comment, not always accurate, appears in R. Berkeley, *A Spy's London* (London, 1994), pp.99–101.

52 KV 2/2258/98y.

53 KV 2/2258/90b on Stanford's presence.

54 KV 2/2257/80a, Special Branch report, 18 October 1939.

55 KV 2/2257/78A.

56 KV2/2257/80a.

57 KV2/2258/99a.

58 Details of Kent's trial can be found in Fascism in Great Britain Collection, USSC, MF 1. The transcript of Wolkoff's trial is not yet in the public domain. A sanitised version of the Kent-Wolkoff affair appears in The Earl Jowitt, *Some were Spies* (London, 1954). See also Simpson, *In the Highest Degree Odious*, pp.146–162 and Appendix IV, and Griffiths, *Patriotism Perverted*, ch.15. Clough, *State Secrets* and T. Hennessey and C. Thomas, *Spooks: The Unofficial History of MI5* (London, 2009), pp.187–199, are more recent expressions of interest.

59 Hope, "Fascism, the Security Service," pp.1–5; Clough, *State Secrets;* Dorril, *Blackshirt*, pp.197–198, 262–265 particularly. Taylor contributed to *The Blackshirt* on industrial issues. He is strikingly absent from Andrew, *Defence of the Realm*.

60 CRIM 1/1230/48.

61 Knight, *Crime Cargo*, p.195.

62 Stewart, "Fellow Travellers of the Right," p.400, on his knowing Joyce, presumably through the Right Club. Intelligence operatives confused their Grahams, referring repeatedly to Sir Ronald Graham, former Ambassador to Italy, whereas the son of the Duke of Montrose should have been in their sights. Lord Ronald Graham died in Rhodesia in 1992. Beyond the Right Club he served on the executive committee of Lt Col. Graham Seton-Hutchinson's National Socialist Workers' Party. Mosley Papers, University of Birmingham Special Collections, OMN/B/8/3/2, letter, Brinsley Le Poer Trench to Unity Mitford, undated.

63 KV 2/2474/81B.

64 KV 2/1698.

65 KV 2/1698/36a.

66 HO 45/23666. She was interned briefly on account of her membership. Her heavily-weeded file carries a Home Office minute dated 20 June 1940: "Capt. Maxwell Knight came to see Sir A. Maxwell about this case and asked that she should be released." She was released the day Max intervened. Fay Taylour, who knew her in internment, always believed she was a "Mata Hari" figure. USSC, MS 5/13. Recent comment on her appears in K. Quinlan, *The Secret War between the Wars. MI5 in the 1920s and 1930s* (Woodbridge, 2014), pp.115–119, particularly.

67 Clough, *State Secrets*, pp.31–32 and elsewhere. Quinlan, *Secret War*, pp.119–121.

68 Quinlan, *Secret War*, pp.124–126. J. Miller, *One Girl's War: Personal Exploits of MI5's Most Secret Station* (Brandon, 1986), ch.2, pp.21–37.

69 Griffiths, *Patriotism Perverted*, p.263.

70 Simpson, *In the Highest Degree Odious*, p.154 on the movement of the letter.

71 Griffiths, *Patriotism Perverted*, p.263. Clough, *State Secrets*, p.142.

72 KV 2/2474/81B, 84a. KV 2/543/1b.

73 A copy of the coded version is in KV2/250.

74 Clough, *State Secrets*, pp.130–131, based on the translations in KV 2/678/579a and CRIM 1/1230, Exhibit 17.

75 The reference to refugee Jews in the Pioneer Corps "guaranteed in writing not to be sent into the firing line," sounds odd. But was it accurately translated for MI5? If the original carried that comment, Joyce would have found it difficult to coin any political capital. But if it suggested Jews had been guaranteed they would not be sent into the front line – a bizarre claim – he would have relished that information and reached straightaway for his typewriter and typed an anti-Semitic broadside. He would have been able to dwell on the old anti-Semitic themes of Jewish cowardice and undue influence. A script on British boys being sacrificed in a War created by Jews almost wrote itself, as it had for past anti-Semites. Holmes, *Anti-Semitism*, especially ch.2 for the wider context on Jews and military matters.

76 Imagine his pleasure at being told Churchill was unpopular and viewed as a tool of Baruch. Joyce would have recognised Baruch as Bernard Baruch (1870–1965), the American financier, stock market speculator and Churchill confidant, viewed by anti-Semites as a major force in the Jewish world conspiracy. See Joyce on Barney Baruch in *Twilight over England*, p.89, and for balance, J. Grant, *Bernard M. Baruch: The Adventures of a Wall Street Legend* (New York, 1997).

77 Joyce would have known that on 16 February 1940 this prison ship had been attacked in Norwegian waters by HMS *Cossack*. "What a result! A fine show!" Harold Nicolson wrote. Olson (ed.), *Harold Nicolson: Diaries and Letters*, p.172, entry 1 January 1940. But this incident could be exploited by Joyce and his correspondent clearly hoped he would. The message drew his attention to the fact that *Truth*, a high Tory newspaper with a pro-German, anti-Semitic outlook and close to Neville Chamberlain, had rejected any suggestion of German atrocities on British prisoners before they were freed (*Truth*, 5 and 12 April 1940). From 1930 *Truth's* financial strings had been controlled by Lord Luke of Pavenham. Sir Joseph Ball directed the paper's political stance. On Ball see Matthew and Harrison (eds) *ODNB*, Vol.3, p.567. See also Andrew, *Defence of the Realm*, pp.126, 150; R. B. Cockett, "Ball, Chamberlain and *Truth*," *Historical Journal*, Vol.33 (1990), pp.131–142; and N. J. Crowson (ed.), *Fleet Street Press Barons and Politics: The Journals of Collin Brooks* (Cambridge, 1998). C. Hirshfield, "The Tenacity of a Tradition: *Truth* and the Jews 1877–1957," *Patterns of Prejudice*, Vol.28 (1994), pp.67–85, focuses specifically on the paper's anti-Semitism. Joyce's contact was suggesting that *Truth's* pre-war outlook remained unchanged; the Nazis had sympathisers in high places. About this time Admiral Sir Barry Domvile was attempting to broker an

understanding between Mosley and the paper's editor, Henry Newnham, by way of enlarging 'The Leader's' influence (KV 2/836/247A, p.24). E. Kris and H. Speier, *German Propaganda: Report on Home Broadcasting during the War* (London, 1944), p.330 on Nazi exploitation of the incident.

78 How would Joyce have interpreted the remark that most of his friends remained supportive and "pay gay" was "00 hundred per cent" behind him? He would have realised his pre-war pro-Nazi contacts were still active and understood that P. G. Taylor, otherwise James McGuirk Hughes, was onside. Hughes has just been noticed handing Wolkoff the letter and requesting she despatch it to Berlin. But what were his motives? The writer of the message to Joyce had been deceived. For further evidence of Taylor's capacity to deceive see HO 283/26/67, letter of Anne Beckett to the Advisory Committee, 14 July 1940. As for, "Lewis wants murder you," this part of the message has been widely misunderstood. It has been linked to the boxer Ted 'Kid' Lewis, already noticed as an early BUF member and well-placed to organise Mosley's 'biff boys' against the Reds. But Joyce was never close to that person. The message was referring to Captain C.C. Lewis, whom Joyce had coached for a political career and later worked alongside in the BUF. The families of both men had become friends (private information). Clough, *State Secrets*, pp.135–137 identified the correct Lewis. Simpson, *In the Highest Degree Odious*, p.155 identified the wrong one. Farndale. *Haw-Haw*, p.160 perpetuated that error. Joyce would have been particularly pleased to have the intelligence which came next, telling him "All league sound." It related almost certainly to former members of the National Socialist League, his fifth column group. The writer was advising him his plans were still in place.

79 Members of Joyce's family, the writer was informing him, were being persecuted by Sir John Anderson. This "po-faced right-wing bureaucrat," now Home Secretary and Minister of Home Security, was charged with implementing internment policy. This initiative had led to "Q", Quentin, being detained and "F" and "R", Frank and Robert, losing their jobs. Frank was later interned. Joyce is likely to have mused that without leaving for Berlin in 1939 he would have been among the detainees. He would have been pleased to hear, however, his family was not "in distress." On Anderson see J. Wheeler-Bennett, *John Anderson, Viscount Waverley* (London, 1962). The description of him is from Calder, *The Myth of the Blitz*, p.47.

80 "Master" was John Macnab.

81 "Baphomet [or B.A.P. Home T.] very friendly, wife also." This comment clearly puzzled Hugh Foss when decoding the letter for MI5. Foss's involvement is in CRIM 1/1230/31. That problem has persisted. See Simpson, *In the Highest Degree Odious*, p.155. Farndale, *Haw-Haw*, pp.159–160, provides an incomplete version of the letter which omits the important reference to "Baphomet." On the Templar link and its origins, see M. Barber, *The New Knighthood: A History of the Order of the*

Temple (Cambridge, 1995), pp.320–321. Joyce would often use the terms Baphomet and Baphometry to emphasise his deep disrespect of political opponents or people who had failed to deliver what he had expected or believed was needed. WJ to MJ, 13, 14, 22 December 1945. In *Twilight over England* he wrote of financial interests not only as "the Lords of Judah," but also as the "sons of Baphomet" and "the agents of International Darkness" (p.119). However he did not retain the term for his Jewish enemy alone. He would have recognised "Baphomet" as Mosley – someone with a politically active wife – who had failed to take British fascism forward. His correspondent was suggesting that 'The Leader' could be counted on to support the Nazi war effort. Did Joyce, thinking of their past turbulent relationship and now yearning for a bigger role in a conquered Britain, envisage more conflict in the future?

82 R. Macleod and D. Kelly (eds), *The Ironside Diaries* (London, 1962), for Ironside's reflections at this time. Dorril, *Blackshirt*, pp. 449–450, for comment. KV 2/2258, MI5 memo, 20 June 1940 records Admiral Wolkoff's favourable view of Ironside. HO 45/25568, "WAR. DETENTION OF SUSPECTS," report 78, from the Berkshire Constabulary, on J.F.C. Fuller as the possible British Franco.

83 CRIM 1/1230, Exhibit 17 for the text of the letter which notes "ex-proselites" should read "expense lives."

84 Jowitt, *Some were Spies*, pp.64–76.

85 Jowitt's letter to Wolkoff, 10 May 1954, reminding her she was "fortunate to have been tried *in camera*." Jowitt Papers, House of Lords, JOW 1/8.

86 Jowitt, *Some were Spies*, p.72. His capitals do not appear in the transcribed version.

87 W.H.G. Armytage, *The Rise of the Technocrats: A Social History* (London, 1965), pp.273–275, on PEP. For fascist attitudes to PEP, see British Library of Political and Economic Science, PEP File, A/5/3.

88 Joyce would probably have translated the advice, "Meg's Tuesday talk unpopular with women," as a rebuke to Margaret's efforts. She had no microphone presence and he would have been painfully aware of her limitations.

89 Would Joyce have understood this observation as a reference to Dorothy Eckersley, former supporter of the National Socialist League, involved in his departure to Germany and also in easing him into his new role in Berlin? She was now broadcasting for the Nazis. Would he have thought of another Rundfunk colleague? James Clark, Eckersley's son, had attended National Socialist League meetings; James Clark in conversation with A. Weiss, 27 March 1995 (private archive). Would neither have occurred to him? Would he have recalled another League? Joyce and Margaret Bothamley had both been active in the Nordic League. See Griffiths, *Patriotism Perverted*, p.134. A degree of uncertainty remains.

90 "C.B." has sometimes been taken to mean the Concordia Bureau, part of the Nazi broadcasting network. It might. But that organisation was Büro Concordia, to which "C.B." does not align. And would the writer offer

blessings to an organisation? Was Joyce intended to have a person in mind? Would he have thought of Christian Bauer, his principal pre-war German contact? Or Clement Bruning, a former BUF colleague, already noticed leaving for Germany before Joyce? Bruning, we know, had worked in the World Service before his still unexplained death early in the War.

91 CRIM 1/1230, Exhibit 17.

92 *Ibid.*

93 KV 2/245/249ab; KV 2/247/497a; CRIM 1/1230/36.

94 Simpson, *In the Highest Degree Odious*, p.156. A cameo of Domvile appears in *ibid.* pp.218–221. Domvile's autobiography *From Admiral to Cabin Boy* and HO 45/25716 for career details.

95 "Churchill and the Fascist Plot," Channel 4 TV, 16 March 2013.

96 Clough's *State Secrets*, pp.142, 254. Farndale, *Haw-Haw*, pp.158–163 follows this line.

97 B. Porter, *Plots and Paranoia: A History of Political Espionage in Britain, 1790–1988* (London, 1989), p.177, for the pressures on MI5.

98 Clough, *State Secrets*, especially p.142.

99 C. Holmes and G. Macklin, "Finding Lord Haw-Haw's Friend," *BBC History Magazine*, Vol.8 (June 2007), p.12.

100 KV 2/543/1b, memo, 14 April 1940.

101 KV 2/1221. Interrogation of Donovan by Mr Knight at Latchmere House, 25 August 1940, p.24. Clough, *State Secrets*, p.216. I. Cobain, *Cruel Britannia: A Secret History of Torture* (London, 2012), ch.1, for some detail on Latchmere.

102 Letter, Charles Clarke, Home Office, to Francis Beckett, 16 January 2001, claimed the destruction of Macnab's internment file. But see KV 2/248/24c.

103 KV 2/2474 is crucial.

104 KV 2/2474/90a, 99d on his continuing contact with the BUF, and /91a, p.30 for his keeping the company of P. G. Taylor. KV 2/2474/85g on being in touch with the Joyce family. On the censorship of his correspondence and "Judy," see Macnab's letter, 22 January 1940, inviting her to a meal at the Helvetia Restaurant, "Fascist and Anti-Fascist Activities," USSC microfilm from Imperial War Museum, Reel 2, 89/14/1. KV 2/2474/91a, pp.20–21, especially, on the Advisory Committee's suspicions about his fifth column role.

105 KV 2/2474/165a.

106 Simpson, *In the Highest Degree Odious*, pp.432–433; Griffiths, *Patriotism Perverted*, p.265.

107 Clough, *State Secrets*, p.36; Rand, *Conspiracy*, p.xiv; *The Times*, 4 December 1982.

108 Simpson, *In the Highest Degree Odious*, p.433 discusses. HO 382/13/1 on her citizenship.

109 *The Times*, 6 August 1973, carries a death notice for Anna de Wolkoff. A memorial service was held at the Russian Orthodox Church in Exile at Emperor's Gate, London SW7.

110 USSC, MF 1, Fascism in Great Britain Collection, for Rex v Tyler Gatewood Kent, Central Criminal Court, 7 November 1940, p.200.

111 WJ to MJ, 6 October 1945.

112 In HO45/25690, in a letter to A. P. Herbert MP (21 March 1940) Macnab, clearly seeking martyrdom, bemoaned that unlike Quentin Joyce he had not already been interned.

113 KV 2/2474/85g.

114 KV 2/7474, minute 142, 9 March 1943.

115 HO 45/25690, Special Branch letter, 2 April 1940, on Macnab's conversion.

116 Macnab became a naturalised citizen of Spain where he died in 1977.

117 HO 144/22707.

118 HO 45/25698 and HO 283/26.

119 Simpson, *In the Highest Degree Odious*, p.174.

120 HO 45/25696/840165/2, pp.8 and 14, Advisory Committee and Captain Ramsay. See also HO 45/25696/840165/9, Birkett to Home Office, 21 June 1940.

121 HO 45/236684.

122 HO 144/22158.

123 The Friends of Oswald Mosley have compiled lists of interned BUF members. See USSC, MS 201, 6/1(a), MS 271, 6/1(b), MS 346, 6/1(c), MS 371, 6/1(d).

124 Mosley appears as such in Nancy Mitford's novel *Wigs on the Green* (London, 1935).

125 *Evening Standard*, 27 July 1939.

126 Crowson (ed.), *Fleet Street, Press Barons and Politics*, p.252, entry, 24 August 1939.

127 HO 144/21382, Special Branch report, 16 September 1939.

128 HO 144/21381/284.

129 Griffiths, *Patriotism Perverted*, *passim*.

130 Griffiths, "A Note on Mosley," pp.675–688.

131 Intercepted letter, 31 December 1939, in KV 2/884, 12A. After wartime military service during which he became a prisoner of the Japanese, Coast returned to London, wrote on his experiences – *The Railroad of Death* appeared in 1946 – and also entered the Foreign Office. He subsequently left the Civil Service, where he held a junior post in Bangkok, went to Thailand and became a strong supporter of Indonesian independence. Back later in England he pursued a successful career as a theatrical agent and impresario. See www.johncoast.org/biography. Accessed 15 November 2014. On Beamish, see Kosmin, "Colonial Careers," pp.16–23 and Lebzelter, "Henry Hamilton Beamish," in Lunn and Thurlow (eds), *British Fascism*, pp.41–56.

132 HO 45/24895/4.

133 KV 4/185, Guy Liddell's diary, 30 January 1940.

134 KV 2/884/17B, report, 5 March 1940, of meeting at Criterion restaurant. His audience included Sir Barry Domvile, Major-General J.F.C.

Fuller, Lady Mosley, P. G. Taylor, Henry Williamson, Anna Wolkoff and Francis Yeats-Brown. KV 2/884/13A, anonymous source to War Office, 23 February 1940 for further evidence on Mosley's activities.

135 Griffiths, *Patriotism Perverted*, pp.183–189.

136 KV 4/185, Guy Liddell's diary, 30 January 1940.

137 *Ibid.* 25 September 1939.

138 Griffiths, "A Note on Mosley," pp.675–688.

139 Pryce-Jones, *Treason of the Heart*, p.168.

140 KV 2/884–888. HO 283/9–19.

141 KV 2/1363–1364. Mosley, *A Life of Contrasts*, pp.169 ff on her internment.

142 "*Diana* – Our Friend," *Comrade*, No.56 (2003).

143 KV 2/884/38G. See also KV 2/884/48A, on her role as Mosley's intermediary with Hitler before the War and, following the British Government's introduction of internment, as a link between internees and their comrades outside. de Courcy, *Diana Mosley*, pp.346–347, for her continuing extremism.

144 When this book was in proof Paul Willetts published *Rendezvous at the Russian Tea Rooms: The Spy Hunter, the Fashion Designer and the Man from Moscow* (London, 2015). It is extremely strong on the wartime atmosphere in London and puts more flesh on many but not all of the leading characters in the Wolkoff affair. However, it carries questionable assumptions about Joyce, fails to identify the real author of the message sent to him in Berlin and leaves unsaid some of the important ramifications of the episode, particularly for Joyce and John Macnab.

PART V
Retribution

18

THE RECKONING BEGINS

For he might have been a Roosian
A French or Turk or Proosian
Or perhaps Itali-an
Or perhaps Itali-an.
But in spite of all temptations
To belong to other nations
He remains an Englishman!
He remains an Englishman!
["For he is an Englishman." Libretto
from W. S. Gilbert and A. Sullivan,
H.M.S. Pinafore. First performed 1878.]

1

Joyce had always been active, busy and vigorous. But the episode in
the wood at Flensburg had ended all that. He was now seriously
disabled and in urgent need of medical treatment. He was therefore
transported by British army personnel to a military hospital. Albert
Cantor, a stretcher bearer, vividly remembers that journey. The driver
deliberately hit every bump on the road. Joyce was being made to pay
for his wartime taunts and threats. Cantor also remembers administering a shot of morphine, "not in the best tradition of the Medical
Corps." and placing a wound card around the prisoner's neck which

read: "Lord Haw-Haw . . . Traitor."[1] A Jew had wounded Joyce. Lieutenant Perry, born Horst Pinschewer in Berlin in 1922, had arrived in Britain as a refugee in the 1930s and been interned under Regulation 18b before joining the services.[2] Another Jew, Cantor, was now administering to Joyce's needs. Had he known, the unrepentant anti-Semite would have been apoplectic.[3]

Contemporary photographs capture Joyce's arrival at the hospital surrounded by a throng of soldiers, curious to 'see' the familiar voice. Here was a slice of history in the making. Some shouted "Traitor! Why not make him walk?"[4] On entering the hospital he certainly created a stir among fellow patients. Gunner Kenneth Nichols from Sheffield recalls Joyce entering the ward surrounded by guards with bayonets.[5]

Lt Col. Martin Fallon, Commanding Officer of the Surgical Division, now took charge of the prisoner's welfare.[6] Fallon's son later claimed his father was to operate on Joyce.[7] But on 28 May 1945 he passed into the immediate care of Major Buckley Hamer of the 52nd Field Surgical Unit and his anaesthetist Major Bill Scrivener. After ascertaining their patient had been hit in the right buttock they operated just before midnight in front of a large audience with Hamer recording their work under the heading, "Traitor. Joyce W," and signing the record book: "CSW (T+T) Rt. Buttock." He was later photographed holding up the bullet he had just removed. Once again, the military had described Joyce as a traitor, though no formal charges had yet been laid.[8]

Joyce's wounds were more extensive than previously recognised.[9] His haggard, pale appearance when soon afterwards he arrived in England, reflected much more than his meagre diet during the dying days of Nazism.

Confined to a hospital bed, probably cursing his bad luck at being captured, Joyce was surrounded by people from Ireland. Surgeon Fallon was Irish.[10] Nurse Maureen Murphy came from Galway and her colleague Peggy Slattery from Limerick.[11] L/Sgt James Melia, with Oldham connections, now guarding a precious prisoner, offered Joyce a reminder of days in the North-West.[12]

Fallon, concerned that Joyce should be properly treated, repeatedly refused to hand him over for questioning.[13] He described his patient as "a most engaging personality entirely free of inhibitions and ready to talk to anyone on anything."[14] However, the British popular press did not echo such generosity.[15] When Joyce left hospital he would receive some support, if only from people who had shared his pre-war political world. But the driver who purposely hit every pothole on the road reflected the feelings of a wider constituency. So did John Leslie. He had been sailing nearby with Reginald Murley when Joyce was admitted to hospital. Visiting him on their return, Leslie reminded Joyce of happier times when he had been attracted to one of Leslie's cousins.[16] "Oh yes, such a nice girl," the patient replied. Leslie continued their conversation but before taking his leave could not resist saying: "Well, I hope they hang you."[17] Brigadier Roscoe Harvey, who met Joyce in hospital, was even blunter. He viewed him as "a filthy bastard and a bloody traitor!" whom he "had half a mind to finish . . . off."[18]

2

How would the British authorities respond? Though not appreciating for some time the work needed to combat Nazi propaganda, they quickly realised that acts of treason would require attention, and lawyers began discussing a number of key issues on 7 September 1939.[19] Should propaganda for the enemy be treated as treasonable? Should sabotage and espionage alone be actionable? Could aliens commit treason? Sharp differences emerged on this last point between the DPP and Treasury Counsel – and legal opinion remained divided when Joyce went on trial. These confidential discussions, which preceded the 1940 Treason Act, aimed to bring the law into line with the twentieth century. However, those present could hardly have envisaged a case as complicated as Joyce's. Yet, ominously for him, one leading authority argued it was preferable "some few offenders" should escape the extreme penalty to improve the chances of "obtaining a conviction in a proper case."[20]

3

By 1941, when Joyce openly announced his identity on air, Britain's key fascists had already been detained.[21] He had slipped through this net. But he was not forgotten. A 1945 MI5 report noted that a number of his broadcasts had been recorded, "with a view to their being made available." Evidence was being collected for future use against him. This exercise had involved the Director of Public Prosecutions and MI5, assisted by BBC technicians and Special Branch officers.[22]

These recordings by Joyce and other renegades are now in the British Library, though a marked deterioration has occurred in sound quality owing to the conditions under which the security service stored this material.[23] However, several fragments have been restored by skilled technicians in the National Sound Archive.[24]

The official printed sources on this initiative call for more attention than they have so far received.[25] These secret files reveal that on 11 September 1941 the security service had contacted the Director of Public Prosecutions regarding Joyce, "the most notable" of the broadcasters, believing "a considerable public outcry" would erupt if he were not put on trial at the end of the War. Viewing him as a British subject, MI5 sought guidance on whether evidence from "responsible persons" who had known Joyce before the War, and "carefully recorded gramophone records" would be sufficient to warrant legal proceedings.[26]

The Director responded cautiously. At a secret meeting in Broadcasting House on 13 November 1942 he advised testimony would be needed from "responsible persons" familiar with Joyce's voice who had been "listening on an ordinary wireless receiving set to a broadcast proved to be given from Germany by Haw-Haw, which was simultaneously recorded." This process had to be repeated on six occasions.[27]

Soon afterwards two Special Branch officers with shorthand skills who had carried out surveillance on Joyce in the 1930s, and could recognise his voice, were enrolled.[28] Their work began in 1943 and early that year the DPP wrote to MI5:

> The arrangements [currently in place] are admirable on the technical side, but you may remember [we] had emphasised the necessity of a witness or witnesses *simultaneously* identifying the recorded voice as being that of William Joyce. The present statements and the proposed recording results do not seem . . . to furnish that element of proof of Joyce's offence.[29]

Detective Inspector Albert Hunt, later a decisive witness at Joyce's trial, became heavily involved in this monitoring role, along with Sergeant J. Buswell.[30] Aware of the DPP's concerns, they listened to Joyce on 30 January, 8 April and 12 July.[31] However, not everything went smoothly. In February, the officers were unable to read back their shorthand and requested permission to listen again to the January broadcast. But the recordings had already been sealed.[32]

Personal papers, previously unseen, some since withdrawn by the police, underline the shakiness of the whole exercise. Attempts to make sense of Joyce's talks led to substantial revisions and amendments of the shorthand notes.[33] But agreed-upon, cleaned-up versions were finally produced.[34]

By the beginning of 1944 MI5 believed it had assembled a case.[35] But D. B. Somervell, the Attorney-General, and L. A. Byrne, Senior Prosecuting Counsel to the Treasury, were not convinced. They advised that Joyce's broadcasts might have damaged British wartime morale but in law it would be difficult to demonstrate he had offered assistance to the enemy or impeded the operation of His Majesty's forces.[36] The security service continued to disagree.[37]

Another recording was made on 30 August 1944. Still believing in Special Branch's shorthand expertise, the authorities again called on Inspector Hunt, this time assisted by Sergeant C. Rhodes.[38]

In November that year the Director of Public Prosecutions, MI5 and Special Branch, decided to assemble all the available evidence against Joyce and his wife. The Director anticipated "a leading state trial" the importance of which "could not be exaggerated."[39] The evidence against Joyce was mounting. No wonder MI5 waited impatiently to interview him.

4

On 31 May 1945, soon after Joyce's doctors had agreed to visitors, Captain Jim Skardon of the Intelligence Corps descended on 74 General Hospital, Lüneberg.[40] Skardon had joined the police in August 1925 and rose to become Inspector before the War took him into Intelligence. A superb sleuth and skilled interrogator, he resigned from the force in August 1947 and joined MI5.[41]

When focusing on Soviet penetration he broke down Klaus Fuchs, the atom bomb spy, and, given more time, might have exposed Kim Philby.[42] Earlier, when sifting through files at Radio Luxembourg, he had found a receipt in Joyce's name relating to talks transmitted in 1943. But had the wounded man made these broadcasts? He would soon find out.

5

The hospital is the setting for an historic interrogation. Will the prisoner prove difficult? Confessions often arise from tiredness after days and nights of close, persistent questioning. Joyce is not tired and might prove hard to break down. If he resists, Skardon holds the Luxembourg receipts. But the man unable to remain silent when he sees British soldiers gathering firewood once again cannot control his tongue.[43] With his sense of historical destiny, he feels an urgent need to impress. Skardon quickly realises Joyce feeds on an audience. He can relax, sit back, and puff on his ever-present pipe, allow the prisoner to talk, have his fix.

Joyce draws attention to his roots in America but cannot resist claiming to be British, remarking, "We were always treated as British during the period of my stay in England, whether we were or not."[44] Sir Hartley Shawcross will soon be able to exploit this remark. Joyce asserts he has always had the future of Britain and its Empire in mind and defends his decision to leave for Germany on these grounds. He also emphasises his growing concern during the War to save Europe from the virulent disease of Bolshevism. "Whatever opinion may be formed at the present time with regard to my conduct," he affirms, "I submit that the final judgement cannot be properly passed until it is seen whether Britain can win the peace."[45]

His statement also includes a personal dimension. He attempts to shield the already-detained Margaret. In earlier, more confident times, dreaming of a Nazi victory, he had claimed in *Twilight over England* that their leaving for Berlin amounted to a joint decision.[46] He was associating her with what he believed then to be a triumphant ideology, granting her a place in the victor's history books. However, in his 'confession,' he takes full responsibility for their decision.[47]

His testimony, carefully noted by Skardon, is strikingly different from Margaret's claim: "We were forced to work for the Nazi Party." She will remain detached from the enormity of her actions; her immediate concern at the War's end, apart from not having time to fix her hair, will centre on a lost copy of *Henry V*.[48]

6

Skardon must have been surprised how smoothly it went. He wrote up his report and despatched it to London, where the stage was being prepared for the prisoner's return. As a first step Joyce was moved from Germany to Brussels, where he remained between 10 and 16 June. While there, on 15 June a new law on treason received the Royal Assent in London. Previously, at least two witnesses had been required to testify to a single alleged act of treason or, alternatively, separate witnesses had to vouch for two such deeds. Under the new legislation the prosecution could rely on one witness testifying to one single act.[49] Joyce's name had appeared in a memorandum to the Attorney-General suggesting the new law should cover all alleged acts of treason since 3 September 1939.[50] It had also featured in parliamentary debates.[51] This simplified legal procedure was to exercise a major influence at his forthcoming trial.

7

Joyce had to be returned to Britain before any legal proceedings against him could begin. This task was entrusted to Commander Leonard Burt of Scotland Yard, who had been seconded during the War to the Intelligence service. Taking no chances, the authorities allocated three armed guards for the journey. Burt believed his mother's death "had been brought about largely through the fear and worry induced by Joyce's broadcasts." But on the RAF Dakota he came to admire Joyce's "courage and his blazing sincerity."[52] His prisoner-passenger reciprocated such feelings.[53]

During the flight Joyce requested the pilot pass over the military graves in Belgium commemorating the fallen of the Great War. On seeing so many white crosses, he remarked that Germany and England, "the two countries which should be closest together, in blood, ideals, ambitions," should never have been at war. A little later, spotting Dover's cliffs, on which he had written in *National Socialism Now*, and last seen in 1939 on his way to Germany, he wrote in a guard's autograph book: "We are about to pass over the white chalk cliffs, England's bulwark. It is a sacred moment in my life – and I can only say whatever my fate may be – God bless Old England on the lee."[54]

"Whatever my fate may be." Burt claimed his passenger was "coolly reconciled . . . to being hanged."[55] This honest assessment is wrong. Joyce believed he had a defence. He had never betrayed Britain's interests. He had said as much to Skardon. A report from the US Embassy in Berlin to the Secretary of State in Washington on 21 July 1941 makes it clear he also had another card to play:

> He has been heard to say that no matter how the war turns out he will be all right, i.e. if Germany wins he can remain here as a good German citizen. If Germany loses, he believes that by virtue of his birth in Brooklyn, he will be able to inflict himself upon the United States.[56]

In any case, Burt's observation is to anticipate. Joyce had not yet been formally arrested and charged.

That situation soon changed. When Joyce's plane touched down on 16 June 1945 Chief Inspector Frank Bridges made an arrest and informed the prisoner he would be taken to Bow Street to face a charge of treason. Joyce, now under caution, replied "Yes, thank you." Later that day when the charge was read over to him, he responded with: "I have heard [it] and taken cognisance of it," adding "To-day I shall not add anything to the statement I have made to the military authorities."[57] When it became clear Germany had lost the War, Joyce had noticed many contemporaries wracked by worry. By contrast, he wrote: "I feel quite serene, not a bit worried."[58] But after being officially arrested and charged? Whatever his emotions, he was powerless to halt the legal process.

On 20 November 1943, to the sound of much initial fury, Oswald Mosley had been freed from internment. According to a contemporary report, "There could hardly have been more commotion if Hitler had been turned loose."[59] One member of the public grumbled, "If he had been an ordinary bloke he wouldn't have been released." Another remarked cynically, "Money talks." Yet, "Why release a man who should be condemned to death as a traitor?" Mosley's treatment also raised wider questions: for example, would "the butchers of Berlin" be leniently treated?[60] Not only had Mosley and his wife been released: 'The Leader' was already planning his future. He remained anxious to resume normal political business "as soon as possible."[61] Beckett and Macnab had been freed.[62]

Joyce did not enjoy that sweetness. He faced the bleak prospect his life might soon be finished forever.

Notes

1 Albert Cantor to author, 6 October 1996.
2 Perry, *When Life*, for autobiographical reflections.
3 When more aware of the events surrounding his capture, Joyce remarked that Perry's birth name was not "echt deutsch." The vicious anti-Semite was for once mounting a coded attack on a Jew. He followed it with a personal remark in his more usual vein. WJ to MJ, 8 November 1945.
4 Albert Cantor provided me with a copy of one such shot. *Belfast Telegraph*, 30 May 1945, recorded the soldiers' shouts.
5 Kenneth Nichols to author, 30 December 2002.
6 Nigel Fallon's letter, *The Times*, 16 February 1995, David Hamer's reply in *ibid*. 28 February 1995.
7 Nigel Fallon to author, 30 August 1995.
8 D. Hamer to author, 19 October 1995, copy of the original.
9 D. Hamer to author, 19 October 1995, copy of B. Hamer's records.
10 Obituary of Martin Fallon, provided by Nigel Fallon.
11 *Irish Times*, 14 July 1945.
12 *Oldham Chronicle*, 5 June 1945, for Joyce being guarded by L/Sgt James Melia.
13 *British Medical Association News Review*, 10 May 1995, p.23.
14 Detail from the Fallon family file. Copy in author's possession.
15 *Daily Express*, 30 May 1945; *Daily Mirror*, 30 May 1945.
16 Is this John Leslie, the inter-war activist in the Greenshirts who wrote "Against the Bankers, Fascism and War," in the West London papers? Joyce would have known this person. YCAL, MSS Box 32, Folder 1337, John Macnab to Ezra Pound, 17 August 1936.
17 Based on Sir Reginald Murley to D. Hamer, 3 March 1995 (copy in author's possession) which refers to an operation before a large audience.

18 T. Fitzgeorge-Parker, *Roscoe: The Bright Shiner. The Biography of Brigadier Roscoe Harvey DSO* (London, 1987), p.237.

19 This file attracted an initial closure date of 2024. Catalogued in the National Archives as HO 45/22329 (read under privileged access in the Home Office as file 700324).

20 700324/2–16, particularly.

21 Simpson, *In the Highest Degree Odious* remains the fullest published account. The Government also interned aliens who had escaped shortly before from the Greater Germany. P. and L. Gillman, *"Collar the Lot!" How Britain Interned and Expelled its Wartime Refugees* (London, 1980). B. Wasserstein, *Britain and the Jews of Europe, 1939–1945* (Oxford, 1979), ch.3, summarises.

22 HO 45/25780/65, MI5 report on William Joyce, 13 June 1945.

23 The recordings include broadcasts by Margaret Joyce and Norman Baillie-Stewart.

24 National Sound Archive, CD R 0023717, BD 1–4.

25 Cole, *Lord Haw-Haw*, and Kenny, *Germany Calling*, remain silent on this important exercise; Farndale, *Haw-Haw*, pp.231–232, carries brief comment; Martland, *Lord Haw-Haw*, pp.60–61, for a short, undeveloped reference.

26 KV 4/117, letter to DPP, 11 September 1941.

27 KV 4/117, minutes of meeting at Broadcasting House, 13 November 1942. Marked SECRET.

28 KV 4/117, memo, 14 December 1942.

29 KV 4/117, DPP to MI5, 28 January 1943.

30 HO 45/25780, MI5 report on William Joyce, 13 June 1945.

31 National Sound Archive, CD R 0023717, BD 1–4, holds the recordings of 8 April and 12 July. Hunt also testified against Norman Baillie-Stewart; *The Times*, 10 January 1946.

32 KV 4/117, MI5 report, 2 February 1943.

33 Metropolitan Police Archive, London, Buswell Papers (uncatalogued and unclassified and some now removed).

34 The cleaned-up versions of what they believed to have heard, can be found in KV2/250.

35 KV 4/117, MI5 to BBC, 15 January 1944.

36 KV 4/117, Treasury Counsel, 19 May 1944.

37 KV 4/117, memo, 24 June 1944.

38 HO 45/25780, MI5 report on William Joyce, 13 June 1945.

39 KV 2/245/355a, note, W. E. Hinchley Cooke, 11 November 1944, reporting DPP opinions.

40 Cole, *Lord Haw-Haw*, p.250, has it as Scardon. So does Selwyn, *Hitler's Englishman*, p.167.

41 Personal file of 114258, William James Skardon, Metropolitan Police Archives.

42 *The Times*, 12 March 1987 and 23 March 1987, for Skardon's obituary notices. *Sunday Times*, 1 June 1980, reported that his former employers

had prevented publication of an auto-biography. Andrew, *Defence of the Realm*, discusses Skardon but remains discreetly silent on any unpublished typescript.

43 *Commander Burt of Scotland Yard*, by himself (London, 1958), p.4, on Joyce's loquacity.

44 HO 45/25780/547–548.

45 HO 45/25780/547–548.

46 Joyce, *Twilight over England*, p.10.

47 HO 45/22405, statement of 31 May 1945.

48 *Irish Times*, 9 June 1945.

49 *Parliamentary Debates* (Lords), Vol.136 (1944–45), cols. 266 and 649, 30 May 1945 and 15 June 1945, respectively.

50 LCO 2/3073, memo, to Attorney-General, 19 January 1945. HO 45/25154 for further reference to Joyce's case.

51 *Parliamentary Debates* (Lords), Vol.136 (1944–45), 30 May 1945, col. 268.

52 *Commander Burt*, pp.4, 3.

53 WJ to MJ, 10 August 1945 for Burt, "that excellent fellow."

54 All from *Commander Burt*, p.1 and facing p.30.

55 *Ibid*. p.3

56 NARA RG 59/DF 1940–1944, 862.20200/32, Box 5456, 250/34/07/01.

57 Hall (ed.), *Trial*, p.82.

58 KV 2/250, 24 March 1945.

59 INF 1/292/391, weekly report, 23–30 November 1943. See also File Report 1990, "Mosley and After," 1 January 1944 and File Report 2011, "Mosley and After," 5 February 1944, Mass Observation Archive, University of Sussex. *Union Jack*, 20 November 1943 and 2 December 1945 note hostility from the armed forces. See also the CP leaflet, *Put Mosley back in Prison* (London, 1943); "Fascist No. 1 and his wife are out. Democracy is flagrantly flouted" (p.2). Joyce had welcomed Mosley's release, praising him for his "gallant fight against international Jewry." *Reynold's News*, 21 November 1943.

60 HO 262/6, "Fascism and the release of Sir Oswald Mosley: reports, memoranda and correspondence, 1939–1944."

61 Skidelsky, *Oswald Mosley*, p.481. Macklin, *Deeply Dyed*, for a detailed account of the post-war Mosley.

62 Simpson, *In the Highest Degree Odious*, pp.388 ff discusses releases. For Macnab, missing from his account, see KV 2/2474//188b. Macnab's internment was suspended on 25 September 1944.

19

JOYCE ON TRIAL

Treason doth never prosper, what's the reason? For if it prosper, none dare call it Treason. [Sir John Harrington, *The Most Elegant and Witty Epigrams. . . .* Book 4, Epigram 5 'Of Treason' (London, 1618).]

1

Until the 1960s, readers of popular Sunday newspapers could often feast on the ghosted confessions of condemned murderers. Joyce had not murdered but like Neville Heath and John Haigh, his notorious killer contemporaries, he faced the prospect of being hanged. This fact alone created a prurient interest in his circumstances, and voyeurs and revenge seekers did not have long to wait for his case to begin.

On 18 June 1945, forty-eight hours after leaving Belgium, Joyce appeared at Bow Street. Described as thirty-nine, and of no fixed address, he was charged with having

committed high treason in that between September 2 1939 and May 29 1945 being a person owing allegiance to his Majesty the King, he adhered to the King's enemies elsewhere than in the King's realm to wit in the German realm contrary to the Treason Act, 1351.

After referring to him as "small of stature," and dressed in "a shabby dark grey suit, with a much creased collar and tie," *The Times* also remarked that his "greying hair" had been "closely cropped."[1] How could this insignificant-looking figure have created such fear among British radio listeners?

H.A.K. Morgan and R. I. Jackson appeared for the Director of Public Prosecutions. But it was intimated Laurence Austin Byrne, Senior Treasury Counsel, would later take over.[2] He was already familiar with Joyce's case following wartime meetings with MI5. At this point Joyce did not enjoy legal representation. However, the hearing afforded him an opportunity to apply for legal aid, which he did.[3] Not that this source alone would provide all the funds for his long-continued defence.[4]

"Looking in better health," Joyce was next put before a magistrate on 25 June.[5] The court heard from Inspector Albert Hunt of Special Branch, whose knowledge of the accused stretched back to 1934.[6] Captain Alexander Adrian Lickorish, who had detained Joyce at Flensburg, appeared. Captain Jim Skardon of MI5, who had listened to Joyce's 'confession' at Lüneberg, was in court. A photograph taken en route to the hearing showed a smart, smiling Lickorish, cigarette smouldering away between his fingers, alongside a tall, moustached, pipe-sucking Skardon, both dressed in full military uniform.[7] The court also heard from Samuel Lopez Salzedo, a "slender and distinguished old gentleman of Spanish-Jewish descent," who translated the key German documents that were produced in court.[8]

The lawyers soon drew their battle lines. C.B.V. Head of Ludlow and Co, referring to Joyce's American birth certificate, questioned whether his client had ever owed any allegiance to the Crown.[9] The prosecution countered that whenever the accused had been required to declare his nationality, he had claimed to be British.[10] This conflict was to rage throughout what became a protracted legal battle. On 28 June the magistrate, Sir Bertrand Watson, ruled Joyce had a *prima facie* case to answer and formally committed him for trial at the Old Bailey. Head requested a defence certificate and announced he had retained Derek Curtis-Bennett KC, and James Burge.[11]

In the middle of July Joyce's lawyers, including his newly appointed lead counsel, G. O. Slade KC – who was also to represent John Amery against a charge of treason – appeared before Mr Justice Charles, to request a postponement.[12] Their client's nationality had become significant and they needed to consult material from the United States. Joyce had begun to play his American card. He might have believed an individual's identity could be defined in the imagination. But, nobody's fool, he knew that in law documentary evidence would prove vital. His clinging to an American birth certificate says it all.[13] The security service was already worried that this document might destroy the case it had carefully prepared against him.[14] For the prosecution Laurence Byrne raised no objection to this postponement. The trial was rescheduled for September.[15] The Crown probably welcomed the delay. Its Law Officers were approaching a complex case with some hesitation and uncertainty.[16]

In Brixton, where he was first detained, Joyce received treatment for his wounds and a scalp infection. From his prison cell he soon started to write letters – he still felt that need to 'talk' – and receive visitors. His parents were dead. But Quentin often came. Margaret's mother arrived from Crumpsall in Lancashire. John Beckett, R. Barnett and Cpl McNeil Sloane, all former political colleagues, soon called.[17] John Macnab could often be glimpsed visiting his dearest friend. 'Master' had remained close to Joyce's family and, before being interned, had done his best to secure Quentin's release from detention. He now transferred his energies to the more daunting task of assisting William.[18] He helped Joyce's solicitor and offered to give evidence on his friend's behalf.[19] Margaret Joyce, detained until 30 November 1945 at Forest Prison in Belgium, did not appear with these early visitors. Nevertheless, she and her husband conducted an intense correspondence.[20] And so the days passed. Joyce wrote letters, read novels, played chess, talked to, or more probably at, the prison staff. They and his fifty or so correspondents made up his new audience. But this daily round could not disguise that he had reached a decisive moment in his life.

2

Some omens were hardly encouraging. In July 1945 F. A. Voigt, the "incorruptible" and erudite editor of the *Nineteenth Century*, brought a "very serious," successful action against the *News Chronicle*, the *Daily*

News and the journalist Cedric Belfrage. He alleged they had repeated a libel, that the *Nineteenth Century* was "Lord Haw-Haw's favourite paper." This case underlined the stench Joyce's name now gave off.[21] An anonymous early correspondent who wrote to him in prison, "Cheer up, the worst is yet to come," caught much of the prevailing public mood.[22]

When Germany surrendered unconditionally in May 1945, "an instinct for revenge and punishment was stronger than that of generosity." Many believed the Nazi elite must pay for their actions and, following the Nuremberg proceedings which began on 20 November 1945, the majority were executed.[23] Joyce's close association with Nazism guaranteed he was vulnerable. Reflecting as much, in early May 1945 *John Bull* carried a fantasy feature, "My Conquest of Britain. The Fuehrer speaks from Buckingham Palace," in which Ribbentrop appeared as Gauleiter and Joyce as one of his deputies. This portrayal, and its claim that an Allied victory had saved Britain from "black-shirted bullies" like Joyce, suggested plenty of storm clouds threatened.[24]

The proceedings at the Old Bailey opened on 17 September 1945. "The fray is joined," Joyce wrote to Margaret.[25] Arnold Leese, veteran fascist and rabid anti-Semite, viewed the date as ominous. It was the Day of Atonement, a clear signal to him that the Jews were fully in charge.[26]

Six years earlier Joyce had left London for Berlin, and in his 1940 broadcasts had rejoiced as the Luftwaffe carried out its nightly raids. Now, had he been able to see anything on his escorted journey from Brixton, he would have noticed the resulting devastation. "The skeletons of the beautiful Wren's Churches" were, in Terence Rattigan's words, often "the only landmarks in a desert of rubble."[27] This damage came close up to the Old Bailey: "the pillared building rose from a vast wasteland of grass and wildflowers," and as a defence against recent air attacks, "the Central Criminal Court remained almost dark inside throughout the day because of the black-out paint."[28]

The courtroom was tightly packed. In a drab post-war London, swathes of which, a fascist novelist wrote, had a "weary forgotten trollop's look," Joyce's trial offered a diversion.[29] There would be a tale to tell one's children or grandchildren. Five extremely keen spectators had spent the previous evening queuing on the pavement.[30] Representatives from the police and Intelligence services were present, along with aldermen and sheriffs invited by the Common Council of the City of London. A sprinkling of diplomats attended. Joyce's predicament drew a full house.

The court rose for the judge's entry. Scarlet-robed, bewigged, carrying his traditional white gloves, Mr Justice Tucker moved purposefully to his place. Joyce was then brought up from the cells. Many court spectators were now catching their first glimpse of the prisoner, known to most of them only by his voice. He bowed to this traditionally garbed figure before him.

Tucker, born in Pietermaritzburg in 1888, was educated at Winchester and Oxford. He had been a pupil of Rayner Goddard, later Lord Chief Justice. Malcolm Muggeridge, present at Tyler Kent's trial in 1940 when Tucker had declared Joyce a traitor, recalled him as "a strange, remote, barely human figure; glasses on beaked nose, layers of wig and folds of cloth about his withered person, fingers tapping, or scribbling down a word or two."[31] However, the portrait of him as "Wykehamist, with the legendary manners, Oxonian, with the legendary graces, barrister, with the legendary style, judge, with the legendary *gravitas*," reveals the esteem in which he was held by other lawyers. In 1950 Tucker entered the House of Lords as a life peer and Lord of Appeal in Ordinary.[32] He retired in 1961 and died in 1975.[33] Shortly before Joyce's case, he had officiated at the Central Criminal Court when counsel had requested a postponement of John Amery's treason trial.[34]

Sir Hartley Shawcross, Attorney-General since 4 August 1945, led for the Crown.[35] He was assisted by Laurence Byrne, already known to us, and Gerald Howard, later Tory MP for Cambridgeshire.[36] In his new post Shawcross would also soon be prosecuting Nazi war criminals at Nuremberg. He had been born in Giessen near Frankfurt am Main in 1902, where his father worked as a university lecturer in English, and by 1945 had become one of the most respected and powerful lawyers in Britain.

His matinée-idol appearance, his honeyed voice, and his outstanding legal ability had already made him one of the highest-paid barristers of the day. Establishing himself on the Northern Circuit in the 1930s he became the last of the great advocates – in the line of Patrick Hastings and Norman Birkett – whose speeches had a compelling lucidity.[37]

Yet he never became Lord Chief Justice or Lord Chancellor. He withdrew from politics and the Bar in the course of the 1950s to pursue his business interests. He died in 2003.[38]

These legal figures were strangers to Joyce. But he would already have met his own well-qualified legal team. Gerald Slade, the lead counsel, was just eleven years older than the Attorney-General. However, "with his wing-collar and patriarchal moustache, and the solid intelligence of his sharp eyes and bald dome, [he] might almost have been the Attorney-General's Victorian grandfather."[39] He was dated not only by his appearance. He was also detached from popular opinion, believing apparently that of the two alleged traitors he was committed to defend, the British public would be more sympathetic to Amery – one of Slade's own class – rather than Joyce.[40] He was wrong. Both were to be executed.

Slade's professional career had brought him into contact with individuals who had already touched Joyce's life. He had defended Oswald Mosley when 'The Leader' faced internment.[41] In 1940 he had acted for *Daily Mirror* Newspapers against Mosley. The following year he had represented the *New York Times* when Captain Ramsay had sued for libel.[42] Some Bar contemporaries regarded him as long-winded and lacking in flair – a man who would never speak once if twice would do – but he had carved out a sound reputation in civil and criminal cases, especially the former.[43] In 1948 he became a Judge of the High Court, in the King's Bench Division. Bar gossip had it that he would often take *Archbold*, the criminal lawyers' bible, to bed with him to guarantee he stayed on top of his work. He died at Eastbourne in 1962.[44]

Derek Curtis-Bennett and James Burge acted for Joyce throughout. The former, son of a distinguished lawyer, had taken silk in 1943, the same year as Slade. He often represented underdogs, participated in the renegade trials, and acted later for the mass murderer John Christie and the atom bomb spy Klaus Fuchs. He died in 1956.[45]

Jimmy Burge, "a jovial" and "Pickwickian sort of man," had served between 1941 and 1944 as Deputy Judge Advocate. He took silk in 1965 but well before then was widely regarded as "the leading junior criminal counsel at the Bar." In 1963 he was to represent Dr Stephen Ward in the trial linked to the Profumo scandal.[46] Joyce, rather condescendingly, described him as "a very able junior."[47] Burge was reputedly a role model for John Mortimer's fictional Rumpole of the Bailey.[48] It was a first-class team, as Joyce recognised.[49]

As a person allegedly owing allegiance to the Crown, Joyce faced three counts of treason. First: by broadcasting for the enemy between 18 September 1939 and 29 May 1945. Second: by becoming a naturalised subject of Germany on 26 September 1940 when a state of war existed between that country and "our Lord the King and his subjects." Third: by broadcasting for the King's enemies between 18 September 1939 and 2 July 1940.[50]

After charges had been solemnly read out, Wilfred W. Nops, clerk of the court, asked Joyce how he pleaded. "Not guilty," he replied. The die had been cast for a struggle. But not of the kind many had anticipated. Words had been Joyce's fortune and misfortune. He had relished savaging political opponents. He had always sought an audience, as a fascist activist in Britain, a Nazi radio propagandist in Berlin, a man on the run at Flensburg, when meeting Skardon at Lüneberg, when writing letters from prison. But he stayed silent throughout his trial. One of his contacts later remarked: "Short, muscular, and extremely hyped-up," he would throw back his head and talk incessantly.[51] Yet "not guilty" were his last words in public.[52] His thunderous silence has encouraged conspiracy theorists to claim that his counsel, the prosecution, possibly both, feared he might disclose secrets acquired either from MI5 contacts or during his other political activities.[53] Another suggestion is that his unusual silence was to protect his wife from the authorities.[54] Neither claim has any substance. He had no wish to justify his actions.[55] He would have found it demeaning. Joyce believed he had no charge to answer. He had already told Jim Skardon he had never betrayed Britain's ultimate interests. He would smile inwardly at depriving "the masses" of their prurient interest in hearing him declaim from the dock. He always relished exercising power.[56]

On the morning of 17 September Shawcross might have been nervous in his first challenge as Mr Attorney. However, he masked it well. He recognised that the War had released a powerful flood of emotions but reminded the court that Joyce must be judged "according to the law without fear or favour, affection or ill-will," in other words "coldly, dispassionately, on the evidence and on that alone."[57] His fluent opening address emphasised that not everyone who assisted the King's enemies could be accused of treason. "Only those can be convicted of treason who owe a duty of loyalty and faithfulness to the British Crown."[58] But did Joyce owe that allegiance? If he were born in New York City to a naturalised American father, it might be assumed he could not be touched by the charge. But a complication arose. Joyce had claimed to be British, had applied for, and been granted, a British passport. Not once, not twice, but on three occasions. That process alone placed him under a heavy responsibility:

> Whether the statement that he was born in Ireland was true or not, whether the statement that he was a British subject, whether by birth in Ireland or by birth in America of British parents was true or not, the submission of the Crown is that so long as that British passport continued to be valid, so long as it was held by him, it placed him, in whatever country he chose to go, in exactly the same position under the protection of the British Crown as would be any other British subject holding a British passport properly obtained. It placed him under the protection of the British Crown, it clothed him with the status of a British subject, and it required from him the duty of faithfulness and allegiance to the British Crown in return.[59]

Joyce might have constantly lied or frequently been evasive about his origins. His mother might have whispered softly, incessantly, he was British to his core. But the lawyer, whose mellifluous voice he now listened to, was suggesting that in law a bottom line existed on this tangled point.

The Attorney-General turned to the three counts of the indictment. If the jury believed Joyce could be treated as a British subject, they could convict him on counts one and two. Even if not so convinced, they nevertheless concluded that between 18 September 1939 and 2 July 1940, with his British passport, Joyce had lived under the Crown's protection and owed it a corresponding duty of allegiance, subject to the judge's discretion they could find against him on the third count alone.[60]

The prosecution called its witnesses. Gladys Winifred Isaac, Secretary to the University of London's Military Education Committee, told the court that Joyce had claimed to be British when applying to join the University of London's OTC.[61] Harold Godwin, from the Foreign Office, testified Joyce had made similar claims in his passport applications in 1933, 1938 and 1939.[62] Detective Inspector Albert Hunt, who had listened to some of the wartime broadcasts, again offered details of Joyce's radio work.[63] Captain Alexander Lickorish once more retailed the Flensburg incident and his finding on Joyce two documents confirming his connection to the Nazi state.[64] Captain Jim Skardon relayed again Joyce's statement at Lüneberg.[65] To underline the professional nature of translated German materials, the Crown relied as it had earlier on Samuel Lopez Salzedo, who worked out of Chancery Lane.[66] Chief Inspector Frank Bridges informed the court of Joyce's arrest when he landed in England at "20 minutes past 4 on the afternoon of Saturday, 16th June 1945."[67]

Detective Inspector Hunt's evidence proved vital. He claimed that between 3 September and 10 December 1939 he had been stationed at Folkestone. There one evening, off duty and fiddling with the dials on his wireless, he suddenly found himself listening to Joyce. It was "either in September or early October 1939."[68] He recognised the voice because as a Special Branch Officer he had monitored the pre-war activities of the BUF and the National Socialist League. He claimed Joyce had told his listeners German bombs had destroyed Dover and Folkestone, a boast clearly intended to corrupt civilian morale. If Hunt had recalled correctly, the court had just heard damning evidence of Joyce working for the Nazis when he held a British passport.[69]

Before the 1945 Treason Act, such uncorroborated evidence from a single witness would have been insufficient proof of Joyce's treason. Now it was. As one lawyer remarked, the new Act had "greatly simplified" treason trials.[70] It is disconcerting therefore to reflect on Hunt's vagueness. He could offer Slade neither the precise time nor date of the broadcast. Nor indeed the station: "I do not know [it] I was just tuning in my receiver round the wavelengths when I heard the voice."[71] How convenient. More might have been expected of a senior policeman with a long career in political surveillance. Did he never think of making notes? In his trial notebook Curtis-Bennett quickly wrote that such vagueness "was sufficient to discredit anything else he might say."[72] Such hazy testimony certainly fell far short of the kind of evidence previously demanded by the Director of Public Prosecutions. Yet, "It was on the uncorroborated evidence of one broadcast, whose date and origin were unknown, whose precise content and authorship could not be verified, that Joyce went to the gallows."[73]

When Slade opened long-windedly for the defence, he focused on whether his client could be treated as a British subject. "I am hoping to prove to you conclusively, or as conclusively as one can prove anything," he said, "that the prisoner has never been a British subject at any time throughout his life."[74] He argued "when William Joyce was born . . . on 24th April 1906, in New York City, he was born out of His Majesty's dominions and born of a father who was not a British subject at the time of his birth: in other words, William Joyce was born and always remained a subject of the United States of America, which he still is."[75] Slade had an American birth certificate in his hands which supported his claim.

He called his witnesses. Frank Holland and Quentin Joyce provided details on family background and nationality.[76] Detective Superintendent John Woodmansey of the Lancashire Police affirmed that when Gertrude Joyce came to Lancashire in 1917 after the death of her mother, she had been treated by his force as an alien because of her marriage to an Irish-American.[77] Bernard Reilly, a retired RIC sergeant, was called next. He informed the court that Michael Joyce, who had taken out American citizenship, believed his subsequent failure to re-register had caused his application to lapse.[78] William Yuile Forbes, quaintly described as "an examiner of questioned documents," verified Michael Joyce's signature on several items, especially American naturalisation records.[79] Henry Stebbing, First Secretary at the US Embassy in London, affirmed Joyce's father had indeed sworn an oath of citizenship. "He thereupon, by American law, became an

American citizen without any further formal order or requirement of any description." Any child of his born in the United States would possess that same nationality.[80] As would any of his children born in Britain who later resided in the United States.[81] No wonder the prosecution, the defence, and the US authorities had been desperately anxious to track Michael's life in America. FBI files bulge with such enquiries and detail.[82] Joyce closely followed these complex arguments, often making precise, tidy notes.

The defence had done well and by the end of the second day, bearing in mind Joyce had produced his American birth certificate, the prosecution could no longer sustain the charge he was a British subject. The first two counts had to be dropped from the indictment. Tucker declared: "I think everybody must agree that the evidence which has been tendered is really overwhelming."[83] Those wartime recordings made by MI5 had now to be disregarded.

Discussion then began on the third count: that whilst owing an allegiance to the King, Joyce had committed treason by broadcasting for Germany between 18 September 1939 and 2 July 1940.[84] This legal argument was on-going when the court adjourned. That evening Slade, Curtis-Bennett and Burge knew big hurdles remained in the final straight. But for now they could return to chambers well-pleased with their progress. Joyce was escorted to prison, understandably lifted in spirits, and anxious to say as much when writing to his new literary audience, Margaret particularly.[85]

On 19 September, the final day, a vital decision was needed. Did an alien's obligation to the Crown end on leaving the country? Slade maintained this position. Or did Joyce's holding a British passport between 18 September 1939 and 2 July 1940 demand a continuing obligation to the Crown, even though his alleged treason had been committed abroad? The prosecution favoured this interpretation. The court adjourned to allow Tucker time to consider. Joyce had a distinctly nervous wait. On his return Tucker declared:

> Mr Attorney and Mr Slade, I shall direct the jury on count 3 that on 24th August 1939, when the passport was applied for the prisoner, beyond a shadow of doubt, owed allegiance to the Crown of this country, and that on the evidence given, if they

accept it, nothing happened at the material time thereafter to put an end to the allegiance that he then owed.[86]

It was for counsel to deliver their closing speeches, the judge to sum up, and the jury to reach a verdict.

Slade's "plain and pedestrian" closing address questioned the accuracy of Inspector Hunt's recollections.[87] His evidence gave the defence its key problem. Counsel queried whether Joyce had made a broadcast in 1939 claiming Dover and Folkestone had been destroyed.[88] Echoing the Crown's opening remarks, he told the jury to cast aside all prejudices against his client. "Everyone talks of him as though he were already condemned and convicted."[89] He was not. British justice stood on trial as well as Joyce. They must get it right.

Shawcross argued that the mere act of broadcasting was sufficient to reveal Joyce's adherence to the King's enemies, and emphasised the importance of Hunt's evidence on the destruction of Dover and Folkestone. In those towns any such claim would have been treated as fantastical. However, Joyce's broadcast carried the potential to damage morale elsewhere in the country.[90] Finally, like Slade, Shawcross reminded jurors the prisoner should be tried entirely "according to law and justice according to the evidence."[91]

After these tedious speeches – was a man's life at stake? – Tucker summed up and reminded jurors that to sustain its case, the prosecution must prove that the accused owed allegiance to the King.[92] In his considered opinion "a man who . . . adopts and uses the protection of the sovereign to whom he has already acquired an allegiance, remains under that allegiance and is guilty of treason if he adheres to the King's enemies."[93] Tucker pronounced that aiding and comforting the enemy need involve no more than voluntarily throwing in one's lot with them. When making this emphasis he drew attention to Hunt's evidence and Joyce's contract with the German Radio Office of 18 September 1939.[94] He advised finding Joyce not guilty on counts one and two. "On count 3 you will ask yourselves whether or not the case has been proved to your satisfaction beyond all reasonable doubt."[95] What passed through Joyce's mind at that point? The 'twelve good men and true' retired at 3.37 in the afternoon. Twenty-three minutes later the jury delivered a "guilty" verdict on count three.[96]

"I watched Joyce at that moment," a reporter wrote. "Beads of sweat broke out on his forehead. He licked his lips. The scar that cuts right across his right cheek, from ear to mouth, glowed." Gathering himself "he stiffened, threw back his head defiantly . . . and grinned." The clerk of the court enquired: "Have you anything to say, prisoner, why the court should not give judgement of death, according to law?" The same journalist had "expected an outburst . . . a political speech. But not a word came."[97] Joyce's silence struck other observers as "rather remarkable."[98]

The black cap, the vampire chapeau, now appeared. In the quiet of the court Tucker carefully and slowly smoothed it to rest on his wig. He then delivered the death sentence.[99] Those wartime monitors, who had listened to Joyce's broadcasts and successfully drawn lots to attend his trial, now became agitated. They had never experienced anything quite as disturbing as the black cap ritual and all it implied.[100] John Macnab "buried his face in his hands and wept unashamedly." Quentin Joyce "made the sign of the cross and bowed his head in silent prayer."[101]

3

Round one of the legal proceedings had ended. A pleased Edie Rutherford, a Mass-Observer from Sheffield, remarked "that bxxxxxd Joyce has not got off."[102] But the prosecution had failed to knock him out. His case had longer to run.

On 30 October appeal proceedings began at the Law Courts in the Strand before the Lord Chief Justice, Viscount Caldecote.[103] He was assisted by Sir Travers Humphreys, who had participated in the 1916 Casement treason trial. A member of the judicial Bench since 1928, he was soon to sit on John Amery's case.[104] They were joined by Mr Justice Lynskey, who had been appointed to the King's Bench Division in 1944.[105] He later presided over the Lynskey Tribunal, dominated by the egregious 'Sidney Stanley,' which investigated an alleged corruption case in the Attlee Government.[106] The prosecution and defence teams remained unchanged. Joyce did not receive legal aid. Friends and sympathisers covered his costs.[107]

Joyce appealed on four grounds. His lawyers argued, firstly, "the Court wrongly assumed jurisdiction to try an alien for an offence against British Law committed in a foreign country"; secondly, they claimed the judge had been wrong in law in holding that Joyce owed allegiance to the Crown between September 1939 and 2 July 1940, and so directing the jury; thirdly, no evidence had been produced to show that "the Appellant's passport afforded him, or was capable of affording him any protection, or that [he] ever availed himself or had any intention of availing himself of any such protection"; finally, "if (contrary to the Appellant's contention), any such evidence existed, the issue was one for the jury" and on this point the judge had failed to direct them.[108]

The Lord Chief Justice stated he and his colleagues did not require the Attorney-General's observations on points three and four. But they did on the remainder. Shawcross argued for a degree of legal flexibility. "The incalculable advantage of the whole system of British law," he declared, "was that its principles were capable of adaptation to the new circumstances perpetually arising."[109] He emphasised a British subject could be tried for treason committed abroad, citing the 1916 action against Sir Roger Casement.[110] "The only real question in the present case," he continued, "was whether the person who committed the allegedly treasonable act was one who could commit treason."[111] He submitted that everyone, under a duty of allegiance, could commit that crime.[112] And until Joyce became a German citizen the protection afforded by his British passport meant he owed an allegiance to the Crown.[113]

Joyce, who listened carefully to another discussion of his fate, had an agonising wait for the outcome. Caldecote announced that judgement would be declined until Wednesday, 7 November 1945. When it came, it offered no comfort to the defence. Caldecote briskly dismissed its submission that an alien could never be guilty of treason for acts committed outside the King's realm. It amounted to "a startling proposition."[114] Joyce's actions had been worsened by the fact that even he admitted to being treated as British following his arrival in England and had applied for passports claiming as much.[115] And he had undoubtedly comforted the King's enemies whilst holding a British passport, which could have afforded him the Crown's protection. These observations preceded the four chilling words: "The appeal is dismissed."[116] Joyce was driven back across Waterloo Bridge to Wandsworth.[117] He was rapidly running out of options.

4

On 16 November 1945 the Attorney-General allowed Joyce's appeal to the Lords.[118] Twelve days later, John Amery came up at the Bailey where, to the distress of his family and the consternation of his lawyers, including Slade, he pleaded guilty to treason.[119] Joyce was still ready for a fight.

The hearing in the Lords took place between 10 and 13 December. The setting was Dickensian. "The winter was already bitter and there was a fuel crisis. The five elderly men sat in judgment with rugs wrapped round their legs to keep warm" while "Joyce, guarded by four warders sat in a corner . . . his face yellow with prison pallor." The public's interest had already waned. To many people he was as good as dead. But Macnab and Quentin came to listen.[120]

The Attorney-General and Gerald Howard represented the Crown. After the Court of Appeal hearing Laurence Byrne had been appointed a judge of the High Court; in 1960 he was to preside over the so-called Lady Chatterley case.[121] Joyce drew as before on Slade, Curtis-Bennett and Burge.

The Lord Chancellor, Baron Jowitt of Stevenage, presided over the hearing. Called to the Bar in 1909, he had first entered Parliament as a Liberal. After switching his allegiance, he had served as Attorney-General in the 1929 Labour administration. As Solicitor-General, in 1940 he had led against Anna Wolkoff. After 1945, Attlee appointed him Lord Chancellor. Changing loyalties clearly served him well in career terms. But his contemporary Norman Birkett regarded him as "weak" and "vacillating," wanting to be "all things to all men, spineless and accommodating, without principles or conviction."[122] Jowitt was unlikely to show any enthusiasm for derailing the seemingly inexorable legal journey to Joyce's end.

After listening to already familiar arguments, their Lordships declared they needed time to consider their judgement. On 18 December, four to one, with Lord Porter, later known pejoratively as Lord Passporter, dissenting – he agreed with the defence that the issue of protection afforded by Joyce's passport was for the jury rather than the judge to decide – they dismissed Joyce's appeal.[123] At this point a spectator "with hollow eyes and pinched nose and a muffler round his scrawny neck" – identified later as James Blair, an ex-serviceman from Motherwell – stood up in the public gallery and shouted in Gaelic, before translating into English, "Joyce is innocent. This thing should stop."[124] A dissenting appellate judgement would normally have halted the legal march to the death sentence.[125] In Joyce's case the process continued. The reasons behind their Lordships' decision did not become public until 1 February 1946. By then Joyce was dead.

The Home Secretary could still sanction a reprieve. But Chuter Ede – "my new landlord," Joyce once called him – proved ill-at-ease in the Home Office.[126] He often ate out of the hand of Sir Frank Newsam, the powerful Deputy Under-Secretary who had been instrumental in devising the 1937 Public Order Act and was familiar with Joyce's political career.

The old *Dictionary of National Biography* carries a complimentary entry on Newsam, but many younger colleagues regarded him as "an incorrigible reactionary."[127] He was a certainly a powerful force in the Home Office and dominated more ministers than Chuter Ede. The clerihew, "Sir Frank Newsam/Affected to look gruesome/Which carried great weight/With successive Secretaries of State," says it all.[128] He took a tough line on murderers. The appeals of Derek Bentley, Ruth Ellis and Timothy Evans, were all turned down on his watch and some abolitionists have portrayed him as a Rasputin.[129] He also had little time for traitors and was unmoved by the campaign to save John Amery.[130] On 29 December, ten days after Amery's execution, Newsam compiled a long memorandum on Joyce's case which noted eight of the nine judges had found him guilty. There was "no question of mental unsoundness." And the prisoner could not be excused on the ground he regarded himself as an alien; on the contrary, he had frequently sworn to be British. Moreover in 1940 – in what Newsam called "Twilight over Britain" – Joyce had claimed to be committing treason on a daily basis.[131] He therefore advised the Home Secretary briefly, unambiguously: "I can find no sufficient grounds for recommending any interference with the law."[132] Chuter Ede – what a strange name, Joyce mused – agreed.[133] After tendering his advice Newsam could turn to other Departmental matters, doubtless taking the occasional break to study the racing pages.[134] But he should not be portrayed as a villain.[135] He argued his case coldly, logically, mandarin-like, on the basis of the evidence before him.

When the Home Secretary's decision came through, a sigh of relief could be heard across Whitehall. Joyce was destined for the gallows. The state did not need to introduce its contingency plan of deporting him to Germany, until which time he would have required protection from the public's outrage.[136]

It was not until February 1946, almost one month to the day after Joyce's execution, that the Lords revealed why his appeal had been rejected. Jowitt declared:

> The material facts are these, that being for long resident here and owing allegiance he applied for and obtained a passport, and, leaving the realm, adhered to the King's enemies. It does not matter that he made false representations as to his status, asserting that he was a British subject by birth, a statement that he was afterwards at pains to disprove. It may be that when he first made the statement he thought it was true. Of this there is no evidence. The essential fact is that he got the passport.[137]

Joyce's British passport created a continuing bond between him and the Crown:

> I am clearly of opinion that so long as he holds the passport he is within the meaning of the Statute a man who, if he is adherent to the King's enemies in the realm or elsewhere commits an act of treason.[138]

With this statement the lawyers had concluded their business: not that the legal wrangling had been silenced forever. Far from it.

Notes

1 *The Times*, 19 June 1945.
2 *Who Was Who 1961–1970* (London, 1972), pp.167–168. Obituary, *The Guardian*, 2 November 1965.
3 *The Times*, 19 June 1945.
4 Ian Sayer Archive, Quentin Joyce to "My dear George," 1 October 1945, on the need for funds. Quentin Joyce Archive, for Fr Clement Russell and

Len Sinclair (ex-NSL), offering donations. Russell letter, 7 August 1945, and Sinclair letter, 2 October 1945.

5 *The Times*, 26 June 1945.

6 *Ibid*. reported Col W. E. Hinchley Cooke and E.J.P. Cussen were present to represent the War Office. Both were MI5.

7 Author's possession.

8 West, *Treason* (2000), p.96.

9 Head died soon after his client. *Daily Mirror*, 19 January 1949.

10 *The Times*, 26 June 1945.

11 *Ibid*. 29 June 1945.

12 *Manchester Guardian*, 5 July 1945, on Slade's appointment as the third and leading counsel. Faber, *Speaking for England*, p.489 on his representing Amery.

13 KV 2/248/8a, for him keeping safe his US birth certificate.

14 KV 2/246/457B, one of many sources.

15 *The Times*, 19 July 1945.

16 Lauterpacht Archive, Law Officers to Professor Hersch Lauterpacht, August 1945.

17 KV 2/246/433A.

18 HO 45/25690 on his campaign for Quentin Joyce.

19 KV 2/246/423A.

20 Kenneth Self (MI5) censored her letters. When not wielding his blue pencil, he would buy for her on the Brussels black market. *Daily Telegraph*, 11 June 1998 for his obituary.

21 *Nineteenth Century and After*, No. DCCCX (August 1944), p.49 and *ibid*. No. DCCCXXII (August 1945), pp.49–70. Matthew and Harrison (eds), *ODNB*, Vol.56, pp.588–590 on Voigt.

22 KV 2/247/518a, letter, 7 July 1945.

23 J. and A. Tusa, *The Nuremberg Trial* (London, 1983), p.13.

24 *John Bull*, 12 May 1945. *It Happened Here*, Kevin Brownlow and Andrew Mollo's 1964 film of Britain under the Nazis; K. Brownlow, *How It Happened Here* (London, 1968); L. Deighton, *SS-GB. Nazi-Occupied Britain 1941* (London, 1978); N. Longmate, *If Britain Had Fallen* (London, 1992); C.J. Sansom, *Dominion* (London, 2012).

25 WJ to MJ, 17 September 1945.

26 *Gothic Ripples*, No.4, 13 October 1945, p.3.

27 Rattigan, British Library, Add MS 74490, f.19.

28 Selwyn, *Hitler's Englishman*, p.174; Waller, *London 1945*, p.8.

29 C. Dee (pseud.), *No Complaints in Hell* (London, 1949), p.257.

30 *Manchester Guardian*, 18 September 1945.

31 Muggeridge, *Chronicles*, p.108.

32 Rawlinson in Matthew and Harrison (eds), *ODNB*, Vol.55, p.497.

33 Obituary in *The Times*, 18 November 1975; Matthew and Harrison (eds), *ODNB*, Vol.55, pp.496–497.

34 *The Times*, 13 September 1945.

35 On the Joyce trial see H. Shawcross, *Life Sentence: The Memoirs of Hartley Shawcross* (London, 1995), pp.78–83.

36 *Who Was Who 1971–1980* (London, 1981), p.386 for Howard.

37 R. Skidelsky on Shawcross's memoirs, *Sunday Telegraph*, 30 July 1995. For Yevonde's portrait of Shawcross, see Hall (ed.), *Trial*, facing p.144.

38 *The Times*, 11 July 2003, has an obituary. N. Fagan, G. Bryson, C. Elston, *A Century of Liverpool Lawyers* (Liverpool, 2002), pp.131–136.

39 Selwyn, *Hitler's Englishman*, p.183. See portrait facing p.160 in Hall (ed.), *Trial*.

40 Faber, *Speaking for England*, p.489.

41 HO 45/25691/71.

42 *The Times*, 8 November 1940, on the first and *ibid*. 19 July 1941, 24 July and 1 August 1941, on Ramsay's action. KV 2/678/298a on the *New York Times*. On Slade's other work, see Simpson, *In the Highest Degree Odious*, p.85.

43 C.G.L. du Cann, *English Treason Trials* (London, 1964), p.255, for his verbosity. *Ibid*.p.252, for further critical assessment.

44 *Who Was Who 1961–1970*, p.1042.

45 *Who Was Who 1951–1960*, p.270; *The Times* 27 June 1956; S. Curtis-Bennett, *The Curtis-Bennett Chronicle* (Chichester, 1998), pp.45–51.

46 Largely from L. Kennedy, *The Trial of Stephen Ward* (Harmondsworth, 1965), pp.44–45. See also *Who Was Who 1981–1990* (London, 1991), p.105. G. Robertson, *Stephen Ward Was Innocent OK* (London, 2013), on Ward.

47 WJ to MJ, 3 July 1945.

48 *The Times*, 15 September 1990.

49 WJ to MJ, 14 July 1945. Quentin Joyce Archive, for Quentin to Gilbert Brooke, 11 July 1945, on the "very fine line-up."

50 Hall (ed.), *Trial*, pp.43–44. On the third day of the trial, when it had been shown Joyce was not a British subject, and charges one and two had been discounted, Shawcross argued, and the judge agreed, that in these counts the word "person" should be amended to "British subject."

51 "Germany Calling," BBC Radio 4, 16 May 1991. James Clark's evidence.

52 Hall (ed.), *Trial*, p.45.

53 Imperial War Museum, Wiseman Papers, Box 1, Folder 3, 86/1/1, S. Darwin Fox to Frank Wiseman, 4 January 1946.

54 Farndale, *Haw-Haw*, pp.303, 342–343.

55 WJ to MJ, 21 December 1945 for wanting to be "above" rather than involved "in" the legal proceedings.

56 WJ to MJ, 6 October 1945.

57 Hall (ed.) *Trial*, p.46.

58 *Ibid*. p.48.

59 *Ibid*. p.52.

60 *Ibid*. pp.58–59.

61 *Ibid*. pp.59–62.

62 *Ibid*. pp.62–65.

63 *Ibid*. pp.65–71.

64 *Ibid*. pp.71–72.

65 *Ibid.* pp.72 ff.
66 *Ibid.* pp.77–82 and KV 2/248/31A.
67 Hall (ed.), *Trial*, p.82.
68 *Ibid.* p.65.
69 *Ibid.* pp.65–71.
70 *The Times*, 19 June 1945.
71 Hall (ed.), *Trial*, p.70.
72 Curtis-Bennett Archive.
73 Selwyn, *Hitler's Englishman*, p.188.
74 Hall (ed.), *Trial*, p.98.
75 *Ibid.* pp.102–103.
76 *Ibid.* pp.117–127. Quentin Joyce Archive reveals 'Q' furiously busy gathering evidence and, later, arranging accommodation in London for defence witnesses. It also shows that after Joyce's execution Quentin and Macnab also provided gifts for the defence team.
77 Hall (ed.), *Trial*, pp.127–131.
78 *Ibid.* p.131.
79 *Ibid.* pp.131–132.
80 *Ibid.* pp.132–133.
81 *Ibid.* pp.99–102, particularly.
82 NARA FBI file, 65–1.
83 Hall (ed.), *Trial*, p.133. M. Lloyd, *The Passport: The History of Man's Most Travelled Document* (Stroud, 2003), pp.162–169, provides later comment.
84 Hall (ed.), *Trial*, pp. 45,133.
85 WJ to MJ, 18 September 1945, for his hopes being raised.
86 Hall (ed.), *Trial*, p.204.
87 du Cann, *English Treason Trials*, p.255.
88 Hall (ed.), *Trial*, p.207.
89 *Ibid.* p.206.
90 *Ibid.* p211.
91 *Ibid.* p.212.
92 *Ibid.* p.215.
93 *Ibid.* p.222.
94 *Ibid.* pp.212–214.
95 *Ibid.* p.227.
96 *Ibid.* p.228.
97 *Daily Herald*, 20 September 1945.
98 du Cann, *English Treason Trials*, p.257.
99 Hall (ed.), *Trial*, p.228.
100 Lorna Swire to author, 20 November 2004.
101 *Daily Mirror*, 20 September 1945.
102 S. Garfield, *Our Hidden Lives: Diaries of Forgotten Britain 1945–1948* (London, 2004), p.98.
103 Matthew and Harrison (eds), *ODNB*, Vol.29, pp.310–312, on Thomas Inskip (Viscount Caldecote).

104 Matthew and Harrison (eds), *ODNB*, Vol.28, pp.809–810. See also S. Jackson, *The Life and Cases of Mr Justice Humphreys* (London, 1952). His Casement involvement appears in *ibid.* pp.125 ff. D. G. Browne, *Sir Travers Humphreys* (London, 1960), for further detail. Faber, *Speaking for England*, pp.498–512 on Amery.

105 Hall (ed.), *Trial*, p.331. Obituary in *The Times*, 23 December 1957. Fagan, Bryson and Elstom, *Liverpool Lawyers*, pp.114–116. Matthew and Harrison (eds), *ODNB*, Vol.34, pp.907–908.

106 P. Hennessy, *Never Again: Britain 1945–51* (London, 1992), p.446 for 'Stanley' as "a bizarrely hilarious spiv who kept the nation entertained during the five weeks of hearings."

107 Martland, *Lord Haw-Haw*, p.95. The Old Bailey trial cost £221.0s. 8d. The Lords Appeal amounted to £12.2s.10d. Quentin Joyce Archive, Ludlow and Co to Quentin Joyce, 26 October 1945 and 24 December 1945, respectively.

108 Hall (ed.), *Trial*, p.232.

109 *Ibid.* p.238.

110 du Cann, *English Treason Trials*, pp.222–245 on legal issues.

111 Hall (ed.), *Trial*, p.239.

112 *Ibid.* p.239.

113 *Ibid.* p.240.

114 *Ibid.* p.243.

115 *Ibid.* pp. 245–246.

116 *Ibid.* p.248.

117 Selwyn, *Hitler's Englishman*, p.208.

118 HO 45/22406/117.

119 Faber, *Speaking for England*, pp.498–512.

120 Selwyn, *Hitler's Englishman*, p.209.

121 Hall (ed.), *Trial*, p.312. Obituary, *Guardian*, 2 November 1965.

122 Hall (ed.), *Trial*, p.309. Matthew and Harrison (eds), *ODNB* Vol.30, pp.767–769. Birkett's diary, 29 March 1947, E57, 1996, 13, 15, AE9, for his assessment, National Galleries of Justice, Nottingham. Matthew and Harrison (eds), *ODNB*, Vol.59, pp.836–838, on Birkett, and also H. M. Hyde, *Norman Birkett* (London, 1964).

123 Hall (ed.), *Trial*, p.257. On Porter, see Matthew and Harrison (eds), *ODNB*, Vol.44, pp.971–973. *Manchester Guardian*, 14 February 1956, for an obituary.

124 Blair also wrote to the Home Office in Joyce's defence. See HO 45/22405/486–489 and /749–751. Is he the Frederick James Blair who features on the renegades list in WO 204/12556? West, *Treason*, pp.56–57, reported the incident.

125 G. Robertson, *Freedom, The Individual and the Law* (Harmondsworth, 1989), p.173. *Manchester Guardian*, 1 January 1946.

126 WJ to MJ, 4 August 1945, on Ede as landlord. Obituary notice, *The Times*, 12 November 1965, and Matthew and Harrison (eds), *ODNB*, Vol.17, pp.658–660. J. B. Christoph, *Capital Punishment and*

British Politics: The British Movement to Abolish the Death Penalty, 1945–57 (London, 1962), p.36, on Ede and abolition.

127 E. T. Williams and C. S. Nicholls (eds), Dictionary of National Biography, 1961–1970 (Oxford, 1981), pp.791–793. Noel Annan to Brian Simpson, 1 August 1991, USSC, MS 287.

128 Quoted, Simpson, In the Highest Degree Odious, p.42.

129 Christoph, Capital Punishment, p.40. In fact, Ede believed he was "at heart" an abolitionist. Ibid. p.70.

130 HO 144/22823/322–323 for his attitude towards John Amery.

131 Joyce, Twilight Over England, p.9.

132 HO 45 22405/835–836.

133 The Times, 2 January 1946. WJ to MJ, 4 August 1945, reveals Joyce's interest in the Home Secretary's name. Anti-Semites are often obsessed by names in their perpetual quest to identify and expose 'hidden' Jews.

134 Matthew and Harrison (eds), ODNB, Vol.40, p.679, notes he was "an inveterate gambler on horse racing."

135 M. Kenny, "Death is the right price," The Guardian, 23 July 2004, where he appears as "Newsome."

136 HO 382/1/35,37,48.

137 Hall (ed.), Trial, p.263; The Times, 2 February 1946.

138 Hall (ed.), Trial, p.265.

20

THE SCENT OF DEATH
WAS IN THE AIR

I see that Lord Haw-Haw is to be hanged on 3 January . . .
It was quite evident that he would be hanged once he was
arrested. If they wanted to kill him, they ought to have shot
him immediately he was arrested, without all this hypocrisy of
a 'trial.' I have no patience with this lamentable English trait.
[B. Charles, a Mass Observer, Saturday 29 December 1945,
in Simon Garfield, *Our Hidden Lives. The Everyday Diaries of a
Forgotten Britain 1945–1948* (London, 2004), p.157.]

1

His appeals exhausted, yet another battle lost, Joyce's execution,
scheduled for 3 January 1946, moves ever nearer. The evening before,
he plays chess until midnight. He wakes at 6am, drinks a cup of tea,
changes into his blue serge suit, washes, but decides not to shave.[1] He
recants nothing. Albert Pierrepoint, the state's appointed executioner,
despatches him at 9 o'clock that morning.

Haw-Haw's execution leaves no great impression on the busy official
hangman.[2] He describes the prisoner as thirty-nine, 5 feet 5¾ inches in
height and 151 lbs in weight. To execute him efficiently – and Pierrepoint prides himself on being as fast as a whippet – requires a drop of
7 feet and 4 inches.[3] He performs his job without any fuss or hesitation.

2

On a bitterly cold morning just over thirty years after Roger Casement's execution for treason, a crowd of about three hundred people
gather outside Wandsworth, waiting for news.

At the appointed hour three young men raise their hats. Adrian
Earle is one of them. In post-war Oxford he has begun a thesis, allegedly without taking a first degree. This unusual feat is possible because
he has Maurice Bowra's patronage and beyond Oxford has cultivated
Lord Alfred Douglas and Harold Nicolson. He is an unstable character whose rackety lifestyle will land him in prison, where Peter
Wildeblood considers him the wickedest man he has ever met. But
how does this "immensely tall" figure, "the Wykehamist blackmailer,"
relate to Joyce?[4]

To an extent, they share political views. Earle favours aristocrats,
which distances them. But his anti-Labour beliefs provide a bridge.
He might also have fascist sympathies. Finally, and a stronger link, he
is an anti-Semite. Years later he will die in suspicious circumstances
in South America.[5]

A middle-aged woman and her daughter hover in the crowd for
forty-five minutes.[6] In a reminder of Joyce's wartime taunts, they
hear some bystanders chant: "Where is the Ark Royal?"[7] A handful
of sailors shout: "Get it over – hang him as high as you can." Two
men from Glasgow tell reporters: "We had a short holiday due to
us, so we thought we would come to London to be here at Joyce's
end." Their journey has not required quite as much effort as George
Selwyn's expedition to Paris to witness Madame Guillotine during
the French Revolution, but has involved a fair effort, nevertheless.
A woman living near the prison brings her ten-year-old daughter
and two other children to join the throng.[8] Journalists encounter an
Army sapper from Tooting who turns up with his bulldog "in case
the Fascists decide to cause trouble."[9] Rebecca West, busy writing on
Joyce, mingles in the crowd.[10]

Elsewhere a number of religious services are under way. At 8.30
a small congregation gathers at Our Lady of Dolours, Fulham Road,
where the Very Reverend Fr Paul Johnson, who knows Joyce through
John Macnab, is conducting a requiem mass.[11] Macnab is present, along

with Quentin Joyce, John Beckett and Robert Gordon-Canning. The last, a leading Mosleyite and funder of Joyce's defence, has just paid £500 for a granite bust of Hitler previously at the German Embassy.[12] Jeffrey Hamm, Oswald Mosley's faithful political servant, who will labour for years in a barren political wilderness, also attends. An MI5 officer reports that the incensed air soon becomes thick with rabid effusions of support for Joyce the political martyr.[13]

At Sudbury, Fr Clement Russell officiates at another service. This Catholic convert and member of the BUF has attracted MI5's attention during the War for listening to Haw-Haw's broadcasts.[14] More recently, he has contributed towards Joyce's defence costs and conducted a sympathetic correspondence with Quentin Joyce.[15]

At Crowthorne, Berkshire, the newly installed Fr Edward Marshall Keene, known originally as Edmund Dunkerton, is likewise engaged.[16] During the War he had informed the British authorities that Margaret Joyce was broadcasting for the Nazis.[17] But at 8.15 he begins prayers for the dying, starts mass at 8.45 and at 9.03 places the chalice on the altar, having consumed the precious blood.[18]

In Galway a mass is held in the Chapel of St Ignatius's School for someone recalled as a bright, sparkling pupil with an important future.[19] But whose life has ended in a way impossible to have envisaged.

As Pierrepoint steadies him for the drop, Aubrey Lees, one of Joyce's fascist contacts, stands in silence with his wife and that unrepentant Mosleyite, Ronald Creasy.[20] Mosley's diary suggests he is fully occupied that early morning with more mundane matters.[21] 'The Leader,' aware of the sympathy for Joyce among Britain's fascists, nevertheless recognises the dangers in any public show of support.[22] His followers are instructed not to sign petitions for clemency.[23]

3

The newspapers have their say. *The Times* announces briefly, "William Joyce, 39, 'Lord Haw-Haw,' was executed at Wandsworth prison at 9 o'clock."[24] By contrast, in the *Jewish Chronicle*, "an ex-Serviceman" reflecting a widespread opinion in Anglo-Jewry, refers to "that vile traitor and Jew-Baiter" who has been sent to "a shameful and unlamented death."[25] In the *Daily Worker* Peter Phillips reports, "Six months ago I saw thin-lipped, sneering little William Joyce strut into the dock at Bow Street . . . yesterday at 9 am I saw the final end of the final chapter in the history of this Fascist braggart." Displaying a nice turn in invective, he calls him "a twisted-mouthed thug" who had "mocked the people of this country in their darkest hours."[26] A few days later *The Patriot* will link Joyce's fate to the post-war betrayal of Britain by young people now busy emigrating whilst alien immigration proceeds apace, implying such desertions amount to a form of treachery.[27]

4

Could events have turned out differently? Would Joyce's solicitor have been well-advised to follow his early inclination and retain a KC from Ireland "with a great deal of fight in him"? His thoughts turned briefly to the tall, commanding figure of Serjeant Sullivan KC, who had defended Sir Roger Casement.[28] The defence did have some contact with him.[29] But letting the Irishman loose on the court was a different matter. In any case, Joyce believed Sullivan was past his best.[30]

Shortly after Joyce arrived back in England, A. E. McCloskey, who knew him before the War, had offered to serve.[31] But Curtis-Bennett and Burge were first retained and then Slade.[32] Joyce continued to think well of Slade. Others have agreed.[33] However, Rebecca West, present at the trial, was scathing on his performance.[34] Even if there is no need to agree with the conspiracy theorists that he was appointed precisely because he would prove ineffective.[35]

Some might query whether he was well-advised to allow his client to remain silent. But Joyce, believing he had never betrayed Britain, had no intention of submitting to any cross-examination. Indeed, he congratulated himself on his stance and, a few days after hearing the death sentence, recalled Andrew Marvell's lines on the execution of Charles I:

> He nothing common did or mean
> Upon that memorable scene.[36]

Had Joyce decided on a verbal battle he would soon have been in trouble. Slade was probably relieved that he insisted on remaining above the fray.

Joyce's counsel could not compel him to testify. But at times Slade could have been more forceful with the prosecution's witnesses. Harold Godwin, the Assistant Passport Officer, "a man with a nervous disposition," became agitated when Slade invited him to explain why Joyce's passport had been renewed in August 1939.[37] Godwin became "indisposed" and, surprisingly, Slade remarked, "I am so sorry to have distressed you, and I don't desire to ask any further questions."[38] The renewal had been approved on 24 August 1939, by which time, in the event of war, Joyce's name had been pencilled in for internment.[39] Why, therefore, was he allowed to leave the country? Slade was beginning a serious line of enquiry. But he never followed it through.

This crucial passport never appeared in the trial papers. When detained, Joyce's possessions included a copy of Horace. He carried with him *National Socialism Now* and an unfinished typescript, "Matrix," started in May 1945. His other books included Jonah Barrington's *Lord Haw-Haw of Zeesen* and Marlowe's *Doctor Faustus*. He had a Smith and Wesson with five rounds of ammunition. He travelled hopefully with a packet of contraceptives. He retained the divorce decree from his first marriage. He still had his reader's ticket for Kensington Public Library. He kept his American birth certificate safe. But no British passport surfaced.[40]

Slade also allowed Inspector Albert Hunt to slip away. When Joyce was put up on 25 June 1945, *The Times* reported Hunt saying that he had listened to Joyce's broadcasts in 1943 and 1944 – which we know he did as a member of the police team gathering evidence against Joyce.[41] However, the following September at the Old Bailey he claimed – crucially and conveniently, for the prosecution – to have heard a broadcast in September–October 1939, when Joyce still held a British passport.[42] Yet he could offer no convincing supporting evidence. His vital intervention demanded a more rigorous assault.

But the defence faced a major difficulty. Mr Justice Tucker had already described Joyce as a traitor and his appointment is unsettling, though at the time it passed without comment.[43] Today, a judge who had previously pronounced on the guilt of an accused would never be appointed.[44] Joyce did not meet a foul-mouthed, lackey-prosecutor such as Andrei Vyshinsky, Stalin's legal 'voice' in the Soviet show trials of the '30s. He did not encounter someone like that bullying, hysterical racist, Roland Freisler, Hitler's 'blood judge,' who carried out the Nazis' bidding during the War. Or anyone resembling the obedient, vicious Josef Urválek, that lean-faced legal hack who implemented Moscow's agenda in the 1953 Slanský show trial. But 'Natal' Tucker's involvement carried serious consequences for the defence. He leaned heavily towards the prosecution.[45]

When representing the Crown, there is a belief Hartley Shawcross worked from a brief provided by Arnold McNair.[46] He never did. But somewhat anxious in his new role, and acutely aware of the intricacies and importance of Joyce's case, he turned to Hersch Lauterpacht, Whewell Professor of International Law at Cambridge.[47]

Lauterpacht's private papers contain various opinions. One, dated 4 September 1945, was in the prosecution's hands before the trial began. Another, on 1 October, set out an argument for the appeal process.[48] Shawcross clung tenaciously to the script and later, when presenting his adviser with a copy of J. W. Hall's account of the trial, dedicated it in his bold flourishing hand: "To Professor Lauterpacht whose assistance contributed so largely to the success of the legal argument."[49] Others would have viewed it differently. Commenting on the Nuremberg trials, Arnold Leese wrote: "What is the Jew Prof: Lauterpacht doing on the British War Crimes Executive?"[50] If he could have peeked behind the scenes and known of Lauterpacht's connection to Joyce's case, it would have fed his obsession that the Old Bailey trial began on the Day of Atonement. It is easy to envisage an article by him on Jewish power and sadism.[51] Joyce's response, had he known of Lauterpacht's involvement, can also be easily imagined.

Shawcross's principal legal adviser argued that Joyce's British passport meant he was not "an alien pure and simple" but stood "in a relation of allegiance to the Crown."[52] He further emphasised the "novel situation" introduced by the "advent of broadcasting." Joyce had delivered his radio talks from Germany. But his actions were "consummated in the United Kingdom" and there was abundant authority in criminal law to confirm that what mattered was not the "the locality of the original causation but the place of the final effect."[53]

Joyce's activities should not go unpunished therefore and Lauterpacht proposed that if the Old Bailey case collapsed, "it might be a matter for consideration whether the way ought to be left open for [his prosecution] under the Four Power Agreement." In other words, Joyce should be tried as a major war criminal. Lauterpacht even pondered whether the Soviet Union, "against whom his activities were displayed with particular vigour and venom," might be encouraged to think on these lines.[54] The Soviets, keen to deal with defeated fascists, would not have needed too much persuasion. This suggestion proved a step too far for the British authorities. In the unlikely event of a failed prosecution we know the preferred policy was to deport Joyce to Germany.

When presenting the Crown's case Shawcross did not always operate in top gear. By any standard, however, his opening address was superb. Terence Rattigan made it a focal point in his film script, suggesting the camera should zoom incrementally onto the Attorney-General as he went about his task.[55] Shawcross reminded jurors of those "dark days of 1940 when this country was standing alone against the whole force and might of Nazi Germany." In these dangerous times some people "may have heard" Joyce's broadcasts or believed they had listened to them, and concluded his aim was "to undermine the morale of our people." He fully recognised the British public's subsequent "dislike and detestation" of Joyce's actions. He acknowledged, too, the "not altogether unnatural satisfaction" felt when Joyce had been detained and brought to trial. Shawcross had taken an exceptionally sharp knife to the accused. Yet, cleverly, he advised: "If any of you had feelings of that kind about this man I ask you, as I know you will, to cast them entirely from your minds."[56] It was superbly done.

Shawcross knew throughout he had MI5's weight solidly behind him. Before the proceedings opened, it had compiled a case against Joyce – though no mention occurred during the trial – and never doubted what the outcome should be:

> There can be no question but that JOYCE in broadcasting over the German Radio Nazi propaganda directed against Great Britain and her allies has committed a series of acts of treason. The evidence, which is available to prove his treasonable conduct . . . is thought to render the case against him conclusive.

Joyce's application for a British passport was viewed as particularly significant.[57]

Previously secret files reveal that, determined to secure a conviction, MI5 officers read Joyce's prison correspondence. Realising they might, he wrote in code, though it hardly assumed a sophisticated form.[58] Quentin, heavily involved in his brother's defence, had his mail opened and phone tapped.[59] Any nuggets could then be referred to the prosecution. Mr Head, Joyce's solicitor, had his communications intercepted.[60] At least once an officer approached defence lawyers to gauge their thinking on the case.[61] Behind the wigs and gowns, the forensic battle in public, secret manoeuvres were taking place off stage to secure a conviction. These interventions would have required and received "the personal considered approval" of the Home Secretary. With Joyce no longer at liberty, it is difficult to understand, how MI5's actions related, as they should, to "the prevention and detection of serious crime" or "the preservation of the safety of the State." This murkiness is not helped by the fact that in 1947 the Intelligence community seemingly requested the Home Office to destroy all warrants it had issued for security purposes.[62] Yet enough remains to show MI5 working assiduously in pursuit of its prey.

5

How did Joyce's predicament resonate in public opinion?

The *New Yorker* commissioned Rebecca West to write on his trial, which suggested an American interest in the dramatic events unfolding in London.[63] However, Irish-Americans did not deluge their government with protests. On 2 January 1946 James O'Brien of New York City did send a telegram to Tom Connally, Chairman of the Senate Committee on Foreign Relations. But the Senator delayed forwarding it to the State Department until after the execution.[64] Moscow, another wartime ally, continued to demand that Joyce and other British renegades pay the full price as Nazi war criminals.[65]

The British public became glued to the proceedings, and Home Office files previously retained under the thirty-year rule reveal that there was a thirst for retribution. F. Ebbsworthy even suggested that proceedings should be broadcast to allow the entire country to feel –

and gloat over? – Joyce's predicament.[66] German radio was to carry the main trials at Nuremberg, and people in Eastern Europe would soon be listening to the prosecutions of László Rajk and Rudolf Slanský. But Ebbsworthy's advice was not followed. Nor did the Home Office pursue the offer from A. Jenkins who wrote later, knowing Joyce would be hanged:

> I have just heard the good news regarding Mr W. Joyce. I have been a Miner 10 years out of work 10 years, and 8 as a market gardener. I would like to offer and pay my own expenses to see him off. Hoping you will give a Welsh miner that privalige.[67]

In any event, he requested a ticket to be present at the execution. Reflecting Britain's class differences, one official was totally puzzled by the phrase "to see him off."[68] D. Risk, from Seven Kings in Essex, offered no such ambiguity. On 8 November 1945 he said Joyce "should be shot as a leading Nazi enemy" before emphasising "Mosley is more guilty as a traitor."[69] Yet 'The Leader,' we know, was already resurrecting his political career.

At the same time Joyce received support from other writers, especially political sympathisers. The "tall, thin, dreamy eyed" Duke of Bedford – he assumed the dukedom in 1940 – has been noticed participating in the British People's Party (BPP), started in 1939 by John Beckett, which later pursued an anti-War programme.[70] Beckett and Bedford resumed their links after the War, and the Duke's intervention was possibly influenced by Beckett, who in some respects continued to think highly of Joyce and wrote to him before his execution.[71]

Writing to the Prime Minister, Bedford emphasised "various people have approached me lately protesting very vigourously against the contemplated execution of William Joyce." The prisoner had not betrayed military secrets. He had broadcast for the Nazis. However, Bedford observed that in their propaganda campaigns the British had employed aliens from Hitler's Germany. Also, his activities paled in comparison with the actions of those statesmen who had sanctioned the use of atomic bombs, even knowing the Japanese intended to discuss peace terms. The Duke admitted Joyce's "frequent use of the term 'Jewish' betrayed the exaggerated bigotry characteristic of anti-Semites," but when telling the British people their "real enemies were the international financiers," he "spoke no more than the truth." Bedford's coded anti-Semitism came off the page here. Finally, Bedford hoped that when Joyce claimed the Soviets would be the real beneficiaries of the peace, he would not prove "a prophet of evil." An execution, he concluded, would be sheer hypocrisy.[72] The BPP duly petitioned for clemency, an initiative Douglas Hyde scathingly reported in the *Daily Worker* under the by-line, "Pals of Haw-Haw Launch Petition for Reprieve."[73] The Duke was not finished, however. In 1949 he called Joyce's execution "a dirty piece of work."[74]

Others from the political Right wrote in. Arnold Leese, now resuming his fascist career, contacted the Home Office.[75] 'Count' Potocki urged Joyce should be spared, if only because of information he might have on the 1940 Katyń massacre: "On behalf of the Poles we require [him] as a witness."[76] Sir Ernest Bennett, a former member of the Right Club, worried that Joyce might be hanged on a legal technicality.[77] The Britons Publishing Company, committed since 1919 to a conspiratorial anti-Semitism, argued that the Jews were the real war criminals.[78] None of these submissions made any impression on Frank Newsam or other senior civil servants.

Alexis Gunning, who before the War had written in praise of Nazi Germany, also intervened.[79] On 3 December 1945, now describing himself as a "Professor of Pianoforte, Singing, Conducting, and Composition," he wrote in the name of "outraged Christianity" seeking permission to visit Joyce on Christmas Day. When his request was refused, Gunning retorted, "this tastes of Nazism ... I deeply resent your decision. I shall not forget it and remember it when having to vote."[80]

Among other correspondents, not evidently fascist sympathisers, twelve Preston soldiers emphasised on 14 December 1945 that as an alien Joyce did not owe any allegiance to the King, a claim that had been argued back and forth during his trial. They urged a reprieve and hoped Chuter Ede would show himself "a *real white man*."[81] And a few days later when pleading for Joyce's life, "John Bull," contrasted his actions with "the dastardly crimes of the Belson gang," who fully deserved to be given the rope.[82]

More measured responses also went the Home Secretary. Baron Quickswood, son of the Marquess of Salisbury and former Provost of

Eton, based his intervention, as did the Preston boys, on Joyce's status as an alien. Any guilt rested on "a narrow legal technicality."[83] And a thoughtful letter on 29 December from Perceval Graves, a retired solicitor, emphasised: "To pardon this man would be to uphold the dignity and impartiality of British justice," whereas "to execute him would be to make of him a political martyr."[84]

All these interventions fell on stony ground. As did a late claim by V. Redwood, formerly Assistant Organiser of the United Empire Party, who, basing himself on their pre-war contact, claimed Joyce was not mentally reliable.[85]

These letters were written before Pierrepoint went to work. However, one epistle reached the Home Office after Joyce had been executed. W. H. Shutter appealed for his life almost one month later. This "reasonably phrased letter from an old man of 72," as one official gently put it, provided a bizarre finale to the public's immediate interest.[86]

6

While letters were flowing towards government departments arguing the case for and against Joyce's execution, he could not speak at meetings, write political tracts, or appear on radio. But he still needed an audience. 'Professor' Joyce retained his compulsion to advise, comment, demand, insist and instruct. How did he satisfy these cravings?

Notes

1 *The Star*, 3 January 1946.
2 Pierrepoint's unpublished memoirs carry the briefest of references. Information from Derek Stevens. L. Klein, A *Very English Hangman: The Life and Times of Albert Pierrepoint* (London, 2006), provides an account of his activities.
3 National Galleries of Justice, Nottingham, AAPSM 2000 0008C E 02207 for a list of Pierrepoint's executions. When executing Joyce he was assisted by H. Riley.
4 P. Wildeblood, *Against the Law* (Harmondsworth, 1959), pp.123–124.
5 Information from the late Professor Douglas Johnson; P. Worsthorne, *Tricks of Memory: An Autobiography* (London, 1993), pp.101–108, 110, particularly.

6 *Evening News*, 3 January 1946.

7 *The Star*, 3 January 1946.

8 All from Evening News, 3 January 1946.

9 *Daily Mirror*, 4 January 1946.

10 West, *Treason*, pp.59–60.

11 Cole, *Lord Haw-Haw*, p.304. USSC, MS 338/7/13, for Johnson attempting to lift Macnab's spirits, by saying he had "complete confidence in the safety of William's soul."

12 KV2/878/1005a on his purchase.

13 KV3/50, "Fascist Activities, January/February 1946." *Daily Mirror*, 4 January 1946. After the execution, Quentin Joyce, an habitué of the Café Bleu in Soho, arrived at the restaurant in an agitated state accompanied by Compton Domvile. Nevertheless, he enjoyed a hearty meal there. E.Salvoni, *Elena: A Life in Soho* (London, 1990), p.59.

14 KV3/50. Russell is noticed in M. Carter, *Anthony Blunt: His Lives* (London, 2001), p.284. MI5's interest can now be seen in KV2/3800/12 a. Fr William Saunders informed me of his clerical career and personality.

15 Quentin Joyce Archive, for Russell's beautifully handwritten letters of 7 August, 20 September, 18 November, 21 November, 19 December 1945 and 1 January 1946.

16 Cole, *Lord Haw-Haw*, p. 304.

17 KV 4/118, entry on Margaret Joyce and HO 45/25779/46.

18 Quentin Joyce Archive, letter to Quentin Joyce, 3 January 1946.

19 Cole, *Lord Haw-Haw*, p.304.

20 Letter, Creasy to author, 27 August 1993. *Comrade*, No.59 (2005), p.20 for Creasy's death and a tribute.

21 Mosley Papers, University of Birmingham Special Collections, OMN/B/5/1/1.Blue leather Piccadilly diary for 1946, entry, 3 January: "Turkey and goose sent."

22 KV2/1228.

23 HO 45/24467, report of a meeting, 15 December 1945.

24 *The Times*, 4 January 1946.

25 *Jewish Chronicle*, 4 January 1946.

26 *Daily Worker*, 4 January 1946.

27 *The Patriot*, 10 January 1946.

28 KV 2/246/437b. Matthew and Harrison (eds), *ODNB*, Vol.53, p.297. A. M. Sullivan, *The Last Sergeant: the Memoirs of Serjeant M. Sullivan* (London, 1952).

29 WJ to MJ, 2 November 1945.

30 KV 2/246/437b.

31 KV 2/246/422a.

32 KV 2/246/437b.

33 Selwyn, *Hitler's Englishman*, pp.183–184, 206.

34 B. K. Scott (ed.), *Selected Letters of Rebecca West* (New Haven and London, 2000), pp.205–206, letter to Letitia Fairfield, 25 September 1945.

35 Suggested to me in private conversations.

36 WJ to MJ, 29 September 1945. Lines from "Horatian Ode Upon Crom-well's Return from Ireland."
37 Farndale, *Haw-Haw*, p.114, describes him thus.
38 C. E. Bechhofer Roberts (ed.), *The Trial of William Joyce: With some Notes on other Recent Trials for Treason* (London, 1946), p.43.
39 KV 2/245/176a.
40 KV 2/246/418B, for an inventory; KV 2/248/8A, on the birth certificate.
41 *The Times*, 26 June 1945. In 1943–44 Hunt had been deputed to listen to Joyce's broadcasts.
42 Bechhofer Roberts (ed.), *Trial*, p.44.
43 J.A.G. Griffith, *The Politics of the Judiciary* (London, 1981), on the sup-posed impartiality of judges.
44 *The Guardian*, 8 December 1998, on Lord Hoffmann and Senator Pino-chet's appeal. Hoffmann's work for Amnesty International provoked defence lawyers to allege bias and the setting aside of the judgement which had involved him. See *ibid.* 18 December 1998.
45 Selwyn, *Hitler's Englishman*, p.196.
46 Martland, *Lord Haw-Haw*, pp.88, 92. Matthew and Harrison (eds), *ODNB*, Vol.35, pp.930–931. *The Times*, 24 May 1975 carried an obitu-ary of McNair. Martland says his evidence derived from Professor Kurt Lipstein. But the latter, in a telephone conversation with me, 20 Septem-ber 2004, denied it.
47 C. J. Hamson's entry in Matthew and Harrison (eds.), *ODNB*, Vol.32, pp.714–716. M. Koskenniemi, "Lauterpacht: The Victorian Tradition in International Law," *European Journal of International Law*, Vol.8(1997), pp.215 ff; C. Herzog, "Sir Hersch Lauterpacht: An Appraisal," in *ibid.* p.299. See also more recently and importantly, E. Lauterpacht, *The Life of Sir Hersch Lauterpacht* (Cambridge, 2010), which discusses Joyce's case on pp. 280–283.
48 Lauterpacht Archive.
49 The dedication is dated 1 July 1947. Sir Elihu Lauterpacht kindly pro-vided me with a copy of this letter. Shawcross also felt indebted to the "aid and comfort" he received from Theobald Mathew at the DPP's office. Shawcross to Mathew, 20 September 1945 (private archive).
50 *Gothic Ripples*, No.5, 20 October 1945, p.4.
51 Morell, "Life and Opinions of Arnold Leese," p.60 for Leese on Jews as sadists.
52 Lauterpacht Archive, Opinion, 4 September.
53 *Ibid.*
54 *Ibid.*
55 Rattigan, British Library, Add MS 74490, f.20.
56 Hall (ed.), *Trial*, p.46.
57 HO 45/25780, pp.1, 3. MI5 report, 13 June 1945.
58 KV 2/247/518a, "Notes on the correspondence of William and Margaret Joyce," by C. A. Haines, 14 January 1946.
59 KV 2/246 at many points. Martland, *Lord Haw-Haw*, pp.87–88.

60 KV 2/247/502b, KV 2/249/101a.

61 KV 2/246/437b, D. H. Sinclair's memorandum, 28 June 1945, on contact with Joyce's solicitor.

62 *Report of the Committee of Privy Councillors appointed to enquire into the interception of communications*, Cmnd.283, Vol.15 (1956–57), especially pp.130, 143.

63 C. Rollyson, *Rebecca West: A Saga of the Century* (London, 1995), p.209.

64 NARA File RG 59 862.20200/1–746. Reel 26 of 41.

65 KV 2/247/502a, BBC digests from Radio Moscow, 5 June 1945, 19 September 1945.

66 HO 45/22405/892. Spelling as in original. The retributive thirst was noted in "Criminal Law. Treason. Effects of Passports on Allegiance of Aliens," *University of Chicago Law Review*, Vol.13 (1946), p.367.

67 HO 45/22406/13. Spelling as in original.

68 *Ibid.*

69 HO 45/22405/707.

70 Bedford's appearance derives from *News Review*, 7 March 1940, p.11.

71 Oral evidence, Francis Beckett, for John Beckett's continuing regard for Joyce. Confirmed in KV 2/1519/624. KV 2/1519/629b and 629c for Beckett's warm "Goodbye William" letter, 19 December 1945 and /629c for Joyce's reply on the 29th.

72 All from HO 45/22406/53. Spelling as in original.

73 *Daily Worker*, 11 December 1945. HO 45/22406/221–234 on other signed petitions though a number derived from fascists or fascist sympathisers.

74 H. W. S. Russell, *The Years of Transition* (London, 1949), p.219.

75 HO 45/22405/543 for his intervention, end of December 1945. He corresponded directly with Joyce. Ian Sayer Archive, for Joyce to Leese, 12 July 1945.

76 HO 45/22406/201–202. Risk, "It is the choice of the Gods," pp.8–9 for his interest in Katyń. Potocki has been noticed in contact with Joyce in the 1930s.

77 HO 45/22406/208–212.

78 HO 45/22405/334–335.

79 *News from Germany*, No.10, June 1939, pp.35–36, for his pre-war views.

80 HO 45/22406/161.

81 HO 45/22406/62–69.

82 HO 45/22405/521. Spelling as in original.

83 HO 45/22406/177–181B.

84 HO 45/22405/355–356.

85 HO 45/22405/397, telephone call, 2 January 1946.

86 HO 45/22406/293 and 297.

21

LAST DAYS IN PRISON

No traitor will admit his treachery: in his own mind his conduct is perfectly justifiable. To him, it is his opponents who are traitors. [A. M. Meerloo, "A Study of Treason," *British Journal of Psychology*, Vol. XXV (January 1945), p.27.]

1

Throughout all those tense days and long nights leading up to his trial, appeals and execution, Joyce engaged in a furious correspondence from Brixton, Wormwood Scrubs and Wandsworth. He never exposed everything he felt and knew.[1] But these letters, never before fully excavated, throw a revealing light on his life and final thoughts.

Before the War he had formed close ties with the Scrimgeours. Alex Scrimgeour, his most important backer, was dead but Ethel Scrimgeour – frail, snow-white-haired, apocalyptic-looking and soon to die of scurvy – kept in touch.[2] Father Edmund Dunkerton, who knew Joyce from Ireland, picked up his pen. Aubrey Lees, long-standing fascist, sent off letters.[3] MI5 estimated Joyce had approximately fifty-eight correspondents.[4]

Quentin Joyce visited his brother in prison, supported Margaret and played a vital role in assisting the defence.[5] He wound up his business to concentrate on these pressing tasks.[6] Joyce's letters to Margaret are full of admiration for him. Here he is writing in August 1945: "Since June 18th . . . [Quentin] has been concentrating on my case and helping Head very industriously. He is a great lad, and not so simply trusting as he used to be."[7] But it was in vain, and Quentin had been badly shaken by the verdict at the Old Bailey.[8] It was absolutely proper 'Q' should become his brother's executor.[9]

2

Joyce's final letters show him reading voraciously. He turned to Aldington, Bennett, Buchan, Forester, Dennis Wheatley and the lesser-known Francis Beeding.[10] He enjoyed *Hatter's Castle by* A. J. Cronin, remarking "it should be studied by all bad-tempered and conceited husbands."[11] He was well-placed to be the judge of that. He revisited past pleasures by turning to Dryden.[12] Ever fancying himself as a critic, he dismissed Hector Bolitho's biography of Edward VII as "a wretched book, if ever there was one."[13] He also tossed aside *Gone with the Wind*, citing its "sickly idealizing of the South" and the "odious personality" of its heroine.[14] Literature had always been one of Joyce's "magic casements," and he soon appreciated how "scandalously lucky" he was in the range of books available in the prison library.[15] Lost in reading, he could indulge to his heart's content in smoking, another big passion. But alcohol, once another constant and favourite companion, was restricted. Those endless boozy hazy nights with Bacchus and the "purple stainèd mouth" were now no more.[16]

After being discharged from Brixton prison hospital, where he was first held, an avidly reading, chain-smoking Joyce created in his small cell at Wormwood Scrubs, then Wandsworth, a largely self-centred world. In this bare universe he became fiercely attached to certain objects, including a tin fish bought towards the end of the War in Hamburg.[17] Through such items, often of little intrinsic worth, we give meaning to our lives. Possessions carry memories. A similar reassurance came through prison-issue Lifebuoy soap, probably a reminder of less traumatic days.[18]

Prison officials provided much of his everyday company. He particularly enjoyed discussions with the Church of England chaplain in Wormwood Scrubs and regretted losing touch in September 1945 when he became "Wandsworth William."[19] But this new home offered similar company in Hugh Smith.[20] Smith, "a *real* white man," an excellent "counsellor, comforter and friend," now had to listen to 'Professor' Joyce's views on "philosophy, psychology, telepathy and kindred topics."[21] An audience of one was better than no audience at all. Chess with the warders also helped the dragging time to pass.[22] Did he recall pre-war tussles with Macnab? Did he think of Berlin and playing against the Indian nationalist Subhas Chandra Bose?[23]

Joyce soon became habituated to this restricted world, just as Abé's woman adjusted to her hole in the sands.[24] "One thing I like about prison here," he wrote early on from Brixton jail, is "the pleasant sense of being in an organization which functions perfectly at every point."[25] His life had often been bound up with routine. He had recently spent countless hours in the Funkhaus and his regimented personality now assisted his adjustment to the confines of prison life. As did the political distance he felt from post-war Britain. "There is no longer anything in this country that I particularly want to see, much as I like the people," he wrote to Margaret. "My memories of the Grünewald are good enough for me."[26] Not quite on a par with Goebbels's stark proclamation that a world without Hitler offered nothing.[27] But a clear sign of his alienation. The arthritic Britain he had striven to destroy had survived. He wanted no part of it.

3

Many letters naturally focus on the legal proceedings. Leonard Burt had remarked that his prisoner on the Dakota was reconciled to being executed. But no hint of such resignation appears in the prison correspondence. Joyce wrote defiantly to Margaret in June 1945: "Be sure lassie that I am going to fight hard: and, if need be, more battles than one."[28] His upbeat mood doubtless derived partly from having an American birth certificate, a fact both he and his friends had advertised early in the War. His jaunty defiance came through again the following August.[29] And it persisted into September: "Our problem is not nearly so hard as an 'Observer' Crossword Puzzle," he told Margaret.[30] Also, since uncertainty is often more troublesome than certainty, he greeted the Old Bailey proceedings with some relief.

The verdict there went against him. But Joyce never blamed his lawyers.[31] He believed Slade had "handled the defence most admirably."[32] Indeed, "I have nothing but praise for [him] and [Curtis-Bennett] and my confidence in them has increased."[33] This bullishness continued for some time. "Slade's performance [at the appeal hearing] . . . was . . . beyond praise" he told Ethel Scrimgeour on 4 November 1945, "he has publicly demonstrated the justice of my cause."[34] Again the outcome disappointed him. However, Joyce remained confident his appeal to the Lords would be successful.[35] Not until after this latest hearing did his mood begin to change. "Now, beloved, you may know the decision ere you get this letter. I am not optimistic," he confided to Margaret on 13 December.[36] For once, he had read the runes correctly.

Joyce believed counsel had not fired every round in his defence, but had "fought very hard against overwhelming odds."[37] However, contrary to a remark Slade made before Tucker, he denied ever intending to return to Britain if the Germans had been victorious[38] Evidence already heard from Bill Shirer and confirmed by Jim Clark, suggests he would have done just that.[39] But when that prospect had vanished, he did not want his prior intentions advertised.[40]

He formed a quite different impression of Hartley Shawcross.[41] Mr Justice Tucker – or "Ucker" as he appears in the letters – featured alongside Shawcross on the devil's side. At first Joyce knew nothing of Tucker.[42] But, once aware the judge had labelled him a traitor during the Kent-Wolkoff trial, he recognised he had been dealt a poor hand.[43] Having been subjected to the intricacies of the English legal system, and by now fancying himself as a lawyer, he believed Tucker was incapable of grasping the complex legal matters his case had raised.[44] He was also critical of Lord Wright, one of the appeal judges, remarking savagely that, in comparison, Shawcross was a "sucking dove of innocence."[45] But Joyce's chief grievance, abiding bitterness, arose from his being despatched to the gallows without knowing why the death sentence had been upheld. "Quel ramp!" he exploded.[46]

Joyce had long clung to a Manichean view of the world. Individuals, events, had to be painted in black or white and, as he moved "nearer to the edge of beyond," Slade, Curtis-Bennett and Burge featured on the side of 'good'; Shawcross, Tucker and Wright represented the world's darker forces.[47]

4

In prison Joyce continued to receive Holy Communion from the Church of England.[48] But he resisted all clerical attempts to capture his soul.[49] The priests were wasting their pearls. 'Professor' Joyce pronounced: "Much as I admire the Church, much as I should like to rejoin it, I just cannot. I prefer voluntary to compulsory faith: and I have no sympathy with needless disputes on dogma arising from Oriental mysticism eg the Immaculate Conception."[50] Aveling and Spearman, his gods from the world of academic psychology, had provided the world with far more insight into the human condition than any College of Cardinals.[51]

Father Edmund Dunkerton, who has been observed saying a mass for Joyce's soul, was one of these disappointed clerics.[52] Believing that after 1945 a fierce battle was raging between God and Lucifer, this Walter Mitty-like character took himself off to the Cistercians at Caldey Island, where he remained until his death in 1979.[53] With time to contemplate, did images of Joyce ever flash through his mind?

Macnab, another devout Catholic, remained nervously anxious to recover his dearest friend for the Roman Church. However, he, too, faced disappointment. On Christmas Eve 1945 Joyce informed Margaret he had told 'Master' he "would not take out a false passport to travel to Heaven, tho' to him I did not put it so frivolously."[54] Even so, their great friendship survived this disappointment. "And that is good," Joyce wrote.[55]

5

As Joyce continued to reflect on eternity, he planned in some detail a commemorative service to keep his memory alive.[56] But who would have attended apart from Macnab, Quentin, possibly other family members and a few diehard fascists? The War's wounds were still bleeding and any service would have met with fierce opposition. Joyce's suggestion showed how far removed he had become from

British opinion and also his obsessive self-regard, which often sharply separated him from reality. For this always-doomed grand commemorative occasion he requested music by Grieg and Wagner, to whose works he had long been attached. He asked for the *Horst-Wessel-Lied* and the *Alte Kameraden* march. But, significantly, nothing Irish.[57]

When still hoping for an acquittal and swallowing his opposition to Irish nationalism, Joyce told Margaret that Ireland would be "the only place for us to live."[58] His hopes dashed, he reflected on what ideally should happen to his body after his execution. He wanted to be cremated and his ashes cast into the sea, preferably off Flensburg or Beachy Head, a part of the Sussex landscape he had come to love.[59] A burial in Galway never featured in these thoughts. Ireland might serve as a refuge – probably short-term – but it was no final resting place.

Wherever his remains should finish up, Joyce believed life did not end with the body's destruction.[60] His interest in and knowledge of psychology – evident since the 1930s – convinced him of it.[61] At the same time, he became obsessed about retaining a physical presence in the world to do his bidding, to ensure his everlasting memory, his immortality and his place in history. Margaret became his vehicle.[62] By the War's end he was confiding in his notebook that she was sexually useless. She had a memory like a sieve. She was a general liability. She was someone he could happily discard.[63] But in prison he persuaded himself their ties would never be fully broken. "I know nothing can ever separate us for long – and *wherever* we go we shall take *memories* with us."[64] In his version of "Lo I am with you always, even unto the end of the world," he promised to remain constantly at her side, aiding her, supporting her, guiding her.[65] This growing belief catered to his massive egotism, the supreme sense of self-importance he had carried from childhood. While appointing her as his biographer, Joyce dared to hope that Margaret would be guided by his influence from behind the curtain, and across the great divide she would continue to live his life after his body had left. It had to be so. For years he had believed he was being prepared for some great task.[66] It could not all shrink and shrivel into nothing. A god never died. On the eve of his execution he was still insisting on a continuing bond with the woman who had shared his tumultuous life, someone he had loved – in his way – but had always preached at, often humiliated, sometimes thrashed.[67]

Joyce's life had been dominated by politics, and he believed that through his continuing spiritual link from beyond the veil to Margaret, and his guiding of "Freja," his National Socialist colleague, as he called her in the letters, a full recognition of his struggles, his correctness, would eventually emerge. And she went some way towards satisfying his fantasies. With thoughts of Margaret as future biographer whirling in his mind, and pleased his parents had been spared the ordeal of his trial and execution, knowing the tragedy would have overwhelmed them, Joyce went stoically to his death.[68]

6

Joyce's letters reveal more than his adjustments to prison life and reflections on his fate. The politico did not cease to be politically conscious, looking only to the past, neglecting the present, and disregarding a future he would never witness. His letters, though hardly comparable to Antonio Gramsci's prison notebooks, underline his continuing passionate interest in contemporary politics.

The atomic bombing of Hiroshima and Nagasaki and its implications for the world soon caught his attention. Not that he always fully grasped the Bomb's significance. He once chided Margaret for exaggerating its horrors.[69] He also treated the subject with a degree of tasteless levity.[70] His preaching could sometimes be far too much, far too clever. Nella Last, housewife and diarist, never doubted that "this atomic bomb business is so dreadful."[71] But Joyce tried to diminish it by focusing on civilian losses inflicted by more conventional weapons, such as the recent firebombing of Hamburg, the last base of his radio operations.[72] In that respect he might be regarded as a pioneer Revisionist. An emphasis on Germany's wartime suffering, designed to divert attention from Nazi war crimes, soon became woven into post-war fascist ideology.[73]

The Nazis ultimately responsible for war crimes soon appeared in the dock at Nuremberg. But Joyce – again anticipating Revisionist literature – quickly dismissed their trials as the vengeful justice of the victors.[74] He also criticised the treatment of alleged war criminals in former occupied countries, claiming a determined search was underway to find a legal pretext for their eventual executions.[75]

Among Nazi officials put on trial were those little gods, former controllers of the concentration and death camps. Following the liberation of these kingdoms of death, visual images of dead bodies and cadaverous survivors soon came on display.[76] And André Singer's 2014 documentary, *Night Will Fall*, which includes footage from the long-suppressed *German Concentration Camps Factual Survey*, brings home a sense of that horror to later generations.[77] Even so, in 1945, some in Britain suggested the Jews had brought their fate upon themselves.[78] And Joyce certainly tried to puncture any sense of outrage. He believed it was important to remember camp officials had not been recruited from the best specimens of humanity; they were hardly typical Germans. Moreover, "Most of the inmates were probably of an order not only unknown, but unconceived in the British imagination (not a defence but a simple fact)."[79] He also claimed that late in the War, as the Nazi state scrambled desperately to survive, it could never have guaranteed the fate of camp inmates hostile to Germany and its ideals. In these quite exceptional circumstances he acknowledged the failure to provide adequate food supplies. But his sympathies lay with the German people, now burdened with a terrible stigma.[80] As ever, he showed no feelings for the countless victims of Nazi tyranny.

While defending German policy, he nevertheless criticised members of the Nazi hierarchy. Josef Goebbels, his everlasting hero, a true god, remained a noticeable exception.[81] But Joachim von Ribbentrop's appearance as that "Swine Ribbentrop" or "Ribbentripe," was a reminder of wartime frictions between the Foreign Office and the Propaganda Ministry.[82] Joyce also savaged in his inimitable style the "purulent" Fritz Hesse, former Head of the English Department of the Foreign Ministry, despite Hesse's success in securing the royalty payments for *Dämmerung über England*.[83]

Joyce either dismissed from his memory or wrote off his recent renegade colleagues. He never grieved for Subhas Chandra Bose.[84] He continued to snipe against old adversaries: "I have to laugh at the idea of me, Amery and Baillie-Stuart being in the one room. Oh Dear!"[85] He retained his low opinion of the lesser-known renegade broadcasters.[86] He never changed his caustic views on the British Free Corps.[87] "Ye gods! – What a 'Kameradschaft!'"[88]

Refocusing from the past to the present, Joyce regretted Germany had become "kaput!"[89] He agreed with Clement Attlee, the British Prime Minister, that a "Great Void" now existed at the heart of Europe.[90] The door to the West had been thrown wide open to a growing Soviet influence, to those devils with their vile concentration camps and the blood of Katyń dripping from their hands.[91] His anxieties here, shared by others, often emerged in his letters to Ethel Scrimgeour.[92]

This recurrent anti-Soviet sentiment amounted to one of Joyce's final political obsessions. Another, reflecting his long-standing anti-Semitism, led him to rail against Jew power in Britain. When discussing nationalisation, a key plank of the post-war Labour government's economic policy, he emphasised – dressing up old themes in a new garb – that no state ownership had been proposed for the retail trades. "So why should Sieff and Marx worry?"[93] With their influence in the state's new planning mechanisms, the power of Jews could only increase.[94] And, he believed, they retained their conspiratorial thirst for power.

Joyce's continuing anti-Jewish obsessions spilled over into events that directly affected him. He would often describe Sir Hartley Shawcross as "Old Hot Cross Buns" or "Hot Cross."[95] But a more sinister tone appeared when he endowed the Attorney-General with Sephardic qualities.[96] He transformed Shawcross into "the Cheetham Vishinski," a vindictive Jewish lawyer working for Jewry.[97] The Attorney-General was not Jewish. But Joyce's contrary belief meshed with his paranoid political outlook. He believed that Jews, obsessed by materialism – how often had he made that claim? – could purchase almost everything in life. But principles lay beyond them. Awkward idealistic individuals, deaf to the world's moneyed voices, had to be destroyed, silenced. And Joyce proclaimed – correctly – he had never "uttered a single word of apology, much less recantation."[98] No-one could ever buy him. He had to be put to death.

Standard histories of the Second World War rightly emphasise the wholesale destruction of Europe's Jewish communities. Yet Joyce never dwelt on this human tragedy. He was never kept awake on his simple prison bed by images of persecuted Jews. He believed international Jewry had retained its power. His crusade against it, all those years of intense vituperative campaigning, had ended in failure. However, keeping faith with his long-held belief in the power of the will, he maintained that at some future point the human spirit would triumph over the dark malign forces of Jewish and Marxist materialism.[99] But he would not live to witness it.

More immediately, he believed his execution by the Jews amounted to a death with honour.[100] It was like a soldier's end at Stalingrad.[101] In a farewell message handed to Quentin, he wrote:

In death, as in this life, I defy the Jews who caused this last war: and I defy the power of Darkness which they represent. I warn the British people against the aggressive imperialism of the Sowjet Union.

His tirade continued:

May Britain be great once again; and, in the hour of the greatest danger to the West, may the standard of the Hakenkreuz be raised from the dust, crowned with the historic words "Ihr habt doch gesiegt". I am proud to die for my ideals; and I am sorry for the sons of Britain who have died without knowing why.[102]

On that defiant note, the kind of inflammatory statement many had expected to hear at his trial, Joyce departed from the political arena which had consumed so much of his remarkable energy and passion.

Notes

1 KV 2/247/516a for the correspondence passing through PO Box 500, SW1.
2 WJ to ES, 2 July 1945. West, *Treason*, p.41 describes Scrimgeour.
3 HO 45/25728 and HO 283/45 on Lees. *The Times*, 24 April 2004, reported the discovery and auction of their letters.
4 KV 2/247/518a.
5 WJ to MJ, 3 July 1945. Kenny, *Germany Calling*, p.247 on his assisting Margaret. When visiting, did Quentin ever think of his own wartime internment in Wandsworth? KV2/2894.
6 WJ to MJ, 1 September 1945.

7 WJ to MJ, 16 August 1945. WJ to ES, 8 October 1945, on Quentin's "shining example of loyalty."

8 As Joyce fully recognised. WJ to MJ, 20 September 1945.

9 WJ to MJ, 18 December 1945.

10 WJ to MJ, 3 August 1945.

11 WJ to MJ, 30 August 1945.

12 WJ to MJ, 15 November 1945, 19 December 1945.

13 WJ to MJ, 1 September 1945.

14 WJ to MJ, 3 August 1945.

15 WJ to MJ, 3 August 1945.

16 WJ to MJ, 24 July 1945.

17 WJ to MJ, 16 July 1945.

18 WJ to MJ, 4 September 1945.

19 WJ to MJ, 24 September 1945 and 28 September 1945 on his transfer.

20 *Crockford's Clerical Directory for 1947* (London, 1947), p.1221 on Smith.

21 Quentin Joyce Archive, Aubrey Lees to Quentin, New Year's Day, 1946. WJ to MJ, 4 October 1945. After Joyce's execution Quentin sent Smith a gift by way of appreciation for his support.

22 WJ to MJ, 21 September 1945.

23 WJ to MJ, 27 August 1945. M. Bose, *The Lost Hero* (London, 1982).

24 K. Abé, *The Woman in the Dunes* (New York, 1964).

25 All from WJ to MJ, 25 August 1945.

26 WJ to MJ, 23 September 1945.

27 Reuth, *Goebbels*, p.342.

28 WJ to MJ, 26 June 1945.

29 WJ to MJ, 7 August 1945.

30 WJ to MJ, 12 September 1945.

31 WJ to MJ, 13 and 20 September 1945.

32 WJ to MJ, 21 September 1945.

33 WJ to MJ, 21 September 1945. Ian Sayer Archive for Quentin Joyce sharing his brother's opinion of Slade (letter to "My dear George," 1 October 1945).

34 WJ to ES, 4 November 1945.

35 WJ to ES, 4 November 1945.

36 WJ to MJ, 13 December 1945.

37 WJ to MJ, 20 December 1945, 26 December 1945.

38 Hall (ed.), *Trial*, p.167 for Slade's remark. A. Roberts, "Hitler's England: What if Germany had Invaded Britain in May 1940?" in N. Ferguson (ed.), *Virtual History: Alternatives and Counterfactuals* (Basingstoke, 1997), p.313, argued similarly, imagining him as the BBC's Director-General.

39 "Germany Calling," Radio 4, 16 May 1991.

40 WJ to MJ, 15 December 1945.

41 WJ to MJ, 15 December 1945.

42 WJ to MJ, 12 September 1945.

43 WJ to MJ, 6 October 1945.

44 WJ to MJ, 20 September 1945.

45 WJ to MJ, 14 December 1945.

46 WJ to MJ, 31 December 1945.

47 WJ to MJ, 2 January 1946 on moving towards the edge.

48 USSC, MS 238/7/13.

49 WJ to MJ, 28 December 1945.

50 WJ to MJ, 30 July 1945, 5 November 1945.

51 WJ to MJ, 24 December 1945.

52 WJ to ED, 23 December 1945.

53 Brother Robert of the Caldey community provided personal details.

54 WJ to MJ, 24 December 1945.

55 WJ to MJ, 26 December 1945.

56 WJ to MJ, 28 December 1945.

57 WJ to MJ, 28 December 1945.

58 WJ to MJ, 3 August 1945 and WJ to ES, 6 August 1945.

59 WJ to MJ, 25 December 1945, on Flensburg and Beachy Head. WJ to ES, 23 June, 2 July, 6 August 1945 on Sussex.

60 WJ to MJ, 6 October 1945.

61 WJ to MJ, 24 December 1945. He referred to the work of Aveling and Spearman.

62 WJ to MJ, 30 December 1945.

63 KV 2/250, 15 April 1945 on her memory.

64 WJ to MJ, 17 September 1945. Quentin Joyce Archive, Joyce to Quentin, 1 January 1946, on a continuing unity with all his family after death. Creasy Collection, Joyce to Aubrey Lees, 28 December 1945, for this sense of unity also embracing his former political comrades.

65 WJ to MJ, 29 December 1945.

66 WJ to MJ, 30 December 1945.

67 WJ to MJ, 2 January 1946.

68 Creasy Collection, Joyce to Aubrey Lees, 19 October 1945. WJ to ES, 11 July 1945. Quentin Joyce Archive, letter to Quentin, 1 January 1946.

69 WJ to MJ, 20 August 1945.

70 WJ to MJ, letter of 17 August 1945 ending with "atomic love" and, particularly, his letter to Margaret on 20 August 1945.

71 Last, *Nella Last's War*, p.301, entry, 8 August 1945.

72 WJ to ES, 14 August 1945.

73 D. Irving, *The Destruction of Dresden* (London, 1963), might be regarded as a pioneer influence.

74 WJ to MJ, 8 October 1945, 26 December 1945. R. Harwood, *Did Six Million really Die?* (Richmond, 1974?), p.9, offers similar Revisionist statement.

75 WJ to MJ, 16 October 1945. D. Lipstadt, *Denying the Holocaust* (New York, 1994), pp.44, 129–132 on Revisionist claims.

76 J. Reilly, *Belsen: The Liberation of a Concentration Camp* (London, 1998).

77 Reviewed in *The Times*, 19 September 2014.

78 T. Kushner, *The Holocaust and the Liberal Imagination: A Social and Cultural History* (Oxford, 1994), pp.205–269.

79 WJ to MJ, 27 September 1945.

80 WJ to MJ, 27 September 1945. Lipstadt, *Denying the Holocaust*, p.22, on German guilt.

81 WJ to MJ, 6 October 1945.

82 WJ to MJ, 18 July 1945, 1 August 1945.

83 WJ to MJ, 25 July 1945, 1 August 1945.

84 WJ to MJ, 27 August 1945.

85 WJ to MJ, 27 August 1945. Spelling as in original.

86 WJ to MJ, 9 October 1945, 20 December 1945.

87 WJ to MJ, 4 September 1945, 28 September 1945.

88 WJ to MJ, 4 September 1945.

89 WJ to MJ, 11 October 1945.

90 WJ to MJ, 14 September 1945.

91 Harwood, *Six Million*, p.9 on Katyń and later Revisionist comment.

92 WJ to ES, 20 July 1945; 6 August 1945; 14 August 1945; 11 November 1945. His fear was shared by the British Fascists. See Bleach Archive for Arnold Leese to the Home Secretary 29 December 1945: "The results of this war (the destruction of European civilisation and the advance of Asia to Berlin and beyond), are now apparent to every intelligent citizen."

93 WJ to MJ, 15 August 1945. Spelling as in original and doubtless intended.

94 WJ to MJ, 15 August 1945.

95 WJ to MJ, 17 September 1945, 12 December 1945.

96 WJ to MJ, 17 September 1945.

97 WJ to MJ, 12 December 1945. In late nineteenth and early twentieth-century Manchester, Cheetham Hill was an important area of settlement for Russian Polish Jews. Andrei Vishinsky (1883–1954), noted already as Stalin's prosecutor in the purge trials of the '30s, later briefly became Soviet Foreign Minister.

98 WJ to MJ, 6 October 1945.

99 Quentin Joyce Archive, letter to Quentin Joyce, 1 January 1946.

100 WJ to MJ, 18 December 1945.

101 WJ to MJ, 14 December 1945.

102 Cole, *Lord Haw*-Haw, p.301 quotes this message, received by Quentin, and intended for publication after the execution. The German translates as "You have conquered nevertheless."

22

THE TREATMENT OF RENEGADES

"War sorts us all out and the process is sad and painful –
very sad and very painful for some of us." [John Betjeman,
"SOME COMMENTS IN WARTIME," BBC Home Service,
4 July 1940, in *Trains and Buttered Toast*, ed. Stephen Games
(London, 2007), p.133.]

1

Joyce's fate had been decided so quickly. His trial, his appeals, his lawyers' best efforts, his letters from prison, occupied less than a year in
his life. Captured in May 1945, he was dead by the following January.
He was not the only renegade to be put on trial in Britain. After the
War the business of the courts was swelled by a troop of bedraggled,
though sometimes fiercely unrepentant figures who never imagined
when they enlisted with Hitler that one day they would be standing in the dock at the Old Bailey. In this process Joyce's treatment
contrasted sharply with that of many people only recently working alongside him in Berlin. The court's decision – that as an alien
he could be charged with, and then convicted of an alleged treason committed abroad – has remained both controversial and legally
significant.

2

How did Joyce's case resonate among lawyers? A letter from Hartley Shawcross to Hersch Lauterpacht shows that legal opinion soon became divided. Written in 1947, it ran as follows:

> I think it would be most useful for you to write an article for the Cambridge Law Journal on the Joyce case, especially in view of the singularly ill-informed and critical accounts which have appeared. I haven't the slightest objection to your making any use of the notes which you so kindly prepared for me, and I will arrange to obtain such transcripts as are available.[1]

Lauterpacht responded by effectively restating the prosecution's argument. He still contended that Joyce's British passport guaranteed him the Crown's protection and in return the state required his allegiance. Lauterpacht also reaffirmed an English court possessed the necessary jurisdiction in the case.[2]

At Joyce's trial, the argument for an alien being charged with treason for acts committed abroad had derived from *Foster's Crown Cases*, where one paragraph read:

> Sect.4. And if such alien, seeking the protection of the Crown, and having a family and effects here, should, during a war with his native country, go thither, and there adhere to the King's enemies *for purposes of hostility*, he might be dealt with as a traitor. For he came and settled here under the protection of the Crown; and, though his person was removed for a time, his effects and family continued still under the same protection. This rule was laid down by all the judges assembled at the Queen's command, Jan. 12th 1707.

A marginal note added "MSS Tracy, Price, Dod and Denton."[3]

Before the hearing, Joyce's counsel had requested Leonard Le Marchant Minty to trace its origins and ascertain its precise wording.[4] He drew a blank. Minty understood the Attorney-General's advisers had attempted a similar exercise. Again to no avail.[5]

By the summer of 1946 Minty had devilled further and now wrote:

> My researches have convinced me that there was a resolution of judges of some kind on 12th January 1707–8, but whether, if it were forthcoming, it would bear out the passage in Foster on which so much importance was laid, is open to doubt – at least in my mind.[6]

Minty's work might have influenced Shawcross once again to seek Lauterpacht's assistance.

It was 1955 before Lauterpacht's opinion was first severely tested by a British lawyer. Glanville Williams then entered the debate.[7] Lauterpacht had approached Joyce's case not only as an eminent international jurist with liberal inclinations but also as a Jew, many of whose Galician family had been slaughtered by the Germans.[8] Williams's legal writings contained "two big and simple notions." The law should be "clear, consistent and accessible" and, befittingly for a conscientious objector during the Second World War, should be humane and avoid punishment, unless society's well-being decreed otherwise.[9]

From private conversations Williams believed that in the Joyce case "the great body of contemporaneous opinion at the Bar . . . was against the [courts'] decision." He also claimed that when it became known Joyce was not a British subject, a wave of revulsion against his conviction swept across the country.[10] Private thoughts – as opposed to public written statements – from Bar members are impossible now to gather up. As for popular opinion, the letters despatched to the Home Office – unseen by Williams – rather than suggesting a widespread unease, reveal a more complex response to Joyce's fate.

In presenting his legal argument Williams focused on whether with his British passport Joyce had lived under the Crown's protection and therefore owed it an allegiance, bearing in mind the court had accepted he was born in New York. He made no comment on an English court possessing jurisdiction over an alien for acts committed abroad.

He queried whether when Joyce applied for a passport he ever considered it would protect him. "It is probably not too much to say that the question of diplomatic protection did not enter his head" and "To say that asking for a passport is the same as asking for protection of which one does not think is to create a fiction that should find no place in the criminal law."[11] Williams continued: "The most that can be said is that the passport gave Joyce a possibility of protection *de facto*." But "to argue that *de facto* protection (or the possibility of it)" raised "a correlative duty of allegiance" was "legally unsound."[12] His objection was admittedly technical. But he argued that Joyce had been found guilty and executed on a "pure technicality."[13]

In the mid-1950s another lawyer, also uneasy at the verdict and speaking for others, remarked:

> One would like to think that this general feeling in the profession would result in the decision being confined to the instance that produced it, and would ensure the exercise of judicial ingenuity to limit and avoid the mischiefs that may arise from it.[14]

In 1960, continuing to reflect this legal unease, Louis Blom-Cooper remarked that in the Joyce case, "English law had been less than true to its highest traditions."[15] Fifteen years later, John Foster, "dark and high-coloured and genially menacing, like a Renaissance bravo" – who had served on John Amery's defence team and represented British interests at Nuremberg – spoke much more bluntly.[16] He alleged Joyce's trial had been a "blood hunt."[17] He had become seriously troubled by such post-war developments and, Rebecca West thought, had encouraged Norman Baillie-Stewart in his 1957 legal action against her.[18]

This belief among lawyers that Joyce was executed on a fine legal technicality has shown no signs of going away.[19] In 1995 one commentator declared his conviction was "not a noble moment for the law or the legal system."[20] Two years later, another, dangerously abstracting the trial from its historical context, claimed that the Crown's argument "would be given short shrift today even in the most humble of magistrates' courts."[21]

The verdict certainly left Gerald Slade, who had done his best for Joyce, feeling distinctly uneasy.[22] Hartley Shawcross, his legal opponent, would not be drawn when questioned in 1991.[23] Four years later, however, he defended the outcome, though admitting he was not "particularly proud" of the case. Partly because Joyce had been executed before being informed why his appeal had been dismissed but primarily because the public had not been provided with "a simple, straightforward legal basis" for the court's verdict.[24]

These discussions went beyond lawyers and legal journals. A Foreign Office file containing a long memorandum on Joyce written by Geoffrey Allchin, a Foreign Office official, later HM Ambassador to Luxembourg, remained closed until early 2007 under section 3[4] of the Public Records Act. Dated 1949, but started in February 1946, one month after Joyce's execution, it began:

> It has seemed to me that, as a result of a misunderstanding about passports, the Joyce trial went off the rails with the consequence that the law of treason and the rights of the holder of a British passport are on a dubious footing.[25]

Allchin argued that the law had been "flung wider than most people thought" and wondered how, since the British had denied a French request to detain P. G. Wodehouse for actions outside France, they could charge an alien with treason for acts committed in Germany?[26]

Joyce's trial had gone ahead because he held a British passport. But Allchin argued its mere possession carried no rights to protection and, by implication, its holder did not automatically owe any allegiance to the Crown. His argument here closely anticipated Glanville Williams's four years later. "A miscarriage of justice" had therefore occurred. Allchin had not worried unduly at the time "except from the point of view of English justice," since he believed Joyce had deserved execution "as a traitor to the United States." It was only later he realised Joyce had become German before the United States had entered the War.[27]

Allchin's memorandum, which was 'lost' in the Foreign Office for two years, reappeared when the law on British nationality was being considered.[28] Joyce Gutteridge, a Foreign Office legal advisor, now drafted a belated reply.[29] Whilst critical of the opinion that possession of a passport *entitled* its holder to the Crown's protection, she concluded that any holder was eligible to receive it and therefore did owe a continuing allegiance.[30]

A month before his execution Joyce, drawing on Dryden's *The Hind and the Panther*, believed no such semantic legal arguments would ever save him:

> What weight of ancient witness can prevail
> When private reason hold the public scale?[31]

As one lawyer argued soon after Joyce's case, in treason trials it was only too easy to "lean forward rather than backward in 'finding' the law to meet [the] case."[32] Even though a distinguished seventeenth-century jurist had cautioned that consequently the law could be made to stretch "as far as the wit and invention of [the] accusers" would wish and "the odiousness and detestation" of the accused would allow.[33] And in the shadow of the War few among the British public shed any tears for Joyce. It was not only that death had recently visited many of their lives. After his traumas in Ireland, he had begun a new life across the water, always claiming to be British. Against this background, to many contemporaries his wartime activities smacked of betrayal: he was a repulsive character, who deserved to be executed. Put to a national vote in 1945–46, that would almost certainly have been the verdict.[34] The state's response was consistent with such sentiment.

3

Writing on wartime traitors in 1944, William Connor asked: "What shall be their fate?"[35] Joyce, we know, was not alone in being executed. John Amery and Theodore Schurch went to the gallows.[36] The broadcaster Walter Purdy and the soldier-traitor Thomas Heller Cooper, both former BUF members, were also sentenced to death, having been charged with treason, but reprieved.[37] Purdy, who admitted "I realise I have been a traitor and a rat," was sent down for life. Released after nine years, he became Robert Wallace Pointer and died in 1982.[38] Cooper, with SS connections and boasts about killing Jews, received a life sentence. Freed in 1953, he died in 1987.[39]

Other renegades, charged under Defence Regulations rather than Treason legislation, received sentences that varied considerably, without any apparent reason. Women generally fared better than men.

Dorothy Eckersley, that avid pre-war fellow traveller, implicated in Joyce's departure to Berlin and launching his radio career there, was given twelve months.[40] "Justice smiled on her."[41] Her son, James Clark, also fared relatively well. In view of his youth and his mother's influence over him, he was bound over for two years.[42] Dorothy Eckersley died in 1971, by which time the Roman Catholic Church had replaced her political enthusiasms. James Clark is still alive.[43]

Such leniency hardly delighted Eckersley's investigators. After being captured, she protested, duplicitous as ever, she had not assisted the Nazis one ha'pporth.[44] However, this calculated deception did not fool her interrogator Reginald Spooner, a Scotland Yard officer attached to MI5, who remarked delicately: "I don't think she told me quite all she was able to."[45]

This display of generosity towards Eckersley infuriated John Macnab. In November 1945, burning up the page to Margaret Joyce, he exclaimed:

> It seems curious that one broadcaster being a foreigner should be sentenced to death, while others, being British and accused of assisting the enemy of their own country in war-time should be charged under a non-capital law, and granted bail to walk about the streets in freedom in the meantime.[46]

Macnab would always have pleaded long and hard for Joyce. But on this occasion his arrows were well and truly aimed.

Margaret Bothamley, a Nazi favourite, who remained in wartime contact with Joyce, must have sighed with relief at her treatment. In 1934, when defending the Oranienburg concentration camp, she wrote to *The Times*: "I hold no brief for Germany. I have no political or personal purpose to further."[47] She was, in short, an accomplished liar. She would later claim her sole aim as a broadcaster was to protect the English, her "children" as she called them, from their political fate.[48] Reginald Spooner, also Bothamley's interrogator, realised how wily she could be.[49] However, she was handed a mere one-year sentence in the second division.[50] Wealthy rentiers should not mix with common criminals. "A light sentence I felt," Barry Domvile noted in his diary.[51] By 1948 she was dead.[52]

Susan Hilton, ex–BUF, likewise had reason to be grateful. She admitted broadcasting for the enemy and went to jail for eighteen months.[53] She later established contact with Rebecca West and from 1959 until at least 1974 posted off a stream of chatty letters, which studiously avoided political topics. She died in 1983.[54]

The leniency displayed towards James Clark shows women renegades were not alone in escaping lightly. This generosity also extended to the paranoid Henry Wicks. He was given four years.[55] By 1949 he was free. Having earlier bombarded Hitler, Himmler and Mussolini with missives, he later conducted a diarrhoeic correspondence with Rebecca West, who must have trembled at the prospect of another letter from him arriving on her doorstep.[56] Much later he was in contact with David Irving.[57] Wicks died on 2 April 1979.

Jack Trevor – disgraced ex-officer, heavy drinker, small-time actor, vicious anti-Semite, washed-up admirer of Margaret Joyce – fared even better. His sentence of three years' penal servitude for aiding the enemy was set aside on appeal. By "construing the offence's requirement of 'intent' in an unusually specific and narrow fashion," Rayner Goddard, the Lord Chief Justice, decided the prosecution had failed to prove its case.[58] MI5 was not best pleased.[59] Trevor tasted prison bread for only a few months and before dying in Deal in 1976 must often have realised how fortunate he had been.[60]

Aware that Norman Baillie-Stewart, Joyce's former rival, was obsessed with all things German, the British considered deporting him to Germany. However, the Attorney-General advised that the Allied Control Commission remained fully committed to proceeding against Nazi collaborators. When this disgraced ex-officer appeared at the Old Bailey the capital charge of treason was dropped, on condition he pleaded guilty to aiding the enemy. As a result, he received a much lighter sentence than he deserved. On 10 January 1946, after describing him as "one of the worst citizens that any country has ever produced," the judge imprisoned him for five years.[61] Released in 1949, he soon left for Ireland and always remained alert against any accusation he was a traitor.[62] These libel threats ended with his death in Dublin in 1966.[63]

The sharp contrast between Joyce's fate and that of other renegades was particularly underlined by the case of Edward Bowlby, only recently in Joyce's company at Flensburg but who, after being captured, followed Wicks and Trevor in playing down any such links.[64] Bowlby had been born in Cork in 1911 and travelled to Germany in April 1939. Five years later, realising Hitler had lost the War, and needing to save his neck, he had applied – unsuccessfully – for Irish papers. Frank Newsam wanted him in the dock but his Home Office colleague Ernest Holderness minuted: "There is always some embarrassment in trying to try an Irishman for treachery."[65] Bowlby walked free. But the DPP advised – there are shades here of P. G. Wodehouse's case – that if he came to live in Britain he would be put on trial. Wisely, he returned to Ireland.[66] But there is an unexpected, previously unrecognised twist to his story. In 1947 he obtained an Irish passport, returned to England and worked as a schoolteacher. He died in Tooting in 1959.[67] He never appeared in court.

4

The wartime career of P. G. Wodehouse, whose name has appeared yet again, is controversial and often misrepresented.[68]

In May 1940 the well-known, much-admired author was not in America, where he spent much of his time, but at Le Touquet with his wife, the redoubtable Ethel, a pet parrot and his Pekinese, when this comfortable domestic scene was suddenly shattered by the arrival of German troops. Wodehouse was detained, soon despatched to an internment camp at Tost and held there between September 1940 and June 1941. Aware that their propaganda to America had been ineffective, the Germans decided to release him and put him behind a microphone. They calculated their gesture would also impress the Americans. "I was playing cricket when the Sonder Führer asked me to pack a bag," Wodehouse recalled.[69] He did not have to be asked twice. The Germans whisked him to Berlin. With many hotels fully booked, they settled him in the bustling, luxurious five-star Adlon, which offered him the lifestyle he craved and to which he had grown accustomed.[70] Werner Plack, "something of a playboy" and inclined "to drink too much," whom Wodehouse had known in Hollywood, played a key role in reeling him in. This enigmatic, puffy-faced German also helped to net John Amery and Gerald Hewitt.[71]

Alerted by Plack that Wodehouse had just arrived in an exuberant still-triumphant Berlin, Harry Flannery, the fiercely anti-Nazi CBS correspondent there, sniffed the prospect of a scoop.[72] He rapidly contacted the author in the Adlon – "the crossroads where journalists, diplomats, spies and government officials all congregated" – and persuaded him to go on air.[73] In this interview on 27 June 1941, soon after the Wehrmacht had rolled menacingly into the Soviet Union, Wodehouse uttered a number of crushingly naive and injudicious remarks.[74] He spoke as if there were no War, no human suffering in a world then being savagely torn apart. "I'm living here at the Adlon – have a suite up on the third floor, a very nice one, too . . . and I can come and go as I please," he remarked, quite content with life.[75] If Flannery had not protected him he would have been even more indiscreet.[76] Wodehouse sounded here like Joyce's colleague, Leonard Banning. Or, even more, the Scottish fascist renegade, Alexander Fraser Grant, who, writing to his parents in 1941, remarked: "Keeping very well . . . Have everything I need. Still golfing? Would enjoy a game."[77]

Following this faux pas, Wodehouse gave five radio talks for the Nazis between 28 June and 6 August 1941 that were to haunt him for the rest of his life.[78] Berlin presented him as a non-Nazi but his talks infuriated the public in Britain and America. He became widely viewed as Hitler's stooge and soon realised he had been "criminally foolish."[79] Wodehouse might also have appeared on Nazi radio at other times. More than once, Wolf Mittler claimed to have interviewed him during his time in Berlin.[80]

Even so, a wartime report from the US Embassy in Berlin remarked Wodehouse was not "a deliberate traitor" even if "the fire of patriotism [did] not burn too fiercely in his breast." Rather, "his sole objective and greatest interest [appeared] to be the increase of his income and the enjoyment of as many of the comforts of life as may be available."[81] Wodehouse was the materialist; Joyce the fanatical ideologue.

Wodehouse's later defenders, often belonging to his literary fan club, have maintained he "didn't have a treacherous fibre in his body."[82] This political innocent was always fully absorbed in his novels. So say Malcolm Muggeridge – unreliable on this point – and, more surprisingly, George Orwell.[83] Delivering the broadcasts was admittedly "a loony thing to do," one biographer concedes, but he was no fascist lackey.[84] A recent television programme claims he was 'set up.'[85] A naïve soul, he was easily lured into making incautious statements.[86]

However, a study of the Amerys has delicately suggested that Wode-house's case might not be quite so straightforward.[87] It is true that before the War 'Plum' had written a thinly disguised portrait of Oswald Mosley as "Roderick Spode," head of the Black Shorts, an unflattering image which could hardly have pleased 'The Leader.'[88] But this novel has no bearing on the wartime charge. The most it shows is that Wode-house did not take politics seriously. The key question remains: was he prepared to give succour to the Nazis, if offered the right terms? Put differently, was the historian Richard Cobb on the correct lines when writing that Wodehouse, "a lousy writer," should have been hanged as a traitor?[89]

When MI5 interrogated Wodehouse in September 1944 at the Hôtel Bristol in Paris, to which he and his wife had moved a year earlier – they had been reunited on 27 July 1941 – not every scrap of evidence on his wartime life was to hand. Major E.J.P. Cussen, the MI5 case officer, nevertheless concluded: "I am bound to say that I have some misgivings as to the account given by Wodehouse of this all-important stage in his activities."[90] Joyce confessed all; Wodehouse held back. Contrary to some belief, Cussen did not grant Wodehouse a clean bill of health. The following month more disquiet surfaced in Whitehall when the redoubtable Frank Newsam advised: "I cannot believe he does not know who the 'enemy' is when Great Britain is at war with Germany."[91]

These feelings of unease increased in 1946 as more Intelligence material emerged, especially on Wodehouse's financial dealings with the Nazis.[92] This later information has so far been curiously over-looked by the writer's admirers and defenders.[93] When considering this evidence, MI5's Gilbert Wakefield wondered whether when the Nazis transferred Wodehouse to Paris in 1943 he remained on their payroll. Echoing Cussen, Wakefield remarked that the author's "delib-erate concealment" during earlier interrogations increased "one's disinclination to accept his statement as the whole truth."[94] But in '46–'47 it proved difficult for MI5 to verify this new incoming detail and, in any case, by now the heat was rapidly evaporating from the renegade problem. Wodehouse was allowed to slip away.

There appears to be no record of Joyce and Wodehouse ever meeting in wartime Berlin. Yet the War did link their lives.[95] Not because, as once suggested, the British authorities pursued Wodehouse and other marginal broadcasters solely to make Joyce's prosecution appear less exceptional.[96] This claim is baseless. But there is a connection.

Following Mr Justice Tucker's judgement at Joyce's trial, Hartley Shawcross advised in 1945 that if Wodehouse came to Britain he would be open to prosecution.[97] Tucker had laid down that any kind of talk, if likely to assist the Germans rather than the Allies, meant the broadcaster could be tried for treason.[98]

Wodehouse knew as much.[99] So did his relatives.[100] However, Shawcross emphasised that if the author decided to live abroad the authorities would not pursue him.[101] Discretion proved the better part of valour. A somewhat anxious Wodehouse – "older, out of touch, and no longer sure of his place in the world" – left France for what would be a long, productive, prosperous life in the United States.[102] But, contrary to what his major biographer has suggested, the official file was not closed long ago.[103] Some attitudes in government towards Wodehouse's behaviour – which in Shawcross's words helped to guarantee him an "exceedingly comfortable war" – did soften as time passed by, but "there was never any final decision not to prosecute."[104] Consequently, Wodehouse had a long wait for the knighthood, which was bestowed on him in 1975 at his home in America by the British Ambassador only a few weeks before he died.[105] For many years Joyce's shadow hovered close. The activities of a bruising, unrepentant fascist and a much admired, superbly gifted comic writer had become inextricably entangled.

5

The remarkable generosity accorded more important renegades contrasts sharply with the treatment of William Albert Colledge and Francis Paul Maton, both second-rank ex-army broadcasters. Colledge received penal servitude for life and was discharged from service with ignominy. What a short straw he had drawn. He even had the ineffectual Margaret Joyce to coach him in his broadcasting career.[106] Maton, a worshipper of Joyce in Berlin, was sent down for ten years.[107]

Other lesser-known broadcasters were similarly treated. After his capture in Paris, ex-BUF member Gerald Percy Sandys Hewitt tried to ingratiate himself with the Allies by writing a radio script.[108] "FINITA LA COMEDIA, MR JOYCE: YOU NEED A WELL-EARNED REST!"[109] When, this "thick-set white-faced man, clean shaven and wearing horn-rimmed spectacles" appeared later at the Old Bailey, he appeared fully contrite – or was it merely a clever tactic? – and pleaded guilty to assisting the Nazis. However, he had seriously miscalculated. He was imprisoned for twelve years.[110] This "worm," as Joyce called him, died in 1969.[111]

The former Mosleyite, Benson Railton Metcalfe Freeman, was also handed a stiff sentence. Derek Curtis-Bennett led for the defence and did his best. But his unpleasant, egotistical client went to prison for ten years.[112] Totally unrepentant, he poured scorn on the court's decision, alleging that the verdict "just shows how rotten this democratic country is. The Germans would have had the honesty to shoot me."[113] After serving his sentence, Freeman slithers away from the history books.

Leonard Banning, Mr Black in Rebecca West's *The Meaning of Treason*, who indecently enlisted with the Nazis in September 1939 and after only a brief hesitation served throughout the War, received a relatively harsh sentence of ten years.[114]

On his release in 1950 he contacted Rebecca West, saying he hoped to resume a career teaching English on the Continent, possibly in Paris. He also expressed an interest in becoming an author: as John Brown he had written that fascist classic, *Woe for my Comrades*. He now sought her advice on two novels. "Man out of Jail" he intended to base on his time in prison and "Scene of my Crime" on his life in wartime Germany.[115] West found a draft of the former slightly disappointing.[116] Neither proposal seems to have appeared. But Banning, who worked later for a Viennese news agency, acted as a stringer for the *Sunday Express* and offered occasional items to the BBC, did dash off two potboilers. *How I fooled the World* and *Return to Istanbul* appeared in the 1970s under the name John Banning.[117]

However, he might have pursued another life, early traces of which can be glimpsed in a 1946 Home Office file that attracted an initial closure date of 2026.[118] Its sensitivity – though parts can be glimpsed in open files – probably relates to Banning's prison letters pleading for an opportunity to serve his "fellow countrymen" and earn their future respect. One letter requested that information he had obtained on the Polish consul in London be passed to MI5.[119] As with Joyce, that opaque link between fascists and the security service begins to feature.

Banning continued to believe he possessed special insights.[120] He remained politically alert, now calling himself a "Germanophile," which, decoded, means that like Joyce he still clung to his fascist beliefs. And, as "a superior being," he was convinced fascism would sweep to power on the wave of a future economic crisis.[121]

However, the authorities would have realised his offer to serve, perhaps also cleverly designed to secure his release, might be exploited. He had Nazi contacts and spoke German. Did the British respond? Was his reporting from Central Europe a useful 'cover'? Or was he a risk too far? Banning retains his tantalising features to the end. His family believe he took out German citizenship but have no details on his date of death.[122]

6

On 10 July 1940 Harold Laski, leading political scientist and Labour Party activist, "little Laski" to the fascists, had delivered a memorial lecture in London which argued against imposing the death penalty for political offences.[123]

> Any cause for which men and women are prepared to die is one which, however wrong or mistaken we believe it to be, corresponds to a deeply-felt experience in them. To kill them because they act upon their convictions does not justify the preference thereby emphasised for your experience over theirs; it merely explains that there is more power of coercion behind your experience.[124]

When he gave his lecture Joyce was gloating on Nazi radio about Britain's imminent destruction. Invasion threatened. The Luftwaffe was visiting overhead. Britain's Nazis were salivating. And Laski – "too good to live in this wicked world," as Rebecca West put it – knew how difficult it would be later to control atavistic impulses.[125] But he argued the country's "shattered fabric" would be restored only by clinging to its rational values.[126]

Five years later Britain's leading liberal newspaper also argued that "killing men is not the way to root out false opinions."[127] However, such views did not enjoy a universal currency.[128]

Against this background, Britain's management of its renegade problem proved controversial and inconsistent, and Joyce's treatment remained stubbornly at the centre of this debate. The many light sentences, together with the small number of executions, showed that while a thirst for revenge could be found among the public and MI5 lobbied for harsh treatment, lawyers were reluctant to follow suit. After Wicks had received four years, Theobald Mathew, writing to Rebecca West from the DPP's office, called his sentence "reasonable enough."[129] Even Nazi supporters given long sentences were often released early and many renegades – especially more prominent public figures – never appeared in court.[130]

By 1947 certainly, tensions had subsided – as Harold Nicolson had predicted they would.[131] As the country began to rebuild under Labour, Rayner Goddard, the Lord Chief Justice, made it clear such prosecutions should cease. His reluctance to punish even hard and fast cases had been evident earlier at Jack Trevor's appeal. The DPP was similarly inclined. Theobald Mathew believed a "fairly calm and reasonable effort" had been made to grapple with "a thoroughly troublesome problem."[132] Joyce would have seriously disagreed. But Mathew was clearly relieved when the files could be bundled up and consigned to the archives.

Notes

1 Lauterpacht Archive, Shawcross to Lauterpacht, 6 January 1947.
2 H. Lauterpacht, "Allegiance, Diplomatic Protection and Criminal Jurisdiction over Aliens," *Cambridge Law Journal*, Vol.9 (1945–1947), p.330.
3 *Foster's Crown Cases* (third ed., London, 1809), p.183.
4 Minty, BSc, BCom, PhD, practised at the Central Criminal Court and on the South-East circuit.
5 L. le M. Minty, "LOOKING IN A DARK ROOM FOR A BLACK HAT THAT ISN'T THERE," *Juridical Review*, Vol.58 (1946), pp.120–122.

6 Minty, "LOOKING IN A DARK ROOM," p.121.

7 P. R. Glazebrook, "Glanville Williams, 1911–1997," *Proceedings of the British Academy*, Vol.115 (2002), pp.411–435. See obituary, *The Times*, 14 April 1997.

8 Lauterpacht, *Lauterpacht* and M. Koskenniemi, "Hersch Lauterpacht (1897–1960)," in J. Beatson and R. Zimmerman (eds.), *Jurists Uprooted: German-speaking Émigré Lawyers in Twentieth-Century Britain* (Oxford, 2004), pp.601–61.

9 J. R. Spencer in Matthew and Harrison (eds), *ODNB*, Vol.59, p.195.

10 G. Williams, "The Correlation of Allegiance and Protection," *Cambridge Law Journal*, Vol.10 (1950), p.54.

11 *Ibid.* p.74.

12 *Ibid.* p.56.

13 *Ibid.* p.75.

14 J.V. Barry, "Treason, Passports and the Ideal of a Fair Trial," *Res Judicatae* (1955–57), p.305.

15 *Guardian*, 24 April 1960.

16 West, *Treason*, pp.235–236.

17 On Foster, see Matthew and Harrison (eds.), *ODNB*, Vol.20, p.515. He made the comment in "Lord Haw-Haw," BBC1, TV, 29 December 1975.

18 West to Mathew, 13 April 1957 (private archive).

19 Robertson, *Freedom*, p.173.

20 S. Gardiner, "Trial of William Joyce," *New Law Journal*, 22 September 1995, p.1386.

21 T. Gleeson, "Passport to Treason," *Justice of the Peace and Local Government Review*, Vol.161, 22 November 1997, p.1086.

22 *The Observer*, 11 February 1962.

23 National Sound Archive, C 465/05/01–05, F 2710–4.

24 Shawcross, *Life Sentence*, pp.82, 83.

25 FO 372/6897. *Who Was Who 1961–1970*, p.17.

26 *Daily Telegraph*, 3 December 1944, for the French interest in Wodehouse. Noted in FO 369/3509.

27 FO 372/6877.

28 V. Bevan, *The Development of British Immigration Law* (London, 1986), pp.112–115, particularly.

29 Daughter of the distinguished jurist H. C. Gutteridge.

30 FO 372/6877, memo, 14 September 1949.

31 WJ to MJ, 19 December 1945. J. Kinsley (ed.), *Dryden's Poems* (London, 1964), p.350.

32 S. C. Biggs, "Treason and the Trial of William Joyce," *University of Toronto Law Journal*, Vol.1, (1947), p.193.

33 Sir Matthew Hale, *Historia Placitorum Coronae*, Vol.1 (London, 1971 ed.), pp.86–87.

34 *Daily Telegraph*, 13 December 2003.

35 William Connor (Cassandra), "What shall be their fate?" *Crusader*, Issue 13, August 1944.

36 Faber, *Speaking for England*, pp.498–512, on Amery. *The Times*, 5 January 1946, on Schurch.

37 *The Times*, 7 February 1946, for Purdy's reprieve. *Ibid.* 21 February 1946, for Heller Cooper's. See later, *Daily Mail*, 16 December 2000 (on Purdy) and *Sunday Times*, 16 June 1996 (on Heller Cooper). The latter features in Walters, *The Traitor*. It has been suggested his mother being German influenced his successful appeal. A. Lyon, "From Dafydd ap Gryffydd to Lord Haw-Haw. The Concept of Allegiance in the Law of Treason," *Cambrian Law Journal*, Vol.33 (2002), p.52.

38 *Daily Telegraph*, 21 November 1945 for his confession. Murphy, *Letting the Side Down*, pp.215–216; *Daily Mail*, 16 December 2000.

39 *Sunday Times*, 16 June 1996 reported he had gone to Japan. He died on 25 November 1987. See Metropolitan Police War Crimes Unit to *Sunday Times*, 8 January 1997. Letter obtained through an FOI request, May 2014.

40 Murphy, *Letting the Side Down*, p.218.

41 *Evening Standard*, 11 December 1945.

42 Murphy, *Letting the Side Down*, p.218.

43 Kenny, *Germany Calling*, pp.256–257 for generous comment on both.

44 *The Times*, 2 November 1945.

45 CRIM 1/1736, interview, 2 July 1945.

46 KV 2/346, J. Macnab to M. Joyce, 18 November 1945. Sceptical of Eckersley's defence, he was also trying to lift Margaret's spirits.

47 *The Times*, 6 April 1934.

48 CRIM 1/1763, statement, 2 February 1946.

49 CRIM 1/1763/55.

50 Murphy, *Letting the Side Down*, p.218.

51 DOM 58, Domvile diary, 27 March 1946.

52 General Register Office, England and Wales.

53 Murphy, *Letting the Side Down*, pp.218–219.

54 RWC, Tulsa SC, 23:2; *Daily Mail*, 1 May 1998 and *The Times*, 19 May 1998, for recent attempts to rehabilitate her reputation.

55 CRIM 1/1767.

56 RWC, Tulsa SC, 59:3.

57 M.C.V. Egan, *The Bridge of Deaths* (Bloomington, Ind., 2011), pp.122–123, and www.fpp.co.uk/speeches/011192.html and www.fpp.co.uk/speeches/281092.html. Wicks's death from www.genealogists'forum.co.uk. Accessed 13 October 2013.

58 Matthew and Harrison (eds), *ODNB*, Vol.22, p.550. F. Bresler, *Lord Goddard: A Biography* (London, 1977), pp.304–305.

59 KV 2/624/198a. G. R. Rubin, "New Light on Steane's Case," *Journal of Legal History*, Vol.24 (2003), pp.143–164, which uses Intelligence files and shows MI5 had grounds for its concerns.

60 Gently treated, too, in Bergmeier and Lotz, *Hitler's Airwaves*, pp.93–95.

61 *The Times*, 11 January 1946, for the Judge's remark. In 1948 his case attracted the attention of the Freedom Defence Committee which believed MI5 had unduly influenced the proceedings. *Bulletin*, No.6 (1948), p.3, and *ibid*. No.7 (1948), p.6.

62 Baillie-Stewart, *Officer in the Tower*, pp.250–251 on his legal actions. FA OE 3/7 for a 1963 threat against J. A. Cole. Rebecca West did not escape his attentions. *The Times*, 6 April 1957. See also RWC, Tulsa SC, 5:4 "Baillie-Stewart v Pan Books and others. Opinion of W. O'B Fitzgerald" (undated). In response West turned to the DPP, Theobald Mathew. West to Mathew, 3 January 1957, 3 April 1957 (private archive). Her January letter noted Kenneth Berry, ex-British Free Corps, and Evelyn Waugh were also agitated about her work.

63 Bergmeier and Lotz, *Hitler's Airwaves*, pp.92–93. KV 2/174–192. *The Times*, 8 June 1966 for an obituary.

64 HO 45/25789, statement by Bowlby, 24 May 1945.

65 HO 45/25789, minute, 7 September 1944. See also R. M. Douglas, "Joyce Family Values: Treason, Nationality and the Case of Lord Haw-Haw's Irish Cousin," *War and Society*, Vol.33 (2014), pp.208–228.

66 Murphy, *Letting the Side Down*, p.210; HO 45/25789.

67 Kenny, *Germany Calling*, p. 228, on his passport. Death certificate, Charles Edward John Salvin Bowlby, Metropolitan Borough of Wandsworth.

68 R. McCrum, *P. G. Wodehouse: A Life* (London, 2004), is the major Wodehouse biography.

69 KV 2/74, statement 9 September 1941.

70 I. R. Guernsey, *Free Trip to Berlin* (Toronto, 1943), pp.174 ff on Wodehouse in Berlin.

71 KV 2/3550/19, p.1 on his personality and other details.

72 I. Sproat, *Wodehouse at War* (Bath, 1981), p.11. Flannery has already been noticed bringing in 1941 with the Joyces.

73 Harsch, *At the Hinge of History*, p.41.

74 HO45/22385 contains the transcript.

75 Flannery, *Assignment to Berlin*, p.245.

76 *Ibid*.

77 KV 2/424/69a.

78 HO 45/22385 for the talks. Sproat, *Wodehouse at War*, pp.107 ff. Roger Milner's play, "Beyond a Joke," premiered at the Yvonne Arnaud Theatre, Guildford in 2000, presented his actions in an unfavourable light. See comment in *Sunday Telegraph*, 6 August 2000.

79 HO 45/22385, Wodehouse to Home Office, 4 September 1944.

80 "Germany Calling," Historia Video, 1997. Wolf Mittler in conversation with D. Blakeway, nd. Private Collection.

81 US Embassy in Berlin to Secretary of State, 21 July 1941. NARA, RG59 BOX 5496 250/34/07/01.

82 Farndale, *Haw-Haw*, p.339.

83 Muggeridge, *Chronicles*, pp.230–231. During the War Muggeridge, working for MI6, was attached to the case of Wodehouse and his wife, Ethel. He described the latter as a mixture of "Mistress Quickly, Florence Nightingale, and Lady Macbeth" (p.231). She captivated him. Indeed, he became too close to both. His oft-repeated testimony reflected this intimacy. KV 2/75, Rothschild to Petrie, 29 September 1944, for concerns at Muggeridge's relationship. Muggeridge is portrayed in Colin Shindler's radio play on Wodehouse's problem, "How to be an Alien with no previous experience," BBC Radio 4, 15 December 2010. Orwell's 1945 essay, "In Defence of P. G. Wodehouse," is printed in S. Orwell and I Angus (eds.), *The Collected Essays, Journalism and Letters of George Orwell*, Vol.3, *As I Please 1943–1945* (London, 1968), pp.388–403.

84 McCrum, *Wodehouse*, pp.301 ff.

85 "Wodehouse in Exile," BBC 4 TV, 25 March 2013.

86 "Heil Wodehouse?" http://yoyogod.20m.com. Accessed 17 February 2006. Sproat, *Wodehouse at War*.

87 Faber, *Speaking for England*, p.460, on Wodehouse possibly being closer to the Nazis than often assumed.

88 P. G. Wodehouse, *The Code of the Woosters* (London, 1953, first ed., 1938), p.118 particularly.

89 A. Horne (ed.), *Telling Lives* (London, 2001), p.354.

90 HO 45/22385, report, E.J.P. Cussen, 28 September 1944, p.8.

91 HO 45/22385, memo, 23 October 1944.

92 FO 369/3509, British Embassy, Paris, to Foreign Office, 25 November 1946.

93 McCrum's *Wodehouse*, p.323, glosses over this evidence.

94 KV 2/75/242b, memo, Wakefield [MI5], 27 February 1947.

95 McCrum, *Wodehouse*, p.205 and elsewhere, plays down any connection. Cole, *Lord Haw-Haw*, fails to connect the two. Selwyn, *Hitler's Englishman*, pp.177, 191, does link them, but not significantly. Kenny, *Germany Calling*, carries no reference to Wodehouse. Farndale, *Haw- Haw*, p.339, remarks, without any evidence, that the authorities could hardly turn a blind eye to Wodehouse's role if Joyce were convicted.

96 Farndale, *Haw-Haw*, p.339.

97 KV 2/75/204a, DPP to the Attorney-General, 3 October 1945. Attorney-General to Mathew, 1 November 1945.

98 HO45/22385. Hall (ed.), *Trial*, p.223.

99 KV 2/75, Wodehouse to Cussen, 1 February 1945, for his awareness of the situation.

100 HO 45/22385, Home Office memo, 17 October 1945.

101 KV 2/75, Shawcross to Mathew, 1 November 1945.

102 McCrum, *Wodehouse*, p.361, on his feelings.

103 *Ibid*. p.346. Repeated in S. Ratcliffe (ed.), *P. G. Wodehouse: A Life in Letters* (London, 2011), pp.339–340 and 359–360.

104 LO 2/1166, Shawcross memo, 8 August 1947 and Beckett to Armstrong, 24 January 1978, respectively.

105 *The Times*, 2 January 1975. LO 2/1166, Armstrong to Beckett, 8 February 1978.

106 *The Times*, 15 May 1946 and WO 71/1131. Bulloch, *Treason*, p.55 carries detail.

107 KV 2/264 and WO 71/1117.

108 Fredborg, *Behind the Steel Wall*, p.242, ". . . when the regime collapses we shall witness the phenomenon that nobody was ever a Nazi by conviction."

109 KV 2/426.

110 *Daily Mirror*, 6 March 1945; HO 45/24474; KV 2/426; KV 2/427. His anti-Joyce script is in KV 2/426. Hastings, Duke of Bedford, *The Years of Transition* (London, 1949), p.219, discussed Hewitt, though not by name. See also his intervention in the Lords. *Parliamentary Debates* (Lords), Vol.146, 18 March 1947, cols 462–470. Bulloch, *Treason*, pp.69–72 referred to Hewitt's case.

111 KV 2/250, 6 March 1945.

112 Murphy, *Letting the Side Down*, p.222.

113 West, *Treason*, p.134.

114 RWA, YCAL, GEN MSS, 105, Box 12, Folder 533, Mathew to West, 20 June 1946.

115 RWC, Tulsa SC, 5:8, letters from Banning to West, 17 March 1950, 28 July 1950, 10 August and an undated communication.

116 RWC, Tulsa SC, 5.8, letter, 31 August 1950. Another reader with whom she shared the typescript described Banning as being "too coquettish" with his readers, a trait that persisted.

117 J. Banning, *How I Fooled the World* (London, 1974) and *Goodbye to Istanbul* (London, 1977).

118 HO 45/24475.

119 Letter, 22 April 1946, a second, undated, from Tortworth prison, and his letter on the Polish Consul, dated 14 June 1947, all from HO 45/24475.

120 Letter to V.E.A. Banning, early in 1947, which the prison authorities refused to send. HO 45/24475.

121 HO 45/24475, letter to his brother, 1 March 1947 and Prison Medical Officer's report, 3 January 1950.

122 Private information, 21 January 2008.

123 *The Blackshirt*, 22–28 July 1933, on "Little Laski."

124 H. J. Laski, *Political Offences and the Death Penalty* (London, 1940), p.4.

125 West to Laski, 21 December 1947 (private archive).

126 Laski, *Political Offences*, p.11.

127 *Manchester Guardian*, 19 December 1945.

128 West, *Treason* (2000), p.31 on how the War had affected the British public. Christoph, *Capital Punishment and British Politics*; V. Bailey, "The Shadow of the Gallows: The Death Penalty and the British Government, 1945–51," www.historycooperative.org, accessed 28 June 2005;

D. Kynaston, *Austerity Britain 1945–51* (London, 2007), pp.267–269, on capital punishment at this time.

129 RWA, YCAL, GEN MSS,105, Box 12, Folder 553, Mathew to West, 31 May 1946.

130 Murphy, *Letting the Side Down*, pp.216, 217, 219. The writer J. S. Barnes (WO 204/12841), art critic Sisley Huddleston (WO 204/12326) – whose entry, like P. G. Wodehouse's, carries the comment ("do not detain unless special circumstances require it") – and Lt Col. Cyril Rocke (HO 45/25783 and FO 371/23826), were among those who escaped any action.

131 H. Nicolson, *Comments, 1944–1948* (London, 1948), p.99, written 1 June 1945.

132 RWC, Tulsa SC, 33.8, Mathew to West, 25 June 1947.

PART VI
Judgements

23

PERSPECTIVES

Perhaps one day a writer will invent a life and present it simply in the form of a sequence of documents, without emphasis or commentary: birth certificate, school reports, driver's licence, life-assurance policy, requests for overdue library books, laundry lists, home-contents insurance inventory, shopping lists, unfilled prescriptions, unredeemed petrol-station vouchers, a passport application filled out in a false name but never sent in, and a final sequence of bills from doctors and nursing agencies, climaxing with a startlingly high invoice from a fashionable mortician. Upon such a structure one could impose one's own consolatory fictions of achievement and development. On the one hand to have done such deeds! On the other: to have paid such a price! And our own lives, by contrast: how boring, how riskless, and how very, very preferable! [John Lanchester, *The Debt to Pleasure* (London, 1997), p.194.]

1

Joyce's life had taken him from being a fresh-faced expectant school-boy in Galway to a career operating as a fully fledged fascist politico in Britain, totally consumed by a hatred of Jews. It had then led him into Hitler's camp. Viewed by the British as a traitor, he paid the ulti-mate price for his political commitment.

Francis Aveling, briefly Joyce's research supervisor, wrote in *Personality and the Will*:

> We are not mere idle spectators, passively contemplating ourselves and the continually unrolling panorama of our experience. We are essentially busy with our experience and with ourselves; we are performers on the stage of actual life and living.[1]

Joyce's life reflected as much. He was a 'doer,' always keen to "seize the day." He married twice, had children, conducted innumerable affairs and with a brutish insensitivity told Margaret he could unleash any woman's deep carnal desires.[2] He worked professionally as a teacher. He skated, boxed, fenced, played billiards, enjoyed playing cards, relished a game of chess, liked walking in the rain and turned his hand to cricket.[3] He loved to act, read greedily and widely, had an interest in music, was always ready to sing and played the piano by ear.[4] He drank – often too deeply – whether it be beer, gin, hock, kummel or cheap wines from Spain.[5] But politics dominated his life.

This political obsession surfaced in a December 1942 radio interview with Erika Schirmer, who had helped to launch him on his broadcasting career. She said having him on her programme was "a special treat." His many listeners would hopefully discover something of the man behind the microphone. However, he must have disappointed them. "That's rather difficult," he told her. "I work practically the whole day."[6]

Fascism, which replaced his lost Catholicism, became Joyce's chosen creed.[7] Amid the social-economic and political turmoil of the early twentieth century, some young idealistic contemporaries including John Cornford, Ralph Fox and Rose Cohen, embraced Marxism. Joyce, also hoping to build a better, different future, moved in a sharply opposite direction. Communists became his hated enemies. He told Schirmer: "National Socialism is the greatest doctrine since the time of the Renaissance . . . it's an irresistible force. Those who try to resist it can only get the worst of the bargain."[8] In Britain, he and his fascist comrades saw themselves on a sacred mission to save society.[9] Their gatherings sometimes appeared like revivalist meetings.

If this campaign involved violence, so be it. Joyce never shirked a street fight. "Brave? Oh yes, he was brave all right."[10] The War, raging about him at the time of Schirmer's interview, marked an extension of that crusade to create a new world, a secular paradise.

Towards the end of the War Joyce had lost faith in some Nazis. "They might be masons or in enemy pay," he remarked savagely in March 1945 on the staff who surrounded Goebbels, "Half of them look like Yids and the other like idiots . . . anyhow they let [him] down."[11] The following month he bemoaned, "most of the Germans, not all, are bloody fools."[12] Much of Hitler's intended paradise then lay in jagged ruins and his own future looked perilously bleak. But Joyce's belief in fascism never wavered: "My sacrifice, I firmly believe, will not be in vain: and one day, out of the ruins of Europe, there will emerge in full triumph the ideal for which I have fought – National Socialism as the saviour of the West." Eventually "the materialistic tyranny of Jewry and the menace of Sowjet Imperialism" would be vanquished. Drawing yet again on a belief which had captured him by the '30s, he claimed: "in the history of the human race . . . the spirit has always, in the end, triumphed over the material."[13]

His fascism became inseparable from a crude, lacerating anti-Semitism. His books, journalism and speeches in the 1930s and 1940s portrayed the Jews as a dangerous misfortune, a constant menacing threat, and he told Schirmer, "I would sooner see a beaten Britain, free from the domination of the old financial order, than a victorious Britain that was in practice only a Jewish-American colony."[14]

Joyce's treason followed on from that momentous 1939 departure to Germany and his unwavering wartime commitment to the Nazis. Sitting opposite Schirmer he was looking forward with confidence to a challenging future under Hitler, when Europe's fate would finally be determined. It was not to be.

2

Why did he pursue this wreckage of a life? What drove his short political career?

Joyce's politics in both Britain and Germany constantly reflected the meshing together of social and personal influences. As a prelude to digging more deeply into what motivated him, more needs to be said here about his "strange" personality.[15]

A. K. Chesterton, a fascist comrade from the 1930s, emphasised it was something future biographers and historians must consider if ever they wanted to understand Joyce's life.[16] He was not alone in noticing Joyce's distinctive traits. Bill Shirer, recalling their contact in Berlin, remarked that he "obviously craved recognition."[17] And Wolf Mittler – who also knew Joyce in Germany – soon realised he was simply not amenable to argument.[18] The 'Professor,' knowing everything, must always have his views respected.[19] Little wonder he was often alone.[20]

Joyce's biographers have briefly noticed something similar. Rebecca West concluded he was "never weak in self-esteem" and displayed an unusual interest in conquering the world.[21] To Jack Cole he had a sense of "mission."[22] Francis Selwyn viewed him as "a leader rather than a follower."[23] To Mary Kenny he revealed a "strong sense" of self.[24] Nigel Farndale, called him "above all" off centre, "an eccentric."[25] Yet none probed deeper, even though these traits significantly affected Joyce's political career.

Such characteristics suggest an insufferable know-all. Which Joyce was. However, his personality cannot be reduced to one dimension alone.[26]

Terence Rattigan's film script acknowledged Joyce's many-sidedness. It remarked on his "brilliance of mind and wit," and "inexhaustible, demoniacal energy," but also noticed those "moments of sudden, purposeless inertia" when the "'Man of Destiny,'" became "the child who needs to be told by his doting mother when to cross the road."[27]

This complexity in Joyce's make-up is further underlined by differences between his private and public persona. Gabriel García Márquez once remarked that in our private, public and secret worlds we can become different people, and so it was with Joyce. Even in private he could quickly become unbearably self-opinionated. "Don't think my darling sweetheart that, to use Queen Victoria's phrase, I am addressing you as if you were a publick meeting," he wrote to Margaret in 1945.[28] Little wonder she rebelled. But he also had his gentler moments. Heather Iandolo cherishes a fond memory of him singing Irish songs such as *The Bonnets of Bonnie Dundee*.[29] Later, when settling down with John Macnab, that "rather touching . . . besotted

Scotsman," in one of their rented London flats, whether drinking, discussing literature, listening to Wagner on the Yagerphone, playing chess, or just smoking, the craic was good.[30] "In these quieter moments, when he put aside his jackboots and parade ground swagger," then "a humble person, not without charm and a delicate sense of irony" emerged.[31] Commander Leonard Burt and Lt Col Fallon, who met him briefly at the end of the War outside the political arena, when he had been stripped of all influence, found him engaging. After writing *The Meaning of Treason* Rebecca West received readers' letters recounting some personal kindness Joyce had shown them.[32]

Joyce's political life was strikingly different, however, and never remarkable for its "quieter moments."[33] Politics attracted him because it held out the prospect of control, power, re-ordering the world.[34] It catered to his sense of an "unyielding specialness."[35] Everybody requires a degree of self-regard to function effectively.[36] And if society is ever to function and develop, individuals have "to cut through indecision and . . . take a lead"[37] But Joyce's politics revealed something stronger, qualitatively different.

As a child he has been noticed hero-worshipping Napoleon, a man of destiny. Here was an early role model for him. He knew better than Oswald Mosley – or indeed anyone – how to lead fascism in Britain and was always ruthlessly ready to sweep aside his contemporaries. As Viceroy of India – a lofty post for which we know he had ambitions – he claimed he would have quickly sorted out the wretched Indian nationalists and put them firmly back in their place. He was the far-sighted politico who, believing he had correctly deciphered the political runes of the 1930s, was fully persuaded Britain's future lay with Nazism. His calculated departure to Berlin reflected that belief. When 'confessing' to Jim Skardon at Lüneberg, appearing later in the dock at the Old Bailey, even when facing a possible death sentence, he showed not the slightest interest in denying any of his past or issuing a grovelling apology. His actions had always been correct; he had represented Britain's best interests. He had no case to answer, no wish to speak in his defence. A god must always remain above the battle. It was absolutely fitting, he believed, that he should receive a biography, slavishly compiled by his helot Margaret, which dwelt on his many political insights and recorded his greatness for posterity.

Considering such evidence – and more could be added – some would say his political life can be summed up by: "I love me."[38] Those observations by earlier biographers noting that he never lacked self-esteem, wanted to conquer the world, had a sense of mission, are correct. They have been echoed here in references to Joyce as "an egotistical pedant," someone consumed by "self-importance," and "supremely self-obsessed," a "man without a soul" who was "always convinced of his talents." Now a more refined assessment is called for. His life might be regarded as a case study in hubris.[39] Expressing it differently, the "unusual degree of self-reference" in his articles, books, journalism, radio talks and speeches, and which affected both his political – and personal – behaviour, would suggest Joyce was a narcissist.[40] Here certainly was a politico whose career was increasingly, remorselessly, driven by "self-love, self-reference, self-absorption, self-idealisation and self-aggrandisement."[41] Indeed, he ticks the key boxes recognised today by clinicians when identifying patients suffering from a narcissistic personality disorder.[42]

It is impossible through psychoanalysis to uncover the long-buried experiences which might have helped to create his narcissism. It is a moot point whether biographers should ever fish in such dark waters.[43] The part played by his genetic composition also remains elusive. However, his early suffocating relationship with his mother was one likely important influence. In New York and Galway, she made Joyce – for some years her treasured only child – the key receptacle of all her compensatory hopes and yearnings. She spoilt him, fussed over him, and placed him at the centre of the universe. No wonder that as a young boy he became consumed by a powerful sense of self-importance and could never suffer fools easily, traits which he continued to display throughout his adult life. Think how easily he dismissed his renegade contemporaries in Berlin and his brutal, scathing criticism of Margaret when he declared she had been a wife unworthy of such a great man.

3

Joyce's social experiences then interacted with his narcissism to propel him along his political paths.[44]

His fascism can be linked partly to events in Ireland. The lives of the Joyce family were turned completely upside down by the attacks nationalist forces mounted on them in Galway and later by Westminster's capitulation to the demands of the nationalists. They were "more English than the English"; their "burning patriotism and aggressive anglophilia were embarrassing and painfully theatrical."[45] But they were made to suffer. Joyce never forgave those politicians responsible.[46] He had believed with the poet that:

> Safe were those evenings of the pre-war world
> When firelight shone on green linoleum[47]

For him they were no more. Much of his later politics can be traced back to this bedrock.

When Joyce left Ireland he had not totally given up on British society, despite his feeling of betrayal. He hoped at first the Die-Hard Tories would restore Britain's position in the world, shaken by the effect of the Great War and threatened by its consequences – the rise of socialism, and nationalist stirrings in the Empire. But he soon moved beyond this political position.

He had arrived in London as an eager, super-patriotic young man, ready to do his bit for the country. Just as he had been on its periphery in Galway. Yet in his professional life he met with rejection after rejection. His frustrated efforts to build a career, as a soldier, a doctor, an academic, a civil servant, rubbed salt into his increasingly raw wounds. He knew how important he was. His mother had frequently told him so. Why could others not realise it? Would he ever make the personal progress he craved? Was the old world worth saving when he could be treated like this?

At this crucial time 'significant others' – too long in the shadows – caught him and helped to direct his political journey from Toryism to a fully-fledged fascism. The race scientist G. P. Mudge was one of them. Max Knight was another. The historian F.J.C. Hearnshaw influenced his early political thinking. And he wove ideas from the psychologists Francis Aveling and Charles Edward Spearman into the growing fabric of his fascism. Joyce's reading of Thomas Carlyle also had its effect. Reflecting such influences, by the early '30s he had given up on democracy and the old parties. He was ready to join Mosley. At the same time, glancing from London to Europe, he became aware that fascism, emphasising authority and youth, was busy transforming much of the political landscape. In the '20s and '30s his eyes were being opened much wider in London than they ever had been in Galway.

Joyce's personality facilitated his political conversion to fascism. In *Dictatorship*, written for the BUF, he remarked: "The inheritance of mental and physical characteristics, the existence of insuperable differences of environment, the laws of biology and psychology, make it impossible that there should exist any real equality between men." In turn, he believed that the superior had an obligation to serve the state.[48] A personal dimension lurked behind this abstract prose. He was writing essentially about himself. Fascism, which cast aside equality in favour of hierarchy and rejected democracy for a disciplined authoritarianism, appealed to his narcissism. It would allow him to become a political god. He yearned increasingly to operate alongside powerful politicians who dealt in human destinies.

4

Like much anti-Jewish hostility, Joyce's anti-Semitism had its social roots.[49] When he moved from Galway to London, encountered those cumulative rejections that dumped him where he believed he should never be, grew frustrated that others could not recognise his talents, in other words became 'lost in translation,' influences in London were directing him towards anti-Semitism.

His years in the British Fascists exposed him a Jew–hatred linked to its anti-Bolshevism. When he read H. A. Gwynne's *Morning Post*, as he often did in the early '20s, he would have noticed its emphasis on the threat of Jew-power.[50] When keeping the company of G. P. Mudge, who helped to direct him towards fascism, he would have listened to an obsessive Jew-hatred and heard allegations of unchangeable bio-logical differences between Aryans and Jews.[51] When reading Thomas Carlyle he would have discovered further anti-Semitic sentiment.[52] He would also soon have detected that widespread amorphous antipathy towards Jews in London which cut across class divisions.[53] A tang of anti-Semitism hovered in the air. It found him. He breathed it in. Then, as his accounts of the Lambeth incident and the thieving tutor at Birkbeck showed, he found the Jews.[54] By the mid-1930s he had become completely consumed by Jew-hatred.[55]

He became particularly receptive to such sentiments on account of his narcissism. There is a recognised link between certain personality types and anti-Semitism.[56] And Joyce's attitudes were not, as psychologists would say, "merely conformative" or "mildly ethnocentric," but essential to "the economy" of his life.[57] He demanded order, hierarchy, and clarity, with no shades of grey. His personal map divided society into good and evil. Staunch friends who realised and understood 'the truth' stood on one side, implacable enemies, intent on the corruption and destruction of his precious world, on the other. Fascism versus Communism, Aryan versus Jew, White civilisation versus the Orient, Europe versus the Steppes, came as an integrated package. He was "an almost textbook example of the classically prejudiced personality."[58] His rigidity, a child of his narcissism, guaranteed he retained his views to the end.[59]

5

Joyce's path towards treason was more complex than often suggested. By 1939 he had suffered many professional disappointments, had become frustrated by fascism's lack of progress in Britain and did not need MI5 to tell him he was threatened with internment or possibly deportation.[60] But these emphases alone are insufficient to account for his decision to turn his back on Britain and work for Hitler. The Nazis amounted to his one remaining political hope.[61] By the late '30s he believed Britain could become a great nation again only under their tutelage.[62] He did not go to Berlin on impulse, was not exhibiting the sheer recklessness of a "chancer."[63] He was following a carefully thought-out and, as it transpired, mistaken strategy. Believing he had always held Britain's interests at heart, at Lüneberg he had presented himself to Jim Skardon as a patriot. Another MI5 officer, while fully recognising the complexity of Joyce's position, nevertheless concluded his treason was "obvious."[64]

Joyce also thought he could embrace Hitler with impunity because, unlike fellow-travelling contemporaries in Britain, he possessed an American birth certificate, and when he decided to leave for Berlin in August 1939 no-one envisaged the United States ever becoming involved in a European war. He would be safe.

His narcissism further helps to explain his decision to enlist with Hitler. What Maxwell Knight called in 1934 his "natural aptitude for intrigue" is a key narcissistic trait.[65] Early signs of his "taste for deceit" his "loyalty towards betrayal" came when he informed on Irish nationalists.[66] With his decisive messianic move to Germany, his intriguing there against Britain, he was continuing with his long personal history of duplicity.

Joyce's personality helped to drive his treason in another sense. With his overpowering self-belief he was convinced destiny had decreed that in Berlin he would assume a decisive role in determining Britain's future. His unshakeable belief that at Hitler's side, he would have helped to defeat the Allies within four years, offers a staggering insight into his narcissistic personality.[67] Looking ahead, as a recognised, respected servant of Nazism he doubtless expected his political career would soar far above those Quislings the Nazis would need to recruit in a subjugated Britain – which, to him, was exactly how it should be. His dreams dashed, his hopes shattered, he denied any such personal ambitions. But his remark to James Clark as they luxuriated in the first flush of Germany's wartime success, about soon sitting down at the table of a grateful nation, would suggest quite the opposite.[68]

6

Throughout Joyce's life his politics were predicated on the belief, "all about was mine." Like the child in the poem he wanted to be god, or king of the world. Those children who read or listened to Stevenson's verses grew up, died, their lives largely forgotten. But Joyce found it impossible to accept he should go the way of ordinary mortals, that his life's thin texture should end absolutely; his final hubristic obsession in the condemned cell was that he must remain a continuing influence in the world.

7

What does Joyce's career reveal about fascism, anti-Semitism and trea-son in twentieth century Britain?

He features regularly but not prominently in general histories of British fascism.[69] That neglect is also mirrored in a biography of Diana Mosley which paints him as a plotter, a schemer, – which he was – but essentially crazy, a writer of nonsense and no more.[70] This reductionist portrait would have brought a smile to Lady Mosley's lips.[71] Bad, mad, unable to organise, what a miserable little creature he was. Diana, the goddess of the BUF, had ignored Joyce entirely in her autobiography.[72] And in his memoirs Mosley had quickly dismissed this "offensive little beast."[73] Yet Joyce deserves more.

By 1936–37 he was exercising a substantial influence on the BUF.[74] To a degree many fascist foot soldiers regarded him as the second-in-command, though the post of deputy leader never existed.[75] A history of the movement – and British fascism – without him would be a strange concoction indeed. Through his contributions to the BUF's journals and newspapers and his many speaking engagements he soon became an important propagandist. His time in the NSL offered more of the same. During the '30s, when carrying the fascist message to the country, relishing the cut and thrust of public meetings, dealing vig-orously with hecklers, telling audiences they would hear him out and brawling with the Reds, he never made any original contribution to fascist ideology. In his later prison correspondence, however, he can be found anticipating certain key ideas of post-war Revisionism.

Joyce's career is also a reminder of the links between British fas-cism and Nazism. He had acquired some Nazi contacts when in the BUF. Then in the late '30s he became increasingly immersed in the Brown International. Some Westminster politicians might be viewed as Hitlerite sympathisers.[76] Joyce and many activists in The Link and the Right Club displayed a much sharper political edge. They were Ber-lin's friends. They recognised the *couleur du temps*. Hitler would decide Europe's future. They yearned to be involved in this action. From 1937 onwards, he remained feverishly busy in this semi-secret political milieu.

Mosleyites have claimed that with his pro-Nazi views Joyce was an unrepresentative figure, essentially 'not one of us.'[77] Admittedly, some

British fascists never lifted their political eyes beyond the national scene. But more sinister international links cannot be wiped from the picture. Mosley remained keen during the '30s to cultivate the Nazis, but after the War he and his supporters have been anxious to suppress this embarrassing detail. Yet pre-war documents reveal his assiduous, secret, at times sycophantic wooing of Berlin, and 'The Leader's' sympathies persisted even after the War had begun.[78] Imagine his fan club's delight that many histories of British fascism have omitted such detail.[79] Mosleyites have thereby been allowed almost free rein to indulge their criticisms of Joyce, the overt tool of the Nazis.

Joyce's political life also opens the door, if only slightly, on the links between British fascism and MI5. The security service monitored fascist groups and, during the War, vigorously pressed for the widespread internment of their supporters. But this historical relationship was far more complex. MI5 glimpsed recruitment opportunities. Fascists could offer information on the Communists, a shared enemy.[80] Joyce's activities reflected this accommodation. Through Maxwell Knight he was for some time in contact with MI5, though the exact nature of their relationship is unlikely ever to emerge.

Finally, whereas some fascists never enlisted in more than one group, Joyce and others forged interlocking links and helped to build a fascist tradition in pre-war Britain. A number of activists continued that work after the War.[81] Yet ironically, after slavishly devoting his entire life to the cause and dying for it, in Britain Joyce seriously damaged it. In the War anyone even slightly connected to him became classed as a security risk. And this traitorous legacy lingered after his execution. In 1947 when Jeffrey Hamm, that colourless, cadaverous admirer of Oswald Mosley, addressed a meeting in East London, hecklers shouted: "What about William Joyce?"[82] That same year Alexander Raven Thomson was told in no uncertain terms: "They should have hanged you with William Joyce."[83] The concerted attempts by Mosley and his supporters to distance themselves from Joyce are easy to understand.

8

Joyce's anti-Semitism conjures up yet again Oswald Mosley's ghost. 'The Leader's' followers have pilloried Joyce as a disloyal member of the BUF, whose Jew-hatred brought their movement into disrepute. Such sentiment, they have loudly asserted, never featured in their politics.

Mosley's autobiography proclaimed he had never been an anti-Semite. He had attacked Jews for what they did, not for what they were.[84] Norman St John Stevas, writing in *The Times*, found this defence "convincing."[85] But 'The Leader's' claim is fraudulent.[86] Old men can forget, sometimes deliberately.

Mosley's current admirers want us to believe that the BUF always functioned as a cosy multi-cultural organisation, "open to all races."[87] How different from Joyce, who in his tutorial venture with John Macnab would teach only Aryans. What a contrast with the man who in 1936 lamented the Britain he loved being poisoned and ruined by a "Jewish negroid culture."[88] Yet Mosleyite claims tell us little about what was happening in the 1930s.

On occasions, when 'The Leader' came under pressure, he would depart from his calculated coded script on Jews as aliens and cosmopolitans, and descend into crude anti-Semitic comment.[89] His movement also displayed overt anti-Semitism and not only, as some believe, after Viscount Rothermere had withdrawn his support in 1934.[90] Joyce did not introduce Jew-hatred into the movement, and it persisted after the great purge in 1937. Years later Richard Reynell Bellamy's "We marched with Mosley," the unpublished official history of the BUF, is shot through with such sentiment, often in coded language. But sometimes, say when discussing Leslie Hore-Belisha – in Bellamy's view a slick and silky Jew, too clever by half – it features more directly.[91]

The counter claims by Mosley and his fan club are easily understood. For their political survival British fascists have increasingly needed to distance themselves from an ideology linked to tragedies like Belsen – and Auschwitz.[92] For years they have lived in stout denial of their anti-Semitism. But their slate cannot be wiped clean. To capitulate before the claims of 'The Leader,' his family, former political colleagues, present-day acolytes, and writers seduced by such sources, that it never stained the annals of the BUF, would be a craven surrender of the historical record. Jew-hatred is a dark thread firmly stitched into the fabric of British fascism.

Joyce's anti-Semitism calls for more than a debate with Mosley and his kind. He was remarkable as an important carrier of that crude tradition of Jew-hatred in Britain. His hostility was always overt. He never displayed any ambiguity.[93] He was also a "violent anti-Semite."[94] As such, he operated in the same tradition as Joseph Banister, whose *England under the Jews*, was one of the fiercest expressions of Jew-hatred in twentieth-century Europe.[95]

Joyce expressed his ceaseless, raging venom against Jews within a biological, racist framework. In the late nineteenth and early twentieth centuries, Arnold White had fussed over what he believed were the economic and cultural dangers posed by Jewish immigration. However, by the inter-war years, his views had become passé in anti-Semitic circles. Joyce personified the new racist trend. "If a Jew happened to change his faith to Buddhist," he told a Bath audience in 1935, "our attitude towards him would be exactly the same."[96] Jews were programmed to behave as they did and he deplored "their enmity to white civilisation."[97] Sir Richard Burton had remarked earlier of Disraeli that conversion could not wash away blood.[98] Joyce would have agreed. This biological rigidity endowed his anti-Semitism with a frightening dynamic. But the would-be-doctor, the psychologist manqué, keenly interested in human attributes, never hesitated to travel along this route.

His hatred was further sharpened by taking on board another recent development, that the world faced a conspiracy driven by Jews.[99] This racist, conspiratorial Jew-hatred which fitted his rigid personality with its inability to tolerate any of life's essential hazy greyness, clearly carried serious implications. It took him right to the anti-Semitic edge.[100] In October 1936 he was suggesting Jewish Communists might be shot in the streets.[101] Two months later he would proclaim: "So long as money is the master of us . . . The Jews are our masters and our enemy, and we must get rid of them."[102] Early in the War, he was advocating that Britain's Jews should have been hanged from lamp-posts.[103] The international reach of these "oleaginous parasites from the East" these "greasy" and "sneering" Orientals with their "cruel, remorseless, calculating depravity" complicated how to deal with them. But, unarguably, like Arnold Leese and some members of The Britons, he had moved towards an exterminatory position.[104]

He never commented directly on the Holocaust yet, despite Margaret Joyce's self-serving claim to the contrary, it never troubled him.[105] He hated Jews to the end of his days. They were the devils in his political religion.

9

Joyce was a fascist and, in Anthony Julius's words, a conspiracist anti-Semite.[106] But the public know him better as a traitor.

There had been earlier cases of treason in twentieth-century Britain. In 1903 Arthur Alfred Lynch, an Australian of Irish descent, stood accused of taking an oath to the Boer Republic during the South African War. He was convicted and sentenced to death, but later reprieved. His story has now been virtually forgotten.[107]

The same cannot be said of Roger Casement's life. During the Great War he had arrived in Germany and was encouraged to raise an Irish Legion to fight the Allies. This plan failed. In 1916 the Germans then transported him to Ireland to ferry arms to the separatists. This chaotic enterprise ended disastrously. That same year the British detained him, tried him, stripped him of his knighthood and hanged him in Pentonville.[108] In 1965, several years before Joyce's reburial in Galway, Casement's remains had been returned to Ireland where he is recalled as a martyr to the nationalist cause.

A small number of traitors were hanged in Britain during the Second World War.[109]

After the War, the executions of John Amery and Theodore Schurch, and the near-executions of Walter Purdy and Thomas Heller Cooper, reveal Joyce's treason was not unique in this conflict among those who had lived in Britain. Leonard Banning, Margaret Bothamley, James Clark, Dorothy Eckersley and Henry Wicks, along with other members of that renegade crew who worked for the Nazis in wartime Berlin, reveal that a commitment to Hitler sucked in others. Fortunately for them, they were charged under Defence Regulations rather than treason legislation. Think, too, of those POWs in the British Free Corps, and Susan Hilton, who broadcast, and worked, for the Gestapo.[110] But none captured the public's imagination as Joyce did.

Nazi supporters who hovered closer to home provide the wider context of his wartime treachery. Pre-war fellow travellers such as

Serocold Skeels and Elwin Wright, as well as John Macnab, entrusted by Joyce with carrying out a key subversive role, fall into this category.[111] As do those sympathisers, exposed in the recently released reports of Jack King (Eric Roberts).[112]

This potential fifth column has usually been written off.[113] But Hitlerite sympathisers with greater social clout waited silently, expectantly in the wings. The Arthur Bryants, the Barry Domviles, the A. P. Lauries, the 'Jock' Ramsays, the Charles Saroléas, lay biding their opportunity. With any successful invasion they would have scrambled for influence, even if they were unlikely to have stayed the course.[114]

Bryant, incorrigible social climber, inveterate clubman, widely viewed as one of Britain's patriotic historians, but *au fond* a fascist sympathiser fortunate to escape internment, would soon have been in difficulties. Before the War he had tried to place his fascist contacts in important positions.[115] But the Nazis would have torn down many of the structures through which he operated.[116] A similar question mark hangs over Domvile, a great admirer of Joyce's Berlin broadcasts. He politicked alongside Skeels, Wright and others but had more channels of communication to the political establishment. He was ardently pro-Nazi and a rabid anti-Semite who thought "Mosley magnificent, Hitler a marvel."[117] But he confessed: "They are so damned intense, these Germans."[118] It is doubtful whether A.P. Laurie, an assiduous paid worker for the Nazis, would have lasted long. Nor would Captain Ramsay, who in 1940 was busy compiling "a special blacklist" of Jews to be dealt with "'when the time comes.'"[119] Saroléa, the cigar-loving, drippingly wealthy, egocentric, notoriously troublesome University of Edinburgh professor, would also have found life difficult.[120] This member of the Right Club might have been indecently eager to be a guest of honour at a *parteitag* at Nuremberg. The Nazis might have 'sweet-talked' him with "you are a true friend of ours in our struggle against Jewish insolence and bolshevic imperialism."[121] But even Domvile, ever alert for potential allies, soon tired of him.[122]

These individuals would not have been alone in offering support.[123] The prominent medievalist John Hooper Harvey, writing to Arnold Leese on 19 April 1940 remarked: "I don't want to be ruled by Germany or other foreigners but at a pinch even that is preferable to being ground to pulp under the heel of the Jewish financier and his pimps and proselytes."[124]

Mosley and his followers have staunchly defended themselves against any such collaborationist accusations.[125] Quick to condemn Joyce as a traitor, they have protested that throughout the War they remained staunch patriots. Photographs and obituary notices in *Comrade* reveal some BUF followers did sacrifice their lives for the country. But even in uniform not all changed their political spots. In 1944 when Tom Mitford, brother of Unity and Diana and a serving British army officer, met James Lees-Milne in Brooks's he affirmed he remained a Nazi sympathiser and had volunteered for Far East service because, Lees-Milne wrote, "he does not want to go to Germany killing German civilians whom he likes. He prefers to kill Japanese whom he does not like."[126] What kind of post-war world did he have in his sights? Not that it mattered. In 1945 he was killed in action in Burma. Consider, too, Robin Pinckard's letter to Quentin Joyce on 22 February 1943:

> You will note that I am now in the Army. The life is OK and I feel grand. I do not however feel enthusiastic about giving *anything* towards helping the bastard Reds and the old Jewish clique. I am afraid the news doesnt look too good from the Russian front, but we must look forward to a successful counter-offensive in the Spring. If there is a God I am sure a Russian atheistic victory would never be achieved. I think its a damn disgrace that when we are short of food that supplies should be sent to Reds. Still we must look forward to a victory for Fascism.[127]

Today's fascist sympathisers are keen to bury such sentiments.

In the event of a Nazi takeover it is highly unlikely that Robert Saunders, Dorset yeoman and staunch Mosley man, would have sought or secured any glittering prizes. But in the dying embers of 1939, after a day shooting rabbits and rooks, he wrote:

> So passes 1939 – what has 1940 in store? Much suffering & misery. . . . *But many big opportunities. That at least one can foresee.* May 1940 be a great Year for Mosley & British Union.[128]

His musings became unfulfilled dreams after the British government extended its internment policy and Germany failed to launch its expected invasion.

The key question, however, relates to Joyce and Mosley. 'The Leader' and his fan club have always insisted that Nazism, what Mosley delicately termed "the international mind," had been killed off in the BUF's 1937 purge, with Joyce as the major casualty.[129] Yet in late 1939 and early 1940 Mosley has been traced entering into contact with fellow-travelling groups to strengthen his hand in anticipation of a Nazi conquest. No absolute dividing line can be drawn between Mosley's support for Hitler's Germany and Joyce's.[130]

Such treason-leaning activity of Britain's fascists and fellow travellers has received far less publicity than the activities of "Stalin's Englishmen." A treason charge can be levelled in the absence of war but under existing legislation it is unlikely these Communist agents would have been convicted.[131] However, they are widely viewed as traitors, and a mountain of literature on them continues to accumulate.[132] Some of it is constantly recycled, full of Cold War propaganda, and often consists of crumbs operatives have cast down to carefully chosen sources. Such disclosures perpetuate the image of a treacherous political Left and build on the 1924 picture in the infamous Zinoviev Letter.[133]

Yet Britain's Nazi supporters should not be allowed slip out of sight, even if they exercised less influence than Soviet agents.[134] Joyce featured as a significant foreground figure on this canvas. When engaged in treason in Germany he never shouldered a rifle, he never defended Berlin's hastily erected barricades. His treachery came when he broadcast for the Nazis, wrote in their cause, acted for them as a recruiting sergeant, served as interpreter at the trials of British prisoners.[135] In particular, by 1940 he had become a broadcasting star.[136] His prominence was such that in 1941 he became the subject of Elliot Paul's novel on the Haw-Haw phenomenon.[137]

Totally committed to Hitler, Joyce followed a dedicated, punishing schedule in the Funkhaus.[138] He wrote his scripts and composed talks for others, and the Propaganda Ministry held his work in high esteem. But he does not feature in German wartime sources as a major figure in the Third Reich's *dramatis personae*. He never met Hitler and never shook Goebbels's hand.[139] He worked within narrow political parameters and, like Rose Cohen in Stalin's Moscow, remained determined to stay leader of the pack that had descended from Britain.[140]

Joyce, though operating in Germany, developed a much more significant presence in wartime Britain, when aiding the King's enemies and pumping the Nazi message on the radio, he attempted to terrorise his British listeners. When Rebecca West listened to him, with her evening's gin and lemon following some "high drama" with servants at Ibstone, she might have pondered a future commission.[141] When Fr Clement Russell, priest and fascist, tuned in, he could dream rosily of a future under Hitler.[142] Other people were affected more dramatically. Think of the five agonising weeks Wilfred Ashton's wife endured after Joyce claimed her husband's ship, HMS *Bellona*, had been sunk, whereas it was steaming on to Murmansk.[143] What passed through Sarah Bellamy's mind late one night in working-class Sheffield before putting her head in a gas oven after listening to one of his threatening broadcasts?[144] Joyce's apologists need to reflect long and hard on such evidence.[145] Relatives of servicemen and women were not easily reconciled to his boasting of Nazi successes, his taunts on Allied losses, his confident prediction that Britain was finished. To say no-one was required to listen is to misunderstand the atmosphere of war, the human need to know.[146] His broadcasts rankled even after the War. He certainly sank the *Ark Royal* too often and too soon.[147] But his taunt: "Where is the *Ark Royal?*" still disturbs one elderly Sheffield woman. She had a brother serving on board.[148]

Some people listened not out of anticipation, curiosity or fear, but as part of their job. BBC monitors thought Joyce possessed an excellent microphone manner, could express different emotions and had a clear gift for mimicry.[149] Radio technology had lifted his profile more than he or anyone in 1939 had thought possible. The undergraduate stage performer had discovered a new powerful outlet for his talents. The often-repeated claim that his influence on public morale in Britain was always "virtually nil" has no credibility.[150]

He was not always effective. In the BUF he often proclaimed at great length. 'Professor' Joyce's two hours' lecture and ninety minutes of questions, at Chiswick in 1934, was not unusual.[151] This tendency could be controlled on air. He had his timed slot. Other traits proved harder to remedy. While fully aware of his talents, BBC monitors remarked on his "humourless, scornful and patronising" style.[152]

He also needed, as ever, to bully audiences, dominate them, and create a sense of fear and menace.[153] This raw diet proved strikingly successful when, in exultant tones following early German military successes, he could play on Britain's vulnerabilities. But Joyce's finest hour as a radio star, a traitor-propagandist, a "Mister Radiola," soon came and went.[154]

Joyce carried other limitations to Berlin. He posed as an authority on Britain and convinced Goebbels, who knew little of the Anglo-Saxon world.[155] But did he fully understand the country where he had lived for nearly twenty years? Nikolaus Pevsner on England's churches and George Mikes on its quaint customs, reveal outsiders offering penetrating insights. But Joyce's rigidity, his blinkered vision, restricted his capacity for similar nuance and reflection. By the late '30s he had acquired a congealed view of world politics and wanted to force his opinions into the ears of others. By then he was impatient for Britain to collapse and added nothing to his ideological stock when working as a traitor in Berlin. *Twilight over England* appeared there in 1940, but much of it had already been drafted in London. He took a political creed to Naziland and with his rigid personality lacked the flexibility that wartime propaganda increasingly required.

Joyce's shortcomings – and the whole of the Nazi propaganda machine – appeared particularly as Germany was forced onto the defensive. He was spitting in the wind when attempting on instructions to detach the British from the Americans, whatever problems came with the US influx.[156] The Nazis also failed to split the Anglo-Soviet alliance. After 1941 support for the Soviets surged to undreamt-of heights in Britain.[157] The Red Flag flew over Selfridge's; the Soviet Ambassador was elected to the Athenaeum.[158] Maisky, savaged by Joyce in a pre-war lecture to the Nordic League, circulated among the clubland elite.[159] Any attempt to drive a wedge between the Soviets and their allies called for subtlety. Even then it was never likely to work. But Joyce, who had already banked years of fierce opposition to Jewish Bolshevism, would have found that approach difficult. He always wanted to wield the sledgehammer in his political life. Just as he did privately with Margaret. She must have tired of hearing: "I tell you *again*, Freja, *most insistently*."[160]

10

Joyce's story moves rapidly from high youthful ideals to disappointment, and self-destruction. He backed the losing side. He fancied himself as a prophet of history, and, as he predicted, Britain emerged weakened by the War; America's influence increased; the coalition of the Western Allies and the USSR collapsed; Soviet Communism gained enormous leverage. But his biggest bet did not come home. Britain did not become Germanised.[161] The messianic fervour which in August 1939 took him to Berlin appeared at first to have paid off. But his world soon turned sour once more. Another initiative had come to nothing. Those dramatic events between 1941 and 1943 marked the beginning of the end, and his fate was quickly sealed when the Third Reich rather than lasting a thousand years crumbled in little more than a decade.

His greatest gamble led not to a major post in a Nazified Britain, but the dock at the Old Bailey, charged with treason. How ironic that John Macnab, his closest friend and personal financier, who worshipped Joyce as a man of destiny, helped to seal his fate when on two occasions – by his indiscretion in Belgium in 1938 and by his writing the Wolkoff letter in 1940 – he tied his dearest William to the Nazi cause.[162]

But could the holder of an American birth certificate commit treason against the Crown? Legal opinion divided sharply then and now. However, in the autumn and winter of 1945 Joyce discovered how infinitely flexible English law could be. Representatives of a world he despised, desperately wanted to replace, held him responsible.[163] Appearing before Mr Justice Tucker, who had already declared him a traitor, encountering a skilled Attorney-General closely advised by Hersch Lauterpacht, having to contend with the covert manoeuvrings of MI5, as well as a strong current of popular opinion, it would have needed a miracle for him to walk free.

Across formerly occupied Europe marked inconsistencies occurred in the treatment of renegades.[164] In France Robert Brasillach's life ended with him shot and slumped against a wall at Fort Montrouge: Sacha Guitry, who had wallowed at the feet of the Nazis, was merely sanctioned.[165] Louis Darquier de Pellepoix, Vichy's Commissioner for

Jewish Affairs, was left alone to pursue a new life in Spain.[166] Coco Chanel, who allegedly spied for the Germans, was never charged with collaboration.[167]

Britain witnessed similar inconsistencies. Sustained by his undoubted courage and thoroughly unrepentant, Joyce, prisoner 3229, was sent to his death. But not before he had condemned the Jews, those malign powers of darkness. They, he declared defiantly, had manoeuvred him into his fate. In contrast, Margaret Bothamley and Dorothy Eckersley received only short prison sentences. Edward Bowlby, W. E. Percival, Lt Col Cyril Rocke and others were never brought before the courts.

11

Throughout his political career Joyce had searched above all for power. He had chased it relentlessly and was always prepared to deal, even double deal, along the way. This obsessive quest controlled and consumed him.[168] He lived his life almost entirely a political odyssey right up to the moment he met Albert Pierrepoint on a cold January morning in 1946. That consummate tradesman had his rope at the ready and, ever-anxious to give satisfaction to his employers, slipped its noose over Joyce's head, released a lever, broke his neck and left him swinging in space and darkness.

Notes

1 F. Aveling, *Personality and the Will* (London and Cambridge, 1931), p.242.
2 WJ to MJ, 29 October 1945.
3 WJ to MJ 21 December 21 September 1945 on chess. WJ to ES, 14 August 1945, on cricket.
4 Seabrook, *All the Devils are Here*, p.102, using evidence from Heather Iandolo.
5 USSC, MS 238/7/11 finds John Macnab providing a number of insights.
6 Wiener Library, microfilms, Reel 111, press cuttings collection, broadcast on Zeesen, 6 December 1942.
7 Farndale, *Haw-Haw*, p.48.
8 Wiener Library, microfilms, reel 111.
9 A. Mitchell, "Mosley, British Fascism and Religious Imagery: Fascist Hagiography and Myth-Making," in C. Binfield (ed.), *Sainthood Revisioned: Studies in Hagiography and Biography* (Sheffield, 1995), pp.107–108.

10 R. W. Jones, "I was a Blackshirt Menace," *The Spectator*, 6 August 1983, p.11.

11 KV 2/250, 14 March 1945.

12 KV 2/250, 22 April 1945.

13 Quentin Joyce Archive, letter to Quentin, 1 January 1946.

14 Wiener Library, microfilms, reel 111.

15 Rattigan, British Library, Add MS 74490, f.25

16 "The Enigma of William Joyce," pp.7–8.

17 Shirer, *20th Century Journey*, p.601.

18 Wolf Mittler in conversation with D. Blakeway, nd (private collection).

19 "The Enigma of William Joyce," p.2. James Clark, conversation with A. Weiss, 27 March 1993.

20 B. Bager, "I Broadcast for Goebbels," *Sunday Dispatch*, 28 November 1943 and also Wolf Mittler, taped conversation with D. Blakeway, nd, discusses Joyce in Germany (private collection).

21 West, *Treason*, pp.95, 72.

22 Cole, *Lord Haw-Haw*, p.55.

23 Selwyn, *Hitler's Englishman*, p.21.

24 Kenny, *Germany Calling*, p.39.

25 Farndale, *Haw-Haw*, pp.6–7.

26 A. C. Elms, *Uncovering Lives: The Uneasy Alliance of Biography and Psychology* (Oxford, 1994), pp.11–12 sounds an appropriate cautionary note on simplistic labelling.

27 Rattigan, British Library, Add MS 74490, f.25.

28 WJ to MJ, 6 November 1945.

29 Interviewed by Francis Beckett, *Guardian*, 1 December 2005.

30 Creasy Collection, W. Joyce to A. Lees, 19 November 1945, on the importance of Wagner. See, by way of comparison, N. Lyndon, "The Monstrous Mosleys," *Daily Mail*, 16 August 2003, remarking that in private the Mosleys could be agreeable companions but this image changed rapidly when the ground shifted to politics. British Library, Add MS 74490, f. 15., for Rattigan on Macnab.

31 "The Enigma of William Joyce," p.7.

32 RWC, Tulsa SC, 33:8, Rebecca West to Theobald Mathew, 18 December 1947.

33 "The Enigma of William Joyce," p.7.

34 A. Temperley, "Can I have your attention, please?" *FT Weekend Magazine*, 4/5 September 2010, p.28.

35 A. P. Morrison (ed.), *Essential Papers on Narcissism* (New York and London, 1986), p.3.

36 Mollon, *The Fragile Self*, p.77.

37 M. Brearley, "Leadership and Narcissism," lecture, Addenbroke's Hospital, Cambridge, 16 September 2010. "Ego Mania," Channel 4 TV, 5 February 2007, supported this argument.

38 T. Bower, "The Three Words that make every Tycoon," *Mail on Sunday Magazine*, 20 March 2011, pp.36–37.

39 D. Owen, *The Hubris Syndrome. Bush, Blair and the Intoxication of Power* (London, 2012).

40 Kernberg, *Borderline Conditions*, p.227. T. Millon, "Narcissism," in R. J. Corsini (ed.), *Encyclopaedia of Psychology* (New York, 1994), p.450 for related personality characteristics.

41 J. Brunner, "Pride and Memory: Nationalism, Narcissism, and the Historians' Debates in Germany and Israel," *History and Memory*, Vol.9 (1997), p.261, writing not on Joyce but narcissistic types generally. See also K. MacDonald, on Tony Blair, in *The Times*, 14 December 2009 and, generally, Owen, *Hubris*.

42 The symptoms of narcissistic personality disorder are: 1) a grandiose sense of self-importance; 2) a preoccupation with fantasies of unlimited success, power and brilliance; 3) a belief he or she is special; 4) a capacity for arrogance and haughtiness; 5) a need for excessive admiration; 6) a sense of entitlement; 7) an envy of the strong and powerful who can be perceived as gods; 8) a generally exploitative approach towards others; 9) an absence of empathy in interpersonal relationships. *Diagnostic and Statistical Manual* (Washington, DC. 2000), p.717. A new edition has recently been published (2013). "Ego Mania," Channel 4 TV, 5 February 2007. See also Vaknin, *Malignant Self Love*. *The Times*, 30 June 2005 for possible tragic consequences.

43 Anthony Seldon queried why Robert Service needed to take a psychiatrist's opinion whilst researching his biography of Leon Trotsky, "Start the Week," BBC Radio 4, 12 October 2009.

44 J. Higham, *Strangers in the Land: Patterns of Nativism in American Life, 1860–1925* (New York, 1963), p.403, considers the thought patterns of figures who shared some of Joyce's characteristics.

45 M. Boveri, *Treason in the Twentieth Century* (London, 1961), p.165.

46 Skidelsky, *Oswald Mosley*, p.343.

47 J. Betjeman, *Summoned by Bells* (London, 1976), p.4.

48 Joyce, *Dictatorship*, p.2.

49 R. Brown, *Prejudice* (Oxford, 1995), pp.31–37, emphasises social influences in the formation of anti-Semitism.

50 Kenny, *Germany Calling*, p.72, on his likely reading of the *Post*. Holmes, *Anti-Semitism*, ch.9 on Gwynne. Wilson, *History and Politics of the Morning Post*, ch.6.

51 Mudge, *Menace to the English Race*, and in *Jewry ueber alles; Jewry ueber alles or The Hidden Hand Exposed; The Hidden Hand or the Jewish Peril*.

52 A. Julius, *Trials of the Diaspora: A History of Anti-Semitism* (Oxford, 2010), pp.414–415.

53 Holmes, *Anti-Semitism*, ch.13; J. Vincent, "The case for Mosley," pp.350–351; R. Griffiths, "The Reception of Bryant's *Unfinished Victory*: Insights into British Public Opinion in early 1940", *Patterns of Prejudice*, Vol.38 (2004), p.23.

54 Voigt, *Unto Caesar*, pp.133–134.

55 *Catholic Herald*, 16 February 1940. The following issue carried a letter supporting the claim.

56 G. W. Allport, *The Nature of* Prejudice (New York, 1958, abridged version), notes this "organic" hatred (p.371). T. W. Adorno (ed.), *The Authoritarian Personality* (New York, London, 1950).

57 Allport, *Prejudice*, p.371; Young-Bruehl, *Anatomy of Prejudices*, pp.230–238; Cole, *Lord Haw-Haw*, p.302.

58 Baker, *Ideology of Obsession*, p.181.

59 Vaknin, *Malignant Self Love*, pp.118–119, for narcissistic rigidity.

60 E. Jones, "The Psychology of Quislingism," *International Journal of Psycho-Analysis*, Vol. 22 (1941), pp.1–6. A. M. Meerloo, "A Study of Treason," *British Journal of Psychology*, Vol.25 (1945), pp. 27–33 on traitors having grudges. For later studies see Pincher, *Treachery*; Pryce-Jones, *Treason of the Heart*; E. Carlton, *Treason: Meaning and Motives* (Aldershot, 1998).

61 West, *Treason*, p.46.

62 T.D.B. Kimpton (MI5) superbly summarised Joyce's position. KV 2/1513/246 a, letter, 5 March 1941.

63 Claimed in *Scotland on Sunday*, 29 May 2005.

64 KV 2/1513/246a.

65 KV 2/245/Ib, report, 21 September 1934. Vaknin, *Malignant Self Love*, p.402, on narcissistic personality traits that could lead to treachery.

66 A novelist's words in a different context. J. Hone, *The Private Sector* (New York, 1972), p.124.

67 KV 2/250, 29 March 1945.

68 James Clark in "Germany Calling," BBC Radio 4, 16 May 1991.

69 Cross, *Fascists in Britain*, pp.80–81; Thurlow, *Fascism in Britain*, pp.131, 142.

70 Dalley, *Diana Mosley*, pp.139–140, 156–157.

71 Macklin, *Deeply Dyed*, p.117, for fierce criticism of this anodyne source. See also D. Pryce-Jones, "Fascism was never chic," *The Times*, 30 September 1999, for comment on the book's naivety.

72 Mosley, *A Life of Contrasts*.

73 Mosley, *My Life*, p.311, for a passing reference. HO 283/13/63 for the beastly Joyce. Even later, Mosley was attempting to distance himself from Joyce. He suggested the "little man's" insignificance by pointedly telling a BBC researcher that he had never read Jack Cole's 1964 biography. Mosley Papers, University of Birmingham Special Collections, OMN/B/2/4, letter, 24 September 1974, to Caroleen Conquest. *Mosley's Blackshirts*, pp.23–24, 34, contains similar sentiment from Robert Saunders and John Charnley, respectively.

74 KV 2/245/1a.

75 OMN/B/7/2/8.

76 Kershaw, *Making Friends with Hitler*.

77 John Warburton, then the leading figure in the Friends of Oswald Mosley, reiterated this theme during my meetings with him.

78 Griffiths, "A Note on Mosley," pp.675–688, particularly pp.676–677,688.

79 Dorril, *Blackshirt*, writes against the earlier trend.

80 Hope, "British Fascism and the State," pp.72–83; *idem*, "Fascism and the State in Britain," pp.367–380. Andrew, *Defence of the Realm*, is unrevealing.

81 Macklin, *Deeply Dyed*, at various points.

82 HO 45/24469, meeting, I June 1947.

83 M. Beckman, *The 43 Group* (London, 1992), p.76. *On Guard*, 1 July 1947 provides more evidence on Joyce's reputation being used against post-war fascists.

84 Mosley, *My Life*, pp.336–337.

85 *The Times*, 21, 24, 25, 26, 28, 29, 30, 31 October 1968 and 1, 4, 5, 7 November 1968.

86 Mandle, *Anti-Semitism and the British Union of Fascists*, exposes Mosley's anti-Semitism.

87 *Mosley's Blackshirts*, p.38.

88 *Jewish Chronicle*, 18 December 1936.

89 Holmes, *Anti-Semitism*, p.180. R. Thurlow, "The Black Knight: Reactions to a Mosley Biography," *Patterns of Prejudice*, Vol.9 (1975), p. 17.

90 Holmes, *Anti-Semitism*; Linehan, *East London for Mosley*.

91 R. R. Bellamy, "We marched with Mosley," pp.677 and 707–713, especially p.712, USSC, unpublished ts. For Hore-Belisha's problems at the hands of anti-Semites, see A. J. Trythall, "The Downfall of Leslie Hore-Belisha," *Journal of Contemporary History*, Vol.16 (1981), pp.391–411. Perhaps Bellamy's hostility was fired by an awareness that Hore-Belisha had allegedly provided funds for the BUF before thinking the better of it. KV 2/880/129a on Hore-Belisha's alleged support.

92 It has already been noticed that the responses among the general public in Britain were not always straightforward. See Kushner, *The Holocaust and the Liberal Imagination*. W. I. Hitchcock, *Liberation: The Bitter Road to Freedom. Europe 1944–1945* (London, 2008), pp. 289–295 and 339–365 on the liberation of Belsen and Auschwitz, respectively. For anniversary comment on the former see *The Times*, 16 April 2005, "When Belsen was Liberated the Holocaust hit Home in Britain."

93 A. Lindemann, *Esau's Tears* (Cambridge, 1997) notes the ambiguity present in some anti- Semitism.

94 Pryce-Jones, *Unity Mitford*, p.77.

95 Holmes, *Anti-Semitism*, pp.39–42.

96 *Bath Chronicle and Herald*, 4 April 1935.

97 *Jewish Chronicle*, 18 December 1936.

98 *Lord Beaconsfield: A Sketch* (London, 1882?), p.4.

99 Holmes, *Anti-Semitism*, ch.9.

100 Joyce, *Fascism and Jewry*, p.8.

101 DPP 2/407, report, 9 October 1936.

102 *Jewish Chronicle*, 18 December 1936 and his *Fascism and Jewry*, p.8.

103 Joyce, *Twilight over England*, p.70.

104 Imagery from KV 2/245/340b, report of Joyce's broadcast, 28 August 1944. Holmes, *Anti-Semitism*, at several points, for exterminatory sentiment in Britain.

105 KV 2/250, 7 March 1945.

106 Julius, *Diaspora*, p.51.

107 A. Lynch, *My Life Story* (London, 1934); Matthew and Harrison (eds), *ODNB*, Vol.34, pp.873–875. *Rex v Lynch* (London, 1903?) for his trial and du Cann, *English Treason Trials*, pp.233, 235, 243, 263.

108 Older sources include Sullivan, *The Last Sergeant* pp.264–274. See also Weale, *Patriot Traitors*, part 1; R. MacColl, *Roger Casement: A New Judgment* (London, 1956); R. Sawyer, *Casement: The Flawed Hero* (London, 1984). See also M.V. Llosa, *The Dream of the Celt* (London, 2012).

109 J. Bulloch, *MI5* (London, 1963), pp.173–174, discusses cases involving Armstrong, Kay, Scott Ford and Job.

110 KV2/423, MI5 report, 14 November 1945, on Hilton's activities.

111 KV 2/2474. Advisory Committee hearing, 29 July 1940.

112 KV2/3800 offers detail. The agent has been named only recently as Eric Roberts. See *The Times*, 24 October 2014.

113 Langdon-Davies, *Fifth Column*. Thurlow, "The Evolution of the Mythical British Fifth Column," pp.477–498.

114 Griffiths, *Patriotism Perverted*. See also his "The Reception of 'Unfinished Victory,'" pp.18–36.

115 File C 66, Bryant Archive, King's College, London, for a letter from Lord Halifax, 5 April 1939, indicating Bryant's attempt to place Billy Luttman-Johnson in government work. A letter from the same minister on 14 June 1939 reveals Bryant trying something similar for Francis Yeats Brown.

116 Roberts, *Eminent Churchillians* (1994 ed.), pp.287–322.

117 KV 2/835/60a.

118 DOM 55, Domvile diary, 6 February 1938.

119 *Daily Telegraph*, 8 August 1939 on Laurie being paid by the Nazis. KV 2/840, report, 21 February 1940, on Ramsay's list.

120 Johnson, "'A good European and a sincere racist.'"

121 University of Edinburgh, Saroléa Collection, File 84, Uetrecht, Hauptarchiv to Saroléa, 17 January 1939. Spelling as in original. This character sketch derives from Domvile's diary and Saroléa's correspondence (File 85) of his papers.

122 DOM 56, Domvile diary, 3 August 1939.

123 HO 45/25568–72, on potential collaborators.

124 HO 45/25571. G. Macklin, "The two lives of John Hooper Harvey," *Patterns of Prejudice*, Vol.42 (2008), pp.167–190.

125 O. Mosley, *My Answer* (Ramsbury, 1946), pp.11–12, set the agenda. See therefore *Action*, 13 June 1958, "The Facts about William Joyce."

126 Lees-Milne, *Prophesying Peace*, p.131, diary, 22 August 1944, 12 November 1944. *Comrade*, No.57 (2004), p.12, gives a simpler portrait.

127 HO 283/43/7. Spelling as in the original. *Daily Worker*, 22 February 1944, reported that Pinckard faced a charge of interfering with the telecommunications network in Britain. "I have a big perpetual grievance against this country," the account quoted him as saying. After the War his case was taken up by the Freedom Defence Committee: *Bulletin*, No.2 (1946), p.2, *ibid.* No.3 (1946), p.3, and *ibid.* No.4 (1946), p.6.

128 USSC, MS 119/F5. Saunders, diary, 31 December 1939. My italics.

129 HO 283/13/61.This defence appeared much earlier in *Action*, 6 June 1940.

130 HO 283/13/61–65 on the Joyce–Mosley conflict. H. Dalton, *The Fateful Years. Memoirs 1931–1945* (London, 1957), p.336, recalled Churchill saying in 1940 that a Nazi takeover of Britain would result in the country being ruled by "Mosley or some such person." J.F.C. Fuller's name also circulated. The latter's biographer has claimed it was "inherently improbable that so distinguished a solder would have given aid and comfort to the enemies of his country." Trythall, *'Boney' Fuller*, p.217. But see HO 45/25568 for Fuller coveting a position similar to Pétain's. Lloyd George was reckoned another candidate. A. P. Laurie engaged in a long correspondence to convince him of German aims. Correspondence, Lloyd George papers, House of Lords Library, LG11/6/1. On Lloyd George in Hitler's work, see A. Hitler, *Mein Kampf* [in weekly parts], (London, nd), p.412. Hattersley, *The Great Outsider*, pp.623–627, on the Welsh Wizard's pre-war contact with Hitler. In the Wolkoff letter, Field Marshal Ironside's name had entered the frame.

131 V. MacCallum, "Warning Shot, *"Law Society Gazette*, 98/45, 22 November 2001, p.19: Edward Garnier QC in the *Daily Telegraph*, 2 November 2001; Lyon, "From Dafydd ap Gruffyd to Lord Haw-Haw," p.36.

132 See the later editions of Rebecca West's, *The Meaning of Treason* as well as Carter, *Blunt, Andrew, Defence of the Realm* and Pincher, *Treachery*. See also A. Boyle, *The Climate of Treason* (London, 1979); R. Cecil, *A Divided Life: A Biography of Donald Maclean* (London, 1988); J. Costello, *Mask of Treachery* (London, 1988); P. Knightley, *Philby: The Life and Times of the KGB Masterspy* (London, 1988); N. West and O. Tsarev, *The Crown Jewels* (London, 1998); M. Y. Modin, *My Five Cambridge Friends* (London, 2001). "I spied for Stalin at War Office, publisher confessed," *The Times*, 30 October 2004 on James MacGibbon. On John Cairncross see his *The Enigma Spy. The Story of the Man who changed the course of World War Two* (London, 1997) and *Scotland on Sunday*, 17 April 2005. On Scott (Arthur Wynn), see *The Times*, 13, 14 May 2009. C. Pincher, *Dangerous to Know* (London, 2014) revisits earlier work. There is also now B. Macintyre, *A Spy among Friends* (London, 2014), on Philby.

133 Bennett, *'A most extraordinary and mysterious business,'* on the Zinoviev affair. N. West, *Venona: The Greatest Soviet of the Cold War* (London, 1999), pp.14–16.

134 V. G. Kiernan, "On Treason," in his *Poets, Politics and the People*, ed. H. J. Kaye (London, 1989), pp.193–203. First published in *London Review of Books*, 25 June 1987, p.3.

135 *Manchester Guardian*, 30 April 1945, on Joyce as interpreter.

136 *Life*, 22 April 1940, pp.39, 42.

137 Rutledge, *Death of Lord Haw-Haw*.

138 Vaknin, *Malignant Self Love*, pp.118–119, on narcissism and obsessive routine.

139 KV 2/250, 24 March 1945.

140 Beckett, *Stalin's British Victims*, p.25.

141 Rollyson, *Rebecca West*, p.173, discusses the West household. West, *Treason* (2000), p.3, on her drink of an evening.

142 Hamm, *Action Replay*, p.154.

143 Private information.

144 *The Star*, 17 January 1940.

145 Kenny, *Germany Calling*, pp.243–244, plays down his wartime treason.

146 *Ibid.* p.243, claiming no-one had to listen.

147 *Manchester Guardian*, 14 August 1942. C. Graves, *Londoner's Life* (London, 1942), p.38.

148 Private testimony.

149 O. Renier and V. Rubinstein, *Assigned to Listen: The Evesham Experience 1930–43* (London, 1986), p.67.

150 F. H. Loxley to N. Acheson. 19 May 1991 and other correspondence attempts to argue against Joyce's effectiveness (private archive).

151 *Brentford Times*, 23 March 1934.

152 Renier and Rubinstein, *Assigned to Listen*, p.67. James Clark noticed something similar. James Clark in discussion with A. Weiss, 27 March 1995 (private archive).

153 In "The Enigma of William Joyce." A. K. Chesterton also noticed such drawbacks.

154 D. Britton, *Baptised in the Blood of Millions* (Manchester, 2000) p.40.

155 Bramsted, *Goebbels*, p.403. von Oven, *Mit Goebbels bis zum Ende*, Vol.1, p.182.

156 Ziegler, *London at War*, pp.215–222. Hylton, Darkest Hour, pp.30–35, Gardiner, *Wartime*, pp.468–484. Calder, *The People's War*, pp.308–311 provided earlier comment on the Americans, and see E. Smithies, *Crime in Wartime: A Social History of Crime in World War II* (London, 1982).

157 F. D. Klingender, *Russia – Britain's Ally 1812–1942* (London, 1942). P. Jordan, *Russian Glory* (London, 1942).

158 Ziegler, *London at War*, ch.9, pp.223 ff.

159 G. Bilainkin, *Maisky. Ten Years Ambassador* (London, 1944), chs 12–13; *Memoirs of a Soviet Ambassador* (London, 1967) for Maisky's reflections.

160 WJ to MJ, 29 December 1945. My emphases.

161 G. Orwell, *Inside the Whale and other Essays* (Harmondsworth, 1966), p.90. In "England your England," written in 1941, he predicted that those who wanted England "Russianized" or "Germanized" would be disappointed.

162 *Evening News*, 3 January 1946, for Macnab on Joyce as a man of destiny.

163 Ludovic Kennedy, "Lord Haw-Haw," BBC1, TV, 29 December 1975, for critical comment.

164 Judt, *Postwar*, ch. 2, brilliantly summarises the atmosphere. I. Deák, J. Gross, T. Judt, *The Politics of Retribution in Europe* (Princeton, 2000). K. Lowe, *Savage Continent. Europe in the Aftermath of World War II* (London, 2012). Joyce took a keen interest in European renegades; WJ to MJ,

12 September 1945 (Ferdonnet), 16 October 1945 (Laval), 19 December 1945 (Mussert), 18 July, 16 and 24 October 1945 (Quisling).

165 A.Y. Kaplan, *The Collaborator. The Trial and Execution of Robert Brasillach* (Chicago, 2000). H. R. Lottman, *The Purge* (New York, 1986), espec. p.260 on Guitry.

166 C. Callil, *Bad Faith. A Forgotten History of Faith and Fatherland* (London, 2006).

167 H.Vaughan, *Sleeping with the Enemy: Coco Chanel, Nazi Agent* (London, 2011); *The Times*, 2 December 2014 and *Daily Mirror*, 3 December 2014.

168 In KV 2/245/1b. Maxwell Knight correctly described the young Joyce as a "politico."

PART VII

Epilogue

24

'LIFE' AFTER DEATH

It seemed part of some larger pattern, accidents forming themselves into a dance of association. Fathers and daughters, fathers and sons, infidelities, the illusions we sometimes call memory. Past errors harped on, or made good by spurious confession. Bodies littered down the years, mostly forgotten except by the perpetrators. History turning sour, or fading away like old photographs. Endings . . . no rhyme or reason to them. They just happened. You died, or disappeared, or were forgotten. You became nothing more than a name on the back of an old photo, and sometimes not even that. [Ian Rankin, *Black and Blue* (London, 1998), p.461.]

1

Before his execution Joyce had brooded constantly in Wandsworth and found it difficult to accept he might become forgotten, a seed dispersed by the unruly winds of time. He need hardly have fretted. Many renegade contemporaries were to sink quickly, decisively, into historical obscurity. But he has remained alive in the collective memory of the British public.[1]

Today some loyalties are less clear-cut.[2] However, among the older generation Joyce's memory can still trigger strong feelings. A magazine feature in 1996 which contrasted his actions with the exploits of a wartime VC was intended to 'speak' volumes.[3] And a proposal the following year by Oldham Council to erect a plaque on a Brompton Street house where he had lived in the 1920s was greeted with outrage. One secretary of an ex-servicemen's association protested: "It is an affront to everyone who served in the Second World War." Another threatened: "It would be torn down in minutes."[4] The Council wisely retreated.[5] Today no plaques recall Joyce's time in Britain. After all, *The Sun* trumpeted a few years later, Joyce was hated in Britain.[6]

Yet there is a paradox. In sketches and biographies this committed fascist, this vicious anti-Semite, this unrepentant traitor, has increasingly been portrayed in a much softer light. Rebecca West was severely critical of Joyce, but later writers – A. K. Chesterton, J. A. Cole, Francis Selwyn, Mary Kenny and Nigel Farndale – have been more forgiving. His image has been sanitised. Several years ago an author casting a critical eye over the manufactured portrait of Oswald Mosley remarked, "some stories are repeated so often that they eventually become accepted as undisputed facts."[7] A reader of Joyce biographies should be equally wary. After offering a new challenging version of Joyce's life, a number of questions remain: why have these more restrained portraits emerged and what blanks and errors do they contain?

2

By the early twentieth century Rebecca West had gained a reputation as a novelist. In 1941 she had also written *Black Lamb and Grey Falcon*, a widely acclaimed book on Yugoslavia. Soon afterwards, when attending the Nuremberg hearings, she had become deeply interested in the fate of Nazi war criminals. Joyce also captured her attention at this time, and in September 1945 West wrote on his trial for the *New Yorker*.[8] In 1947 an essay by her on treachery appeared in *Harper's Magazine*.[9] That same year her soon-to-become classic study, *The Meaning of Treason*, came out in the United States.[10] Published in Britain in 1949, it focused on Joyce. But it also discussed that motley crew of renegade broadcasters and tattered remnants of the British Free Corps who shuffled through the English courts at the War's end. It was well received.[11] Subsequent editions, incorporating detail on later traitors, have attracted similar praise.[12]

Since her death in 1983 West's standing has barely dimmed. Bernard Levin wrote: "None of her novels is wholly successful as a work of art," before adding "Her reportage is of an altogether different quality; at its best it has few equals in all journalism."[13] Biographies appearing later have marked a further step towards her literary canonisation.[14]

West argued that the state protected its citizens and in return required their allegiance. Here, unspoken, was "a beautiful contract."[15]

> The children who go from their homes with strangers because they have been given cakes and sweets are unsustained by pride when the unkindness falls on them. They know well that they have done wrong. A person should be loyal to his father and mother, to his brothers and sisters, to his friends, to his town or village, to his province, to his country; and a person should do nothing for a bribe, even if it takes the form of a promise that he should live instead of die.[16]

Yet fascism's international focus inclined its followers towards betrayal.[17] She believed increasingly the same could be said of Communism.[18]

She also pronounced, "All men should have a drop of treason in their veins if the nations are not to go soft like so many sleepy pears."[19] Society needed to be constantly challenged, invigorated. But betraying one's country trespassed beyond that boundary. Those venturing into that dangerous, forbidden territory placed themselves under enormous pressures. "It is the essence of treachery," she emphasised, "that those who commit it would still be severely punished if the law forgot its duty to provide deterrents to crime and did not lay a finger on them."[20] With Joyce the state demanded and secured the ultimate sacrifice, and West challenged those observers who hesitated to support this verdict.[21]

The Meaning of Treason rested on impressive foundations. West "had not only reported the trials, she had worked like a biographer and historian, reading government records and interviewing members of the traitors' families and their friends."[22] She had trawled widely, sometimes in privileged waters. Theobald Mathew, a friend and one-time family solicitor, then serving as Director of Public Prosecutions, provided detail few if any other writers would have secured.[23] Biographies of West remain silent on the matter, but she reciprocated by turning state informant, sending him information on individuals she considered Soviet agents, and requesting he transmit her intelligence to MI5.[24] She also enjoyed a particularly close relationship with Hartley Shawcross.[25]

The various editions of *The Meaning of Treason* contain factual inaccuracies.[26] Joyce's' family home was not burned down by Irish nationalists.[27] He did not leave for Germany during the War yet West allowed for this possibility.[28] Mr Head showed no reluctance to accept the defence brief.[29] Joyce was never reconciled to his Roman faith.[30] She suggested, wrongly, he might not have been fully au fait with his family's American links, until informed by lawyers just before his trial.[31] His father was obsessively secretive on this point. But close friends knew of the American card ready and waiting up Joyce's sleeve, which he expected would see him safe whatever the outcome of the War. John Macnab picked off many such errors in the first edition with a mixture of relish and despair.[32]

The book also echoed with silences. Ireland hardly featured. It took virtually sixty years for that gap to be filled. Joyce's formative fascist career in Britain was never fully explored. Nor was his rampant anti-Semitism. The complexity of the Haw-Haw phenomenon was nowhere to be found: that matter was not settled until nearly twenty years later. By circulating among the crowd outside Wandsworth prison West captured some sense of that post-war mood so crucial in understanding how Joyce was treated, but files in the National Archives now provide a much fuller picture.

Her work is clearly no sacred text, free from error or blemish. But she was not interested in fine detail. For historians accuracy is a duty rather than a virtue. But she was writing neither history nor an outline biography. Her indulgence in character sketches suggests she was composing a morality tract.

Hartley Shawcross, Mr Attorney, so "young for the post," was "charming in manner and voice."[33] At the Lords appeal she admired Earl Jowitt as "one of the handsomest men in London, superb in his white full-bottomed wig, its curls lying in rows on his shoulders."[34] Authority appeared magnificent, resplendent. Joyce, by contrast, was "a tiny little creature and, though not very ugly, was exhaustively so."[35] His supporters in court were treated similarly. They were physically ugly people supporting an ugly cause. "There were some women who especially attracted attention by an almost unearthly physical repulsiveness, notably an ageing and floozy blond in a tight Air Force uniform, who sucked sweets and wept as she swung an ankle creased with fat from crossed knees that pressed up against her drooping bosom."[36] John Macnab she portrayed as "a thin man with fierce black eyes blazing behind thick glasses, a tiny fuzz of black hair fancifully arranged on his prematurely bald head, and wrists and ankles as straight as lead piping in their emaciation." He might have been "a spiritualist medium or a believer in the lost ten tribes of Israel."[37] But no-one could take him seriously, could they? Frank Holland, defence witness and friend of Joyce's father, appeared as "an old gentleman, white-haired and shrivelled and deaf and palsied and quavering."[38] What possible weight could attach to his testimony? By their appearances ye shall know them. Character and worth were being suggested by physical presence, as in an Eisenstein film. *The Meaning of Treason* presented a battle between beauty and ugliness, good and evil. The nation's guardians appeared on one side; the traitor and his sympathisers on the other. West, like Joyce, clung to a Manichean view of the world.

In this twentieth-century morality tale Joyce suffered from West's crushing condescension.[39] He had been successful at university. Yet with "brazen snobbery" she wrote:

> He could never by any chance have been invited to join the staff of any school or college of conventional academic prestige, for in spite of all his studies there clung to everything he did or said a curious atmosphere of illiteracy. Only uneducated people accepted easily that he was learned: educated people were always astonished to hear that he had been at a University.[40]

While being condescending, West could partly identify with him. He served as a reminder of "her own sense of rejection."[41] She, too, had grown up as a family darling, rebelled and paid a heavy price.[42] Even so, she simply could not resist pouring a bucket of ethnic hostility over him. He had "the real Donnybrook air," she wrote, "He was a not very fortunate example of the small, nippy, jig-dancing type of Irish peasant."[43] In many ways Joyce was a thoroughly unpleasant character – a bully, a double-dealer, a plotter, a schemer. In his need to dominate an audience, pronounce on everybody and everything he could quickly become exceedingly tiresome.[44] But in mocking him as an illiterate Irish peasant West reveals more about herself than about Joyce.

Her book has been labelled "idiosyncratic" as well as "solipsistic and overwrought."[45] Not to say "legally illiterate."[46] Yet it impressed many contemporaries and a devoted fan club still exists. But even with later editions *The Meaning of Treason* is not definitive.[47] Errors, gaps, speculative fancies, remained.[48]

3

Dead in Wandsworth's grounds, Joyce could not respond. But Margaret, his appointed biographer, was alive. She had sighed with relief when detained by British troops but would not have done if knowing that MI5, Jim Skardon particularly, wanted her in court.[49] She might have been in serious trouble. Yet she escaped lightly.

Her case proved complicated. If Joyce were American, did she lose British nationality when they married in 1937? After he became a naturalised German in 1940 did she have that same status? The best minds in the Home Office and the DPP wrestled with these nice legal problems. They concluded she had not ceased to be British on marriage. However, following Joyce's naturalisation in Berlin she, too, had become a German citizen.[50]

Against this complex background any prosecution faced problems. Under the 1925 Criminal Justice Act she could claim that when leaving for Germany and working there, she had been acting under the influence of her husband. Joyce had admitted as much to Skardon. Here was an early case of marital coercion.[51] There was another issue. She had first broadcast in late 1939 but the earliest recordings dated from November 1940, by which time she was German. It will be recalled she was not introduced as Margaret Joyce on Nazi radio until December 1942.[52]

Brought from Belgium to Holloway prison in November 1945, Margaret never appeared in court. The British authorities suggested she had been spared on compassionate grounds but the decision clearly had more tangled roots.[53]

'Margaret Schmidt' was removed from London to Brussels on 5 January 1946.[54] Complaining bitterly, she was despatched to Germany on 20 March.[55] She knew hardly anyone there and, long exposed to Joyce's searing anti-Bolshevism, was fearful of ever falling into Soviet hands.[56] She would have preferred to settle in Éire but the Home Office objected.[57] It relished even less her presence in Britain and was able to prevent it.[58] Her transfer to Germany occurred against this background. The Foreign Office often wanted her moved.[59] However, the Home Office remained implacably opposed to her return.[60] Yet it acknowledged that when the British Nationality Act became law in 1948 she would enjoy a legal right to re-enter the country, unless by then she had specifically renounced her British citizenship.[61] She returned to Britain in 1955. Seven years later in Casablanca she married Donald May, an accountant, alcoholic and convicted fraudster, whom she had met in a bar in Germany.[62] They lived later at 29 Dunraven Road, Shepherd's Bush. Margaret, a chronic alcoholic, died in Hammersmith from cirrhosis of the liver on 19 February 1972.[63]

Wherever she went, whatever she did, she carried that wearisome legacy Joyce had laid upon her in their increasingly urgent prison correspondence. My memory must not fade. My significance must be recognised. My insights must never be lost. Margaret possessed some first-hand knowledge of Joyce's life and, as will soon become clear, knew how to protect her dead man's reputation. But writing the book of his life was a different matter entirely. Her brief pencilled scrawlings on a packet of Kastellas reveal how ill-equipped she was for that task.[64]

Her dead husband's surviving family, friends, and former political comrades, also yearned for a critique of West. In rather uncertain poetry, one of them wrote:

> No traitors—men unprofitably bold!
> Far nobler too, who lies encased in lime's
> Acid sincere, than those who great through gold

> Die in their dotage flattered by the "Times"
> And it were no great matter to decide
> Which better, the condemner or the crucified?[65]

But who might produce such a biography? John Beckett had part-nered Joyce in the BUF and the National Socialist League. They had split forces before the War. However, he continued in some ways to admire his old comrade. Beckett was also an experienced journalist. But after the War, scrambling to survive on life's precipice, always searching for the next shilling, he made no attempt to write. Not that the dead man's surviving inner circle would have wanted it. Fierce loyalty remained their order of the day and Beckett's pre-war renun-ciation of the National Socialist League would not have been for-gotten. Other fascists, faithful to Mosley, would have retained some knowledge of Joyce's life but, keen to distance themselves from his memory, they were unlikely ever to step forward.[66] Nor would they have been welcomed. Joyce's small surviving circle avoided any close contact with them.[67] Fascism's fratricidal streak persisted. Old battles, political differences, rumbled on.

John Macnab remained desperately anxious to massage his friend's memory and on the day of the execution Beckett had urged him to write a biography, remarking, "You knew him so well for a lengthy period and have access to and contact with all the necessary people and documents."[68] Later, in Franco's Spain, still under close security surveillance by the British, Macnab busied himself with writing – he even wrote an ode in praise of Hermann Göring – and broadcast-ing on Radio Nacional.[69] During this time he and Margaret kept in touch and through her he would have become familiar with a par-ticular version of Joyce's life in Nazi Germany. Moreover, by 1957 he had established contact with at least one leading London publishing house.[70] Yet he never wrote that biography. Perhaps he would have found it a painful task, if only because of his central involvement in the 1940 Wolkoff business which helped to guarantee Joyce's execu-tion. The search continued.

A. K. Chesterton, decorated soldier, fascist, journalist and theatre critic, eventually accepted the challenge.[71] In 1936 he had written an adulatory portrait of Mosley.[72] However, on leaving the BUF, he had savaged 'The Leader' and his fawning worshippers in a pamphlet published in 1938 by the National Socialist League.[73] This breach between Chesterton and Mosley was never repaired.[74] Fully aware of the conflict, Joyce remarked significantly in November 1945, "of course, his sympathy is entirely with us."[75] Thereby conveniently forgetting that in the early 1930s he had attempted to have Chesterton classified insane.[76] As early as December 1946, before *The Meaning of Treason* had appeared, Chesterton was promising – probably prompted by Quentin Joyce – he would soon "get cracking" on a biography.[77] But he obviously shelved the idea. Sections of the British press had already associated him with Joyce, implying he had similar treasonous tendencies, and writing a biography might have further fuelled such comment.[78]

Nothing appeared for another seven years. By then some of the vindictive fury generated by the War had faded and, also importantly, Chesterton had gained a number of useful Fleet Street contacts. Between 1944 and 1953 he had served as deputy editor and chief leader writer on *Truth*. He had also gained entrée to the Beaverbrook press, writing for the *Daily Express* and the *Sunday Express* and spent nine months in 1953 as the 'Beaver's' personal journalist, ghosting *Don't Trust to Luck*, which came out in 1954.[79] He now had a platform.

Chesterton fired his salvo in the *Sunday Express* in the summer of 1953.[80] His timing was excellent. A new edition of *The Meaning of Treason* had appeared in 1952. In his calculated counter-attack he introduced arguments and details from Margaret and Macnab which, until now, have seeped uncritically into all subsequent biographies.

He emphasised that as an American Joyce had never owed any allegiance to the Crown, even though holding a British passport. His execution had turned on a legal technicality. West had supported the hanging. Chesterton presented it as an illegal killing.

Influenced by Macnab's suspect claim that Joyce was interested in immediate naturalisation should he leave for Berlin, Chesterton stressed how badly he had been let down by Christian Bauer.

He suggested finally that Margaret and Joyce had desperately wanted to return to England before the War began, but were denied by the lowering circumstances of early September 1939. Here is the origin of that often painted picture of two young people at the mercy of fate, tragic victims of circumstance.[81]

As an alleged believer in the "absolute values of the nation state," Chesterton claimed to have rejected a Nazi invitation to engage in propaganda work.[82] But he had just defended Joyce, whose fascism was based on racist internationalism, in a way that underlined how deeply the dead man's closest allies had been stung by West's portrait.

He pulled his punches in this hack enterprise. "It was understood," Macnab wrote later to Alf Flockhart, "Mr Chesterton would not say – and I am sure he did not wish to say – anything that would hurt [Joyce's relatives and friends]."[83] Later writers have been insufficiently alert to his bias and special pleading.

However, any quiet satisfaction in the Joyce camp was tinged with disappointment. Chesterton had intended a fuller study but the *Sunday Express* spiked his proposal.[84] That sympathetic biography, thoughts of which had helped to sustain Joyce in the condemned cell, had still failed to appear. Rebecca West's glittering literary reputation virtually guaranteed her smooth access to a publisher. It was proving difficult for anyone associated with British fascism to put out a counterblast.[85]

4

Margaret, incapable of writing a biography, turned to someone else to salvage what her dead husband had desperately craved. She and John Alfred Cole had met in Sennelager Camp. He was serving there as Chief Interrogator in what Arnold Leese called "this Ruhr concentration camp."[86] Margaret had been despatched to Sennelager on her return to Germany.

Jack Cole's association with Faber and Faber began in 1935 with *Come Dungeon Dark*. After the publication of *My Host Michael*, just over twenty years later, he suggested his next project might involve a novel set in the GDR. But he floated another idea, which Alan Pringle, a legendary Faber editor, described as follows:

A book about Lord Haw-Haw based on his unpublished letters and on unpublished material to be supplied to J. A. Cole by

Mrs Joyce (The story behind this).The curious world of British renegades in Berlin, of which J.A. Cole has first hand experience, having arrested one.The author to be Mrs Joyce but the writing to be done by J.A. Cole. Serialisation possibilities. But would it be better if the author were J.A. Cole?[87]

Pringle was unsure about a market for the book and worried over Margaret Joyce's involvement. "It would be much better if the book were not only written by you but had your name on it as the author," he emphasised, and it had to be an "objective" and "critical" work rather than "some kind of apologia." He agreed with Cole's suggestion that in addition to Joyce it should discuss "that curious world of British renegades in Berlin."[88]

Against this background the biography started to take shape and in 1959, with work now under way, Cole wrote to Pringle:

I could not, of course, produce the book at all without Mrs J's good will. Apart from that, she is supplying material about their personal life in Germany (but not about [Joyce's] work, on which she is not very well informed), some introductions and some illustrations. She can have nothing to do with a considerable part of the book, which will have to cover the Fascist movement here, the operation of German wartime broadcasting, the broadcasts themselves, the public reaction to [Joyce], the trial and the implications of the case. All the writing and possibly three quarters of the material gathering will fall to me.[89]

He requested seventy-five per cent of all book royalties and all other English language rights. At this stage nothing was clear-cut. He would be seeing his chief source soon and told Pringle, "She will very probably have ideas of her own about terms, so we may well have to amend our proposals."[90] But Cole had a strong hand and Margaret knew it. When the parties signed their contracts in the summer of 1959, he had become the sole author.[91]

A drink-soddened Margaret – who renounced all interests in September 1971 – was probably relieved to be shot of the weighty biographical albatross Joyce had thrust upon her.[92] And she must have been pleased that her prints, favourable to his memory, lay all over the manuscript.

Cole submitted his typescript in 1964. When Pringle read it he immediately became enthusiastic: "everybody here . . . is so keen on it that we want a blurb which will treat it as a book of general importance, as we mean to do ourselves."[93] What had produced this buzz of excitement?

Morley Kennerley, a Faber director, provides the answer. He wrote: "People in this country will be speechless with amazement when they learn that Joyce was not Lord Haw-Haw." The recently received typescript emphasised for the first time that the Nazis had employed a number of broadcasters who fitted the Haw-Haw stereotype. Kennerley continued: "Hardly anything written about Joyce before has been correct, and this really applies to what Rebecca West has written about him."[94] This evident sense of excitement also reflected something else. Margaret had granted Cole access to her husband's prison letters. Rebecca West had not seen this evidence. "The letters are very valuable indeed," Kennerley emphasised, "and it is imperative that they do not get into the press at this time, for this would greatly lessen the impact of the book when it is published."[95] A word of caution here. Unknown to Faber, Cole was permitted only a restricted access to this material. He worked from a sample Margaret had carefully selected and censored.[96] Some items which reflected badly on her dead husband did slip through her net but to the best of Margaret's ability she was attempting to protect Joyce's reputation.

The typescript came without a title. But author and publisher settled on *Lord Haw-Haw – and William Joyce. The Full Story*.[97] By now believing in the book, Faber attempted its serialisation, paying little attention to the author's reluctance to feature in "the posh papers."[98] The *Sunday Telegraph* declined the offer.[99] As did the *Sunday Times*.[100] The *Evening Standard* could not be persuaded.[101] The *News of the World* followed suit.[102] However, the *Sunday Express* paid £1000 for the delivery of four articles.[103] With attendant publicity on radio and television the biography appeared in 1964.[104]

The *Sunday Telegraph* called it "brilliant."[105] *The Guardian* and *The Times* liked it.[106] *The Times Literary Supplement* found it "singularly fascinating reading."[107] Respecting Cole's wishes, the publishers tried to ensure Rebecca West was denied a review copy.[108] Nevertheless, the book did face some criticism. Cole was especially stung by Philip Toynbee's remark in *The Observer* that he was "surprisingly naïve in his understanding of politics."[109] However, Faber could exploit Toynbee's more favourable comments and Cole must have felt generally comfortable with his notices. His earlier literary efforts had led to him being described as "a lightweight but respectable amateur author."[110] He had now achieved much greater recognition. Surrounded by Joyce *curiosa* he saw himself as the big hunter who had tracked down his man.[111] Enjoying his new – found status, he remained ever – vigilant against any unauthorised use of his material.[112] Rebecca West's presence loomed large here and in 1965 he contacted Faber on the blurb to Penguin's new edition of *The Meaning of Treason*. He believed it contained a major inaccuracy regarding his own book.[113]

Cole died in 1990. The appearance of a paperback edition of his book three years earlier testified to the continuing fascination of the saga he had spun. Margaret and Macnab's involvement mentioned in the first edition had disappeared from view.

Lord Haw-Haw focused largely on the Joyces' personal life. Misspelling Cole's name, Rebecca West remarked haughtily it even proved useful on this account.[114] But only in passing did it notice Joyce's "ego-inflating" tendencies.[115] And, while recognising he was high risk as a husband, his persistent wife-beating stayed well hidden.[116] With Margaret loyal to her dead husband's memory, and the ever-faithful Macnab hovering in the background, Will's portrait had to be painted without exposing too many cracks and faults.

Joyce's Irish background hardly featured in the book. A short jig with "The Merry Joyces" said it all.[117] And Joyce's fascist politics in Britain were soon passed over. Reflecting Cole's interest in Germany, he was clearly impatient to have his subject in wartime Berlin. Even though, contrary to what he had proposed – and Faber advised – those renegades working there alongside Joyce remained invisible. Thereafter, the narrative drew heavily on the prison letters. In no sense therefore does it give "the full story" of Joyce's life, nor indeed is it "a fine primary source."[118] Cole played to his strengths. The letters were his scoop. He knew very well they would set his work apart from Rebecca West's.

Leave these silences and noticeable gaps. Did he further contribute to that revised image of Joyce which first surfaced with Chesterton in the *Sunday Express*? If so, how and why?

Philip Toynbee's remark that political naivety affected Cole's treatment of British fascism needs to be revisited here. Cole's anodyne approach reflected something else. The BUF had expressed an interest in his earlier work. Joyce himself can be found praising *Come Dungeon Dark* in the 1935 *Fascist Quarterly* as a work "of psychological skill and literary humour" that dwelt "on every page" with "the inner recesses of the social-democratic pseudo-intellectual mind."[119] Three years later the author's next book, *Just back from Germany*, was also favourably reviewed in BUF circles and could be bought in British Union's London bookshops in Great Smith Street and Fetter Lane.[120] Which is not surprising; after visiting Hitler's paradise Cole described National Socialism as an ideology that might accurately reflect German public opinion.[121] He was not merely naïve. He was one of the many pre-war writers seduced by Nazism. To an extent that he defended its concentration camps.[122] He even expressed some sympathy with Hitler's anti-Semitic policies.[123]

Another important influence also played on his narrative. Margaret Joyce, attractive, vivacious, seriously well-dressed, drew men to her and she and Cole enjoyed a close relationship, even if they never became lovers. Why otherwise address him as "Dear Ducky"?[124] Morley Kennerley at Faber hinted as much, remarking Cole knew her "intimately."[125] Other staff there echoed him.[126] Biographers who nestle too close to their subject's family and friends risk becoming seriously compromised.

Yet Margaret's evidence rested at the heart of the new book, even though William had recently lamented her memory was like a sieve.[127] She, and the equally partial Macnab, had offered Cole an intriguing story; he gave far less weight to other evidence. In the first edition he stated that neither Margaret nor Macnab had interfered with his work.[128] But he remained insufficiently alert to their calculated manoeuvres. They were on a concerted mission to overturn Rebecca West's portrait of Joyce, even if detail had to be tainted to this end. They were fabricating history. Philip Toynbee, sensing something, wondered whether the biography amounted to a "whitewash," but hesitated to go further.[129] Four emphases Margaret fed to Cole suggest Toynbee had glimpsed – though darkly – something significant.

It is in Cole we first encounter Margaret's picture of a dithering, persecuted Joyce leaving London for Berlin only after being tipped off by an MI5 officer that he was about to be interned.[130] By neglecting to emphasise that he took this decision because he had been totally seduced by Hitler's vision for Europe, she is searching here for our sympathy.

A previously unnoticed puzzle exists in the telling of this episode. Before we know our history we need to know our historian. Yet Jack Cole remains a grey figure, almost faceless. His autobiography is a model of discretion.[131] Staff at Faber knew he worked in the BBC's German language service and appeared well-informed on contemporary politics. Some there wondered if he had Intelligence connections. Shortly before his widow died in May 2000 she told me he had indeed undertaken work for MI5 and after "poor Jack's" death his pied-à-terre in Fleet Street had been visited to ensure nothing untoward had been left lying around. Was her unprompted remark an unreliable aside? Possibly, I thought. But Cole did have an apartment in town, Flat 12, Crane Court, Fleet Street, EC4.[132] Soon afterwards a more informed source confirmed that Cole did indeed have security service connections.[133] Why then did he advertise Margaret Joyce's unsupported and unlikely story? That puzzle has to be left, to say more of the three remaining distortions.

In the *Sunday Express* A. K. Chesterton had already reported Margaret's misleading claim that in late August 1939, as the threat of war increased, she and Joyce, feeling totally isolated in Berlin, were extremely anxious to return to Britain. That fantasy now reappeared in Cole.[134] Margaret advanced this fiction with one eye cocked towards the historical record, to improve their post-War reputations when any enthusiasm for National Socialism was frowned upon.

She also offered another cleverly designed story – since widely repeated – aimed at distancing Joyce from the worst excesses of Nazi anti-Semitism. He had worked enthusiastically, faithfully, throughout the War for a state that ruthlessly killed millions. Yet Margaret reports him becoming visibly upset when suddenly glimpsing an old Jew in a Berlin street wearing the compulsory Judenstern, the Yellow Star.

Jack Cole swallowed this fantasy.[135] "A tattered coat upon a stick" can generate sympathy. But the exterminatory anti-Semite who hated Jews to the end would never have felt any such emotion on seeing this bent figure.[136]

Finally, in a further attempt to gain sympathy for Joyce – in this instance as someone once again betrayed by authority – she introduced into the narrative of his life the fantastic U-boat story, claiming that as Germany fragmented a submarine was intended to surface off Hamburg and whisk Haw-Haw to safety in Ireland.[137] Joyce himself never promoted this story. In the Reich's closing days he clearly heard the gossip then taking place on people being transported to safety on submarines but wrote soon afterwards that all the survival strategies suggested to him personally were either "Mad!" or "very nebulous," and later sighed resignedly, "we have to depend on others."[138] We know that in the end he and Margaret were left to fend for themselves.

When offering her observations Margaret realised that after the War Joyce's strident, defiant Nazism had no purchase. She determined therefore to give him a make-over. Had he survived with his old views he would have cut a lonely and tragic figure in post-war politics. Today, 'Lord Haw-Haw,' Blood and Honour's disc jockey, named after that "far sighted hero" who had opened "our nation's eyes to the truth of our situation using the airwaves," appeals to only the smallest constituency.[139] At the same time, she was providing some justification of her own wartime life.

Margaret never did write the biography "Wandsworth William" had obsessively dreamed about. Next best, though, and reflecting his continuing influence over her, she had just guided a book which enjoyed a wide circulation. Often badly treated in her marriage, she had inherited a deep obligation from Joyce and felt compelled to fulfil it. She had acted just in time. Many past traumas might have lingered daily to haunt her. However, often befuddled, floating on a sea of alcohol, some details had doubtless slipped away. And – important, too – she had lived almost twenty years without Joyce's domineering presence and that relentless strident insistence on his greatness.

The Meaning of Treason had provided the thesis but the antithesis had just gained greater currency. Chesterton had attempted to effect this change quite deliberately in the *Sunday Express*. He was a fascist and in hock to the Joyce camp. With 'Master's' help particularly, Margaret had just taken the process a stage further by influencing a susceptible Jack Cole.

5

Since then, Joyce's life has since continued to attract interest. Radio and television programmes have been made on him.[140] And a steady succession of books has appeared. Francis Selwyn's *Hitler's Englishman*, heavily reliant on existing sources, came out in 1987.[141] Five years later the Imperial War Museum produced an edition of *Twilight over England*.[142] Then in 2003 the National Archives published a collection of Intelligence documents on part of his career.[143] All testify to the public's continuing fascination.

6

Between 2003 and 2005 two new biographies also appeared. And key emphases in the new canon of Joyce's life, already formed by 1964 – however dubious, fantastical even – have persisted in these later reflections. This remark is not intended to suggest a continuing conspiracy. But a powerful reason – though not the only one – for these more recent mellowed portraits arises from their uncritical reliance on those earlier texts by Chesterton and Cole.

The journalist Mary Kenny realised that tracing Joyce's life involved far more than a pilgrimage to Kew to blow away many years of accumulated dust from security service files. And her *Germany Calling*, which appeared in 2003, unearthed a commendable mass of detail on Joyce's important and previously neglected years in Ireland, and on his family. Her determined efforts here will stand the test of time. She proceeded to argue, correctly, his early experiences created a mind-set which continued to influence his politics.[144] Hers was also the first Joyce biography to reference its sources.[145]

Dangers abound, though, in 'Irishing' him. Joyce's politics became heavily coloured by his time in London. His succession of acute professional disappointments there, those powerful ideological currents that surrounded him in the capital, his growing list of contacts in the British Fascists, the BUF, the National Socialist League and, crucially, the Nazi fellow – travelling groups, all combined to have their effect on his politics. None of which is seriously explored.

More significantly, when *Germany Calling* discussed the three main features in Joyce's political career – his fascism, his anti-Semitism and his treachery – its criticism was remarkably restrained.

His fascism came shorn of its inherent brutalism. Was that ideology ever "perfectly harmless" or "worthy?"[146] No wonder the Friends of Oswald Mosley believed the BUF had been afforded "a very fair hearing."[147]

Joyce's "pathological" Jew-hatred was unreservedly deplored. It amounted to the "most disagreeable" aspect of his political career. But attempting again to "somewhat mitigate his faults," it was emphasised his hostility essentially reflected a widely held belief among his contemporaries.[148] His sentiments certainly did reveal that widespread anti-Jewish sentiment in pre-war Britain.[149] But wait. While his anti-Semitism mirrored such antipathy, it became qualitatively different.[150] At Birkbeck he would leave the refectory whenever a Jew entered.[151] Later, when aware of the Holocaust if not its fine detail, he displayed no remorse. The Jews remained his great racial enemy. He has been observed recommending these sub-men, these parasitic Orientals, must be shot in the streets, eliminated, hanged from lamp-posts. He was an exterminatory anti-Semite, as few in inter-war Britain were. Kenny claims he would have recanted if exposed to the horrors of Auschwitz.[152] That outcome would have been most unlikely. In order "To change [his hatred], the whole pattern of [his] life would have to be altered."[153]

Joyce's treason was treated as less culpable than his anti-Semitism.[154] But in wartime Britain, especially during the dark threatening days of 1940 – and even after in some cases – his sneering mockery mattered enormously. The British public shed few tears for him when he was executed. No attempt is made to explain why.[155]

In 1953 Chesterton had been deliberately defending a comrade. In 1964 Jack Cole had Margaret hovering at his elbow, and, at a distance, Macnab. All were long dead. Why in 2003 had Joyce been presented in this way?

John Warburton, BUF veteran and for many years the leading figure in the Friends of Oswald Mosley, acted as one influence. To Kenny he was "actually, a nice man – a George Formby Lancastrian with a stand-up comedian's humour."[156] But there was much more to him than that. Generous to certain researchers – and even more to some favoured others – he acted as gatekeeper to key BUF sources, performed an important role in preserving its history, and invariably displayed charm, grace and a sense of humour. But it always paid to be vigilant when dealing with him. He never wavered from his political agenda, to spin a history of fascism without its barbarous and treasonable features. Warburton displayed absolutely no public sympathy for Joyce but by drawing heavily on his evidence, *Germany Calling* softened the ideology to which Joyce enthusiastically, wholeheartedly committed himself.

The book is also described significantly as "a personal biography" where Kenny admits to identifying in some respects with Joyce. Their Irish connections, their dislike of compromise – described as an English trait – their common interest in "smoking, drinking, talking, debating and arguing into the night," as well as their having to meet deadlines, are all mentioned.[157] Joyce even became a familiar spirit who entered the author's reveries.[158] What one reviewer called a "determinedly sympathetic" biography was always likely, therefore.[159] Kenny's portrait also reflected a deep Christian preparedness to forgive Joyce his political sins.[160]

Joyce's politics had always revealed a totally ruthless streak – which at times spilled over into his private life – but much of that viciousness was missing because yet again his family had been busy at work.[161] A gentle, deeply religious Heather Iandolo has worked tirelessly for many years to improve her father's reputation.[162] And she was the book's "first source."[163] Heather was a mere child when Joyce disappeared from her life. Later, desperately searching for him, she has increasingly idealised an object lost many years ago.[164] When defending him, she is inclined to emphasise he "only made speeches," he "never killed anyone."[165] Kenny repeats that defence.[166] Yet as Mr Justice Tucker declared at Joyce's trial and prosecutors decided at Nuremberg when hearing the case against Julius Streicher, words count.[167] War converts them into powerful weapons often with destructive consequences.

Lastly, Margaret Joyce, dead now almost forty years, was still making her presence felt with some but not all of her familiar, deliberately suspect evidence.[168]

Joyce's ruthless knowing critical streak would undoubtedly have pounced on some of these emphases.[169] But this latest portrait would have given him some satisfaction. Kenny openly admitted he was "not a particularly nice man."[170] But her overall picture remains, in a reviewer's words, "somewhat indulgent."[171] Rebecca West would hardly have recognised the Joyce she knew.

7

Two years later Nigel Farndale, journalist, novelist, writer on the 1949 Yangtze incident, produced a biography of Joyce authorised by Heather Iandolo.[172] By drawing heavily on official files, yet giving few references, *Haw-Haw: The Tragedy of William and Margaret Joyce* had more on Joyce's time in Berlin, especially his relationship there with Margaret. And by noticing both in Britain and Germany his heavy drinking, perpetual womanising – Joyce's string of lovers make cameo appearances – as well as his taste for marital violence, it offered a less restrained portrayal of the private Joyce than earlier biographies.

But when its focus switched to Joyce's political life and his "repellent" views, important gaps soon appeared.[173] Ireland scarcely featured.[174] His time in British fascism in the 1920s was rapidly dismissed.[175] His days in the BUF were rather better served.[176] But those crucial years between '37 and '39, so vital in influencing his departure to Berlin, were dashed off at speed.[177] Why waste time, it is asked, on "small swivel-eyed" groups?[178] Furthermore, Joyce's anti-Semitism was never properly explored. He was more than a contemptible xenophobe; he was an exterminatory Jew-hater.[179] Finally, Joyce's icy sin of treason, particularly his notorious broadcasts, were subordinated to the compelling, rapidly moving story of his and Margaret's personal traumas in Berlin.[180] And Joyce's renegade colleagues there – a vital piece of the jigsaw in which he was daily committing treason – were largely ignored, as they had been in earlier biographies.[181]

At the same time, Farndale's *Haw-Haw* supplemented that picture of Joyce first painted by Chesterton and Cole. Two influences in particular, one old, one new, were at work here.

Margaret Joyce's fantasies, aimed at attracting sympathy – by now well known to us – are given yet another airing. How persistent they have been. The story of Maxwell Knight's alleged tip-off that sent Joyce scurrying to Germany in 1939;[182] the claim that in late August 1939 if not stranded in Berlin the Joyces would have returned to London;[183] the Berlin Jew fable;[184] and finally the U-boat fantasy, first mentioned in Cole, were all paraded.[185] Farndale added to the Max Knight episode by offering – without any evidence – a telling conversation between Max and "Joycey."[186]

Joyce had always been his own relentless myth machine.[187] His personality demanded it and those close to him picked up where he had left off, advancing claims to improve his image. When 'Master' co-operated with A. K. Chesterton in 1953 he insisted his evidence was subject to Margaret's and Quentin Joyce's approval and they had "*a right in my opinion, to veto anything they object to.*"[188] Yet, unknowingly, Farndale was often drinking heavily from these tainted wells.

Farndale has no truck with Joyce's political views. But his conspiratorial approach also has the effect – intended or not – of further presenting the arch-intriguer sympathetically, as a figure ultimately destroyed by the security service. Rather than recognising that John Macnab wrote the Wolkoff letter in 1940, attention is switched to Max Knight. Max, it is claimed, "almost certainly" fabricated the message, trapped Wolkoff into sending it, and thereby converted her into an enemy agent.[189] To secure her conviction, Joyce needed to be labelled a traitor and Mr Justice Tucker duly obliged.[190] The security service did intervene in events. But to portray Knight as the shadowy off-stage manipulator deliberately sealing Joyce's fate ignores the immense complexities of this important wartime episode. The whiff of conspiracy is too strong in all of this.[191]

Joyce's execution also received a quite remarkable conspiratorial twist. Kenny had written earlier of his redemptive walk to the gallows – though not all readers and reviewers were persuaded.[192] His behaviour was now elevated to an even nobler level by suggesting a secret deal had been brokered with MI5. If he remained silent on his security service links, the authorities would spare Margaret from prosecution.[193] He duly sacrificed himself, god-like.[194] The media understandably swooped on this 'marmalade dropper,' sensationalism masquerading as history.[195] But Joyce's prison correspondence and official files reveal that neither his unusual silence nor Margaret's fate reflected any such deal.

Joyce never did realise his early professional ambitions. He found it difficult to sustain fulfilling relationships; Alex Scrimgeour and John Macnab were among the few exceptions. He died young in tragic circumstances. In many respects it was clearly a disappointing and sad life. That much can be recognised. It is also the case that in private – when dropping his bullying and pedantry – he could be an engaging companion. But when operating as a politico another persona quickly came on display. We have seen that he was constantly scheming and unashamedly exploitative. In pursuit of his goals he was always ruthless, frequently vicious, often violent. He believed in killing Jews. He was dangerous. In Farndale's *Haw-Haw* that side of him was at some risk of disappearing from view.

8

The sharp contrast between Rebecca West presenting Joyce as someone engaged in a "peculiarly odious form of treachery" and the later portraits of him is quite remarkable.[196] These more recent writings have reflected not only a reliance on partial sources but also a changing social background.

West continued to defend Joyce's execution, but from the 1950s no longer treated him as a great bogey figure. When focusing on Soviet agents, she claimed that in comparison his career possessed a decidedly "lace and lavender" tinge.[197] When her original reflections appeared, a bloody war had just ended. A pinched-faced, exhausted Britain could still hear Joyce's sneering, mocking broadcasts. The whistle and crash of Hitler's bombs continued to echo in the country's ears. Dead bodies lay spread-eagled under rubble. Many were mourning family and friends, killed in active service. And Britain retained the death penalty. Here was the background against which she wrote and Joyce was executed. By the late twentieth century his career could still stir strong emotions. But for the younger generation especially, the sad and bitter memories of the War had lost their cutting edge. Who in 1945–1946 would have written: "it is possible, with some effort, to regard aspects of [his treason] in an almost sympathetic light?"[198] Also, the country had lived for nearly forty years without capital punishment. These social shifts and the fact he was convicted and executed on a controversial point of law have all influenced how, increasingly, he has been presented.[199]

9

None of these portraits would have slaked Joyce's thirst to be lauded as a major historical figure. That worshipping biography could have appeared in a Nazi Britain. When the country was being rebuilt, Jew-free, Socialists executed or tamed, the City's influence ended, the old parliamentary elite vanquished, the slightest criticism of fascism firmly repressed, he would have relished the power of feeding his imagined achievements and rampant fantasies to authors who came knocking on his door. Rather than luxuriating in this glorious Nazi future, but facing execution, he consoled himself with: "It is better to die for the truth than to live for lies," adding "What a saga my life would make!"[200] Everyone, friend or foe, can agree on that. Forgotten? No. He remains 'alive.'

Notes

1 Literature testifies to his 'longevity.' Noël Coward had him delivering a Christmas broadcast in *Peace in Our Time* (London, 1947), p.25. As "Frolich" Henry Williamson introduced him into *The Phoenix Generation* (London, 1965). He featured as a threatening voice in V. Pemberton, *Our Street* (London, 1993) and as head of Nazi radio in O. Sheers, *Resistance* (London, 2007), pp.250–251. More recently he surfaced in A. MacLeod, *Unexploded* (London, 2013), longlisted for the Man Booker Prize. Thomas Kilroy's play, "Double Cross," first performed in Derry on 13 February 1986, saw the character of Joyce occupying a central role. See T. Kilroy, *Double Cross* (Oldcastle, 1986). Soon afterwards Savoy Books in Manchester converted Joyce into a cult figure in *Lord Horror* (Manchester, 1990). See also their later publications, Britton, *Baptised in the Blood of Millions*, the same author's *La Squab* (Manchester, 2012) and D. Britton and J. Coulthard, *Lord Horror. Reverbstorm* (Manchester, 2013), and graphic works such as *Hard Core Horror*, Nos 1–5. On Savoy books see B. Noys, "Fascinating (British) Fascism: David Britton's Lord Horror," *Rethinking History*, Vol. 6 (2002), pp.305–318 and P. Gravett, "From Iky Mo to Lord Horror: Representations of Jews in British Comics," *Journal of Graphic Novels and Comics*, Vol.1 (2010), pp.5–16.

2 Max Hastings, *Sunday Telegraph*, 16 November 2003, on loyalties becoming less congealed.

3 *This England*, Summer 1994, p.18.

4 *The Times*, 5 June 1997.

5 *Daily Telegraph*, 5 June 1997.

6 *The Sun*, 23 August 2002.

7 Griffiths, "A Note on Mosley," p.675, on the manufacturing of Oswald Mosley's image as a patriot.

8 "The Crown versus William Joyce," *New Yorker*, 29 September 1945, pp.30–40. Rollyson, *Rebecca West*, p.209.

9 R. West, "The Meaning of Treason," *Harper's Magazine*, Vol.195 (1947), pp.289–293.

10 R. West, *The Meaning of Treason* (New York, 1947).

11 See reviews in *Time and Tide*, 17 September 1949; *Glasgow Herald*, 22 September 1949; *The Spectator*, 23 September 1949; *New Statesman and Nation*, 24 September 1949; *Cavalcade*, 1 October 1949.

12 C. Ricks, "Treason's Reasons," *Sunday Times*, 18 February 1982, and P. Beer in *London Review of Books*, 6–9 May 1982, pp 14–16. Later editions appeared in 1952, in 1965 to take account of the activities of Guy Burgess and Donald Maclean and in 1982 to accommodate Anthony Blunt's. A paperback version appeared in 2000.

13 Lord Blake and C. S. Nicholls (eds.), *Dictionary of National Biography, 1981–1985* (Oxford, 1986) p.421.

14 Rollyson, *Rebecca West*; V. Glendinning, *Rebecca West: A Life* (New York, 1987); L. Gibb, *West's World. The Extraordinary Life of Dame Rebecca West* (London, 2013).

15 Note to 1949 edition, p.vi.

16 West, *Treason*, p.328.

17 *Ibid*. p.214.

18 Evident in the increasing focus on the treacherous Left in later editions of *Treason*.

19 West, *Treason* (2000), p.413.

20 West, *Treason*, p.252.

21 RWA, YCAL, MSS 1245, for West's critical observations on those opposed to Joyce's execution. West, *Treason*, pp.61 ff.

22 Rollyson, *Rebecca West*, p.225.

23 RWA, YCAL, MSS, Box 12, Folder 553 Mathew to West, 15 January 1946, 22 February 1946, and RWC, Tulsa SC, 33.8. Mathew to West, 28 February 1946. See also West to Mathew, 2 January 1963, 7 March 1963, 3 January 1964 (private archive).

24 West to Mathew, 10 March 1952, for their correspondence, which continued into 1954. Mathew forwarded the letters from "our mutual friend" to MI5's Dick White. Theobald Mathew to MI5, 28 June 1954 (all from private archive). Now confirmed in the recent release, KV2/3792. *Ibid* (report by Hanley of MI5, 26 January 1951) described her as "rather pompous" and someone who saw herself as "the high-priestess of Anti-Communism."

25 RWC, Tulsa SC, 46.7, Shawcross to West, 9 July 1946; West to Shawcross, 12 October 1950; Shawcross to West, 30 October 1950.

26 *The Law Times*, 3 February 1950. Weale, *Renegades* (2002 ed.), p.xv.

27 West, *Treason*, p.20, and 2000 ed., p.19.

28 West, *Treason*, p.26, and retained in 2000 ed., p.25.

29 West, *Treason*, pp.7–8.

30 West, *Treason* (2000), p.49.

31 West, *Treason*, pp.11–12.

32 USSC, MS 338/7/12, Macnab's critique of West.

33 West, *Treason*, p.9.

34 *Ibid*. pp.39–40.

35 *Ibid*. p.4. In private she was even more damning. He was "a poor little runt." Letter to Letitia Fairfield, 25 September 1945, in Scott (ed.), *Selected Letters*, p.206.

36 West, *Treason*, p.7.

37 West, *Treason* (2000), p.16.

38 West, *Treason*, p.12.

39 *Ibid*. p.5.

40 *Ibid*. p.80. Weale, *Renegades* (2002 ed.), p.xv recognises her snobbery.

41 Rollyson, *Rebecca West*, p.207.

42 *Ibid*. p.267, 209.

43 West, *Treason*, p.7. Rollyson, *Rebecca West*, pp.208–209 on West's problems with her own Irishness.

44 James Clark to Derek Denton, 12 June 1997. Denton Archive.

45 Keene, *Treason*, p.16.

46 W. Simon, "The Evolution of Treason," *Tulane Law Review*, Vol.35 (1961), p.669.

47 *Glasgow Herald*, 22 September 1949, described The *Meaning of Treason* as the work of "a reporter of the highest quality" rather than a historical study.

48 Keene, *Treason*, p.16.

49 KV 2/253/59a, Skardon's note, 27 June 1945.

50 Sir Oscar Dowson's note, 2 October 1945 and Theobald Mathew (DPP) to MI5, 10 October 1945, both in KV 2/253/80z. See also HO 213/383.

51 HO 213/383.

52 KV 2/253/48a.

53 KV 2/253/100B.

54 KV 2/253/95c.

55 HO 45/25779/14.

56 HO 382/1/10.

57 HO 45/25779/16.

58 HO 45/25779/20.

59 HO 382/1/91, for example.

60 HO 382/1/78, 77.

61 HO 382/1/68–9 contains a detailed discussion of her nationality.

62 Kenny, *Germany Calling*, pp.19, 247 on her later life. *Daily Express*, 6 June 1962 for her marriage.

63 Death certificate, 24 February 1972, Hammersmith Register Office.

64 KV 2/346, No.3.

65 Desmond Stewart "For Political Martyrs," *People's Post*,Vol.3, May 1947.

66 HO 45/862171/183, report on a Christmas meeting, Royal Hotel, WCI, 15 December 1945 and Metropolitan Police report, 21 December 1945.

67 USSC, MS 181/3/35,39. Correspondence between Macnab and L. A. Flockhart.

68 KV 2/1519/624.

69 KV2/ 2474/ 306a, 334a.

70 Heinemann published *The Bulls of Iberia* in 1957. Macnab's translation of René Guénon, *Le Symbolisme de la Croix*, appeared the following year under the imprint of Luzac and Co. *Spain under the Crescent Moon* (Louisville, Ky, 1999), is a posthumous work. Edited by William Stoddart, it draws from Macnab's talks on Moorish Spain broadcast to North America.

71 Baker, *Ideology of Obsession*. In his late political incarnation, in 1967 Chesterton helped to establish the National Front.

72 Chesterton, *Oswald Mosley*.

73 Chesterton, *Why I Left Mosley*.

74 Baker, *Ideology of Obsession*, pp.188–189.

75 KV 2/247/518a, letter, 14 November 1945.

76 KV 2/245, memo, 3 April 1935.

77 Quentin Joyce Archive, letter to Quentin, 7 December 1946.

78 *Daily Worker*, 20 August 1943 and *Jewish Chronicle*, 27 August 1943.

79 A rewritten version of Beaverbrook's *Success*, first published in 1921.

80 A. K. Chesterton, "How men who play high stakes trip up over trifles," *Sunday Express*, 12 July 1953.

81 All from Chesterton, "How men who play for high stakes."

82 Baker, *Ideology of Obsession*, p.130.

83 USSC, MS 181/3/39, John Macnab to L. A. Flockhart, 14 July 1953.

84 Bleach Archive contains drafts of three articles.

85 Quentin Joyce Archive. Quentin's correspondence (December 1947–January 1948) with Charles Curran, editor of the *Evening Standard*, illustrates some of the difficulty.

86 *Gothic Ripples*, No.21, 8 September 1946, p.2.

87 FA, memo, A. Pringle, 9 November 1956. All references to Cole and Faber are from FA, file AP14/38.

88 FA, Pringle to Cole, 16 November 1956.

89 FA, Cole, to Pringle, 28 April 1959.

90 FA, Cole to Pringle, 28 April 1959.

91 FA, letter, 15 June 1959.

92 FA, letter Margaret May to Faber, 22 September 1971, thereby giving up her interest just as a film based on Cole's book was being discussed.

93 FA, Pringle to Cole, 21 February 1964.

94 FA, Kennerley to Goad, 6 January 1964.

95 FA, Kennerley to Goad, 20 May 1964.

96 Information, James Clark.
97 FA, 9 March 1964.
98 FA, memo, by Goad, 15 January 1964.
99 FA, *Sunday Telegraph* to Faber, 20 May 1964.
100 FA, *Sunday Times* to Faber, 28 May 1964.
101 FA, *Evening Standard* to Faber, 2 July 1964.
102 FA, *News of the World* to Faber, 8 May 1964.
103 FA, *Sunday Express* to Faber, 8 August 1964.
104 Cole, *Lord Haw-Haw.*
105 *Sunday Telegraph*, 1 November 1964.
106 *Guardian*, 30 October 1964; *The Times*, 19 November 1964.
107 *The Times Literary Supplement*, 12 November 1964.
108 FA, Goad to Kennerley, 13 May 1964.
109 *The Observer*, 1 November 1964. FA, Goad to Pringle, 29 January 1965.
110 CSC 11/150, memo, 8 August 1961.
111 Cole to Pringle, 5 May 1965, refers to his collection. FA.
112 FA, internal memo, 6 October 1965 for a complaint against a BBC pro-
     gramme, "A World of Sound," 5 July 1965. Cole received compensation
     of four guineas.
113 FA, Cole to Pringle, 5 May 1965. Penguin Books to Faber, 19 May 1965.
114 West, *Treason* (2000), p.10.
115 Cole, *Lord Haw-Haw*, p. 58.
116 *Ibid.* p.55.
117 *Ibid.* pp.17–25.
118 Kenny, *Germany Calling*, p.248 on its primary source value.
119 *Fascist Quarterly*, Vol. 1 (1935), pp.510–511.
120 *Action*, 18 June 1938 and 2 July 1938.
121 J. A. Cole, *Just back from Germany* (London, 1938), pp.145–146.
122 *Ibid.* pp.289–290.
123 Cole, *Just back from Germany*, p.256. Schwarz, "British Visitors to
     National Socialist Germany," pp.502, 506, notes Cole's travels there.
124 Stewart, "Fellow Travellers of the Right," p.400.
125 FA, Kennerley to Goad, 6 January 1964.
126 Private information.
127 KV 2/250, 15 April 1945.
128 Cole, *Lord Haw-Haw* (1964), p.7.
129 *The Observer*, 1 November 1964 for "Hitler's Voice in Britain."
130 Cole, *Lord Haw-Haw*, p.86
131 J. A. Cole, *The View from the Park* (London, 1979), draws a line in 1929.
132 FA, Brooksbank to Cole, 12 May 1964.
133 Private information.
134 Cole, *Lord Haw-Haw*, pp.95–99.
135 *Ibid.* pp.197–198.
136 DPP 2/407, report, 9 October 1936, on shooting Jewish Communists.
     See also Joyce, *Fascism and Jewry*, p.8, and his *Twilight over England*, p.70.
137 Cole, *Lord Haw-Haw* p.229.

138 Joyce's observations are from KV2/250, 13, 24 and 25 April 1945.

139 *Blood and Honour*, No.32 (2005), pp.8–9.

140 Christopher Olgiati's television documentary, BBC1, TV, 29 December 1975 and Nigel Acheson's excellent 1991 radio programmes made full use of new witnesses. The latter can be heard on National Sound Archive, B8209/01 and B8234/04. Contrast National Sound Archive, "Let Justice Be Done – Treason, the Case of William Joyce," 1CE0000 364–369, BBC Home Service Broadcast, 7 October 1948. *Lord Haw-Haw* was transmitted on the History Channel on 9 and 15 June 2005. It also carried *Great Crimes and Trials: Lord Haw-Haw*, 10 July 2005. Fastnet Films, Ireland released a TV programme, *Hitler's Irishman: The Story of Lord Haw-Haw*, on 8 May 2005.

141 Selwyn, *Hitler's Englishman*.

142 Charman (ed.), *Twilight*.

143 Martland, *Lord Haw-Haw*.

144 Kenny, *Germany Calling*, p.3.

145 H. Newman, "Germany Calling! Germany Calling!" BA Dissertation, Monash University, 1998, p.9, reveals a student's frustration when reading texts on Joyce that carried no footnotes.

146 Kenny, *Germany Calling*, p.98.

147 *Comrade*, No.57 (2004), pp.10–11. See, by contrast, its hostility to Farndale's later biography, *ibid.* No.60 (2006), pp.17–18.

148 Alan Judd, in *Daily Telegraph*, 13 December 2003 on the tendency to mitigate Joyce's faults.

149 Kenny, *Germany Calling*, pp. 5–6 on Joyce's anti-Semitism.

150 M. Banton, *Race Relations* (London, 1967), pp.298–299 emphasises the distinction between antipathy and prejudice.

151 *Irish Times*, 21 June 1945. Recollection of the Rev. P.W. Webb.

152 Kenny, *Germany Calling*, p.244 on Joyce's Jew-hatred. See critical comment by P. Laity, "Uneasy Listening," *London Review of Books*, 8 July 2004, p.24.

153 Allport, *Nature of Prejudice*, p.384, commenting on prejudiced personalities such as Joyce.

154 Kenny, *Germany Calling*, pp.243–244.

155 Alan Judd's review, *Daily Telegraph*, 13 December 2003.

156 *Guardian*, 4 September 2004; Daily *Telegraph*, 2 September 2004. See also Kenny's portrait in *The Oldie*, No.177 (2003), pp.34–35. *Comrade*, No.58 (2004), for "Goodbye Johnny."

157 Kenny, *Germany Calling*, pp.3–4. See Joyce's *National Socialism Now*, p.60 for "Compromise is the only form of treachery that the Irishman is never prepared to pardon."

158 Kenny, *Germany Calling*, p.3; Laity, "Uneasy Listening," p.23.

159 Laity, "Uneasy Listening," p.23. Kenny's spirited response appeared in *ibid.* 5 August 2004, p.4.

160 Hastings, *Sunday Telegraph*, 16 November 2003, on the "Christian charity of a remarkable order."

161 Laity, "Uneasy Listening," p.24.

162 She has been noticed campaigning for the transfer of his remains to Galway. She contributed to "Dear Old Daddy," RTÉ, 15 September 1999, appeared on Saturday Live, BBC Radio 4, 13 June 2009, supported Nigel Farndale's work. See also her interview with Francis Beckett, *The Guardian*, 5 December 2005. Her latest campaign is to secure a pardon for her father. *Daily Express*, 22 May 2011.

163 Kenny, *Germany Calling*, p.10.

164 *Daily Express*, 11 February 1995. "Her parents divorced when she was seven and she never saw Joyce again." Mrs Iandolo offered this detail to the reporter.

165 *Kent Today*, 21 October 1996.

166 Kenny, *Germany Calling*, p.243.

167 J. E. Persico, *Nuremberg: Infamy on Trial* (London, 1994 ed.), p.493 on Streicher's case.

168 Kenny, *Germany Calling*, pp.123, 137–138, 183–184 and 213.

169 Laity, "Uneasy Listening," p.23.

170 Kenny, *Germany Calling*, p.5.

171 Hastings, *Sunday Telegraph*, 16 November 2003, on the book's indulgence.

172 Farndale, *Haw-Haw*.

173 *Ibid*. p.3 on Joyce's repulsive views.

174 *Ibid*. pp.45–50.

175 *Ibid*. pp.54–58 on British Fascists.

176 *Ibid*. pp.67–90, 103–104, Joyce drifting in and out of the BUF's history.

177 *Ibid*. pp.110–111. It is no surprise that the reviewer in *Scotland on Sunday*, 29 May 2005 found no convincing explanation in Farndale of why Joyce went to Berlin.

178 Farndale, *Haw-Haw*, p.110.

179 *Ibid*. p.11.

180 *Ibid*. p.3 on treason's sin. Byron Rogers's review in *The Spectator*, 9 July 2005, notices the neglect of the broadcasts.

181 There are no references to Banning, Tester, Trevor or Wicks. Farndale touches slightly on Amery and Baillie-Stewart, and even less on Bothamley, Eckersley and Purdy.

182 Farndale, *Haw-Haw*, p.114. Cole, *Lord Haw*-Haw, p.86. Kenny, *Germany Calling*, p.123, where Knight is the "spymaster."

183 Farndale, pp.123–125.

184 *Ibid*. p.215

185 *Ibid*. p.261.

186 *Ibid*. p.114.

187 Also attempted by Kim Philby. See M. Scanlon, "Philby and His Fictions," *Dalhousie Review*, Vol.62 (1982–83), p.536. "Philby's autobiography is more usefully regarded as fiction." There are other examples of "fakery" in S. Vice, *Textual Deceptions: False Memoirs and Literary Hoaxes in the Contemporary Era* (Edinburgh, 2014).

188 USSC, MS 238/7/11.

189 Farndale, *Haw-Haw*, pp.158–159.

190 *Ibid*. p.168.

191 *Ibid*. pp.156–168. Aaronovitch, *Voodoo Histories*, on conspiratorial history.

192 *Sunday Telegraph*, 16 November 2003.

193 Farndale, *Haw-Haw*, p.303.

194 *Ibid*. p.328.

195 *Sunday Telegraph*, 8 May 2005. It featured on the "Today" programme, BBC Radio 4, 27 May 2005.

196 West, *Treason* (2000), p.29.

197 West to Harold Laski, 21 December 1947, on the Soviet threat (private archive). For "lace and lavender" see West to Theobald Mathew, 13 July 1963 (private archive).

198 Farndale, *Haw-Haw*, p.2

199 Selwyn, *Hitler's Englishman*, pp.221–222; Kenny, *Germany Calling*, pp.243–244; Farndale, *Haw-Haw*, p.323.

200 WJ to MJ, 25 December 1945. RWC, Tulsa SC, 9.8. Capra to West, 1 June 1960, for Frank Capra's interest in filming the *Meaning of Treason*. Terence Rattigan has been noticed writing a film script. *The Times*, 10 March 2004 for later interest in a film of Joyce's life.

SELECT BIBLIOGRAPHY

Searching for Lord Haw-Haw carries extensive endnotes, therefore I have restricted this bibliography to a selection of published written material. The inclusion of an item does not signify that I agree with its arguments. But each source adds detail or context to the texture of William Joyce's short life.

P. Aldag (pseud.) *Das Judentum in England* (Berlin, 1943).

G. W. Allport, *The Nature of Prejudice* (New York, 1958 ed.).

C. Andrew, *In Defence of the Realm. The Authorized History of MI5* (London, 2009).

F. Aveling, *Personality and the Will* (London and Cambridge, 1931).

D. Baker, *Ideology of Obsession: A.K. Chesterton and British Fascism* (London, 1996).

J. W. Baird, *The Mythical World of Nazi Propaganda* (Minneapolis, 1974).

J. Barrington, *Lord Haw-Haw of Zeesen* (London, 1939).

F. Beckett, *The Rebel who Lost His Cause. The Tragedy of John Beckett* (London, 1999).

A. Beevor, *Stalingrad* (London, 1998).

R. R. Bellamy, *We Marched With Mosley. The Authorised History Of The British Union Of Fascists* (London, 2013).

R. Benewick, *Political Violence and Public Order: A Study of British Fascism* (London, 1969). Revised as *The Fascist Movement in Britain* (London, 1972).

H.J.P. Bergmeier and R. E. Lotz, *Hitler's Airwaves. The Inside Story of Nazi Radio Broadcasting and Propaganda Swing* (New Haven and London, 1997).

W. A. Boelcke (ed.), *The Secret Conferences of Dr Goebbels. The Nazi Propaganda War 1939–43* (New York, 1970).

P. Brendon, *The Dark Valley. A Panorama of the 1930s* (London, 2000).

J. Brown (pseud.), *Woe for My Comrades* (Berne, 1944).

K. Brownlow, *How It Happened Here* (London, 1968).

P. Burrin, "Political Religion: The Relevance of a Concept," *History and Memory*, Vol. 9 (1997).

A. Calder, *The People's War: Britain 1939–45* (London, 1969 and subsequent eds).

C.G.L. du Cann, *English Treason Trials* (London, 1964).

B. Clough, *State Secrets: The Kent-Wolkoff Affair* (Hove, 2006).

C. Cross, *The Fascists in Britain* (London, 1961).

J. A. Cole, *Lord Haw-Haw – and William Joyce. The Full Story* (London, 1964: pbk ed., 1987).

M. Constantine (pseud.), *Swastika Night* (London, 1940 ed. First published 1937).

N. Cohn, *Warrant for Genocide* (London, 1967 and Harmondsworth, 1970).

Diagnostic and Statistical Manual (Washington DC., 2000 and later eds).

M. Doherty, *Nazi Wireless Propaganda. Lord Haw-Haw and British Public Opinion in the Second World War* (Edinburgh, 2000).

D. O'Donoghue, *Hitler's Irish Voices. The Story of German Radio's Wartime Irish Service* (Belfast, 1998).

S. Dorril, *Blackshirt: Sir Oswald Mosley and British Fascism* (London, 2006).

J. C. Edwards, *Berlin Calling. American Broadcasters in Service to the Reich* (New York, 1991).

H. Ettlinger, *The Axis on the Air* (New York, 1943).

R. J. Evans, *The Third Reich at War 1939–1945* (London, 2008).

D. Faber, *Speaking for England. Leo, Julien and John Amery: The Tragedy of a Political Family* (London, 2005).

N. Farndale, *Haw-Haw: The Tragedy of William and Margaret Joyce* (London, 2005: pbk ed., 2006).

H. W. Flannery, *Assignment to Berlin* (London, 1942).

R. F. Foster, *The Oxford History of Ireland* (Oxford, 1989).

A. Fredborg, *Behind the Steel Wall* (London, 1944).

R. Andreas-Friedrich, *Berlin Underground 1939–1945* (London, 1948).

J. Gardiner, *Wartime Britain 1939–1945* (London, 2004).

H. Gibbs, *The Spectre of Communism* (London, 1936).

J. V. Gottlieb and T. P. Linehan (eds), *The Culture of Fascism: Visions of the Far Right in Britain* (London, 2004).

P. Gravett, "From Iky Mo to Lord Horror: Representations of Jews in British Comics," *Journal of Graphic Novels and Comics*, Vol. 1 (2010).

R. Griffin, "British Fascism: The Ugly Duckling," in M. Cronin (ed.), *The Failure of British Fascism* (London, 1996).

R. Griffiths, *Fellow Travellers of the Right; British Enthusiasts for Nazi Germany* (London, 1980).

R. Griffiths, *Patriotism Perverted: Captain Ramsay, the Right Club and British Anti-Semitism 1939–40* (London, 1998).

R. Griffiths, "A Note on Mosley, the 'Jewish War' and Conscientious Objection," *Journal of Contemporary History*, Vol. 40 (2005).

H. A. Gwynne (ed.), *The Cause of World Unrest* (London, 1920).

J.W. Hall (ed.), *The Trial of William Joyce* (London, 1946).

J. C. Harsch, *At the Hinge of History. A Reporter's Story* (Athens, Ga, 1993).

M. Hastings, *All Hell Let Loose: The Second World War 1939–1945* (London, 2011).

F.J.C. Hearnshaw, *A Survey of Socialism* (London, 1929).

C. Holmes, "New Light on the 'Protocols of Zion,' *Patterns of Prejudice*, Vol. VI (1977).

C. Holmes, *Anti-Semitism in British Society 1876–1939* (London, 1979).

C. Holmes, "Finding Lord Haw-Haw's Friend," *BBC History Magazine*, Vol. 8 (June 2007).

C. Husbands, "East End Racism 1900–1980: Continuities in Vigilantist and Extreme Right-Wing Behaviour," *The London Journal*, Vol. 8 (1982).

D. Irving, *Goebbels. Mastermind of the Third Reich* (London, 1996).

D. Pryce-Jones, *Treason of the Heart: From Thomas Paine to Kim Philby* (London, 2011).

W. Joyce, *Dictatorship* (London, 1933).

W. Joyce, *Fascism and India* (London, 1933?).

W. Joyce, "Quis Separabit?" *Fascist Quarterly*, Vol.2 (1936).

W. Joyce, "Thomas Carlyle – National Socialist," *Fascist Quarterly*, Vol.2 (1936).

W. Joyce, *Fascism and Jewry* (London, 1936?).

W. Joyce, *National Socialism Now* (London, 1937).

W. Joyce, *Twilight over England* (Metairie, La, nd). The original is: *Dämmerung über England* (Berlin, 1940).

A. A. Kallis, *Nazi Propaganda and the Second World War* (London, 2005).

U. von Kardoff, *Diary of a Nightmare: Berlin 1942–1945* (London, 1965).

M. Kenny, *Germany Calling. A Personal Biography of William Joyce, 'Lord Haw-Haw'* (Dublin, 2003).

O. Kernberg, *Borderline Conditions and Pathological Narcissism* (New Jersey, 1990).

I. Kershaw, *Hitler 1889–1936: Hubris* (London, 1998).

I. Kershaw, *Hitler 1936–1945: Nemesis* (London, 2000).

I. Kershaw, *Fateful Choices: Ten Decisions that Changed the World, 1939–1941* (London, 2007).

I. Kershaw, *The End. Hitler's Germany 1944–45* (London, 2011).

V. G. Kiernan, "On Treason," in his *Poets, Politics and the People*, ed. H.J. Kaye (London, 1989).

T. Kilroy, *Double Cross* (Oldcastle, 1986).

H. R. Knickerbocker, *Die Schwarzhemden in England und Englands wirtschaftlichen Aufsteig* (Berlin, 1934).

H. von Kotze (ed.), *Heeresadjutant bei Hitler 1938–1943. Aufzeichnungen des Majors Engel* (Stuttgart, 1974).

T. Kushner, *The Persistence of Prejudice: Antisemitism in British Society during the Second World War* (Manchester, 1989).

D. Kynaston, *Austerity Britain 1945–51* (London, 2007).

H. Laski, *Political Offences and the Death Penalty* (London, 1940).

H. Lauterpacht, "Allegiance, Diplomatic Protection and Criminal Jurisdiction over Aliens," Cambridge *Law Journal*, Vol.9 (1945–1947).

T. P. Linehan, *East London for Mosley: The British Union of Fascists in East London and South West Essex* (London, 1996).

T. P. Linehan, *British Fascism 1918–39: Parties, Ideology and Culture* (Manchester, 2000).

K. Lowe, *Savage Continent. Europe in the Aftermath of World War II* (London, 2012).

J. Lukacs, *Five Days in London, May 1940* (New Haven and Yale, 1999).

K. Lunn, "The Impact and Ideology of British Fascism in the 1920s," in T. Kushner and K.Lunn (eds), *Traditions of Intolerance: Historical Perspectives on Fascism and Race Discourse in Britain* (Manchester, 1989).

A. Lynch, *My Life Story* (London, 1934).

A. Lyon, "From Dafydd ap Gryffdd to Lord Haw-Haw. The Concept of Allegiance in the Law on Treason," *Cambrian Law Journal*, Vol.33 (2003).

G. Macklin, *Very Deeply Dyed in Black. Sir Oswald Mosley and the Resurrection of British Fascism after 1945* (London, 2007).

W. F. Mandle, *Anti-Semitism and the British Union of Fascists* (London, 1968).

E. Maresch, *Katyń* (Stroud, 2000).

P. Martland, *Lord Haw Haw. The English Voice of Nazi Germany* (London, 2003).

A. Masters, *The Man who was M: The Life of Maxwell Knight* (London, 1986).

R. McCrum, *P. G. Wodehouse. A Life* (London, 2004).

L. le M. Minty, "LOOKING IN A DARK ROOM FOR A BLACK HAT THAT ISN'T THERE," *Juridical Review*, Vol.58 (1946).

W. Mittler, *Anzac Tattoo: Eine Reise durch Niemansland* (Percha, 1987).

R. Moorhouse, *Berlin at War. Life and Death in Hitler's Capital 1939–45* (London, 2010).

R. Moorhouse, *The Devil's Alliance : Hitler's Pact with Stalin* (London, 2014)

F. Mullally, *Fascism inside England* (London, 1946).

S. Murphy, *Letting the Side Down. British Traitors of the Second World War* (Stroud, 2003).

B. Noys, "Fascinating (British) Fascism: David Britton's Lord Horror," *Rethinking History*, Vol.6 (2002).

R. Overy, *The Morbid Age. Britain between the Wars* (London, 2009).

M. Pugh, '*Hurrah for the Blackshirts!' Fascists and Fascism in England between the Wars* (London, 2005).

P. Rand, *Conspiracy of One* (Guildford, Conn., 2013).

A. Roberts, "Hitler's England: What if Germany had invaded Britain in May 1940?" in N. Ferguson, *Virtual History: Alternatives and Counterfactuals* (Basingstoke, 1997).

C. Rollyson, *Rebecca West: A Saga of the Century* (London, 1995).

C. J. Rolo, *Radio Goes To War* (London, 1943).

C. E. Bechhofer Roberts (ed.), *The Trial of William Joyce with some other Recent Trials for Treason* (London, 1946).

R. Saikia, *The Red Book: The Membership List of the Right Club* (London, 2010).

F. Selwyn, *Hitler's Englishman. The Crime of Lord Haw-Haw* (Harmondsworth, 1993 ed. First published 1987).

W. L. Shirer, *Berlin Diary: The Journal of a Foreign Correspondent 1939–1941* (London, 1941).

W. L. Shirer, *The Traitor* (New York, 1950 ed.).

W. L. Shirer, *This Is Berlin* (London, 1999).

A.W.B. Simpson, *In the Highest Degree Odious: Detention without Trial in Wartime Britain* (Oxford, 1994 ed.).

R. Skidelsky, *Oswald Mosley* (London, 1975 and subsequent eds).

C. E. Spearman, *The Abilities of Man* (London, 1927).

N. Baillie-Stewart, *The Officer in the Tower* (London, 1967).

A. Tester, *England – Quo Vadis?* (Bukarest, nd).

R. Thurlow, *Fascism in Britain. A History 1918–1985* (Oxford, 1987), revised as *Fascism in Britain: from Oswald Mosley's Blackshirts to the National Front* (London, 1998).

R. Thurlow, *Fascism in Modern Britain* (Stroud, 2000).

S. Vaknin, *Malignant Self-Love: Narcissism Revisited* (Prague and Skopje, 2007).

A. Weale, *Patriot Traitors: Roger Casement, John Amery and the Real Meaning of Treason* (London, 2001).

R. West, *The Meaning of Treason* (London, 1949 and subsequent eds).

P. Willetts, *Rendezvous at the Russian Tea Rooms. The Spy Hunter, the Fashion Designer and the Man from Moscow* (London, 2015), appeared when my book was in press.

G. Williams, "The Correlation of Allegiance and Protection," *Cambridge Law Journal*, Vol. 10 (1950).

H. Williamson, *The Phoenix Generation* (London, 1965).

INDEX

[Page references in **bold** denote images]

PLACES

SUBJECTS